D0139629

THE OXFORD

W. E. B. DU BOIS READER

Edited by

Eric J. Sundquist

New York   Oxford
OXFORD UNIVERSITY PRESS
1996

OXFORD UNIVERSITY PRESS

Oxford   New York
Athens   Auckland   Bangkok   Bombay
Calcutta   Cape Town   Dar es Salaam   Delhi
Florence   Hong Kong   Istanbul   Karachi
Kuala Lumpur   Madras   Madrid   Melbourne
Mexico City   Nairobi   Paris   Singapore
Taipei   Tokyo   Toronto

and associated companies in

Berlin   Ibadan

Copyright © 1996 by Oxford University Press, Inc.

Published by Oxford University Press, Inc.
198 Madison Avenue, New York, New York 10016

Oxford is a registered trademark of Oxford University Press

All rights reserved. No part of this publication may be reproduced,
stored in a retrieval system, or transmitted, in any form or by any means,
electronic, mechanical, photocopying, recording, or otherwise,
without the prior permission of Oxford University Press.

A Negro within the Nation. Reprinted with permission from *Current History*
magazine (June 1935). © 1935, Current History, Inc.

Negro Art and Literature (1924) from *The Gifts of Black Folks* (1924). The Propaganda of History (1935)
from *Black Reconstruction in America, 1860–1880* (1935). Reprinted by permission of Kraus
International Publications.

The Concept of Race (1940) from *Dusk of Dawn* (1940). Reprinted by permission of
David G. Du Bois.

Toussaint L'Ouverture (1961), original title: "African and the French Revolution." Reprinted
from *Freedomways* Magazine, Summer 1961.

The following are reprinted by permission of *The Crisis Magazine*.

"On Being Crazy" (1923); issue 26, June 1923
"The Name 'Negro' " (1928); March 1928
"On Being Ashamed of Oneself" (1933); issue 40, Sept. 1933
"Charles Young" (1922); Feb. 1922
"Robert E. Lee" (1928); March 1928
"Criteria of Negro Art" (1926); issue 32, Oct. 1926
"Americanization" (1922); issue 24, Aug. 1922
"The Negro and Communism" (1931); issue 38, Sept. 1931
"Little Portraits of Africa" (1924); issue 27, April 1924

W. E. B. Du Bois "The Realities of Africa" *Foreign Affairs* 1943. Reprinted by permission of *Foreign
Affairs* (July 1943). Copyright (1943) by the Council on Foreign Relations, Inc.

The Autobiography of W. E. B. Du Bois, copyright 1968 by International Publishers Co., Inc.; *The World
of Africa,* copyright 1965 International Publishers Co., Inc.

Library of Congress Cataloging-in-Publication Data
Du Bois, W. E. B. (William Edward Burghardt), 1868–1963.
[Selections. 1996]
The Oxford W. E. B. Du Bois reader / edited by Eric J. Sundquist.
p.   cm.
Includes bibliographical references (p.   ).

ISBN: 978-0-19-509178-6

1. Afro-Americans.   2. United States—Race relations.
I. Sundquist, Eric J.   II. Title.
E185.97.D73A25   1996
305.896'073—dc20   95-21307

Printed in the United States of America
on acid-free paper

Original Sources of Publication

The Conservation of Races
  American Negro Academy Occa-sional Papers, no. 2 (1897)
The Present Outlook for the Dark Races of Mankind
  Church Review 17 (October 1900)
The Song of the Smoke
  The Horizon 1 (February 1907)
The First Universal Races Congress
  The Independent 70 (August 24, 1911)
In Black
  The Crisis 20 (October 1920)
The Superior Race
  Smart Set 70 (April 1923)
On Being Crazy
  The Crisis 26 (June 1923)
The Name "Negro"
  The Crisis 34 (March 1928)
On Being Ashamed of Oneself
  The Crisis 40 (September 1933)
The Concept of Race
  from Du Bois, *Dusk of Dawn* (1940)
Jefferson Davis as a Representative of Civilization
  Harvard Graduation Speech, 1890
Booker T. Washington
  The Dial (July 16, 1901)
Abraham Lincoln
  Voice of the Negro 4 (June 1907)
John Brown
  from Du Bois, *John Brown* (1909)
Charles Young
  The Crisis 23 (February 1922)
Marcus Garvey
  orig. title: "Back to Africa," *Century Magazine* 105 (February 1923)
Robert E. Lee
  The Crisis 34 (March 1928)
A Tribute to Carter Woodson
  Masses and Mainstream 3 (June 1950)
Paul Robeson
  Negro Digest 7 (March 1950)
Joseph Stalin
  National Guardian (March 16, 1953)

Kwame Nkrumah
  orig. pub. date 1957; from Du Bois, *The World and Africa* (1967)
Gandhi and the American Negro
  Gandhi Marg 1 (July 1957)
Toussaint L'Ouverture
  orig. title: "Africa and the French Revolution," *Freedomways* 1 (Summer 1961)
On The Souls of Black Folk
  The Independent (November 17, 1904)
The Star of Ethiopia
  orig. title: "The People of Peoples and Their Gifts to Men," *The Crisis* 6 (November 1913)
Negro Art
  The Crisis 22 (June 1921)
Negro Art and Literature
  from Du Bois, *The Gift of Black Folks* (1924)
Criteria of Negro Art
  The Crisis 32 (October 1926)
Phillis Wheatley and African American Culture
  orig. title: "The Vision of Phillis the Blessed (An Allegory of Negro American Literature in the Eighteenth and Nineteenth Centuries," *Fisk News* 14 (May 1941)
The Humor of Negroes
  Mark Twain Quarterly 5 (Winter 1942–43)
What is the Negro Problem?
  from Du Bois, *The Philadelphia Negro* (1899)
The Training of the Negro for Social Power
  Outlook 75 (October 17, 1903)
The Future of the Negro Race in America
  The East and the West 2 (January 1904)
The Niagara Movement
  Address at founding of Niagara Movement, pamphlet, 1906
Triumph
  The Crisis 2 (September 1911)

Contents

Contents

CHAPTER **4**

Literature and Art

303

CHAPTER **5**

Politics, Economics, and Education

344

Contents

C H A P T E R 6
Darkwater **(1920)**
481

C H A P T E R 7
Africa and Colonialism
624

THE OXFORD

W. E. B. Du Bois Reader

W. E. B. Du Bois and the Autobiography of Race

At the outset of his last sustained autobiographical writing, a work undertaken in the late 1950s but published posthumously in 1968, W. E. B. Du Bois, having just provided a capsule summary of his recent invigorating trip to the Soviet Union and China, offers the following reflection on his work:

> I mention this trip in some detail because it was one of the most important trips that I had ever taken, and had wide influence on my thought. To explain this influence, my Soliloquy becomes an autobiography. Autobiographies do not form indisputable authorities. They are always incomplete, and often unreliable. Eager as I am to put down the truth, there are difficulties; memory fails especially in small details, so that it becomes finally but a theory of my life, with much forgotten and misconceived, with valuable testimony but often less than absolutely true, despite my intention to be frank and fair.
>
> Who and what is this I, which in the last year looked on a torn world and tried to judge it? Prejudiced I certainly am by my twisted life; by the way in which I have been treated by my fellows; by what I myself have thought and done. I have passed through changes by reason of my growth and willing; by my surroundings without; by knowledge and ignorance. What I think of myself, now and in the past, furnishes no certain document proving what I really am. Mostly my life today is a mass of memories with vast omissions, matters which are forgotten accidentally or by deep design.

Taking note of the remarkable ideological gulf between the views presented in his most recent autobiography, *Dusk of Dawn*, some twenty years earlier and those of the *Autobiography*, conceived at the height of the cold war and Du Bois's estrangement from the United States, he adds: "One must then see these varying views as contradictions to truth, and not as final and complete authority. This book then is the Soliloquy of an old man on what he dreams his life has been as he sees

3

it slowly drifting away; and what he would like others to believe" (Du Bois, *Autobiography*, 12–13).

One justifiably wonders if this is not the introduction to a work of postmodern antiteleology, a radical empowerment of black subjectivity in the African diaspora, cut loose from any national identity or historical matrix. Or perhaps—as one might deduce from the volume's hyperbolic praise of communist regimes—it is intended to forecast some future state of social totality in which liberal individualism has been all but annihilated. In either event, the assumption that autobiography is premised on some notion of authenticity, even if it turns out to be self-serving or distorted by the writer, has here been swiftly undercut.

No one imagines that autobiography is transparent. At the least, any autobiography is a narrative, a single story selected from a set of possible lives to cast the protagonist in a particular light. In the instance of a more self-conscious or devious autobiographer, his text might be likened to a map wherein manifold routes are evident even as many others remain concealed. In the end, no doubt, each autobiography calls up its own set of metaphors—confession, trial and triumph, messianic personification, or some combination of like narrative modes. What stands out in the case of Du Bois—for whom all of these figures of self-dramatization are apt—is not the number of autobiographical works with which he may be credited. Nor is it simply the astonishing fact that, living to the age of ninety-five and writing to the bitter end, the span of his narrated life begins during the presidency of Andrew Johnson and ends just short of the presidency of Lyndon Johnson. As the passage cited above indicates, what is notable about Du Bois is the fundamental mutability of his conception of the represented life itself. Insofar as it initiates a final life story the burden of which is intellectual (soon to be actual) exile from the United States and a tragic defense of totalitarianism, the passage from the *Autobiography* has obvious political and moral implications. His final ideological choice, needless to say, brought to sudden intensity Du Bois's long-evolving view that all language—all art, as he usually put it—is a form of propaganda. From this perspective, the *Autobiography*, an ultimate confession of dissent from the very membership in American democracy that Du Bois had passionately sought throughout his life, illustrates the theory that it endorses. But Du Bois's political apostasy—he at long last joined the Communist Party in 1961 and immediately moved to Ghana, where he died in 1963—could hardly have been predicted, even a decade earlier; and the plaintive, even mournful quality of this late prose surely springs from the author's deep disappointment and anger that his many decades of struggle for black civil and political equality had seemed to produce so little result. That he was mistaken—his contribution to African American freedom had been immense—does little to mitigate the pain of his final soliloquy.

Despite its inherent contradiction of the ideology espoused in the

Autobiography, Du Bois's choice of the term "soliloquy" is especially appropriate, for his whole writing life had, in fact, been a dramatic performance in which the first person, the often grandiloquent "I," was at center stage. Although the motives had shifted over time, irrevocably during the cold war, the underlying significance of Du Bois's typically self-centered writing remained constant. In writing his own life, however, Du Bois was at all times writing the story of his people—all those people belonging to the "race" or "nation" he grouped under the amorphous category of "Negro." Had he himself never contended that he was writing not just his own life but the "autobiography of a race," the fact would have been nonetheless evident as early as *The Souls of Black Folk*, which preceded the *Autobiography* by sixty years. Not least because he was a man in whom various paradoxes of marginality were combined, he attempted to make his life and his racial advocacy representative of all African Americans, indeed of all Africans in the diaspora. The course of his variegated public life as a historian, a sociologist, a teacher, a cofounder of the National Association for the Advancement of Colored People (NAACP), a magazine editor, a novelist, a governmental envoy, a Pan-Africanist, a spokesman for socialism, and an opponent of anticommunism underscored Du Bois's claim to incarnate in himself the biography of his race. If the *Autobiography* is in one sense a characteristic Du Boisian performance—grandiose, almost martial in the rectitude and sweep of its judgments—the subordination of race as the defining category of Du Bois's argumentation marks a divergence, not unprecedented but nonetheless abrupt, from the evident motives of his theory of himself, of Africans in the diaspora, and of the global economic structure from his nineteenth-century writings on.

Race is a concept of great ambiguity and power in Du Bois's thought—the power, one could say, deriving precisely from the ambiguity. Both are at their highest pitch in his most complete and theoretically sophisticated autobiography, *Dusk of Dawn*, published in 1940. Although Du Bois at this time was enamoured of the Russian Revolution, a view dating from his initial trip to the Soviet Union in 1926, and of Marxist doctrine, up to that point most clearly articulated in his massive 1935 study *Black Reconstruction in America*, he could nonetheless forthrightly proclaim: "I was not and am not a communist. I do not believe in the dogma of inevitable revolution in order to right economic wrong" (Du Bois, *Dusk*, 302). In *Dusk of Dawn* race, not class, remains the driving force in Du Bois's theory of world colonialism, but not because race itself functions for him in any commonplace or predictable way. It is already apparent, for instance, that the first-person presence guiding the drama of *The Souls of Black Folk* and *Darkwater*, however chaotic is the generic identity of those cases, has been partially overtaken by conceptualized ideological forces such as "science," "empire," "propaganda," and the "colored world." To be sure, *Dusk of Dawn* re-

mains organized, in both its autobiographical narrative line and its dia-
chronic argument for the continuity of African culture, according to an
abiding racialist substratum, but the close relationship between "race"
and the speaking "I" of Du Bois has clearly begun to decay.

What is one to make, for instance, of the volume's enigmatic subti-
tle: *An Essay Toward the Autobiography of a Race Concept?* This strange
phrase is, in fact, a fit summary of the wealth of Du Bois's thinking
and writing over the half century preceding World War II. A passage
deeper in the text demonstrates why. Following a series of chapters
devoted to theories of race and racial superiority, the history of colonialism, and the potential economic and cultural benefits of African
American self-segregation in the face of the realities of Jim Crow, Du
Bois writes:

> My discussions of the concept of race, and of the white and colored
> worlds, are to be regarded as digressions from the history of my life; rather
> my autobiography is a digressive illustration and exemplification of what
> race has meant in the world of the nineteenth and twentieth centuries. It
> is for this reason that I have named and tried to make this book an autobi-
> ography of race rather than merely a personal reminiscence, with the idea
> that [the] peculiar racial situation and problems could best be explained in
> the life history of one who has lived them. My living gains its importance
> from the problems and not the problems from me. (Du Bois, *Dusk*, 221)

Here the life lived and the voice speaking in the autobiographical
soliloquy are subordinated not to some hypothesized redemptive
power of the state, as in the *Autobiography*, but to the commanding
figure that Du Bois said time and again governed the history of the
twentieth century and inscribed into a well-known aphorism, "the
problem of the twentieth century is the problem of the color line,"
which first achieved prominence in *The Souls of Black Folk* in 1903. Du
Bois had already employed the figure in "The Present Outlook for the
Dark Races of Mankind" (1900), where he directed his audience at the
third annual meeting of the American Negro Academy to recognize
that "the color line belts the world and that the social problem of the
twentieth century is to be the relation of the civilized world to the
darker races of mankind" (Du Bois, *Reader*, 48). He would repeat it
again in "Worlds of Color," an essay on colonialism first published in
Foreign Affairs in 1925 and reprinted the same year in Alain Locke's
famous anthology *The New Negro;* in *Black Folk Then and Now* (1939), a
Marxist updating of his landmark 1915 study *The Negro*, his reconceptu-
alization of the color line as a vertical rather than horizontal marking
would be complete: "The proletariat of the world consists . . . overwhelmingly of the dark workers of Asia, Africa, the islands of the sea,
and South and Central America. These are the ones who support a
superstructure of wealth, luxury, and extravagance. . . . The problem

of the twentieth century is the problem of the color line" (Du Bois, *Black Folk*, 283). Less a boundary or legal barrier in Du Bois's mind than a figure with temporal and geographical dimensionality, a figure that segregates and grounds at the same time, the color line at length became a means to account for the unorthodox character of his autobiography in the preface to *Dusk of Dawn:* "My life [has] had its significance and its only deep significance because it was part of a Problem; but that problem was, as I continue to think, the central problem of the greatest of the world's democracies and so the Problem of the future world" (Du Bois, *Dusk*, vii–viii).

With the requisite appearance of self-abnegation, a rhetorical strategy at which the stubborn and rather egotistical Du Bois was adept, he organizes a grand theory of modern history around the experiences of his own life. Yet there is nothing at all false about this claim. To understand the various meanings that the "autobiography of race" held for Du Bois is to understand who he is and why he is a central figure in American literary and intellectual history. In his encompassing forecast of the cross-cultural studies of literature and historical events that would become commonplace by the end of the twentieth century, Du Bois himself is a central figure in the black Atlantic diaspora that Paul Gilroy has designated a "counterculture of modernity" (Gilroy, 34–40), and his exceptional range of writing summarizes the modern exile of African Americans, at once figurative and historically actual, in which the legacy of slavery and reiterated migrations from bondage to freedom form the subtance of a nation's story.

From the very beginning of his public life Du Bois modeled himself on powerful public figures, at once to imitate their personal strength (and not a little of their glory) and to find in them a vehicle for his own racial leadership. His first exemplar was the German chancellor Otto von Bismarck, whose leadership he celebrated in his 1888 commencement address at Fisk University: "He had made a nation out of a mass of bickering peoples. He had dominated the whole development with his strength until he crowned an emperor at Versailles. This foreshadowed in my mind the kind of thing that American Negroes must do, marching forth with strength and determination under trained leadership" (Du Bois, *Dusk*, 32). To speak for American blacks required that Du Bois adopt the mantle of no less a figure than Frederick Douglass and compete with powerful men such as Booker T. Washington and Marcus Garvey. And it required that he negotiate a number of clashing positions within a racial community torn apart by prejudice without and bickering within. In finding the voice of his own leadership, Du Bois had to balance his northern birth against his desire to speak also for the black South; his elite intellectual tastes against his commitment to the equal importance of folk art; his immersion in a political tradition of liberal individualism against his evolving belief that socialism promised a more just world; his hope to link African America's liberation to anticolonial movements in Africa against the view of some Africans that he had little to offer them; and his own mixed-race heritage against the suspicions of those American blacks who considered him, by reason of his birth and his privileged education, inherently a traitor to the racial cause. In such a maelstrom of competing interests, all exacerbated by the fact that Du Bois came of age at the height of white America's denial of equality to blacks through segregation and vigilante violence, it is no surprise, perhaps, that he quickly took on something of a prophetic voice and determined to make the narrative of his own life a virtual saga of the march toward freedom. Du Bois's contemporary, the black historian William Ferris, was not far from the mark when he referred to *The Souls of Black Folk* as "the political Bible of the Negro race" and Du Bois himself as "the long-looked-for political Messiah, the Moses that will lead them out of the Egypt of peonage, across the Red Sea of Jim Crow legislation, through the wilderness of disfranchisement and restricted opportunity and into the promised land of liberty of opportunity and equality of rights" (Ferris, I, 274–76). Between Frederick Douglass and Martin Luther King, Jr., no black American was more suited, or more wanted, to lead the Exodus.

Born in Great Barrington, Massachusetts, in 1868, the year the Fourteenth Amendment to the Constitution was adopted, Du Bois spent his life attempting to make the equal protection clause of the amendment a reality for black Americans. He grew to young adulthood in a context that offered him many more advantages than were available to most African Americans, but also in a familial situation that seems to have left a deep mark on his personality and hence on the shape of his autobiographies. On more than one occasion, whether through confusion or design, Du Bois concealed or to some degree altered the facts of his genealogy. Descended from Dutch and African on his mother's side and from French Huguenot and African on his father's (the Africans were slaves two generations previous in both instances), Du Bois would in *Darkwater* speak of his "flood of Negro blood, a strain of French, a bit of Dutch, but, thank God! no 'Anglo-Saxon' " (Du Bois, *Reader*, 488). But Du Bois's familial origins also marked him in a more direct way. His father, himself illegitimate, committed bigamy when he married Du Bois's mother, and he then disappeared when his son was two years old. The ambiguity of his paternity may have prompted the variable accounts that Du Bois would later give of his genealogy at the same time that it kindled his interest in tracing his roots through the medium of the African song, purportedly passed down from his great-great-grandmother, which he cites in many of his autobiographical works (Davis, 106–14; Lewis, 21–27, 46–47). In a number of later writings featuring African American or anticolonial messiahs, Du Bois would make his heroes' illegitimacy a sign of special power, frequently a mix of Christ's virgin birth and an out-of-wedlock birth resulting from the rape of a woman of color. However much he veiled the facts of his own beginnings, that is to say, Du Bois transformed them into a rhetorical drama in which his own life and messianic leadership were encoded in the lives of his created saviors.

The college years that Du Bois spent at Fisk University in Nashville, Tennessee, from 1885 to 1888 introduced him to life in the Black Belt of the South. Especially his summers teaching in rural Tennessee showed him both a world of desperate poverty and a world of cultural resilience anchored in the history of slavery. Without the experience of an education at a southern black college, it is questionable whether Du Bois would ever have written *The Souls of Black Folk*, his histories of the slave trade and Reconstruction, or any number of works in which the several regions and societies of the black diaspora are linked and grounded in the black South. Without the years at Fisk, that is to say, it is questionable whether Du Bois would have been Du Bois. One has only to think, for instance, of his first trip to Africa in 1923. Du Bois found the Christmas singing he heard in Monrovia to be a transfiguration of mission revival hymns into an "unknown tongue—liquid and sonorous . . . tricked out and expounded with cadence and rhythm," and the music seemed to Du Bois to carry the "same rhythm I heard first in Tennessee forty years ago: the air is raised and carried by men's strong voices, while floating above in obbligato, come the high mellow voices of women—it is the ancient African art of part singing, so curiously and insistently different" (Du Bois, *Reader*, 88–89). His experience in the South grounded Du Bois in a black world that had known slavery and knew well its lingering burden of sharecropping impoverishment and white oppression on a scale unlike that in other parts of the nation, but that also embodied a racial heritage of African American culture—ancestral beliefs, songs, stories, art forms, kinship relations—unique among blacks in America. Without his time in the South, Du Bois might not have found the common thread in his historical scholarship, his political activism, and his cultivation of a nationalism that sought to unite Africans in the Atlantic diaspora.

Du Bois took a second undergraduate degree at Harvard in 1890 and in 1895 became the first African American to earn a doctoral degree there, writing a quickly published thesis entitled *The Suppression of the African Slave Trade to the United States of America, 1638–1870* (1896), which remained a standard work in the field for many decades. Before completing his work at Harvard, Du Bois studied for two years at the University of Berlin, where he absorbed a good deal of the prevailing nineteenth-century theories of racial destiny and historical progress. In his Harvard graduate training under such men as William James, George Santayana, and Nathaniel Shaler, Du Bois derived his views of the historical basis of social analysis and the psychological complexities of identity; at Berlin he learned from Gustav Schmoller how political economies might determine social structure and from Henrich von

Treitschke, despite his overt racism, how national histories might be understood to represent the evolutionary progress of racial groups. Readers of Du Bois have located his intellectual roots in the Puritan substructure of American thought, the grand historical tradition derived from Hegel, and the late-nineteenth-century flowering of pragmatism (Lewis, 56–149; Rampersad, 1–67; West, 138–50), No single intellectual tradition explains Du Bois, but all played a part in the unique perspective and searching intensity that he brought to bear on the problem of the color line.

While teaching at the University of Pennsylvania, following an initial year as a classics instructor at the all-black Wilberforce University, Du Bois finished a second study destined to remain a landmark in its field. The first modern work of sociology devoted to an urban black population, *The Philadelphia Negro* (1899) combined scientific, demographic rigor with Du Bois's growing insight into both the overt and the subtle effects of racial discrimination. From 1897 to 1910, Du Bois taught history and economics at Atlanta University, where he edited *The Horizon* from 1907 to 1910 and oversaw a multivolume study of African Americans that was known collectively as the *Atlanta University Studies* and devoted to topics such as the family, religion, crime, health, agriculture, business, and the arts. It was here that he began to promote black higher education as the foundation of racial progress and developed his well-known advocacy of what he called the "Talented Tenth": "developing the Best of this race that they may guide the Mass away from the contamination and death of the Worst, in their own and other races" (Du Bois, "The Talented Tenth," 33). Du Bois left Atlanta in 1910 to become a cofounder of the NAACP and editor of its magazine, *The Crisis*, which grew to have 100,000 subscribers by the end of World War I. A number of the major literary figures of the Harlem Renaissance were promoted in *The Crisis*, and all of Du Bois's significant positions were initially aired in his editorials, essays, and reviews. For twenty-four years, Du Bois's writings in the magazine and elsewhere—combined with his full-length studies in biography, politics, and the arts, his first two novels, and his writings on Africa— made his the leading intellectual voice of black America. His editorial independence made *The Crisis* very successful even as it estranged him from other leaders in the NAACP, who resented his arrogance, his mixing of domestic and international affairs, and his unpredictable ideological reversals.

In addition to modeling himself on representative leaders such as Bismarck or intellectuals such as Goethe, Du Bois clearly gathered intellectual energy by his antagonism to rival black leaders, most notably Booker T. Washington and Marcus Garvey. As Harold Cruse has noted, with rhetorical exaggeration, "out of this amazing historic, triangular feud came everything of intellectual, spiritual, cultural, and political value to the American Negro" (Cruse, 334). Du Bois's battle against Washington was predicated on his antagonism toward Washington's accommodation to white racism in a notorious speech given at the Atlanta States Cotton and Industrial Exposition in 1895—widely known as Washington's "Atlanta Compromise" for its willingness to sacrifice political and educational rights in favor of white paternalism. Combined with his own growing influence, first as one of the conveners in 1905 of the Niagara Movement (an early civil rights organization) and then as a cofounder of the NAACP, Du Bois's attack on Washington in *The Souls of Black Folk* and elsewhere also put him at war with Washington's "Tuskegee Machine," a loose conglomerate of politicians, journalists, and educators dedicated to advancing Washington's programs.

If Du Bois lacked Washington's ability to wear the mask of subservience in order to achieve his greater purposes, he also lacked Marcus Garvey's charisma. As leader of the Universal Negro Improvement Association (UNIA), Garvey, a Jamaican immigrant, exerted great influence over African Americans, especially in Harlem, from 1916 to the early 1920s. Publicized in his newspaper, *Negro World*, Garvey's UNIA set itself against the Communist Party, which disavowed racial separatism in favor of an integrated class struggle, and advanced black political self-determination and the affirmation of African cultural history through an anticolonialist philosophy of "Africa for the Africans." Garvey's promotion of voluntary repatriation to Africa foundered when his steamship company, the Black Star Line, failed and he was convicted of mail fraud and deported to Jamaica after serving two years in prison. Even though their versions of Pan-Africanism were not dissimilar, Garvey's implausible schemes and his intense nationalism—he argued that racial mixing was "race suicide" and went as far as to seek a rapprochement with the Ku Klux Klan—turned Du Bois's initial admiration for him to scorn.

Coincident with his rise as a sociologist, essayist, educator, and creative writer, Du Bois was a leading participant in the Pan-African movement, and his extensive writings about Africa, even though they were based principally on secondary scholarship and marked by romantic preconceptions, are of increasing interest to readers today. He served as secretary of the First Pan-African Congress in 1900 and in 1911 was a key voice in the First Universal Races Congress in London. He attended successive Pan-African conferences in 1919, 1921, and 1923, all of them held in Europe, and in 1924 he traveled to Liberia as a special (and largely ceremonial) envoy of President Coolidge. The Pan-African conferences devoted to the effects of World War I on the European partitioning of Africa produced stirring anticolonial documents calling for political independence and economic self-determination of which Du Bois was a principal author. The 1945 Pan-African Conference, in which his part was principally symbolic, is an index of the changes Du Bois's own thinking had undergone over the decades between the two world wars. Looking forward to the 1955 Afro-Asian Conference in Bandung, Indonesia, often considered the benchmark of anticolonialism, the 1945 conference in Manchester, England, led by the West Indian George Padmore and featuring African representatives such as Jomo Kenyatta and Kwame Nkrumah, adopted a socialist labor and political program and threatened violent overthrow of colonial rule. Taken together, the conferences themselves had few practical results, and even though Du Bois's role in them was less prominent than he often claimed, they were instrumental in his intellectual development. Long interested in discovering an African foundation for black American culture, Du Bois quite early in his career found in Pan-Africanism a vehicle that gave his struggle for African American equality a global dimension.

Quick on the heels of the death of Booker T. Washington in 1915, the onset of World War I thrust Du Bois to center stage as a spokesman for black Americans. In a controversial 1918 *Crisis* editorial, "Close Ranks," he asked African Americans patriotically to put aside racial demands in order to further the military effort. Du Bois was willing to accept segregated armed forces in order to ensure the commissioning of black officers. Even as Du Bois was taken to task by staunch leftists such as Chandler Owen and A. Phillip Randolph for a seeming accommodation to racism, however, his own optimism about this strategy proved short-lived. The riots and oppressive labor measures that greeted returning black veterans prompted some of Du Bois's most bitter words, the best example of which is the 1919 editorial "Returning Soldiers" and its accompanying documents exposing overt racism in the U.S. military command abroad. Du Bois's anger that African American military service and support for the war had not resulted in civil rights or economic advances fixed in his own writings a polemical strain that soon came to full flower in *Darkwater*.

Much as his visit to Africa gave Du Bois experiential as well as ideological grounding for his Pan-Africanism, his trip to the Soviet Union galvanized his long-standing inclination to see the historical situation of American blacks in the context of a global economic structure. His major work of scholarship in the next decade, *Black Reconstruction in America*, with its unusual mix of biblical prose and Marxist analysis, was decades ahead of its time in offering a sweeping revisionist interpretation of the role of blacks in the Civil War and Reconstruction, and of the national economic interests served by sectional reunion at the expense of civil rights. Against the grain of early-twentieth-century views of Reconstruction—namely, that by promoting black political and economic rights too quickly it had led to disaster—Du Bois had advanced his thesis in "Reconstruction and Its Benefits," a 1910 address before the American Historical Association that was so heterodox that it went virtually unnoticed (Lewis, 383–85). Even in its grand form as *Black Reconstruction*, Du Bois's interpretation would not begin to find sympathy among professional historians for another generation. His claim that southern slaves were something like an organized proletariat whose "general strike" initiated a war against the capitalist system of slavery (an idea derived from the theories of Georges Sorel) is highly debatable. But his well-researched account of the failure of Reconstruction, as well as his evisceration of the racist underpinnings of the views held by the day's leading historians, such as William A. Dunning and James F. Rhodes, charted the way for the massive reinterpretation of Reconstruction undertaken by scholars years later, and the volume remains a centerpiece of what David Blight has called Du Bois's "struggle for American historical memory" (Blight, 45–71). By the 1930s Du Bois had become skeptical enough of his own integrationist philosophy that he wrote a number of essays advocating separate education for African Americans and black development of self-segregated economic and social structures—a "nation within a nation," as he called it. At this point Du Bois remained openly critical of the Communist Party (and contemptuous of the International's notion that a separate African American state might be created in the Black Belt of the South), rightly contending that its appeal to blacks was divisive and exploitive, but his views constituted a clear dissent from the philosophy of the NAACP. Du Bois felt that his separatist programs were not a capitulation to racism but rather a stage in African American development that would ultimately lead to equality.

After his break with the NAACP Du Bois returned to teach again at Atlanta University, where he founded the respected journal *Phylon* in 1940. In 1944, the seventy-six-year-old Du Bois once more joined the NAACP, this time in a research rather than an editorial position, but almost immediately found himself at odds with its director, Walter White. Although he contributed some important essays and worked on behalf of the NAACP in the early years of the United Nations, Du Bois was dismissed from his position in 1948. From the 1930s on, Du Bois's Marxism had become more and more pronounced. His participation in the Cultural and Scientific Conference for World Peace in 1949 and his work on behalf of the Stockholm Appeal, a petition to ban atomic weapons, were activities deemed by the U.S. government to be against national interests in the cold war. Refusing to comply with a governmental demand that they register as agents of a foreign principal—namely, the Soviet Union—Du Bois and others faced a criminal indictment in 1951. Although the charges were dismissed, the traumatic event, recounted in his short work *In Battle for Peace* (1952), persuaded the elderly Du Bois that his long struggle for justice in the United States may have come to nothing. Already openly sympathetic to the Soviet Union and Communist China, where he soon traveled and met on friendly terms with Mao Tse-tung, Du Bois at last joined the Communist Party in 1961. In the same year, at the age of ninety-three, Du Bois moved to the recently independent Ghana, which he had visited at the invitation of its leader, Kwame Nkrumah, the year before, ostensibly to oversee a long-delayed scholarly project entitled *Encyclopedia Africana*. There he died in 1963, the day before the March on Washington long advocated by A. Philip Randolph and finally led by Martin Luther King, Jr.

Ernest Hemingway once remarked that all modern American literature comes from Mark Twain's *Adventures of Huckleberry Finn*. Just as plausibly, one could claim that modern African American literature and intellectual history descend from *The Souls of Black Folk*. Central themes and episodes of Du Bois's book are echoed in James Weldon Johnson's *Autobiography of an Ex-Coloured Man* (1912), Jean Toomer's *Cane* (1923), Richard Wright's *Black Boy* (1945), J. Saunders Redding's *Stranger and Alone* (1950), Ralph Ellison's *Invisible Man* (1952), and Alice Walker's *Meridian* (1976), to name only a few works. Johnson remarked that the book "had a greater effect upon and within the Negro race in America than any other single book published in this country since *Uncle Tom's Cabin*," and Claude McKay reported that it "shook me like an earthquake. Dr. Du Bois stands on a pedestal illuminated in my mind. And the light that shines there comes from my first reading of *The Souls of Black Folk*." In 1956, Langston Hughes wrote to Du Bois: "I have just read again your *The Souls of Black Folk*—for perhaps the tenth time—the first time having been some forty years ago when I was a child in Kansas. Its beauty and power are as moving and as meaningful as ever" (Du Bois, *Correspondence*, 3: 401; Johnson, 203; McKay, 110). More recently, Gerald Early has gathered twenty contemporary African American responses to the legacy of *The Souls of Black Folk* in a volume entitled *Lure and Loathing: Essays on Race, Identity, and the Ambivalence of Assimilation* (1993). Even though its roots lie in sources as diverse as Phillis Wheatley, Ralph Waldo Emerson, and William James, Du Bois's famous theory of "double consciousness" became a defining trope of multicultural study. One finds it adopted explicitly, for instance, in Richard Wright's remarks at the 1956 Congress of Negro Writers and Artists in Paris when he spoke of the "contradiction of being both Western and a man of color" (Legum, 99), and one hears its themes echoed as well in works springing from other traditions such as Vine Deloria, Jr.'s, *Custer Died for Your Sins* (1969) or Gloria Anzaldúa's *Borderlands/La Frontera: The New Mestiza* (1987). Like Twain and his great book, Du Bois and his are touchstones of such importance that American writing is difficult to imagine in their absence.

To a group of previously published and then revised essays on various aspects of black life from slavery through the post-Reconstruction era, Du Bois added several new chapters on life "within the veil" of African America when he came to compose *The Souls of Black Folk*. The resulting volume is a peculiar generic mix whose unity of argument is sometimes as perplexing as it is powerful. A master-work of many dimensions—a first-rate history of post–Civil War race relations in the South; a pathbreaking essay in sociological and economic analysis; a brief for black education; and a study in comparative European American and African American cultures—*The Souls of Black Folk* is the preeminent modern text of African American cultural consciousness. In his commentary on the transforming power of black music, from slave culture through post-Reconstruction modernity, Du Bois discovered a deep spiritual foundation for his social and economic analysis, one that would for many years to come make his work unique in its blending of poetics and politics—what he later argued was the necessary union of art and propaganda. As in *Darkwater*, Du Bois includes coherent fragments of autobiography in *The Souls of Black Folk*; but here as elsewhere in his major writings, the life is primarily an occasion for theorizing about the relationship between biography and culture, for making the representative experience a means to recover a people's spiritual roots and erect the temple of their nationhood.

The educated Du Bois sought an ideal of culture beyond the color line where, as a famous passage puts it, "wed with Truth," he could "dwell above the Veil . . . sit with Shakespeare, move arm in arm with Balzac and Dumas, and summon Aristotle and Aurelius, all to meet him "graciously with no scorn or condescension" (Du Bois, *Reader*, 156–57). In placing the spirituals at the center of *The Souls of Black Folk*, however, he did not contradict this vision but instead brought it to life. The unreconciled tension between the African American songs and the epigraphic texts from the Western tradition illustrate the trap of divided identity in which Du Bois himself was caught: How could he balance the cultivation of white, European cultural forms against the preserved beliefs and cultural patterns of black America that had originated in slavery? Interwoven with his argument against Booker T. Washington, his tribute to Alexander Crummel, his moving story of his infant son's death, and his multifaceted recitation of the transition in African American life from slavery to Reconstruction to the modern age of segregation, the black spirituals anchored the written saga of *The Souls of Black Folk* in the true history of the African diaspora even as they illuminated its resistance to full recovery.

In a brief commentary published a year after *The Souls of Black Folk*, Du Bois characterized the book's style as "tropical—African," and he explained the "intimate tone of self-revelation" that runs throughout the book, in contrast to a more traditional impersonality and judiciousness, as a function of the fact that "the blood of my fathers spoke through me and cast off the English restraint of my training and surroundings" (Du Bois, *Reader*, 305). Combined with his assertion that even as a child he knew that these "weird old songs in which the soul of the black slave spoke to men" were something personal, something he recognized as being "of me and mine," such a claim suggests that one of the first things Du Bois imbibed from the sorrow songs was

15

their combined historical and prophetic structure (Du Bois, *Reader*, 231). In the theoretical use to which he put the enigmatic bars of music, and in tying himself to the bardic role that he found to have descended from the African priest to the African American preacher, Du Bois infused his volume's rich experiment in autobiography, political history, and social essay with a power comparable to that of the African *griots*, the communal genealogists and historians who sang of their people's historical events, and of their kings and rulers, in a repertoire of song that was constantly subject to innovation. Like the anonymous collective composers of the slave spirituals in James Weldon Johnson's famous poem "O Black and Unknown Bards" (1908) or the archetype of the bardic preacher, "Singing Johnson," whose talents Johnson described first in fictional form in *The Autobiography of an Ex-Coloured Man* and then in biographical form in *The Book of American Negro Spirituals* (1925), Du Bois moved in the direction of a lived scriptural story that had sources in the African chants of tribal law, historical narrative, and folk story.

What might be called the book's crisis point of cultural recovery appears in Du Bois's reproduction of the African song first sung in his family, he says, by his grandfather's grandmother, who was stolen from Africa by a Dutch trader. Her song ("Do bana coba gene me, gene me . . .") had traveled down the generations for 200 years, "and we sing it to our children, knowing as little as our fathers what its words may mean, but knowing well the meaning of its music" (Du Bois, *Reader*, 233). The story of his great-great-grandmother reappears throughout Du Bois's autobiographical writings, its telling mutable and its accuracy questionable. Especially in *The Souls of Black Folk*, though, it grounds Du Bois's bardic history of black American life in a symbolic, if not a demonstrably actual, African world—a world of hypothesized ancestral memory reached, in Du Bois's case, by a reenacted typological escape from what he calls the "Egypt of the Confederacy" (Du Bois, *Reader*, 165). Because it cannot be translated, the African song evokes the coded language of the slave spirituals, thus joining Du Bois's work as a cultural critic to the anonymous lives of those unknown bards and common folk from whose toil have sprung the present generations and the beginnings of African American culture. Founding both modern African American literature and Du Bois's own writing career, *The Souls of Black Folk* established the coherence of African American culture as a set of values and expressions that were not annihilated by slavery but nurtured by its "voice of exile" (Du Bois, *Reader*, 233).

Although Du Bois espoused a moderate form of Afrocentrism at times placed in the service of a racial polemic, his views of Africa were the complicated product of the time in which he wrote. Africa was at once a source of genealogical identity, a complex of potential nation states struggling for liberation from colonial rule, and a puzzling semiotic system that stretched beyond continental boundaries to define blackness throughout the New World. Du Bois was frequently romantic or semi-mystical in his pronouncements about Africa and about black Americans' relationship to Africa, and it may be noted that in *The World and Africa* (1946), his last extended work on Africa, he entitled a section devoted to the premodern history of West Africa "Atlantis," the mythic lost continent of antiquity. At least one prominent scholar has concluded that because of his abiding romanticism, Du Bois missed a chance to give Pan-Africanism a rational, scholarly basis (Geiss, 259–61), but others have been quick to admire Du Bois's fundamental role in helping to establish Africa and the African diaspora as fields of study grounded in careful research and critical study. As much as he himself tended to idealize a lost African past or an anticipated future—in both instances he envisioned the achievement of a utopian social-ism—he would have been embarrassed by the essentialist, and some-times patently racist, claims of some of the more radical versions of late-twentieth-century Afrocentrism. Even though his extended writ-ings about Africa—as distinct from his many editorials and short essays on topical events—were largely based on the growing secondary litera-ture about the continent that had been produced by both black and white historians since the late nineteenth century, Du Bois wished his polemical views to be anchored in fact. Important as it may have been as an act of political protest, moreover, Du Bois's self-exile to Ghana in his last years is hard to construe either as evidence that he had reached the culmination of a lifelong pursuit of his true African identity or, what is even less likely, as an endorsement of repatriation. Except that he hated his nation's cold war ideology enough to renounce his citizen-ship and endorse communist dictatorships, Du Bois never ceased to be an *American* African.

From the outset, Du Bois's famous conception of double conscious-ness opened him to accusations of Eurocentrism and dictated a neces-sary ambivalence in his views of Africa. It also made him acutely aware of the democratic implications of race theory. Unable to find a sound basis for a scientific theory of race but reluctant to give up a critical feature of his rhetorical argument for racial unity, Du Bois returned frequently to quasi-mystical notions such as "genius" and "common memory." Yet the source or location of such phenomena remained maddeningly indefinite. "Race" and "Africa" were no more synony-mous for Du Bois than were "race" and "nation." Nevertheless, the two pairs of terms were not clearly separable. In his sociological writ-ing, even as early as *The Philadelphia Negro*, economic and environmen-tal factors played a large role in Du Bois's view of the constructedness of race—that is, his belief that prejudice against blacks, in addition to shaping opportunity and behavior, inevitably participates in defining racial identity. By the 1930s such extrinsic factors become more domi-nant in all of Du Bois's writings, but in his cultural and historical works, at least through *Darkwater* and *The Gift of Black Folk* (1924), he clung to distinct modes of racialism.

The fundamental ambiguity in Du Bois's view of race appears first in "The Conservation of the Races," a paper presented to the American Negro Academy, which Du Bois founded with Alexander Crummell, an African American Episcopalian missionary who returned to the United States after many years of service in Africa. Defining "race" and "nation" as virtually identical, Du Bois still found himself unable to discard all traces of race as a phenomenon of color with biological roots. Race here comprises a "vast family of human beings" infused with a common purpose or idea—a world-spirit, or *volksgeist*, to cite the German notion that Du Bois had absorbed during his study abroad. In maintaining that black Americans are to take their "just place in the van of Pan-Negroism," Du Bois established a familial link to Africa that gave them a role in the unfolding, progressive drama of history where, in Hegelian fashion, one might see manifest "the race idea, the race spirit, the race ideal" (Du Bois, *Reader*, 40–43). What mattered more than a stable definition of race was the language with which Du Bois might articulate the fact that "Negro" meant nothing that could be measured, and hence subjected to pseudoscientific denigration, but nevertheless described a clearly definable historical experience. By the time he published *The Negro* in 1915, Du Bois said forthrightly that races were "continually changing and developing, amalgamating and differentiating." As a continent but also as a geosocial entity that had produced the "family" to which Du Bois belonged, Africa is therefore "the Land of the Blacks," the homeland of "the darker part of the human family, which is separated from the rest of mankind by no absolute physical line, but which nevertheless forms, as a mass, a social group distinct in history, appearance, and to some extent in spiritual gift" (Du Bois, *Reader*, 629, 631). As he himself came closer and closer to reading race as an environmental index of civilization or culture, he increasingly transfigured his ideas of "soul" and "nation" into expressions of labor, artisanship, geography, or sociopolitical life, allowing them to acquire a more vital Pan-African shape even as they were modified to fit Du Bois's commitment to American pluralism.

Without in any way diminishing the exceptional history of Africans in America, brought in chains and singled out for harsh servitude, Du Bois wished to place black Americans on the same cultural plane with other immigrant groups. If he was not quite ready to follow William Ferris in proclaiming a new race of "Negrosaxons" (Ferris, I, 296–311), his views were not far from those of Randolph Bourne, a leading proponent of pluralism, who eschewed Anglo-Saxon dominance and argued that "America is coming to be, not a nationality, but a transnationality, weaving back and forth, with the other lands, of many threads of all sizes and colors" (Bourne, 297). In *The Gift of Black Folk: The Negroes in the Making of America*, a historical survey of African

Americans throughout American history, with particular emphasis on literature and the arts, Du Bois kept intact some of his racialist premises (arguing, for instance, that "the peculiar spiritual quality which the Negro has injected in[to] American life and civilization . . . [is] a sensuous, tropical love of life, in vivid contrast to the cool and cautious New England reason"), but he intended most of all to measure the African's contribution to a pluralist mosaic. "America is conglomerate," not English or even European, he writes in a preface that echoes Bourne on several fronts; the nation represents "a coming together of the peoples of the world." In publishing his volume in a Knights of Columbus–sponsored "Racial Contribution Series" devoted to bolstering "national solidarity," Du Bois put African exclusion and race prejudice in the United States on a par with antagonism toward Irish Catholics, Jews, and other immigrant minorities (Du Bois, *Gift*, 320, i–ii, 1).

The spectrum of opinion in which Du Bois wrote is best understood, that is, not as African American alone but as embracing both advertisements for assimilation such as Mary Antin's *The Promised Land* (1912) and socialist critiques such as Carlos Bulosan's *America Is in the Heart* (1946). Du Bois was well aware that "Americanization" could easily become a code word for race hate and race crimes, and at no moment did he advocate mere capitulation to the dominant culture. But neither, as he wrote in a famous passage in *The Souls of Black Folk*, would he renounce Shakespeare and Goethe as models or "bleach" his Africanity in a flood of European American culture (Du Bois, *Reader*, 102). Steering a course between extremes, Du Bois formulated racial identity as a necessary set of paradoxes, and the shared "kingdom of culture" to which he aspired anticipated nothing so much as Leopold Senghor's "civilization of the universal," a theory wherein race consciousness—*negritude*, in Senghor's case—arises not from attachment to color as such but instead from an awareness and a defense of those black cultural values that contribute to the "dynamic symbiosis" of all human civilization (Senghor, 96–98).

Like Emerson before him, Du Bois was also fascinated by the personal force and the epochal meaning of "representative men." Bismarck, Goethe, Toussaint L'Ouverture, Abraham Lincoln, and even Jefferson Davis elicited Du Bois's ecumenical admiration for their capacity to express the defining beliefs of the cultures for which they stood. As the president of the Confederacy, Jefferson Davis in particular might seem a counterintuitive choice for Du Bois's study. But just as European colonialist writers have provided important points of departure for critiques by modern Africans—Joseph Conrad for Chinua Achebe or Karen Blixen (Isak Dineson) for Ngugi wa Thiong'o (Achebe, 1–20; Ngugi, 132–35)—Jefferson Davis was a figure in whom Du Bois might reveal the "moral obtuseness and refined brutality" of the South. At the same time, however, Davis, like Bismarck in Du

Bois's eyes, was the incarnation of his region's "stalwart manhood and heroic character" (Du Bois, *Reader*, 244). As a Teutonic hero, Davis certainly offered nothing to African Americans; but as the moral and political embodiment of his people, he offered intriguing possibilities to the young Du Bois.

By Du Bois's estimation, such figures were exponents of racial spirit, bridging the distance between the timeless mystique of racialism and pragmatic action within the real time of history. "We see the Pharaohs, Caesars, Toussaints, and Napoleons of history," he writes, "and forget the vast races of which they were but epitomized expressions" (Du Bois, *Reader*, 40). This revealing passage moves the question of race in nationalist directions, forecasts Du Bois's notion of the Talented Tenth who will lead the race forward, and as a result presages his own messianic conception of himself. To be the "epitomized expression" of African Americans would not override, but would rather contain in vital tension, the conflicts of double consciousness. As the epitome of his race, Du Bois set himself the formidable task of representing not just Africans in America but, by implication, the whole "vast family" of Africa—what Marcus Garvey would later appropriately refer to as "scattered Ethiopia"—as though it were an integral part of his own self.

Du Bois's late-nineteenth-century education at Fisk, Harvard, and Berlin would have taught him almost nothing about Africa, which remained for the vast majority of Europeans and Americans (including most black Americans) the "dark continent," a place of superstition and savagery (McCarthy, 59–119). But well before he integrated his extensive independent study into a series of books and essays on the African diaspora, Du Bois included African history and culture in his analysis of race. In his very first position as a young writer, from 1883 to 1885, Du Bois contributed local Massachusetts news to Thomas Fortune's *New York Globe*, a newspaper that printed much material on Africa and editorial commentary on early Pan-Africanism. As *The Souls of Black Folk* demonstrated, African retentions like those Du Bois found in the African American church and spirituals were as much a theoretical matrix that could be extended to other disciplines as a set of practices that had left their mark on post–Civil War black culture. The sociological studies published during his early years at Atlanta University showed Du Bois's growing perception of the links between Africa and black American culture, while in the *Horizon*, which he edited from 1907 until 1910, when he joined the NAACP and launched *The Crisis*, Du Bois printed both brief accounts of contemporary African events and early versions of some of the two-pronged lyric assaults on racism and colonialism that would later be folded into *Darkwater*.

The advent of Africa as a historical subject coincided both with the imperial scramble by European colonial powers to divide the spoils of Africa and with the rise of segregation in the United States. In his own work, Du Bois drew in proportionate measure from the available writings by white explorers, colonial administrators, and historians such as Harry H. Johnston, as well as from African American scholarship such as George Washington Williams's *History of the Negro Race in America* (1883), William T. Alexander's *History of the Colored Race in America* (1887), Pauline Hopkins's *Primer of Facts Pertaining to the Early Greatness of the African Race* (1905), and William Ferris's *The African Abroad* (1913). Among black Americans in particular, the research sparked by the founding of the Negro Society for Historical Research by John E. Bruce and Arthur Schomburg in 1911, and the Association for the Study of Negro Life and History by Carter Woodson in 1915, capped a remarkable revitalization of African American intellectual history in which Du Bois himself was centrally involved. In the decade before World War I, Du Bois immersed himself in the study of Africa and produced two interlocked works—*The Negro*, one of the most important surveys of African (and African American) history in the early twentieth century, and "The African Roots of the War," a classic anticolonial essay first printed in the *Atlantic Monthly* in 1915 and later incorporated into *Darkwater*. Like Du Bois's subsequent volumes that revised its central materials, *The Gift of Black Folk* and *Black Folk Then and Now*, *The Negro* combined history, ethnology, and cultural study, tracing a transgeographical Negro history from ancient Africa through contemporary black worlds of the Caribbean and the United States.

Revisionist writing about Africa and Africans in the diaspora at the turn of the century had to respond to several key elements of racist historiography. *The Negro* was among a number of books that countered the prevailing view that whatever greatness had been achieved in African civilization had come from outside influences or the infusion of non-Negro blood. Arguments about the importance of black African civilizations dated in the United States from the first colonizationist movement in the early nineteenth century, and during the antebellum era Henry Highland Garnet, James W. C. Pennington, Frederick Douglass, and Martin Delany, among others, appealed to the writings of Homer, Herodotus, and other classical writers to argue that Egypt and Ethiopia had been great and progressive black civilizations. In the age of Jim Crow, however, with violence against African Americans accelerating, with many African Americans themselves shunning reminders of the past as counterproductive to racial progress, and with popular and high culture alike infused with racist characterizations of blacks, the need to authenticate Africa as part of world civilization, perhaps its cradle, was as compelling as the task was hard. *The Negro* appeared at the high noon of racialist theory and white supremacy, when the advocacy of Teutonic, Aryan, and Anglo-Saxon superiority heralded in such works as Madison Grant's *The Passing of the Great Race* (1916) and Lothrop Stoddard's *The Rising Tide of Color* (1920) combined romantic historicism with pseudoscientific quantification to eliminate the "darker races" from the scheme of civilization (Gossett, 84–122; Higham, 131–59; Moses, 251–71). The restoration to prominence of African civilizations was a necessary counter to the stereotypes of plantation mythology, which buttressed sociological predictions that African Americans, if uncontrolled by slavery or rigid segregation, would regress to savagery, and to ethnological doubts about the value or even the existence of African retentions. Serious historians depicted slavery as a benign, if not beneficent, institution that had rescued blacks from primitive, non-Christian life in Africa, and most scholars agreed with the southern historian U. B. Phillips's statement that black Americans were "as completely broken from their tribal stems as if they had been brought from the planet Mars" (Phillips, 160). Even influential black leaders such as Booker T. Washington and Henry Turner maintained that slavery might be seen as a providential step in the regeneration of Africans and Africa. Whether Washington actually held such a view or was slyly accommodating his argument to the day's pervasive neo-Confederate predilections, a large number of African Americans themselves lacked any pride in the legacy of slave culture and renounced all things African. Within this historical moment, *The Negro* attempted to raise African Americans from a provincial American minority context and make them exponents of opposition to international racial imperialism (Toll, 170).

The study of black history undertaken by Du Bois and others promised to recover latent African sources of spiritual belief, restore a source of communal pride at a moment when African American rights were under the greatest assault since slavery, and create a reservoir of ideas to spur new conceptualizations of race consciousness. Du Bois's main contribution lay not in the originality of his scholarship but rather in the argument, first advanced in *The Negro* and elaborated more impressively in his essays and creative work, that Africa was literally at the center of the triumph of a modern industrial economy. World War I, as noted above, brought Du Bois's thought to a new and more far-reaching maturity, providing a bridge between his involvement in organizing and writing declarations of African rights for the Pan-African Conferences, and his stewardship of the NAACP between 1910 and 1934, where he focused the greatest part of his energy on racial injustice within the United States. His outrage that patriotic service in the military did not bring racial justice for blacks in America was matched by his disappointment that the League of Nations did not adequately address the problem of colonial rule. Both at home and abroad, one might say, the war was at the historical center of Du Bois's conception of Pan-Africanism, or Ethiopianism, for it crystallized his apprehension of the parallels between the struggle for racial equality in America and anticolonial independence movements in Africa.

Both a philosophy with diverse intellectual roots in nineteenth-century black history and a loose political movement that served to unite scattered cultures of resistance in the African diaspora, Ethiopianism is a concept that illuminates a good deal of Du Bois's writing, even though he himself seldom referred directly to its principal advocates or ideas. Based on varying interpretations of Psalms 68: 31, "Princes shall come out of Egypt, [and] Ethiopia shall soon stretch forth her hands to God," Ethiopianism portrayed colonized Africa or enslaved Africans in the diaspora as prepared for providential delivery from bondage. In a more radical interpretation the scripture could be seen to prophesy a black millennium, a violent seizure of freedom through acts of revolt sanctioned by God and led, literally or figuratively, by an anticolonial redeemer from within Africa or, in some interpretations, from America. As forerunners to more overtly political organizations such as the South African Native Congress, which was founded in 1912 and became the African National Congress in the 1920s, the Ethiopian separatist churches were thus credibly feared to form an underground movement whose purpose was to overthrow colonial rule.

Although Ethiopianism had specific sources in anticolonial African church movements with which Du Bois was familiar, and although it can be traced to American black nationalists such as Robert Alexander Young, who had entitled his 1829 jeremiad against slavery and the denial of black rights "The Ethiopian Manifesto," two near contemporaries of the young Du Bois, Edward Blyden and Henry Turner, are of special note in his intellectual genealogy. For the West Indian theorist Blyden, Ethiopian thought was a vehicle for the reversal of Western thought and the cultivation of what he called "African Personality," a phrase that later became important to the proponents of *negritude*. In "Ethiopia Stretching Out Her Hands Unto God; or, Africa's Service to the World," a discourse first delivered in the United States in 1880, Blyden interpreted the scripture in the first instance to refer to Africa's piety, kindness, and fidelity, and to its people's vast economic service to the world, like that of the Hebrews, whom he considered a model for nationhood that he was to explore further in his Zionist volume *The Jewish Question* (1898). Africa therefore acted as a "spiritual conservatory" against the materialism of the civilized world and was the inheritance of Africans throughout the diaspora. In America, Blyden argued, the black man is forced to "surrender his race integrity," whereas in Africa "his wings develop, and he soars into an atmosphere of exhaustless truth for him" (Blyden, 130–49).

For Blyden African Personality entailed a condemnation of both biological and cultural absorption of blacks by the dominant white race. And it was just this strain in Blyden's thought that the West African writer and political theorist J. E. Casely Hayford featured in *Ethiopia Unbound* (1911) when he set Blyden's Africanist ideas against what he said was the assimilationist American mentality of Du Bois. "The African in America is in a worse plight than the Hebrew in Egypt," wrote

Casely Hayford. "The one preserved his language, his manners and customs, his religion and household gods; the other has committed national suicide, and at present it seems as if the dry bones of the vision have no life in them" (Casely Hayford, 172–73). Committed throughout his life to the ideals of integration and pluralism, Du Bois rejected Blyden's essentialism. But his conception of black "soul" nonetheless derived something from Blyden's "Personality," just as Du Bois's attempts to revitalize black America's sense of its African past appears to have borrowed something from Casely Hayford (not least, perhaps, the unorthodox generic miscellany of *Darkwater*). It is also likely that Du Bois owed something to the African American minister Henry Turner, whose most important address, entitled "The American Negro and His Fatherland," embraced a nationalist doctrine of "Africa for the Africans" (Turner, 195–98). Anticipating by two decades Marcus Garvey's call for black repatriation to Africa and his general theory of "African Fundamentalism," Turner's address is one of many texts of the period that underline the relationship between Jewish Zionism and what was often referred to as "Black Zionism" or "African Zionism," a parallel that was especially important in the evolution of Du Bois's thought.

Debates among African Americans about Africa as the rightful home of those blacks descended from slavery paralleled contemporary arguments among American Jews about whether America or Palestine should be the new Zion of Slavic and European immigrants. Extending a central analogy of antislavery rhetoric—the slaves' delivery from pharaonic bondage—Du Bois would write in 1919, for example, that "the African movement means to us what the Zionist movement must mean to the Jews, the centralization of the race effort and the recognition of a racial fount" (Du Bois, *Reader*, 639). Whereas Turner's and Garvey's Zionism meant a return to the homeland, at least in principle, Du Bois envisioned a spiritual rather than a geographical domain—a "nation" that consisted primarily of a transhistorical consciousness outside of actual land or the literal black body. The figurative "Ethiopia" was for Du Bois an uncolonized territory of the spirit, the black soul that had not been extinguished by slavery or imperialism and that could never be fully assimilated to European American culture, at least so long as racial equality remained unrealized. The younger Du Bois did not escape expressing the commonplace anti-Semitism of his era. When he revised *The Souls of Black Folk* in 1953, however, he eliminated several pointed references to Jews as exploiters of poor blacks in the postwar South; he endorsed the founding of Israel in 1948; and his post–World War II essays (such as "The Negro and the Warsaw Ghetto," written for *Jewish Life* in 1952) reflect a more penetrating consciousness of the array of modern racism. Although the coming enormity of the Holocaust made the parallel nonsense, in *Dusk of Dawn* Du Bois had predicted that the advancement of African American civil rights and economic power could create a backlash: "we may be expelled from the United States as the Jew is being expelled from Germany" (Du Bois, *Dusk*, 306).

In the end the analogy failed, just as Du Bois's attempt to embrace the "colored" or the oppressed races of the world as a single racial collective continually betrayed the most profound misunderstanding. The diverse "worlds of color" had no unity, and Du Bois's repeated attempts to discover one in the multitudinous conflicts of Africa, China, Japan, India, and Latin America often led to implausible contentions—for instance, that Japan's militarist expansionism in the years leading toward World War II was an attempt to rescue Manchuria from the West and save its racial purity. Although such grand theories did not hold up, Du Bois's appeal to the model of Zionism was genuine, and the metaphor of a racial fount captures well his idea of the role played by the diaspora in constructing the double consciousness of Africans in the New World. His black Zionism, moreover, superimposed on the Exodus of post-Emancipation African American history the potential salvation of heroic leadership—namely, his own—in the protean figure of the black messiah. At times a literal Christ and at times more a prophet of the coming millennium, the iconic figure of the messiah in Du Bois's work has always a strong autobiographical component. Especially in the essays and poems that he wrote during and immediately after World War I—a number of which went into *Darkwater* in 1920—he found in the Black Christ a forceful expression of his messianic vision and a means of organizing a Pan-African political aesthetic.

In its radical rejection of the archetype of Negro submissiveness central to plantation mythology, the Black Christ dated at least from Nat Turner, the great cultural counterweight to the mass popularity of Uncle Tom. By the end of the nineteenth century, a number of black historians and ministers began to turn against the consensus reading of Christ as the model for black forebearance in order to promote a more militant resistance to oppression (Fullinwider, 26–46). In this respect, the Black messiah acted as a retort to the cultural revival of the New South, where Confederate heroes were seen as examples of manly Christianity, even figures of the Passion waging a holy war against the "Negro problem." The white supremacist appropriation of messianism reached its apogee in the Christian iconography and violent rituals of the Ku Klux Klan, immortalized in such popular forms as Thomas Dixon's novel *The Clansman* (1905) and D. W. Griffith's film adaptation *The Birth of a Nation* (1915), one part of the NAACP response to which was Du Bois's own 1915 pageant of black history, *The Star of Ethiopia* (Lewis, 509). For Du Bois and other black writers of the early twentieth century, the sacrificial theology of racial violence had to be turned inside out. Like the militant Christ associated with the liberation theology of Latin American and Latino Catholicism—one thinks of the Aztec Christ invoked at the conclusion of Rudolfo Gonzales's epic labor poem *I Am Joaquin* (1967)—Du Bois's Black Christ was an inspiring symbol in the fight against segregation and colonialism. Lynching, poverty, and discrimination were his crucifixion, and resistance, not docility, was the message of his new parables.

The figure of the messianic leader was latent in Du Bois's comments in *The Souls of Black Folk* about the survival of the priest's role in the African American community; it reappeared strongly in his 1909 study of John Brown. Asked to write a biography for the series Beacon Biographies of Eminent Americans—Du Bois was first approached to write on Frederick Douglass, but confusion on the publisher's part had resulted in assignment of the Douglass volume to Booker T. Washington—Du Bois suggested Nat Turner before compromising on John Brown. The step from Turner to Brown is not remarkable, however, for Du Bois located in the white abolitionist the same charismatic leadership that one imagines he would have dramatized in the case of Nat Turner.

In *The Negro* Du Bois would speak of Toussaint L'Ouverture as "the greatest of American Negroes" (Du Bois, *The Negro*, 103), and half a century later he returned to Toussaint's role as the father of black liberation movements in an essay entitled "Africa and the French Revolution" written for *Freedomways* in 1961. In *John Brown* he allies the Haitian Revolution to the American from an alternative perspective. Du Bois had already invoked Brown in his address to the Niagara Movement when it convened at Harper's Ferry in 1906, and in an addendum to the 1957 edition of *John Brown* Du Bois would attempt to claim him as a prophet of Marxist utopianism. Half a century earlier, however, Brown is presented as a Christ-like martyr conceived in the throes of Toussaint's revolt. In the cataclysm envisioned in John Brown's raid, says Du Bois, Toussaint's war brought the revolutionary spirit of the diaspora, the "shudder of Haiti," to the soil of the United States: "The vision of the damned was stirring the western world and stirring black men as well as white. Something was forcing the issue—call it what you will, the Spirit of God or the spell of Africa. It came like some great grinding ground swell,—vast, indefinite, immeasurable but mighty, like the dark low whispering of some infinite disembodied voice—a riddle of the Sphinx (Du Bois, *John Brown*, 93). If Toussaint was to become the base of Pan-African consciousness for later Marxist historians such as C. L. R. James, whose monumental *Black Jacobins* (1938) launched a far-reaching reinterpretation of Caribbean history comparable in its scope to Du Bois's revisionist *Black Reconstruction*, and for *negritude* writers such as Aimé Césaire, who wrote the story of Toussaint the liberator into his surrealist epic *Cahier d'un retour au pays natal* (1939) and argued that "Haiti was the cradle of Negritude" (Césaire, 74), Du Bois made the energizing assertion that Toussaint's spirit had become incarnate in a militant white American abolitionist.

The many strands of Du Bois's anticolonial thinking coalesce in the narrative melange of *Darkwater: Voices from Within the Veil,* a combination of essays, poetry, polemic, and life writing. In its compelling arrangement of texts and arguments in many registers, *Darkwater* is a book that records the reassembling of racial identity "out of the refractions and discontinuities of exile," if one may borrow an apt formulation from an allied context (Said, 361). Once again, as in *The Souls of Black Folk,* building his vision out of the rudiments of his own autobiography, Du Bois now fuses protest against American race riots, lynchings, and economic injustice with anticolonial Pan-African advocacy. The revisions in previously published material in this case serve to foreground Du Bois's messianic identification with the black prophet-savior. Take as an example "The Hands of Ethiopia," a new version of Du Bois's landmark 1915 essay "The African Roots of the War." In its initial version Du Bois anticipated Lenin's *Imperialism, the Highest Stage of Capitalism* (1916) in advancing the dubious argument, derived from J. A. Hobson, that imperial nations realized enormous profits by exporting surplus capital to "backward" countries. The revised essay places less emphasis on economic statistics and Du Bois's forecast of Lenin, and instead advances a philosophy of "Africa for Africans." The concluding paragraph of the essay, identical in both forms, speaks of black Africa as "prostrated, raped, and shamed," and figures her as an impoverished black woman "weeping and waiting, with her sons on her breast" (Du Bois, *Reader,* 520).

What is an incidental element in "The African Roots of the War," however, becomes by the juxtaposition of the essay with Du Bois's poem "The Riddle of the Sphinx" a commanding analogy for the colonial devastation of the "body" of the African continent. In the figure of the raped woman borne back by her multiple attackers who stifle her sighs (an interesting adumbration of Yeats made more pointed by the poem's further allusion to a militant black Christ born in an Easter uprising), Du Bois offers his most significant delineation to date of the soil of colonized Africa as an extension of the sharecropping peonage of Black Belt America. In *Darkwater,* as in allied stories such as "The Gospel According to Mary Brown" (1919) or "The Son of God" (1933) and the novel *Dark Princess* (1928), Du Bois replaced the immaculate conception with sexual violation, not in order blasphemously to revel in it but rather to make illegitimacy the source of the redemption carried in martyrs and messianic leaders. Fusing the two senses of "labor" that his attacks on industrial exploitation and the "damnation of women" had addressed, Du Bois compressed Christmas and Easter into a single conceptual moment. Whereas Marcus Garvey made his nationalism the vehicle for a civil religion based incongruously on capitalism and repatriation to Africa, Du Bois's subversion of Christian typology was meant to forge from personal anxiety about his own quasi-illegitimacy, from autobiographical acts of ancestral recovery, and from political struggle a visionary philosophy of race consciousness. In such saviors born within the veil of American segregation, Du Bois brought forth antislavery, anticolonial equivalents to the revolutionary Caliban evident in C. L. R. James's Toussaint and other insurgent figures created by Caribbean writers in answer to European accounts of New World history (Lamming, 118–50; Retamar, 3–55).

As I have already indicated, *Dusk of Dawn* represents something of a way station in the course of Du Bois's written representations of himself. Taken as a whole, it is his most comprehensive autobiographical statement and the capstone to his displacement of liberalism by Marxism. At the same time, it is a work in which the very idea of race has become deracinated. Du Bois's tilt toward Marxism in the late 1920s resulted in a pathbreaking work of revisionist history, *Black Reconstruction*, and a series of essays devoted to black education and self-segregated economic development that are one of the strongest twentieth-century briefs for racial separatism. His prevailing trope of this period, the idea of a "nation within a nation," is, among other things, a structural reinterpretation of double consciousness: what previously belonged abstractly to the realm of personal psychology or an internalized matrix of culture is now superimposed on an economic and political geography. Whether as an *imperium in imperio* (to cite the common phrase adopted by Sutton Griggs as the title of his 1899 nationalist novel about the creation of a secret black state hidden within Texas) or as a catch phrase promoting black buying from black storeowners, the concept of a nation within resonated in the case of Du Bois with his ambiguous notion of the African identity as a "hidden self" within, or constituting, the soul of African Americans (Sundquist, 570–75).

In an age of strict segregation, the economic and political preservation of the black community lay in harnessing its powers and holding them in reserve for the future. For Du Bois, however, the cultivation of separatist strategies was no contradiction to his ultimate goal of integration. His adaptation of his theory of the Talented Tenth to a socialist and separatist model, in which educated blacks would provide the leadership of a new industrial organization, was not intended to negate his long-standing commitment to integration and cultural pluralism. Nor was his contention that a "Negro university" in the United States is justified in using "that variety of the English idiom which [African Americans] understand" and founding its curriculum "on a knowledge of the history of their people in Africa and in the United States"—a view in harmony with the last generation of moderate thought about Afrocentric education—inherently contradictory to social and economic assimilation (Du Bois, *Reader*, 416).

In his writing of the 1930s, when racial and economic separatism functioned as a prelude to collectivist political activism, Du Bois's personification of messianic leadership likewise waned. In *Black Reconstruction*, for instance, the place of the magnified black or abolitionist hero seems to have been usurped by the black masses; lacking a revolutionary figure comparable to Toussaint, Du Bois depicted the slaves themselves as a proletarian collective rising up in defiance of slave masters and world economic oppressors alike. Because it incorporates many traditional aspects of autobiography, *Dusk of Dawn* returns us to the commanding and directive life of the hero—that is, Du Bois himself—but the effects of the Depression and stirrings of the coming world war against fascism are now interwoven into Du Bois's narrative staging of his ongoing "autobiography of a race concept." A summary reinterpretation of the transformation of Du Bois's thought over the course of the 1930s, specifically its accommodation of Marxism to his goals of integration and pluralism, *Dusk of Dawn* recomposes the autobiographical dimensions of *The Souls of Black Folk* and *Darkwater* in large blocks of polemic, to a great degree replacing the searching lyricism of the earlier works with a Du Boisian version of scientific materialism, an odd wedding of Marxist doctrine and poetic cadence. *Dusk of Dawn* ends not with a beautiful tribute to slave culture (as in *The Souls of Black Folk*) or an apocalyptic meditation on segregation (as in *Darkwater*) but with Du Bois's announcement of the "Basic American Creed," an eleven-part program that somewhat awkwardly ties a philosophy of the Talented Tenth to belief in "the ultimate triumph of some form of Socialism the world over" (Du Bois, *Dusk*, 321).

In keeping with the book's scrutiny of his earlier life and beliefs in light of his mature Marxist perspective, Du Bois recapitulates and analyzes the development of his own racial philosophy in the sequential argument of the chapter entitled "The Concept of Race." After a brief critique of scientific vews of race, he begins by sketching his own genealogical history, complete with family tree. Repeating the anecdote about the inherited song "Do bana coba," but noting that there was almost nothing African in the speech or customs of his immediate family, Du Bois now attributes his sense of Africanity to his "later learning and reaction" to the racial assumptions of whites and to his time in the South: "I felt myself African by 'race,' " he says, "and by that token was African and an integral member of the group of dark Americans who were called Negroes." Here Du Bois depicts himself wavering on the border of the kind of essentialist definition that animated, without finally determining, the early arguments of "The Conservation of Races" and *The Souls of Black Folk*. Quickly, however, the privileged power of "reaction" to racism in the formation of racial identity is now brought to the fore. Du Bois recalls that when he applied in 1908 for membership in the Massachusetts Society of the Sons of the American Revolution on the basis of his great-great-grandfather's war record, his application was denied because he could not produce a birth certificate of the man who had, of course, been a slave stolen from Africa. He then glibly remarks, "my membership was, therefore, suspended," and proceeds to quote Countee Cullen's refrain, "What is Africa to me?" as a searching counterpoint to the denationalization he has just described (Du Bois, *Reader*, 86). Africa, which Du Bois admits affords "a tie which I can feel better than I can explain," becomes a means to provide "membership" in a nation that has been denied in the United States. And one could as well say "citizenship," for the clear burden of this anecdote is to remind his readers that the evisceration of the Fourteenth and Fifteenth amendments, culminating in *Plessy* v. *Ferguson* (1896), returned blacks in many ways to the stateless condition described for them in the infamous pre–Civil War ruling of Justice Roger Taney in *Dred Scott* v. *Sandford* (1857), which declared that African Americans had no rights that whites were bound to respect.

Whether or not he intended the further word play, Du Bois's choice of "suspended" is more than appropriate. The paradox of double consciousness is not so much that it describes two (or more) potential modes of identity at war with one another, but that it describes a suspension between them—a condition of statelessness or *homelessness*, as it is often called in contemporary writing on the cultures of exile, which Du Bois anticipated with telling accuracy, as he did more recent conceptions of a nation or a people as ideological constructions or rhetorical strategies (Bhabha, 145). It is no mistake, then, that the argument of this key chapter in *Dusk of Dawn* hinges on a combination of tenuous ethnographic evidence—Du Bois proceeds to contend, in a passage already cited, that the Christmas singing in Monrovia echoed the sorrow songs he had heard forty years earlier in Tennessee—and autobiographical longing reconceived as political theory. Africa is "my fatherland," Du Bois asserts; but he dismisses the mere physical characteristics of race, the "badge of color," as having little meaning either to accurate science or to Negroes. Instead, he argues that what unites blacks and ties them to Africa is the fact that they "have suffered a common disaster and have one long memory" (Du Bois, *Reader*, 87). Or, as James Baldwin would later put it in an essay devoted to the 1956 Conference of Negro Writers and Artists at the Sorbonne: "What they held in common was their precarious, their unutterably painful relation to the white world . . . their ache to come into the world as men" (Baldwin, 35). Baldwin was skeptical that this was equivalent to a cultural bond. Perhaps because he was close enough to the experience of slavery, however, or because he was temporally proximate to the colonial devastation of African culture through the artificial creation of new political and economic nations, Du Bois, unlike Baldwin, often made Africa the cultural as well as the emotional centerpiece of racial identity.

And yet, such a common bond was not for Du Bois "African" or "black" alone, and he maintained that the world color line "binds together not simply the children of Africa, but extends through yellow

Asia and into the South Seas. It is this unity that draws me to Africa" (Du Bois, *Reader*, 87). His willingness to extend this vague "nationhood" to virtually all people of color, as well as his corollary that precolonized Africa provided a condition of communal harmony, raises unavoidable problems. It may be, as Martin Luther King, Jr., argued, that Du Bois "did not make a mystique out of blackness," that he "was proud of his people, not because their color endowed them with some vague greatness but because their concrete achievements in struggle had advanced humanity . . . in all its hues, black, white, yellow, red and brown" (King, 18). As Kwame Anthony Appiah has argued, however, Du Bois's Pan-Colored hypothesis nearly evacuates his claim of black race solidarity of any meaning; and the appeal to "a common disaster" and "one long memory" hides a lingering biological conception of race beneath the surface of the sociohistorical explanation (Appiah, 41). Against more ardent proponents of *negritude*, Du Bois stood forth as a dissenter from racial determinism; but against those who would construct race purely of cultural predispositions and habits, Du Bois legitimated an irrational faith in African "memory" by dissolving historical differences among the world's nonwhite groups. Even after fifty years, it might seem, Du Bois had neither found a way to avoid the temptation of racial essentialism nor devised a solution to the puzzle of nationalism.

It was his 1923 visit to Africa as an official envoy to Liberia that afforded Du Bois the realization, as he now recalls it, that the "income-bearing value of race prejudice was the cause and not the result of theories of race inferiority" both in the colonized world and in America during the decades since the collapse of the cotton kingdom (Du Bois, *Reader*, 94). Having determined that slavery created racism, not the reverse, Du Bois recasts his most ethereal earlier conceptions of Africa into a form of economic, rather than racial, primitivism. All his previous romantic idealizations of Africa—from his first poems of Pan-African *negritude*, "The Song of the Smoke" (1907) and "A Day in Africa" (1908), to his arguments in "What Is Civilization?" (1925), *The Gift of Black Folk*, and *Black Folk Then and Now*, where the utopian socialism of the African village appears as an antidote to the destructive, capitalized industrialism of modernity—are refashioned in *Dusk of Dawn* as though to illustrate his progress from nineteenth-century racialism to modern Marxism. In a famous expression of his Victorian sensibilities, Du Bois had stated in "The Primitive Black Man" (1924) that during two months in West Africa, when he routinely saw "children quite naked and women usually naked to the waist," he witnessed "less of sex dalliance and appeal than I see daily on Fifth Avenue" (Du Bois, *Writings in Periodicals*, II, 231). This passage reappears more or less verbatim in *Dusk of Dawn*, but joined to it are further speculations about the pleasure of unindustrialized, uncapitalized work in Africa, the whole creating a luminous, strangely naive proof that the "communalism of the African clan can be transferred to the Negro American group" (Du Bois, *Dusk*, 219).

Surprisingly, the autobiographical presence is not erased but, if anything, more pronounced in *Dusk of Dawn*, for Du Bois's own pedagogy becomes that of black America. His unequivocal commitment to an art of overt ideology was first announced in 1926, following his first trip to Africa and his increasing admiration for the Soviet Union, when he delivered an address on the "Criteria of Negro Art" in which he claimed, against the "wailing of the purists," that "all Art is propaganda and ever must be" (Du Bois, *Reader*, 328). The Russian Revolution, he would write in *Dusk of Dawn*, "was the foundation stone of my fight for black folk; it explained me" (Du Bois, *Dusk*, 285). This formulation is a succinct index of the way in which the whole of the volume functions as a rewriting of previous self-conceptions. In "The Concept of Race," the idealization in both economic and cultural terms allows Du Bois to create of Africa an imaginary homeland (to borrow a phrase from Salman Rushdie) against which the colonizing world in general and the United States in particular can be set for comparison. *Dusk of Dawn* represents the conjunction of Du Bois's propagandistic theory of culture and his desperate belief that a philosophy of separatism—a cultivation of what is referred to in this case as "The Colored World Within"—can find sustenance in Africa's anticolonial recovery of its own cultural unity. So long as discriminatory racial laws and economic practices exist, he suggests, so long as African Americans are excluded from American nationhood, they will be drawn toward Africa—most of all, perhaps, toward an inaccurately idealized Africa—by pure force of reaction to political and economic racism.

The chapter culminates in one of the most haunting passages in all of Du Bois's work, a portrait of the pain of segregation that underlies double consciousness:

> It is difficult to let others see the full psychological meaning of caste segregation. It is as though one, looking out from a dark cave in a side of an impending mountain, sees the world passing and speaks to it; speaks courteously and persuasively, showing them how these entombed souls are hindered in their natural movement, expression, and development; and how their loosening from prison would be a matter not simply of courtesy, sympathy, and help to them, but aid to all the world. One talks on evenly and logically in this way, but notices that the passing throng does not even turn its head, or if it does, glances curiously and walks on. It gradually penetrates the minds of the prisoners that the people passing do not hear; that some thick sheet of invisible but horribly tangible plate glass is between them and the world. They get excited; they talk louder; they gesticulate. Some of the passing stop in curiosity; these gesticulations seem so pointless; they laugh and pass on. They still either do not hear at all, or hear but dimly, and even what they hear, they do not understand. Then the people within may become hysterical. They may scream and hurl

themselves against the barriers, hardly realizing in their bewilderment that they are screaming in a vacuum unheard and that their antics may actually seem funny to those outside looking in. They may even, here and there, break through in blood and disfigurement, and find themselves faced by a horrified, implacable, and quite overwhelming mob of people frightened for their own very existence. (Du Bois, *Reader*, 95)

The effect of this tragic incarceration, this "group imprisonment," is to make an individual provincial; he "neglects the wider aspects of national life and human existence" and focuses on "his inner group"; he "thinks of himself not as an individual but as a group man, a 'race' man." Having at best partial citizenship in the United States, black Americans in the age of Jim Crow had good reason to seek their national identity, as well as their racial consciousness, elsewhere than in America. Over the course of the chapter, Du Bois not only creates a forceful cyclical argument that enfolds his own representative life into the history of the African diaspora and the literal and emotional violence of contemporary American segregation; he also displays the crucial but ephemeral nature of the transgeographical "nation," a world of exile in his case synonymous with the autobiographical self, in which African Americans are forced to seek their only hope of justice.

"The Plot" of *Dusk of Dawn*, as the opening chapter calls the coincidence between events in Du Bois's life and the unfolding of parallel events in world history, is far more coherently autobiographical than either *The Souls of Black Folk* or *Darkwater*. By the same token, its resemblance to the biography of John Brown reminds us that it is almost the story of someone else—that is, an objectification of the author as exemplary of diasporic historical and economic forces resonant in the passage with which the Brown text had opened: "the mystic spell of Africa is and ever was over all America" (Du Bois, *Reader*, 256). In the centrality of Du Bois himself—"one who expressed in life and action and made vocal to many, a single whirlpool of social entanglement and inner psychological paradox," as he puts it—and in his continual rehearsal of historical events whose meaning has only now become clear to him through the prism of Marxist analysis, we find at once an adoption of conventional autobiographical form and its renunciation (Du Bois, *Dusk*, 3). Du Bois's own messianic pretensions are subordinated here to the scripture itself; the prophet is folded into his prophecy.

By the time Du Bois composed the *Autobiography*—it would be published in abridged form in the Soviet Union, China, and East Germany before it appeared posthumously in the West, after the manuscript was retrieved from Accra in the wake of the 1966 military coup that ousted Kwame Nkrumah from power—the elision is complete. Soliloquy and propaganda have become one, not just in the routine sense that Du Bois is now more unapologetically a spokesman for communism, but also in the formal sense that the text itself has swallowed the last surviving features of liberal individualism still present in earlier texts, even in *Dusk of Dawn*. The famous "Credo" of *Darkwater*, a popular set of aphorisms, has given way in the *Autobiography* to a structurally parallel interlude entitled "Communism," in which Du Bois announces his revised creed: "I now state my conclusion frankly and clearly: I believe in communism . . . I shall therefore hereafter help the triumph of communism in every honest way that I can. . . . This is the excuse for this writing which I call a Soliloquy" (Du Bois, *Autobiography*, 57–58).

All is now seen through a new lens. The "startling miracle" of Sputnik, Du Bois writes, has "taught the United States the superiority of Soviet thought and calculation," while Elvis Presley's "motions of copulation on the public stage," in an ideological updating of Du Bois's long-standing prudery, is a clear sign of capitalism's degeneracy (Du Bois, *Autobiography*, 414–16). Here and elsewhere during a period darkened by his aversion to cold war ideology and his harassment by the government—the subject of surveillance like a number of Americans of the left, his actions were charted by the FBI and his passport was withheld by the State Department—Du Bois went out of his way to denigrate the failed promise of American democracy and to laud the twentieth century's most ruthless totalitarian regimes. He said of Harry Truman that "he ranks with Adolph Hitler as one of the greatest killers of our day" (Rampersad, 256). By comparison, Joseph Stalin was easier to defend. In honor of the fortieth anniversary of the Bolshevik Revolution in 1957, Du Bois wrote in a Soviet magazine: "On occasion, human nature is horrible and human beings beastly, but the world progresses; men reel and stagger forward; and never before in the history of man, have they made so gallant and successful struggle as in the Soviet Union since the Revolution of 1917" (Du Bois, *Correspondence*, 3: 415). Mao Tse-tung he deemed the architect of a brave new world—"Mistakes are but stepping stones upon which one may climb higher and higher," Mao told the admiring Du Bois (Du Bois, S. G., 286)–and postcolonial Africans, he thought, might look to Fidel Castro for model governments: "They will make up their own minds on communism and not listen solely to American lies. The latest voice to reach them is from Cuba" (Du Bois, *World and Africa*, 338).

Such concessions in the name of "progress," if applied, say, to slavery or colonial rule in Africa, would, of course, have been anathema to Du Bois. From the perspective of the late twentieth century, Du Bois's embrace of such regimes is nearly as perplexing as his sudden willingness to rewrite not just the past, as in his reinscriptions of autobiography into world economic history in *Dusk of Dawn*, but also the present, as in his assertion now that *Brown* v. *Board of Education* would not have been possible without "the world pressure of communism led by the Soviet Union" (Du Bois, *Autobiography*, 333). Despite his own ideological shift, however, Du Bois did not discard the guiding messianic paradigm of his life story. The climax of the *Autobiography*, as well as his intellectual life—though one might better call it an anticlimax—is Du Bois's indictment and trial for failing to register as the agent of a foreign power during his participation in the Cultural and Scientific Conference for World Peace and his work on behalf of the Stockholm Appeal. Although the charges were dismissed, the traumatic event, recounted in his short work *In Battle for Peace* (1952), provided the final act for his self-dramatization in the *Autobiography*. The experience of "this fantastic accusation and criminal process," wrote Du Bois, freed him from the "racial provincialism" of his previous views. Such a process of liberation, of course, was well underway by the 1930s, but the trial became nothing less than the occasion of Du Bois's own ideological passion play. Now hounded by the government—from Du Bois's point of view it was the United States, not the Soviet Union, that was tyrannical—he depicts himself as an outcast within the black community as well, ignored by those African Americans who have sacrificed the saving potential of "ancient African communism" to their desire to "follow in the footsteps of western acquisitive society, with its exploitation of labor, its monopoly of land and resources, and with private profit for the smart and unscrupulous in a world of poverty, disease, and ignorance, as the natural end of human culture." His glorification of Stalin and Mao sprang most not from Du Bois's flattered sense that his views were being taken seriously by key world figures or simply from his renewed admiration of the sort of power he had found seventy years earlier in Bismarck. Rather, in a battle of ideological wills that Du Bois could not afford to lose, an old man at odds with his country and his people represents the oblivion that has begun to overtake his own national leadership as a silencing of his voice by both the government and the African American community: "the colored children ceased to hear my name" (Du Bois, *Autobiography*, 391–95).

In the chapters devoted to his trial, his travels in the Soviet Union and China, his speeches on behalf of Paul Robeson or Kwame Nkrumah, and the views that at last led to his renunciation of U.S. citizenship, Du Bois frames himself as a political prisoner of America's cold war paranoia. The book fittingly concludes, whether by Du Bois's own intentions alone or through the subsequent editorial intervention of Herbert Aptheker, with a mystical jeremiad spoken in the form of a rapt benediction "to the Almighty Dead, into whose pale approaching faces, I stand and stare." In a great cadenza of prose not unlike but far exceeding comparable perorations in *The Souls of Black Folk* and *Darkwater*, Du Bois writes: "Hell lies about us in our Age: blithely we push into its stench and flame. Suffer us not, Eternal Dead to stew in this Evil—the Evil of South Africa, the Evil of Mississippi; the Evil of Evils which is what we hope to hold in Asia and Africa, in the southern Americas and islands of the Seven Seas. . . . Let then the Dreams of the Dead rebuke the Blind who think that what is will be forever and teach them that what was worth living for must live again and that which merited death must stay dead. Teach us, Forever Dead, there is no Dream but Deed, there is no Deed but Memory" (Du Bois, *Autobiography*, 422–23).

Although his religious skepticism is augmented in the *Autobiography* by communist secularism, Du Bois is far from giving up the language of allegory. The proliferation of personified figures, evident in the capitalized phrases, indicates the degree to which Du Bois has been absorbed by historical—and now eschatological—forces. The represented life, which for so long had brilliantly encoded the autobiography of a whole people, perhaps more so than any American's before or since, here gives way to a nearly sacred lamentation of failure. Preparing for exile from the nation of which he had never been a true citizen, Du Bois looked beyond his coming African repatriation to a world of transcendence. Words failed him, one could say, but in spirit he returned to the multivalent meanings of the simple sorrow songs, casting his own fate in a form that combined the escape from bondage and the vision of an afterlife in which the long sought "common memory" of African diaspora culture was to be achieved. Unanticipated and coincidental though it was—and not without pathos as a parting gesture of political protest—Du Bois's final journey to Africa was indeed the return to a lost homeland and the last act in his complex representation of his own life, nothing less than the autobiography of a race.

CHAPTER 1

Concepts of Race

L ittle that Du Bois wrote could not be placed under the heading "concepts of race." Whether he was writing or speaking on political, cultural, economic, or social issues, Du Bois wove meditations on the meaning of race into his editorials, position papers, and scholarly projects. He recognized early on that the ambiguities and complexities of race as a category were responsible for the misuse of race in scientific and political theory. Yet that same ambiguity allowed him to derive the utmost rhetorical force and imaginative breadth from race and from related concepts such as "soul," "genius," "folk," and "nation." Having inherited the prevailing nineteenth-century belief in racialism—the view that people belong to broad, often national groups defined by shared physical, emotional, and intellectual traits—Du Bois never quite discarded his own initial view that race had some biological basis, but he constantly refined his own definitions over time, arguing more and more clearly that race must be understood principally as a cultural and political concept.

"The Conservation of Races," first presented in 1897 as an address before the American Negro Academy, which Du Bois had founded with Alexander Crummell, is one of Du Bois's most important early attempts to define the parameters of race and to identify races as evolving historically. Like "The Present Outlook for the Dark Races of Mankind" (1900) and "The First Universal Races Congress" (1911), an essay occasioned by a London conference devoted to the discussion of race and racism on a global scale, "The Conservation of Races" is steeped in the argument that nations are primarily formed and driven by the "race spirit." In a later extract from *Dusk of Dawn* entitled "The Concept of Race" (1940), one finds the entire array of contexts in which race functioned as a key part of Du Bois's work, from familial genealogy to the struggle against segregation to geopolitical theory to the philosophy of Afrocentrism. In this essay Du Bois records the transformation that his own conception of race underwent as economic and Marxist structures of argument became central to his thinking.

The importance of Africa to Du Bois—a later section of this volume is devoted to representative selections from his writing about Africa and Pan-Africanism—lay in good part in its acting as a point of reference for racial identity. Defining Africa as the "land of the blacks" and employing the term "Negro" positively to denote both Africans and blacks in the New World diaspora, Du Bois frequently mixed a critique of racism with proclamations of race pride. Much of his creative writing, whether in hybrid works such as *The Souls of Black Folk* and *Darkwater* or in individual poems and novels, addresses the problem of racial solidarity and challenges African Americans to believe in their own heritage and accomplishments as a race. An early poem, "The Song of the Smoke" (1907), looks forward to the Caribbean *negritude* movement of the 1940s and 1950s, and to the Black Power movement of 1960s America in its evocation of blackness as a source of unity and beauty. Du Bois was especially intent on combatting the stereotypes that sprang from doctrines of racial inferiority, as in his attack on racist caricature in "In Black" (1920) or his satiric dialogues on white supremacy in "The Superior Race" and "On Being Crazy" (1923). In a brief 1928 editorial for *The Crisis* Du Bois replied to a student who had written to rebuke the magazine for using what he considered a denigrating term. Du Bois argued that, like all such names, the word "Negro" ought to be defined by how blacks, not whites, used it. The same motive underlies "On Being Ashamed of Oneself" (1933), where Du Bois explores the role played by the interplay between racism and race pride in the contemporary struggle for civil rights and racial justice. In this essay, as in so many of his writings on the power of race in individual and communal self-conceptions, Du Bois turned the "problem" of color, of being black, into a source of historical empowerment and creative inspiration.

THE CONSERVATION OF RACES

The American Negro has always felt an intense personal interest in discussions as to the origins and destinies of races: primarily because back of most discussions of race with which he is familiar, have lurked certain assumptions as to his natural abilities, as to his political, intellectual and moral status, which he felt were wrong. He has, consequently, been led to deprecate and minimize race distinctions, to believe intensely that out of one blood God created all nations, and to speak of human brotherhood as though it were the possibility of an already dawning tomorrow.

Nevertheless, in our calmer moments we must acknowledge that human beings are divided into races; that in this country the two most extreme types of the world's races have met, and the resulting problem as to the future relations of these types is not only of intense and living interest to us, but forms an epoch in the history of mankind.

It is necessary, therefore, in planning our movements, in guiding our future development, that at times we rise above the pressing, but smaller questions of separate schools and cars, wage-discrimination and lynch law, to survey the whole question of race in human philosophy and to lay, on a basis of broad knowledge and careful insight, those large lines of policy and higher ideals which may form our guiding lines and boundaries in the practical difficulties of everyday. For it is certain that all human striving must recognize the hard limits of natural law, and that any striving, no matter how intense and earnest, which is against the constitution of the world, is vain. The question, then, which we must seriously consider is this: what is the real meaning of race; what has, in the past, been the law of race development, and what lessons has the past history of race development to teach the rising Negro people?

When we thus come to inquire into the essential difference of races we find it hard to come at once to any definite conclusion. Many criteria of race differences have in the past been proposed, as color, hair, cranial measurements and language. And manifestly, in each of these respects, human beings differ widely. They vary in color, for instance, from the marble-like pallor of the Scandinavian to the rich, dark brown of the Zulu, passing by the creamy Slav, the yellow Chinese, the light brown Sicilian and the brown Egyptian. Men vary, too, in the texture of hair from the obstinately straight hair of the Chinese to the obstinately tufted and frizzled hair of the Bushman. In measurement of heads, again, men vary; from the broad-headed Tartar to the medium-headed European and the narrow-headed Hottentot; or, again in language, from the highly-inflected Roman tongue to the monosyllabic Chinese. All these physical characteristics are patent enough, and if they agreed with each other it would be very easy to classify mankind. Unfortunately for scientists, however, these criteria of race are most exasperatingly intermingled. Color does not agree with texture of hair, for many of the dark races have straight hair; nor does color agree with the breadth of the head, for the yellow Tartar has a broader head than the German; nor, again, has the science of language as yet succeeded in clearing up the relative authority of these various and contradictory criteria.

The final word of science, so far, is that we have at least two, perhaps three, great families of human beings—the whites and Negroes, possibly the yellow race. That other races have arisen from the intermingling of the blood of these two. This broad division of the world's races which men like [Thomas Henry] Huxley and [Friedrich] Raetzel have introduced as more nearly true than the old five-race scheme of [Johann-Friedrich] Blumenbach, is nothing more than an acknowledgement that, so far as purely physical characteristics are concerned, the differences between men do not explain all the differences of their history. It declares, as Darwin himself said, that great as is the physical unlikeness of the various races of men, their likenesses are greater, and upon this rests the whole scientific doctrine of human brotherhood.

Although the wonderful developments of human history teach that the grosser physical differences of color, hair and bone go but a short way toward explaining the different roles which groups of men have played in human progress, yet there are differences—subtle, delicate and elusive, though they may be—which have silently but definitely separated men into groups. While these subtle forces have generally followed the natural cleavage of common blood, descent and physical peculiarities, they have at other times swept across and ignored these. At all times, however, they have divided human beings into races, which, while they perhaps transcend scientific definition, nevertheless, are clearly defined to the eye of the historian and sociologist.

If this be true, then the history of the world is the history, not of individuals, but of groups, not of nations, but of races, and he who ignores or seeks to override the race idea in human history ignores and overrides the central thought of all history. What, then, is a race? It is a vast family of human beings, generally of common blood and language, always of common history, traditions and impulses, who are both voluntarily and involuntarily striving together for the accomplishment of certain more or less vividly conceived ideals of life.

Turning to real history, there can be no doubt, first, as to the widespread, nay, universal, prevalence of the race idea, the race spirit, the race ideal, and as to its efficiency as the vastest and most ingenious invention for human progress. We, who have been reared and trained under the individualistic philosophy of the Declaration of Independence and the laissez-faire philosophy of Adam Smith, are loath to see and loath to acknowledge this patent fact of human history. We see the Pharaohs, Caesars, Toussaints and Napoleons of history and forget the vast races of which they were but epitomized expressions. We are apt to think in our American impatience, that while it may have been true in the past that closed race groups made history, that here in conglomerate America *nous avons changé tout cela*—we have changed all that, and have no need of this ancient instrument of progress. This assumption of which the Negro people are especially fond cannot be established by a careful consideration of history.

We find upon the world's stage today eight distinctly differentiated races, in the sense in which history tells us the word must be used. They are the Slavs of Eastern Europe, the Teutons of middle Europe, the English of Great Britain and America, the Romance nations of Southern and Western Europe, the Negroes of Africa and America, the Semitic people of Western Asia and Northern Africa, the Hindoos of Central Asia and the Mongolians of Eastern Asia. There are, of course, other minor race groups, [such] as the American Indians, the Esquimaux and the South Sea Islanders; these larger races, too, are far from homogeneous; the Slav includes the Czech, the Magyar, the Pole and the Russian; the Teuton includes the German, the Scandinavian and the Dutch; the English include the Scotch, the Irish and the conglomerate American. Under Romance nations the widely-differing Frenchman, Italian, Sicilian and Spaniard are comprehended. The term Negro is, perhaps, the most indefinite of all, combining the Mulattoes and Zamboes of America and the Egyptians, Bantus and Bushmen of Africa. Among the Hindoos are traces of widely differing nations, while the great Chinese, Tartar, Korean and Japanese families fall under the one designation—Mongolian.

The question now is: What is the real distinction between these nations? Is it the physical differences of blood, color and cranial measurements? Certainly we must all acknowledge that physical differences play a great part, and that, with wide exceptions and qualifications, these eight great races of today follow the cleavage of physical race distinctions; the English and Teuton represent the white variety of mankind; the Mongolian, the yellow; the Negroes, the black. Between these are many crosses and mixtures, where Mongolian and Teuton have blended into the Slav, and other mixtures have produced the Romance nations and the Semites. But while race differences have followed mainly physical race lines, yet no mere physical distinctions would really define or explain the deeper differences—the cohesiveness and continuity of these groups. The deeper differences are spiritual, psychical, differences—undoubtedly based on the physical, but infinitely transcending them. The forces that bind together the Teuton nations are, then, first, their race identity and common blood; secondly, and more important, a common history, common laws and religion, similar habits of thought and a conscious striving together for certain ideals of life. The whole process which has brought about these race differentiations has been a growth, and the great characteristic of this growth has been the differentiation of spiritual and mental differences between great races of mankind and the integration of physical differences.

The age of nomadic tribes of closely related individuals represents the maximum of physical differences. They were practically vast families, and there were as many groups as families. As the families came together to form cities the physical differences lessened, purity of blood was replaced by the requirement of domicile, and all who lived within the city bounds became gradually to be regarded as members of the group; i.e., there was a slight and slow breaking down of physical barriers. This, however, was accompanied by an increase of the spiritual and social differences between cities. This city became husbandmen; this, merchants; another, warriors; and so on. The *ideals of life* for which the different cities struggled were different.

When at last cities began to coalesce into nations there was another breaking down of barriers which separated groups of men. The larger and broader differences of color, hair and physical proportions were not by any means ignored, but myriads of minor differences disappeared, and the sociological and historical races of men began to approximate the present division of races as indicated by physical researches. At the same time the spiritual and psychical differences of race groups which constituted the nations became deep and decisive. The English nation stood for constitutional liberty and commercial freedom; the German nation for science and philosophy; the Romance nations stood for literature and art, and the other race groups are striving, each in its own way, to develop for civilization its particular message, its particular ideal, which shall help to guide the world nearer and nearer that perfection of human life for which we all long, that "one far-off Divine event."

This has been the function of the race differences up to the present time. What shall be its function in the future? Manifestly some of the great races of today—particularly the Negro race—have not as yet given to civilization the full spiritual message which they are capable of giving. I will not say that the Negro race has as yet given no message to the world, for it is still a mooted question among scientists as to just how far Egyptian civilization was Negro in its origin; if it was not wholly Negro, it was certainly very closely allied. Be that as it may, however, the fact still remains that the full, complete Negro message of the whole Negro race has not as yet been given to the world: that the messages and ideal of the yellow race have not been completed, and that the striving of the mighty Slavs has but begun.

The question is, then: how shall this message be delivered; how shall these various ideals be realized? The answer is plain: by the development of these race groups, not as individuals, but as races. For the development of Japanese genius, Japanese literature and art, Japanese spirit, only Japanese, bound and welded together, Japanese inspired by one vast ideal, can work out in its fullness the wonderful message which Japan has for the nations of the earth. For the development of Negro genius, of Negro literature and art, of Negro spirit, only Negroes bound and welded together, Negroes inspired by one vast ideal, can work out in its fullness the great message we have for humanity. We cannot reverse history; we are subject to the same natural laws as other races, and if the Negro is ever to be a factor in the world's history—if among the gaily-colored banners that deck the broad ramparts of civilization is to hang one uncompromising black, then it must be placed there by black hands, fashioned by black heads and hallowed by the travail of two hundred million black hearts beating in one glad song of jubilee.

For this reason, the advance guard of the Negro people—the eight million people of Negro blood in the United States of America—must soon come to realize that if they are to take their just place in the van of Pan-Negroism, then their destiny is *not* absorption by the white Americans. That if in America it is to be proven for the first time in the modern world that not only are Negroes capable of evolving individual men like Toussaint the Saviour, but are a nation stored with wonderful possibilities of culture, then their destiny is not a servile imitation of Anglo-Saxon culture, but a stalwart originality which shall unswervingly follow Negro ideals.

It may, however, be objected here that the situation of our race in America renders this attitude impossible; that our sole hope of salvation lies in our being able to lose our race identity in the commingled blood of the nation; and that any other course would merely increase the friction of races which we call race prejudice, and against which we have so long and so earnestly fought.

Here, then, is the dilemma, and it is a puzzling one, I admit. No Negro who has given earnest thought to the situation of his people in America has failed, at some time in life, to find himself at these crossroads; has failed to ask himself at some time: what, after all, am I? Am I an American or am I a Negro? Can I be both? Or is it my duty to cease to be a Negro as soon as possible and be an American? If I strive as a Negro, am I not perpetuating the very cleft that threatens and separates black and white America? Is not my only possible practical aim the subduction of all that is Negro in me to the American? Does my black blood place upon me any more obligation to assert my nationality than German, or Irish or Italian blood would?

It is such incessant self-questioning, and the hesitation that arises from it, that is making the present period a time of vacillation and contradiction for the American Negro; combined race action is stifled, race responsibility is shirked, race enterprises languish, and the best blood, the best talent, the best energy of the Negro people cannot be marshaled to do the bidding of the race. They stand back to make room for every rascal and demagogue who chooses to cloak his selfish devilry under the veil of race pride.

Is this right? Is it rational? Is it good policy? Have we in America a distinct mission as a race—a distinct sphere of action and an opportunity for race development, or is self-obliteration the highest end to which Negro blood dare aspire?

If we carefully consider what race prejudice really is, we find it, historically, to be nothing but the friction between different groups of people; it is the difference in aim, in feeling, in ideals of two different races; if, now, this difference exists touching territory, laws, language, or even religion, it is manifest that these people cannot live in the same territory without fatal collision; but if, on the other hand, there is substantial agreement in laws, language and religion; if there is a satisfactory adjustment of economic life, then there is no reason why, in the same country and on the same street, two or three great national ideals might not thrive and develop, that men of different races might not strive together for their race ideals as well, perhaps even better, than in isolation.

Here, it seems to me, is the reading of the riddle that puzzles so many of us. We are Americans, not only by birth and by citizenship, but by our political ideals, our language, our religion. Farther than that, our Americanism does not go. At that point, we are Negroes, members of a vast historic race that from the very dawn of creation has slept, but half awakening in the dark forests of its African fatherland. We are the first fruits of this new nation, the harbinger of that black tomorrow which is yet destined to soften the whiteness of the Teutonic today. We are that people whose subtle sense of song has given America its only American music, its only American fairy tales, its only touch of pathos and humor amid its mad money-getting plutocracy. As such, it is our duty to conserve our physical powers, our intellectual endowments, our spiritual ideals; as a race we must strive by race organization, by race solidarity, by race unity to the realization of that broader humanity which freely recognizes differences in men, but sternly deprecates inequality in their opportunities of development.

For the accomplishment of these ends we need race organizations: Negro colleges, Negro newspapers, Negro business organizations, a Negro school of literature and art, and an intellectual clearing house, for all these products of the Negro mind, which we may call a Negro Academy. Not only is all this necessary for positive advance, it is absolutely imperative for negative defense. Let us not deceive ourselves at our situation in this country. Weighted with a heritage of moral iniquity from our past history, hard pressed in the economic world by foreign immigrants and native prejudice, hated here, despised there and pitied everywhere; our one haven of refuge is ourselves, and but one means of advance, our own belief in our great destiny, our own implicit trust in our ability and worth.

There is no power under God's high heaven that can stop the advance of eight thousand thousand honest, earnest, inspired and united people. But—and here is the rub—they *must* be honest, fearlessly criticizing their own faults, zealously correcting them; they must be *earnest*. No people that laughs at itself, and ridicules itself, and wishes to God it was anything but itself ever wrote its name in history; it *must* be inspired with the Divine faith of our black mothers, that out of the blood and dust of battle will march a victorious host, a mighty nation, a peculiar people, to speak to the nations of earth a Divine truth that shall make them free. And such a people must be united; not merely united for the organized theft of political spoils, not united to disgrace religion with whoremongers and ward-heelers; not united merely to protest and pass resolutions, but united to stop the ravages of consumption among the Negro people, united to keep black boys from loafing, gambling and crime; united to guard the purity of black women and to reduce that vast army of black prostitutes that is today marching to hell; and united in serious organizations, to determine by careful conference and thoughtful interchange of opinion the broad lines of policy and action for the American Negro.

This is the reason for being which the American Negro Academy has. It aims at once to be the epitome and expression of the intellect of the black-blooded people of America, the exponent of the race ideals of one of the world's great races. As such, the Academy must, if successful, be:

a. Representative in character.

b. Impartial in conduct.

c. Firm in leadership.

It must be representative in character; not in that it represents all interests or all factions, but in that it seeks to comprise something of the *best* thought, the most unselfish striving and the highest ideals. There are scattered in forgotten nooks and corners throughout the land, Negroes of some considerable training, of high minds, and high motives, who are unknown to their fellows, who exert far too little influence. These the Negro Academy should strive to bring into touch with each other and to give them a common mouthpiece.

The Academy should be impartial in conduct; while it aims to exalt the people it should aim to do so by truth—not by lies, by honesty—not by flattery. It should continually impress the fact upon the Negro people that they must not expect to have things done for them—they *must do for themselves;* that they have on their hands a vast work of self-reformation to do, and that a little less complaint and whining, and a little more dogged work and manly striving would do us more credit and benefit than a thousand Force or Civil Rights bills.

Finally, the American Negro Academy must point out a practical path of advance to the Negro people; there lie before every Negro to-day hundreds of questions of policy and right which must be settled and which each one settles now, not in accordance with any rule, but by impulse or individual preference; for instance: what should be the attitude of Negroes toward the educational qualification for voters? What should be our attitude toward separate schools? How should we meet discriminations on railways and in hotels? Such questions need not so much specific answers for each part as a general expression of policy, and nobody should be better fitted to announce such a policy than a representative honest Negro Academy.

All this, however, must come in time after careful organization and long conference. The immediate work before us should be practical and have direct bearing upon the situation of the Negro. The historical work of collecting the laws of the United States and of the various states of the Union with regard to the Negro is a work of such magnitude and importance that no body but one like this could think of undertaking it. If we could accomplish that one task we would justify our existence.

In the field of sociology an appalling work lies before us. First, we must unflinchingly and bravely face the truth, not with apologies, but with solemn earnestness. The Negro Academy ought to sound a note of warning that would echo in every black cabin in the land: *unless we conquer our present vices they will conquer us;* we are diseased, we are developing criminal tendencies, and an alarmingly large percentage of our men and women are sexually impure. The Negro Academy should stand and proclaim this over the housetops, crying with Garrison: *I will not equivocate, I will not retreat a single inch, and I will be heard.* The Academy should seek to gather about it the talented, unselfish men, the pure and noble-minded women, to fight an army of devils that disgraces our manhood and our womanhood. There does not stand today upon God's earth a race more capable in muscle, in intellect, in morals, than the American Negro, if he will bend his energies in the right direction; if he will

> Burst his birth's invidious bar
> And grasp the skirts of happy chance,
> And breast the blows of circumstance,
> And grapple with his evil star.

In science and morals, I have indicated two fields of work for the Academy. Finally, in practical policy, I wish to suggest the following *Academy Creed:*

1. We believe that the Negro people, as a race, have a contribution to make to civilization and humanity, which no other race can make.

2. We believe it the duty of the Americans of Negro descent, as a body, to maintain their race identity until this mission of the Negro people is accomplished, and the ideal of human brotherhood has become a practical possibility.

3. We believe that, unless modern civilization is a failure, it is entirely feasible and practicable for two races in such essential political, economic and religious harmony as the white and colored people of America, to develop side by side in peace and mutual happiness, the peculiar contribution which each has to make to the culture of their common country.

4. As a means to this end we advocate, not such social equality between these races as would disregard human likes and dis-

likes, but such a social equilibrium as would, throughout all the complicated relations of life, give due and just consideration to culture, ability, and moral worth, whether they be found under white or black skins.

5. We believe that the first and greatest step toward the settlement of the present friction between the races—commonly called the Negro problem—lies in the correction of the immorality, crime and laziness among the Negroes themselves, which still remains as a heritage from slavery. We believe that only earnest and long continued efforts on our own part can cure these social ills.

6. We believe that the second great step toward a better adjustment of the relations between the races should be a more impartial selection of ability in the economic and intellectual world, and a greater respect for personal liberty and worth, regardless of race. We believe that only earnest efforts on the part of the white people of this country will bring much needed reform in these matters.

7. On the basis of the foregoing declaration, and firmly believing in our high destiny, we, as American Negroes, are resolved to strive in every honorable way for the realization of the best and highest aims, for the development of strong manhood and pure womanhood, and for the rearing of a race ideal in America and Africa, to the glory of God and the uplifting of the Negro people.

THE PRESENT OUTLOOK FOR THE DARK RACES OF MANKIND

In bringing to you and your friends the official greetings of the American Negro Academy at this their third annual meeting, it is my purpose to consider with you the problem of the color line not simply as a national and personal question but rather in its larger world aspect in time and space. I freely acknowledge that in the red heat of a burning social problem like this, when each one of us feels the bitter sting of proscription, it is a difficult thing to place one's self at that larger point of view and ask with the cold eye of the historian and social philosopher: What part is the color line destined to play in the twentieth century? And yet this is the task I have laid out for you this evening, and one which you must take up for yourselves; for, after all, the secret of social progress is wide and thorough understanding of the social forces which move and modify your age.

It is but natural for us to consider that our race question is a purely national and local affair, confined to nine millions Americans and settled when their rights and opportunities are assured, and yet a glance over the world at the dawn of the new century will convince us that this is but the beginning of the problem—that the color line belts the world and that the social problem of the twentieth century is to be the relation of the civilized world to the dark races of mankind. If we start eastward to-night and land on the continent of Africa we land in the center of the greater Negro problem—of the world problem of the black man. The nineteenth century of the Christian era has seen strange transformation in the continent where civilization was born twice nineteen centuries before the Christ-child. We must not overlook or forget the marvelous drama that is being played on that continent to-day, with the English at the North and on the cape, the Portuguese and Germans on the East and West coasts, the French in Guinea and the Saharah [sic], Belgium in the Congo, and everywhere the great seething masses of the Negro people. Two events of vast significance to the future of the Negro people have taken place in the year 1899—the recapture of Khartoum and the Boer war, or in other words the determined attempt to plant English civilization at two centers in the heart of Africa. It is of interest to us because it means the wider extension among our own kith and kin of the influence of that European nation whose success in dealing with underdeveloped races has been far greater than any others. Say what we will of England's rapacity and injustice (and much can be said), the plain fact remains that no other European nation—and America least of all—has governed its alien subjects with half the wisdom and justice that England has. While then the advance of England from the cape to Cairo is no unclouded good for our people, it is at least a vast improvement on Arab slave traders and Dutch brutality. Outside of America the greatest field of contrast between whites and Negroes to-day is in South Africa, and the situation there should be watched with great interest. We must not forget that the deep-lying cause of the present Boer war is the abolition of Negro slavery among the Cape Dutch by England. The great Trek or migration of the Transvaal Boers followed and in the Free State no Negro has to-day a third of the rights which he enjoys in Georgia—he cannot hold land, cannot live in town, has practically no civil status, and is in all but name a slave. Among the English his treatment is by no means ideal and yet there he has the advantage of school, has the right of suffrage under some circumstances, and has just courts before which he may plead his cause. We watch therefore this war with great interest and must regard the triumph of England as a step toward the solution of the greater Negro problem. In the Congo Free State we see the rapid development of trade and industry, the railroad has crept further in toward the heart of Africa and the slave trade has at least been checked. Liberia stands hard pressed by France but she has begun to pay interest on the English debt and shows in some ways signs of industrial development along with her political decline. Leaving our black brothers of Africa we travel northward to our brown cousins of Egypt: rescued from war and rapine, slavery and centuries of misrule they are to-day enjoying stable government under England and rapid industrial advancement. Crossing the Red Sea we come upon the brown and yellow millions of Asia. Those who have left their maps in their school days would best, in curiosity, look now and then at the modern development of the mother continent. On the north Russia creeping down far beyond the limits set by your schoolday geographies. On the south English India creeping up. On the west the still lively corpse of Turkey, the still wild deserts of Arabia and dreary Persia; on the east the vast empire of China and the island kingdom of Japan. This continent deserves more than a passing notice from us for it is a congeries of race and color problems. The history of Asia is but the history of the moral and physical degeneration which follows the unbridled injustice of conquerors toward the conquered—of advanced toward undeveloped races—of swaggering braggadocio toward dumb submission. The brown Turanians of India were overborne by their yellow conquerors and the resulting caste system to keep the despised down was the very cause of that wide-spread discontent and internal dissension which welcomed the armies and government of England. So too when the case was reversed and the dark Turks swept over the white inhabitants of Asia Minor and southern Europe, it was the unjust determination to keep down the conquered, to recognize among Armenians no rights which a Turk was bound to respect. It was this that ultimately paralyzed the pristine vigor of the Ottoman and leaves them to-day beggars at the gates of Europe. And finally if we turn to China we have again an example of that marvelous internal decay that overcomes the nation which trifles with Truth and Right and Justice, and makes force and fraud and dishonesty and caste distinction the rule of its life and government. The one bright spot in Asia to-day is the island empire of Japan, and her recent admission to the ranks of modern civilized nations by the abolition of foreign consular courts within her borders is the greatest concession to the color line which the nineteenth century has seen. Outside Japan we see in English India alone a fairly honest attempt to make in some degree the welfare of the lowest classes of an alien race a distinct object of government. A system of education with a well-equipped university at the head has long been established for the natives and in the last few years some natives have been admitted to administrative positions in government. The cordial sympathy shown toward Queen Victoria's black and brown subjects at the late jubilee has borne golden fruit.

Crossing the Pacific we come to South America where the dark blood of the Indian and Negro has mingled with that of the Spaniard and the whole has been deluged by a large German and Italian migration. The resulting social conditions are not clear to the student. The color line has been drawn here perhaps less than in any other continent and yet the condition of the dark masses is far from satisfactory. We must not forget these dark cousins of ours, for their uplifting, and the establishment of permanent government and for industrial conditions is the work of the new century.

At last, after this hasty and inadequate survey we come back to our own land. The race question in America has reached an acute and in some respects a critical stage. Tracing the Negro question historically we can divide it as follows:

Up to about 1774 there was on the whole acquiescence in Negro slavery.

From the inception of the Revolution up until 1820 or 1830, the best thought of the nation believed in the abolition of slavery and were casting about for the best way to accomplish this.

From 1830 to 1850 economic revolution led to apathy on the part of the nation and a growing disposition to defend the institution.

From 1850 to 1865 came the rise and triumph of the abolition movement.

From 1865 to 1880 an attempt was made to clothe the Negro with full civil and political right.

From 1880 to 1890 there was a growing sympathy with the South and apathy toward the Negro.

1890—Today the era of criticism and the beginning of the movement for social reform and economic regeneration.

In this we can see progress—tremendous progress from the times when New England deacons invested their savings in slave trade ventures, passed the Dred Scott decision and the fugitive slave act down to the lynchings and discriminating laws of to-day. To be sure the actual status to-day, far from being ideal, is in many respects deplorable and far beyond those ideals of human brotherhood which from time to time have animated the nature; and yet we must be prepared in the progress of all reformatory movements for periods of exhalation and depression, of rapid advance and retrogression, of hope and fear. The Negro problem in America curiously illustrates this. Away back in the seventeenth century Massachusetts arose in wrath and denounced the slave trade, and the Pennsylvanian Quakers asked: "Is slavery according to the Golden Rule?" and yet 50 years later, Massachusetts slave traders swarmed on the coast of Africa and the Quakers held 10,000 slaves. Toward the end of the eighteenth century the conscience of the nation was again aroused. Darien, Georgia, where the Delegall riot recently occurred, declared its abhorrence of the unnatural practice of slavery. Jefferson denounced the institution as a crime against liberty, and the day of freedom seemed dawning; and yet fifty years later a cargo of black bondsmen were landed near Darien, Georgia, and the Vice President of the Confederacy declared Negro slavery the corner-stone of the new-born nation. So again the dreams of Garrison, Brown, Phillips and Sumner seemed about to be realized after the war when the Negro was free, enfranchised and protected in his civil rights, and yet a generation later finds the freedman in economic serfdom, practically without a vote, denied in many cases common law rights and subject to all sorts of petty discrimination. Notwithstanding all this the progress of the nation toward a settlement of the Negro is patent—the movement with all its retrogression is a spiral, not a circle, and as long as there is motion there is hope. At the same time we must indulge in no fantastic dreams, simply because in the past this nation has turned back from its errors against the Negro and tardily sought the higher way is no earnest for the future. Error that ends in progress is none the less error—none the less dangerously liable to end in disaster and wrong. It behooves us then here, to study carefully and seek to under-stand the present social movement in America as far as it affects our interests and to ask what we can do to ensure the ultimate triumph of right and justice. There is no doubt of the significance of the present attitude of the public mind toward us; it is the critical rebound that follows every period of moral exhalation; the shadow of doubt that creeps silently after the age of faith; the cold reasoning that follows gloomy idealism. Nor is this a thing to be unsparingly condemned. The human soul grasping—striving after dearly conceived ideals, needs ever the corrective and guiding power of sober afterthought. Human fancy must face plain facts. This is as true of nations as of men. We find great waves of sympathy seizing mankind at times and succeeded by cold criticism and doubt. Sometimes this latter reaction chokes and postpones reform or even kills it and lets the blind world flounder on. At the other times it leads to more rational and practical measures than mere moral enthusiasm could possibly offer. It is not the critic as such that the idealist must oppose but only that attitude of human criticism and doubt which neglects and denies all ideals. This is curiously illustrated in the modern world's attitude toward poverty: first came stern unbending morality: the pauper, the tramp, it said ras-cals and drones every one of them—punish them. Then came the cen-tury of sympathy crying as it saw dumb toil and hopeless suffering and the paradox of progress and poverty:

> Down all the stretch of Hell to its last gulf
> There is no shape more terrible than this—
> More tongued with censure of the world's blind greed
> More filled with signs and portents for the soul,
> More fraught with menace to the universe.

So the world sympathized until there came the era of calm criticism and doubt. Are all paupers pitiable? What makes men poor? Is the cause always the same? Is poverty or the fear of it an unmixed evil? Will not sympathy with the failures in the race of life increase the number of failures? Will not the strengthening of the weak weaken the strong and the enriching of the poor pauperize the rich? Today, in the world of social reform, we stand as it were between these two attitudes seeking some mode of reconciliation. The ideals of human betterment in our day could ill afford to lose the scientific attitude of statistics and sociology and science without ideas would lose half its excuse for being.

This then is the state of mind of the age that is called to settle the Negro problem in America and in the world. The abolitionists with their pure and lofty ideals of human brotherhood and their fine hate of dark damnation of national wrong and injustice, have left this generation a priceless heritage, and from their heights of enthusiasm was bound to come a reaction, and the natural recoil was hastened by sympathy with the stricken and conquered South, by horror at the memory of civil strife, by growing distrust of universal suffrage, and by deepseated doubt as to the capabilities and desert of the Negro. Here then we have the ideal and the criticism—the still presistent thrust for a broader and deeper humanity, the still powerful doubt as to what the Negro can and will do. The first sign of reconciliation between these two attitudes is the growth of a disposition to study the Negro problem honestly, and to inaugurate measures of social reform in the light of the scientific study. At the same time this disposition is still weak and largely powerless in the face of the grosser and more unscrupulous forces of reaction, and the vital question is: which of these two forces is bound to triumph?

In our attitude toward this battle we must make no tactical mistake, we must recognize clearly the questions at issue. They have changed since the abolition controversy and arguments suited to that time run strangely by the point to-day; the question is now not as to slavery, not as to human equality, not as to universal suffrage, but rather as to individual efficiency, the proper utilization of the manifestly different endowments of men, and the proper limitation to-day is not so much of rights as of duties—not so much of desires as of abilities—not so much of leveling down the successful to the dead level of the masses, as of giving to individuals among the masses the opportunity to reach the highest.

Here we must take our stand. We must inveigh against any drawing of the color line which narrows our opportunity of making the best of ourselves and we must continually and repeatedly show that we are capable of taking hold of every opportunity offered. I need hardly advert to the fact that denial of legal rights and curtailment of industrial opening does make our opportunities to-day exceptionally narrow. At the same time widespread laziness, crime, and neglect of family life show that we fall far short of taking advantage of the opportunities we have.

But most significant of all at this period is the fact that the colored population of our land is, through the new imperial policy, about to be doubled by our own ownership of Porto [sic] Rico, and Hawaii, our protectorate of Cuba, and conquest of the Philippines. This is for us and for the nation the greatest event since the Civil War and demands attention and action on our part. What is to be our attitude toward these new lands and toward the masses of dark men and women who inhabit them? Manifestly it must be an attitude of deepest sympathy and strongest alliance. We must stand ready to guard and guide them with our vote and our earnings. Negro and Filipino, Indian and Porto [sic] Rican, Cuban and Hawaiian, all must stand united under the stars and stripes for an America that knows no color line in the freedom of its opportunities. We must remember that the twentieth century will find nearly twenty millions of brown and black people under the protection of the American flag, a third of the nation, and that on the success and efficiency of the nine millions of our own number depends the ultimate destiny of Filipinos, Porto [sic] Ricans, Indians and Hawaiians, and that on us too depends in a large degree the attitude of Europe toward the teeming millions of Asia and Africa.

No nation ever bore a heavier burden that we black men of America, and if the third millennium of Jesus Christ dawns, as we devoutly believe it will, upon a brown and yellow world out of whose advancing civilization the color line has faded as mists before the sun—if this be the goal toward which every free born American Negro looks, then mind you, my hearers, its consummation depends on you, not on your neighbor but on you, not on Southern lynchers or Northern injustice, but on you. And that we may see just what this task means and how men have accomplished similar tasks, I turn to the one part of the world which we have not visited in our quest of the color line—Europe.

There are three significant things in Europe of to-day which must attract us: the Jew and Socialist in France, the Expansion of Germany and Russia, and the race troubles of Austria. None of these bring us directly upon the question of color; and yet nearly all touch it indirectly. In France we have seen the exhibition of a furious racial prejudice mingled with deep-lying economic causes, and not the whole public opinion of the world was able to secure an entirely satisfactory outcome. The expansion of military Germany is a sinister thing, for with all her magnificent government and fine national traits, her dealings with undeveloped races hitherto have been conspicuous failures. Her contact with the blacks of east and west Africa has been marked by a long series of disgraceful episodes, and we cannot view with complacency her recent bullying of Hayti [sic] and her high-handed seizure of Chinese territory. The development of Russia is the vast unknown quantity of the European situation and has been during the 19th century. Her own great population of Slavs stands midway racially between the white Germans and the yellow Tartar, and this makes the whole progress of the Bear a faint reflection of the color line. With the advance of Russia in Asia, the completion of the great trans-Siberian railway, and the threatened seizure of Korea, comes the inevitable clash of the Slav with the yellow masses of Asia. Perhaps a Russia-Japanese war is in the near future. At any rate a gigantic strife across the color line is impending during the next one hundred years. In Austria we see to-day the most curious and complicated race conflict between Germans, Hungarians, Czechs, Jews and Poles, the outcome of which is puzzling. Finally in the lesser countries of Europe the race question as affecting the darker peoples is coming to the fore. In the question of the status of Turkey and the Balkan States, in the ventures of Italy in Africa and China, in the black membership of the Catholic church, indeed a survey of the civilized world at the end of the 19th century but confirms the proposition with which I started—the world problem of the 20th century is the Problem of the Color line—the question of the relation of the advanced races of men who happen to be white to the great majority of the undeveloped or half developed nations of mankind who happen to be yellow, brown, or black. . . .

THE SONG OF THE SMOKE

I am the Smoke King
I am black!
I am swinging in the sky,
I am wringing worlds awry;
I am the thought of the throbbing mills,
I am the soul of the soul-toil kills,
Wraith of the ripple of trading rills;
Up I'm curling from the sod,
I am whirling home to God;
   I am the Smoke King
   I am black.

I am the Smoke King,
I am black!
I am wreathing broken hearts,
I am sheathing love's light darts;
   Inspiration of iron times
   Wedding the toil of toiling climes,
   Shedding the blood of bloodless crimes—
Lurid lowering 'mid the blue,

Torrid towering toward the true,
   I am the Smoke King,
   I am black.

I am the Smoke King,
   I am black!
I am darkening with song,
I am hearkening to wrong!
   I will be black as blackness can—
   The blacker the mantle, the mightier the man!
   For blackness was ancient ere whiteness began.
I am daubing God in night,
I am swabbing Hell in white:
   I am the Smoke King
   I am black.

I am the Smoke King
   I am black!
I am cursing ruddy morn,
I am hearsing hearts unborn:
   Souls unto me are as stars in a night,
   I whiten my black men—I blacken my white!
   What's the hue of a hide to a man in his might?
Hail! great, gritty, grimy hands—
Sweet Christ, pity toiling lands!
   I am the Smoke King
   I am black.

THE FIRST UNIVERSAL RACES CONGRESS

Of the two thousand international meetings that have taken place in the last seventy-five years there have been few that have so touched the imagination as the Universal Races Congress of this summer.

Such a meeting may be viewed in many lights: as a meeting of widely separated men, as a reunion of East and West, as a glance across the color line or as a sort of World Grievance Committee. Perhaps it was in part something of each of these. There was, however, one thing that this congress could do of inestimable importance. Outside the discussion of racial problems, it could make clear the present state of scientific knowledge concerning the meaning of the term "race."

This the congress did and this was its most important work. There were practically no reports of new anthropological knowledge. There were, however, several reviews and restatements in popular terms of the present *dicta* of the science in the matter of human races, exprest with a clearness, force and authority that deserve especial mention.

The scientific men who contributed papers to the congress, and who were with few exceptions there in person to take part in the discussions, were, many of them, of the first rank: Von Luschan and Von Ranke, of Germany; Sergi, of Italy; Myers, Lyde and Hadden, of England, and Boas, of America, are all well known; among the other speakers were the Indian scholar, Seal; Lacerda, of Brazil; Fino of France, and Reinsch, of America. All those mentioned, save Boas, were present in person.

To realize the full meaning of the statements made by these men one must not forget the racial philosophy upon which America has long been nursed. The central idea of that philosophy has been that there are vast and, for all practical purposes, unbridgeable differences between the races of men, the whites representing the higher nobler stock, the blacks the lower meaner race. Between the lowest races (who are certainly undeveloped and probably incapable of any considerable development) and the highest, range the brown and yellow peoples with various intermediate capacities.

The proofs of these assumptions have been repeatedly pointed out; the high civilization of the whites, the lack of culture among the blacks, the apparent incapacity for self-rule in many non-Europeans, and the stagnation of Asia. The reasons for this condition were variously stated: some assumed separate development for each race, while others spoke as tho the various races represented different stages in the same general development, with thousands of years between, the Negro remaining nearest the ape, the whites furthest from the common ancestor.

Had these assumptions remained merely academic opinions it would not be necessary to recall them, but they have become the scientific sanction for wide-spread and decisive political action—like the disfranchisement of American Negroes, the subjection of India and the partition of Africa. Under the aegis of this philosophy strong arguments have justified human slavery and peonage, conquest, enforced ignorance, the dishonoring of women and the exploitation of children. It was divine to enslave Negroes; Mexican peonage is the only remedy for laziness; powerful nations must rule the mass of men who are not fit and cannot be fitted to rule themselves; colored women must not be expected to be treated like white, and if commerce is arranged so as to make the dark world toil for the luxury and ease of the white, this is but the law of nature.

As I sat in the great hall of the University of London, I wondered how many of those audiences of five, six and seven hundred who daily braved the sweltering heat of a midsummer meeting realized how epoch-making many of the words quietly spoken there were, and how far they went toward undermining long and comfortably cherished beliefs.

The anthropologists were not rash in statement. They spoke with full realization of the prevalent attitude of Europeans toward other races. Some, like Von Luschan, took pains to emphasize separate racial development for the sake of the "hassenkampf," but he began with the sweeping assertion that "mankind is one":

> "Fair and dark races, long and short-headed, intelligent and primitive, all come from one stock. Favorable circumstances and surroundings, especially a good environment . . . caused one group to advance more quickly than another."

Moreover both he and Von Ranke, Sergi and others ridiculed the possibility of a "science" of race, or, indeed, of the possibility or desirability of drawing complete racial lines: "The question of the number of human races," said Von Luschan, "has quite lost its *raison d'être*, and has become a subject of philosophical speculation, rather than of scientific research. It is of no more importance to know how many races there are than to know how many angels dance on the point of a needle!"

Especial insistence was made against regarding races as unchangeable accomplished facts; they were, in the words of Boas and Seal, "growing developing entities" and "the old idea of the absolute stability of racial types must evidently be given up; and with it the belief in the hereditary superiority of certain types over others."

This brought the discussion to the crucial point, for granted that human beings form a family thru which it is difficult to draw absolute lines, yet does not the present advancement of the various groups of men correspond on the whole with their physical characteristics? No proposition was more emphatically denied than this. In physique, said Seal, quoting Weisbach, "each race has its share of the characteristics of inferiority," and it is impossible to arrange the main groups of men in an ascending scale of physical development. Lyde, of Oxford, added that even color, which is today made the greatest of racial barriers, is with little doubt "entirely a matter of climatic control."

Nevertheless there are tremendous differences in the present condition of the various groups of men—whence do they arise and how permanent are they? Practically every anthropologist present laid the chief stress on environment in explaining these differences; not simply physical environment but the even more important social environment in which the individual is educated. Von Luschan traced dark-skinned primitive man from Southern Asia to the Negro and Negroid toward the Northwest, the Indo-European toward the North and the Mongol toward the Northeast. "We have thus the three chief varieties of mankind," he said, "all branching off the same primitive stock, diverging from each other for thousands of years, but all three forming a complete unity, intermarrying in all directions without the slightest decrease of fertility." Sir Harry Johnston emphasized this early interpenetration of primitive races and found traces of Negro blood from Asia to Ireland. Others like Reinsch showed that the differences that arose among the scattered branches of men were due at first to physical environment, and pointed out the way in which the contrasting geography of Greece and Africa, and Europe and Asia, had influenced the history of their inhabitants.

Had not this long difference of environment left traces in the characters of races so ingrained as to be today practically ineradicable? Myers, of Oxford, asserted, in answer to this, that the mental characteristics of the majority of Europe were today essentially the same as those of the primitive peoples of the earth; that such differences as exist are due to present social and physical environment and that therefore "the progressive development of all primitive people must be conceded if the environment can be appropriately changed."

From the papers submitted to the congress and from his own studies, Gustav Spiller, the secretary, stated that a fair interpretation of the scientific evidence would support these propositions:

1.   It is not legitimate to argue from differences in physical characteristics to difference in mental characteristics.

2.   Physical and mental characteristics of races are not permanent, nor are they modifiable only thru long ages. On the contrary they are capable of being profoundly modified in a few generations by changes in education, public sentiment and environment generally.

3.   The status of a race at any particular time offers no index as to its innate or inherited capacities.

As to race mixture all the anthropologists said that there were no "pure" races and that modern peoples were all more or less mixt. Nevertheless while many of these mixtures were obviously beneficial, it was not clear whether all racial mixtures would be. Certainly it was unscientific to assert that mulattoes and Eurasians were degenerate in the absence of all scientific data. Lacerda, of Brazil, showed the high proportion of mulattoes in the population of Brazil and the leading role they had played in emancipating the slaves, in establishing the republic and in the literary and political life of the day. Sir Charles Bruce and Sir Sidney Olivier made somewhat similar statements concerning the West Indies.

It would be too much to say that all anthropologists today would subscribe to the main conclusions of those who attended the Races Congress or that the doctrine of inevitable race superiority is dead. On the other hand there is good reason to affirm with Finot, in the brochure which he gave to the congress:

> The conception of races as of so many watertight compartments into which human beings can be crammed as if they were so many breeds of horses or cattle, has had its day. The word race will doubtless long survive, even tho it may have lost all meaning. From time immemorial men have taken far more pains to damn their souls than would have sufficed to save them. Hence they will be certain to preserve this most scientific term which incites to hatred and unjustifiable contempt for our fellow men, instead of replacing it by some word implying the brotherhood of man.

The congress itself recorded its judgment on the matter of race differences by

> Urging the vital importance at this juncture of history of discountenancing race prejudice, as tending to inflict on humanity incalculable harm, and as based on generalizations unworthy of an enlightened and progressive age.

IN BLACK

It was in Chicago. John Haynes Holmes was talking.

He said: "I met two children—one as fair as the dawn—the other as beautiful as the night." Then he paused. He had to pause for the audience guffawed in wild merriment. Why?

It was a colored audience. Many of them were black. Some black faces there were as beautiful as the night.

Why did they laugh?

Because the world had taught them to be ashamed of their color.

Because for 500 years men had hated and despised and abused black folk.

And now in strange, inexplicable transposition the rising blacks laugh at themselves in nervous, blatant, furtive merriment.

They laugh because they think they are expected to laugh—because all their poor hunted lives they have heard "black" things laughed at.

Of all the pitiful things of this pitiful race problem, this is the pitifullest. So curious a mental state tends to further subtleties. Colored folk, like all folk, love to see themselves in pictures; but they are afraid to see the types which the white world has caricatured. The whites obviously seldom picture brown and yellow folk, but for five centuries they have exhausted every ingenuity of trick, of ridicule and caricature on black folk: "grinning" Negroes, "happy" Negroes, "gold dust twins," "Aunt Jemimas," "solid" headed tacks—everything and anything to make Negroes ridiculous. As a result if THE CRISIS puts a black face on its cover our 500,000 colored readers do not see the actual picture—they see the caricature that white folks intend when *they* make a black face. In the last few years a thoughtful, clear eyed artist, Frank Walts, has done a number of striking portraits for THE CRISIS. Mainly he has treated black faces: and regularly protests have come to us from various colored sources. His lovely portrait of the bright-eyed boy, Harry Elam, done in thoughtful sympathy, was approved by few Negroes. Our photograph of a woman of Santa Lucia, with its strength and humor and fine swing of head, was laughed at by many.

Why?

"O—er—it was not because they were black," stammer some of my office companions, "but they are *too* black. No people were ever so—"

Nonsense! Do white people complain because their pictures are too white? They ought to, but they do not. Neither do we complain if we are photographed a shade "light."

No. It is not that we are ashamed of our color and blood. We are instinctively and almost unconsciously ashamed of the caricatures done of our darker shades. Black *is* caricature in our half conscious thought and we shun in print and paint that which we love in life. How good a dark face looks to us in a strange white city! How the black soldiers, despite their white French sweethearts, yearned for their far-off "brown-skins." A mighty and swelling human consciousness is leading us joyously to embrace the darker world, but we remain afraid of black pictures because they are the cruel reminders of the crimes of Sunday "comics" and "Nigger" minstrels.

Off with these thought-chains and inchoate soul-shrinkings, and let us train ourselves to see beauty in black.

THE SUPERIOR RACE

I

When the obsession of his race consciousness leaves him, my white friend is quite companionable; otherwise he is impossible. He has a way of putting an excessive amount of pity in his look and of stating as a general and incontrovertible fact that it is "horrible" to be an Exception. By this he means me. He is more than certain that I prove the rule. He is not a bright person, but of that famous average, standardized and astonished at anything that even seems original. His thesis is simple: The world is composed of Race superimposed on Race; classes superimposed on classes; beneath the whole thing is "Our Family" in capitals, and under that is God. God seems to be a cousin, or at least a blood relative of the Van Diemans.

"Of course," he says, "you know Negroes are inferior."

I admit nothing of the sort, I maintain. In fact, having known with considerable intimacy, both male and female, the people of the British Isles, of Scandinavia, of Russia, of Germany, north and south, of the three ends of France and the two ends of Italy; specimens from the Balkans and black and white Spain; the three great races of Asia and the melange of Africa, without mentioning America, I sit here and maintain that black folk are much the superior of white.

"You are either joking or mad," he says.

Both and neither. This race talk is, of course, a joke, and frequently it has driven me insane and probably will permanently in the future; and yet, seriously and soberly, we black folk are the salvation of mankind.

He regards me with puzzled astonishment and says confidentially:

"Do you know that sometimes I am half afraid that you really believe this? At other times I see clearly the inferiority complex."

The former after lunch, I reply, and the latter before.

"Very well," he says, "let's lunch."

Where? I ask quizzically, we being at the time in the roaring Forties.

"Why-oh, well!—their refusal to serve you lunch at least does not prove your superiority."

Nor yet theirs, I answer; but never mind, come with me to Second Avenue.

We start again with the salad.

"Now, superiority consists of what?" he argues.

Life is, I remark, (1) Beauty and health of body, (2) Mental clearness and creative genius, (3) Spiritual goodness and receptivity, (4) Social adaptability and constructiveness.

"Not bad," he answers. "Not bad at all. Now I contend that the white race conspicuously excels in one, two and four and is well abreast even in three."

And I maintain that the black race excels in one, three and four and is well abreast in two.

"Sheer nonsense and pure balderdash! Compare the Venus of Milo and the Apollo Belvedere with a Harlem or Beale Street couple."

With a Fifth Avenue Easter parade or a Newport Dance. In short, compare humanity at its best or worst with the Ideal, and humanity suffers. But black folk in most attributes of physical beauty, in line and height and curve, have the same norms as white and differ only in small details of color, hair and curve of countenance. Now can there be any question but that as colors bronze, mahogany, coffee and gold are far lovelier than pink, gray and marble? Hair is a matter of taste. Some will have it drab and stringy and others in a gray, woven, unmoving mass. Most of us like it somewhere between, in tiny tendrils, smoking curls and sweeping curves. I have loved all these varieties in my day. I prefer the crinkly kind, almost wavy, in black brown and glistening. In faces I hate straight features; needles and razors may be sharp—but beautiful, never.

"All that is personal opinion. I prefer the colors of heaven and day: sunlight hair and blue eyes, and straight noses and thin lips, and that incomparable air of haughty aloofness and aristocracy."

And I, on the contrary, am the child of twilight and night, and choose intricately curly hair, black eyes, full and luscious features, and that air of humility and wonder which streams from moonlight. Add to this, voices that caress instead of rasp, glances that appeal rather then repel, and a sinuous litheness of movement to replace Anglo-Saxon stalking—there you have my ideal. Of course you can bury any human body in dirt and misery and make it horrible. I have seen the East End of London.

"Beauty seems to be simply opinion, if you put it that way."

To be sure. But whose opinion?

"Bother beauty. Here we shall never agree. But, after all, I doubt if it makes much difference. The real point is Brains: clear thinking, pure reason, mathematical precision and creative genius. Now, with *blague*, stand and acknowledge that here the white race is supreme."

Quite the contrary. I know no attribute in which the white race has more conspicuously failed. This is white and European civilization; and as a system of culture it is idiotic, addle-brained, unreasoning, topsy-turvy, without precision, and its genius chiefly runs to marvelous contrivances for enslaving the many and enriching the few. I see absolutely no proof that the average ability of the white man's brain to think clearly is any greater than that of the yellow man or of the black man. If we take even that doubtful but widely heralded test, the frequency of individual creative genius (when a real racial test should be the frequency of ordinary common sense)—if we take the Genius as the saviour of mankind, it is only possible for the white race to prove its own incontestable superiority by appointing both judge and jury and summoning only its own witnesses.

I freely admit that, according to white writers, white teachers, white historians and white molders of public opinion,, nothing ever happened in the world of any importance that could not or should not be labeled "white." How silly. I place black iron welding and village democracy and yellow printing and state building side by side with white representative government and the steam engine, and unhesitatingly give the palm to the first. I hand the first vast conception of the solar system to the Africanized Egyptians, the creation of Art to the Chinese, and then let Europe rave over the Factory system.

"But is not well-being more widely diffused among white folk than among yellow and black, and general intelligence more common?"

Momentarily true; and why? Ask the geography of Europe, the African Slave Trade and the Imperial Industrialization of the nineteenth-century white man. Turn the thing around and let mountain and sea protect and isolate a continuous tradition of culture among yellow and black for one thousand years, while simultaneously they bleed the world of its brawn and wealth, and you will have exactly what we have today, under another name and color.

"Precisely. Then, at least, the white race is more advanced and no more blameworthy than others because, as I insist, its native intelligence is greater. It is germ plasm—seed—that I am talking about. Do you believe in heredity?"

Not blindly; but I should be mildly surprised to see a dog born of a cat.

"Exactly; or a genius born of a fool."

No, no; on the contrary, I rather expect fools of geniuses and geniuses of fools. And while I stoutly maintain that cattiness and dogginess are as far apart as the East from the West, on the other hand I just as strongly believe that the human ass and superman have much in common and can often, if not always, spawn each other.

"Is it possible that you have never heard of the Jukes, or of the man who married first an idiot and then a prune?"

It is not possible; they have been served up to me ad infinitum. But they are nothing. I know greater wonders: Lincoln from Nancy Hanks, Dumas from a black beast of burden, Kant from a saddler, and Jesus Christ from a manger.

"All of which, instead of disproving, is exact and definite proof of the persistence of good blood."

Precisely, and of the catholicity of its tastes; the method of proof is this: When anything good occurs, it is proof of good blood; when anything bad occurs, it is proof of bad blood. Very well. Now good and bad, native endowment and native deficiency, do not follow racial lines. There is good stock in all races and the outcropping of bad individuals, too; and there has been absolutely no proof that the white race has any larger share of the gifted strains of human heritage than the black race or the yellow race. To be sure, good seed proves itself in the flower and fruit, but the failure of seed to sprout is no proof that it is not good. It may be proof simply of the absence of manure—or its excessive presence.

Granted, that when time began, there was hidden in a Seed that tiny speck that spelled the world's salvation, do you think today it would manifest itself crudely and baldly in a dash of skin color and a crinkle of hair? Is the subtle mystery of life and consciousness and of ability portrayed in any such slapdash and obvious marks of difference?

"Go out upon the street; choose ten white men and ten colored men. Which can best carry on and preserve American civilization?"

The whites.

"Well, then!"

You evidently consider that a compliment. Let it pass. Go out upon the street and choose ten men and ten women. Which could best run a Ford car? The men, of course; but—hold. Fly out into the sky and look down upon ten children of Podunk and ten children of Chicago. Which would know most about elevated railroads, baseball, zoology and movies?

"The point is visible, but beyond that, outside of mere experience and education, and harking back to native gift and intelligence, on your honor, which has most, white folk or black folk?"

There you have me deep in the shadows, beyond the benign guidance of words. Just what is gift and intelligence, especially of the native sort? And when we compare the gift of one human soul with that of another, are we not seeking to measure incommensurable things; trying to lump things like sunlight and music and love? And if a certain shadowy Over-soul can really compare the incomparable with some transcendental yardstick, may we not here emerge into a super-equality of man? At least this I can quite believe.

"But it is a pious belief, not more."

Not more; but a pious belief outweighs an impious unbelief.

II

Admitting that the problem of native human endowment is obscure, there is no corresponding obscurity in spiritual values. Goodness and unselfishness; simplicity and honor; tolerance, susceptibility to beauty in form, color and music; courage to look truth in the face; courage to live and suffer in patience and humility, and forgiveness and in hope; eagerness to turn, not simply the other cheek, but the face and the bowed back; capacity to love. In all these mighty things, the greatest things in the world, where do black folk and white folk stand?

Why, man of mine, you would not have the courage to live one hour as a black man in America, or as a Negro in the whole wide world. Ah, yes, I know what you whisper to such accusation. You say dryly that if we had good sense, we would not live either; and that the fact that we do submit to life as it is and yet laugh and dance and dream is but another proof that we are idiots.

This is the truly marvelous way in which you prove your superiority by admitting that our love of life can only be intelligently explained on the hypothesis of inferiority. What finer tribute is possible to our courage?

What great works of Art have we made? Very few. The Pyramids, Luqsor, the Bronzes of Benin, the Spears of the Bongo. "When Malinda

Sings" and the Sorrow Song she is always singing. Oh, yes, and the love of her dancing.

But art is not simply works of art; it is the spirit that knows Beauty, that has music in its soul and the color of sunsets in its headkerchiefs; that can dance on a flaming world and make the world dance, too. Such is the soul of the Negro.

Why, do you know the two finest things in the industry of the West, finer than factory, shop or ship? One is the black laborers' Saturday off. Neither the whip of the driver, nor starvation wage, nor the disgust of the Yankee, nor the call of the cotton crop, had yet convinced the common black variety of plantation laborer that one day in the week is enough for rest and play. He wants two days. And, from California to Texas, from Florida to Trinidad, he takes two days while the planter screams and curses. They have beaten the English slavey, the French and German peasants and the North Italian contadini into twelve-hour, six day slaves. They crushed the Chinese and Indian coolie into a twenty-four-hour beast of burden; they have even made the American, free, white and twenty-one, believe that daily toil is one of the Ten Commandments. But not the Negro. From Monday to Friday the field hand is a slave; then for forty-eight golden hours he is free, and through these same forty-eight hours he may yet free the dumb, driven cattle of the world.

Then the second thing, laughter. This race has the greatest of the gifts of God, laughter. It dances and sings; it is humble; it longs to learn; it loves men; it loves women. It is frankly, baldly, deliciously human in an artificial and hypocritical land. If you will hear men laugh, go to Guinea, "Black Bottom," "Niggertown," Harlem. If you want to feel humor too exquisite and subtle for translation, sit invisibly among a gang of Negro workers. The white world has its gibes and cruel caricatures; it has its loud guffaws, but to the black world alone belongs the delicious chuckle.

"But the State; the modern industrial State. Wealth of work, wealth of commerce, factory and mine, skyscrapers; New York, Chicago, Johannesburg, Lyons and Liverpool."

This is the best expression of the civilization in which the white race finds itself today. This is what the white world means by culture.

"Does it not excel the black and yellow race here?"

It does. But the excellence here raises no envy; only regrets. If this vast Frankenstein monster really served its makers; if it were their minister and not their master, god and king; if their machines gave us rest and leisure, instead of the drab uniformity of uninteresting drudgery; if their factories gave us gracious community of thought and feeling; beauty enshrined, free and joyous; if their work veiled them with tender sympathy at human distress and wide tolerance and understanding—then, all hail, White Imperial Industry. But it does not. It is a Beast! Its creators even do not understand it, cannot curb or guide it.

They, themselves, are but hideous, groping higher Hands, doing their bit to oil the raging, devastating machinery which kills men to make cloth, prostitutes women to rear buildings and eats little children.

Is this superiority? It is madness. We are the supermen who sit idly by and laugh and look at civilization. We, who frankly want the bodies of our mates and conjure no blush to our bronze cheeks when we own it. We, who exalt the Lynched above the Lyncher and the Worker above the Owner and the Crucified above Imperial Rome.

"But why have you black and yellow men done nothing better or even as good in the history of the world?"

We have, often.

"I never heard of it."

Lions have no historians.

"It is idiotic even to discuss it. Look around and see the pageantry of the world. It belongs to white men; it is the expression of white power; it is the product of white brains. Who can have the effrontery to stand for a moment and compare with this white triumph, yellow and brown anarchy and black savagery?"

You are obsessed by the swiftness of the gliding of the sled at the bottom of the hill. You say: What tremendous power must have caused its speed, and how wonderful is Speed. You think of the rider as the originator and inventor of that vast power. You admire his poise and *sang froid*, his utter self-absorption. You say: Surely here is the Son of God and he shall reign forever and forever.

You are wrong, quite wrong. Away back on the level stretches of the mountain tops in the forests, amid drifts and driftwood, this sled was slowly and painfully pushed on its little hesitating start. It took power, but the power of sweating, courageous men, not of demi-gods. As the sled slowly started and gained momentum, it was the Law of Being that gave it speed, and the grace of God that steered its lone, scared passengers. Those passengers, white, black, red and yellow, deserve credit for their balance and pluck. But many times it was sheer good luck that the made road did not land the white man in the gutter, as it had others so many times before, and as it may him yet. He has gone farther than others because of others whose very falling made hard ways iced and smooth for him to traverse. His triumph is a triumph not of himself alone, but of humankind, from the pusher in the primeval forests to the last flier through the winds of the twentieth century.

III

And so to leave our parable and come to reality. Great as has been the human advance in the last one thousand years, it is, so far as native human ability, so far as intellectual gift and moral courage are concerned, nothing as compared with any one of ten and more millenniums before, far back in the forests of tropical Africa and in hot India, where brown and black humankind first fought climate and disease and bugs and beasts; where man dared simply to live and propagate himself. There was the hardest and greatest struggle in all the human world. If in sheer exhaustion or in desperate self-defense during this last moment of civilization he has rested, half inert and blinded with the sweat of his efforts, it is only the silly onlooker who sees but the passing moment of time, who can think of him as subhuman and inferior.

All this is Truth, but unknown, unapprehended Truth. Indeed, the greatest and most immediate danger of white culture, perhaps least sensed, is its fear of the Truth. Its childish belief in the efficacy of lies as a method of human uplift. The lie is defensible; it has been used widely and often profitably among humankind. But it may be doubted if ever before in the world so many intelligent people believed in it so deeply. We deliberately and continuously deceive not simply others, but ourselves as to the truth about them, us and the world. We have raised Propaganda to capital "P" and elaborated an art, almost a science of how one may make the world believe what is not true, provided the untruth is a widely wished-for thing like the probable extermination of Negroes, the failure of the Chinese Republic, the incapacity of India for self-rule, the failure of [the] Russian Revolution. When in other days the world lied, it was to a world that expected lies and consciously defended them; when the world lies today it is to a world that pretends to be true.

"In other words, according to you, white folk are about the meanest and lowest on earth."

They are human, even as you and I.

"Why don't you leave them then? Get out, go to Africa or to the North Pole; shake the dust of their hospitality from off your feet?"

There are abundant reasons. First, they have annexed the earth and hold it by transient but real power. Thus by running away, I shall not only not escape them, but succeed in hiding myself in out of the way places where they can work their deviltry on me without photograph, telegraph or telephone. But even more important than this: I am as bad as they are. In fact, I am related to them and they have much that belongs to me—this land, for instance, for which my fathers starved and fought; I share their sins; in fine, I am related to them.

"By blood?"

By blood.

"Then you are railing at yourself. You are not black; you are no Negro."

And you? Yellow blood and black has deluged Europe in days past even more than America yesterday. You are not white, as the measurements of your head will show.

"What then becomes of all your argument, if there are no races and we are all so horribly mixed as you maliciously charge?"

Oh, my friend, can you not see that I am laughing at you? Do you suppose this world of men is simply a great layer cake with superimposed slices of inferior and superior races, interlaid with mud?

No, no. Human beings are infinite in variety, and when they are agglutinated in groups, great and small, the groups differ as though they, too, had integrating souls. But they have not. The soul is still individual if it is free; the group is a social, sometimes an historical fact. And all that I really have been trying to say is that a certain group that I know and to which I belong, as contrasted with the group you know and to which you belong, and in which you fanatically and glorifyingly believe, bears in its bosom just now the spiritual hope of this land because of the persons who compose it and not by divine command.

"But what is this group; and how do you differentiate it; and how can you call it 'black' when you admit it is not black?"

I recognize it quite easily and with full legal sanction: the black man is a person who must ride "Jim Crow" in Georgia.

ON BEING CRAZY

It was one o'clock and I was hungry. I walked into a restaurant, seated myself and reached for the bill-of-fare. My table companion rose.

"Sir," said he, "do you wish to force your company on those who do not want you?"

No, said I, I wish to eat.

"Are you aware, Sir, that this is social equality?"

Nothing of the sort, Sir, it is hunger,—and I ate.

The day's work done, I sought the theatre. As I sank into my seat, the lady shrank and squirmed.

I beg pardon, I said.

"Do you enjoy being where you are not wanted?" she asked coldly.

Oh no I said.

"Well you are not wanted here."

I was surprised. I fear you are mistaken, I said. I certainly want the music and I like to think the music wants me to listen to it.

"Usher," said the lady, "this is social equality."

No, madame, said the usher, it is the second movement of Beethoven's Fifth Symphony.

After the theatre, I sought the hotel where I had sent my baggage. The clerk scowled.

"What do you want?" he asked.

Rest, I said.

"This is a white hotel," he said.

I looked around. Such a color scheme requires a great deal of cleaning, I said, but I don't know that I object.

"We object," said he.

Then why—, I began, but he interrupted.

"We don't keep 'niggers'," he said, "we don't want social equality."

Neither do I. I replied gently, I want a bed.

I walked thoughtfully to the train. I'll take a sleeper through Texas. I'm a bit dissatisfied with this town.

"Can't sell you one."

I only want to hire it, said I, for a couple of nights.

"Can't sell you a sleeper in Texas," he maintained. "They consider that social equality."

I consider it barbarism, I said, and I think I'll walk.

Walking, I met a wayfarer who immediately walked to the other side of the road where it was muddy. I asked his reasons.

" 'Niggers' is dirty," he said.

So is mud, said I. Moreover I added, I am not as dirty as you—at least, not yet.

"But you're a 'nigger', ain't you?" he asked.

My grandfather was so-called.

"Well then!" he answered triumphantly.

Do you live in the South? I persisted, pleasantly.

"Sure," he growled, "and starve there."

I should think you and the Negroes might get together and vote out starvation.

"We don't let them vote."

We? Why not? I said in surprise.

" 'Niggers' is too ignorant to vote."

But, I said, I am not so ignorant as you.

"But you're a 'nigger'."

Yes, I'm certainly what you mean by that.

"Well then!" he returned, with that curiously inconsequential note of triumph. "Moreover," he said, "I don't want my sister to marry a nigger."

I had not seen his sister, so I merely murmured, let her say, no.

"By God you shan't marry her, even if she said yes."

But,—but I don't want to marry her, I answered a little perturbed at the personal turn.

"Why not!" he yelled, angrier than ever.

Because I'm already married and I rather like my wife.

"Is she a 'nigger'?" he asked suspiciously.

Well, I said again, her grandmother—was called that.

"Well then!" he shouted in that oddly illogical way.
I gave up. Go on, I said, either you are crazy or I am.
"We both are," he said as he trotted along in the mud.

THE NAME "NEGRO"

Dear Sir:

I am only a high school student in my Sophomore year, and have not the understanding of you college educated men. It seems to me that since THE CRISIS is the Official Organ of the National Association for the Advancement of Colored People which stand for equality for all Americans, why would it designate, and segregate us as "Negroes," and not as "Americans."

The most piercing thing that hurts me in this February CRISIS, which forced me to write, was the notice that called the natives of Africa, "Negroes," instead of calling them "Africans," or "natives".

The word, "Negro," or "nigger," is a white man's word to make us feel inferior. I hope to be a worker for my race, that is why I wrote this letter. I hope that by the time I become a man, that this word, "Negro," will be abolished.

ROLAND A. BARTON.

My dear Roland:

Do not at the outset of your career make the all too common error of mistaking names for things. Names are only conventional signs for identifying things. Things are the reality that counts. If a thing is despised, either because of ignorance or because it is despicable, you will not alter matters by changing its name. If men despise Negroes, they will not despise them less if Negroes are called "colored" or "Afro-Americans."

Moreover, you cannot change the name of a thing at will. Names are not merely matters of thought and reason; they are growths and habits. As long as the majority of men mean black or brown folk when they say "Negro," so long will Negro be the name of folks brown and black. And neither anger nor wailing nor tears can or will change the name until the name-habit changes.

But why seek to change the name? "Negro" is a fine word. Etymologically and phonetically it is much better and more logical than "African" or "colored" or any of the various hyphenated circumlocutions. Of course, it is not "historically" accurate. No name ever was historically accurate: neither "English," "French," "German," "White," "Jew," "Nordic" nor "Anglo-Saxon." They were all at first nicknames, misnomers, accidents, grown eventually to conventional habits and achieving accuracy because, and simply because, wide and continued usage rendered them accurate. In this sense "Negro" is quite as accurate, quite as old and quite as definite as any name of any great group of people.

Suppose now we could change the name. Suppose we arose tomorrow morning and lo! instead of being "Negroes," all the world called us "Cheiropolidi"—do you really think this would make a vast and momentous difference to you and to me? Would the Negro problem be suddenly and eternally settled? Would you be any less ashamed of being descended from a black man, or would your schoolmates feel any less superior to you? The feeling of inferiority is in you, not in any name. The name merely evokes what is already there. Exorcise the hateful complex and no name can ever make you hang your head.

Or, on the other hand, suppose that we slip out of the whole thing by calling ourselves "Americans." But in that case, what word shall we use when we want to talk about those descendants of dark slaves who are largely excluded still from full American citizenship and from complete social privilege with white folk? Here is Something that we want to talk about; that we do talk about; that we Negroes could not live without talking about. In that case, we need a name for it, do we not? In order to talk logically and easily and be understood. If you do not believe in the necessity of such a name, watch the antics of a colored newspaper which has determined in a fit of New Year's Resolutions not to use the word "Negro!"

And then too, without the word that means Us, where are all those spiritual ideals, those inner bonds, those group ideals and forward strivings of this mighty army of 12 millions? Shall we abolish these with the abolition of a name? Do we want to abolish them? Of course we do not. They are our most precious heritage.

Historically, of course, your dislike of the word Negro is easily explained: "Negroes" among your grandfathers meant black folk; "Colored" people were mulattoes. The mulattoes hated and despised the blacks and were insulted if called "Negroes". But we are not insulted—not you and I. We are quite as proud of our black ancestors as of our white. And perhaps a little prouder. What hurts us is the mere memory that any man of Negro descent was ever so cowardly as to despise any part of his own blood.

Your real work, my dear young man, does not lie with names. It is not a matter of changing them, losing them, or forgetting them. Names are nothing but little guideposts along the Way. The Way would be there and just as hard and just as long if there were no guideposts—but not quite as easily followed! Your real work as a Negro lies in two directions: *First,* to let the world know what there is fine and genuine about the Negro race. And *secondly,* to see that there is nothing about that race which is worth contempt; your contempt, my contempt; or the contempt of the wide, wide world.

Get this then, Roland, and get it straight even if it pierces your soul: a Negro by any other name would be just as black and just as white; just as ashamed of himself and just as shamed by others, as today. It is not the name—it's the Thing that counts. Come on, Kid, let's go get the Thing!

ON BEING ASHAMED OF ONESELF

AN ESSAY ON RACE PRIDE

My Grandfather left a passage in his diary expressing his indignation at receiving an invitation to a "Negro" picnic. Alexander Du Bois, born in the Bahamas, son of Dr. James Du Bois of the well-known Du Bois family of Poughkeepsie, N.Y., had been trained as a gentleman in the Cheshire School of Connecticut, and the implications of a Negro picnic were anathema to his fastidious soul. It meant close association with poverty, ignorance and suppressed and disadvantaged people, dirty and with bad manners.

This was in 1856. Seventy years later, Marcus Garvey discovered that a black skin was in itself a sort of patent to nobility, and that Negroes ought to be proud of themselves and their ancestors, for the same or analogous reasons that made white folk feel superior.

Thus, within the space of three-fourths of a century, the pendulum has swung between race pride and race suicide, between attempts to build up a racial ethos and attempts to escape from ourselves. In the years between emancipation and 1900, the theory of escape was dominant. We were, by birth, law and training, American citizens. We were going to escape into the mass of Americans in the same way that the Irish and Scandinavians and even the Italians were beginning to disappear. The process was going to be slower on account of the badge of color; but then, after all, it was not so much the matter of physical assimilation as of spiritual and psychic amalgamation with the American people.

For this reason, we must oppose all segregation and all racial patriotism; we must salute the American flag and sing "Our Country 'Tis of Thee" with devotion and fervor, and we must fight for our rights with [a] long and carefully planned campaign; uniting for this purpose with all sympathetic people, colored and white.

This is still the dominant philosophy of most American Negroes and it is [in] back of the objection to even using a special designation like "Negro" or even "Afro-American" or any such term.

But there are certain practical difficulties connected with this program which are becoming more and more clear today. First of all comes the fact that we are still ashamed of ourselves and are thus estopped from valid objection when white folks are ashamed to call us human. The reasons, of course, are not as emphatic as they were in the case of my grandfather. I remember a colored man, now ex-patriate, who made this discovery in my company, some twenty-five years ago. He was a handsome burning brown, tall, straight and well-educated, and he occupied a position which he had won, across and in spite of the color line. He did not believe in Negroes, for himself or his family, and he planned elaborately to escape the trammels of race. Yet, he had responded to a call for a meeting of colored folk which touched his interests, and he came. He found men of his own caliber and training; he found men charming and companionable. He was thoroughly delighted. I know that never before, or I doubt if ever since, he had been in such congenial company. He could not help mentioning his joy continually and reiterating it.

All colored folk had gone through the same experience, for more and more largely in the last twenty-five years, colored America has discovered itself: has discovered groups of people, association with whom is a poignant joy and despite their ideal of American assimilation, in more and more cases and with more and more determined object they seek each other.

That involves, however, a drawing of class lines inside the Negro race, and it means the emergence of a certain social aristocracy, who by reasons of looks and income, education and contact, form the sort of upper social group which the world has long known and helped to manufacture and preserve. The early basis of this Negro group was simply color and a bald imitation of the white environment. Later, it tended, more and more, to be based on wealth and still more recently on education and social position.

This leaves a mass of untrained and uncultured colored folk and even of trained but ill-mannered people and groups of impoverished workers of whom this upper class of colored Americans are ashamed. They are ashamed both directly and indirectly, just as any richer or better sustained group in a nation is ashamed of those less fortunate and withdraws its skirts from touching them. But more than that, because the upper colored group is desperately afraid of being represented before American whites by this lower group, or being mistaken for them, or being treated as though they were part of it, they are pushed to the extreme of effort to avoid contact with the poorest classes of Negroes. This exaggerates, at once, the secret shame of being identified with such people and the anomaly of insisting that the physical characteristics of these folk, which the upper class shares, are not the stigmata of degradation.

When, therefore, in offense or defense, the leading group of Negroes must make common cause with the masses of their own race, the embarrassment or hesitation becomes apparent. They are embarrassed and indignant because an educated man should be treated as a Negro, and that no Negroes receive credit for social standing. They are ashamed and embarrassed because of the compulsion of being classed with a mass of people over whom they have no real control and whose action they can influence only with difficulty and compromise and with every risk of defeat.

Especially is all natural control over this group difficult—I mean control of law and police, of economic power, of guiding standards and ideals, of news propaganda. On this comes even greater difficulty because of the incompatibility of any action which looks toward racial integrity and race action with previous ideals. What are we really aiming at? The building of a new nation or the integration of a new group into an old nation? The latter has long been our ideal. Must it be changed? Should it be changed? If we seek new group loyalty, new pride of race, new racial integrity—how, where, and by what method shall these things be attained? A new plan must be built up. It cannot be the mere rhodomontade and fatuous propaganda on which Garveyism was based. It has got to be far-sighted planning. It will involve increased segregation and perhaps migration. It will be pounced upon and aided and encouraged by every "nigger-hater" in the land.

Moreover, in further comment on all this, it may be pointed out that this is not the day for the experiment of new nations or the emphasis of racial lines. This is, or at least we thought it was, the day of the Inter-nation, of Humanity, and the disappearance of "race" from our vocabulary. Are we American Negroes seeking to move against or into the face of this fine philosophy? Here then is the real problem, the real new dilemma between rights of American citizens and racial pride, which faces American Negroes today and which is not always or often clearly faced.

The situation is this: America, in denying equality of rights, of employment and social recognition to American Negroes, has said in the past that the Negro was so far below the average nation in social position, that he could not be recognized until he had developed further. In the answer to this, the Negro has eliminated five-sixths of his illiteracy, according to official figures, and greatly increased the number of colored persons who have received education of the higher sort. They still are poor, with a large number of delinquents and dependents. Nevertheless, their average situation in this respect has been greatly improved and, on the other hand, the emergence and accomplishment of colored men of ability has been undoubted. Notwithstanding this, the Negro is still a group apart, with almost no social recognition, subject to insult and discrimination, with income and wage far below the average of the nation and the most deliberately exploited industrial class in America. Even trained Negroes have increasing difficulty in making a living sufficient to sustain a civilized standard of life. Particularly in the recent vast economic changes, color discrimination as it now goes on, is going to make it increasingly difficult for the Negro to remain an integral part of the industrial machine or to increase his participation in accordance with his ability.

The integration of industry is making it more and more possible for executives to exercise their judgment in choosing for key positions, persons who can guide the industrial machine, and the exclusion of persons from such positions merely on the basis of race and color or even Negro descent is a widely recognized and easily defended prerogative. All that is necessary for any Christian American gentleman of high position and wide power to say in denying place and promotion to an eligible candidate is: "He is of Negro descent." The answer and excuse is final and all but universally accepted. For this reason, the Negro's opportunity in State directed industry and his opportunity in the great private organization of industry, if not actually growing less, is certainly much smaller than his growth in education and ability. Either the industry of the nation in the future is to be conducted by private trusts or by government control. There seems in both to be little or no chance of advancement for the Negro worker, the educated artisan and the educated leader.

On the other hand, organized labor is giving Negroes less recognition today than ever. It has practically excluded them from all the higher lines of skilled work, on railroads, in machine-shops, in manufacture and in the basic industries. In agriculture, where the Negro has theoretically the largest opportunity, he is excluded from successful participation, not only by conditions common to all farmers, but by special conditions due to lynching, lawlessness, disfranchisement and social degradation.

Facing these indisputable facts, there is on the part of the leaders of public opinion in America, no effective response to our agitation or organized propaganda. Our advance in the last quarter century has been in segregated, racially integrated institutions and efforts and not in effective entrance into American national life. In Negro churches, Negro schools, Negro colleges, Negro business and Negro art and literature our advance has been determined and inspiring; but in industry, general professional careers and national life, we have fought battle after battle and lost more often than we have won. There seems no hope that America in our day will yield in its color or race hatred any substantial ground and we have no physical nor economic power, nor any alliance with other social or economic classes, that will force compliance with decent civilized ideals in Church, State, industry or art.

The next step, then, is certainly one on the part of the Negro and it involves group action. It involves the organization of intelligent and earnest people of Negro descent for their preservation and advancement in America, in the West Indies and in Africa; and no sentimental distaste for racial or national unity can be allowed to hold them back from a step which sheer necessity demands.

A new organized group action along economic lines, guided by intelligence and with the express object of making it possible for Negroes to earn a better living and, therefore, more effectively to support agencies for social uplift, is without the slightest doubt the next step. It will involve no opposition from white America[ns] because they do not believe we can accomplish it. They expect always to be able to crush, insult, ignore and exploit 12,000,000 individual Negroes without intelligent organized opposition. This organization is going to involve deliberate propaganda for race pride. That is, it is going to start out by convincing American Negroes that there is no reason for them being ashamed of themselves; that their record is one which should make them proud; that their history in Africa and the world is a history of effort, success and trial, comparable with that of any other people.

Such measured statements can and will be exaggerated. There will be those who will want to say that the black race is the first and greatest of races, that its accomplishments are most extraordinary, that its desert is most obvious and its mistakes negligible. This is the kind of talk we hear from people with the superiority complex among the white and the yellow race.

We cannot entirely escape it, since it is just as true, and just as false, as such statements among other races; but we can use intelligence in modifying and restraining it. We can refuse deliberately to lie about our history, while at the same time taking just pride in Nefertari, Askia, Moshesh, Toussaint and Frederick Douglass, and testing and encouraging belief in our own ability by organized economic and social action.

There is no other way; let us not be deceived. American Negroes will be beaten into submission and degradation if they merely wait unorganized to find some place voluntarily given them in the new reconstruction of the economic world. They must themselves force their race into the new economic set-up and bring with them the millions of West Indians and Africans by peaceful organization for normative action or else drift into greater poverty, greater crime, greater helplessness until there is no resort but the last red alternative of revolt, revenge and war.

THE CONCEPT OF RACE

I want now to turn aside from the personal annals of this biography to consider the conception which is after all my main subject. The concept of race lacks something in personal interest, but personal interest in my case has always depended primarily upon this race concept and I wish to examine this now. The history of the development of the race concept in the world and particularly in America, was naturally reflected in the education offered me. In the elementary school it came only in the matter of geography when the races of the world were pictured: Indians, Negroes and Chinese, by their most uncivilized and bizarre representatives; the whites by some kindly and distinguished-looking philanthropist. In the elementary and high school, the matter was touched only incidentally, due I doubt not to the thoughtfulness of the teachers; and again my racial inferiority could not be dwelt upon because the single representative of the Negro race in the school did not happen to be in any way inferior to his fellows. In fact it was not difficult for me to excel them in many ways and to regard this as quite natural.

At Fisk, the problem of race was faced openly and essential racial equality asserted and natural inferiority strenuously denied. In some cases the teachers expressed this theory; in most cases the student opinion naturally forced it. At Harvard, on the other hand, I began to face scientific race dogma: first of all, evolution and the "Survival of the Fittest." It was continually stressed in the community and in classes that there was a vast difference in the development of the whites and the "lower" races; that this could be seen in the physical development of the Negro. I remember once in a museum, coming face to face with a demonstration: a series of skeletons arranged from a little monkey to a tall well-developed white man, with a Negro barely outranking a chimpanzee. Eventually in my classes stress was quietly transferred to brain weight and brain capacity, and at last to the "cephalic index."

In the graduate school at Harvard and again in Germany, the emphasis again was altered, and race became a matter of culture and cultural history. The history of the world was paraded before the observation of students. Which was the superior race? Manifestly that which had a history, the white race; there was some mention of Asiatic culture, but no course in Chinese or Indian history or culture was offered at Harvard, and quite unanimously in America and Germany, Africa was left without culture and without history. Even when the matter of mixed races was touched upon their evident and conscious inferiority was mentioned. I can never forget that morning in the class of the great Heinrich von Treitschke in Berlin. He was a big aggressive man, with an impediment in his speech which forced him to talk rapidly lest he stutter. His classes were the only ones always on time, and an angry scraping of feet greeted a late comer. Clothed in black, big, bushy-haired, peering sharply at the class, his words rushed out in a flood: "Mulattoes," he thundered, "are inferior." I almost felt his eyes boring into me, although probably he had not noticed me. "Sie fühlen sich niedriger!" "Their actions show it," he asserted. What contradiction could there be to that authoritative dictum?

The first thing which brought me to my senses in all this racial discussion was the continuous change in the proofs and arguments advanced. I could accept evolution and the survival of the fittest, provided the interval between advanced and backward races was not made too impossible. I balked at the usual "thousand years." But no sooner had I settled into scientific security here, than the basis of race distinction was changed without explanation, without apology. I was skeptical about brain weight; surely much depended upon what brains were weighed. I was not sure about physical measurements and social inquiries. For instance, an insurance actuary published in 1890 incontrovertible statistics showing how quickly and certainly the Negro race was dying out in the United States through sheer physical inferiority. I lived to see every assumption of Hoffman's "Race Traits and Tendencies" contradicted; but even before that, I doubted the statistical method which he had used. When the matter of race became a question of comparative culture, I was in revolt. I began to see that the cultural equipment attributed to any people depended largely on who estimated it; and conviction came later in a rush as I realized what in my education had been suppressed concerning Asiatic and African culture.

It was not until I was long out of school and indeed after the World War that there came the hurried use of the new technique of psychological tests, which were quickly adjusted so as to put black folk absolutely beyond the possibility of civilization. By this time I was unimpressed. I had too often seen science made the slave of caste and race hate. And it was interesting to see Odum, McDougall and Brigham eventually turn somersaults from absolute scientific proof of Negro inferiority to repudiation of the limited and questionable application of any test which pretended to measure innate human intelligence.

So far I have spoken of "race" and race problems quite as a matter of course without explanation or definition. That was our method in the nineteenth century. Just as I was born a member of a colored family, so too I was born a member of the colored race. That was obvious and no definition was needed. Later I adopted the designation "Negro" for the race to which I belong. It seemed more definite and logical. At the same time I was of course aware that all members of the Negro race were not black and that the pictures of my race which were current were not authentic nor fair portraits. But all that was incidental. The world was divided into great primary groups of folk who belonged naturally together through heredity of physical traits and cultural affinity.

I do not know how I came first to form my theories of race. The process was probably largely unconscious. The differences of personal appearance between me and my fellows, I must have been conscious of when quite young. Whatever distinctions came because of that did not irritate me; they rather exalted me because, on the whole, while I was still a youth, they gave me exceptional position and a chance to excel rather than handicapping me.

Then of course, when I went South to Fisk, I became a member of a closed racial group with rites and loyalties, with a history and a corporate future, with an art and philosophy. I received these eagerly and expanded them so that when I came to Harvard the theory of race separation was quite in my blood. I did not seek contact with my white fellow students. On the whole I rather avoided them. I took it for granted that we were training ourselves for different careers in worlds largely different. There was not the slightest idea of the permanent subordination and inequality of my world. Nor again was there any idea of racial amalgamation. I resented the assumption that we desired it. I frankly refused the possibility while in Germany and even in America gave up courtship with one "colored" girl because she looked quite white, and I should resent the inference on the street that I had married outside my race.

All this theory, however, was disturbed by certain facts in America, and by my European experience. Despite everything, race lines were not fixed and fast. Within the Negro group especially there were people of all colors. Then too, there were plenty of my colored friends who resented my ultra "race" loyalty and ridiculed it. They pointed out that I was not a "Negro," but a mulatto; that I was not a Southerner but a Northerner, and my object was to be an American and not a Negro; that race distinctions must go. I agreed with this in part and as an ideal, but I saw it leading to inner racial distinction in the colored group. I resented the defensive mechanism of avoiding too dark companions in order to escape notice and discrimination in public. As a sheer matter of taste I wanted the color of my group to be visible. I hotly championed the inclusion of two black school mates whose names were not usually on the invitation list to our social affairs. In Europe my friendships and close contact with white folk made my own ideas waver. The eternal walls between races did not seem so stern and exclusive. I began to emphasize the cultural aspects of race.

It is probably quite natural for persons of low degree, who have reached any status, to search feverishly for distinguished ancestry, as a sort of proof of their inherent desert. This is particularly true in America and has given rise to a number of organizations whose membership depends upon ancestors who have made their mark in the world. Of course, it is clear that there must be here much fable, invention and wishful thinking, facilitated by poor vital statistics and absence of written records. For the mass of Americans, and many Americans who have had the most distinguished careers, have been descended from people who were quite ordinary and even less; America indeed has meant the breaking down of class bars which imprisoned personalities and capabilities and allowing new men and new families to emerge. This is not, as some people assume, a denial of the importance of heredity and family. It is rather its confirmation. It shows us that the few in the past who have emerged are not necessarily the best; and quite certainly are not the only ones worthy of development and distinction; that, on the contrary, only a comparatively few have, under our present economic and social organization, had a chance to show their capabilities.

I early began to take a direct interest in my own family as a group and became curious as to that physical descent which so long I had taken for granted quite unquestioningly. But I did not at first think of any but my Negro ancestors. I knew little and cared less of the white forebears of my father. But this chauvinism gradually changed. There is, of course, nothing more fascinating than the question of the various types of mankind and their intermixture. The whole question of heredity and human gift depends upon such knowledge; but ever since the African slave trade and before the rise of modern biology and sociology, we have been afraid in America that scientific study in this direction might lead to conclusions with which we were loath to agree; and this fear was in reality because the economic foundation of the modern world was based on the recognition and preservation of so-called racial distinctions. In accordance with this, not only Negro slavery could be justified, but the Asiatic coolie profitably used and the labor classes in white countries kept in their places by [a] low wage.

It is not singular then that here in America and in the West Indies, where we have had the most astonishing modern mixture of human types, scientific study of the results and circumstances of this mixture has not only lagged but been almost non-existent. We have not only not studied race and race mixture in America, but we have tried almost by legal process to stop such study. It is for this reason that it has occurred to me just here to illustrate the way in which Africa and Europe have been united in my family. There is nothing unusual about this interracial history. It has been duplicated thousands of times; but on the one hand, the white folk have bitterly resented even a hint of the facts of this intermingling; while black folk have recoiled in natural hesitation and affected disdain in admitting what they know.

I am, therefore, relating the history of my family and centering it around my maternal great-great-grandfather, Tom Burghardt, and my paternal grandfather, Alexander Du Bois.

Absolute legal proof of facts like those here set down is naturally unobtainable. Records of birth are often nonexistent, proof of paternity is exceedingly difficult and actual written record [is] rare. In the case of my family I have relied on oral tradition in my mother's family and direct word and written statement from my paternal grandfather; and upon certain general records which I have been able to obtain. I have no doubt of the substantial accuracy of the story that I am to tell.

Of my own immediate ancestors I knew personally only four: my mother and her parents and my paternal grandfather. One other I knew at second hand—my father. I had his picture. I knew what my mother told me about him and what others who had known him said. So that in all, five of my immediate forebears were known to me. Three others, my paternal great-grandfather and my maternal great-grandfather and great-great-grandfather, I knew about through persons who knew them and through records; and also I knew many of my collateral relatives and numbers of their descendants. My known ancestral family, therefore, consisted of eight or more persons. None of these had reached any particular distinction or were known very far beyond their own families and localities. They were divided into whites, blacks and mulattoes, most of them being mulattoes.

My paternal great-grandfather, Dr. James Du Bois, was white and descended from Chrétien Du Bois who was a French Huguenot farmer and perhaps artisan and resided at Wicres near Lille in French Flanders. It is doubtful if he had any ancestors among the nobility, although his white American descendants love to think so. He had two, possibly three, sons of whom Louis and Jacques came to America to escape religious persecution. Jacques went from France first to Leiden in the Netherlands, where he was married and had several children, including a second Jacques or James. In 1674 that family came to America and settled at Kingston, New York. James Du Bois appears in the Du Bois family genealogy as a descendant of Jacques in the fifth generation, although the exact line of descent is not clear; but my grandfather's written testimony establishes that James was a physician and a landholder along the Hudson and in the West Indies. He was born in 1750, or later. He may have been a loyalist refugee. One such refugee, Isaac Du Bois, was given a grant of five hundred acres in Eleuthera after the Revolutionary War.

The career of Dr. James Du Bois was chiefly as a plantation proprietor and slave owner in the Bahama Islands with his headquarters at Long Cay. Cousins of his named Gilbert also had plantations near. He never married, but had one of his slaves as his common-law wife, a small brown-skinned woman born on the island. Of this couple two sons were born, Alexander and John. Alexander, my grandfather, was born in 1803, and about 1810, possibly because of the death of the mother, the father brought both these boys to America and planned to give them the education of gentlemen. They were white enough in appearance to give no inkling of their African descent. They were entered in the private Episcopal school at Cheshire, Connecticut, which still exists there and has trained many famous men. Dr. James Du Bois used often to visit his sons there, but about 1812, on his return from a visit, he had a stroke of apoplexy and died. He left no will and his estate descended to a cousin.

The boys were removed from school and bound out as apprentices, my grandfather to a shoemaker. Their connection with the white Du

Bois family ceased suddenly, and was never renewed. Alexander Du Bois thus started with a good common school and perhaps some high school training and with the instincts of a gentleman of his day. Naturally he passed through much inner turmoil. He became a rebel, bitter at his lot in life, resentful at being classed as a Negro and yet implacable in his attitude toward whites. Of his brother, John, I have only a picture. He may have been the John Du Bois who helped Bishop Payne to purchase Wilberforce University.

If Alexander Du Bois, following the footsteps of Alexander Hamilton, had come from the West Indies to the United States, stayed with the white group and married and begotten children among them, anyone in after years who had suggested his Negro descent would have been unable to prove it and quite possibly would have been laughed to scorn, or sued for libel. Indeed the legal advisers of the publishers of my last book could write: "We may assume as a general proposition that it is libelous to state erroneously that a white man or woman has colored blood." Lately in Congress the true story, in a WPA [Works Progress Administration] history, of miscegenation affecting a high historic personage raised a howl of protest.

Alexander Du Bois did differently from Hamilton. He married into the colored group and his oldest son allied himself with a Negro clan but four generations removed from Africa. He himself first married Sarah Marsh Lewis in 1823 and then apparently set out to make his way in Haiti. There my father was born in 1825, and his elder sister, Augusta, a year earlier, either there or just as the family was leaving the United States. Evidently the situation in Haiti did not please my grandfather or perhaps the death of his young wife when she was scarcely thirty turned him back to America. Within a year he married Emily Basset who seems to have been the widow of a man named Jacklyn and lived in New Milford. Leonard Bacon, a well-known Congregational clergyman, performed his second marriage.

The following year, Alexander began his career in the United States. He lived in New Haven, Springfield, Providence, and finally in New Bedford. For some time, he was steward on the New York-New Haven boat and insisted on better treatment for his colored help. Later about 1848 he ran a grocery store at 23 Washington Street, New Haven, and owned property at different times in the various cities where he lived. By his first wife, my grandmother, he had two children, and by his second wife, one daughter, Henrietta. Three or four children died in infancy. Alexander was a communicant of Trinity Parish, New Haven, and was enrolled there as late as 1845; then something happened, because in 1847 he was among that group of Negroes who formed the new colored Episcopal Parish of St. Luke, where he was for years their senior warden. Probably this indicates one of his bitter fights and rebellions, for nothing but intolerable insult would have led him into a seg-

regated church movement. Alexander Crummell was his first rector
here.

As I knew my grandfather, he was a short, stern, upstanding man,
sparing but precise in his speech and stiff in manner, evidently long
used to repressing his feelings. I remember as a boy of twelve, watching his ceremonious reception of a black visitor, John Freedom; his
stately bow, the way in which the red wine was served and the careful
almost stilted conversation. I had seen no such social ceremony in my
simple western Massachusetts home. The darkened parlor with its
horsehair furniture became a very special and important place. I was
deeply impressed. My grandfather evidently looked upon me with a
certain misgiving if not actual distaste. I was brown, the son of his
oldest son, Alfred, and Alfred and his father had never gotten on together.

The boy Alfred was a throwback to his white grandfather. He was
small, olive-skinned and handsome and just visibly colored, with curly
hair; and he was naturally a play-boy. My only picture of him shows
him clothed in the uniform of the Union Army; but he never actually
went to the front. In fact, Alfred never actually did much of anything.
He was gay and carefree, refusing to settle long at any one place or
job. He had a good elementary school training but nothing higher. I
think that my father ran away from home several times. Whether he
got into any very serious scrapes or not, I do not know, nor do I know
whether he was married early in life; I imagine not. I think he was
probably a free lance, gallant and lover, yielding only to marital bonds
when he found himself in the rather strict clannishness of my mother's
family. He was barber, merchant and preacher, but always irresponsible and charming. He had wandered out from eastern New England
where his father lived and come to the Berkshire valley in 1867 where
he met and married my brown mother.

The second wife of Alexander Du Bois died in 1865. His oldest
daughter, Augusta, married a light mulatto and has descendants today
who do not know of their Negro blood. Much later Alexander Du Bois
married his third wife, Annie Green, who was the grandmother that I
knew, and who knew and liked my father Alfred, and who brought
me and my grandfather together. Alexander Du Bois died December 9,
1887, at the age of eighty-four, in New Bedford, and lies buried today
in Oak Grove Cemetery near the Yale campus in New Haven, in a
lot which he owned and which is next to that of Jehudi Ashmun of
Liberian fame.

My father, by some queer chance, came into western Massachusetts and into the Housatonic Valley at the age of forty-two and there
met and quickly married my brown mother who was then thirty-six
and belonged to the Burghardt clan. This brings us to the history of
the black Burghardts.

In 1694, Rev. Benjamin Wadsworth, afterwards president of Harvard College, made a journey through western Massachusetts, and says in regard to the present site of the town of Great Barrington, "Ye greatest part of our road this day was a hideous, howling wilderness." Here it was that a committee of the Massachusetts General Court confirmed a number of land titles in 1733–34, which had previously been in dispute between the English, Dutch, and Indians. In the "fifth division" of this land appears the name of a Dutchman, who signed himself as "Coenraet Borghghardt." This Borghghardt, Bogoert or Burghardt family has been prominent in Dutch colonial history and its descendants have been particularly identified with the annals of the little town of about five thousand inhabitants which today still lies among the hills of middle Berkshire.

Coenrod Burghardt seems to have been a shrewd pushing Dutchman and is early heard of in Kinderhook, together with his son John. This family came into possession of an African Negro named Tom, who had formerly belonged to the family of Etsons (Ettens?) and had come to the Burghardts by purchase or possibly by marriage. This African has had between one hundred and fifty and two hundred descendants, a number of whom are now living and reach to the eighth generation.

Tom was probably born about 1730. His granddaughter writes me that her father told her that Tom was born in Africa and was brought to this country when he was a boy. For many years my youthful imagination painted him as certainly the son of a tribal chief, but there is no warrant for this even in family tradition. Tom was probably just a stolen black boy from the West African Coast, nameless and lost, either a war captive or a tribal pawn. He was probably sent overseas on a Dutch ship at the time when their slave trade was beginning to decline and the vast English expansion to begin. He was in the service of the Burghardts and was a soldier in the Revolutionary War, going to the front probably several times; of only one of these is there official record when he appeared with the rank of private on the muster and payroll of Colonel John Ashley's Berkshire County regiment and Captain John Spoor's company in 1780. The company marched northward by order of Brigadier-General Fellows on an alarm when Fort Anne and Fort George were taken by the enemy. It is recorded that Tom was "reported a Negro." (Record Index of the Military Archives of Massachusetts)

Tom appears to have been held as a servant and possibly a legal slave first by the family of Etsons or Ettens and then to have come into the possession of the Burghardts who settled at Great Barrington. Eventually, probably after the Revolutionary War, he was regarded as a freeman. There is [a] record of only one son, Jacob Burghardt, who continued in the employ of the Burghardt family, and was born apparently about 1760. He is listed in the census of 1790 as "free" with two in his family. He married a wife named Violet who was apparently newly arrived from Africa and brought with her an African song which became traditional in the family. After her death, Jacob married Mom Bett, a rather celebrated figure in western Massachusetts history. She had been freed under the Bill of Rights of 1780 and the son of the judge who freed her wrote, "Even in her humble station, she had, when occasion required it, an air of command which conferred a degree of dignity and gave her an ascendancy over those of her rank, or color. Her determined and resolute character, which enabled her to limit the ravages of Shays's mob, was manifested in her conduct and deportment during her whole life. She claimed no distinction, but it was yielded to her from her superior experience, energy, skill and sagacity. Having known this woman as familiarly as I knew either of my parents, I cannot believe in the moral or physical inferiority of the race to which she belonged. The degradation of the African must have been otherwise caused than by natural inferiority."

Family tradition has it that her husband, Jacob, took part in suppressing this Shays's Rebellion. Jacob Burghardt had nine children, five sons of whom one was my grandfather, and four daughters. My grandfather's brothers and sisters had many children: Harlow had ten and Ira also ten; Maria had two. Descendants of Harlow and Ira still survive. Three of these sons, Othello, Ira, Harlow, and one daughter Lucinda settled on South Egremont plain near Great Barrington, where they owned small adjoining farms. A small part of one of these farms I continue to own.

Othello was my grandfather. He was born November 18, 1791, and married Sarah Lampman in 1811. Sarah was born in Hillsdale, New York, in 1793, of a mother named Lampman. There is no record of her father. She was probably the child of a Dutchman perhaps with Indian blood. This couple had ten children, three sons and seven daughters. Othello died in 1872 at the age of eighty-one and Sarah or Sally in 1877 at the age of eighty-six. Their sons and daughters married and drifted to town as laborers and servants. I thus had innumerable cousins up and down the valley. I was brought up with the Burghardt clan and this fact determined largely my life and "race." The white relationship and connections were quite lost and indeed unknown until long years after. The black Burghardts were ordinary farmers, laborers and servants. The children usually learned to read and write. I never heard or knew of any of them of my mother's generation or later who were illiterate. I was, however, the first one of the family who finished in the local high school. Afterward, one or two others did. Most of the members of the family left Great Barrington. Parts of the family are living and are fairly prosperous in the Middle West and on the Pacific Coast. I have heard of one or two high school graduates in the Middle West branch of the family.

This, then, was my racial history and as such it was curiously complicated. With Africa I had only one direct cultural connection and that was the African melody which my great-grandmother Violet used to sing. Where she learned it, I do not know. Perhaps she herself was born in Africa or had it of a mother or father stolen and transported. But at any rate, as I wrote years ago in the "Souls of Black Folk," "coming to the valleys of the Hudson and Housatonic, black, little, and lithe, she shivered and shrank in the harsh north winds, looked longingly at the hills, and often crooned a heathen melody to the child between her knees, thus:

> Do bana coba, gene me, gene me!
> Do bana coba, gene me, gene me!
> Ben d' nuli, nuli, nuli, nuli, ben d' le.

The child sang it to his children and they to their children's children, and so two hundred years it has traveled down to us and we sing it to our children, knowing as little as our fathers what its words may mean, but knowing well the meaning of its music."

Living with my mother's people I absorbed their culture patterns and these were not African so much as Dutch and New England. The speech was an idiomatic New England tongue with no African dialect; the family customs were New England, and the sex mores. My African racial feeling was then purely a matter of my own later learning and reaction; my recoil from the assumptions of the whites; my experience in the South at Fisk. But it was none the less real and a large determinant of my life and character. I felt myself African by "race" and by that token was African and an integral member of the group of dark Americans who were called Negroes.

At the same time I was firm in asserting that these Negroes were Americans. For that reason and on the basis of my great-great-grandfather's Revolutionary record I was accepted as a member of the Massachusetts Society of the Sons of the American Revolution, in 1908. When, however, the notice of this election reached the headquarters in Washington and was emphasized by my requesting a national certificate, the secretary, A. Howard Clark of the Smithsonian Institution, wrote to Massachusetts and demanded "proof of marriage of the ancestor of Tom Burghardt and record of birth of the son." He knew, of course, that the birth record of a stolen African slave could not possibly be produced. My membership was, therefore, suspended.

Countee Cullen sings:

> What is Africa to me:
> Copper sun or scarlet sea,
> Jungle star or jungle track,
> Strong bronzed men, or regal black

Women from whose loins I sprang
When the birds of Eden sang?
One three centuries removed
From the scenes his fathers loved,
Spicy grove, cinnamon tree,
What is Africa to me?

What is Africa to me? Once I should have answered the question simply: I should have said "fatherland" or perhaps better "motherland" because I was born in the century when the walls of race were clear and straight; when the world consisted of mutally exclusive races; and even though the edges might be blurred, there was no question of exact definition and understanding of the meaning of the word. One of the first pamphlets that I wrote in 1897 was on "The Conservation of Races" wherein I set down as the first article of a proposed racial creed: "We believe that the Negro people as a race have a contribution to make to civilization and humanity which no other race can make."

Since then the concept of race has so changed and presented so much of contradiction that as I face Africa I ask myself: what is it between us that constitutes a tie which I can feel better than I can explain? Africa is, of course, my fatherland. Yet neither my father nor my father's father ever saw Africa or knew its meaning or cared overmuch for it. My mother's folk were closer and yet their direct connection, in culture and race, became tenuous; still, my tie to Africa is strong. On this vast continent were born and lived a large portion of my direct ancestors going back a thousand years or more. The mark of their heritage is upon me in color and hair. These are obvious things, but of little meaning in themselves; only important as they stand for real and more subtle differences from other men. Whether they do or not, I do not know nor does science know today.

But one thing is sure and that is the fact that since the fifteenth century these ancestors of mine and their other descendants have had a common history; have suffered a common disaster and have one long memory. The actual ties of heritage between the individuals of this group, vary with the ancestors that they have in common and many others: Europeans and Semites, perhaps Mongolians, certainly American Indians. But the physical bond is least and the badge of color relatively unimportant save as a badge; the real essence of this kinship is its social heritage of slavery; the discrimination and insult; and this heritage binds together not simply the children of Africa, but extends through yellow Asia and into the South Seas. It is this unity that draws me to Africa.

When shall I forget the night I first set foot on African soil? I am the sixth generation in descent from forefathers who left this land. The moon was at the full and the waters of the Atlantic lay like a lake. All the long slow afternoon as the sun robed herself in her western scarlet with veils of misty cloud, I had seen Africa afar. Cape Mount—that mighty headland with its twin curves, northern sentinel of the realm of Liberia—gathered itself out of the cloud at half past three and then darkened and grew clear. On beyond flowed the dark low undulating land quaint with palm and breaking sea. The world grew black. Africa faded away, the stars stood forth curiously twisted—Orion in the zenith—the Little Bear asleep and the Southern Cross rising behind the horizon. Then afar, ahead, a lone light shone, straight at the ship's fore. Twinkling lights appeared below, around, and rising shadows. "Monrovia," said the Captain.

Suddenly we swerved to our left. The long arms of the bay enveloped us and then to the right rose the twinkling hill of Monrovia, with its crowning star. Lights flashed on the shore—here, there. Then we sensed a darker shading in the shadows; it lay very still. "It's a boat," one said. "It's two boats!" Then the shadow drifted in pieces and as the anchor roared into the deep, five boats outlined themselves on the waters—great ten-oared barges with men swung into line and glided toward us.

It was nine at night—above, the shadows, there the town, here the sweeping boats. One forged ahead with the flag—stripes and a lone star flaming behind, the ensign of the customs floating wide; and bending to the long oars, the white caps of ten black sailors. Up the stairway clambered a soldier in khaki, aide-de-camp of the President of the Republic, a customhouse official, the clerk of the American legation—and after them sixty-five lithe, lean black stevedores with whom the steamer would work down to Portuguese Angola and back. A few moments of formalities, greetings and good-bys and I was in the great long boat with the President's aide—a brown major in brown khaki. On the other side, the young clerk and at the back, the black barelegged pilot. Before us on the high thwarts were the rowers: men, boys, black, thin, trained in muscle and sinew, little larger than the oars in thickness, they bent their strength to them and swung upon them.

One in the center gave curious little cackling cries to keep up the rhythm, and for the spurts and the stroke, a call a bit thicker and sturdier; he gave a low guttural command now and then; the boat, alive, quivering, danced beneath the moon, swept a great curve to the bar to breast its narrow teeth of foam—"t'chick-a-tickity, t'chick-a-tickity," sang the boys, and we glided and raced, now between boats, now near the landing—now cast aloft at the dock. And lo! I was in Africa.

Christmas Eve, and Africa is singing in Monrovia. They are Krus and Fanti—men, women and children, and all the night they march and sing. The music was once the music of mission revival hymns. But it is that music now transformed and the silly words hidden in an unknown tongue—liquid and sonorous. It is tricked out and expounded with cadence and turn. And this is that same rhythm I heard first in Tennessee forty years ago: the air is raised and carried by men's strong voices, while floating above in obbligato, come the high mellow voices of women—it is the ancient African art of part singing, so curiously and insistently different.

So they come, gay appareled, lit by transparency. They enter the gate and flow over the high steps and sing and sing and sing. They saunter round the house, pick flowers, drink water and sing and sing and sing. The warm dark heat of the night steams up to meet the moon. And the night is song.

On Christmas Day, 1923, we walk down to the narrow, crooked wharves of Monrovia, by houses old and gray and step-like streets of stone. Before is the wide St. Paul River, double-mouthed, and beyond, the sea, white, curling on the sand. Before us is the isle—the tiny isle, hut-covered and guarded by a cotton tree, where the pioneers lived in 1821. We board the boat, then circle round—then up the river. Great bowing trees, festoons of flowers, golden blossoms, star-faced palms and thatched huts; tall spreading trees lifting themselves like vast umbrellas, low shrubbery with gray and laced and knotted roots—the broad, black, murmuring river. Here a tree holds wide fingers out and stretches them over the water in vast incantation; bananas throw their wide green fingers to the sun. Iron villages, scarred clearings with gray, sheet-iron homes staring, grim and bare, at the ancient tropical flood of green.

The river sweeps wide and the shrubs bow low. Behind, Monrovia rises in clear, calm beauty. Gone are the wharves, the low and clustered houses of the port, the tight-throated business village, and up sweep the villas and the low wall, brown and cream and white, with great mango and cotton trees, with lighthouse and spire, with porch and pillar and the color of shrubbery and blossom.

We climbed the upright shore to a senator's home and received his wide and kindly hospitality—curious blend of feudal lord and modern farmer—sandwiches, cake, and champagne. Again we glided up the drowsy river—five, ten, twenty miles and came to our hostess, a mansion of five generations with a compound of endless native servants and cows under the palm thatches. The daughters of the family wore, on the beautiful black skin of their necks, the exquisite pale gold chains of the Liberian artisan and the slim, black little granddaughter of the house had a wide pink ribbon on the thick curls of her dark hair, that lay like sudden sunlight on the shadows. Double porches, one above the other, welcomed us to ease. A native man, gay with Christmas and a dash of gin, sang and danced in the road. Children ran and played in the blazing sun. We sat at a long broad table and ate duck, chicken, beef, rice, plantain, collards, cake, tea, water and Madeira wine. Then we went and looked at the heavens, the uptwisted sky—Orion and

Cassiopeia at zenith; the Little Bear beneath the horizon, now unfamiliar sights in the Milky Way—all awry, a-living—sun for snow at Christmas, and happiness and cheer.

The shores were lined with old sugar plantations, the buildings rotting and falling. I looked upon the desolation with a certain pain. What had happened, I asked? The owners and planters had deserted these homes and come down to Monrovia, but why? After all, Monrovia had not much to offer in the way of income and occupation. Was this African laziness and inefficiency? No, it was a specimen of the way in which the waves of modern industry broke over the shores of far-off Africa. Here during our Civil War, men hastened to raise sugar and supply New York. They built their own boats and filled the river and sailed the sea. But afterwards, Louisiana came back into the Union, colored Rillieux invented the vacuum pan; the sugar plantations began to spread in Cuba and the Sugar Trust monopoly of refining machinery, together with the new beet sugar industry, drove Liberia quickly from the market. What all this did not do, the freight rates finished. So sugar did not pay in Liberia and other crops rose and fell in the same way.

As I look back and recall the days, which I have called great—the occasions in which I have taken part and which have had for me and others the widest significance, I can remember none like the first of January, 1924. Once I took my bachelor's degree before a governor, a great college president, and a bishop of New England. But that was rather personal in its memory than in any way epochal. Once before the assembled races of the world I was called to speak in London in place of the suddenly sick Sir Harry Johnston. It was a great hour. But it was not greater than the day when I was presented to the President of the Negro Republic of Liberia.

Liberia had been resting under the shock of world war into which the Allies forced her. She had asked and been promised a loan by the United States to bolster and replace her stricken trade. She had conformed to every preliminary requirement and waited when waiting was almost fatal. It was not simply money, it was world prestige and protection at a time when the little republic was sorely beset by creditors and greedy imperial powers. At the last moment, an insurgent Senate peremptorily and finally refused the request and strong recommendation of President Wilson and his advisers, and the loan was refused. The Department of State made no statement to the world, and Liberia stood naked, not only well-nigh bankrupt, but peculiarly defenseless amid scowling and unbelieving powers.

It was then that the United States made a gesture of courtesy; a little thing, and merely a gesture, but one so unusual that it was epochal. President Coolidge, at the suggestion of William H. Lewis, a leading colored lawyer of Boston, named me, an American Negro traveler, Envoy Extraordinary and Minister Plenipotentiary to Liberia—the highest rank ever given by any country to a diplomatic agent in black Africa. And it named this Envoy the special representative of the President of the United States to the President of Liberia, on the occasion of his inauguration; charging the Envoy with a personal word of encouragement and moral support. It was a significant action. It had in it nothing personal. Another appointee would have been equally significant. But Liberia recognized the meaning. She showered upon the Envoy every mark of appreciation and thanks. The Commander of the Liberian Frontier Force was made his special aide, and a sergeant, his orderly. At ten a.m. New Year's morning, 1924, a company of the Frontier Force, in red fez and khaki, presented arms before the American Legation and escorted Solomon Porter Hood, the American Minister Resident, and myself as Envoy Extraordinary and my aide to the Presidential Mansion—a beautiful white, verandaed house, waving with palms and fronting a grassy street.

Ceremonials are old and to some antiquated and yet this was done with such simplicity, grace and seriousness that none could escape its spell. The Secretary of State met us at the door, as the band played the impressive Liberian National hymn, and soldiers saluted:

> All hail! Liberia, hail!
> In union strong, success is sure.
> We cannot fail.
> With God above,
> Our rights to prove,
> We will the world assail.

We mounted a broad stairway and into a great room that stretched across the house. Here in semi-circle were ranged the foreign consuls and the cabinet—the former in white, gilt with orders and swords; the latter in solemn black. Present were England, France, Germany, Spain, Belgium, Holland, and Panama, to be presented to me in order of seniority by the small brown Secretary of State with his perfect poise and ease. The President entered—frock-coated with the star and ribbon of a Spanish order on his breast. The American Minister introduced me, and I said:

"The President of the United States has done me the great honor of designating me as his personal representative on the occasion of your inauguration. In so doing, he has had, I am sure, two things in mind. First, he wished publicly and unmistakably to express before the world the interest and solicitude which the hundred million inhabitants of the United States of America have for Liberia. Liberia is a child of the United States, and a sister Republic. Its progress and success is the progress and success of democracy everywhere and for all men; and the United States would view with sorrow and alarm any misfortune which might happen to this Republic and any obstacle that was placed in her path.

"But special and peculiar bonds draw these two lands together. In America live eleven million persons of African descent; they are citizens, legally invested with every right that inheres in American citizenship. And I am sure that in this special mark of the President's favor, he has had in mind the wishes and hopes of Negro Americans. He knows how proud they are of the hundred years of independence which you have maintained by force of arms and by brawn and brain upon the edge of this mighty continent; he knows that in the great battle against color caste in America, the ability of Negroes to rule in Africa has been and ever will be a great and encouraging reenforcement. He knows that the unswerving loyalty of Negro Americans to their country is fitly accompanied by a pride in their race and lineage, a belief in the potency and promise of Negro blood which makes them eager listeners to every whisper of success from Liberia, and eager helpers in every movement for your aid and comfort. In a special sense, the moral burden of Liberia and the advancement and integrity of Liberia is the sincere prayer of America."

And now a word about the African himself—about this primitive black man: I began to notice a truth as I entered southern France. I formulated it in Portugal. I knew it as a great truth one Sunday in Liberia. And the Great Truth was this: efficiency and happiness do not go together in modern culture. Going south from London, as the world darkens it gets happier. Portugal is deliciously dark. Many leading citizens would have difficulty keeping off a Georgia "Jim Crow" car. But, oh, how lovely a land and how happy a people! And so leisurely. Little use of trying to shop seriously in Lisbon before eleven. It isn't done. Nor at noon; the world is lunching or lolling in the sun. Even after four p.m. one takes chances, for the world is in the Rocio. And the banks are so careless and the hotels so leisurely. How delightfully angry Englishmen get at the "damned, lazy" Portuguese!

But if this of Portugal, what of Africa? Here darkness descends and rests on lovely skins until brown seems luscious and natural. There is sunlight in great gold globules and soft, heavy-scented heat that wraps you like a garment. And laziness; divine, eternal, languor is right and good and true. I remember the morning; it was Sunday, and the night before we heard the leopards crying down there. Today beneath the streaming sun we went down into the gold-green forest. It was silence—silence the more mysterious because life abundant and palpitating pulsed all about us and held us drowsy captives to the day. Ahead the gaunt missionary strode, alert, afire, with his gun. He apologized for the gun, but he did not need to, for I saw the print of a leopard's hind foot. A monkey sentinel screamed, and I heard the whir of the horde as they ran.

Then we came to the village; how can I describe it? Neither London, nor Paris, nor New York has anything of its delicate, precious beauty. It was a town of the Veys and done in cream and pale purple—still, clean, restrained, tiny, complete. It was no selfish place, but the central abode of fire and hospitality, clean-swept for wayfarers, and best seats were bare. They quite expected visitors, morning, noon, and night; and they gave our hands a quick, soft grasp and talked easily. Their manners were better than those of Park Lane or Park Avenue. Oh, much better and more natural. They showed breeding. The chief's son—tall and slight and speaking good English—had served under the late Colonel Young. He made a little speech of welcome. Long is the history of the Veys and comes down from the Eastern Roman Empire, the great struggle of Islam and the black empires of the Sudan.

We went on to other villages—dun-colored, not so beautiful, but neat and hospitable. In one sat a visiting chief of perhaps fifty years in a derby hat and a robe, and beside him stood a shy young wife done in ebony and soft brown, whose liquid eyes would not meet ours. The chief was taciturn until we spoke of schools. Then he woke suddenly—he had children to "give" to a school. I see the last village fading away; they are plastering the wall of a home, leisurely and carefully. They smiled a good-by—not effusively, with no eagerness, with a simple friendship, as we glided under the cocoa trees and into the silent forest, the gold and silent forest.

And there and elsewhere in two long months I began to learn: primitive men are not following us afar, frantically waving and seeking our goals; primitive men are not behind us in some swift foot-race. Primitive men have already arrived. They are abreast, and in places ahead of us; in others behind. But all their curving advance line is contemporary, not prehistoric. They have used other paths and these paths have led them by scenes sometimes fairer, sometimes uglier than ours, but always toward the Pools of Happiness. Or, to put it otherwise, these folk have the leisure of true aristocracy—leisure for thought and courtesy, leisure for sleep and laughter. They have time for their children—such well-trained, beautiful children with perfect, unhidden bodies. Have you ever met a crowd of children in the east of London or New York, or even on the Avenue at Forty-second or One Hundred and Forty-second Street, and fled to avoid their impudence and utter ignorance of courtesy? Come to Africa, and see well-bred and courteous children, playing happily and never sniffling and whining.

I have read everywhere that Africa means sexual license. Perhaps it does. Most folk who talk sex frantically have all too seldom revealed their source material. I was in West Africa only two months, but with both eyes wide. I saw children quite naked and women usually naked to the waist—with bare bosom and limbs. And in those sixty days I saw less of sex dalliance and appeal than I see daily on Fifth Avenue. This does not mean much, but it is an interesting fact.

The primitive black man is courteous and dignified. If the platforms of Western cities had swarmed with humanity as I have seen the platforms swarm in Senegal, the police would have a busy time. I did not see one respectable quarrel. Wherefore shall we all take to the Big Bush? No. I prefer New York. But my point is that New York and London and Paris must learn of West Africa and may learn.

The one great lack in Africa is communication—communication as represented by human contact, movement of goods, dissemination of knowledge. All these things we have—we have in such crushing abundance that they have mastered us and defeated their real good. We meet human beings in such throngs that we cannot know or even understand them—they become to us inhuman, mechanical, hateful. We are choked and suffocated, tempted and killed by goods accumulated from the ends of the earth; our newspapers and magazines so overwhelm us with knowledge—knowledge of all sorts and kinds from particulars as to our neighbors' underwear to Einstein's mathematics—that one of the great and glorious joys of the African bush is to escape from "news."

On the other hand, African life with its isolation has deeper knowledge of human souls. The village life, the forest ways, the teeming markets, bring in intimate human knowledge that the West misses, sinking the individual in the social. Africans know fewer folk, but know them infinitely better. Their intertwined communal souls, therefore, brook no poverty nor prostitution—these things are to them ununderstandable. On the other hand, they are vastly ignorant of what the world is doing and thinking, and of what is known of its physical forces. They suffer terribly from preventable disease, from unnecessary hunger, from the freaks of the weather.

Here, then, is something for Africa and Europe both to learn; and Africa is eager, breathless, to learn—while Europe? Europe laughs with loud guffaws. Learn of Africa? Nonsense. Poverty cannot be abolished. Democracy and firm government are incompatible. Prostitution is world old and inevitable. And Europe proceeds to use Africa as a means and not as an end; as a hired tool and welter of raw materials and not as a land of human beings.

I think it was in Africa that I came more clearly to see the close connection between race and wealth. The fact that even in the minds of the most dogmatic supporters of race theories and believers in the inferiority of colored folk to white, there was a conscious or unconscious determination to increase their incomes by taking full advantage of this belief. And then gradually this thought was metamorphosed into a realization that the income-bearing value of race prejudice was the cause and not the result of theories of rare inferiority; that particularly in the United States the income of the Cotton Kingdom based on black slavery caused the passionate belief in Negro inferiority and the determination to enforce it even by arms.

I have wandered afield from miscegenation in the West Indies to race blending and segregation in America and to a glimpse of present Africa. Now to return to the American concept of race. It was in my boyhood, as I have intimated, an adventure. In my youth, it became the vision of a glorious crusade where I and my fellows were to match our mettle against white folk and show them what black folk could do. But as I grew older the matter became more serious and less capable of jaunty settlement. I not only met plenty of persons equal in ability to myself but often with greater ability and nearly always with greater opportunity. Racial identity presented itself as a matter of trammels and impediments as "tightening bonds about my feet." As I looked out into my racial world the whole thing verged on tragedy. My "way was cloudy" and the approach to its high goals by no means straight and clear. I saw the race problem was not as I conceived, a matter of clear, fair competition, for which I was ready and eager. It was rather a matter of segregation, of hindrance and inhibitions, and my struggles against this and resentment at it began to have serious repercussions upon my inner life.

It is difficult to let others see the full psychological meaning of caste segregation. It is as though one, looking out from a dark cave in a side of an impending mountain, sees the world passing and speaks to it; speaks courteously and persuasively, showing them how these entombed souls are hindered in their natural movement, expression, and development; and how their loosening from prison would be a matter not simply of courtesy, sympathy, and help to them, but aid to all the world. One talks on evenly and logically in this way, but notices that the passing throng does not even turn its head, or if it does, glances curiously and walks on. It gradually penetrates the minds of the prisoners that the people passing do not hear; that some thick sheet of invisible but horribly tangible plate glass is between them and the world. They get excited; they talk louder; they gesticulate. Some of the passing world stop in curiosity; these gesticulations seem to pointless; they laugh and pass on. They still either do not hear at all, or hear but dimly, and even what they hear, they do not understand. Then the people within may become hysterical. They may scream and hurl themselves against the barriers, hardly realizing in their bewilderment that they are screaming in a vacuum unheard and that their antics may actually seem funny to those outside looking in. They may even, here and there, break through in blood and disfigurement, and find themselves faced by a horrified, implacable, and quite overwhelming mob of people frightened for their own very existence.

It is hard under such circumstances to be philosophical and calm, and to think through a method of approach and accommodation between castes. The entombed find themselves not simply trying to make the outer world understand their essential and common humanity but even more, as they become inured to their experience, they have to keep reminding themselves that the great and oppressing world out-

95

side is also real and human and in its essence honest. All my life I have had continually to haul my soul back and say, "All white folk are not scoundrels nor murderers. They are, even as I am, painfully human."

One development continually recurs: any person outside of this wall of glass can speak to his own fellows, can assume a facile championship of the entombed, and gain the enthusiastic and even gushing thanks of the victims. But this method is subject to two difficulties: first of all, not being possibly among the entombed or capable of sharing their inner thought and experience, this outside leadership will continually misinterpret and compromise and complicate matters, even with the best of will. And secondly, of course, no matter how successful the outside advocacy is, it remains impotent and unsuccessful until it actually succeeds in freeing and making articulate the submerged caste.

Practically, this group imprisonment within a group has various effects upon the prisoner. He becomes provincial and centered upon the problems of his particular group. He tends to neglect the wider aspects of national life and human existence. On the one hand he is unselfish so far as his inner group is concerned. He thinks of himself not as an individual but as a group man, a "race" man. His loyalty to this group idea tends to be almost unending and balks at almost no sacrifice. On the other hand, his attitude toward the environing race congeals into a matter of unreasoning resentment and even hatred, deep disbelief in them and refusal to conceive honesty and rational thought on their part. This attitude adds to the difficulties of conversation, intercourse, understanding between groups.

This was the race concept which has dominated my life, and the history of which I have attempted to make the leading theme of this book. It had as I have tried to show all sorts of illogical trends and irreconcilable tendencies. Perhaps it is wrong to speak of it at all as "a concept" rather than as a group of contradictory forces, facts and tendencies. At any rate I hope I have made its meaning to me clear. It was for me as I have written first a matter of dawning realization, then of study and science; then a matter of inquiry into the diverse strands of my own family; and finally consideration of my connection, physical and spiritual, with Africa and the Negro race in its homeland. All this led to an attempt to rationalize the racial concept and its place in the modern world.

CHAPTER 2

The Souls of Black Folk

The *Souls of Black Folk*, first published in 1903, was last revised by Du Bois in 1953. Over the course of its life in the twentieth century, the book has been published in numerous editions and sold hundreds of thousands of copies. It has been cited by many African American writers and intellectuals as the most formative reading experience of their lives and is now widely taught in literature and African American Studies courses. "The problem of the twentieth century is the problem of the color line," wrote Du Bois in one of the book's most famous passages. It would be fair to say of *The Souls of Black Folk* that it is likewise *the* African American book of the twentieth century. Its well-known aphoristic ideas—the problem of the color line and the notion of "double consciousness"—were not invented by Du Bois, strictly speaking, but his brilliant oratorical prose gave them such urgency that they have remained ingrained in twentieth-century writing in just the formulations he created.

The book is composed of a group of nine previously published and revised essays—"Of Our Spiritual Strivings," "Of the Dawn of Freedom," "Of Mr. Booker T. Washington and Others," "Of the Meaning of Progress," "Of the Training of Black Men," "Of the Black Belt," "Of the Quest of the Golden Fleece," "Of the Sons of Master and Man," and "Of the Faith of the Fathers" had already appeared in journals such as *Atlantic Monthly, The Dial,* and *World's Work*—and five new essays that Du Bois wrote when asked by the publisher A. C. McClurg if he would like to gather some of his essays into a publishable book. Du Bois's revisions have been studied in some detail by several scholars (Aptheker, "Introduction," 5–45; Stepto, 52–91), and it is evident that although the volume remains a collection of disparate essays and genres, Du Bois achieved an undeniable formal and thematic unity. Most remarkable is the book's successful integration of African American history, political critique, and sociology with forays into autobiography ("Of the Black Belt," "Of the Passing of the First-Born"), fiction ("Of the Coming of John"), eulogy ("Of Alexander Crummell"), and musicology ("The Sorrow Songs"). The chapters devoted to the history of the black South during Reconstruction and the late nineteenth century are still among the most succinct and penetrating analyses of the human dimensions of the failure of Reconstruction to offer plausible, sustained remedies to the illiteracy and poverty spawned by racism. In Du Bois's presentation, the harsh life of contemporary sharecroppers is not far removed from slavery, both in memory and in contemporary experience, and the argument of the book returns time and again to the economic legacy of slavery as the principal cause of present problems in African American families and communities. Du Bois uses mythology, literary allusion, passionate declamation, statistics, case studies, historical narrative, personal confession, and music itself to advance his complex but coherent contention that the political and economic subordination of a great part of America's citizens, merely on account of their race, is a moral catastrophe, and that the law and custom of segregation is bound to create a disordered society founded on unconstitutional principles.

Reviews of *The Souls of Black Folk* were largely quite favorable, but many readers took their cue—whether pro or con—from Du Bois's notorious attack on Booker T. Washington. As the president of Tuskegee Institute, the well-known author of *Up from Slavery*, and the most famous black leader in America, Washington wielded enormous influence. It was precisely what he took to be Washington's misuse of his power—namely, his accommodation to segregation and the dictates of white supremacy—that Du Bois made the centerpiece of his critique in "Of Mr. Booker T. Washington and Others." Editors and reviewers associated with Washington's Tuskegee Machine dealt harshly with the young Du Bois, but it is perhaps safe to say that the controversy added to his book's fame and certainly helped to boost Du Bois to a position of rivalry with Washington. Not just in the chapter on Washington but throughout the book Du Bois vigorously promoted an agenda of black male suffrage (he was later a staunch advocate of women's voting rights as well), equal protection under the law, and access to higher education, whether in integrated or black colleges. Something more than manual arts, argued Du Bois, was necessary to make African Americans capable and responsible citizens. And indeed, the high intellectual and stylistic pitch of *The Souls of Black Folk* was itself a demonstration of the importance and power of education, an illustration of how the Talented Tenth of African Americans must lead the way in the arts as well as in business, science, and the professions.

In this regard, it is most remarkable that Du Bois, while advancing his thesis on so many fronts, also chose to place African American music at the heart of American culture by declaring the slave spirituals the most important national art produced to date. By pairing his literary and musical epigraphs and grounding the arguments of his chapters in the unprinted words of fifteen selected spirituals (the last chapter cites two), Du Bois created a half-written, half-sung text of brilliant complexity and enduring beauty (Sundquist, 457–539). The historical tensions surrounding Du Bois's choice to anchor his text in an elaborate assertion of the importance of the slave spirituals to American cultural history became a significant part of his achievement. Spirituals were being collected and published in great numbers by the turn of the century, but this was accompanied by a sense that black music was about to be lost as the older generations died and as the black middle class sought to distance itself from all reminders of slavery, relegating the songs' social message and artistic value to a receding historical moment. Moreover, those older African Americans who had known the spirituals under the regime of slavery frequently remarked that new versions of the songs, performed or collected in volumes, were but pale imitations of the originals—a view taken to its theoretical limit by Zora Neale Hurston, who contended in her landmark essay "Spirituals and Neo-Spirituals" that "there never has been a presentation of genuine Negro spirituals to any audience anywhere" (Hurston, 223–24).

In Du Bois's use of the spirituals, then, complex questions of cultural progress and decline are entangled with the task of preserving and celebrating African American artistry. The same balance of demands—to transcend the pain and liabilities of the past while remembering and restoring the power of the African American heritage—runs throughout *The Souls of Black Folk*. No work before or since has met the challenge so well.

CONTENTS

THE AFTERTHOUGHT

NOTES BY MONICA M. ELBERT

THE SOULS OF BLACK FOLK

The Forethought

Herein lie buried many things which if read with patience may show the strange meaning of being black here in the dawning of the Twentieth Century. This meaning is not without interest to you, Gentle Reader; for the problem of the Twentieth Century is the problem of the color-line.

I pray you, then, receive my little book in all charity, studying my words with me, forgiving mistake and foible for sake of the faith and passion that is in me, and seeking the grain of truth hidden there.

I have sought here to sketch, in vague, uncertain outline, the spiritual world in which ten thousand thousand Americans live and strive. First, in two chapters I have tried to show what Emancipation meant to them, and what was its aftermath. In a third chapter I have pointed out the slow rise of personal leadership, and criticised candidly the leader who bears the chief burden of his race to-day. Then, in two other chapters I have sketched in swift outline the two worlds within and without the Veil, and thus have come to the central problem of training men for life. Venturing now into deeper detail, I have in two chapters studied the struggles of the massed millions of the black peasantry, and in another have sought to make clear the present relations of the sons of master and man.

Leaving, then, the world of the white man, I have stepped within the Veil, raising it that you may view faintly its deeper recesses,—the meaning of its religion, the passion of its human sorrow, and the struggle of its greater souls. All this I have ended with a tale twice told but seldom written.

Some of these thoughts of mine have seen the light before in other guise. For kindly consenting to their republication here, in altered and extended form, I must thank the publishers of *The Atlantic Monthly, The World's Work, The Dial, The New World*, and the *Annals of the American Academy of Political and Social Science*.

Before each chapter, as now printed, stands a bar of the Sorrow Songs,—some echo of haunting melody from the only American music which welled up from black souls in the dark past. And, finally, need I add that I who speak here am bone of the bone and flesh of the flesh of them that live within the Veil?

W. E. B. Du B.

Atlanta, Ga., Feb. 1, 1903.

CHAPTER I

Of Our Spiritual Strivings

O water, voice of my heart, crying in the sand,
  All night long crying with a mournful cry,
As I lie and listen, and cannot understand
    The voice of my heart in my side or the voice of the sea,
  O water, crying for rest, is it I, is it I?
  All night long the water is crying to me.

Unresting water, there shall never be rest
  Till the last moon droop and the last tide fail,
And the fire of the end begin to burn in the west;
    And the heart shall be weary and wonder and cry like the sea,
  All life long crying without avail,
    As the water all night long is crying to me.

Arthur Symons

Between me and the other world there is ever an unasked question: unasked by some through feelings of delicacy; by others through the difficulty of rightly framing it. All, nevertheless, flutter round it. They approach me in a half-hesitant sort of way, eye me curiously or compassionately, and then, instead of saying directly, How does it feel to be a problem? they say, I know an excellent colored man in my town; or, I fought at Mechanicsville; or, Do not these Southern outrages make your blood boil? At these I smile, or am interested, or reduce the boiling to a simmer, as the occasion may require. To the real question, How does it feel to be a problem? I answer seldom a word.

And yet, being a problem is a strange experience,—peculiar even for one who has never been anything else, save perhaps in babyhood and in Europe. It is in the early days of rollicking boyhood that the revelation first bursts upon one, all in a day, as it were. I remember well when the shadow swept across me. I was a little thing, away up in the hills of New England, where the dark Housatonic winds between Hoosac and Taghkanic to the sea. In a wee wooden schoolhouse, something put it into the boys' and girls' heads to buy gorgeous visiting-cards—ten cents a package—and exchange. The exchange was merry, till one girl, a tall newcomer, refused my card,—refused it peremptorily, with a glance. Then it dawned upon me with a certain suddenness that I was different from the others; or like, mayhap, in heart and life and longing, but shut out from their world by a vast veil. I had thereafter no desire to tear down that veil, to creep through; I held all beyond it in common contempt, and lived above it in a region of blue sky and great wandering shadows. That sky was bluest when I could beat my mates at examination-time, or beat them at a foot-race, or even beat their stringy heads. Alas, with the years all this fine contempt began to fade; for the worlds I longed for, and all their dazzling opportunities, were theirs, not mine. But they should not keep these prizes, I said; some, all, I would wrest from them. Just how I would do it I could never decide: by reading law, by healing the sick, by telling the wonderful tales that swam in my head,—some way. With other black boys the strife was not so fiercely sunny: their youth shrunk into tasteless sycophancy, or into silent hatred of the pale world about them and mocking distrust of everything white; or wasted itself in a bitter cry, Why did God make me an outcast and a stranger in mine own house? The shades of the prison-house closed round about us all: walls strait and stubborn to the whitest, but relentlessly narrow, tall, and unscalable to sons of night who must plod darkly on in resignation, or beat unavailing palms against the stone, or steadily, half hopelessly, watch the streak of blue above.

After the Egyptian and Indian, the Greek and Roman, the Teuton and Mongolian, the Negro is a sort of seventh son, born with a veil, and gifted with second-sight in this American world,—a world which yields him no true self-consciousness, but only lets him see himself through the revelation of the other world. It is a peculiar sensation, this double-consciousness, this sense of always looking at one's self through the eyes of others, of measuring one's soul by the tape of a world that looks on in amused contempt and pity. One ever feels his twoness,—an American, a Negro; two souls, two thoughts, two unreconciled strivings; two warring ideals in one dark body, whose dogged strength alone keeps it from being torn asunder.

The history of the American Negro is the history of this strife—this longing to attain self-conscious manhood, to merge his double self into a better and truer self. In this merging he wishes neither of the older selves to be lost. He would not Africanize America, for America has too much to teach the world and Africa. He would not bleach his Negro soul in a flood of white Americanism, for he knows that Negro blood has a message for the world. He simply wishes to make it possible for a man to be both a Negro and an American, without being cursed and spit upon by his fellows, without having the doors of Opportunity closed roughly in his face.

This, then, is the end of his striving: to be a co-worker in the kingdom of culture, to escape both death and isolation, to husband and use his best powers and his latent genius. These powers of body and mind have in the past been strangely wasted, dispersed, or forgotten. The shadow of a mighty Negro past flits through the tale of Ethiopia the Shadowy and of Egypt the Sphinx. Throughout history, the powers

of single black men flash here and there like falling stars, and die sometimes before the world has rightly gauged their brightness. Here in
America, in the few days since Emancipation, the black man's turning
hither and thither in hesitant and doubtful striving has often made his
very strength to lose effectiveness, to seem like absence of power, like
weakness. And yet it is not weakness,—it is the contradiction of double aims. The double-aimed struggle of the black artisan—on the one
hand to escape white contempt for a nation of mere hewers of wood
and drawers of water, and on the other hand to plough and nail and
dig for a poverty-stricken horde—could only result in making him a
poor craftsman, for he had but half a heart in either cause. By the
poverty and ignorance of his people, the Negro minister or doctor was
tempted toward quackery and demagogy; and by the criticism of the
other world, toward ideals that made him ashamed of his lowly tasks.
The would-be black *savant* was confronted by the paradox that the
knowledge his people needed was a twice-told tale to his white neighbors, while the knowledge which would teach the white world was
Greek to his own flesh and blood. The innate love of harmony and
beauty that set the ruder souls of his people a-dancing and a-singing
raised but confusion and doubt in the soul of the black artist; for the
beauty revealed to him was the soul-beauty of a race which his larger
audience despised, and he could not articulate the message of another
people. This waste of double aims, this seeking to satisfy two unreconciled ideals, has wrought sad havoc with the courage and faith and
deeds of ten thousand thousand people,—has sent them often wooing
false gods and invoking false means of salvation, and at times has even
seemed about to make them ashamed of themselves.

Away back in the days of bondage they thought to see in one divine
event the end of all doubt and disappointment; few men ever worshipped Freedom with half such unquestioning faith as did the American Negro for two centuries. To him, so far as he thought and dreamed,
slavery was indeed the sum of all villainies, the cause of all sorrow, the
root of all prejudice; Emancipation was the key to a promised land of
sweeter beauty than ever stretched before the eyes of wearied Israelites.
In song and exhortation swelled one refrain—Liberty; in his tears and
curses the God he implored had Freedom in his right hand. At last it
came,—suddenly, fearfully, like a dream. With one wild carnival of
blood and passion came the message in his own plaintive cadences:—

> "Shout, O children!
> Shout, you're free!
> For God has bought your liberty!"

Years have passed away since then,—ten, twenty, forty; forty years
of national life, forty years of renewal and development, and yet the

swarthy spectre sits in its accustomed seat at the Nation's feast. In vain do we cry to this our vastest social problem:—

> "Take any shape but that, and my firm nerves
> Shall never tremble!"

The Nation has not yet found peace from its sins; the freedman has not yet found in freedom his promised land. Whatever of good may have come in these years of change, the shadow of a deep disappointment rests upon the Negro people,—a disappointment all the more bitter because the unattained ideal was unbounded save by the simple ignorance of a lowly people.

The first decade was merely a prolongation of the vain search for freedom, the boon that seemed ever barely to elude their grasp,—like a tantalizing will-o'-the-wisp, maddening and misleading the headless host. The holocaust of war, the terrors of the Ku-Klux Klan, the lies of carpet-baggers, the disorganization of industry, and the contradictory advice of friends and foes, left the bewildered serf with no new watchword beyond the old cry for freedom. As the time flew, however, he began to grasp a new idea. The ideal of liberty demanded for its attainment powerful means, and these the Fifteenth Amendment gave him. The ballot, which before he had looked upon as a visible sign of freedom, he now regarded as the chief means of gaining and perfecting the liberty with which war had partially endowed him. And why not? Had not votes made war and emancipated millions? Had not votes enfranchised the freedmen? Was anything impossible to a power that had done all this? A million black men started with renewed zeal to vote themselves into the kingdom. So the decade flew away, the revolution of 1876 came, and left the half-free serf weary, wondering, but still inspired. Slowly but steadily, in the following years, a new vision began gradually to replace the dream of political power,—a powerful movement, the rise of another ideal to guide the unguided, another pillar of fire by night after a clouded day. It was the ideal of "book-learning"; the curiosity, born of compulsory ignorance, to know and test the power of the cabalistic letters of the white man, the longing to know. Here at last seemed to have been discovered the mountain path to Canaan; longer than the highway of Emancipation and law, steep and rugged, but straight, leading to heights high enough to overlook life.

Up the new path the advance guard toiled, slowly, heavily, doggedly; only those who have watched and guided the faltering feet, the misty minds, the dull understandings, of the dark pupils of these schools know how faithfully, how piteously, this people strove to learn. It was weary work. The cold statistician wrote down the inches of progress here and there, noted also where here and there a foot had slipped or some one had fallen. To the tired climbers, the horizon was ever dark, the mists were often cold, the Canaan was always dim and far away. If, however, the vistas disclosed as yet no goal, no resting-place, little but flattery and criticism, the journey at least gave leisure for reflection and self-examination; it changed the child of Emancipation to the youth with dawning self-consciousness, self-realization, self-respect. In those sombre forests of his striving his own soul rose before him, and he saw himself,—darkly as through a veil; and yet he saw in himself some faint revelation of his power, of his mission. He began to have a dim feeling that, to attain his place in the world, he must be himself, and not another. For the first time he sought to analyze the burden he bore upon his back, that dead-weight of social degradation partially masked behind a half-named Negro problem. He felt his poverty; without a cent, without a home, without land, tools, or savings, he had entered into competition with rich, landed, skilled neighbors. To be a poor man is hard, but to be a poor race in a land of dollars is the very bottom of hardships. He felt the weight of his ignorance,—not simply of letters, but of life, of business, of the humanities; the accumulated sloth and shirking and awkwardness of decades and centuries shackled his hands and feet. Nor was his burden all poverty and ignorance. The red stain of bastardy, which two centuries of systematic legal defilement of Negro women had stamped upon his race, meant not only the loss of ancient African chastity, but also the hereditary weight of a mass of corruption from white adulterers, threatening almost the obliteration of the Negro home.

A people thus handicapped ought not to be asked to race with the world, but rather allowed to give all its time and thought to its own social problems. But alas! while sociologists gleefully count his bastards and his prostitutes, the very soul of the toiling, sweating black man is darkened by the shadow of a vast despair. Men call the shadow prejudice, and learnedly explain it as the natural defence of culture against barbarism, learning against ignorance, purity against crime, the "higher" against the "lower" races. To which the Negro cries Amen! and swears that to so much of this strange prejudice as is founded on just homage to civilization, culture, righteousness, and progress, he humbly bows and meekly does obeisance. But before that nameless prejudice that leaps beyond all this he stands helpless, dismayed, and well-nigh speechless; before that personal disrespect and mockery, the ridicule and systematic humiliation, the distortion of fact and wanton license of fancy, the cynical ignoring of the better and the boisterous welcoming of the worse, the all-pervading desire to inculcate disdain for everything black, from Toussaint to the devil,—before this there rises a sickening despair that would disarm and discourage any nation save that black host to whom "discouragement" is an unwritten word.

But the facing of so vast a prejudice could not but bring the inevitable self-questioning, self-disparagement, and lowering of ideals which ever accompany repression and breed in an atmosphere of contempt and hate. Whisperings and portents came borne upon the four winds: Lo! we are diseased and dying, cried the dark hosts; we cannot write, our voting is vain; what need of education, since we must always cook and serve? And the Nation echoed and enforced this self-criticism, saying: Be content to be servants, and nothing more; what need of higher culture for half-men? Away with the black man's ballot, by force or fraud,— and behold the suicide of a race! Nevertheless, out of the evil came something of good,—the more careful adjustment of education to real life, the clearer perception of the Negroes' social responsibilities, and the sobering realization of the meaning of progress.

So dawned the time of *Sturm und Drang:* storm and stress today rocks our little boat on the mad waters of the world-sea; there is within and without the sound of conflict, the burning of body and rending of soul; inspiration strives with doubt, and faith with vain questionings. The bright ideals of the past,—physical freedom, political power, the training of brains and the training of hands,—all these in turn have waxed and waned, until even the last grows dim and overcast. Are they all wrong,—all false? No, not that, but each alone was oversimple and incomplete,—the dreams of a credulous race-childhood, or the fond imaginings of the other world which does not know and does not want to know our power. To be really true, all these ideals must be melted and welded into one. The training of the schools we need to-day more than ever,—the training of deft hands, quick eyes and ears, and above all the broader, deeper, higher culture of gifted minds and pure hearts. The power of the ballot we need in sheer self-defence,—else what shall save us from a second slavery? Freedom, too, the long-sought, we still seek,—the freedom of life and limb, the freedom to work and think, the freedom to love and aspire. Work, culture, liberty,—all these we need, not singly but together, not successively but together, each growing and aiding each, and all striving toward that vaster ideal that swims before the Negro people, the ideal of human brotherhood, gained through the unifying ideal of Race; the ideal of fostering and developing the traits and talents of the Negro, not in opposition to or contempt for other races, but rather in large conformity to the greater ideals of the American Republic, in order that some day on American soil two world-races may give each to each those characteristics both so sadly lack. We the darker ones come even now not altogether empty-handed: there are to-day no truer exponents of the pure human spirit of the Declaration of Independence than the American Negroes; there is no true American music but the wild sweet melodies of the Negro slave; the American fairy tales and folklore are Indian and African; and, all in all, we black men seem the sole oasis of simple faith and reverence in a dusty desert of dollars and smartness. Will America be poorer if she replace her brutal dyspeptic blundering with light-hearted but determined Negro humility? or her coarse and cruel wit with loving jovial good-humor? or her vulgar music with the soul of the Sorrow Songs?

Merely a concrete test of the underlying principles of the great republic is the Negro Problem, and the spiritual striving of the freedmen's sons is the travail of souls whose burden is almost beyond the measure of their strength, but who bear it in the name of an historic race, in the name of this the land of their fathers' fathers, and in the name of human opportunity.

And now what I have briefly sketched in large outline let me on coming pages tell again in many ways, with loving emphasis and deeper detail, that men may listen to the striving in the souls of black folk.

CHAPTER **II**

Of the Dawn of Freedom

Careless seems the great Avenger;
  History's lessons but record
One death-grapple in the darkness
  'Twixt old systems and the Word;
Truth forever on the scaffold,
  Wrong forever on the throne;
Yet that scaffold sways the future,
  And behind the dim unknown
Standeth God within the shadow
  Keeping watch above His own.

Lowell

The problem of the twentieth century is the problem of the color-line,—the relation of the darker to the lighter races of men in Asia and Africa, in America and the islands of the sea. It was a phase of this problem that caused the Civil War; and however much they who marched South and North in 1861 may have fixed on the technical points of union and local autonomy as a shibboleth, all nevertheless knew, as we know, that the question of Negro slavery was the real cause of the conflict. Curious it was, too, how this deeper question ever forced itself to the surface despite effort and disclaimer. No sooner had Northern armies touched Southern soil than this old question, newly guised, sprang from the earth,—What shall be done with Negroes? Peremptory military commands, this way and that, could not answer the query; the Emancipation Proclamation seemed but to broaden and intensify the difficulties; and the War Amendments made the Negro problems of to-day.

It is the aim of this essay to study the period of history from 1861 to 1872 so far as it relates to the American Negro. In effect, this tale of the dawn of Freedom is an account of that government of men called the Freedmen's Bureau,—one of the most singular and interesting of the attempts made by a great nation to grapple with vast problems of race and social condition.

The war has naught to do with slaves, cried Congress, the President, and the Nation; and yet no sooner had the armies, East and West, penetrated Virginia and Tennessee than fugitive slaves appeared within their lines. They came at night, when the flickering camp-fires shone like vast unsteady stars along the black horizon: old men and thin, with gray and tufted hair; women, with frightened eyes, dragging whimpering hungry children; men and girls, stalwart and gaunt,—a horde of starving vagabonds, homeless, helpless, and pitiable, in their dark distress. Two methods of treating these newcomers seemed equally logical to opposite sorts of minds. Ben Butler, in Virginia, quickly declared slave property contraband of war, and put the fugitives to work; while Fremont, in Missouri, declared the slaves free under martial law. Butler's action was approved, but Fremont's was hastily countermanded, and his successor, Halleck, saw things differently. "Hereafter," he commanded, "no slaves should be allowed to come into your lines at all; if any come without your knowledge, when owners call for them deliver them." Such a policy was difficult to enforce; some of the black refugees declared themselves freemen, others showed that their masters had deserted them, and still others were captured with forts and plantations. Evidently, too, slaves were a source of strength to the Confederacy, and were being used as laborers and producers. "They constitute a military resource," wrote Secretary Cameron, late in 1861; "and being such, that they should not be turned over to the enemy is too plain to discuss." So gradually the tone of the army chiefs changed; Congress forbade the rendition of fugitives, and Butler's "contrabands" were welcomed as military laborers. This complicated rather than solved the problem, for now the scattering fugitives became a steady stream, which flowed faster as the armies marched.

Then the long-headed man with care-chiselled face who sat in the White House saw the inevitable, and emancipated the slaves of rebels on New Year's, 1863. A month later Congress called earnestly for the

Negro soldiers whom the act of July, 1862, had half grudgingly allowed to enlist. Thus the barriers were levelled and the deed was done. The stream of fugitives swelled to a flood, and anxious army officers kept inquiring: "What must be done with slaves, arriving almost daily? Are we to find food and shelter for women and children?"

It was a Pierce of Boston who pointed out the way, and thus became in a sense the founder of the Freedmen's Bureau. He was a firm friend of Secretary Chase; and when, in 1861, the care of slaves and abandoned lands devolved upon the Treasury officials, Pierce was specially detailed from the ranks to study the conditions. First, he cared for the refugees at Fortress Monroe; and then, after Sherman had captured Hilton Head, Pierce was sent there to found his Port Royal experiment of making free workingmen out of slaves. Before his experiment was barely started, however, the problem of the fugitives had assumed such proportions that it was taken from the hands of the over-burdened Treasury Department and given to the army officials. Already centres of massed freedmen were forming at Fortress Monroe, Washington, New Orleans, Vicksburg and Corinth, Columbus, Ky., and Cairo, Ill., as well as at Port Royal. Army chaplains found here new and fruitful fields; "superintendents of contrabands" multiplied, and some attempt at systematic work was made by enlisting the able-bodied men and giving work to the others.

Then came the Freedmen's Aid societies, born of the touching appeals from Pierce and from these other centres of distress. There was the American Missionary Association, sprung from the *Amistad*, and now full-grown for work; the various church organizations, the National Freedmen's Relief Association, the American Freedmen's Union, the Western Freedmen's Aid Commission,—in all fifty or more active organizations, which sent clothes, money, school-books, and teachers southward. All they did was needed, for the destitution of the freedmen was often reported as "too appalling for belief," and the situation was daily growing worse rather than better.

And daily, too, it seemed more plain that this was no ordinary matter of temporary relief, but a national crisis; for here loomed a labor problem of vast dimensions. Masses of Negroes stood idle, or, if they worked spasmodically, were never sure of pay; and if perchance they received pay, squandered the new thing thoughtlessly. In these and other ways were camp-life and the new liberty demoralizing the freedmen. The broader economic organization thus clearly demanded sprang up here and there as accident and local conditions determined. Here it was that Pierce's Port Royal plan of leased plantations and guided workmen pointed out the rough way. In Washington the military governor, at the urgent appeal of the superintendent, opened confiscated estates to the cultivation of the fugitives, and there in the shadow of the dome gathered black farm villages. General Dix gave over estates to the freedmen of Fortress Monroe, and so on, South and

West. The government and benevolent societies furnished the means of cultivation, and the Negro turned again slowly to work. The systems of control, thus started, rapidly grew, here and there, into strange little governments, like that of General Banks in Louisiana, with its ninety thousand black subjects, its fifty thousand guided laborers, and its annual budget of one hundred thousand dollars and more. It made out four thousand pay-rolls a year, registered all freedmen, inquired into grievances and redressed them, laid and collected taxes, and established a system of public schools. So, too, Colonel Eaton, the superintendent of Tennessee and Arkansas, ruled over one hundred thousand freedmen, leased and cultivated seven thousand acres of cotton land, and fed ten thousand paupers a year. In South Carolina was General Saxton, with his deep interest in black folk. He succeeded Pierce and the Treasury officials, and sold forfeited estates, leased abandoned plantations, encouraged schools, and received from Sherman, after that terribly picturesque march to the sea, thousands of the wretched camp followers.

Three characteristic things one might have seen in Sherman's raid through Georgia, which threw the new situation in shadowy relief: the Conqueror, the Conquered, and the Negro. Some see all significance in the grim front of the destroyer, and some in the bitter sufferers of the Lost Cause. But to me neither soldier nor fugitive speaks with so deep a meaning as that dark human cloud that clung like remorse on the rear of those swift columns, swelling at times to half their size, almost engulfing and choking them. In vain were they ordered back, in vain were bridges hewn from beneath their feet; on they trudged and writhed and surged, until they rolled into Savannah, a starved and naked horde of tens of thousands. There too came the characteristic military remedy: "The islands from Charleston south, the abandoned rice-fields along the rivers for thirty miles back from the sea, and the country bordering the St. John's River, Florida, are reserved and set apart for the settlement of Negroes now made free by act of war." So read the celebrated "Field-order Number Fifteen."

All these experiments, orders, and systems were bound to attract and perplex the government and the nation. Directly after the Emancipation Proclamation, Representative Eliot had introduced a bill creating a Bureau of Emancipation; but it was never reported. The following June a committee of inquiry, appointed by the Secretary of War, reported in favor of a temporary bureau for the "improvement, protection, and employment of refugee freedmen," on much the same lines as were afterwards followed. Petitions came in to President Lincoln from distinguished citizens and organizations, strongly urging a comprehensive and unified plan of dealing with the freedmen, under a bureau which should be "charged with the study of plans and execution of measures for easily guiding, and in every way judiciously and humanely aiding, the passage of our emancipated and yet to be emancipated blacks from the old condition of forced labor to their new state of voluntary industry."

Some half-hearted steps were taken to accomplish this, in part, by putting the whole matter again in charge of the special Treasury agents. Laws of 1863 and 1864 directed them to take charge of and lease abandoned lands for periods not exceeding twelve months, and to "provide in such leases, or otherwise, for the employment and general welfare" of the freedmen. Most of the army officers greeted this as a welcome relief from perplexing "Negro affairs," and Secretary Fessenden, July 29, 1864, issued an excellent system of regulations, which were afterward closely followed by General Howard. Under Treasury agents, large quantities of land were leased in the Mississippi Valley, and many Negroes were employed; but in August, 1864, the new regulations were suspended for reasons of "public policy," and the army was again in control.

Meanwhile Congress had turned its attention to the subject; and in March the House passed a bill by a majority of two establishing a Bureau for Freedmen in the War Department. Charles Sumner, who had charge of the bill in the Senate, argued that freedmen and abandoned lands ought to be under the same department, and reported a substitute for the House bill attaching the Bureau to the Treasury Department. This bill passed, but too late for action by the House. The debates wandered over the whole policy of the administration and the general question of slavery, without touching very closely the specific merits of the measure in hand. Then the national election took place; and the administration, with a vote of renewed confidence from the country, addressed itself to the matter more seriously. A conference between the two branches of Congress agreed upon a carefully drawn measure which contained the chief provisions of Sumner's bill, but made the proposed organization a department independent of both the War and the Treasury officials. The bill was conservative, giving the new department "general superintendence of all freedmen." Its purpose was to "establish regulations" for them, protect them, lease them lands, adjust their wages, and appear in civil and military courts as their "next friend." There were many limitations attached to the powers thus granted, and the organization was made permanent. Nevertheless, the Senate defeated the bill, and a new conference committee was appointed. This committee reported a new bill, February 28, which was whirled through just as the session closed, and became the act of 1865 establishing in the War Department a "Bureau of Refugees, Freedmen, and Abandoned Lands."

This last compromise was a hasty bit of legislation, vague and uncertain in outline. A Bureau was created, "to continue during the present War of Rebellion, and for one year thereafter," to which was given "the supervision and management of all abandoned lands and the control of all subjects relating to refugees and freedmen," under "such rules and regulations as may be presented by the head of the Bureau and approved by the President." A Commissioner, appointed by the President and Senate, was to control the Bureau, with an office force not exceeding ten clerks. The President might also appoint assistant commissioners in the seceded States, and to all these offices military officials might be detailed at regular pay. The Secretary of War could issue rations, clothing, and fuel to the destitute, and all abandoned property was placed in the hands of the Bureau for eventual lease and sale to ex-slaves in forty-acre parcels.

Thus did the United States government definitely assume charge of the emancipated Negro as the ward of the nation. It was a tremendous undertaking. Here at a stroke of the pen was erected a government of millions of men,—and not ordinary men either, but black men emasculated by a peculiarly complete system of slavery, centuries old; and now, suddenly, violently, they come into a new birthright, at a time of war and passion, in the midst of the stricken and embittered population of their former masters. Any man might well have hesitated to assume charge of such a work, with vast responsibilities, indefinite powers, and limited resources. Probably no one but a soldier would have answered such a call promptly; and, indeed, no one but a soldier could be called, for Congress had appropriated no money for salaries and expenses.

Less than a month after the weary Emancipator passed to his rest, his successor assigned Major-Gen. Oliver O. Howard to duty as Commissioner of the new Bureau. He was a Maine man, then only thirty-five years of age. He had marched with Sherman to the sea, had fought well at Gettysburg, and but the year before had been assigned to the command of the Department of Tennessee. An honest man, with too much faith in human nature, little aptitude for business and intricate detail, he had had large opportunity of becoming acquainted at first hand with much of the work before him. And of that work it has been truly said that "no approximately correct history of civilization can ever be written which does not throw out in bold relief, as one of the great landmarks of political and social progress, the organization and administration of the Freedmen's Bureau."

On May 12, 1865, Howard was appointed; and he assumed the duties of his office promptly on the 15th, and began examining the field of work. A curious mess he looked upon: little despotisms, communistic experiments, slavery, peonage, business speculations, organized charity, unorganized almsgiving,—all reeling on under the guise of helping the freedmen, and all enshrined in the smoke and blood of war and the cursing and silence of angry men. On May 19 the new government—for a government it really was—issued its constitution; commissioners were to be appointed in each of the seceded States, who were to take charge of "all subjects relating to refugees and freedmen," and all relief and rations were to be given by their consent

112

alone. The Bureau invited continued coöperation with benevolent societies, and declared: "It will be the object of all commissioners to introduce practicable systems of compensated labor," and to establish
schools. Forthwith nine assistant commissioners were appointed. They
were to hasten to their fields of work; seek gradually to close relief
establishments, and make the destitute self-supporting; act as courts of
law where there were no courts, or where Negroes were not recognized in them as free; establish the institution of marriage among ex-
slaves, and keep records; see that freedmen were free to choose their
employers, and help in making fair contracts for them; and finally, the
circular said: "Simple good faith, for which we hope on all hands for
those concerned in the passing away of slavery, will especially relieve
the assistant commissioners in the discharge of their duties toward the
freedmen, as well as promote the general welfare."

No sooner was the work thus started, and the general system and
local organization in some measure begun, than two grave difficulties
appeared which changed largely the theory and outcome of Bureau
work. First, there were the abandoned lands of the South. It had long
been the more or less definitely expressed theory of the North that all
the chief problems of Emancipation might be settled by establishing
the slaves on the forfeited lands of their masters,—a sort of poetic justice, said some. But this poetry done into solemn prose meant either
wholesale confiscation of private property in the South, or vast appropriations. Now Congress had not appropriated a cent, and no sooner
did the proclamations of general amnesty appear than the eight hundred thousand acres of abandoned lands in the hands of the
Freedmen's Bureau melted quickly away. The second difficulty lay in
perfecting the local organization of the Bureau throughout the wide
field of work. Making a new machine and sending out officials of duly
ascertained fitness for a great work of social reform is no child's task;
but this task was even harder, for a new central organization had to be
fitted on a heterogeneous and confused but already existing system of
relief and control of ex-slaves; and the agents available for this work
must be sought for in an army still busy with war operations,—men in
the very nature of the case ill fitted for delicate social work,—or among
the questionable camp followers of an invading host. Thus, after a
year's work, vigorously as it was pushed, the problem looked even
more difficult to grasp and solve than at the beginning. Nevertheless,
three things that year's work did, well worth the doing: it relieved a
vast amount of physical suffering; it transported seven thousand fugitives from congested centres back to the farm; and, best of all, it inau-
gurated the crusade of the New England school-ma'am.

The annals of this Ninth Crusade are yet to be written,—the tale of
a mission that seemed to our age far more quixotic than the quest of
St. Louis seemed to his. Behind the mists of ruin and rapine waved the
calico dresses of women who dared, and after the hoarse mouthings of

the field guns rang the rhythm of the alphabet. Rich and poor they were, serious and curious. Bereaved now of a father, now of a brother, now of more than these, they came seeking a life work in planting New England schoolhouses among the white and black of the South. They did their work well. In that first year they taught one hundred thousand souls, and more.

Evidently, Congress must soon legislate again on the hastily organized Bureau, which had so quickly grown into wide significance and vast possibilities. An institution such as that was well-nigh as difficult to end as to begin. Early in 1866 Congress took up the matter, when Senator Trumbull, of Illinois, introduced a bill to extend the Bureau and enlarge its powers. This measure received, at the hands of Congress, far more thorough discussion and attention than its predecessor. The war cloud had thinned enough to allow a clearer conception of the work of Emancipation. The champions of the bill argued that the strengthening of the Freedmen's Bureau was still a military necessity; that it was needed for the proper carrying out of the Thirteenth Amendment, and was a work of sheer justice to the ex-slave, at a trifling cost to the government. The opponents of the measure declared that the war was over, and the necessity for war measures past; that the Bureau, by reason of its extraordinary powers, was clearly unconstitutional in time of peace, and was destined to irritate the South and pauperize the freedmen, at a final cost of possibly hundreds of millions. These two arguments were unanswered, and indeed unanswerable: the one that the extraordinary powers of the Bureau threatened the civil rights of all citizens; and the other that the government must have power to do what manifestly must be done, and that present abandonment of the freedmen meant their practical re-enslavement. The bill which finally passed enlarged and made permanent the Freedmen's Bureau. It was promptly vetoed by President Johnson as "unconstitutional," "unnecessary," and "extrajudicial," and failed of passage over the veto. Meantime, however, the breach between Congress and the President began to broaden, and a modified form of the lost bill was finally passed over the President's second veto, July 16.

The act of 1866 gave the Freedmen's Bureau its final form,—the form by which it will be known to posterity and judged of men. It extended the existence of the Bureau to July, 1868; it authorized additional assistant commissioners, the retention of army officers mustered out of regular service, the sale of certain forfeited lands to freedmen on nominal terms, the sale of Confederate public property for Negro schools, and a wider field of judicial interpretation and cognizance. The government of the unreconstructed South was thus put very largely in the hands of the Freedmen's Bureau, especially as in many cases the departmental military commander was now made also assistant commissioner. It was thus that the Freedmen's Bureau became a full-fledged government of men. It made laws, executed them and interpreted them; it laid and collected taxes, defined and punished crime, maintained and used military force, and dictated such measures as it thought necessary and proper for the accomplishment of its varied ends. Naturally, all these powers were not exercised continuously nor to their fullest extent; and yet, as General Howard has said, "scarcely any subject that has to be legislated upon in civil society failed, at one time or another, to demand the action of this singular Bureau."

To understand and criticise intelligently so vast a work, one must not forget an instant the drift of things in the later sixties. Lee had surrendered, Lincoln was dead, and Johnson and Congress were at loggerheads; the Thirteenth Amendment was adopted, the Fourteenth pending, and the Fifteenth declared in force in 1870. Guerrilla raiding, the ever-present flickering after-flame of war, was spending its force against the Negroes, and all the Southern land was awakening as from some wild dream to poverty and social revolution. In a time of perfect calm, amid willing neighbors and streaming wealth, the social uplifting of four million slaves to an assured and self-sustaining place in the body politic and economic would have been a herculean task; but when to the inherent difficulties of so delicate and nice a social operation were added the spite and hate of conflict, the hell of war; when suspicion and cruelty were rife, and gaunt Hunger wept beside Bereavement,—in such a case, the work of any instrument of social regeneration was in large part foredoomed to failure. The very name of the Bureau stood for a thing in the South which for two centuries and better men had refused even to argue,—that life amid free Negroes was simply unthinkable, the maddest of experiments.

The agents that the Bureau could command varied all the way from unselfish philanthropists to narrow-minded busybodies and thieves; and even though it be true that the average was far better than the worst, it was the occasional fly that helped spoil the ointment.

Then amid all crouched the freed slave, bewildered between friend and foe. He had emerged from slavery,—not the worst slavery in the world, not a slavery that made all life unbearable, rather a slavery that had here and there something of kindliness, fidelity, and happiness,—but withal slavery, which, so far as human aspiration and desert were concerned, classed the black man and the ox together. And the Negro knew full well that, whatever their deeper convictions may have been, Southern men had fought with desperate energy to perpetuate this slavery under which the black masses, with half-articulate thought, had writhed and shivered. They welcomed freedom with a cry. They shrank from the master who still strove for their chains; they fled to the friends that had freed them, even though those friends stood ready to use them as a club for driving the recalcitrant South back into loyalty. So the cleft between the white and black South grew. Idle to say it never should have been; it was as inevitable as its results were pitiable. Curiously incongruous elements were left arrayed against each other,—the North, the government, the carpet-bagger, and the slave, here; and there, all the South that was white, whether gentleman or vagabond, honest man or rascal, lawless murderer or martyr to duty.

Thus it is doubly difficult to write of this period calmly, so intense was the feeling, so mighty the human passions that swayed and blinded men. Amid it all, two figures ever stand to typify that day to coming ages,—the one, a gray-haired gentleman, whose fathers had quit themselves like men, whose sons lay in nameless graves; who bowed to the evil of slavery because its abolition threatened untold ill to all; who stood at last, in the evening of life, a blighted, ruined form, with hate in his eyes;—and the other, a form hovering dark and moth-erlike, her awful face black with the mists of centuries, had aforetime quailed at that white master's command, had bent in love over the cradles of his sons and daughters, and closed in death the sunken eyes of his wife,—aye, too, at his behest had laid herself low to his lust, and borne a tawny man-child to the world, only to see her dark boy's limbs scattered to the winds by midnight marauders riding after "cursed Niggers." These were the saddest sights of that woful day; and no man clasped the hands of these two passing figures of the present-past; but, hating, they went to their long home, and, hating, their children's children live to-day.

Here, then, was the field of work for the Freedmen's Bureau; and since, with some hesitation, it was continued by the act of 1868 until 1869, let us look upon four years of its work as a whole. There were, in 1868, nine hundred Bureau officials scattered from Washington to Texas, ruling, directly and indirectly, many millions of men. The deeds of these rulers fall mainly under seven heads: the relief of physical suffering, the overseeing of the beginnings of free labor, the buying and selling of land, the establishment of schools, the paying of boun-ties, the administration of justice, and the financiering of all these ac-tivities.

Up to June, 1869, over half a million patients had been treated by Bureau physicians and surgeons, and sixty hospitals and asylums had been in operation. In fifty months twenty-one million free rations were distributed at a cost of over four million dollars. Next came the difficult question of labor. First, thirty thousand black men were transported from the refuges and relief stations back to the farms, back to the criti-cal trial of a new way of working. Plain instructions went out from Washington: the laborers must be free to choose their employers, no fixed rate of wages was prescribed, and there was to be no peonage or forced labor. So far, so good; but where local agents differed *toto cœlo* in capacity and character, where the *personnel* was continually chang-ing, the outcome was necessarily varied. The largest element of success lay in the fact that the majority of the freedmen were willing, even eager, to work. So labor contracts were written,—fifty thousand in a single State,—laborers advised, wages guaranteed, and employers supplied. In truth, the organization became a vast labor bureau,—not perfect, indeed, notably defective here and there, but on the whole successful beyond the dreams of thoughtful men. The two great obstacles which confronted the officials were the tyrant and the idler,—the slaveholder who was determined to perpetuate slavery under another name; and the freedman who regarded freedom as perpetual rest,—the Devil and the Deep Sea.

In the work of establishing the Negroes as peasant proprietors, the Bureau was from the first handicapped and at last absolutely checked. Something was done, and larger things were planned; abandoned lands were leased so long as they remained in the hands of the Bureau, and a total revenue of nearly half a million dollars derived from black tenants. Some other lands to which the nation had gained title were sold on easy terms, and public lands were opened for settlement to the very few freedmen who had tools and capital. But the vision of "forty acres and a mule"—the righteous and reasonable ambition to become a landholder, which the nation had all but categorically promised the freedmen—was destined in most cases to bitter disappointment. And those men of marvellous hindsight who are to-day seeking to preach the Negro back to the present peonage of the soil know well, or ought to know, that the opportunity of binding the Negro peasant willingly to the soil was lost on that day when the Commissioner of the Freedmen's Bureau had to go to South Carolina and tell the weeping freedmen, after their years of toil, that their land was not theirs, that there was a mistake—somewhere. If by 1874 the Georgia Negro alone owned three hundred and fifty thousand acres of land, it was by grace of his thrift rather than by bounty of the government.

The greatest success of the Freedmen's Bureau lay in the planting of the free school among Negroes, and the idea of free elementary education among all classes in the South. It not only called the schoolmistresses through the benevolent agencies and built them schoolhouses, but it helped discover and support such apostles of human culture as Edmund Ware, Samuel Armstrong, and Erastus Cravath. The opposition to Negro education in the South was at first bitter, and showed itself in ashes, insult, and blood; for the South believed an educated Negro to be a dangerous Negro. And the South was not wholly wrong; for education among all kinds of men always has had, and always will have, an element of danger and revolution, of dissatisfaction and discontent. Nevertheless, men strive to know. Perhaps some inkling of this paradox, even in the unquiet days of the Bureau, helped the bayonets allay an opposition to human training which still to-day lies smouldering in the South, but not flaming. Fisk, Atlanta, Howard, and Hampton were founded in these days, and six million dollars were expended for educational work, seven hundred and fifty thousand dollars of which the freedmen themselves gave of their poverty.

Such contributions, together with the buying of land and various other enterprises, showed that the ex-slave was handling some free capital already. The chief initial source of this was labor in the army, and his pay and bounty as a soldier. Payments to Negro soldiers were at first complicated by the ignorance of the recipients, and the fact that the quotas of colored regiments from Northern States were largely filled by recruits from the South, unknown to their fellow soldiers. Consequently, payments were accompanied by such frauds that Congress, by joint resolution in 1867, put the whole matter in the hands of the Freedmen's Bureau. In two years six million dollars was thus distributed to five thousand claimants, and in the end the sum exceeded eight million dollars. Even in this system fraud was frequent; but still the work put needed capital in the hands of practical paupers, and some, at least, was well spent.

The most perplexing and least successful part of the Bureau's work lay in the exercise of its judicial functions. The regular Bureau court consisted of one representative of the employer, one of the Negro, and one of the Bureau. If the Bureau could have maintained a perfectly judicial attitude, this arrangement would have been ideal, and must in time have gained confidence; but the nature of its other activities and the character of its *personnel* prejudiced the Bureau in favor of the black litigants, and led without doubt to much injustice and annoyance. On the other hand, to leave the Negro in the hands of Southern courts was impossible. In a distracted land where slavery had hardly fallen, to keep the strong from wanton abuse of the weak, and the weak from gloating insolently over the half-shorn strength of the strong, was a thankless, hopeless task. The former masters of the land were peremptorily ordered about, seized, and imprisoned, and punished over and again, with scant courtesy from army officers. The former slaves were intimidated, beaten, raped, and butchered by angry and revengeful men. Bureau courts tended to become centres simply for punishing whites, while the regular civil courts tended to become solely institutions for perpetuating the slavery of blacks. Almost every law and method ingenuity could devise was employed by the legislatures to reduce the Negroes to serfdom,—to make them the slaves of the State, if not of individual owners; while the Bureau officials too often were found striving to put the "bottom rail on top," and give the freedmen a power and independence which they could not yet use. It is all well enough for us of another generation to wax wise with advice to those who bore the burden in the heat of the day. It is full easy now to see that the man who lost home, fortune, and family at a stroke, and saw his land ruled by "mules and niggers," was really benefited by the passing of slavery. It is not difficult now to say to the young freedman, cheated and cuffed about, who has seen his father's head beaten to a jelly and his own mother namelessly assaulted, that the meek shall inherit the earth. Above all, nothing is more convenient than to heap on the Freedmen's Bureau all the evils of that evil day, and damn it utterly for every mistake and blunder that was made.

All this is easy, but it is neither sensible nor just. Some one had blundered, but that was long before Oliver Howard was born; there was criminal aggression and heedless neglect, but without some system of control there would have been far more than there was. Had that control been from within, the Negro would have been re-enslaved, to all intents and purposes. Coming as the control did from without, perfect men and methods would have bettered all things; and even with imperfect agents and questionable methods, the work accomplished was not undeserving of commendation.

Such was the dawn of Freedom; such was the work of the Freedmen's Bureau, which, summed up in brief, may be epitomized thus: For some fifteen million dollars, beside the sums spent before 1865, and the dole of benevolent societies, this Bureau set going a system of free labor, established a beginning of peasant proprietorship, secured the recognition of black freedmen before courts of law, and founded the free common school in the South. On the other hand, it failed to begin the establishment of good-will between ex-masters and freedmen, to guard its work wholly from paternalistic methods which discouraged self-reliance, and to carry out to any considerable extent its implied promises to furnish the freedmen with land. Its successes were the result of hard work, supplemented by the aid of philanthropists and the eager striving of black men. Its failures were the result of bad local agents, the inherent difficulties of the work, and national neglect.

Such an institution, from its wide powers, great responsibilities, large control of moneys, and generally conspicuous position, was naturally open to repeated and bitter attack. It sustained a searching Congressional investigation at the instance of Fernando Wood in 1870. Its archives and few remaining functions were with blunt discourtesy transferred from Howard's control, in his absence, to the supervision of Secretary of War Belknap in 1872, on the Secretary's recommendation. Finally, in consequence of grave intimations of wrongdoing made by the Secretary and his subordinates, General Howard was court-martialed in 1874. In both of these trials the Commissioner of the Freedmen's Bureau was officially exonerated from any wilful misdoing, and his work commended. Nevertheless, many unpleasant things were brought to light,—the methods of transacting the business of the Bureau were faulty; several cases of defalcation were proved, and other frauds strongly suspected; there were some business transactions which savored of dangerous speculation, if not dishonesty; and around it all lay the smirch of the Freedmen's Bank.

Morally and practically, the Freedmen's Bank was part of the Freedmen's Bureau, although it had no legal connection with it. With the prestige of the government back of it, and a directing board of unusual respectability and national reputation, this banking institution had made a remarkable start in the development of that thrift among black folk which slavery had kept them from knowing. Then in one sad day came the crash,—all the hard-earned dollars of the freedmen disappeared; but that was the least of the loss,—all the faith in saving went too, and much of the faith in men; and that was a loss that a Nation which to-day sneers at Negro shiftlessness has never yet made good. Not even ten additional years of slavery could have done so much to throttle the thrift of the freedmen as the mismanagement and bankruptcy of the series of savings banks chartered by the Nation for their especial aid. Where all the blame should rest, it is hard to say; whether the Bureau and the Bank died chiefly by reason of the blows of its selfish friends or the dark machinations of its foes, perhaps even time will never reveal, for here lies unwritten history.

Of the foes without the Bureau, the bitterest were those who attacked not so much its conduct or policy under the law as the necessity for any such institution at all. Such attacks came primarily from the Border States and the South; and they were summed up by Senator Davis, of Kentucky, when he moved to entitle the act of 1866 a bill "to promote strife and conflict between the white and black races . . . by a grant of unconstitutional power." The argument gathered tremendous strength South and North; but its very strength was its weakness. For, argued the plain common-sense of the nation, if it is unconstitutional, unpractical, and futile for the nation to stand guardian over its helpless wards, then there is left but one alternative,—to make those wards their own guardians by arming them with the ballot. Moreover, the path of the practical politician pointed the same way; for, argued this opportunist, if we cannot peacefully reconstruct the South with white votes, we certainly can with black votes. So justice and force joined hands.

The alternative thus offered the nation was not between full and restricted Negro suffrage; else every sensible man, black and white, would easily have chosen the latter. It was rather a choice between suffrage and slavery, after endless blood and gold had flowed to sweep human bondage away. Not a single Southern legislature stood ready to admit a Negro, under any conditions, to the polls; not a single Southern legislature believed free Negro labor was possible without a system of restrictions that took all its freedom away; there was scarcely a white man in the South who did not honestly regard Emancipation as a crime, and its practical nullification as a duty. In such a situation, the granting of the ballot to the black man was a necessity, the very least a guilty nation could grant a wronged race, and the only method of compelling the South to accept the results of the war. Thus Negro suffrage ended a civil war by beginning a race feud. And some felt gratitude toward the race thus sacrificed in its swaddling clothes on the altar of national integrity; and some felt and feel only indifference and contempt.

Had political exigencies been less pressing, the opposition to government guardianship of Negroes less bitter, and the attachment to the slave system less strong, the social seer can well imagine a far better policy,—a permanent Freedmen's Bureau, with a national system of Negro schools; a carefully supervised employment and labor office; a system of impartial protection before the regular courts; and such institutions for social betterment as savings-banks, land and building associations, and social settlements. All this vast expenditure of money and brains might have formed a great school of prospective citizenship, and solved in a way we have not yet solved the most perplexing and persistent of the Negro problems.

That such an institution was unthinkable in 1870 was due in part to certain acts of the Freedmen's Bureau itself. It came to regard its work as merely temporary, and Negro suffrage as a final answer to all present perplexities. The political ambition of many of its agents and *protégés* led it far afield into questionable activities, until the South, nursing its own deep prejudices, came easily to ignore all the good deeds of the Bureau and hate its very name with perfect hatred. So the Freedmen's Bureau died, and its child was the Fifteenth Amendment.

The passing of a great human institution before its work is done, like the untimely passing of a single soul, but leaves a legacy of striving for other men. The legacy of the Freedmen's Bureau is the heavy heritage of this generation. To-day, when new and vaster problems are destined to strain every fibre of the national mind and soul, would it not be well to count this legacy honestly and carefully? For this much all men know: despite compromise, war, and struggle, the Negro is not free. In the backwoods of the Gulf States, for miles and miles, he may not leave the plantation of his birth; in well-nigh the whole rural South the black farmers are peons, bound by law and custom to an economic slavery, from which the only escape is death or the penitentiary. In the most cultured sections and cities of the South the Negroes are a segregated servile caste, with restricted rights and privileges. Before the courts, both in law and custom, they stand on a different and peculiar basis. Taxation without representation is the rule of their political life. And the result of all this is, and in nature must have been, lawlessness and crime. That is the large legacy of the Freedmen's Bureau, the work it did not do because it could not.

I have seen a land right merry with the sun, where children sing, and rolling hills lie like passioned women wanton with harvest. And there in the King's Highway sat and sits a figure veiled and bowed, by which the traveller's footsteps hasten as they go. On the tainted air broods fear. Three centuries' thought has been the raising and unveiling of that bowed human heart, and now behold a century new for the duty and the deed. The problem of the Twentieth Century is the problem of the color-line.

121

CHAPTER **III**

Of Mr. Booker T. Washington and Others

From birth till death enslaved; in word, in deed, unmanned!

Hereditary bondsmen! Know ye not
Who would be free themselves must strike the blow?

Byron

Easily the most striking thing in the history of the American Negro since 1876 is the ascendancy of Mr. Booker T. Washington. It began at the time when war memories and ideals were rapidly passing; a day of astonishing commercial development was dawning; a sense of doubt and hesitation overtook the freedmen's sons,—then it was that his leading began. Mr. Washington came, with a simple definite programme, at the psychological moment when the nation was a little ashamed of having bestowed so much sentiment on Negroes, and was concentrating its energies on Dollars. His programme of industrial education, conciliation of the South, and submission and silence as to civil and political rights, was not wholly original; the Free Negroes from 1830 up to wartime had striven to build industrial schools, and the American Missionary Association had from the first taught various trades; and Price and others had sought a way of honorable alliance with the best of the Southerners. But Mr. Washington first indissolubly linked these things; he put enthusiasm, unlimited energy, and perfect faith into this programme, and changed it from a by-path into a veritable Way of Life. And the tale of the methods by which he did this is a fascinating study of human life.

It startled the nation to hear a Negro advocating such a programme after many decades of bitter complaint; it startled and won the applause of the South, it interested and won the admiration of the North; and after a confused murmur of protest, it silenced if it did not convert the Negroes themselves.

To gain the sympathy and coöperation of the various elements comprising the white South was Mr. Washington's first task; and this, at the time Tuskegee was founded, seemed, for a black man, well-nigh impossible. And yet ten years later it was done in the word spoken at Atlanta: "In all things purely social we can be as separate as the five fingers, and yet one as the hand in all things essential to mutual progress." This "Atlanta Compromise" is by all odds the most notable thing in Mr. Washington's career. The South interpreted it in different ways: the radicals received it as a complete surrender of the demand for civil and political equality; the conservatives, as a generously conceived working basis for mutual understanding. So both approved it, and to-day its author is certainly the most distinguished Southerner since Jefferson Davis, and the one with the largest personal following.

Next to this achievement comes Mr. Washington's work in gaining place and consideration in the North. Others less shrewd and tactful had formerly essayed to sit on these two stools and had fallen between them; but as Mr. Washington knew the heart of the South from birth and training, so by singular insight he intuitively grasped the spirit of the age which was dominating the North. And so thoroughly did he learn the speech and thought of triumphant commercialism, and the ideals of material prosperity, that the picture of a lone black boy poring over a French grammar amid the weeds and dirt of a neglected home soon seemed to him the acme of absurdities. One wonders what Socrates and St. Francis of Assisi would say to this.

And yet this very singleness of vision and thorough oneness with his age is a mark of the successful man. It is as though Nature must needs make men narrow in order to give them force. So Mr. Washington's cult has gained unquestioning followers, his work has wonderfully prospered, his friends are legion, and his enemies are confounded. To-day he stands as the one recognized spokesman of his ten million fellows, and one of the most notable figures in a nation of seventy millions. One hesitates, therefore, to criticise a life which, beginning with so little, has done so much. And yet the time is come when one may speak in all sincerity and utter courtesy of the mistakes and shortcomings of Mr. Washington's career, as well as of his triumphs, without being thought captious or envious, and without forgetting that it is easier to do ill than well in the world.

The criticism that has hitherto met Mr. Washington has not always been of this broad character. In the South especially has he had to walk warily to avoid the harshest judgments,—and naturally so, for he is dealing with the one subject of deepest sensitiveness to that section. Twice—once when at the Chicago celebration of the Spanish-American War he alluded to the color-prejudice that is "eating away the vitals of the South," and once when he dined with President Roosevelt—has the resulting Southern criticism been violent enough to threaten seriously his popularity. In the North the feeling has several times forced itself into words, that Mr. Washington's counsels of submission overlooked certain elements of true manhood, and that his educational programme was unnecessarily narrow. Usually, however, such criticism has not found open expression, although, too, the spiritual sons of the Abolitionists have not been prepared to acknowledge that the schools founded before Tuskegee, by men of broad ideals and self-sacrificing spirit, were wholly failures or worthy of ridicule. While, then, criticism has not failed to follow Mr. Washington, yet the prevailing public opinion of the land has been but too willing to deliver the solution of a wearisome problem into his hands, and say, "If that is all you and your race ask, take it."

Among his own people, however, Mr. Washington has encountered the strongest and most lasting opposition, amounting at times to bitterness, and even to-day continuing strong and insistent even though largely silenced in outward expression by the public opinion of the nation. Some of this opposition is, of course, mere envy; the disappointment of displaced demagogues and the spite of narrow minds. But aside from this, there is among educated and thoughtful colored men in all parts of the land a feeling of deep regret, sorrow, and apprehension at the wide currency and ascendancy which some of Mr. Washington's theories have gained. These same men admire his sincerity of purpose, and are willing to forgive much to honest endeavor which is doing something worth the doing. They coöperate with Mr. Washington as far as they conscientiously can; and, indeed, it is no ordinary tribute to this man's tact and power that, steering as he must between so many diverse interests and opinions, he so largely retains the respect of all.

But the hushing of the criticism of honest opponents is a dangerous thing. It leads some of the best of the critics to unfortunate silence and paralysis of effort, and others to burst into speech so passionately and intemperately as to lose listeners. Honest and earnest criticism from those whose interests are most nearly touched,—criticism of writers by readers, of government by those governed, of leaders by those led,—this is the soul of democracy and the safeguard of modern society. If the best of the American Negroes receive by outer pressure a leader whom they had not recognized before, manifestly there is here a certain palpable gain. Yet there is also irreparable loss,—a loss of that peculiarly valuable education which a group receives when by search and criticism it finds and commissions its own leaders. The way in which this is done is at once the most elementary and the nicest problem of social growth. History is but the record of such group-leadership; and yet how infinitely changeful is its type and character! And of all types and kinds, what can be more instructive than the leadership of a group within a group?—that curious double movement where real progress may be negative and actual advance be relative retrogression. All this is the social student's inspiration and despair.

Now in the past the American Negro has had instructive experience in the choosing of group leaders, founding thus a peculiar dynasty which in the light of present conditions is worth while studying.

When sticks and stones and beasts form the sole environment of a people, their attitude is largely one of determined opposition to and conquest of natural forces. But when to earth and brute is added an environment of men and ideas, then the attitude of the imprisoned group may take three main forms,—a feeling of revolt and revenge; an attempt to adjust all thought and action to the will of the greater group; or, finally, a determined effort at self-realization and self-development despite environing opinion. The influence of all of these attitudes at various times can be traced in the history of the American Negro, and in the evolution of his successive leaders.

Before 1750, while the fire of African freedom still burned in the veins of the slaves, there was in all leadership or attempted leadership but the one motive of revolt and revenge,—typified in the terrible Maroons, the Danish blacks, and Cato of Stono, and veiling all the Americas in fear of insurrection. The liberalizing tendencies of the latter half of the eighteenth century brought, along with kindlier relations between black and white, thoughts of ultimate adjustment and assimilation. Such aspiration was especially voiced in the earnest songs of Phyllis, in the martyrdom of Attucks, the fighting of Salem and Poor, the intellectual accomplishments of Banneker and Derham, and the political demands of the Cuffes.

Stern financial and social stress after the war cooled much of the previous humanitarian ardor. The disappointment and impatience of the Negroes at the persistence of slavery and serfdom voiced itself in two movements. The slaves in the South, aroused undoubtedly by vague rumors of the Haytian revolt, made three fierce attempts at insurrection,—in 1800 under Gabriel in Virginia, in 1822 under Vesey in Carolina, and in 1831 again in Virginia under the terrible Nat Turner. In the Free States, on the other hand, a new and curious attempt at self-development was made. In Philadelphia and New York color-prescription led to a withdrawal of Negro communicants from white churches and the formation of a peculiar socio-religious institution among the Negroes known as the African Church,—an organization still living and controlling in its various branches over a million of men.

Walker's wild appeal against the trend of the times showed how the world was changing after the coming of the cotton-gin. By 1830 slavery seemed hopelessly fastened on the South, and the slaves thoroughly cowed into submission. The free Negroes of the North, inspired by the mulatto immigrants from the West Indies, began to change the basis of their demands; they recognized the slavery of slaves, but insisted that they themselves were freemen, and sought assimilation and amalgamation with the nation on the same terms with other men. Thus, Forten and Purvis of Philadelphia, Shad of Wilmington, Du Bois of New Haven, Barbadoes of Boston, and others, strove singly and together as men, they said, not as slaves; as "people of color," not as "Negroes." The trend of the times, however, refused them recognition save in individual and exceptional cases, considered them as one with all the despised blacks, and they soon found themselves striving to keep even the rights they formerly had of voting and working and moving as freemen. Schemes of migration and colonization arose among them; but these they refused to entertain, and they eventually turned to the Abolition movement as a final refuge.

Here, led by Remond, Nell, Wells-Brown, and Douglass, a new period of self-assertion and self-development dawned. To be sure, ultimate freedom and assimilation was the ideal before the leaders, but the assertion of the manhood rights of the Negro by himself was the main reliance, and John Brown's raid was the extreme of its logic. After the war and emancipation, the great form of Frederick Douglass, the greatest of American Negro leaders, still led the host. Self-assertion, especially in political lines, was the main programme, and behind Douglass came Elliot, Bruce, and Langston, and the Reconstruction politicians, and, less conspicuous but of greater social significance Alexander Crummell and Bishop Daniel Payne.

Then came the Revolution of 1876, the suppression of the Negro votes, the changing and shifting of ideals, and the seeking of new lights in the great night. Douglass, in his old age, still bravely stood for the ideals of his early manhood,—ultimate assimilation *through* self-assertion, and on no other terms. For a time Price arose as a new leader, destined, it seemed, not to give up, but to re-state the old ideals in a form less repugnant to the white South. But he passed away in his prime. Then came the new leader. Nearly all the former ones had become leaders by the silent suffrage of their fellows, had sought to lead their own people alone, and were usually, save Douglass, little known outside their race. But Booker T. Washington arose as essentially the leader not of one race but of two,—a compromiser between the South, the North, and the Negro. Naturally the Negroes resented, at first bitterly, signs of compromise which surrendered their civil and political rights, even though this was to be exchanged for larger chances of economic development. The rich and dominating North, however, was not only weary of the race problem, but was investing largely in Southern enterprises, and welcomed any method of peaceful coöperation. Thus, by national opinion, the Negroes began to recognize Mr. Washington's leadership; and the voice of criticism was hushed.

Mr. Washington represents in Negro thought the old attitude of adjustment and submission; but adjustment at such a peculiar time as to make his programme unique. This is an age of unusual economic development, and Mr. Washington's programme naturally takes an economic cast, becoming a gospel of Work and Money to such an extent as apparently almost completely to overshadow the higher aims of life. Moreover, this is an age when the more advanced races are coming in closer contact with the less developed races, and the race-feeling is therefore intensified; and Mr. Washington's programme practically accepts the alleged inferiority of the Negro races. Again, in our own land, the reaction from the sentiment of war time has given impetus to race-prejudice against Negroes, and Mr. Washington withdraws many of the high demands of Negroes as men and American citizens. In other periods of intensified prejudice all the Negro's tendency to self-assertion has been called forth; at this period a policy of submission is advocated. In the history of nearly all other races and peoples the doctrine preached at such crises has been that manly self-respect is worth more than lands and houses, and that a people who voluntarily surrender such respect, or cease striving for it, are not worth civilizing.

In answer to this, it has been claimed that the Negro can survive only through submission. Mr. Washington distinctly asks that black people give up, at least for the present, three things,—

First, political power,

Second, insistence on civil rights,

Third, higher education of Negro youth,—and concentrate all their energies on industrial education, the accumulation of wealth, and the conciliation of the South. This policy has been courageously and insistently advocated for over fifteen years, and has been triumphant for perhaps ten years. As a result of this tender of the palm-branch, what has been the return? In these years there have occurred:

1. The disfranchisement of the Negro.

2. The legal creation of a distinct status of civil inferiority for the Negro.

3. The steady withdrawal of aid from institutions for the higher training of the Negro.

These movements are not, to be sure, direct results of Mr. Washington's teachings; but his propaganda has, without a shadow of doubt, helped their speedier accomplishment. The question then comes: Is it possible, and probable, that nine millions of men can make effective progress in economic lines if they are deprived of political rights, made a servile caste, and allowed only the most meagre chance for developing their exceptional men? If history and reason give any distinct answer to these questions, it is an emphatic *No.* And Mr. Washington thus faces the triple paradox of his career:

1. He is striving nobly to make Negro artisans business men and property-owners; but it is utterly impossible, under modern competitive methods, for workingmen and property-owners to defend their rights and exist without the right of suffrage.

2. He insists on thrift and self-respect, but at the same time counsels a silent submission to civic inferiority such as is bound to sap the manhood of any race in the long run.

3. He advocates common-school and industrial training, and depreciates institutions of higher learning; but neither the Negro common-schools, nor Tuskegee itself, could remain open a day were it not for teachers trained in Negro colleges, or trained by their graduates.

This triple paradox in Mr. Washington's position is the object of criticism by two classes of colored Americans. One class is spiritually descended from Toussaint the Savior, through Gabriel, Vesey, and Turner, and they represent the attitude of revolt and revenge; they hate the white South blindly and distrust the white race generally, and so far as they agree on definite action, think that the Negro's only hope lies in emigration beyond the borders of the United States. And yet, by the irony of fate, nothing has more effectually made this programme seem hopeless than the recent course of the United States toward weaker and darker peoples in the West Indies, Hawaii, and the Philippines,—for where in the world may we go and be safe from lying and brute force?

The other class of Negroes who cannot agree with Mr. Washington has hitherto said little aloud. They deprecate the sight of scattered counsels, of internal disagreement; and especially they dislike making their just criticism of a useful and earnest man an excuse for a general discharge of venom from small-minded opponents. Nevertheless, the questions involved are so fundamental and serious that it is difficult to see how men like the Grimkes, Kelly Miller, J. W. E. Bowen, and other representatives of this group, can much longer be silent. Such men feel in conscience bound to ask of this nation three things:

1. The right to vote.
2. Civic equality.
3. The education of youth according to ability.

They acknowledge Mr. Washington's invaluable service in counselling patience and courtesy in such demands; they do not ask that ignorant black men vote when ignorant whites are debarred, or that any reasonable restrictions in the suffrage should not be applied; they know that the low social level of the mass of the race is responsible for much discrimination against it, but they also know, and the nation knows, that relentless color-prejudice is more often a cause than a result of the Negro's degradation; they seek the abatement of this relic of barbarism, and not its systematic encouragement and pampering by all agencies of social power from the Associated Press to the Church of Christ. They advocate, with Mr. Washington, a broad system of Negro common schools supplemented by thorough industrial training; but they are surprised that a man of Mr. Washington's insight cannot see that no such educational system ever has rested or can rest on any other basis than that of the well-equipped college and university, and they insist that there is a demand for a few such institutions throughout the South to train the best of the Negro youth as teachers, professional men, and leaders.

This group of men honor Mr. Washington for his attitude of conciliation toward the white South; they accept the "Atlanta Compromise" in its broadest interpretation; they recognize, with him, many signs of promise, many men of high purpose and fair judgment, in this section;

they know that no easy task has been laid upon a region already tottering under heavy burdens. But, nevertheless, they insist that the way to truth and right lies in straightforward honesty, not in indiscriminate flattery; in praising those of the South who do well and criticising uncompromisingly those who do ill; in taking advantage of the opportunities at hand and urging their fellows to do the same, but at the same time in remembering that only a firm adherence to their higher ideals and aspirations will ever keep those ideals within the realm of possibility. They do not expect that the free right to vote, to enjoy civic rights, and to be educated, will come in a moment; they do not expect to see the bias and prejudices of years disappear at the blast of a trumpet; but they are absolutely certain that the way for a people to gain their reasonable rights is not by voluntarily throwing them away and insisting that they do not want them; that the way for a people to gain respect is not by continually belittling and ridiculing themselves; that, on the contrary, Negroes must insist continually, in season and out of season, that voting is necessary to modern manhood, that color discrimination is barbarism, and that black boys need education as well as white boys.

In failing thus to state plainly and unequivocally the legitimate demands of their people, even at the cost of opposing an honored leader, the thinking classes of American Negroes would shirk a heavy responsibility,—a responsibility to themselves, a responsibility to the struggling masses, a responsibility to the darker races of men whose future depends so largely on this American experiment, but especially a responsibility to this nation,—this common Fatherland. It is wrong to encourage a man or a people in evil-doing; it is wrong to aid and abet a national crime simply because it is unpopular not to do so. The growing spirit of kindliness and reconciliation between the North and South after the frightful differences of a generation ago ought to be a source of deep congratulation to all, and especially to those whose mistreatment caused the war; but if that reconciliation is to be marked by the industrial slavery and civic death of those same black men, with permanent legislation into a position of inferiority, then those black men, if they are really men, are called upon by every consideration of patriotism and loyalty to oppose such a course by all civilized methods, even though such opposition involves disagreement with Mr. Booker T. Washington. We have no right to sit silently by while the inevitable seeds are sown for a harvest of disaster to our children, black and white.

First, it is the duty of black men to judge the South discriminatingly. The present generation of Southerners are not responsible for the past, and they should not be blindly hated or blamed for it. Furthermore, to no class is the indiscriminate endorsement of the recent course of the South toward Negroes more nauseating than to the best thought of the South. The South is not "solid"; it is a land in the ferment of social change, wherein forces of all kinds are fighting for supremacy; and to praise the ill the South is to-day perpetrating is just as wrong as to condemn the good. Discriminating and broad-minded criticism is what the South needs,—needs it for the sake of her own white sons and daughters, and for the insurance of robust, healthy mental and moral development.

To-day even the attitude of the Southern whites toward the blacks is not, as so many assume, in all cases the same; the ignorant Southerner hates the Negro, the workingmen fear his competition, the money-makers wish to use him as a laborer, some of the educated see a menace in his upward development, while others—usually the sons of the masters—wish to help him to rise. National opinion has enabled this last class to maintain the Negro common schools, and to protect the Negro partially in property, life, and limb. Through the pressure of the money-makers, the Negro is in danger of being reduced to semi-slavery, especially in the country districts; the workingmen, and those of the educated who fear the Negro, have united to disfranchise him, and some have urged his deportation; while the passions of the ignorant are easily aroused to lynch and abuse any black man. To praise this intricate whirl of thought and prejudice is nonsense; to inveigh indiscriminately against "the South" is unjust; but to use the same breath in praising Governor Aycock, exposing Senator Morgan, arguing with Mr. Thomas Nelson Page, and denouncing Senator Ben Tillman, is not only sane, but the imperative duty of thinking black men.

It would be unjust to Mr. Washington not to acknowledge that in several instances he has opposed movements in the South which were unjust to the Negro; he sent memorials to the Louisiana and Alabama constitutional conventions, he has spoken against lynching, and in other ways has openly or silently set his influence against sinister schemes and unfortunate happenings. Notwithstanding this, it is equally true to assert that on the whole the distinct impression left by Mr. Washington's propaganda is, first, that the South is justified in its present attitude toward the Negro because of the Negro's degradation; secondly, that the prime cause of the Negro's failure to rise more quickly is his wrong education in the past; and, thirdly, that his future rise depends primarily on his own efforts. Each of these propositions is a dangerous half-truth. The supplementary truths must never be lost sight of: first, slavery and race-prejudice are potent if not sufficient causes of the Negro's position; second, industrial and common-school training were necessarily slow in planting because they had to await the black teachers trained by higher institutions,—it being extremely doubtful if any essentially different development was possible, and certainly a Tuskegee was unthinkable before 1880; and, third, while it is a great truth to say that the Negro must strive and strive mightily to help himself, it is equally true that unless his striving be not simply seconded, but rather aroused and encouraged, by the initiative of the richer and wiser environing group, he cannot hope for great success.

In his failure to realize and impress this last point, Mr. Washington is especially to be criticised. His doctrine has tended to make the whites, North and South, shift the burden of the Negro problem to the Negro's shoulders and stand aside as critical and rather pessimistic spectators; when in fact the burden belongs to the nation, and the hands of none of us are clean if we bend not our energies to righting these great wrongs.

The South ought to be led, by candid and honest criticism, to assert her better self and do her full duty to the race she has cruelly wronged and is still wronging. The North—her co-partner in guilt—cannot salve her conscience by plastering it with gold. We cannot settle this problem by diplomacy and suaveness, by "policy" alone. If worse come to worst, can the moral fibre of this country survive the slow throttling and murder of nine millions of men?

The black men of America have a duty to perform, a duty stern and delicate,—a forward movement to oppose a part of the work of their greatest leader. So far as Mr. Washington preaches Thrift, Patience, and Industrial Training for the masses, we must hold up his hands and strive with him, rejoicing in his honors and glorying in the strength of this Joshua called of God and of man to lead the headless host. But so far as Mr. Washington apologizes for injustice, North or South, does not rightly value the privilege and duty of voting, belittles the emasculating effects of caste distinctions, and opposes the higher training and ambition of our brighter minds,—so far as he, the South, or the Nation, does this,—we must unceasingly and firmly oppose them. By every civilized and peaceful method we must strive for the rights which the world accords to men, clinging unwaveringly to those great words which the sons of the Fathers would fain forget: "We hold these truths to be self-evident: That all men are created equal; that they are endowed by their Creator with certain unalienable rights; that among these are life, liberty, and the pursuit of happiness."

CHAPTER **IV**

Of the Meaning of Progress

Willst Du Deine Macht verkünden,
Wähle sie die frei von Sünden,
Steh'n in Deinem ew'gen Haus!
Deine Geister sende aus!
Die Unsterblichen, die Reinen,
Die nicht fühlen, die nicht weinen!
Nicht die zarte Jungfrau wähle,
Nicht der Hirtin weiche Seele!

Schiller

Once upon a time I taught school in the hills of Tennessee, where the broad dark vale of the Mississippi begins to roll and crumple to greet the Alleghanies. I was a Fisk student then, and all Fisk men thought that Tennessee—beyond the Veil—was theirs alone, and in vacation time they sallied forth in lusty bands to meet the county school-commissioners. Young and happy, I too went, and I shall not soon forget that summer, seventeen years ago.

First, there was a Teachers' Institute at the county-seat; and there distinguished guests of the superintendent taught the teachers fractions and spelling and other mysteries,—white teachers in the morning, Negroes at night. A picnic now and then, and a supper, and the rough world was softened by laughter and song. I remember how— But I wander.

There came a day when all the teachers left the Institute and began the hunt for schools. I learn from hearsay (for my mother was mortally afraid of fire-arms) that the hunting of ducks and bears and men is wonderfully interesting, but I am sure that the man who has never hunted a country school has something to learn of the pleasures of the chase. I see now the white, hot roads lazily rise and fall and wind before me under the burning July sun; I feel the deep weariness of heart and limb as ten, eight, six miles stretch relentlessly ahead; I feel my heart sink heavily as I hear again and again, "Got a teacher? Yes." So I walked on and on—horses were too expensive—until I had wandered beyond railways, beyond stage lines, to a land of "varmints" and rattlesnakes, where the coming of a stranger was an event, and men lived and died in the shadow of one blue hill.

Sprinkled over hill and dale lay cabins and farmhouses, shut out from the world by the forests and the rolling hills toward the east. There I found at last a little school. Josie told me of it; she was a thin, homely girl of twenty, with a dark-brown face and thick, hard hair. I had crossed the stream at Watertown, and rested under the great willows; then I had gone to the little cabin in the lot where Josie was resting on her way to town. The gaunt farmer made me welcome, and Josie, hearing my errand, told me anxiously that they wanted a school over the hill; that but once since the war had a teacher been there; that she herself longed to learn,—and thus she ran on, talking fast and loud, with much earnestness and energy.

Next morning I crossed the tall round hill, lingered to look at the blue and yellow mountains stretching toward the Carolinas, then plunged into the wood, and came out at Josie's home. It was a dull frame cottage with four rooms, perched just below the brow of the hill, amid peach-trees. The father was a quiet, simple soul, calmly ignorant, with no touch of vulgarity. The mother was different,—strong, bustling, and energetic, with a quick, restless tongue, and an ambition to live "like folks." There was a crowd of children. Two boys had gone away. There remained two growing girls; a shy midget of eight; John, tall, awkward, and eighteen; Jim, younger, quicker, and better looking; and two babies of indefinite age. Then there was Josie herself. She seemed to be the centre of the family: always busy at service, or at home, or berry-picking; a little nervous and inclined to scold, like her mother, yet faithful, too, like her father. She had about her a certain fineness, the shadow of an unconscious moral heroism that would willingly give all of life to make life broader, deeper, and fuller for her and hers. I saw much of this family afterwards, and grew to love them for their honest efforts to be decent and comfortable, and for their knowledge of their own ignorance. There was with them no affectation. The mother would scold the father for being so "easy"; Josie would roundly berate the boys for carelessness; and all knew that it was a hard thing to dig a living out of a rocky side-hill.

I secured the school. I remember the day I rode horseback out to the commissioner's house with a pleasant young white fellow who wanted the white school. The road ran down the bed of a stream; the sun laughed and the water jingled, and we rode on. "Come in," said the commissioner,—"come in. Have a seat. Yes, that certificate will do. Stay to dinner. What do you want a month?" "Oh," thought I, "this is lucky"; but even then fell the awful shadow of the Veil, for they ate first, then I—alone.

The schoolhouse was a log hut, where Colonel Wheeler used to shelter his corn. It sat in a lot behind a rail fence and thorn bushes, near the sweetest of springs. There was an entrance where a door once was, and within, a massive rickety fireplace; great chinks between the logs served as windows. Furniture was scarce. A pale blackboard crouched in the corner. My desk was made of three boards, reinforced at critical points, and my chair, borrowed from the landlady, had to be returned every night. Seats for the children—these puzzled me much. I was haunted by a New England vision of neat little desks and chairs, but, alas! the reality was rough plank benches without backs, and at times without legs. They had the one virtue of making naps dangerous,—possibly fatal, for the floor was not to be trusted.

It was a hot morning late in July when the school opened. I trembled when I heard the patter of little feet down the dusty road, and saw the growing row of dark solemn faces and bright eager eyes facing me. First came Josie and her brothers and sisters. The longing to know, to be a student in the great school at Nashville, hovered like a star above this child-woman amid her work and worry, and she studied doggedly. There were the Dowells from their farm over toward Alexandria,—Fanny, with her smooth black face and wondering eyes; Martha, brown and dull; the pretty girl-wife of a brother, and the younger brood.

There were the Burkes,—two brown and yellow lads, and a tiny haughty-eyed girl. Fat Reuben's little chubby girl came, with golden face and old-gold hair, faithful and solemn. 'Thenie was on hand early,—a jolly, ugly, good-hearted girl, who slyly dipped snuff and looked after her little bow-legged brother. When her mother could spare her, 'Tildy came,—a midnight beauty, with starry eyes and tapering limbs; and her brother, correspondingly homely. And then the big boys,—the hulking Lawrences; the lazy Neills, unfathered sons of mother and daughter; Hickman, with a stoop in his shoulders; and the rest.

There they sat, nearly thirty of them, on the rough benches, their faces shading from a pale cream to a deep brown, the little feet bare and swinging, the eyes full of expectation, with here and there a twinkle of mischief, and the hands grasping Webster's blue-back spelling-book. I loved my school, and the fine faith the children had in the wisdom of their teacher was truly marvellous. We read and spelled together, wrote a little, picked flowers, sang, and listened to stories of the world beyond the hill. At times the school would dwindle away, and I would start out. I would visit Mun Eddings, who lived in two very dirty rooms, and ask why little Lugene, whose flaming face seemed ever ablaze with the dark-red hair uncombed, was absent all last week, or why I missed so often the inimitable rags of Mack and Ed. Then the father, who worked Colonel Wheeler's farm on shares, would tell me how the crops needed the boys; and the thin, slovenly mother, whose face was pretty when washed, assured me that Lugene must mind the baby. "But we'll start them again next week." When the Lawrences stopped, I knew that the doubts of the old folks about book-learning had conquered again, and so, toiling up the hill, and getting as far into the cabin as possible, I put Cicero "pro Archia Poeta" into the simplest English with local applications, and usually convinced them—for a week or so.

On Friday nights I often went home with some of the children,— sometimes to Doc Burke's farm. He was a great, loud, thin Black, ever working, and trying to buy the seventy-five acres of hill and dale where he lived; but people said that he would surely fail, and the "white folks would get it all." His wife was a magnificent Amazon, with saffron face and shining hair, uncorseted and barefooted, and the children were strong and beautiful. They lived in a one-and-a-half-room cabin in the hollow of the farm, near the spring. The front room was full of great fat white beds, scrupulously neat; and there were bad chromos on the walls, and a tired centre-table. In the tiny back kitchen I was often invited to "take out and help" myself to fried chicken and wheat biscuit, "meat" and corn pone, stringbeans and berries. At first I used to be a little alarmed at the approach of bedtime in the one lone bedroom, but embarrassment was very deftly avoided. First, all the children nodded and slept, and were stowed away in one great pile of goose feathers; next, the mother and father discreetly slipped away to the kitchen while I went to bed; then, blowing out the dim light, they retired in the dark. In the morning all were up and away before I thought of awaking. Across the road, where fat Reuben lived, they all went outdoors while the teacher retired, because they did not boast the luxury of a kitchen.

I liked to stay with the Dowells, for they had four rooms and plenty of good country fare. Uncle Bird had a small, rough farm, all woods and hills, miles from the big road; but he was full of tales,—he preached now and then,—and with his children, berries, horses, and wheat he was happy and prosperous. Often, to keep the peace, I must go where life was less lovely; for instance, 'Tildy's mother was incorrigibly dirty, Reuben's larder was limited seriously, and herds of untamed insects wandered over the Eddingses' beds. Best of all I loved to go to Josie's, and sit on the porch, eating peaches, while the mother bustled and talked: how Josie had bought the sewing-machine; how Josie worked at service in winter, but that four dollars a month was "mighty little" wages; how Josie longed to go away to school, but that it "looked like" they never could get far enough ahead to let her; how the crops failed and the well was yet unfinished; and, finally, how "mean" some of the white folks were.

For two summers I lived in this little world; it was dull and humdrum. The girls looked at the hill in wistful longing, and the boys fretted and haunted Alexandria. Alexandria was "town,"—a straggling, lazy village of houses, churches, and shops, and an aristocracy of Toms, Dicks, and Captains. Cuddled on the hill to the north was the village of the colored folks, who lived in three- or four-room unpainted cottages, some neat and homelike, and some dirty. The dwellings were scattered rather aimlessly, but they centered about the twin temples of the hamlet, the Methodist, and the Hard-Shell Baptist churches. These, in turn, leaned gingerly on a sad-colored schoolhouse. Hither my little world wended its crooked way on Sunday to meet other worlds, and gossip, and wonder, and make the weekly sacrifice with frenzied priest at the altar of the "old-time religion." Then the soft melody and mighty cadences of Negro song fluttered and thundered.

I have called my tiny community a world, and so its isolation made it; and yet there was among us but a half-awakened common consciousness, sprung from common joy and grief, at burial, birth, or wedding; from a common hardship in poverty, poor land, and low wages; and, above all, from the sight of the Veil that hung between us and Opportunity. All this caused us to think some thoughts together; but these, when ripe for speech, were spoken in various languages. Those whose eyes twenty-five and more years before had seen "the glory of the coming of the Lord," saw in every present hindrance or help a dark fatalism bound to bring all things right in His own good time. The mass of those to whom slavery was a dim recollection of childhood found the world a puzzling thing: it asked little of them, and they answered with little, and yet it ridiculed their offering. Such a paradox they could not understand, and therefore sank into listless indifference, or shiftlessness, or reckless bravado. There were, however, some—such as Josie, Jim, and Ben—to whom War, Hell, and Slavery were but childhood tales, whose young appetites had been whetted to an edge by school and story and half-awakened thought. Ill could they be content, born without and beyond the World. And their weak wings beat against their barriers,—barriers of caste, of youth, of life; at last, in dangerous moments, against everything that opposed even a whim.

The ten years that follow youth, the years when first the realization comes that life is leading somewhere,—these were the years that passed after I left my little school. When they were past, I came by chance once more to the walls of Fisk University, to the halls of the chapel of melody. As I lingered there in the joy and pain of meeting old school-friends, there swept over me a sudden longing to pass again beyond the blue hill, and to see the homes and the school of other days, and to learn how life had gone with my school-children; and I went.

Josie was dead, and the gray-haired mother said simply, "We've had a heap of trouble since you've been away." I had feared for Jim. With a cultured parentage and a social caste to uphold him, he might have made a venturesome merchant or a West Point cadet. But here he was, angry with life and reckless; and when Farmer Durham charged him with stealing wheat, the old man had to ride fast to escape the stones which the furious fool hurled after him. They told Jim to run away; but he would not run, and the constable came that afternoon. It grieved Josie, and great awkward John walked nine miles every day to see his little brother through the bars of Lebanon jail. At last the two came back together in the dark night. The mother cooked supper, and Josie emptied her purse, and the boys stole away. Josie grew thin and silent, yet worked the more. The hill became steep for the quiet old father, and with the boys away there was little to do in the valley. Josie helped them to sell the old farm, and they moved nearer town. Brother Dennis, the carpenter, built a new house with six rooms; Josie toiled a year in Nashville, and brought back ninety dollars to furnish the house and change it to a home.

When the spring came, and the birds twittered, and the stream ran proud and full, little sister Lizzie, bold and thoughtless, flushed with the passion of youth, bestowed herself on the tempter, and brought home a nameless child. Josie shivered and worked on, with the vision of schooldays all fled, with a face wan and tired,—worked until, on a summer's day, some one married another; then Josie crept to her mother like a hurt child, and slept—and sleeps.

I paused to scent the breeze as I entered the valley. The Lawrences have gone,—father and son forever,—and the other son lazily digs in the earth to live. A new young widow rents out their cabin to fat Reuben. Reuben is a Baptist preacher now, but I fear as lazy as ever, though his cabin has three rooms; and little Ella has grown into a bouncing woman, and is ploughing corn on the hot hillside. There are babies a-plenty, and one half-witted girl. Across the valley is a house I did not know before, and there I found, rocking one baby and expecting another, one of my schoolgirls, a daughter of Uncle Bird Dowell. She looked somewhat worried with her new duties, but soon bristled into pride over her neat cabin and the tale of her thrifty husband, the horse and cow, and the farm they were planning to buy.

My log schoolhouse was gone. In its place stood Progress; and Progress, I understand, is necessarily ugly. The crazy foundation stones still marked the former site of my poor little cabin, and not far away, on six weary boulders, perched a jaunty board house, perhaps twenty by thirty feet, with three windows and a door that locked. Some of the window-glass was broken, and part of an old iron stove lay mournfully under the house. I peeped through the window half reverently, and found things that were more familiar. The blackboard had grown by about two feet, and the seats were still without backs. The county owns the lot now, I hear, and every year there is a session of school. As I sat by the spring and looked on the Old and the New I felt glad, very glad, and yet—

After two long drinks I started on. There was the great double log-house on the corner. I remembered the broken, blighted family that used to live there. The strong, hard face of the mother, with its wilderness of hair, rose before me. She had driven her husband away, and while I taught school a strange man lived there, big and jovial, and people talked. I felt sure that Ben and 'Tildy would come to naught from such a home. But this is an odd world; for Ben is a busy farmer in Smith County, "doing well, too," they say, and he had cared for little 'Tildy until last spring, when a lover married her. A hard life the lad had led, toiling for meat, and laughed at because he was homely and crooked. There was Sam Carlon, an impudent old skinflint, who had definite notions about "niggers," and hired Ben a summer and would not pay him. Then the hungry boy gathered his sacks together, and in broad daylight went into Carlon's corn; and when the hard-fisted farmer set upon him, the angry boy flew at him like a beast. Doc Burke saved a murder and a lynching that day.

The story reminded me again of the Burkes, and an impatience seized me to know who won in the battle, Doc or the seventy-five acres. For it is a hard thing to make a farm out of nothing, even in fifteen years. So I hurried on, thinking of the Burkes. They used to have a certain magnificent barbarism about them that I liked. They were never vulgar, never immoral, but rather rough and primitive, with an unconventionality that spent itself in loud guffaws, slaps on the back, and naps in the corner. I hurried by the cottage of the misborn Neill boys. It was empty, and they were grown into fat, lazy farmhands. I saw the home of the Hickmans, but Albert, with his stopping shoulders, had passed from the world. Then I came to the Burkes' gate and peered through; the inclosure looked rough and untrimmed, and yet there were the same fences around the old farm save to the left, where lay twenty-five other acres. And lo! the cabin in the hollow had climbed the hill and swollen to a half-finished six-room cottage.

The Burkes held a hundred acres, but they were still in debt. Indeed, the gaunt father who toiled night and day would scarcely be happy out of debt, being so used to it. Some day he must stop, for his massive frame is showing decline. The mother wore shoes, but the lion-like physique of other days was broken. The children had grown up. Rob, the image of his father, was loud and rough with laughter. Birdie, my school baby of six, had grown to a picture of maiden beauty, tall and tawny. "Edgar is gone," said the mother, with head half bowed,—"gone to work in Nashville; he and his father couldn't agree."

Little Doc, the boy born since the time of my school, took me horseback down the creek next morning toward Farmer Dowell's. The road and the stream were battling for mastery, and the stream had the better of it. We splashed and waded, and the merry boy, perched behind me, chattered and laughed. He showed me where Simon Thompson had bought a bit of ground and a home; but his daughter Lana, a plump, brown, slow girl, was not there. She had married a man and a farm twenty miles away. We wound on down the stream till we came to a gate that I did not recognize, but the boy insisted that it was "Uncle Bird's." The farm was fat with the growing crop. In that little valley was a strange stillness as I rode up; for death and marriage had stolen youth and left age and childhood there. We sat and talked that night after the chores were done. Uncle Bird was grayer, and his eyes did not see so well, but he was still jovial. We talked of the acres bought,— one hundred and twenty-five,—of the new guest-chamber added, of Martha's marrying. Then we talked of death: Fanny and Fred were gone; a shadow hung over the other daughter, and when it lifted she was to go to Nashville to school. At last we spoke of the neighbors, and as night fell, Uncle Bird told me how, on a night like that, 'Thenie came wandering back to her home over yonder, to escape the blows of her husband. And next morning she died in the home that her little bow-legged brother, working and saving, had bought for their widowed mother.

My journey was done, and behind me lay hill and dale, and Life and Death. How shall man measure Progress there where the dark-faced Josie lies? How many heartfuls of sorrow shall balance a bushel of wheat? How hard a thing is life to the lowly, and yet how human and real! And all this life and love and strife and failure,—is it the twilight of nightfall or the flush of some faint-dawning day?

Thus sadly musing, I rode to Nashville in the Jim Crow car.

CHAPTER V

Of the Wings of Atalanta

> O black boy of Atlanta!
>   But half was spoken;
> The slave's chains and the master's
>   like are broken;
> The one curse of the races
>   Held both in tether;
> They are rising—all are rising—
>   The black and white together.
>
> *Whittier*

South of the North, yet north of the South, lies the City of a Hundred Hills, peering out from the shadows of the past into the promise of the future. I have seen her in the morning, when the first flush of day had half-roused her; she lay gray and still on the crimson soil of Georgia; then the blue smoke began to curl from her chimneys, the tinkle of bell and scream of whistle broke the silence, the rattle and roar of busy life slowly gathered and swelled, until the seething whirl of the city seemed a strange thing in a sleepy land.

Once, they say, even Atlanta slept dull and drowsy at the foot-hills of the Alleghanies, until the iron baptism of war awakened her with its sullen waters, aroused and maddened her, and left her listening to the sea. And the sea cried to the hills and the hills answered the sea, till the city rose like a widow and cast away her weeds, and toiled for her daily bread; toiled steadily, toiled cunningly,—perhaps with some bitterness, with a touch of *réclame*,—and yet with real earnestness, and real sweat.

It is a hard thing to live haunted by the ghost of an untrue dream;

to see the wide vision of empire fade into real ashes and dirt; to feel the pang of the conquered, and yet know that with all the Bad that fell on one black day, something was vanquished that deserved to live, something killed that in justice had not dared to die; to know that with the Right that triumphed, triumphed something of Wrong, something sordid and mean, something less than the broadest and best. All this is bitter hard; and many a man and city and people have found in it excuse for sulking, and brooding, and listless waiting.

Such are not men of the sturdier make; they of Atlanta turned resolutely toward the future; and that future held aloft vistas of purple and gold:—Atlanta, Queen of the cotton kingdom; Atlanta, Gateway to the Land of the Sun; Atlanta, the new Lachesis, spinner of web and woof for the world. So the city crowned her hundred hills with factories, and stored her shops with cunning handiwork, and stretched long iron ways to greet the busy Mercury in his coming. And the Nation talked of her striving.

Perhaps Atlanta was not christened for the winged maiden of dull Bœotia; you know the tale,—how swarthy Atalanta, tall and wild, would marry only him who out-raced her; and how the wily Hippomenes laid three apples of gold in the way. She fled like a shadow, paused, startled over the first apple, but even as he stretched his hand, fled again; hovered over the second, then, slipping from his hot grasp, flew over river, vale, and hill; but as she lingered over the third, his arms fell round her, and looking on each other, the blazing passion of their love profaned the sanctuary of Love, and they were cursed. If Atlanta be not named for Atalanta, she ought to have been.

Atalanta is not the first or the last maiden whom greed of gold has led to defile the temple of Love; and not maids alone, but men in the race of life, sink from the high and generous ideals of youth to the gambler's code of the Bourse; and in all our Nation's striving is not the Gospel of Work befouled by the Gospel of Pay? So common is this that one-half think it normal; so unquestioned, that we almost fear to question if the end of racing is not gold, if the aim of man is not rightly to be rich. And if this is the fault of America, how dire a danger lies before a new land and a new city, lest Atlanta, stooping for mere gold, shall find that gold accursed!

It was no maiden's idle whim that started this hard racing; a fearful wilderness lay about the feet of that city after the War,—feudalism, poverty, the rise of the Third Estate, serfdom, the re-birth of Law and Order, and above and between all, the Veil of Race. How heavy a journey for weary feet! what wings must Atalanta have to flit over all this hollow and hill, through sour wood and sullen water, and by the red waste of sun-baked clay! How fleet must Atalanta be if she will not be tempted by gold to profane the Sanctuary!

The Sanctuary of our fathers has, to be sure, few Gods,—some sneer, "all too few." There is the thrifty Mercury of New England, Pluto of the North, and Ceres of the West; and there, too, is the half-forgotten Apollo of the South, under whose ægis the maiden ran,— and as she ran she forgot him, even as there in Bœotia Venus was forgot. She forgot the old ideal of the Southern gentleman,—that new-world heir of the grace and courtliness of patrician, knight, and noble; forgot his honor with his foibles, his kindliness with his carelessness, and stooped to apples of gold,—to men busier and sharper, thriftier and more unscrupulous. Golden apples are beautiful—I remember the lawless days of boyhood, when orchards in crimson and gold tempted me over fence and field—and, too, the merchant who has dethroned the planter is no despicable *parvenu*. Work and wealth are the mighty levers to lift this old new land; thrift and toil and saving are the high-ways to new hopes and new possibilities; and yet the warning is needed lest the wily Hippomenes tempt Atalanta to thinking that golden apples are the goal of racing, and not mere incidents by the way.

Atlanta must not lead the South to dream of material prosperity as the touchstone of all success; already the fatal might of this idea is beginning to spread; it is replacing the finer type of Southerner with vulgar money-getters; it is burying the sweeter beauties of Southern life beneath pretence and ostentation. For every social ill the panacea of Wealth has been urged,—wealth to overthrow the remains of the slave feudalism; wealth to raise the "cracker" Third Estate; wealth to employ the black serfs, and the prospect of wealth to keep them work-ing; wealth as the end and aim of politics, and as the legal tender for law and order; and, finally, instead of Truth, Beauty, and Goodness, wealth as the ideal of the Public School.

Not only is this true in the world which Atlanta typifies, but it is threatening to be true of a world beneath and beyond that world,—the Black World beyond the Veil. To-day it makes little difference to At-lanta, to the South, what the Negro thinks or dreams or wills. In the soul-life of the land he is to-day, and naturally will long remain, un-thought of, half forgotten; and yet when he does come to think and will and do for himself,—and let no man dream that day will never come,—then the part he plays will not be one of sudden learning, but words and thoughts he has been taught to lisp in his race-childhood. Today the ferment of his striving toward self-realization is to the strife of the white world like a wheel within a wheel: beyond the Veil are smaller but like problems of ideals, of leaders and the led, of serfdom, of poverty, of order and subordination, and, through all, the Veil of Race. Few know of these problems, few who know notice them; and yet there they are, awaiting student, artist, and seer,—a field for some-body sometime to discover. Hither has the temptation of Hippomenes penetrated; already in this smaller world, which now indirectly and anon directly must influence the larger for good or ill, the habit is forming of interpreting the world in dollars. The old leaders of Negro opinion, in the little groups where there is a Negro social consciousness, are being replaced by new; neither the black preacher nor the black teacher leads as he did two decades ago. Into their places are pushing the farmers and gardeners, the well-paid porters and artisans, the businessmen,—all those with property and money. And with all this change, so curiously parallel to that of the Other-world, goes too the same inevitable change in ideals. The South laments to-day the slow, steady disappearance of a certain type of Negro,—the faithful, courteous slave of other days, with his incorruptible honesty and dignified humility. He is passing away just as surely as the old type of Southern gentleman is passing, and from not dissimilar causes,—the sudden transformation of a fair far-off ideal of Freedom into the hard reality of bread-winning and the consequent deification of Bread.

In the Black World, the Preacher and Teacher embodied once the ideals of this people,—the strife for another and a juster world, the vague dream of righteousness, the mystery of knowing; but to-day the danger is that these ideals, with their simple beauty and weird inspiration, will suddenly sink to a question of cash and a lust for gold. Here stands this black young Atalanta, girding herself for the race that must be run; and if her eyes be still toward the hills and sky as in the days of old, then we may look for noble running; but what if some ruthless or wily or even thoughtless Hippomenes lay golden apples before her? What if the Negro people be wooed from a strife for righteousness, from a love of knowing, to regard dollars as the be-all and end-all of life? What if to the Mammonism of America be added the rising Mammonism of the reborn South, and the Mammonism of this South be reinforced by the budding Mammonism of its half-awakened black millions? Whither, then, is the new-world quest of Goodness and Beauty and Truth gone glimmering? Must this, and that fair flower of Freedom which, despite the jeers of latter-day striplings, sprung from our fathers' blood, must that too degenerate into a dusty quest of gold,— into lawless lust with Hippomenes?

The hundred hills of Atlanta are not all crowned with factories. On one, toward the west, the setting sun throws three buildings in bold relief against the sky. The beauty of the group lies in its simple unity:— a broad lawn of green rising from the red street with mingled roses and peaches; north and south, two plain and stately halls; and in the midst, half hidden in ivy, a larger building, boldly graceful, sparingly decorated, and with one low spire. It is a restful group,—one never looks for more; it is all here, all intelligible. There I live, and there I hear from day to day the low hum of restful life. In winter's twilight, when the red sun glows, I can see the dark figures pass between the halls to the music of the night-bell. In the morning, when the sun is golden, the clang of the day-bell brings the hurry and laughter of three hundred young hearts from hall and street, and from the busy city below,—children all dark and heavy-haired,—to join their clear young voices in the music of the morning sacrifice. In a half-dozen class-rooms they gather then,—here to follow the love-song of Dido, here to listen to the tale of Troy divine; there to wander among the stars, there to wander among men and nations,—and elsewhere other well-worn ways of knowing this queer world. Nothing new, no time-saving de-vices,—simply old time-glorified methods of delving for Truth, and searching out the hidden beauties of life, and learning the good of liv-ing. The riddle of existence is the college curriculum that was laid be-fore the Pharaohs, that was taught in the groves by Plato, that formed the *trivium* and *quadrivium,* and is to-day laid before the freedmen's sons by Atlanta University. And this course of study will not change; its methods will grow more deft and effectual, its content richer by toil of scholar and sight of seer; but the true college will ever have one goal,—not to earn meat, but to know the end and aim of that life which meat nourishes.

The vision of life that rises before these dark eyes has in it nothing mean or selfish. Not at Oxford or at Leipsic, not at Yale or Columbia, is there an air of higher resolve or more unfettered striving; the deter-mination to realize for men, both black and white, the broadest possi-bilities of life, to seek the better and the best, to spread with their own hands the Gospel of Sacrifice,—all this is the burden of their talk and dream. Here, amid a wide desert of caste and proscription, amid the heart-hurting slights and jars and vagaries of a deep race-dislike, lies this green oasis, where hot anger cools, and the bitterness of disap-pointment is sweetened by the springs and breezes of Parnassus; and here men may lie and listen, and learn of a future fuller than the past, and hear the voice of Time:

"Entbehren sollst du, sollst entbehren."

They made their mistakes, those who planted Fisk and Howard and Atlanta before the smoke of battle had lifted; they made their mis-takes, but those mistakes were not the things at which we lately laughed somewhat uproariously. They were right when they sought to found a new educational system upon the University: where, forsooth, shall we ground knowledge save on the broadest and deepest knowl-edge? The roots of the tree, rather than the leaves, are the sources of its life; and from the dawn of history, from Academus to Cambridge, the culture of the University has been the broad foundation-stone on which is built the kindergarten's A B C.

But these builders did make a mistake in minimizing the gravity of the problem before them; in thinking it a matter of years and decades; in therefore building quickly and laying their foundation carelessly, and lowering the standard of knowing, until they had scattered haphazard through the South some dozen poorly equipped high schools and miscalled them universities. They forgot, too, just as their successors are forgetting, the rule of inequality:—that of the million black youth, some were fitted to know and some to dig; that some had the talent and capacity of university men, and some the talent and capacity of blacksmiths; and that true training meant neither that all should be college men nor all artisans, but that the one should be made a missionary of culture to an untaught people, and the other a free workman among serfs. And to seek to make the blacksmith a scholar is almost as silly as the more modern scheme of making the scholar a blacksmith; almost, but not quite.

The function of the university is not simply to teach breadwinning, or to furnish teachers for the public schools, or to be a centre of polite society; it is, above all, to be the organ of that fine adjustment between real life and the growing knowledge of life, an adjustment which forms the secret of civilization. Such an institution the South of to-day sorely needs. She has religion, earnest, bigoted:—religion that on both sides the Veil often omits the sixth, seventh, and eighth commandments, but substitutes a dozen supplementary ones. She has, as Atlanta shows, growing thrift and love of toil; but she lacks that broad knowledge of what the world knows and knew of human living and doing, which she may apply to the thousand problems of real life to-day confronting her. The need of the South is knowledge and culture,—not in dainty limited quantity, as before the war, but in broad busy abundance in the world of work; and until she has this, not all the Apples of Hesperides, be they golden and bejewelled, can save her from the curse of the Bœotian lovers.

The Wings of Atalanta are the coming universities of the South. They alone can bear the maiden past the temptation of golden fruit. They will not guide her flying feet away from the cotton and gold; for—ah, thoughtful Hippomenes!—do not the apples lie in the very Way of Life? But they will guide her over and beyond them, and leave her kneeling in the Sanctuary of Truth and Freedom and broad Humanity, virgin and undefiled. Sadly did the Old South err in human education, despising the education of the masses, and niggardly in the support of colleges. Her ancient university foundations dwindled and withered under the foul breath of slavery; and even since the war they have fought a failing fight for life in the tainted air of social unrest and commercial selfishness, stunted by the death of criticism, and starving for lack of broadly cultured men. And if this is the white South's need and danger, how much heavier the danger and need of the freedmen's sons! how pressing here the need of broad ideals and true culture, the conservation of soul from sordid aims and petty passions! Let us build the Southern university—William and Mary, Trinity, Georgia, Texas,

Tulane, Vanderbilt, and the others—fit to live; let us build, too, the Negro universities:—Fisk, whose foundation was ever broad; Howard, at the heart of the Nation; Atlanta at Atlanta, whose ideal of scholarship has been held above the temptation of numbers. Why not here, and perhaps elsewhere, plant deeply and for all time centres of learning and living, colleges that yearly would send into the life of the South a few white men and a few black men of broad culture, catholic tolerance, and trained ability, joining their hands to other hands, and giving to this squabble of the Races a decent and dignified peace?

Patience, Humility, Manners, and Taste, common schools and kindergartens, industrial and technical schools, literature and tolerance,—all these spring from knowledge and culture, the children of the university. So must men and nations build, not otherwise, not upside down.

Teach workers to work,—a wise saying; wise when applied to German boys and American girls; wiser when said of Negro boys, for they have less knowledge of working and none to teach them. Teach thinkers to think,—a needed knowledge in a day of loose and careless logic; and they whose lot is gravest must have the carefulest training to think aright. If these things are so, how foolish to ask what is the best education for one or seven or sixty million souls! shall we teach them trades, or train them in liberal arts? Neither and both: teach the workers to work and the thinkers to think; make carpenters of carpenters, and philosophers of philosophers, and fops of fools. Nor can we pause here. We are training not isolated men but a living group of men,—nay, a group within a group. And the final product of our training must be neither a psychologist nor a brickmason, but a man. And to make men, we must have ideals, broad, pure, and inspiring ends of living,—not sordid money-getting, not apples of gold. The worker must work for the glory of his handiwork, not simply for pay; the thinker must think for truth, not for fame. And all this is gained only by human strife and longing; by ceaseless training and education; by founding Right on righteousness and Truth on the unhampered search for Truth; by founding the common school on the university, and the industrial school on the common school; and weaving thus a system, not a distortion, and bringing a birth, not an abortion.

When night falls on the City of a Hundred Hills, a wind gathers itself from the seas and comes murmuring westward. And at its bidding, the smoke of the drowsy factories sweeps down upon the mighty city and covers it like a pall, while yonder at the University the stars twinkle above Stone Hall. And they say that yon gray mist is the tunic of Atalanta pausing over her golden apples. Fly, my maiden, fly, for yonder comes Hippomenes!

CHAPTER **VI**

Of the Training of Black Men

Why, if the Soul can fling the Dust aside,
And naked on the Air of Heaven ride,
   Were't not a Shame—were't not a Shame for him
In this clay carcase crippled to abide?

Omar Khayyám (Fitzgerald)

From the shimmering swirl of waters where many, many thoughts
ago the slave-ship first saw the square tower of Jamestown, have
flowed down to our day three streams of thinking; one swollen from
the larger world here and over-seas, saying, the multiplying of human
wants in culture-lands calls for the world-wide coöperation of men in
satisfying them. Hence arises a new human unity, pulling the ends of
earth nearer, and all men, black, yellow, and white. The larger humanity strives to feel in this contact of living Nations and sleeping hordes
a thrill of new life in the world, crying, "If the contact of Life and Sleep
by Death, shame on such Life." To be sure, behind this thought lurks
the afterthought of force and dominion,—the making of brown men to
delve when the temptation of beads and red calico cloys.

The second thought streaming from the death-ship and the curving
river is the thought of the older South,—the sincere and passionate
belief that somewhere between men and cattle, God created a *tertium
quid*, and called it a Negro,—a clownish, simple creature, at times even
lovable within its limitations, but straitly foreordained to walk within
the Veil. To be sure, behind the thought lurks the afterthought,—some
of them with favoring chance might become men, but in sheer self-
defence we dare not let them, and we build about them walls so high,
and hang between them and the light a veil so thick, that they shall
not even think of breaking through.

And last of all there trickles down that third and darker thought,—
the thought of the things themselves, the confused, half-conscious
mutter of men who are black and whitened, crying "Liberty, Freedom,
Opportunity—vouchsafe to us, O boastful World, the chance of living
men!" To be sure, behind the thought lurks the afterthought,—sup-

pose, after all, the World is right and we are less than men? Suppose this mad impulse within is all wrong, some mock mirage from the untrue?

So here we stand among thoughts of human unity, even through conquest and slavery; the inferiority of black men, even if forced by fraud; a shriek in the night for the freedom of men who themselves are not yet sure of their right to demand it. This is the tangle of thought and afterthought wherein we are called to solve the problem of training men for life.

Behind all its curiousness, so attractive alike to sage and *dilettante*, lie its dim dangers, throwing across us shadows at once grotesque and awful. Plain it is to us that what the world seeks through desert and wild we have within our threshold,—a stalwart laboring force, suited to the semi-tropics; if, deaf to the voice of the Zeitgeist, we refuse to use and develop these men, we risk poverty and loss. If, on the other hand, seized by the brutal afterthought, we debauch the race thus caught in our talons, selfishly sucking their blood and brains in the future as in the past, what shall save us from national decadence? Only that saner selfishness, which Education teaches men, can find the rights of all in the whirl of work.

Again, we may decry the color-prejudice of the South, yet it remains a heavy fact. Such curious kinks of the human mind exist and must be reckoned with soberly. They cannot be laughed away, nor always successfully stormed at, nor easily abolished by act of legislature. And yet they must not be encouraged by being let alone. They must be recognized as facts, but unpleasant facts; things that stand in the way of civilization and religion and common decency. They can be met in but one way,—by the breadth and broadening of human reason, by catholicity of taste and culture. And so, too, the native ambition and aspiration of men, even though they be black, backward, and ungraceful, must not lightly be dealt with. To stimulate wildly weak and untrained minds is to play with mighty fires; to flout their striving idly is to welcome a harvest of brutish crime and shameless lethargy in our very laps. The guiding of thought and the deft coördination of deed is at once the path of honor and humanity.

And so, in this great question of reconciling three vast and partially contradictory streams of thought, the one panacea of Education leaps to the lips of all:—such human training as will best use the labor of all men without enslaving or brutalizing; such training as will give us poise to encourage the prejudices that bulwark society, and to stamp out those that in sheer barbarity deafen us to the wail of prisoned souls within the Veil, and the mounting fury of shackled men.

But when we have vaguely said that Education will set this tangle straight, what have we uttered but a truism? Training for life teaches living; but what training for the profitable living together of black men and white? A hundred and fifty years ago our task would have seemed easier. Then Dr. Johnson blandly assured us that education was need-ful solely for the embellishments of life, and was useless for ordinary vermin. To-day we have climbed to heights where we would open at least the outer courts of knowledge to all, display its treasures to many, and select the few to whom its mystery of Truth is revealed, not wholly by birth or the accidents of the stock market, but at least in part according to deftness and aim, talent and character. This programme, however, we are sorely puzzled in carrying out through that part of the land where the blight of slavery fell hardest, and where we are dealing with two backward peoples. To make here in human education that ever necessary combination of the permanent and the contingent—of the ideal and the practical in workable equilibrium—has been there, as it ever must be in every age and place, a matter of infinite experiment and frequent mistakes.

In rough approximation we may point out four varying decades of work in Southern education since the Civil War. From the close of the war until 1876, was the period of uncertain groping and temporary relief. There were army schools, mission schools, and schools of the Freedman's Bureau in chaotic disarrangement seeking system and co-öperation. Then followed ten years of constructive definite effort toward the building of complete school systems in the South. Normal schools and colleges were founded for the freedmen, and teachers trained there to man the public schools. There was the inevitable tendency of war to underestimate the prejudices of the master and the ignorance of the slave, and all seemed clear sailing out of the wreckage of the storm. Meantime, starting in this decade yet especially developing from 1885 to 1895, began the industrial revolution of the South. The land saw glimpses of a new destiny and the stirring of new ideals. The educational system striving to complete itself saw new obstacles and a field of work ever broader and deeper. The Negro colleges, hurriedly founded, were inadequately equipped, illogically distributed, and of varying efficiency and grade; the normal and high schools were doing little more than common-school work, and the common schools were training but a third of the children who ought to be in them, and training these too often poorly. At the same time the white South, by reason of its sudden conversion from the slavery ideal, by so much the more became set and strengthened in its racial prejudice, and crystallized it into harsh law and harsher custom; while the marvellous pushing forward of the poor white daily threatened to take even bread and butter from the mouths of the heavily handicapped sons of the freedmen. In the midst, then, of the larger problem of Negro education sprang up the more practical question of work, the inevitable economic quandary that faces a people in the transition from slavery to freedom, and especially those who make that change amid hate and prejudice, lawlessness and ruthless competition.

The industrial school springing to notice in this decade, but coming to full recognition in the decade beginning with 1895, was the proffered answer to this combined educational and economic crisis, and an answer of singular wisdom and timeliness. From the very first in nearly all the schools some attention had been given to training in handiwork, but now was this training first raised to a dignity that brought it in direct touch with the South's magnificent industrial development, and given an emphasis which reminded black folk that before the Temple of Knowledge swing the Gates of Toil.

Yet after all they are but gates, and when turning our eyes from the temporary and the contingent in the Negro problem to the broader question of the permanent uplifting and civilization of black men in America, we have a right to inquire, as this enthusiasm for material advancement mounts to its height, if after all the industrial school is the final and sufficient answer in the training of the Negro race; and to ask gently, but in all sincerity, the ever-recurring query of the ages, Is not life more than meat, and the body more than raiment? And men ask this to-day all the more eagerly because of sinister signs in recent educational movements. The tendency is here, born of slavery and quickened to renewed life by the crazy imperialism of the day, to regard human beings as among the material resources of a land to be trained with an eye single to future dividends. Race-prejudices, which keep brown and black men in their "places," we are coming to regard as useful allies with such a theory, no matter how much they may dull the ambition and sicken the hearts of struggling human beings. And above all, we daily hear that an education that encourages aspiration, that sets the loftiest of ideals and seeks as an end culture and character rather than bread-winning, is the privilege of white men and the danger and delusion of black.

Especially has criticism been directed against the former educational efforts to aid the Negro. In the four periods I have mentioned, we find first, boundless, planless enthusiasm and sacrifice; then the preparation of teachers for a vast public-school system; then the launching and expansion of that school system amid increasing difficulties; and finally the training of workmen for the new and growing industries. This development has been sharply ridiculed as a logical anomaly and flat reversal of nature. Soothly we have been told that first industrial and manual training should have taught the Negro to work, then simple schools should have taught him to read and write, and finally, after years, high and normal schools could have completed the system, as intelligence and wealth demanded.

That a system logically so complete was historically impossible, it needs but a little thought to prove. Progress in human affairs is more often a pull than a push, surging forward of the exceptional man, and the lifting of his duller brethren slowly and painfully to his vantage-ground. Thus it was no accident that gave birth to universities centuries before the common schools, that made fair Harvard the first flower of our wilderness. So in the South: the mass of the freedmen at the end of the war lacked the intelligence so necessary to modern working-men. They must first have the common school to teach them to read, write, and cipher; and they must have higher schools to teach teachers for the common schools. The white teachers who flocked South went to establish such a common-school system. Few held the idea of founding colleges; most of them at first would have laughed at the idea. But they faced, as all men since them have faced, that central paradox of the South,—the social separation of the races. At that time it was the sudden volcanic rupture of nearly all relations between black and white, in work and government and family life. Since then a new adjustment of relations in economic and political affairs has grown up,—an adjustment subtle and difficult to grasp, yet singularly ingenious, which leaves still that frightful chasm at the color-line across which men pass at their peril. Thus, then and now, there stand in the South two separate worlds; and separate not simply in the higher realms of social intercourse, but also in church and school, on railway and street-car, in hotels and theatres, in streets and city sections, in books and newspapers, in asylums and jails, in hospitals and graveyards. There is still enough of contact for large economic and group coöperation, but the separation is so thorough and deep that it absolutely precludes for the present between the races anything like that sympathetic and effective group-training and leadership of the one by the other, such as the American Negro and all backward peoples must have for effectual progress.

This the missionaries of '68 soon saw; and if effective industrial and trade schools were impracticable before the establishment of a common-school system, just as certainly no adequate common schools could be founded until there were teachers to teach them. Southern whites would not teach them; Northern whites in sufficient numbers could not be had. If the Negro was to learn, he must teach himself, and the most effective help that could be given him was the establishment of schools to train Negro teachers. This conclusion was slowly but surely reached by every student of the situation until simultaneously, in widely separated regions, without consultation or systematic plan, there arose a series of institutions designed to furnish teachers for the untaught. Above the sneers of critics at the obvious defects of this procedure must ever stand its one crushing rejoinder: in a single generation they put thirty thousand black teachers in the South; they wiped out the illiteracy of the majority of the black people of the land, and they made Tuskegee possible.

Such higher training-schools tended naturally to deepen broader development: at first they were common and grammar schools, then some became high schools. And finally, by 1900, some thirty-four had one year or more of studies of college grade. This development was reached with different degrees of speed in different institutions: Hampton is still a high school, while Fisk University started her college in 1871, and Spelman Seminary about 1896. In all cases the aim was identical,—to maintain the standards of the lower training by giving teachers and leaders the best practicable training; and above all, to furnish the black world with adequate standards of human culture and lofty ideals of life. It was not enough that the teachers of teachers should be trained in technical normal methods; they must also, so far as possible, be broad-minded, cultured men and women, to scatter civilization among a people whose ignorance was not simply of letters, but of life itself.

It can thus be seen that the work of education in the South began with higher institutions of training, which threw off as their foliage common schools, and later industrial schools, and at the same time strove to shoot their roots ever deeper toward college and university training. That this was an inevitable and necessary development, sooner or later, goes without saying; but there has been, and still is, a question in many minds if the natural growth was not forced, and if the higher training was not either overdone or done with cheap and unsound methods. Among white Southerners this feeling is widespread and positive. A prominent Southern journal voiced this in a recent editorial.

> "The experiment that has been made to give the colored students classical training has not been satisfactory. Even though many were able to pursue the course, most of them did so in a parrot-like way, learning what was taught, but not seeming to appropriate the truth and import of their instruction, and graduating without sensible aim or valuable occupation for their future. The whole scheme has proved a waste of time, efforts, and the money of the state."

While most fair-minded men would recognize this as extreme and overdrawn, still without doubt many are asking, Are there a sufficient number of Negroes ready for college training to warrant the undertaking? Are not too many students prematurely forced into this work? Does it not have the effect of dissatisfying the young Negro with his environment? And do these graduates succeed in real life? Such natural questions cannot be evaded, nor on the other hand must a Nation naturally skeptical as to Negro ability assume an unfavorable answer without careful inquiry and patient openness to conviction. We must not forget that most Americans answer all queries regarding the Negro *a priori,* and that the least that human courtesy can do is to listen to evidence.

The advocates of the higher education of the Negro would be the last to deny the incompleteness and glaring defects of the present system: too many institutions have attempted to do college work, the work in some cases has not been thoroughly done, and quantity rather than quality has sometimes been sought. But all this can be said of higher education throughout the land; it is the almost inevitable incident of educational growth, and leaves the deeper question of the legitimate demand for the higher training of Negroes untouched. And this latter question can be settled in but one way,—by a first-hand study of the facts. If we leave out of view all institutions which have not actually graduated students from a course higher than that of a New England high school, even though they be called colleges; if then we take the thirty-four remaining institutions, we may clear up many misapprehensions by asking searchingly, What kind of institutions are they? what do they teach? and what sort of men do they graduate?

And first we may say that this type of college, including Atlanta, Fisk, and Howard, Wilberforce and Lincoln, Biddle, Shaw, and the rest, is peculiar, almost unique. Through the shining trees that whisper before me as I write, I catch glimpses of a boulder of New England granite, covering a grave, which graduates of Atlanta University have placed there, with this inscription:

"IN GRATEFUL MEMORY OF THEIR
FORMER TEACHER AND FRIEND
AND OF THE UNSELFISH LIFE HE
LIVED, AND THE NOBLE WORK HE
WROUGHT; THAT THEY, THEIR
CHILDREN, AND THEIR CHIL-
DREN'S CHILDREN MIGHT BE
BLESSED."

This was the gift of New England to the freed Negro: not alms, but a friend; not cash, but character. It was not and is not money these seething millions want, but love and sympathy, the pulse of hearts beating with red blood;—a gift which to-day only their own kindred and race can bring to the masses, but which once saintly souls brought to their favored children in the crusade of the sixties, that finest thing in American history, and one of the few things untainted by sordid greed and cheap vainglory. The teachers in these institutions came not to keep the Negroes in their place, but to raise them out of the defilement of the places where slavery had wallowed them. The colleges they founded were social settlements; homes where the best of the sons of the freedmen came in close and sympathetic touch with the best traditions of New England. They lived and ate together, studied and worked, hoped and harkened in the dawning light. In actual formal content their curriculum was doubtless old-fashioned, but in educational power it was supreme, for it was the contact of living souls.

From such schools about two thousand Negroes have gone forth with the bachelor's degree. The number in itself is enough to put at rest the argument that too large a proportion of Negroes are receiving higher training. If the ratio to population of all Negro students throughout the land, in both college and secondary training, be counted, Commissioner Harris assures us "it must be increased to five times its present average" to equal the average of the land.

Fifty years ago the ability of Negro students in any appreciable numbers to master a modern college course would have been difficult to prove. To-day it is proved by the fact that four hundred Negroes, many of whom have been reported as brilliant students, have received the bachelor's degree from Harvard, Yale, Oberlin, and seventy other leading colleges. Here we have, then, nearly twenty-five hundred Negro graduates, of whom the crucial query must be made, How far did their training fit them for life? It is of course extremely difficult to collect satisfactory data on such a point,—difficult to reach the men, to get trustworthy testimony, and to gauge that testimony by any generally acceptable criterion of success. In 1900, the Conference at Atlanta University undertook to study these graduates, and published the results. First they sought to know what these graduates were doing, and succeeded in getting answers from nearly two-thirds of the living. The direct testimony was in almost all cases corroborated by the reports of the colleges where they graduated, so that in the main the reports were worthy of credence. Fifty-three per cent of these graduates were teachers,—presidents of institutions, heads of normal schools, principals of city school-systems, and the like. Seventeen per cent were clergymen; another seventeen per cent were in the professions, chiefly as physicians. Over six per cent were merchants, farmers, and artisans, and four per cent were in the government civil-service. Granting even that a considerable proportion of the third unheard from are unsuccessful, this is a record of usefulness. Personally I know many hundreds of these graduates, and have corresponded with more than a thousand; through others I have followed carefully the life-work of scores; I have taught some of them and some of the pupils whom they have taught, lived in homes which they have builded, and looked at life through their eyes. Comparing them as a class with my fellow students in New England and in Europe, I cannot hesitate in saying that nowhere have I met men and women with a broader spirit of helpfulness, with deeper devotion to their life-work, or with more consecrated determination to succeed in the face of bitter difficulties than among Negro college-bred men. They have, to be sure, their proportion of ne'er-do-weels, their pedants and lettered fools, but they have a surprisingly small proportion of them; they have not that culture of manner which we instinctively associate with university men, forgetting that in reality it is the heritage from cultured homes, and that no people a generation removed from slavery can escape a certain unpleasant rawness and *gaucherie*, despite the best of training.

With all their larger vision and deeper sensibility, these men have usually been conservative, careful leaders. They have seldom been agitators, have withstood the temptation to head the mob, and have worked steadily and faithfully in a thousand communities in the South. As teachers, they have given the South a commendable system of city schools and large numbers of private normal-schools and academies. Colored college-bred men have worked side by side with white college graduates at Hampton; almost from the beginning the backbone of Tuskegee's teaching force has been formed of graduates from Fisk and Atlanta. And to-day the institute is filled with college graduates, from the energetic wife of the principal down to the teacher of agriculture, including nearly half of the executive council and a majority of the heads of departments. In the professions, college men are slowly but surely leavening the Negro church, are healing and preventing the devastations of disease, and beginning to furnish legal protection for the liberty and property of the toiling masses. All this is needful work. Who would do it if Negroes did not? How could Negroes do it if they were not trained carefully for it? If white people need colleges to furnish teachers, ministers, lawyers, and doctors, do black people need nothing of the sort?

If it is true that there are an appreciable number of Negro youth in the land capable by character and talent to receive that higher training, the end of which is culture, and if the two and a half thousand who have had something of this training in the past have in the main proved themselves useful to their race and generation, the question then comes, What place in the future development of the South ought the Negro college and college-bred man to occupy? That the present social separation and acute race-sensitiveness must eventually yield to the influences of culture, as the South grows civilized, is clear. But such transformation calls for singular wisdom and patience. If, while the healing of this vast sore is progressing, the races are to live for many years side by side, united in economic effort, obeying a common government, sensitive to mutual thought and feeling, yet subtly and silently separate in many matters of deeper human intimacy,—if this unusual and dangerous development is to progress amid peace and order, mutual respect and growing intelligence, it will call for social surgery at once the delicatest and nicest in modern history. It will demand broad-minded, upright men, both white and black, and in its final accomplishment American civilization will triumph. So far as white men are concerned, this fact is to-day being recognized in the South, and a happy renaissance of university education seems imminent. But the very voices that cry hail to this good work are, strange to relate, largely silent or antagonistic to the higher education of the Negro.

Strange to relate! for this is certain, no secure civilization can be built in the South with the Negro as an ignorant, turbulent proletariat.

Suppose we seek to remedy this by making them laborers and nothing more: they are not fools, they have tasted of the Tree of Life, and they will not cease to think, will not cease attempting to read the riddle of the world. By taking away their best equipped teachers and leaders, by slamming the door of opportunity in the faces of their bolder and brighter minds, will you make them satisfied with their lot? or will you not rather transfer their leading from the hands of men taught to think to the hands of untrained demagogues? We ought not to forget that despite the pressure of poverty, and despite the active discouragement and even ridicule of friends, the demand for higher training steadily increases among Negro youth: there were, in the years from 1875 to 1880, 22 Negro graduates from Northern colleges; from 1885 to 1890 there were 43, and from 1895 to 1900, nearly 100 graduates. From Southern Negro colleges there were, in the same three periods, 143, 413, and over 500 graduates. Here, then, is the plain thirst for training; by refusing to give this Talented Tenth the key to knowledge, can any sane man imagine that they will lightly lay aside their yearning and contentedly become hewers of wood and drawers of water?

No. The dangerously clear logic of the Negro's position will more and more loudly assert itself in that day when increasing wealth and more intricate social organization preclude the South from being, as it so largely is, simply an armed camp for intimidating black folk. Such waste of energy cannot be spared if the South is to catch up with civilization. And as the black third of the land grows in thrift and skill, unless skilfully guided in its larger philosophy, it must more and more brood over the red past and the creeping, crooked present, until it grasps a gospel of revolt and revenge and throws its new-found energies athwart the current of advance. Even to-day the masses of the Negroes see all too clearly the anomalies of their position and the moral crookedness of yours. You may marshal strong indictments against them, but their counter-cries, lacking though they be in formal logic, have burning truths within them which you may not wholly ignore, O Southern Gentlemen! If you deplore their presence here, they ask, Who brought us? When you cry, Deliver us from the vision of intermarriage, they answer that legal marriage is infinitely better than systematic concubinage and prostitution. And if in just fury you accuse their vagabonds of violating women, they also in fury quite as just may reply: The wrong which your gentlemen have done against helpless black women in defiance of your own laws is written on the foreheads of two millions of mulattoes, and written in ineffaceable blood. And finally, when you fasten crime upon this race as its peculiar trait, they answer that slavery was the arch-crime, and lynching and lawlessness its twin abortion; that color and race are not crimes, and yet they it is which in this land receives most unceasing condemnation, North, East, South, and West.

I will not say such arguments are wholly justified,—I will not insist that there is no other side to the shield; but I do say that of the nine millions of Negroes in this nation, there is scarcely one out of the cradle to whom these arguments do not daily present themselves in the guise of terrible truth. I insist that the question of the future is how best to keep these millions from brooding over the wrongs of the past and the difficulties of the present, so that all their energies may be bent toward a cheerful striving and co-operation with their white neighbors toward a larger, juster, and fuller future. That one wise method of doing this lies in the closer knitting of the Negro to the great industrial possibilities of the South is a great truth. And this the common schools and the manual training and trade schools are working to accomplish. But these alone are not enough. The foundations of knowledge in this race, as in others, must be sunk deep in the college and university if we would build a solid, permanent structure. Internal problems of social advance must inevitably come,—problems of work and wages, of families and homes, of morals and the true valuing of the things of life; and all these and other inevitable problems of civilization the Negro must meet and solve largely for himself, by reason of his isolation; and can there be any possible solution other than by study and thought and an appeal to the rich experience of the past? Is there not, with such a group and in such a crisis, infinitely more danger to be apprehended from half-trained minds and shallow thinking than from over-education and over-refinement? Surely we have wit enough to found a Negro college so manned and equipped as to steer successfully between the *dilettante* and the fool. We shall hardly induce black men to believe that if their stomachs be full, it matters little about their brains. They already dimly perceive that the paths of peace winding between honest toil and dignified manhood call for the guidance of skilled thinkers, the loving, reverent comradeship between the black lowly and the black men emancipated by training and culture.

The function of the Negro college, then, is clear: it must maintain the standards of popular education, it must seek the social regeneration of the Negro, and it must help in the solution of problems of race contact and co-operation. And finally, beyond all this, it must develop men. Above our modern socialism, and out of the worship of the mass, must persist and evolve that higher individualism which the centres of culture protect; there must come a loftier respect for the sovereign human soul that seeks to know itself and the world about it; that seeks a freedom for expansion and self-development; that will love and hate and labor in its own way, untrammeled alike by old and new. Such souls aforetime have inspired and guided worlds, and if we be not wholly bewitched by our Rhine-gold, they shall again. Herein the longing of black men must have respect: the rich and bitter depth of their experience, the unknown treasures of their inner life, the strange rendings of nature they have seen, may give the world new points of view and make their loving, living, and doing precious to all human hearts.

And to themselves in these the days that try their souls, the chance to soar in the dim blue air above the smoke is to their finer spirits boon and guerdon for what they lose on earth by being black.

I sit with Shakespeare and he winces not. Across the color line I move arm in arm with Balzac and Dumas, where smiling men and welcoming women glide in gilded halls. From out the caves of evening that swing between the strong-limbed earth and the tracery of the stars, I summon Aristotle and Aurelius and what soul I will, and they come all graciously with no scorn nor condescension. So, wed with Truth, I dwell above the Veil. Is this the life you grudge us, O knightly America? Is this the life you long to change into the dull red hideousness of Georgia? Are you so afraid lest peering from this high Pisgah, between Philistine and Amalekite, we sight the Promised Land?

CHAPTER **VII**

Of the Black Belt

> I am black but comely, O ye daughters of Jerusalem,
> As the tents of Kedar, as the curtains of Solomon.
> Look not upon me, because I am black,
> Because the sun hath looked upon me:
> My mother's children were angry with me;
> They made me the keeper of the vineyards;
> But mine own vineyard have I not kept.
>
> *The Song of Solomon*

Out of the North the train thundered, and we woke to see the crimson soil of Georgia stretching away bare and monotonous right and left. Here and there lay straggling, unlovely villages, and lean men loafed leisurely at the depots; then again came the stretch of pines and clay. Yet we did not nod, nor weary of the scene; for this is historic ground. Right across our track, three hundred and sixty years ago, wandered the cavalcade of Hernando de Soto, looking for gold and the Great Sea; and he and his foot-sore captives disappeared yonder in the grim forests to the west. Here sits Atlanta, the city of a hundred hills, with something Western, something Southern, and something quite its own, in its busy life. And a little past Atlanta, to the southwest, is the land of the Cherokees, and there, not far from where Sam Hose was crucified, you may stand on a spot which is to-day the centre of the Negro problem,—the centre of those nine million men who are America's dark heritage from slavery and the slave-trade.

Not only is Georgia thus the geographical focus of our Negro population, but in many other respects, both now and yesterday, the Negro problems have seemed to be centered in this State. No other State in the Union can count a million Negroes among its citizens,—a population as large as the slave population of the whole Union in 1800; no other State fought so long and strenuously to gather this host of Africans. Oglethorpe thought slavery against law and gospel; but the circumstances which gave Georgia its first inhabitants were not calculated to furnish citizens over-nice in their ideas about rum and slaves. Despite the prohibitions of the trustees, these Georgians, like some of their descendants, proceeded to take the law into their own hands; and so pliant were the judges, and so flagrant the smuggling, and so earnest were the prayers of Whitefield, that by the middle of the eighteenth century all restrictions were swept away, and the slave-trade went merrily on for fifty years and more.

Down in Darien, where the Delegal riots took place some summers ago, there used to come a strong protest against slavery from the Scotch Highlanders; and the Moravians of Ebenezer did not like the system. But not till the Haytian Terror of Toussaint was the trade in men even checked; while the national statute of 1808 did not suffice to stop it. How the Africans poured in!—fifty thousand between 1790 and 1810, and then, from Virginia and from smugglers, two thousand a year for many years more. So the thirty thousand Negroes of Georgia in 1790 were doubled in a decade,—were over a hundred thousand in 1810, had reached two hundred thousand in 1820, and half a million at the time of the war. Thus like a snake the black population writhed upward.

But we must hasten on our journey. This that we pass as we leave Atlanta is the ancient land of the Cherokees,—that brave Indian nation which strove so long for its fatherland, until Fate and the United States Government drove them beyond the Mississippi. If you wish to ride with me you must come into the "Jim Crow Car." There will be no objection,—already four other white men, and a little white girl with her nurse, are in there. Usually the races are mixed in there; but the white coach is all white. Of course this car is not so good as the other, but it is fairly clean and comfortable. The discomfort lies chiefly in the hearts of those four black men yonder—and in mine.

We rumble south in quite a business-like way. The bare red clay and pines of Northern Georgia begin to disappear, and in their place appears a rich rolling land, luxuriant, and here and there well tilled. This is the land of the Creek Indians; and a hard time the Georgians had to seize it. The towns grow more frequent and more interesting, and brand-new cotton mills rise on every side. Below Macon the world grows darker; for now we approach the Black Belt,—that strange land of shadows, at which even slaves paled in the past, and whence come now only faint and half-intelligible murmurs to the world beyond. The "Jim Crow Car" grows larger and a shade better; three rough field-hands and two or three white loafers accompany us, and the newsboy still spreads his wares at one end. The sun is setting, but we can see the great cotton country as we enter it,—the soil now dark and fertile, now thin and gray, with fruit-trees and dilapidated buildings,—all the way to Albany.

At Albany, in the heart of the Black Belt, we stop. Two hundred miles south of Atlanta, two hundred miles west of the Atlantic, and one hundred miles north of the Great Gulf lies Dougherty County, with ten thousand Negroes and two thousand whites. The Flint River winds down from Andersonville, and, turning suddenly at Albany, the county-seat, hurries on to join the Chattahoochee and the sea. Andrew Jackson knew the Flint well, and marched across it once to avenge the Indian Massacre at Fort Mims. That was in 1814, not long before the battle of New Orleans; and by the Creek treaty that followed this campaign, all Dougherty County, and much other rich land, was ceded to Georgia. Still, settlers fought shy of this land, for the Indians were all about, and they were unpleasant neighbors in those days. The panic of 1837, which Jackson bequeathed to Van Buren, turned the planters from the impoverished lands of Virginia, the Carolinas, and east Georgia, toward the West. The Indians were removed to Indian Territory, and settlers poured into these coveted lands to retrieve their broken fortunes. For a radius of a hundred miles about Albany, stretched a great fertile land, luxuriant with forests of pine, oak, ash, hickory, and poplar; hot with the sun and damp with the rich black swamp-land; and here the corner-stone of the Cotton Kingdom was laid.

Albany is to-day a wide-streeted, placid, Southern town, with a broad sweep of stores and saloons, and flanking rows of homes,— whites usually to the north, and blacks to the south. Six days in the week the town looks decidedly too small for itself, and takes frequent and prolonged naps. But on Saturday suddenly the whole county disgorges itself upon the place, and a perfect flood of black peasantry pours through the streets, fills the stores, blocks the sidewalks, chokes the thoroughfares, and takes full possession of the town. They are black, sturdy, uncouth country folk, good-natured and simple, talkative to a degree, and yet far more silent and brooding than the crowds of the Rhine-pfalz, or Naples, or Cracow. They drink considerable quantities of whiskey, but do not get very drunk; they talk and laugh loudly at times, but seldom quarrel or fight. They walk up and down the streets, meet and gossip with friends, stare at the shop windows, buy coffee, cheap candy, and clothes, and at dusk drive home— happy? well no, not exactly happy, but much happier than as though they had not come.

Thus Albany is a real capital,—a typical Southern county town, the centre of the life of ten thousand souls; their point of contact with the outer world, their centre of news and gossip, their market for buying and selling, borrowing and lending, their fountain of justice and law. Once upon a time we knew country life so well and city life so little, that we illustrated city life as that of a closely crowded country district. Now the world has well-nigh forgotten what the country is, and we must imagine a little city of black people scattered far and wide over three hundred lonesome square miles of land, without train or trolley, in the midst of cotton and corn, and wide patches of sand and gloomy soil.

It gets pretty hot in Southern Georgia in July,—a sort of dull, determined heat that seems quite independent of the sun; so it took us some days to muster courage enough to leave the porch and venture out on the long country roads, that we might see this unknown world. Finally we started. It was about ten in the morning, bright with a faint breeze, and we jogged leisurely southward in the valley of the Flint. We passed the scattered box-like cabins of the brick-yard hands, and the long tenement-row facetiously called "The Ark," and were soon in the open country, and on the confines of the great plantations of other days. There is the "Joe Fields place"; a rough old fellow was he, and had killed many a "nigger" in his day. Twelve miles his plantation used to run,—a regular barony. It is nearly all gone now; only straggling bits belong to the family, and the rest has passed to Jews and Negroes. Even the bits which are left are heavily mortgaged, and, like the rest of the land, tilled by tenants. Here is one of them now,—a tall brown man, a hard worker and a hard drinker, illiterate, but versed in farm-lore, as his nodding crops declare. This distressingly new board house is his, and he has just moved out of yonder moss-grown cabin with its one square room.

From the curtains in Benton's house, down the road, a dark comely face is staring at the strangers; for passing carriages are not every-day occurrences here. Benton is an intelligent yellow man with a good-sized family, and manages a plantation blasted by the war and now the broken staff of the widow. He might be well-to-do, they say; but he carouses too much in Albany. And the half-desolate spirit of neglect born of the very soil seems to have settled on these acres. In times past there were cotton-gins and machinery here; but they have rotted away.

The whole land seems forlorn and forsaken. Here are the remnants of the vast plantations of the Sheldons, the Pellots, and the Rensons; but the souls of them are passed. The houses lie in half ruin, or have wholly disappeared; the fences have flown, and the families are wandering in the world. Strange vicissitudes have met these whilom masters. Yonder stretch the wide acres of Bildad Reasor; he died in wartime, but the upstart overseer hastened to wed the widow. Then he went, and his neighbors too, and now only the black tenant remains; but the shadow-hand of the master's grand-nephew or cousin or creditor stretches out of the gray distance to collect the rack-rent remorselessly, and so the land is uncared-for and poor. Only black tenants can stand such a system, and they only because they must. Ten miles we have ridden to-day and have seen no white face.

A resistless feeling of depression falls slowly upon us, despite the gaudy sunshine and the green cotton-fields. This, then, is the Cotton Kingdom,—the shadow of a marvellous dream. And where is the King? Perhaps this is he,—the sweating ploughman, tilling his eighty acres with two lean mules, and fighting a hard battle with debt. So we sit musing, until, as we turn a corner on the sandy road, there comes a fairer scene suddenly in view,—a neat cottage snugly ensconced by the road, and near it a little store. A tall bronzed man rises from the porch as we hail him, and comes out to our carriage. He is six feet in height, with a sober face that smiles gravely. He walks too straight to be a tenant,—yes, he owns two hundred and forty acres. "The land is run down since the boom-days of eighteen hundred and fifty," he explains, and cotton is low. Three black tenants live on his place, and in his little store he keeps a small stock of tobacco, snuff, soap, and soda, for the neighborhood. Here is his gin-house with new machinery just installed. Three hundred bales of cotton went through it last year. Two children he has sent away to school. Yes, he says sadly, he is getting on, but cotton is down to four cents; I know how Debt sits staring at him.

Wherever the King may be, the parks and palaces of the Cotton Kingdom have not wholly disappeared. We plunge even now into great groves of oak and towering pine, with an undergrowth of myrtle and shrubbery. This was the "home-house" of the Thompsons,—slave-barons who drove their coach and four in the merry past. All is silence now, and ashes, and tangled weeds. The owner put his whole fortune into the rising cotton industry of the fifties, and with the falling prices of the eighties he packed up and stole away. Yonder is another grove, with unkempt lawn, great magnolias, and grass-grown paths. The Big House stands in half-ruin, its great front door staring blankly at the street, and the back part grotesquely restored for its black tenant. A shabby, well-built Negro he is, unlucky and irresolute. He digs hard to pay rent to the white girl who owns the remnant of the place. She married a policeman, and lives in Savannah.

Now and again we come to churches. Here is one now,—Shepherd's, they call it,—a great whitewashed barn of a thing, perched on stilts of stone, and looking for all the world as though it were just resting here a moment and might be expected to waddle off down the road at almost any time. And yet it is the centre of a hundred cabin homes; and sometimes, of a Sunday, five hundred persons from far and near gather here and talk and eat and sing. There is a school-house near,—a very airy, empty shed; but even this is an improvement, for usually the school is held in the church. The churches vary from loghuts to those like Shepherd's, and the schools from nothing to this little house that sits demurely on the county line. It is a tiny plank-house, perhaps ten by twenty, and has within a double row of rough unplaned benches, resting mostly on legs, sometimes on boxes. Opposite the door is a square home-made desk. In one corner are the ruins of a stove, and in the other a dim blackboard. It is the cheerfulest schoolhouse I have seen in Dougherty, save in town. Back of the schoolhouse is a lodge-house two stories high and not quite finished. Societies meet there,—societies "to care for the sick and bury the dead"; and these societies grow and flourish.

We had come to the boundaries of Dougherty, and were about to turn west along the county-line, when all these sights were pointed out to us by a kindly old man, black, white-haired, and seventy. Forty-five years he had lived here, and now supports himself and his old wife by the help of the steer tethered yonder and the charity of his black neighbors. He shows us the farm of the Hills just across the county line in Baker,—a widow and two strapping sons, who raised ten bales (one need not add "cotton" down here) last year. There are fences and pigs and cows, and the soft-voiced, velvet-skinned young Memnon, who sauntered half-bashfully over to greet the strangers, is proud of his home. We turn now to the west along the county line. Great dismantled trunks of pines tower above the green cotton-fields, cracking their naked gnarled fingers toward the border of living forest beyond. There is little beauty in this region, only a sort of crude abandon that suggests power,—a naked grandeur, as it were. The houses are bare and straight; there are no hammocks or easy-chairs, and few flowers. So when, as here at Rawdon's, one sees a vine clinging to a little porch, and home-like windows peeping over the fences, one takes a long breath. I think I never before quite realized the place of the Fence in civilization. This is the Land of the Unfenced, where crouch on either hand scores of ugly one-room cabins, cheerless and dirty. Here lies the Negro problem in its naked dirt and penury. And here are no fences. But now and then the crisscross rails or straight palings break into view, and then we know a touch of culture is near. Of course Harrison Gohagen,—a quiet yellow man, young, smooth-faced, and diligent,—of course he is lord of some hundred acres, and we expect to see a vision of well-kept rooms and fat beds and laughing children. For has he not fine fences? And those over yonder, why should they build fences on the rack-rented land? It will only increase their rent.

On we wind, through sand and pines and glimpses of old plantations, till there creeps into sight a cluster of buildings,—wood and brick, mills and houses, and scattered cabins. It seemed quite a village. As it came nearer and nearer, however, the aspect changed: the buildings were rotten, the bricks were falling out, the mills were silent, and the store was closed. Only in the cabins appeared now and then a bit of lazy life. I could imagine the place under some weird spell, and was half-minded to search out the princess. An old ragged black man, honest, simple, and improvident, told us the tale. The Wizard of the North—the Capitalist—had rushed down in the seventies to woo this coy dark soil. He bought a square mile or more, and for a time the field-hands sang, the gins groaned, and the mills buzzed. Then came a change. The agent's son embezzled the funds and ran off with them. Then the agent himself disappeared. Finally the new agent stole even the books, and the company in wrath closed its business and its houses, refused to sell, and let houses and furniture and machinery rust and rot. So the Waters-Loring plantation was stilled by the spell of dishonesty, and stands like some gaunt rebuke to a scarred land.

Somehow that plantation ended our day's journey; for I could not shake off the influence of that silent scene. Back toward town we glided, past the straight and thread-like pines, past a dark tree-dotted pond where the air was heavy with a dead sweet perfume. White slender-legged curlews flitted by us, and the garnet blooms of the cotton looked gay against the green and purple stalks. A peasant girl was hoeing in the field, white-turbaned and black-limbed. All this we saw, but the spell still lay upon us.

How curious a land is this,—how full of untold story, of tragedy and laughter, and the rich legacy of human life; shadowed with a tragic past, and big with future promise! This is the Black Belt of Georgia. Dougherty County is the west end of the Black Belt, and men once called it the Egypt of the Confederacy. It is full of historic interest. First there is the Swamp, to the west, where the Chickasawhatchee flows sullenly southward. The shadow of an old plantation lies at its edge, forlorn and dark. Then comes the pool; pendent gray moss and brackish waters appear, and forests filled with wild-fowl. In one place the wood is on fire, smouldering in dull red anger; but nobody minds. Then the swamp grows beautiful; a raised road, built by chained Negro convicts, dips down into it, and forms a way walled and almost covered in living green. Spreading trees spring from a prodigal luxuriance of undergrowth; great dark green shadows fade into the black background, until all is one mass of tangled semi-tropical foliage, marvellous in its weird savage splendor. Once we crossed a black silent stream, where the sad trees and writhing creepers, all glinting fiery yellow and green, seemed like some vast cathedral,—some green Milan builded of wildwood. And as I crossed, I seemed to see again that fierce tragedy of seventy years ago. Osceola, the Indian-Negro chieftain, had risen in the swamps of Florida, vowing vengeance. His warcry reached the red Creeks of Dougherty, and their war-cry rang from the Chattahoochee to the sea. Men and women and children fled and fell before them as they swept into Dougherty. In yonder shadows a dark and hideously painted warrior glided stealthily on,—another and another, until three hundred had crept into the treacherous swamp. Then the false slime closing about them called the white men from the east. Waist-deep, they fought beneath the tall trees, until the war-cry was hushed and the Indians glided back into the west. Small wonder the wood is red.

Then came the black slaves. Day after day the clank of chained feet marching from Virginia and Carolina to Georgia was heard in these rich swamp lands. Day after day the songs of the callous, the wail of the motherless, and the muttered curses of the wretched echoed from the Flint to the Chickasawhatchee, until by 1860 there had risen in West Dougherty perhaps the richest slave kingdom the modern world ever knew. A hundred and fifty barons commanded the labor of nearly six thousand Negroes, held sway over farms with ninety thousand acres of tilled land, valued even in times of cheap soil at three millions of dollars. Twenty thousand bales of ginned cotton went yearly to England, New and Old; and men that came there bankrupt made money and grew rich. In a single decade the cotton output increased four-fold and the value of lands was tripled. It was the heyday of the *nouveau riche*, and a life of careless extravagance reigned among the masters. Four and six bob-tailed thoroughbreds rolled their coaches to town; open hospitality and gay entertainment were the rule. Parks and groves were laid out, rich with flower and vine, and in the midst stood the low wide-halled "big house," with its porch and columns and great fire-places.

And yet with all this there was something sordid, something forced,—a certain feverish unrest and recklessness; for was not all this show and tinsel built upon a groan? "This land was a little Hell," said a ragged, brown, and grave-faced man to me. We were seated near a roadside blacksmith-shop, and behind was the bare ruin of some master's home. "I've seen niggers drop dead in the furrow, but they were kicked aside, and the plough never stopped. And down in the guard-house, there's where the blood ran."

With such foundations a kingdom must in time sway and fall. The masters moved to Macon and Augusta, and left only the irresponsible overseers on the land. And the result is such ruin as this, the Lloyd "home-place":—great waving oaks, a spread of lawn, myrtles and chestnuts, all ragged and wild; a solitary gate-post standing where once was a castle entrance; an old rusty anvil lying amid rotting bellows and wood in the ruins of a blacksmith shop; a wide rambling old mansion, brown and dingy, filled now with the grandchildren of the slaves who once waited on its tables; while the family of the master has dwindled to two lone women, who live in Macon and feed hungrily off the remnants of an earldom. So we ride on, past phantom gates and falling homes,—past the once flourishing farms of the Smiths, the Gandys, and the Lagores,—and find all dilapidated and half ruined, even there where a solitary white woman, a relic of other days, sits alone in state among miles of Negroes and rides to town in her ancient coach each day.

This was indeed the Egypt of the Confederacy,—the rich granary whence potatoes and corn and cotton poured out to the famished and ragged Confederate troops as they battled for a cause lost long before 1861. Sheltered and secure, it became the place of refuge for families, wealth, and slaves. Yet even then the hard ruthless rape of the land began to tell. The red-clay sub-soil already had begun to peer above the loam. The harder the slaves were driven the more careless and fatal was their farming. Then came the revolution of war and Emancipation, the bewilderment of Reconstruction,—and now, what is the Egypt of the Confederacy, and what meaning has it for the nation's weal or woe?

It is a land of rapid contrasts and of curiously mingled hope and pain. Here sits a pretty blue-eyed quadroon hiding her bare feet; she was married only last week, and yonder in the field is her dark young husband, hoeing to support her, at thirty cents a day without board. Across the way is Gatesby, brown and tall, lord of two thousand acres shrewdly won and held. There is a store conducted by his black son, a blacksmith shop, and a ginnery. Five miles below here is a town owned and controlled by one white New Englander. He owns almost a Rhode Island county, with thousands of acres and hundreds of black laborers. Their cabins look better than most, and the farm, with machinery and fertilizers, is much more business-like than any in the county, although the manager drives hard bargains in wages. When now we turn and look five miles above, there on the edge of town are five houses of prostitutes,—two of blacks and three of whites; and in one of the houses of the whites a worthless black boy was harbored too openly two years ago; so he was hanged for rape. And here, too, is the high whitewashed fence of the "stockade," as the county prison is called; the white folks say it is ever full of black criminals,—the black folks say that only colored boys are sent to jail, and they not because they are guilty, but because the State needs criminals to eke out its income by their forced labor.

The Jew is the heir of the slave-baron in Dougherty; and as we ride westward, by wide stretching cornfields and stubby orchards of peach and pear, we see on all sides within the circle of dark forest a Land of Canaan. Here and there are tales of projects for money-getting, born in the swift days of Reconstruction,—"improvement" companies, wine companies, mills and factories; nearly all failed, and the Jew fell heir. It is a beautiful land, this Dougherty, west of the Flint. The forests are wonderful, the solemn pines have disappeared, and this is the "Oakey Woods," with its wealth of hickories, beeches, oaks, and palmettos. But a pall of debt hangs over the beautiful land; the merchants are in debt to the wholesalers, the planters are in debt to the merchants, the tenants owe the planters, and laborers bow and bend beneath the burden of it all. Here and there a man has raised his head above these murky waters. We passed one fenced stock-farm, with grass and grazing cattle, that looked very homelike after endless corn and cotton. Here and there are black freeholders: there is the gaunt dull-black Jackson, with his hundred acres. "I says, 'Look up! If you don't look up you can't get up,' " remarks Jackson, philosophically. And he's gotten up. Dark Carter's neat barns would do credit to New England. His master helped him to get a start, but when the black man died last fall the master's sons immediately laid claim to the estate. "And them white folks will get it, too," said my yellow gossip.

I turn from these well-tended acres with a comfortable feeling that the Negro is rising. Even then, however, the fields, as we proceed, begin to redden and the trees disappear. Rows of old cabins appear filled with renters and laborers,—cheerless, bare, and dirty, for the most part, although here and there the very age and decay makes the scene picturesque. A young black fellow greets us. He is twenty-two, and just married. Until last year he had good luck renting; then cotton fell, and the sheriff seized and sold all he had. So he moved here, where the rent is higher, the land poorer, and the owner inflexible; he rents a forty-dollar mule for twenty dollars a year. Poor lad!—a slave at twenty-two. This plantation, owned now by a Russian Jew, was a part of the famous Bolton estate. After the war it was for many years worked by gangs of Negro convicts,—and black convicts then were even more plentiful than now; it was a way of making Negroes work, and the question of guilt was a minor one. Hard tales of cruelty and mistreatment of the chained freemen are told but the county authorities were deaf until the free-labor market was nearly ruined by wholesale migration. Then they took the convicts from the plantations, but not until one of the fairest regions of the "Oakey Woods" had been ruined and ravished into a red waste, out of which only a Yankee or a Jew could squeeze more blood from debt-cursed tenants.

No wonder that Luke Black, slow, dull, and discouraged, shuffles to our carriage and talks hopelessly. Why should he strive? Every year finds him deeper in debt. How strange that Georgia, the world-heralded refuge of poor debtors, should bind her own to sloth and misfortune as ruthlessly as ever England did! The poor land groans with its birth-pains, and brings forth scarcely a hundred pounds of cotton to the acre, where fifty years ago it yielded eight times as much. Of this meagre yield the tenant pays from a quarter to a third in rent, and most of the rest in interest on food and supplies bought on credit. Twenty years yonder sunken-cheeked, old black man has labored under that system, and now, turned day-laborer, is supporting his wife and boarding himself on his wages of a dollar and a half a week, received only part of the year.

The Bolton convict farm formerly included the neighboring plantation. Here it was that the convicts were lodged in the great log prison still standing. A dismal place it still remains, with rows of ugly huts filled with surly ignorant tenants. "What rent do you pay here?" I inquired. "I don't know,—what is it, Sam?" "All we make," answered Sam. It is a depressing place,—bare, unshaded, with no charm of past association, only a memory of forced human toil,—now, then, and before the war. They are not happy, these black men whom we meet throughout this region. There is little of the joyous abandon and play-fulness which we are wont to associate with the plantation Negro. At best, the natural good-nature is edged with complaint or has changed into sullenness and gloom. And now and then it blazes forth in veiled but hot anger. I remember one big red-eyed black whom we met by the roadside. Forty-five years he had labored on this farm, beginning with nothing, and still having nothing. To be sure, he had given four children a common-school training, and perhaps if the new fence-law had not allowed unfenced crops in West Dougherty he might have raised a little stock and kept ahead. As it is, he is hopelessly in debt, disappointed, and embittered. He stopped us to inquire after the black boy in Albany, whom it was said a policeman had shot and killed for loud talking on the sidewalk. And then he said slowly: "Let a white man touch me, and he dies; I don't boast this,—I don't say it around loud, or before the children,—but I mean it. I've seen them whip my father and my old mother in them cotton-rows till the blood ran; by—" and we passed on.

Now Scars, whom we met next lolling under the chubby oak-trees, was of quite different fibre. Happy?—Well, yes; he laughed and flipped pebbles, and thought the world was as it was. He had worked here twelve years and has nothing but a mortgaged mule. Children? Yes, seven; but they hadn't been to school this year;—couldn't afford books and clothes, and couldn't spare their work. There go part of them to the fields now,—three big boys astride mules, and a strapping girl with bare brown legs. Careless ignorance and laziness here, fierce hate and vindictiveness there,—these are the extremes of the Negro problem which we met that day, and we scarce knew which we preferred.

Here and there we meet distinct characters quite out of the ordinary. One came out of a piece of newly cleared ground, making a wide detour to avoid the snakes. He was an old, hollow-cheeked man, with a drawn and characterful brown face. He had a sort of self-contained quaintness and rough humor impossible to describe; a certain cynical earnestness that puzzled one. "The niggers were jealous of me over on the other place," he said, "and so me and the old woman begged this piece of woods, and I cleared it up myself. Made nothing for two years, but I reckon I've got a crop now." The cotton looked tall and rich, and we praised it. He curtsied low, and then bowed almost to the ground, with an imperturbable gravity that seemed almost suspicious. Then he continued, "My mule died last week,"—a calamity in this land equal to a devastating fire in town,—"but a white man loaned me another." Then he added, eyeing us, "Oh, I gets along with white folks." We turned the conversation. "Bears? deer?" he answered, "well, I should say there were," and he let fly a string of brave oaths, as he told hunting-tales of the swamp. We left him standing still in the middle of the road looking after us, and yet apparently not noticing us.

The Whistle place, which includes his bit of land, was bought soon after the war by an English syndicate, the "Dixie Cotton and Corn Company." A marvellous deal of style their factor put on, with his servants and coach-and-six; so much so that the concern soon landed in inextricable bankruptcy. Nobody lives in the old house now, but a man comes each winter out of the North and collects his high rents. I know not which are the more touching,—such old empty houses, or the homes of the masters' sons. Sad and bitter tales lie hidden back of those white doors,—tales of poverty, of struggle, of disappointment. A revolution such as that of '63 is a terrible thing; they that rose rich in the morning often slept in paupers' beds. Beggars and vulgar speculators rose to rule over them, and their children went astray. See yonder sad-colored house, with its cabins and fences and glad crops? It is not glad within; last month the prodigal son of the struggling father wrote home from the city for money. Money! Where was it to come from? And so the son rose in the night and killed his baby, and killed his wife, and shot himself dead. And the world passed on.

I remember wheeling around a bend in the road beside a graceful bit of forest and a singing brook. A long low house faced us, with porch and flying pillars, great oaken door, and a broad lawn shining in the evening sun. But the window-panes were gone, the pillars were worm-eaten, and the moss-grown roof was falling in. Half curiously I peered through the unhinged door, and saw where, on the wall across the hall, was written in once gay letters a faded "Welcome."

Quite a contrast to the southwestern part of Dougherty County is the northwest. Soberly timbered in oak and pine, it has none of that half-tropical luxuriance of the southwest. Then, too, there are fewer signs of a romantic past, and more of systematic modern land-grabbing and money-getting. White people are more in evidence here, and farmer and hired labor replace to some extent the absentee landlord and rack-rented tenant. The crops have neither the luxuriance of the richer land nor the signs of neglect so often seen, and there were fences and meadows here and there. More of this land was poor, and beneath the notice of the slave-baron, before the war. Since then his nephews and the poor whites and the Jews have seized it. The returns of the farmer are too small to allow much for wages, and yet he will not sell off small farms. There is the Negro Sanford; he has worked fourteen years as overseer on the Ladson place, and "paid out enough for fertilizers to have bought a farm," but the owner will not sell off a few acres.

Two children—a boy and a girl—are hoeing sturdily in the fields on the farm where Corliss works. He is smooth-faced and brown, and is fencing up his pigs. He used to run a successful cotton-gin, but the Cotton Seed Oil Trust has forced the price of ginning so low that he says it hardly pays him. He points out a stately old house over the way as the home of "Pa Willis." We eagerly ride over, for "Pa Willis" was the tall and powerful black Moses who led the Negroes for a generation, and led them well. He was a Baptist preacher, and when he died two thousand black people followed him to the grave; and now they preach his funeral sermon each year. His widow lives here,—a weazened, sharp-featured little woman, who curtsied quaintly as we greeted her. Further on lives Jack Delson, the most prosperous Negro farmer in the county. It is a joy to meet him,—a great broad-shouldered, handsome black man, intelligent and jovial. Six hundred and fifty acres he owns, and has eleven black tenants. A neat and tidy home nestled in a flower-garden, and a little store stands beside it.

We pass the Munson place, where a plucky white widow is renting and struggling; and the eleven hundred acres of the Sennet plantation, with its Negro overseer. Then the character of the farms begins to change. Nearly all the lands belong to Russian Jews; the overseers are white, and the cabins are bare board-houses scattered here and there. The rents are high, and day-laborers and "contract" hands abound. It is a keen, hard struggle for living here, and few have time to talk. Tired with the long ride, we gladly drive into Gillonsville. It is a silent cluster of farm-houses standing on the cross-roads, with one of its stores closed and the other kept by a Negro preacher. They tell great tales of busy times at Gillonsville before all the railroads came to Albany; now it is chiefly a memory. Riding down the street, we stop at the preacher's and seat ourselves before the door. It was one of those scenes one cannot soon forget:—a wide, low, little house, whose motherly roof reached over and sheltered a snug little porch. There we sat, after the long hot drive, drinking cool water,—the talkative little store-keeper who is my daily companion; the silent old black woman patching pantaloons and saying never a word; the ragged picture of helpless misfortune who called in just to see the preacher; and finally the neat matronly preacher's wife, plump, yellow, and intelligent. "Own land?" said the wife; "well, only this house." Then she added quietly, "We did buy seven hundred acres up yonder, and paid for it; but they cheated us out of it. Sells was the owner." "Sells!" echoed the ragged misfortune, who was leaning against the balustrade and listening, "he's a regular cheat. I worked for him thirty-seven days this spring, and he paid me in cardboard checks which were to be cashed at the end of the month. But he never cashed them,—kept putting me off. Then the sheriff came and took my mule and corn and furniture—" "Furniture?" I asked; "but furniture is exempt from seizure by law." "Well, he took it just the same," said the hard-faced man.

CHAPTER **VIII**

Of the Quest of the Golden Fleece

But the Brute said in his breast, "Till the mills I grind have ceased,
The riches shall be dust of dust, dry ashes be the feast!

   "On the strong and cunning few
   Cynic favors I will strew;
I will stuff their maw with overplus until their spirit dies;
   From the patient and the low
   I will take the joys they know;
   They shall hunger after vanities and still an-hungered go.
Madness shall be on the people, ghastly jealousies arise;
Brother's blood shall cry on brother up the dead and empty skies."

William Vaughn Moody

Have you ever seen a cotton-field white with the harvest,—its golden fleece hovering above the black earth like a silvery cloud edged with dark green, its bold white signals waving like the foam of billows from Carolina to Texas across that Black and human Sea? I have sometimes half suspected that here the winged ram Chrysomallus left that Fleece after which Jason and his Argonauts went vaguely wandering into the shadowy East three thousand years ago; and certainly one might frame a pretty and not far-fetched analogy of witchery and dragon's teeth, and blood and armed men, between the ancient and the modern Quest of the Golden Fleece in the Black Sea.

And now the golden fleece is found; not only found, but, in its birthplace, woven. For the hum of the cotton-mills is the newest and most significant thing in the New South today. All through the Carolinas and Georgia, away down to Mexico, rise these gaunt red buildings, bare and homely, and yet so busy and noisy withal that they scarce seem to belong to the slow and sleepy land. Perhaps they sprang from dragons' teeth. So the Cotton Kingdom still lives; the world still bows beneath her sceptre. Even the markets that once defied the *parvenu* have crept one by one across the seas, and then slowly and reluctantly, but surely, have started toward the Black Belt.

To be sure, there are those who wag their heads knowingly and tell us that the capital of the Cotton Kingdom has moved from the Black to the White Belt,—that the Negro of to-day raises not more than half of the cotton crop. Such men forget that the cotton crop has doubled, and more than doubled, since the era of slavery, and that, even granting their contention, the Negro is still supreme in a Cotton Kingdom larger than that on which the Confederacy builded its hopes. So the Negro forms to-day one of the chief figures in a great world-industry; and this, for its own sake, and in the light of historic interest, makes the field-hands of the cotton country worth studying.

We seldom study the condition of the Negro to-day honestly and carefully. It is so much easier to assume that we know it all. Or perhaps, having already reached conclusions in our own minds, we are loth to have them disturbed by facts. And yet how little we really know of these millions,—of their daily lives and longings, of their homely joys and sorrows, of their real shortcomings and the meaning of their crimes! All this we can only learn by intimate contact with the masses, and not by wholesale arguments covering millions separate in time and space, and differing widely in training and culture. To-day, then, my reader, let us turn our faces to the Black Belt of Georgia and seek simply to know the condition of the black farm-laborers of one county there.

Here in 1890 lived ten thousand Negroes and two thousand whites. The country is rich, yet the people are poor. The keynote of the Black Belt is debt; not commercial credit, but debt in the sense of continued inability on the part of the mass of the population to make income cover expense. This is the direct heritage of the South from the wasteful economies of the slave *régime;* but it was emphasized and brought to a crisis by the Emancipation of the slaves. In 1860, Dougherty County had six thousand slaves, worth at least two and a half millions of dollars; its farms were estimated at three millions,—making five and a half millions of property, the value of which depended largely on the slave system, and on the speculative demand for land once marvellously rich but already partially devitalized by careless and exhaustive culture. The war then meant a financial crash; in place of the five and a half millions of 1860, there remained in 1870 only farms valued at less than two millions. With this came increased competition in cotton culture from the rich lands of Texas; a steady fall in the normal price of cotton followed, from about fourteen cents a pound in 1860 until it reached four cents in 1898. Such a financial revolution was it that involved the owners of the cotton-belt in debt. And if things went ill with the master, how fared it with the man?

The plantations of Dougherty County in slavery days were not as imposing and aristocratic as those of Virginia. The Big House was smaller and usually one-storied, and sat very near the slave cabins. Sometimes these cabins stretched off on either side like wings; sometimes only on one side, forming a double row, or edging the road that turned into the plantation from the main thoroughfare. The form and disposition of the laborers' cabins throughout the Black Belt is to-day the same as in slavery days. Some live in the self-same cabins, others in cabins rebuilt on the sites of the old. All are sprinkled in little groups over the face of the land, centering about some dilapidated Big House where the head-tenant or agent lives. The general character and arrangement of these dwellings remains on the whole unaltered. There were in the county, outside the corporate town of Albany, about fifteen hundred Negro families in 1898. Out of all these, only a single family occupied a house with seven rooms; only fourteen have five rooms or more. The mass live in one- and two-room homes.

The size and arrangements of a people's homes are no unfair index of their condition. If, then, we inquire more carefully into these Negro homes, we find much that is unsatisfactory. All over the face of the land is the one-room cabin—now standing in the shadow of the Big House, now staring at the dusty road, now rising dark and sombre amid the green of the cotton-fields. It is nearly always old and bare, built of rough boards, and neither plastered nor ceiled. Light and ventilation are supplied by the single door and by the square hole in the wall with its wooden shutter. There is no glass, porch, or oramentation without. Within is a fireplace, black and smoky, and usually unsteady with age. A bed or two, a table, a wooden chest, and a few chairs compose the furniture; while a stray show-bill or a newspaper makes up the decorations for the walls. Now and then one may find such a cabin kept scrupulously neat, with merry steaming fireplace and hospitable door; but the majority are dirty and dilapidated, smelling of eating and sleeping, poorly ventilated, and anything but homes.

Above all, the cabins are crowded. We have come to associate crowding with homes in cities almost exclusively. This is primarily because we have so little accurate knowledge of country life. Here in Dougherty County one may find families of eight and ten occupying one or two rooms, and for every ten rooms of house accommodation for the Negroes there are twenty-five persons. The worst tenement abominations of New York do not have above twenty-two persons for every ten rooms. Of course, one small, close room in a city, without a yard, is in many respects worse than the larger single country room. In other respects it is better; it has glass windows, a decent chimney, and a trustworthy floor. The single great advantage of the Negro peasant is that he may spend most of his life outside his hovel, in the open fields.

There are four chief causes of these wretched homes: First, long custom born of slavery has assigned such homes to Negroes; white laborers would be offered better accommodations, and might, for that and similar reasons, give better work. Secondly, the Negroes, used to such accommodations, do not as a rule demand better; they do not know what better houses mean. Thirdly, the landlords as a class have not yet come to realize that it is a good business investment to raise the standard of living among labor by slow and judicious methods; that a Negro laborer who demands three rooms and fifty cents a day would give more efficient work and leave a larger profit than a discouraged toiler herding his family in one room and working for thirty cents. Lastly, among such conditions of life there are few incentives to make the laborer become a better farmer. If he is ambitious, he moves to town or tries other labor; as a tenant-farmer his outlook is almost hopeless, and following it as a makeshift, he takes the house that is given him without protest.

In such homes, then, these Negro peasants live. The families are both small and large; there are many single tenants,—widows and bachelors, and remnants of broken groups. The system of labor and the size of the houses both tend to the breaking up of family groups: The grown children go away as contract hands or migrate to town, the sister goes into service; and so one finds many families with hosts of babies, and many newly married couples, but comparatively few families with half-grown and grown sons and daughters. The average size of Negro families has undoubtedly decreased since the war, primarily from economic stress. In Russia over a third of the bridegrooms and over half the brides are under twenty; the same was true of the antebellum Negroes. To-day, however, very few of the boys and less than a fifth of the Negro girls under twenty are married. The young men marry between the ages of twenty-five and thirty-five; the young women between twenty and thirty. Such postponement is due to the difficulty of earning sufficient to rear and support a family; and it undoubtedly leads, in the country districts, to sexual immorality. The form of this immorality, however, is very seldom that of prostitution, and less frequently that of illegitimacy than one would imagine. Rather, it takes the form of separation and desertion after a family group has been formed. The number of separated persons is thirty-five to the thousand,—a very large number. It would of course be unfair to compare this number with divorce statistics, for many of these separated women are in reality widowed, were the truth known, and in other cases the separation is not permanent. Nevertheless, here lies the seat of greatest moral danger. There is little or no prostitution among these Negroes, and over three-fourths of the families, as found by house-to-house investigation, deserve to be classed as decent people with considerable regard for female chastity. To be sure, the ideas of the mass would not suit New England, and there are many loose habits and notions. Yet the rate of illegitimacy is undoubtedly lower than in Austria or Italy, and the women as a class are modest. The plague-spot in sexual relations is easy marriage and easy separation. This is no sudden development, nor the fruit of Emancipation. It is the plain heritage from slavery. In those days Sam, with his master's consent, "took up" with Mary. No ceremony was necessary, and in the busy life of the great plantations of the Black Belt it was usually dispensed with. If now the master needed Sam's work in another plantation or in another part of the same plantation, or if he took a notion to sell the slave, Sam's married life with Mary was usually unceremoniously broken, and then it was clearly to the master's interest to have both of them take new mates. This widespread custom of two centuries has not been eradicated in thirty years. To-day Sam's grandson "takes up" with a woman without license or ceremony; they live together decently and honestly, and are, to all intents and purposes, man and wife. Sometimes these unions are never broken until death; but in too many cases family quarrels, a roving spirit, a rival suitor, or perhaps more frequently the hopeless battle to support a family, lead to separation, and a broken household is the result. The Negro church has done much to stop this practice, and now most marriage ceremonies are performed by the pastors. Nevertheless, the evil is still deep seated, and only a general raising of the standard of living will finally cure it.

Looking now at the county black population as a whole, it is fair to characterize it as poor and ignorant. Perhaps ten per cent compose the well-to-do and the best of the laborers, while at least nine per cent are thoroughly lewd and vicious. The rest, over eighty per cent, are poor and ignorant, fairly honest and well meaning, plodding, and to a degree shiftless, with some but not great sexual looseness. Such class lines are by no means fixed; they vary, one might almost say, with the price of cotton. The degree of ignorance cannot easily be expressed. We may say, for instance, that nearly two-thirds of them cannot read or write. This but partially expresses the fact. They are ignorant of the world about them, of modern economic organization, of the function of government, of individual worth and possibilities,—of nearly all those things which slavery in self-defence had to keep them from learning. Much that the white boy imbibes from his earliest social atmosphere forms the puzzling problems of the black boy's mature years. America is not another word for Opportunity to *all* her sons.

It is easy for us to lose ourselves in details in endeavoring to grasp and comprehend the real condition of a mass of human beings. We often forget that each unit in the mass is a throbbing human soul. Ignorant it may be, and poverty stricken, black and curious in limb and ways and thought; and yet it loves and hates, it toils and tires, it laughs and weeps its bitter tears, and looks in vague and awful longing at the grim horizon of its life,—all this, even as you and I. These black thousands are not in reality lazy; they are improvident and careless; they insist on breaking the monotony of toil with a glimpse at the great town-world on Saturday; they have their loafers and their rascals; but the great mass of them work continuously and faithfully for a return, and under circumstances that would call forth equal voluntary effort from few if any other modern laboring class. Over eighty-eight per cent of them—men, women, and children—are farmers. Indeed, this is almost the only industry. Most of the children get their schooling after the "crops are laid by," and very few there are that stay in school after the spring work has begun. Child-labor is to be found here in some of its worst phases, as fostering ignorance and stunting physical development. With the grown men of the county there is little variety in work: thirteen hundred are farmers, and two hundred are laborers, teamsters, etc., including twenty-four artisans, ten merchants, twenty-one preachers, and four teachers. This narrowness of life reaches its maximum among the women: thirteen hundred and fifty of these are farm laborers, one hundred are servants and washerwomen, leaving sixty-five housewives, eight teachers, and six seamstresses.

Among this people there is no leisure class. We often forget that in the United States over half the young and adults are not in the world earning incomes, but are making homes, learning of the world, or resting after the heat of the strife. But here ninety-six per cent are toiling; no one with leisure to turn the bare and cheerless cabin into a home, no old folks to sit beside the fire and hand down traditions of the past; little of careless happy childhood and dreaming youth. The dull monotony of daily toil is broken only by the gayety of the thoughtless and the Saturday trip to town. The toil, like all farm toil, is monotonous, and here there are little machinery and few tools to relieve its burdensome drudgery. But with all this, it is work in the pure open air, and this is something in a day when fresh air is scarce.

The land on the whole is still fertile, despite long abuse. For nine or ten months in succession the crops will come if asked: garden vegetables in April, grain in May, melons in June and July, hay in August, sweet potatoes in September, and cotton from then to Christmas. And yet on two-thirds of the land there is but one crop, and that leaves the toilers in debt. Why is this?

Away down the Baysan Road, where the broad flat fields are flanked by great oak forests, is a plantation; many thousands of acres it used to run, here and there, and beyond the great wood. Thirteen hundred human beings here obeyed the call of one,—were his in body, and largely in soul. One of them lives there yet,—a short, stocky man, his dull-brown face seamed and drawn, and his tightly curled hair gray-white. The crops? Just tolerable, he said; just tolerable. Getting on? No—he wasn't getting on at all. Smith of Albany "furnishes" him, and his rent is eight hundred pounds of cotton. Can't make anything at that. Why didn't he buy land? *Humph!* Takes money to buy land. And he turns away. Free! The most piteous thing amid all the black ruin of war-time, amid the broken fortunes of the masters, the blighted hopes of mothers and maidens, and the fall of an empire,—the most piteous thing amid all this was the black freedman who threw down his hoe because the world called him free. What did such a mockery of freedom mean? Not a cent of money, not an inch of land, not a mouthful of victuals,—not even ownership of the rags on his back. Free! On Saturday, once or twice a month, the old master, before the war, used to dole out bacon and meal to his Negroes. And after the first flush of freedom wore off, and his true helplessness dawned on the freedman, he came and picked up his hoe, and old master still doled out his bacon and meal. The legal form of service was theoretically far different; in practice, task-work or "cropping" was substituted for daily toil in gangs; and the slave gradually became a metayer, or tenant on shares, in name, but a laborer with indeterminate wages in fact.

Still the price of cotton fell, and gradually the landlords deserted their plantations, and the reign of the merchant began. The merchant of the Black Belt is a curious institution,—part banker, part landlord, part contractor, and part despot. His store, which used most frequently to stand at the crossroads and become the centre of a weekly village, has now moved to town; and thither the Negro tenant follows him. The merchant keeps everything,—clothes and shoes, coffee and sugar, pork and meal, canned and dried goods, wagons and ploughs, seed and fertilizer,—and what he has not in stock he can give you an order for at the store across the way. Here, then, comes the tenant, Sam Scott, after he has contracted with some absent landlord's agent for hiring forty acres of land; he fingers his hat nervously until the merchant finishes his morning chat with Colonel Sanders, and calls out, "Well, Sam, what do you want?" Sam wants him to "furnish" him,— *i.e.,* to advance him food and clothing for the year, and perhaps seed and tools, until his crop is raised and sold. If Sam seems a favorable subject, he and the merchant go to a lawyer, and Sam executes a chattel mortgage on his mule and wagon in return for seed and a week's rations. As soon as the green cotton-leaves appear above the ground, another mortgage is given on the "crop." Every Saturday, or at longer intervals, Sam calls upon the merchant for his "rations"; a family of five usually gets about thirty pounds of fat side-pork and a couple of bushels of corn-meal a month. Besides this, clothing and shoes must be furnished; if Sam or his family is sick, there are orders on the druggist and doctor; if the mule wants shoeing, an order on the blacksmith, etc. If Sam is a hard worker and crops promise well, he is often encouraged to buy more,—sugar, extra clothes, perhaps a buggy. But he is seldom encouraged to save. When cotton rose to ten cents last fall, the shrewd merchants of Dougherty County sold a thousand buggies in one season, mostly to black men.

The security offered for such transactions—a crop and chattel mortgage—may at first seem slight. And, indeed, the merchants tell many a true tale of shiftlessness and cheating; of cotton picked at night, mules disappearing, and tenants absconding. But on the whole the merchant of the Black Belt is the most prosperous man in the section. So skilfully and so closely has he drawn the bonds of the law about the tenant, that the black man has often simply to choose between pauperism and crime; he "waives" all homestead exemptions in his contract; he cannot touch his own mortgaged crop, which the laws put almost in the full control of the land-owner and of the merchant. When the crop is growing the merchant watches it like a hawk; as soon as it is ready for market he takes possession of it, sells it, pays the land-owner his rent, subtracts his bill for supplies, and if, as sometimes happens, there is anything left, he hands it over to the black serf for his Christmas celebration.

The direct result of this system is an all-cotton scheme of agriculture and the continued bankruptcy of the tenant. The currency of the Black Belt is cotton. It is a crop always salable for ready money, not usually subject to great yearly fluctuations in price, and one which the Negroes know how to raise. The landlord therefore demands his rent in cotton, and the merchant will accept mortgages on no other crop. There is no use asking the black tenant, then, to diversify his crops,— he cannot under this system. Moreover, the system is bound to bankrupt the tenant. I remember once meeting a little one-mule wagon on the River road. A young black fellow sat in it driving listlessly, his elbows on his knees. His dark-faced wife sat beside him, stolid, silent.

"Hello!" cried my driver,—he has a most impudent way of addressing these people, though they seem used to it,—"what have you got there?"

"Meat and meal," answered the man, stopping. The meat lay uncovered in the bottom of the wagon,—a great thin side of fat pork covered with salt; the meal was in a white bushel bag.

"What did you pay for that meat?"

"Ten cents a pound." It could have been bought for six or seven cents cash.

"And the meal?"

"Two dollars." One dollar and ten cents is the cash price in town. Here was a man paying five dollars for goods which he could have bought for three dollars cash, and raised for one dollar or one dollar and a half.

Yet it is not wholly his fault. The Negro farmer started behind,— started in debt. This was not his choosing, but the crime of this happy-go-lucky nation which goes blundering along with its Reconstruction tragedies, its Spanish war interludes and Philippine matinees, just as though God really were dead. Once in debt, it is no easy matter for a whole race to emerge.

In the year of low-priced cotton, 1898, out of three hundred tenant families one hundred and seventy-five ended their year's work in debt to the extent of fourteen thousand dollars; fifty cleared nothing, and the remaining seventy-five made a total profit of sixteen hundred dollars. The net indebtedness of the black tenant families of the whole county must have been at least sixty thousand dollars. In a more prosperous year the situation is far better; but on the average the majority of tenants end the year even, or in debt, which means that they work for board and clothes. Such an economic organization is radically wrong. Whose is the blame?

The underlying causes of this situation are complicated but discernible. And one of the chief, outside the carelessness of the nation in letting the slave start with nothing, is the widespread opinion among the merchants and employers of the Black Belt that only by the slavery of debt can the Negro be kept at work. Without doubt, some pressure was necessary at the beginning of the free-labor system to keep the listless and lazy at work; and even to-day the mass of the Negro laborers need stricter guardianship than most Northern laborers. Behind this honest and widespread opinion dishonesty and cheating of the ignorant laborers have a good chance to take refuge. And to all this must be added the obvious fact that a slave ancestry and a system of unrequited toil has not improved the efficiency or temper of the mass of black laborers. Nor is this peculiar to Sambo; it has in history been just as true of John and Hans, of Jacques and Pat, of all ground-down peasantries. Such is the situation of the mass of the Negroes in the Black Belt to-day; and they are thinking about it. Crime, and a cheap and dangerous socialism, are the inevitable results of this pondering. I see now that ragged black man sitting on a log, aimlessly whittling a stick. He muttered to me with the murmur of many ages, when he said: "White man sit down whole year; Nigger work day and night and make crop; Nigger hardly gits bread and meat; white man sittin' down gits all. *It's wrong.*" And what do the better classes of Negroes do to improve their situation? One of two things: if any way possible, they buy land; if not, they migrate to town. Just as centuries ago it was no easy thing for the serf to escape into the freedom of townlife, even so to-day there are hindrances laid in the way of county laborers. In considerable parts of all the Gulf States, and especially in Mississippi, Louisiana, and Arkansas, the Negroes on the plantations in the back-country districts are still held at forced labor practically without wages. Especially is this true in districts where the farmers are composed of the more ignorant class of poor whites, and the Negroes are beyond the reach of schools and intercourse with their advancing fellows. If such a peon should run away, the sheriff, elected by white suffrage, can usually be depended on to catch the fugitive, return him, and ask no questions. If he escape to another county, a charge of petty thieving, easily true, can be depended upon to secure his return. Even if some unduly officious person insist upon a trial, neighborly comity will probably make his conviction sure, and then the labor due the county can easily be bought by the master. Such a system is impossible in the more civilized parts of the South, or near the large towns and cities; but in those vast stretches of land beyond the telegraph and the newspaper the spirit of the Thirteenth Amendment is sadly broken. This represents the lowest economic depths of the black American peasant; and in a study of the rise and condition of the Negro freeholder we must trace his economic progress from this modern serfdom.

Even in the better-ordered country districts of the South the free movement of agricultural laborers is hindered by the migration-agent laws. The "Associated Press" recently informed the world of the arrest of a young white man in Southern Georgia who represented the "Atlantic Naval Supplies Company," and who "was caught in the act of enticing hands from the turpentine farm of Mr. John Greer." The crime for which this young man was arrested is taxed five hundred dollars for each county in which the employment agent proposes to gather laborers for work outside the State. Thus the Negroes' ignorance of the labor-market outside his own vicinity is increased rather than diminished by the laws of nearly every Southern State.

Similar to such measures is the unwritten law of the back districts and small towns of the South, that the character of all Negroes unknown to the mass of the community must be vouched for by some white man. This is really a revival of the old Roman idea of the patron under whose protection the new-made freedman was put. In many instances this system has been of great good to the Negro, and very often under the protection and guidance of the former master's family, or other white friends, the freedman progressed in wealth and morality. But the same system has in other cases resulted in the refusal of whole communities to recognize the right of a Negro to change his habitation and to be master of his own fortunes. A black stranger in Baker County, Georgia, for instance, is liable to be stopped anywhere on the public highway and made to state his business to the satisfaction of any white interrogator. If he fails to give a suitable answer, or seems too independent or "sassy," he may be arrested or summarily driven away.

Thus it is that in the country districts of the South, by written or unwritten law, peonage, hindrances to the migration of labor, and a system of white patronage exists over large areas. Besides this, the chance for lawless oppression and illegal exactions is vastly greater in the country than in the city, and nearly all the more serious race disturbances of the last decade have arisen from disputes in the county between master and man,—as, for instance, the Sam Hose affair. As a result of such a situation, there arose, first, the Black Belt; and, second, the Migration to Town. The Black Belt was not, as many assumed, a movement toward fields of labor under more genial climatic conditions; it was primarily a huddling for self-protection,—a massing of the black population for mutual defence in order to secure the peace and tranquillity necessary to economic advance. This movement took place between Emancipation and 1880, and only partially accomplished the desired results. The rush to town since 1880 is the counter-movement of men disappointed in the economic opportunities of the Black Belt.

In Dougherty County, Georgia, one can see easily the results of this experiment in huddling for protection. Only ten per cent of the adult population was born in the county, and yet the blacks outnumber the whites four or five to one. There is undoubtedly a security to the blacks in their very numbers,—a personal freedom from arbitrary treatment, which makes hundreds of laborers cling to Dougherty in spite of low wages and economic distress. But a change is coming, and slowly but surely even here the agricultural laborers are drifting to town and leaving the broad acres behind. Why is this? Why do not the Negroes become land-owners, and build up the black landed peasantry, which has for a generation and more been the dream of philanthropist and statesman?

To the car-window sociologist, to the man who seeks to understand and know the South by devoting the few leisure hours of a holiday trip to unravelling the snarl of centuries,—to such men very often the whole trouble with the black fieldhand may be summed up by Aunt Ophelia's word, "Shiftless!" They have noted repeatedly scenes like one I saw last summer. We were riding along the highroad to town at the close of a long hot day. A couple of young black fellows passed us in a mule-team, with several bushels of loose corn in the ear. One was driving, listlessly bent forward, his elbows on his knees,—a happy-go-lucky, careless picture of irresponsibility. The other was fast asleep in the bottom of the wagon. As we passed we notice an ear of corn fall from the wagon. They never saw it,—not they. A rod farther on we noted another ear on the ground; and between that creeping mule and town we counted twenty-six ears of corn. Shiftless? Yes, the personification of shiftlessness. And yet follow those boys: they are not lazy; to-morrow morning they'll be up with the sun; they work hard when they do work, and they work willingly. They have no sordid, selfish, money-getting ways, but rather a fine disdain for mere cash. They'll loaf before your face and work behind your back with good-natured honesty. They'll steal a watermelon, and hand you back your lost purse intact. Their great defect as laborers lies in their lack of incentive to work beyond the mere pleasure of physical exertion. They are careless because they have not found that it pays to be careful; they are improvident because the improvident ones of their acquaintance get on about as well as the provident. Above all, they cannot see why they should take unusual pains to make the white man's land better, or to fatten his mule, or save his corn. On the other hand, the white land-owner argues that any attempt to improve these laborers by increased responsibility, or higher wages, or better homes, or land of their own, would be sure to result in failure. He shows his Northern visitor the scarred and wretched land; the ruined mansions, the worn-out soil and mortgaged acres, and says, This is Negro freedom!

Now it happens that both master and man have just enough argument on their respective sides to make it difficult for them to understand each other. The Negro dimly personifies in the white man all his ills and misfortunes; if he is poor, it is because the white man seizes the fruit of his toil; if he is ignorant, it is because the white man gives him neither time or facilities to learn; and, indeed, if any misfortune happens to him, it is because of some hidden machinations of "white folks." On the other hand, the masters and the masters' sons have never been able to see why the Negro, instead of settling down to be day-laborers for bread and clothes, are infected with a silly desire to rise in the world, and why they are sulky, dissatisfied, and careless, where their fathers were happy and dumb and faithful. "Why, you niggers have an easier time than I do," said a puzzled Albany merchant to his black customer. "Yes," he replied, "and so does yo' hogs."

Taking, then, the dissatisfied and shiftless field-hand as a starting-point, let us inquire how the black thousands of Dougherty have struggled from him up toward their ideal, and what that ideal is. All social struggle is evidenced by the rise, first of economic, then of social classes, among a homogeneous population. To-day the following economic classes are plainly differentiated among these Negroes.

A "submerged tenth" of croppers, with a few paupers; forty per cent who are metayers and thirty-nine per cent of semi-metayers and wage-laborers. There are left five per cent of money-renters and six per cent of freeholders,—the "Upper Ten" of the land. The croppers are entirely without capital, even in the limited sense of food or money to keep them from seed-time to harvest. All they furnish is their labor; the land-owner furnishes land, stock, tools, seed, and house; and at the end of the year the laborer gets from a third to a half of the crop. Out of his share, however, comes pay and interest for food and clothing advanced him during the year. Thus we have a laborer without capital and without wages, and an employer whose capital is largely his employees' wages. It is an unsatisfactory arrangement, both for hirer and hired, and is usually in vogue on poor land with hard-pressed owners.

Above the croppers come the great mass of the black population who work the land on their own responsibility, paying rent in cotton and supported by the crop-mortgage system. After the war this system was attractive to the freedmen on account of its larger freedom and its possibilities for making a surplus. But with the carrying out of the crop-lien system, the deterioration of the land, and the slavery of debt, the position of the metayers has sunk to a dead level of practically unrewarded toil. Formerly all tenants had some capital, and often considerable; but absentee landlordism, rising rack-rent, and falling cotton have stripped them well-nigh of all, and probably not over half of them today own their mules. The change from cropper to tenant was accomplished by fixing the rent. If, now, the rent fixed was reasonable, this was an incentive to the tenant to strive. On the other hand, if the rent was too high, or if the land deteriorated, the result was to discourage and check the efforts of the black peasantry. There is no doubt that the latter case is true; that in Dougherty County every economic advantage of the price of cotton in market and of the strivings of the tenant has been taken advantage of by the landlords and merchants, and swallowed up in rent and interest. If cotton rose in price, the rent rose even higher; if cotton fell, the rent remained or followed reluctantly. If a tenant worked hard and raised a large crop, his rent was raised the next year; if that year the crop failed, his corn was confiscated and his mule sold for debt. There were, of course, exceptions to this,—cases of personal kindness and forbearance; but in the vast majority of cases the rule was to extract the uttermost farthing from the mass of the black farm laborers.

The average metayer pays from twenty to thirty per cent of his crop in rent. The result of such rack-rent can only be evil,—abuse and neglect of the soil, deterioration in the character of the laborers, and a widespread sense of injustice. "Wherever the country is poor," cried Arthur Young, "it is in the hands of metayers," and "their condition is more wretched than that of day-laborers." He was talking of Italy a century ago; but he might have been talking of Dougherty County today. And especially is that true to-day which he declares was true in France before the Revolution: "The metayers are considered as little better than menial servants, removable at pleasure, and obliged to conform in all things to the will of the landlords." On this low plane half the black population of Dougherty County—perhaps more than half the black millions of this land—are to-day struggling.

A degree above these we may place those laborers who receive money wages for their work. Some receive a house with perhaps a garden-spot; then supplies of food and clothing are advanced, and certain fixed wages are given at the end of the year, varying from thirty to sixty dollars, out of which the supplies must be paid for, with interest. About eighteen per cent of the population belong to this class of semi-metayers, while twenty-two per cent are laborers paid by the month or year, and are either "furnished" by their own savings or perhaps more usually by some merchant who takes his chances of payment. Such laborers receive from thirty-five to fifty cents a day during the working season. They are usually young unmarried persons, some being women; and when they marry they sink to the class of metayers, or, more seldom, become renters.

The renters for fixed money rentals are the first of the emerging classes, and form five per cent of the families. The sole advantage of this small class is their freedom to choose their crops, and the increased responsibility which comes through having money transactions. While some of the renters differ little in condition from the metayers, yet on the whole they are more intelligent and responsible persons, and are the ones who eventually become land-owners. Their better character and greater shrewdness enable them to gain, perhaps to demand, better terms in rents; rented farms, varying from forty to a hundred acres, bear an average rental of about fifty-four dollars a year. The men who conduct such farms do not long remain renters; either they sink to metayers, or with a successful series of harvests rise to be land-owners.

In 1870 the tax-books of Dougherty report no Negroes as landholders. If there were any such at that time,—and there may have been a few,—their land was probably held in the name of some white patron,—a method not uncommon during slavery. In 1875 ownership of land had begun with seven hundred and fifty acres; ten years later this had increased to over sixty-five hundred acres, to nine thousand acres in 1890 and ten thousand in 1900. The total assessed property has in this same period risen from eighty thousand dollars in 1875 to two hundred and forty thousand dollars in 1900.

Two circumstances complicate this development and make it in some respects difficult to be sure of the real tendencies; they are the panic of 1893, and the low price of cotton in 1898. Besides this, the system of assessing property in the country districts of Georgia is somewhat antiquated and of uncertain statistical value; there are no assessors, and each man makes a sworn return to a tax-receiver. Thus public opinion plays a large part, and the returns vary strangely from year to year. Certainly these figures show the small amount of accumulated capital among the Negroes, and the consequent large dependence of their property on temporary prosperity. They have little to tide over a few years of economic depression, and are at the mercy of the cotton-market far more than the whites. And thus the land-owners, despite their marvellous efforts, are really a transient class, continually being depleted by those who fall back into the class of renters or metayers, and augmented by newcomers from the masses. Of the one hundred land-owners in 1898, half had bought their land since 1983, a fourth between 1890 and 1893, a fifth between 1884 and 1890, and the rest between 1870 and 1884. In all, one hundred and eighty-five Negroes have owned land in this county since 1875.

If all the black land-owners who had ever held land here had kept it or left it in the hands of black men, the Negroes would have owned nearer thirty thousand acres than the fifteen thousand they now hold. And yet these fifteen thousand acres are a creditable showing,—a proof of no little weight of the worth and ability of the Negro people. If they had been given an economic start at Emancipation, if they had been in an enlightened and rich community which really desired their best good, then we might perhaps call such a result small or even insignificant. But for a few thousand poor ignorant field-hands, in the face of poverty, a falling market, and social stress, to save and capitalize two hundred thousand dollars in a generation has meant a tremendous effort. The rise of a nation, the pressing forward of a social class, means a bitter struggle, a hard and soul-sickening battle with the world such as few of the more favored classes know or appreciate.

Out of the hard economic conditions of this portion of the Black Belt, only six per cent of the population have succeeded in emerging into peasant proprietorship; and these are not all firmly fixed, but grow and shrink in number with the wavering of the cotton-market. Fully ninety-four per cent have struggled for land and failed, and half of them sit in hopeless serfdom. For these there is one other avenue of escape toward which they have turned in increasing numbers, namely, migration to town. A glance at the distribution of land among the black owners curiously reveals this fact. In 1898 the holdings were as follows: Under forty acres, forty-nine families; forty to two hundred and fifty acres, seventeen families; two hundred and fifty to one thousand acres, thirteen families; one thousand or more acres, two families. Now in 1890 there were forty-four holdings, but only nine of these were under forty acres. The great increase of holdings, then, has come in the buying of small homesteads near town, where their owners really share in the town life; this is a part of the rush to town. And for every landowner who has thus hurried away from the narrow and hard conditions of country life, how many field-hands, how many tenants, how many ruined renters, have joined that long procession? Is it not strange compensation? The sin of the country districts is visited on the town, and the social sores of city life to-day may, here in Dougherty County, and perhaps in many places near and far, look for their final healing without the city walls.

CHAPTER IX

Of the Sons of Master and Man

Life treads on life, and heart on heart;
We press too close in church and mart
To keep a dream or grave apart.

Mrs. Browning

The world-old phenomenon of the contact of diverse races of men is to have new exemplification during the new century. Indeed, the characteristic of our age is the contact of European civilization with the world's undeveloped peoples. Whatever we may say of the results of such contact in the past, it certainly forms a chapter in human action not pleasant to look back upon. War, murder, slavery, extermination, and debauchery,—this has again and again been the result of carrying civilization and the blessed gospel to the isles of the sea and the heathen without the law. Nor does it altogether satisfy the conscience of the modern world to be told complacently that all this has been right and proper, the fated triumph of strength over weakness, of righteousness over evil, of superiors over inferiors. It would certainly be soothing if one could readily believe all this; and yet there are too many ugly facts for everything to be thus easily explained away. We feel and know that there are many delicate differences in race psychology, numberless changes that our crude social measurements are not yet able to follow minutely, which explain much of history and social development. At the same time, too, we know that these considerations have never adequately explained or excused the triumph of brute force and cunning over weakness and innocence.

It is, then, the strife of all honorable men of the twentieth century to see that in the future competition of races the survival of the fittest shall mean the triumph of the good, the beautiful, and the true; that we may be able to preserve for future civilization all that is really fine and noble and strong, and not continue to put a premium on greed and impudence and cruelty. To bring this hope to fruition, we are compelled daily to turn more and more to a conscientious study of the phenomena of race-contact,—to a study frank and fair, and not falsified and colored by our wishes or our fears. And we have in the South as fine a field for such a study as the world affords,—a field, to be sure, which the average American scientist deems somewhat beneath his dignity, and which the average man who is not a scientist knows all about, but nevertheless a line of study which by reason of the enormous race complications with which God seems about to punish this nation must increasingly claim our sober attention, study, and thought, we must ask, what are the actual relations of whites and blacks in the South? and we must be answered, not by apology or fault-finding, but by a plain, unvarnished tale.

In the civilized life of to-day the contact of men and their relations to each other fall in a few main lines of action and communication: there is, first, the physical proximity of homes and dwelling-places, the way in which neighborhoods group themselves, and the contiguity of neighborhoods. Secondly, and in our age chiefest, there are the economic relations,—the methods by which individuals coöperate for earning a living, for the mutual satisfaction of wants, for the production of wealth. Next, there are the political relations, the coöperation in social control, in group government, in laying and paying the burden of taxation. In the fourth place, there are the less tangible but highly important forms of intellectual contact and commerce, the interchange of ideas through conversation and conference, through periodicals and libraries; and, above all, the gradual formation for each community of that curious *tertium quid* which we call public opinion. Closely allied with this come the various forms of social contact in everyday life, in travel, in theatres, in house gatherings, in marrying and giving in marriage. Finally, there are the varying forms of religious enterprise, of moral teaching and benevolent endeavor. These are the principal ways in which men living in the same communities are brought into contact with each other. It is my present task, therefore, to indicate, from my point of view, how the black race in the South meet and mingle with the whites in these matters of everyday life.

First, as to physical dwelling. It is usually possible to draw in nearly every Southern community a physical color-line on the map, on the one side of which whites dwell and on the other Negroes. The winding and intricacy of the geographical color line varies, of course, in different communities. I know some towns where a straight line drawn through the middle of the main street separates nine-tenths of the whites from nine-tenths of the blacks. In other towns the older settlement of whites has been encircled by a broad band of blacks; in still other cases little settlements or nuclei of blacks have sprung up amid surrounding whites. Usually in cities each street has its distinctive color, and only now and then do the colors meet in close proximity. Even in the country something of this segregation is manifest in the smaller areas, and of course in the larger phenomena of the Black Belt.

All this segregation by color is largely independent of that natural clustering by social grades common to all communities. A Negro slum may be in dangerous proximity to a white residence quarter, while it is quite common to find a white slum planted in the heart of a respectable Negro district. One thing, however, seldom occurs: the best of the whites and the best of the Negroes almost never live in anything like close proximity. It thus happens that in nearly every Southern town and city, both whites and blacks see commonly the worst of each other. This is a vast change from the situation in the past, when, through the close contact of master and house-servant in the patriarchal big house, one found the best of both races in close contact and sympathy, while at the same time the squalor and dull round of toil among the field-hands was removed from the sight and hearing of the family. One can easily see how a person who saw slavery thus from his father's parlors, and sees freedom on the streets of a great city, fails to grasp or comprehend the whole of the new picture. On the other hand, the settled belief of the mass of the Negroes that the Southern white people do not have the black man's best interests at heart has been intensified in later years by this continual daily contact of the better class of blacks with the worst representatives of the white race.

Coming now to the economic relations of the races, we are on ground made familiar by study, much discussion, and no little philanthropic effort. And yet with all this there are many essential elements in the coöperation of Negroes and whites for work and wealth that are too readily overlooked or not thoroughly understood. The average American can easily conceive of a rich land awaiting development and filled with black laborers. To him the Southern problem is simply that of making efficient workingmen out of this material, by giving them the requisite technical skill and the help of invested capital. The problem, however, is by no means as simple as this, from the obvious fact that these workingmen have been trained for centuries as slaves. They exhibit, therefore, all the advantages and defects of such training; they are willing and good-natured, but not self-reliant, provident, or careful. If now the economic development of the South is to be pushed to the verge of exploitation, as seems probable, then we have a mass of workingmen thrown into relentless competition with the workingmen of the world, but handicapped by a training the very opposite to that of the modern self-reliant democratic laborer. What the black laborer needs is careful personal guidance, group leadership of men with hearts in their bosoms, to train them to foresight, carefulness, and honesty. Nor does it require any fine-spun theories of racial differences to prove the necessity of such group training after the brains of the race have been knocked out by two hundred and fifty years of assiduous education in submission, carelessness, and stealing. After Emancipation, it was the plain duty of some one to assume this group leadership and training of the Negro laborer. I will not stop here to inquire whose duty it was,—whether that of the white ex-master who had profited by upaid toil, or the Northern philanthropist whose persistence brought on the crisis, or the National Government whose edict freed the bondmen; I will not stop to ask whose duty it was, but I insist it was the duty of some one to see that these workingmen were not left along and unguided, without capital, without land, without skill, without economic organization, without even the bald protection of law, order, and decency,—left in a great land, not to settle down to slow and careful internal development, but destined to be thrown almost immediately into relentless and sharp competition with the best of modern workingmen under an economic system where every participant is fighting for himself, and too often utterly regardless of the rights or welfare of his neighbor.

For we must never forget that the economic system of the South to-day which has succeeded the old *régime* is not the same system as that of the old industrial North, of England, or of France, with their trades-unions, their restrictive laws, their written and unwritten commercial customs, and their long experience. It is, rather, a copy of that England of the early nineteenth century, before the factory acts,—the England that wrung pity from thinkers and fired the wrath of Carlyle. The rod of empire that passed from the hands of Southern gentlemen in 1865, partly by force, partly by their own petulance, has never returned to them. Rather it has passed to those men who have come to take charge of the industrial exploitation of the New South,—the sons of poor whites fired with a new thirst for wealth and power, thrifty and avaricious Yankees, shrewd and unscrupulous Jews. Into the hands of these men the Southern laborers, white and black, have fallen; and this to their sorrow. For the laborers as such there is in these new captains of industry neither love nor hate, neither sympathy nor romance; it is a cold question of dollars and dividends. Under such a system all labor is bound to suffer. Even the white laborers are not yet intelligent, thrifty, and well trained enough to maintain themselves against the powerful inroads of organized capital. The results among them, even, are long hours of toil, low wages, child labor, lack of protection against usury and cheating. But among the black laborers all this is aggravated, first, by a race prejudice which varies from a doubt and distrust among the best element of whites to a frenzied hatred among the worst; and, secondly, it is aggravated, as I have said before, by the wretched economic heritage of the freedmen from slavery. With this training it is difficult for the freedman to learn to grasp the opportunities already opened to him, and the new opportunities are seldom given him, but go by favor to the whites.

Left by the best elements of the South with little protection or oversight, he has been made in law and custom the victim of the worst and most unscrupulous men in each community. The crop-lien system which is depopulating the fields of the South is not simply the result of shiftlessness on the part of Negroes, but is also the result of cunningly devised laws as to mortgages, liens, and misdemeanors, which can be made by conscienceless men to entrap and snare the unwary until escape is impossible, further toil a farce, and protest a crime. I have seen, in the Black Belt of Georgia, an ignorant, honest Negro buy and pay for a farm in installments three separate times, and then in the face of law and decency the enterprising Russian Jew who sold it to him pocketed money and deed and left the black man landless, to labor on his own land at thirty cents a day. I have seen a black farmer fall in debt to a white storekeeper, and that storekeeper go to his farm and strip it of every single marketable article,—mules, ploughs, stored crops, tools, furniture, bedding, clocks, looking-glass,—and all this without a warrant, without process of law, without a sheriff or officer, in the face of the law for homestead exemptions, and without rendering to a single responsible person any account or reckoning. And such proceedings can happen, and will happen, in any community where a class of ignorant toilers are placed by custom and race-prejudice beyond the pale of sympathy and race-brotherhood. So long as the best elements of a community do not feel in duty bound to protect and train and care for the weaker members of their group, they leave them to be preyed upon by these swindlers and rascals.

This unfortunate economic situation does not mean the hindrance of all advance in the black South, or the absence of a class of black landlords and mechanics, who, in spite of disadvantages, are accumulating property and making good citizens. But it does mean that this class is not nearly so large as a fairer economic system might easily make it, that those who survive in the competition are handicapped so as to accomplish much less than they deserve to, and that, above all, the *personnel* of the successful class is left to chance and accident, and not to any intelligent culling or reasonable methods of selection. As a remedy for this, there is but one possible procedure. We must accept some of the race prejudice in the South as a fact,—deplorable in its intensity, unfortunate in results, and dangerous for the future, but nevertheless a hard fact which only time can efface. We cannot hope, then, in this generation, or for several generations, that the mass of the whites can be brought to assume that close sympathetic and self-sacrificing leadership of the blacks which their present situation so eloquently demands. Such leadership, such social teaching and example, must come from the blacks themselves. For some time men doubted as to whether the Negro could develop such leaders; but to-day no one seriously disputes the capability of individual Negroes to assimilate the culture and common sense of modern civilization, and to pass it on, to some extent at least, to their fellows. If this is true, then here is the path out of the economic situation, and here is the imperative demand for trained Negro leaders of character and intelligence,—men of skill, men of light and leading, college-bred men, black captains of industry, and missionaries of culture; men who thoroughly comprehend and know modern civilization, and can take hold of Negro communities and raise and train them by force of precept and example, deep sympathy, and the inspiration of common blood and ideals. But if such men are to be effective they must have some power,—they must be backed by the best public opinion of these communities, and able to wield for their objects and aims such weapons as the experience of the world has taught are indispensable to human progress.

Of such weapons the greatest, perhaps, in the modern world is the power of the ballot; and this brings me to a consideration of the third form of contact between whites and blacks in the South,—political activity.

In the attitude of the American mind toward Negro suffrage can be traced with unusual accuracy the prevalent conceptions of government. In the fifties we were near enough the echoes of the French Revolution to believe pretty thoroughly in universal suffrage. We argued, as we thought then rather logically, that no social class was so good, so true, and so disinterested as to be trusted wholly with the political destiny of its neighbors; that in every state the best arbiters of their own welfare are the persons directly affected; consequently that it is only by arming every hand with a ballot,—with the right to have a voice in the policy of the state,—that the greatest good to the greatest number could be attained. To be sure, there were objections to these arguments, but we thought we had answered them tersely and convincingly; if some one complained of the ignorance of voters, we answered, "Educate them." If another complained of their venality, we replied, "Disfranchise them or put them in jail." And, finally, to the men who feared demagogues and the natural perversity of some human beings we insisted that time and bitter experience would teach the most hardheaded. It was at this time that the question of Negro suffrage in the South was raised. Here was a defenceless people suddenly made free. How were they to be protected from those who did not believe in their freedom and were determined to thwart it? Not by force, said the North; not by government guardianship, said the South; then by the ballot, the sole and legitimate defence of a free people, said the Common Sense of the Nation. No one thought, at the time, that the ex-slaves could use the ballot intelligently or very effectively; but they did think that the possession of so great power by a great class in the nation would compel their fellows to educate this class to its intelligent use.

Meantime, new thoughts came to the nation: the inevitable period of moral retrogression and political trickery that ever follows in the wake of war overtook us. So flagrant became the political scandals that reputable men began to leave politics alone, and politics consequently became disreputable. Men began to pride themselves on having nothing to do with their own government, and to agree tacitly with those who regarded public office as a private perquisite. In this state of mind it became easy to wink at the suppression of the Negro vote in the South, and to advise self-respecting Negroes to leave politics entirely alone. The decent and reputable citizens of the North who neglected their own civic duties grew hilarious over the exaggerated importance with which the Negro regarded the franchise. Thus it easily happened that more and more the better class of Negroes followed the advice from abroad and the pressure from home, and took no further interest in politics, leaving to the careless and the venal of their race the exercise of their rights as voters. The black vote that still remained was not trained and educated, but further debauched by open and unblushing bribery, or force and fraud; until the Negro voter was thoroughly inoculated with the idea that politics was a method of private gain by disreputable means.

And finally, now, to-day, when we are awakening to the fact that the perpetuity of republican institutions on this continent depends on the purification of the ballot, the civic training of voters, and the raising of voting to the plane of a solemn duty which a patriotic citizen neglects to his peril and to the peril of his children's children,—in this day, when we are striving for a renaissance of civic virtue, what are we going to say to the black voter of the South? Are we going to tell him still that politics is a disreputable and useless form of human activity? Are we going to induce the best class of Negroes to take less and less interest in government, and to give up their right to take such an interest, without a protest? I am not saying a word against all legitimate efforts to purge the ballot of ignorance, pauperism, and crime. But few have pretended that the present movement for disfranchisement in the South is for such a purpose; it has been plainly and frankly declared in nearly every case that the object of the disfranchising laws is the elimination of the black man from politics.

Now, is this a minor matter which has no influence on the main question of the industrial and intellectual development of the Negro? Can we establish a mass of black laborers and artisans and landholders in the South who, by law and public opinion, have absolutely no voice in shaping the laws under which they live and work? Can the modern organization of industry, assuming as it does free democratic government and the power and ability of the laboring classes to compel respect for their welfare,—can this system be carried out in the South when half its laboring force is voiceless in the public councils and powerless in its own defense? To-day the black man of the South has almost nothing to say as to how much he shall be taxed, or how those taxes shall be expended; as to who shall execute the laws, and how they shall do it; as to who shall make the laws, and how they shall be made. It is pitiable that frantic efforts must be made at critical times to get lawmakers in some States even to listen to the respectful presentation of the black man's side of a current controversy. Daily the Negro is coming more and more to look upon law and justice, not as protecting safeguards, but as sources of humiliation and oppression. The laws are made by men who have little interest in him; they are executed by men who have absolutely no motive for treating the black people with courtesy or consideration; and, finally, the accused law-breaker is tried, not by his peers, but too often by men who would rather punish ten innocent Negroes than let one guilty one escape.

I should be the last one to deny the patent weaknesses and shortcomings of the Negro people; I should be the last to withhold sympathy from the white South in its efforts to solve its intricate social problems. I freely acknowledge that it is possible, and sometimes best, that a partially undeveloped people should be ruled by the best of their stronger and better neighbors for their own good, until such time as they can start and fight the world's battles alone. I have already pointed out how sorely in need of such economic and spiritual guidance the emancipated Negro was, and I am quite willing to admit that if the representatives of the best white Southern public opinion were the ruling and guiding powers in the South to-day the conditions indicated would be fairly well fulfilled. But the point I have insisted upon, and now emphasize again, is that the best opinion of the South to-day is not the ruling opinion. That to leave the Negro helpless and without a ballot to-day is to leave him, not to the guidance of the best, but rather to the exploitation and debauchment of the worst; that this is no truer of the South than of the North,—of the North than of Europe: in any land, in any country under modern free competition, to lay any class of weak and despised people, be they white, black, or blue, at the political mercy of their stronger, richer, and more resourceful fellows, is a temptation which human nature seldom has withstood and seldom will withstand.

Moreover, the political status of the Negro in the South is closely connected with the question of Negro crime. There can be no doubt that crime among Negroes has sensibly increased in the last thirty years, and that there has appeared in the slums of great cities a distinct criminal class among the blacks. In explaining this unfortunate development, we must note two things: (1) that the inevitable result of Emancipation was to increase crime and criminals, and (2) that the police system of the South was primarily designed to control slaves. As to the first point, we must not forget that under a strict slave system there can scarcely be such a thing as crime. But when these variously constituted human particles are suddenly thrown broadcast on the sea of life, some swim, some sink, and some hang suspended, to be forced up or down by the chance currents of a busy hurrying world. So great an economic and social revolution as swept the South in '63 meant a weeding out among the Negroes of the incompetents and vicious, the beginning of a differentiation of social grades. Now a rising group of people are not lifted bodily from the ground like an inert solid mass, but rather stretch upward like a living plant with its roots still clinging in the mould. The appearance, therefore, of the Negro criminal was a phenomenon to be awaited; and while it causes anxiety, it should not occasion surprise.

Here again the hope for the future depended peculiarly on careful and delicate dealing with these criminals. Their offences at first were those of laziness, carelessness, and impulse, rather than of malignity or ungoverned viciousness. Such misdemeanors needed discriminating treatment, firm but reformatory, with no hint of injustice, and full proof of guilt. For such dealing with criminals, white or black, the South had no machinery, no adequate jails or reformatories; its police system was arranged to deal with blacks alone, and tacitly assumed that every white man was *ipso facto* a member of that police. Thus grew up a double system of justice, which erred on the white side by undue leniency and the practical immunity of red-handed criminals, and erred on the black side by undue severity, injustice, and lack of discrimination. For, as I have said, the police system of the South was originally designed to keep track of all Negroes, not simply of criminals; and when the Negroes were freed and the whole South was convinced of the impossibility of free Negro labor, the first and almost universal device was to use the courts as a means of reënslaving the blacks. It was not then a question of crime, but rather one of color, that settled a man's conviction on almost any charge. Thus Negroes came to look upon courts as instruments of injustice and oppression, and upon those convicted in them as martyrs and victims.

When, now, the real Negro criminal appeared, and instead of petty stealing and vagrancy we began to have highway robbery, burglary, murder, and rape, there was a curious effect on both sides the color-line: the Negroes refused to believe the evidence of white witnesses or the fairness of white juries, so that the greatest deterrent to crime, the public opinion of one's own social caste, was lost, and the criminal was looked upon as crucified rather than hanged. On the other hand, the whites, used to being careless as to the guilt or innocence of accused Negroes, were swept in moments of passion beyond law, reason, and decency. Such a situation is bound to increase crime, and has increased it. To natural viciousness and vagrancy are being daily added motives of revolt and revenge which stir up all the latent savagery of both races and made peaceful attention to economic development often impossible.

But the chief problem in any community cursed with crime is not the punishment of the criminals, but the preventing of the young from being trained to crime. And here again the peculiar conditions of the South have prevented proper precautions. I have seen twelve-year-old boys working in chains on the public streets of Atlanta, directly in front of the schools, in company with old and hardened criminals; and this indiscriminate mingling of men and women and children makes the chain-gangs perfect schools of crime and debauchery. The struggle for reformatories, which has gone on in Virginia, Georgia, and other States, is the one encouraging sign of the awakening of some communities to the suicidal results of this policy.

It is the public schools, however, which can be made, outside the homes, the greatest means of training decent self-respecting citizens. We have been so hotly engaged recently in discussing trade-schools and the higher education that the pitiable plight of the public-school system in the South has almost dropped from view. Of every five dollars spent for public education in the State of Georgia, the white schools get four dollars and the Negro one dollar; and even then the white public-school system, save in the cities, is bad and cries for reform. If this is true of the whites, what of the blacks? I am becoming more and more convinced, as I look upon the system of common-school training in the South, that the national government must soon step in and aid popular education in some way. To-day it has been only by the most strenuous efforts on the part of the thinking men of the South that the Negro's share of the school fund has not been cut down to a pittance in some half-dozen States; and that movement not only is not dead, but in many communities is gaining strength. What in the name of reason does this nation expect of a people, poorly trained and hard pressed in severe economic competition, without political rights, and with ludicrously inadequate common-school facilities? What can it expect but crime and listlessness, offset here and there by the dogged struggles of the fortunate and more determined who are themselves buoyed by the hope that in due time the country will come to its senses?

I have thus far sought to make clear the physical, economic, and political relations of the Negroes and whites in the South, as I have conceived them, including, for the reasons set forth, crime and education. But after all that has been said on these more tangible matters of human contact, there still remains a part essential to a proper description of the South which it is difficult to describe or fix in terms easily understood by strangers. It is, in fine, the atmosphere of the land, the thought and feeling, the thousand and one little actions which go to make up life. In any community or nation it is these little things which are most elusive to the grasp and yet most essential to any clear conception of the group life taken as a whole. What is thus true of all communities is peculiarly true of the South, where, outside of written history and outside of printed law, there has been going on for a generation as deep a storm and stress of human souls, as intense a ferment of feeling, as intricate a writhing of spirit, as ever a people experienced. Within and without the sombre veil of color vast social forces have been at work,—efforts for human betterment, movements toward disintegration and despair, tragedies and comedies in social and economic life, and a swaying and lifting and sinking of human hearts which have made this land a land of mingled sorrow and joy, of change and excitement and unrest.

The centre of this spiritual turmoil has ever been the millions of black freedmen and their sons, whose destiny is so fatefully bound up with that of the nation. And yet the casual observer visiting the South sees at first little of this. He notes the growing frequency of dark faces as he rides along,—but otherwise the days slip lazily on, the sun shines, and this little world seems as happy and contented as other worlds he has visited. Indeed, on the question of questions—the Negro problem—he hears so little that there almost seems to be a conspiracy of silence; the morning papers seldom mention it, and then usually in a far-fetched academic way, and indeed almost every one seems to forget and ignore the darker half of the land, until the astonished visitor is inclined to ask if after all there *is* any problem here. But if he lingers long enough there comes the awakening: perhaps in a sudden whirl of passion which leaves him gasping at its bitter intensity; more likely in a gradually dawning sense of things he had not at first noticed. Slowly but surely his eyes begin to catch the shadows of the color-line: here he meets crowds of Negroes and whites; then he is suddenly aware that he cannot discover a single dark face; or again at the close of a day's wandering he may find himself in some strange assembly, where all faces are tinged brown or black, and where he has the vague, uncomfortable feeling of the stranger. He realizes at last that silently, resistlessly, the world about flows by him in two great streams: they ripple on in the same sunshine, they approach and mingle their waters in seeming carelessness,—then they divide and flow wide apart. It is done quietly; no mistakes are made, or if one occurs, the swift arm of the law and of public opinion swings down for a moment, as when the other day a black man and a white woman were arrested for talking together on Whitehall Street in Atlanta.

Now if one notices carefully one will see that between these two worlds, despite much physical contact and daily intermingling, there is almost no community of intellectual life or point of transference where the thoughts and feelings of one race can come into direct contact and sympathy with thoughts and feelings of the other. Before and directly after the war, when all the best of the Negroes were domestic servants in the best of the white families, there were bonds of intimacy, affection, and sometimes blood relationship, between the races. They lived in the same home, shared in the family life, often attended the same church, and talked and conversed with each other. But the increasing civilization of the Negro since then has naturally meant the development of higher classes: there are increasing numbers of ministers, teachers, physicians, merchants, mechanics, and independent farmers, who by nature and training are the aristocracy and leaders of the blacks. Between them, however, and the best element of the whites, there is little or no intellectual commerce. They go to separate churches, they live in separate sections, they are strictly separated in all public gatherings, they travel separately, and they are beginning to read different papers and books. To most libraries, lectures, concerts, and museums, Negroes are either not admitted at all, or on terms peculiarly galling to the pride of the very classes who might otherwise be attracted. The daily paper chronicles the doings of the black world from afar with no great regard for accuracy; and so on, throughout the category of means for intellectual communication,—schools, conferences, efforts, for social betterment, and the like,—it is usually true that the very representatives of the two races, who for mutual benefit and the welfare of the land ought to be in complete understanding and sympathy, are so far strangers that one side thinks all whites are narrow and prejudiced, and the other thinks educated Negroes dangerous and insolent. Moreover, in a land where the tyranny of public opinion and the intolerance of criticism is for obvious historical reasons so strong as in the South, such a situation is extremely difficult to correct. The white man, as well as the Negro, is bound and barred by the color-line, and many a scheme of friendliness and philanthropy, of broad-minded sympathy and generous fellowship between the two has dropped still-born because some busybody has forced the color-question to the front and brought the tremendous force of unwritten law against the innovators.

It is hardly necessary for me to add very much in regard to the social contact between the races. Nothing has come to replace that finer sympathy and love between some masters and house servants which the radical and more uncompromising drawing of the color-line in recent years has caused almost completely to disappear. In a world where it means so much to take a man by the hand and sit beside him, to look frankly into his eyes and feel his heart beating with red blood; in a world where a social cigar or a cup of tea together means more than legislative halls and magazine articles and speeches,—one can imagine the consequences of the almost utter absence of such social amenities between estranged races, whose separation extends even to parks and street-cars.

Here there can be none of that social going down to the people,— the opening of heart and hand of the best to the worst, in generous acknowledgment of a common humanity and a common destiny. On the other hand, in matters of simple almsgiving, where there can be no question of social contact, and in the succor of the aged and sick, the South, as if stirred by a feeling of its unfortunate limitations, is generous to a fault. The black beggar is never turned away without a good deal more than a crust, and a call for help for the unfortunate meets quick response. I remember, one cold winter, in Atlanta, when I refrained from contributing to a public relief fund lest Negroes should be discriminated against, I afterward inquired of a friend: "Were any black people receiving aid?" "Why," said he, "they were *all* black."

And yet this does not touch the kernel of the problem. Human advancement is not a mere question of almsgiving, but rather of sympathy and coöperation among classes who would scorn charity. And here is a land where, in the higher walks of life, in all the higher striving for the good and noble and true, the color-line comes to separate natural friends and co-workers; while at the bottom of the social group, in the saloon, the gambling-hell, and the brothel, that same line wavers and disappears.

I have sought to paint an average picture of real relations between the sons and master and man in the South. I have not glossed over matters for policy's sake, for I fear we have already gone too far in that sort of thing. On the other hand, I have sincerely sought to let no unfair exaggerations creep in. I do not doubt that in some Southern communities conditions are better than those I have indicated; while I am no less certain that in other communities they are far worse.

Nor does the paradox and danger of this situation fail to interest and perplex the best conscience of the South. Deeply religious and intensely democratic as are the mass of the whites, they feel acutely the false position in which the Negro problems place them. Such an essentially honest-hearted and generous people cannot cite the caste-leveling precepts of Christianity, or believe in equality of opportunity for all men, without coming to feel more and more with each generation that the present drawing of the color-line is a flat contradiction to their beliefs and professions. But just as often as they come to this point, the present social condition of the Negro stands as a menace and a portent before even the most open-minded: if there were nothing to charge against the Negro but his blackness or other physical peculiarities, they argue, the problem would be comparatively simple; but what can we say to his ignorance, shiftlessness, poverty, and crime? can a self-respecting group hold anything but the least possible fellowship with such persons and survive? and shall we let a mawkish sentiment sweep away the culture of our fathers or the hope of our children? The argument so put is of great strength but it is not a whit stronger than the argument of thinking Negroes: granted, they reply, that the condition of our masses is bad; there is certainly on the one hand adequate historical cause for this, and unmistakable evidence that no small number have, in spite of tremendous disadvantages, risen to the level of American civilization. And when, by proscription and prejudice, these same Negroes are classed with and treated like the lowest of their people, simply *because* they are Negroes, such a policy not only discourages thrift and intelligence among black men, but puts a direct premium on the very things you complain of,—inefficiency and crime. Draw lines of crime, of incompetency, of vice, as tightly and uncompromisingly as you will, for these things must be proscribed; but a color-line not only does not accomplish this purpose, but thwarts it.

In the face of two such arguments, the future of the South depends on the ability of the representatives of these opposing views to see and appreciate and sympathize with each other's position,—for the Negro to realize more deeply than he does at present the need of uplifting the masses of his people, for the white people to realize more vividly than they have yet done the deadening and disastrous effect of a color-prejudice that classes Phillis Wheatley and Sam Hose in the same despised class.

It is not enough for the Negroes to declare that color-prejudice is the sole cause of their social condition, nor for the white South to reply that their social condition is the main cause of prejudice. They both act as reciprocal cause and effect, and a change in neither alone will bring the desired effect. Both must change, or neither can improve to any great extent. The Negro cannot stand the present reactionary tendencies and unreasoning drawing of the color-line indefinitely without discouragement and retrogression. And the condition of the Negro is ever the excuse for further discrimination. Only by a union of intelligence and sympathy across the color-line in this critical period of the Republic shall justice and right triumph,—

> "That mind and soul according well,
> May make one music as before,
> But vaster."

CHAPTER X

Of the Faith of the Fathers

> Dim face of Beauty haunting all the world,
>   Fair face of Beauty all too fair to see,
> Where the lost stars adown the heavens are hurled,—
>   There, there alone for thee
>   May white peace be.
>
>   .   .   .
>
> Beauty, sad face of Beauty, Mystery, Wonder,
>   What are these dreams to foolish babbling men
> Who cry with little noises 'neath the thunder
>   Of Ages ground to sand,
>   To a little sand.

Fiona Macleod

It was out in the country, far from home, far from my foster home, on a dark Sunday night. The road wandered from our rambling log-house up the stony bed of a creek, past wheat and corn, until we could hear dimly across the fields a rhythmic cadence of song,—soft, thrilling, powerful, that swelled and died sorrowfully in our ears. I was a country school-teacher then, fresh from the East, and had never seen a Southern Negro revival. To be sure, we in Berkshire were not perhaps as stiff and formal as they in Suffolk of olden time; yet we were very quiet and subdued, and I know not what would have happened those clear Sabbath mornings had some one punctuated the sermon with a wild scream, or interrupted the long prayer with a loud Amen! And so most striking to me, as I approached the village and the little plain church perched aloft, was the air of intense excitement that possessed that mass of black folk. A sort of suppressed terror hung in the air and seemed to seize us,—a pythian madness, a demoniac possession, that lent terrible reality to song and word. The black and massive form of the preacher swayed and quivered as the words crowded to his lips and flew at us in singular eloquence. The people moaned and fluttered, and then the gaunt-checked brown woman beside me suddenly leaped straight into the air and shrieked like a lost soul, while round about came wail and groan and outcry, and a scene of human passion such as I had never conceived before.

Those who have not thus witnessed the frenzy of a Negro revival in the untouched backwoods of the South can but dimly realize the religious feeling of the slave; as described, such scenes appear grotesque and funny, but as seen they are awful. Three things characterized this religion of the slave,—the Preacher, the Music and the Frenzy. The Preacher is the most unique personality developed by the Negro on American soil. A leader, a politican, an orator, a "boss," an intriguer, an idealist,—all these he is, and ever, too, the centre of a group of men, now twenty, now a thousand in number. The combination of a certain adroitness with deep-seated earnestness, of tact with consummate ability, gave him his preëminence, and helps him maintain it. The type, of course, varies according to time and place, from the West Indies in the sixteenth century to New England in the nineteenth, and from the Mississippi bottoms to cities like New Orleans or New York.

The Music of Negro religion is that plaintive rhythmic melody, with its touching minor cadences, which, despite caricature and defilement, still remains the most original and beautiful expression of human life and longing yet born on American soil. Sprung from the African forests, where its counterpart can still be heard, it was adapted, changed, and intensified by the tragic soul-life of the slave, until, under the stress of law and whip, it became the one true expression of a people's sorrow, despair, and hope.

Finally the Frenzy or "Shouting," when the Spirit of the Lord passed by, and, seizing the devotee, made him mad with supernatural joy, was the last essential of Negro religion and the one more devoutly believed in than all the rest. It varied in expression from the silent rapt countenance or the low murmur and moan to the mad abandon of physical fervor,—the stamping, shrieking, and shouting, the rushing to and fro and wild waving of arms, the weeping and laughing, the vision and the trance. All this is nothing new in the world, but old as religion, as Delphi and Endor. And so firm a hold did it have on the Negro, that many generations firmly believed that without this visible manifestation of the God there could be no true communion with the Invisible.

These were the characteristics of Negro religious life as developed up the the time of Emancipation. Since under the peculiar circumstances of the black man's environment they were the one expression of his higher life, they are of deep interest to the student of his development, both socially and psychologically. Numerous are the attractive lines of inquiry that here group themselves. What did slavery mean to the African savage? What was his attitude toward the World and Life? What seemed to him good and evil,—God and Devil? Whither went his longings and strivings, and wherefore were his heart-burnings and disappointments? Answers to such questions can come only from a study of Negro religion as a development, through its gradual changes from the heathenism of the Gold Coast to the institutional Negro church of Chicago.

Moreover, the religious growth of millions of men, even though they be slaves, cannot be without potent influence upon their contemporaries. The Methodists and Baptists of America owe much of their condition to the silent but potent influence of their millions of Negro converts. Especially is this noticeable in the South, where theology and religious philosophy are on this account a long way behind the North, and where the religion of the poor whites is a plain copy of Negro thought and methods. The mass of "gospel" hymns which has swept through American Churches and well-nigh ruined our sense of song consists largely of debased imitations of Negro melodies made by ears that caught the jingle but not the music, the body but not the soul, of the Jubilee songs. It is thus clear that the study of Negro religion is not only a vital part of the history of the Negro in America, but no uninteresting part of American history.

The Negro church of to-day is the social centre of Negro life in the United States, and the most characteristic expression of African character. Take a typical church in a small Virginian town: it is the "First Baptist"—a roomy brick edifice seating five hundred or more persons, tastefully finished in Georgia pine, with a carpet, a small organ, and stained-glass windows. Underneath is a large assembly room with benches. This building is the central club-house of a community of a thousand or more Negroes. Various organizations meet here,—the church proper, the Sunday-school, two or three insurance societies, women's societies, secret societies, and mass meetings of various kinds. Entertainments, suppers, and lectures are held beside the five or six regular weekly religious services. Considerable sums of money are collected and expended here, employment is found for the idle, strangers are introduced, news is disseminated and charity distributed. At the same time this social, intellectual, and economic centre is a religious centre of great power. Depravity, Sin, Redemption, Heaven, Hell, and Damnation are preached twice a Sunday with much fervor, and revivals take place every year after the crops are laid by; and few indeed of the community have the hardihood to withstand conversion. Back of this more formal religion, the Church often stands as a real conserver of morals, a strengthener of family life, and the final authority on what is Good and Right.

Thus one can see in the Negro church to-day, reproduced in microcosm, all that great world from which the Negro is cut off by color-prejudice and social condition. In the great city churches the same tendency is noticeable and in many respects emphasized. A great church like the Bethel of Philadelphia has over eleven hundred members, an edifice seating fifteen hundred persons and valued at one hundred thousand dollars, an annual budget of five thousand dollars, and a government consisting of a pastor with several assisting local preachers, an executive and legislative board, financial boards and tax collectors; general church meetings for making laws; subdivided groups led by class leaders, a company of militia, and twenty-four auxiliary societies. The activity of a church like this is immense and far-reaching, and the bishops who preside over these organizations throughout the land are among the most powerful Negro rulers in the world.

Such churches are really governments of men, and consequently a little investigation reveals the curious fact that, in the South, at least, practically every American Negro is a church member. Some, to be sure, are not regularly enrolled, and a few do not habitually attend services; but practically, a proscribed people must have a social centre, and that centre for this people is the Negro church. The census of 1890 shows nearly twenty-four thousand Negro churches in the country, with a total enrolled membership of over two and a half millions, or ten actual church members to every twenty-eight persons, and in some Southern States one in every two persons. Besides these there is the large number who, while not enrolled as members, attend and take part in many of the activities of the church. There is an organized Negro church for every sixty black families in the nation, and in some States for every forty families, owning, on an average, a thousand dollars' worth of property each, or nearly twenty-six million dollars in all.

Such, then, is the large development of the Negro church since Emancipation. The question now is, What have been the successive steps of this social history and what are the present tendencies? First, we must realize that no such institution as the Negro church could rear itself without definite historical foundations. These foundations we can find if we remember that the social history of the Negro did not start in America. He was brought from a definite social environment,—the polygamous clan life under the headship of the chief and the potent influence of the priest. His religion was nature-worship, with profound belief in invisible surrounding influences, good and bad, and his worship was through incantation and sacrifice. The first rude change in this life was the slave ship and the West Indian sugar-fields. The plantation organization replaced the clan and tribe, and the white master replaced the chief with far greater and more despotic powers. Forced and long-continued toil became the rule of life, the old ties of blood relationship and kinship disappeared, and instead of the family appeared a new polygamy and polyandry, which, in some cases, almost reached promiscuity. It was a terrific social revolution, and yet some traces were retained of the former group life, and the chief remaining institution was the Priest or Medicine-man. He early appeared on the plantation and found his function as the healer of the sick, the interpreter of the Unknown, the comforter of the sorrowing, the supernatural avenger of wrong, and the one who rudely but picturesquely expressed the longing, disappointment, and resentment of a stolen and oppressed people. Thus, as bard, physician, judge, and priest, within the narrow limits allowed by the slave system, rose the Negro preacher, and under him the first Afro-American institution, the Negro church. This church was not at first by any means Christian nor definitely organized; rather it was an adaption and mingling of heathen rites among the members of each plantation, and roughly designated as Voodooism. Association with the masters, missionary effort and motives of expediency gave these rites an early veneer of Christianity, and after the lapse of many generations the Negro church became Christian.

Two characteristic things must be noticed in regard to this church. First, it became almost entirely Baptist and Methodist in faith; secondly, as a social institution it antedated by many decades the monogamic Negro home. From the very circumstances of its beginning, the church was confined to the plantation, and consisted primarily of a series of disconnected units; although, later on, some freedom of movement was allowed, still this geographical limitation was always important and was one cause of the spread of the decentralized and democratic Baptist faith among the slaves. At the same time, the visible rite of baptism appealed strongly to their mystic temperament. To-day the Baptist Church is still largest in membership among Negroes, and has a million and a half communicants. Next in popularity came the churches organized in connection with the white neighboring churches, chiefly Baptist and Methodist, with a few Episcopalian and others. The Methodists still form the second greatest denomination, with nearly a million members. The faith of these two leading denominations was more suited to the slave church from the prominence they gave to religious feeling and fervor. The Negro membership in other denominations has always been small and relatively unimportant, although the Episcopalians and Presbyterians are gaining among the more intelligent classes to-day, and the Catholic Church is making headway in certain sections. After Emancipation, and still earlier in the North, the Negro churches largely severed such affiliations as they had had with the white churches, either by choice or by compulsion. The Baptist churches became independent, but the Methodists were compelled early to unite for purposes of episcopal government. This gave rise to the great African Methodist Church, the greatest Negro organization in the world, to the Zion Church and the Colored Methodist, and to the black conferences and churches in this and other denominations.

The second fact noted, namely, that the Negro church antedates the Negro home, leads to an explanation of much that is paradoxical in this communistic institution and in the morals of its members. But especially it leads us to regard this institution as peculiarly the expression of the inner ethical life of a people in a sense seldom true elsewhere. Let us turn, then, from the outer physical development of the church to the more important inner ethical life of the people who compose it. The Negro has already been pointed out many times as a religious animal,—a being of that deep emotional nature which turns instinctively toward the supernatural. Endowed with a rich tropical imagination and a keen, delicate appreciation of Nature, the transplanted African lived in a world animate with gods and devils, elves and witches; full of strange influences,—of Good to be implored, of Evil to be propitiated. Slavery, then, was to him the dark triumph of Evil over him. All the hateful powers of the Under-world were striving against him, and a spirit of revolt and revenge filled his heart. He called up all the resources of heathenism to aid,—exorcism and witchcraft, the mysterious Obi worship with its barbarous rites, spells, and blood-sacrifice even, now and then, of human victims. Weird midnight orgies and mystic conjurations were invoked, the witch-woman and the voodoo-priest became the centre of Negro group life, and that vein of vague superstition which characterizes the unlettered Negro even to-day was deepened and strengthened.

In spite, however, of such success as that of the fierce Maroons, the Danish blacks, and others, the spirit of revolt gradually died away under the untiring energy and superior strength of the slave masters. By the middle of the eighteenth century the black slave had sunk, with hushed murmurs, to his place at the bottom of a new economic system, and was unconsciously ripe for a new philosophy of life. Nothing suited his condition then better than the doctrines of passive submission embodied in the newly learned Christianity. Slave masters early realized this, and cheerfully aided religious propaganda within certain bounds. The long system of repression and degradation of the Negro tended to emphasize the elements in his character which made him a valuable chattel: courtesy became humility, moral strength degenerated into submission, and the exquisite native appreciation of the beautiful became an infinite capacity for dumb suffering. The Negro, losing the joy of this world, eagerly seized upon the offered conceptions of the next; the avenging Spirit of the Lord enjoining patience in this world, under sorrow and tribulation until the Great Day when He should lead His dark children home,—this became his comforting dream. His preacher repeated the prophecy, and his bards sang,—

> "Children, we all shall be free
> When the Lord shall appear!"

This deep religious fatalism, painted so beautifully in "Uncle Tom," came soon to breed, as all fatalistic faiths will, the sensualist side by side with the martyr. Under the lax moral life of the plantation, where marriage was a farce, laziness a virtue, and property a theft, a religion of resignation and submission degenerated easily, in less strenuous minds, into a philosophy of indulgence and crime. Many of the worst characteristics of the Negro masses of to-day had their seed in this period of the slave's ethical growth. Here it was that the Home was ruined under the very shadow of the Church, white and black; here habits of shiftlessness took root, and sullen hopelessness replaced hopeful strife.

With the beginning of the abolition movement and the gradual growth of a class of free Negroes came a change. We often neglect the influence of the freedman before the war, because of the paucity of his numbers and the small weight he had in the history of the nation. But we must not forget that his chief influence was internal,—was exerted on the black world; and that there he was the ethical and social leader. Huddled as he was in a few centres like Philadelphia, New York, and New Orleans, the masses of the freedmen sank into poverty and listlessness; but not all of them. The free Negro leader early arose and his chief characteristic was intense earnestness and deep feeling on the slavery question. Freedom became to him a real thing and not a dream. His religion became darker and more intense, and into his ethics crept a note of revenge, into his songs a day of reckoning close at hand. The "Coming of the Lord" swept this side of Death, and came to be a thing to be hoped for in this day. Through fugitive slaves and irrepressible discussion this desire for freedom seized the black millions still in bondage, and became their one ideal of life. The black bards caught new notes, and sometimes even dared to sing,—

> "O Freedom, O Freedom, O Freedom over me!
> Before I'll be a slave
> I'll be buried in my grave,

And go home to my Lord
And be free."

For fifty years Negro religion thus transformed itself and identified itself with the dream of Abolition, until that which was a radical fad in the white North and an anarchistic plot in the white South had become a religion to the black world. Thus, when Emancipation finally came, it seemed to the freedman a literal Coming of the Lord. His fervid imagination was stirred as never before, by the tramp of armies, the blood and dust of battle, and the wail and whirl of social upheaval. He stood dumb and motionless before the whirl-wind: what had he to do with it? Was it not the Lord's doing, and marvellous in his eyes? Joyed and bewildered with what came, he stood awaiting new wonders till the inevitable Age of Reaction swept over the nation and brought the crisis of to-day.

It is difficult to explain clearly the present critical stage of Negro religion. First, we must remember that living as the blacks do in close contact with a great modern nation, and sharing, although imperfectly, the soul-life of that nation, they must necessarily be affected more or less directly by all the religious and ethical forces that are to-day moving the United States. These questions and movements are, however, overshadowed and dwarfed by the (to them) all-important question of their civil, political, and economic status. They must perpetually discuss the "Negro problem,"—must live, move, and have their being in it, and interpret all else in its light or darkness. With this come, too, peculiar problems of their inner life,—of the status of women, the maintenance of Home, the training of children, the accumulation of wealth, and the prevention of crime. All this must mean a time of intense ethical ferment, of religious heart-searching and intellectual unrest. From the double life every American Negro must live, as a Negro and as an American, as swept on by the current of the nineteenth while yet struggling in the eddies of the fifteenth century,—from this must arise a painful self-consciousness, an almost morbid sense of personality and a moral hesistancy which is fatal to self-confidence. The worlds within and without the Veil of Color are changing, and changing rapidly, but not at the same rate, not in the same way; and this must produce a peculiar wrenching of the soul, a peculiar sense of doubt and bewilderment. Such a double life, with double thoughts, double duties, and double social classes, must give rise to double words and double ideals, and tempt the mind to pretence or to revolt, to hypocrisy or to radicalism.

In some such doubtful words and phrases can one perhaps most clearly picture the peculiar ethical paradox that faces the Negro of to-day and is tingeing and changing his religious life. Feeling that his rights and his dearest ideals are being trampled upon, that the public conscience is ever more deaf to his righteous appeal, and that all the reactionary forces of prejudice, greed, and revenge are daily gaining new strength and fresh allies, the Negro faces no enviable dilemma. Conscious of his impotence, and pessimistic, he often becomes bitter and vindictive; and his religion, instead of a worship, is a complaint and a curse, a wail rather than a hope, a sneer rather than a faith. On the other hand, another type of mind, shrewder and keener and more tortuous too, sees in the very strength of the anti-Negro movement its patent weaknesses, and with Jesuitic casuistry is deterred by no ethical considerations in the endeavor to turn this weakness to the black man's strength. Thus we have two great and hardly reconcilable streams of thought and ethical strivings; the danger of the one lies in anarchy, that of the other in hypocrisy. The one type of Negro stands almost ready to curse God and die, and the other is too often found a traitor to right and a coward before force; the one is wedded to ideals remote, whimsical, perhaps impossible of realization; the other forgets that life is more than meat and the body more than raiment. But, after all, is not this simply the writhing of the age translated into black,— the triumph of the Lie which to-day, with its false culture, faces the hideousness of the anarchist assassin?

To-day the two groups of Negroes, the one in the North, the other in the South, represent these divergent ethical tendencies, the first tending toward radicalism, the other toward hypocritical compromise. It is no idle regret with which the white South mourns the loss of the old-time Negro,—the frank, honest, simple old servant who stood for the earlier religious age of submission and humility. With all his laziness and lack of many elements of true manhood, he was at least open-hearted, faithful, and sincere. To-day he is gone, but who is to blame for his going? Is it not those very persons who mourn for him? Is it not the tendency, born of Reconstruction and Reaction, to found a society on lawlessness and deception, to tamper with the moral fibre of a naturally honest and straightforward people until the whites threaten to become ungovernable tyrants and the blacks criminals and hypocrites? Deception is the natural defence of the weak against the strong, and the South used it for many years against its conquerors; to-day it must be prepared to see its black proletariat turn that same two-edged weapon against itself. And how natural this is! The death of Denmark Vesey and Nat Turner proved long since to the Negro the present hopelessness of physical defence. Political defence is becoming less and less available, and economic defence is still only partially effective. But there is a patent defence at hand,—the defence of deception and flattery, of cajoling and lying. It is the same defence which the Jews of the Middle Age used and which left its stamp on their character for centuries. To-day the young Negro of the South who would succeed cannot be frank and outspoken, honest and self-assertive, but rather he is daily tempted to be silent and wary, politic and sly; he must flatter and be pleasant, endure petty insults with a smile, shut his eyes to wrong; in too many cases he sees positive personal advantage in deception and lying. His real thoughts, his real aspirations, must be guarded in whispers; he must not criticise, he must not complain. Patience, humility, and adroitness must, in these growing black youth, replace impulse, manliness, and courage. With this sacrifice there is an economic opening, and perhaps peace and some prosperity. Without this there is riot, migration, or crime. Nor is this situation peculiar to the Southern United States,—is it not rather the only method by which undeveloped races have gained the right to share modern culture? The price of culture is a Lie.

On the other hand, in the North the tendency is to emphasize the radicalism of the Negro. Driven from his birthright in the South by a situation at which every fibre of his more outspoken and assertive nature revolts, he finds himself in a land where he can scarcely earn a decent living amid the harsh competition and the color discrimination. At the same time, through schools and periodicals, discussions and lectures, he is intellectually quickened and awakened. The soul, long pent up and dwarfed, suddenly expands in new-found freedom. What wonder that every tendency is to excess,—radical complaint, radical remedies, bitter denunciation or angry silence. Some sink, some rise. The criminal and the sensualist leave the church for the gambling-hell and the brothel, and fill the slums of Chicago and Baltimore; the better classes segregate themselves from the group-life of both white and black, and form an aristocracy, cultured but pessimistic, whose bitter criticism stings while it points out no way of escape. They despise the submission and subserviency of the Southern Negroes, but offer no other means by which a poor and oppressed minority can exist side by side with its masters. Feeling deeply and keenly the tendencies and opportunities of the age in which they live, their souls are bitter at the fate which drops the Veil between; and the very fact that this bitterness is natural and justifiable only serves to intensify it and make it more maddening.

Between the two extreme types of ethical attitude which I have thus sought to make clear wavers the mass of the millions of Negroes, North and South; and their religious life and activity partake of this social conflict within their ranks. Their churches are differentiating,— now into groups of cold, fashionable devotees, in no way distinguishable from similar white groups save in color of skin; now into large social and business institutions catering to the desire for information and amusement of their members, warily avoiding unpleasant questions both within and without the black world, and preaching in effect if not in word: *Dum vivimus, vivamus.*

But back of this still broods silently the deep religious feeling of the real Negro heart, the stirring, unguided might of powerful human souls who have lost the guiding star of the past and are seeking in the great night a new religious ideal. Some day the Awakening will come, when the pent-up vigor of ten million souls shall sweep irresistibly toward the Goal, out of the Valley of the Shadow of Death, where all that makes life worth living—Liberty, Justice, and Right—is marked "For White People Only."

CHAPTER XI

Of the Passing of the First-Born

O sister, sister, thy first-begotten,
The hands that cling and the feet that follow,
The voice of the child's blood crying yet,
Who hath remembered me? who hath forgotten?
Thou has forgotten, O summer swallow,
But the world shall end when I forget.

Swinburne

"Unto you a child is born," sang the bit of yellow paper that fluttered into my room one brown October morning. Then the fear of fatherhood mingled wildly with the job of creation; I wondered how it looked and how it felt,—what were its eyes, and how its hair curled and crumpled itself. And I thought in awe of her,—she who had slept with Death to tear a man-child from underneath her heart, while I was unconsciously wandering. I fled to my wife and child, repeating the while to myself half wonderingly, "Wife and child? Wife and child?"— fled fast and faster than boat and steam-car, and yet must ever impatiently await them; away from the hard-voiced city, away from the flickering sea into my own Berkshire Hills that sit all sadly guarding the gates of Massachusetts.

Up the stairs I ran to the wan mother and whimpering babe, to the sanctuary on whose altar a life at my bidding had offered itself to win a life, and won. What is this tiny formless thing, this new-born wail from an unknown world,—all head and voice? I handle it curiously, and watch perplexed its winking, breathing, and sneezing. I did not love it then; it seemed a ludicrous thing to love; but her I loved, my girl-mother, she whom now I saw unfolding like the glory of the morning—the transfigured woman.

Through her I came to love the wee thing, as it grew and waxed strong; as its little soul unfolded itself in twitter and cry and half-formed word, and as its eyes caught the gleam and flash of life. How beautiful he was, with his olive-tinted flesh and dark gold ringlets, his eyes of mingled blue and brown, his perfect little limbs, and the soft voluptuous roll which the blood of Africa had moulded into his features! I held him in my arms, after we had sped far away to our Southern home,—held him, and glanced at the hot red soil of Georgia and the breathless city of a hundred hills, and felt a vague unrest. Why was his hair tinted with gold? An evil omen was golden hair in my life. Why had not the brown of his eyes crushed out and killed the blue?—for brown were his father's eyes, and his father's father's. And thus in the Land of the Color-line I saw, as it fell across my baby, the shadow of the Veil.

Within the Veil was he born, said I; and there within shall he live,—a Negro and a Negro's son. Holding in that little head—ah, bitterly!—the unbowed pride of a hunted race, clinging with that tiny dimpled hand—ah, wearily!—to a hope not hopeless but unhopeful, and seeing with those bright wondering eyes that peer into my soul a land whose freedom is to us a mockery and whose liberty a lie. I saw the shadow of the Veil as it passed over my baby, I saw the cold city towering above the blood-red land. I held my face beside his little cheek, showed him the star-children and the twinkling lights as they began to flash, and stilled with an even-song the unvoiced terror of my life.

So sturdy and masterful he grew, so filled with bubbling life, so tremulous with the unspoken wisdom of a life but eighteen months distant from the All-life,—we were not far from worshipping this revelation of the divine, my wife and I. Her own life builded and moulded itself upon the child; he tinged her every dream and idealized her every effort. No hands but hers must touch and garnish those little limbs; no dress or frill must touch them that had not wearied her fingers; no voice but hers could coax him off to Dreamland, and she and he together spoke some soft and unknown tongue and in it held communion. I too mused above his little white bed; saw the strength of my own arm stretched onward through the ages through the newer strength of his; saw the dream of my black fathers stagger a step onward in the wild phantasm of the world; heard in his baby voice the voice of the Prophet that was to rise within the Veil.

And so we dreamed and loved and planned by fall and winter, and the full flush of the long Southern spring, till the hot winds rolled from the fetid Gulf, till the roses shivered and the still stern sun quivered its awful light over the hills of Atlanta. And then one night the little feet pattered wearily to the wee white bed, and the tiny hands trembled; and a warm flushed face tossed on the pillow, and we knew baby was sick. Ten days he lay there,—a swift week and three endless days, wasting, wasting away. Cheerily the mother nursed him the first days, and laughed into the little eyes that smiled again. Tenderly then she hovered round him, till the smile fled away and Fear crouched beside the little bed.

Then the day ended not, and night was a dreamless terror, and joy and sleep slipped away. I hear now that Voice at midnight calling me from dull and dreamless trance,—crying, "The Shadow of Death! The Shadow of Death!" Out into the starlight I crept, to rouse the gray physician,—the Shadow of Death, the Shadow of Death. The hours trembled on; the night listened; the ghastly dawn glided like a tired thing across the lamplight. Then we two alone looked upon the child as he turned toward us with great eyes, and stretched his string-like hands,—the Shadow of Death! And we spoke no word, and turned away.

He died at eventide, when the sun lay like a brooding sorrow above the western hills, veiling its face; when the winds spoke not, and the trees, the great green trees he loved, stood motionless. I saw his breath beat quicker and quicker, pause, and then his little soul leapt like a star that travels in the night and left a world of darkness in its train. The day changed not; the same tall trees peeped in at the windows, the same green grass glinted in the setting sun. Only in the chamber of death writhed the world's most piteous thing—a childless mother.

I shirk not. I long for work. I pant for a life full of striving. I am no coward, to shrink before the rugged rush of the storm, nor even quail before the awful shadow of the Veil. But hearken, O Death! Is not this my life hard enough,—is not that dull land that stretches its sneering web about me cold enough,—is not all the world beyond these four little walls pitiless enough, but that thou must needs enter here,— thou, O Death? About my head the thundering storm beat like a heartless voice, and the crazy forest pulsed with the curses of the weak; but what cared I, within my home beside my wife and baby boy? Was thou so jealous of one little coign of happiness that thou must needs enter there,—thou, O Death?

A perfect life was his, all joy and love, with tears to make it brighter,—sweet as a summer's day beside the Housatonic. The world loved him; the women kissed his curls, the men looked gravely into his wonderful eyes, and the children hovered and fluttered about him. I can see him now, changing like the sky from sparkling laughter to darkening frowns, and then to wondering thoughtfulness as he watched the world. He knew no color-line, poor dear,—and the Veil, though it shadowed him, had not yet darkened half his sun. He loved the white matron, he loved his black nurse; and in his little world walked souls alone, uncolored and unclothed. I—yea, all men—are larger and purer by the infinite breath of that one little life. She who in simple clearness of vision sees beyond the stars said when he had flown, "He will be happy There; he ever loved beautiful things." And I, far more ignorant, and blind by the web of mine own weaving, sit alone winding words and muttering, "If still he be, and he be There, and there be a There, let him be happy, O Fate!"

Blithe was the morning of his burial, with bird and song and sweet-smelling flowers. The trees whispered to the grass, but the children sat with hushed faces. And yet it seemed a ghostly unreal day,—the wraith of Life. We seemed to rumble down an unknown street behind a little white bundle of posies, with the shadow of a song in our ears. The busy city dinned about us; they did not say much, those pale-faced hurrying men and women; they did not say much,—they only glanced and said, "Niggers!"

We could not lay him in the ground there in Georgia, for the earth there is strangely red; so we bore him away to the northward, with his flowers and his little folded hands. In vain, in vain!—for where, O God! beneath thy broad blue sky shall my dark baby rest in peace,—where Reverence dwells, and Goodness, and a Freedom that is free?

All that day and all that night there sat an awful gladness in my heart,—nay, blame me not if I see the world thus darkly through the Veil,—and my soul whispers ever to me, saying, "Not dead, not dead, but escaped; not bond, but free." No bitter meanness now shall sicken his baby heart till it die a living death, no taunt shall madden his happy boyhood. Fool that I was to think or wish that this little soul should grow choked and deformed within the Veil! I might have known that yonder deep unworldly look that ever and anon floated past his eyes was peering far beyond this narrow Now. In the poise of his little curl-crowned head did there not sit all that wild pride of being which his father had hardly crushed in his own heart? For what, forsooth, shall a Negro want with pride amid the studied humiliations of fifty million fellows? Well sped, my boy, before the world had dubbed your ambition insolence, had held your ideals unattainable, and taught you to cringe and bow. Better far this nameless void that stops my life than a sea of sorrow for you.

Idle words; he might have borne his burden more bravely than we,—aye, and found it lighter too, some day; for surely, surely this is not the end. Surely there shall yet dawn some mighty morning to lift the Veil and set the prisoned free. Not for me,—I shall die in my bonds,—but for fresh young souls who have not known the night and waken to the morning; a morning when men ask of the workman, not "Is he white?" but "Can he work?" When men ask artists, not "Are they black?" but "Do they know?" Some morning this may be, long, long years to come. But now there wails, on that dark shore within the Veil, the same deep voice, *Thou shalt forego!* And all have I foregone at that command, and with small complaint,—all save that

211

fair young form that lies so coldly wed with death in the nest I had builded.

If one must have gone, why not I? Why may I not rest me from this restlessness and sleep from this wide waking? Was not the world's alembic, Time, in his young hands, and is not my time waning? Are there so many workers in the vineyard that the fair promise of this little body could lightly be tossed away? The wretched of my race that line the alleys of the nation sit fatherless and unmothered; but Love sat beside his cradle, and in his ear Wisdom waited to speak. Perhaps now he knows the All-love, and needs not to be wise. Sleep, then, child,—sleep till I sleep and waken to a baby voice and the ceaseless patter of little feet—above the Veil.

CHAPTER **XII**

Of Alexander Crummell

Then from the Dawn it seemed there came, but faint
As from beyond the limit of the world,
Like the last echo born of a great cry,
Sounds, as if some fair city were one voice
Around a king returning from his wars.

Tennyson

This is the history of a human heart,—the tale of a black boy who many long years ago began to struggle with life that he might know the world and know himself. Three temptations he met on those dark dunes that lay gray and dismal before the wonder-eyes of the child: the temptation of Hate, that stood out against the red dawn; the temptation of Despair, that darkened noonday; and the temptation of Doubt, that ever steals along with twilight. Above all, you must hear of the vales he crossed,—the Valley of Humiliation and the Valley of the Shadow of Death.

I saw Alexander Crummell first at a Wilberforce commencement season, amid its bustle and crush. Tall, frail, and black he stood, with simple dignity and an unmistakable air of good breeding. I talked with him apart, where the storming of the lusty young orators could not harm us. I spoke to him politely, then curiously, then eagerly, as I began to feel the fineness of his character;—his calm courtesy, the sweetness of his strength, and his fair blending of the hope and truth of life. Instinctively I bowed before this man, as one bows before the prophets of the world. Some seer he seemed, that came not from the crimson Past or the gray To-come, but from the pulsing Now,—that mocking world which seemed to me at once so light and dark, so splendid and sordid. Four-score years had he wandered in this same world of mine, within the Veil.

He was born with the Missouri Compromise and lay a-dying amid the echoes of Manila and El Caney: stirring times for living, times dark to look back upon, darker to look forward to. The black-faced lad that paused over his mud and marbles seventy years ago saw puzzling vistas as he looked down the world. The slave-ship still groaned across the Atlantic, faint cries burdened the Southern breeze, and the great black father whispered mad tales of cruelty into those young ears. From the low doorway the mother silently watched her boy at play, and at nightfall sought him eagerly lest the shadows bear him away to the land of slaves.

So his young mind worked and winced and shaped curiously a vision of Life; and in the midst of that vision ever stood one dark figure alone,—ever with the hard, thick countenance of that bitter father, and a form that fell in vast and shapeless folds. Thus the temptation of Hate grew and shadowed the growing child,—gliding stealthily into his laughter, fading into his play, and seizing his dreams by day and night with rough, rude turbulence. So the black boy asked of sky and sun and flower the never-answered Why? and loved, as he grew, neither the world nor the world's rough ways.

Strange temptation for a child, you may think; and yet in this wide land to-day a thousand thousand dark children brood before this same temptation, and feel its cold and shuddering arms. For them, perhaps, some one will some day lift the Veil,—will come tenderly and cheerily into those sad little lives and brush the brooding hate away, just as Beriah Green strode in upon the life of Alexander Crummell. And before the bluff, kind-hearted man the shadow seemed less dark. Beriah Green had a school in Oneida County, New York, with a score of mischievous boys. "I'm going to bring a black boy here to educate," said Beriah Green, as only a crank and an abolitionist would have dared to say. "Ohio!" laughed the boys. "Yees," said his wife; and Alexander came. Once before, the black had sought a school, had travelled, cold and hungry, four hundred miles up into free New Hampshire, to Canaan. But the godly farmers hitched ninety yoke of oxen to the abolition schoolhouse and dragged it into the middle of the swamp. The black boy trudged away.

The nineteenth was the first century of human sympathy,—the age when half wonderingly we began to descry in others that transfigured spark of divinity which we call Myself; when clodhopper and peasants, and tramps and thieves, and millionaires and—sometimes—Negroes, became throbbing souls whose warm pulsing life touched us so nearly that we half gasped with surprise, crying, "Thou too! Hast Thou seen Sorrow and the dull waters of Hopelessness? Hast Thou known Life?" And then all helplessly we peered into those Other-worlds, and wailed, "O World of Worlds, how shall man make you one?"

So in that little Oneida school there came to those schoolboys a revelation of thought and longing beneath one black skin, of which they had not dreamed before. And to the lonely boy came a new dawn of sympathy and inspiration. The shadowy, formless thing—the temptation of Hate, that hovered between him and the world—grew fainter and less sinister. It did not wholly fade away, but diffused itself and lingered thick at the edges. Through it the child now first saw the blue and gold of life,—the sun-swept road that ran 'twixt heaven and earth until in one far-off wan wavering line they met and kissed. A vision of life came to the growing boy,—mystic, wonderful. He raised his head, stretched himself, breathed deep of the fresh new air. Yonder, behind the forests, he heard strange sounds; then glinting through the trees he saw, far, far away, the bronzed hosts of a nation calling,—calling faintly, calling loudly. He heard the fateful clank of their chains, he felt them cringe and grovel, and there rose within him a protest and a prophecy. And he girded himself to walk down the world.

A voice and vision called him to be a priest,—a seer to lead the uncalled out of the house of bondage. He saw the headless host turn toward him like the whirling of mad waters,—he stretched forth his hands eagerly, and then, even as he stretched them, suddenly there swept across the vision the temptation of Despair.

They were not wicked men,—the problem of life is not the problem of the wicked,—they were calm, good men, Bishops of the Apostolic Church of God, and strove toward righteousness. They said slowly, "It is all very natural—it is even commendable; but the General Theological Seminary of the Episcopal Church cannot admit a Negro." And when that thin, half-grotesque figure still haunted their doors, they put their hands kindly, half sorrowfully, on his shoulders, and said, "Now,—of course, we—we know how *you* feel about it; but you see it is impossible,—that is—well—it is premature. Sometime, we trust—sincerely trust—all such distinctions will fade away; but now the world is as it is."

This was the temptation of Despair; and the young man fought it doggedly. Like some grave shadow he flitted by those halls, pleading, arguing, half angrily demanding admittance, until there came the final *No;* until men hustled the disturber away, marked him as foolish, unreasonable, and injudicious, a vain rebel against God's law. And then from that Vision Splendid all the glory faded slowly away, and left an earth gray and stern rolling on beneath a dark despair. Even the kind hands that stretched themselves toward him from out the depths of that dull morning seemed but parts of the purple shadows. He saw them coldly, and asked, "Why should I strive by special grace when the way of the world is closed to me?" All gently yet, the hands urged him on,—the hand of young John Jay, that daring father's daring son; the hands of the good folk of Boston, that free city. And yet, with a way to the priesthood of the Church open at last before him, the cloud lingered there; and even when in old St. Paul's the venerable Bishop raised his white arms above the Negro deacon—even then the burden had not lifted from that heart, for there had passed a glory from the earth.

And yet the fire through which Alexander Crummell went did not burn in vain. Slowly and more soberly he took up again his plan of life. More critically he studied the situation. Deep down below the slavery and servitude of the Negro people he saw their fatal weaknesses, which long years of mistreatment had emphasized. The dearth of strong moral character, of unbending righteousness, he felt, was their great shortcoming, and here he would begin. He would gather the best of his people into some little Episcopal chapel and there lead, teach, and inspire them, till the leaven spread, till the children grew, till the world hearkened, till—till—and then across his dream gleamed some faint after-glow of that first fair vision of youth—only an after-glow, for there had passed a glory from the earth.

One day—it was in 1842, and the springtide was struggling merrily with the May winds of New England—he stood at the last in his own chapel in Providence, a priest of the Church. The days sped by, and the dark young clergyman labored; he wrote his sermons carefully; he intoned his prayers with a soft, earnest voice; he haunted the streets and accosted the wayfarers; he visited the sick, and knelt beside the dying. He worked and toiled, week by week, day by day, month by month. And yet month by month the congregation dwindled, week by week the hollow walls echoed more sharply, day by day the calls came fewer and fewer, and day by day the third temptation sat clearer and still more clearly within the Veil; a temptation, as it were, bland and smiling, with just a shade of mockery in its smooth tones. First it came casually, in the cadence of a voice: "Oh, colored folks? Yes." Or perhaps more definitely: "What do you *expect*?" In voice and gesture lay the doubt—the temptation of Doubt. How he hated it, and stormed at it furiously! "Of course they are capable," he cried; "of course they can learn and strive and achieve—" and "Of course," added the temptation softly, "they do nothing of the sort." Of all the three temptations, this one struck the deepest. Hate? He had outgrown so childish a thing. Despair? He had steeled his right arm against it, and fought it with the vigor of determination. But to doubt the worth of his life-work,—to doubt the destiny and capability of the race his soul loved because it was his; to find listless squalor instead of eager endeavor; to hear his own lips whispering, "They do not care; they cannot know; they are dumb driven cattle,—why cast your pearls before swine?"—this, this seemed more than man could bear; and he closed the door, and sank upon the steps of the chancel, and cast his robe upon the floor and writhed.

The evening sunbeams had set the dust to dancing in the gloomy chapel when he arose. He folded his vestments, put away the hymn-books, and closed the great Bible. He stepped out into the twilight, looked back upon the narrow little pulpit with a weary smile, and locked the door. Then he walked briskly to the Bishop, and told the Bishop what the Bishop already knew. "I have failed," he said simply. And gaining courage by the confession, he added: "What I need is a larger constituency. There are comparatively few Negroes here, and perhaps they are not of the best. I must go where the field is wider, and try again." So the Bishop sent him to Philadelphia, with a letter to Bishop Onderdonk.

Bishop Onderdonk lived at the head of six white steps,—corpulent, red-faced, and the author of several thrilling tracts on Apostolic Succession. It was after dinner, and the Bishop had settled himself for a pleasant season of contemplation, when the bell must needs ring, and there must burst in upon the Bishop a letter and a thin, ungainly Negro. Bishop Onderdonk read the letter hastily and frowned. Fortunately, his mind was already clear on this point; and he cleared his brow and looked at Crummell. Then he said, slowly and impressively: "I will receive you into this diocese on one condition: no Negro priest can sit in my church convention, and no Negro church must ask for representation there."

I sometimes fancy I can see that tableau: the frail black figure, nervously twitching his hat before the massive abdomen of Bishop Onderdonk; his threadbare coat thrown against the dark woodwork of the book-cases, where Fox's "Lives of the Martyrs" nestled happily beside "The Whole Duty of Man." I seem to see the wide eyes of the Negro wander past the Bishop's broadcloth to where the swinging glass doors of the cabinet glow in the sunlight. A little blue fly is trying to cross the yawning keyhole. He marches briskly up to it, peers into the chasm in a surprised sort of way, and rubs his feelers reflectively; then he essays its depths, and, finding it bottomless, draws back again. The dark-faced priest finds himself wondering if the fly too has faced its Valley of Humiliation, and if it will plunge into it,—when lo! it spreads its tiny wings and buzzes merrily across, leaving the watcher wingless and alone.

Then the full weight of his burden fell upon him. The rich walls wheeled away, and before him lay the cold rough moor winding on through life, cut in twain by one thick granite ridge,—here, the Valley of Humiliation; yonder, the Valley of the Shadow of Death. And I know not which be darker,—no, not I. But this I know: in yonder Vale of the Humble stand today a million swarthy men, who willingly would

> ". . . bear the whips and scorns of time,
> The oppressor's wrong, the proud man's contumely,
> The pangs of despised love, the law's delay,
> The insolence of office, and the spurns
> That patient merit of the unworthy takes,"

all this and more would they bear did they but know that this were sacrifice and not a meaner thing. So surged the thought within that lone black breast. The Bishop cleared his throat suggestively; then, recollecting that there was really nothing to say, considerately said nothing, only sat tapping his foot impatiently. But Alexander Crummell said, slowly and heavily: "I will never enter your diocese on such terms." And saying this, he turned and passed into the Valley of the Shadow of Death. You might have noted only the physical dying, the shattered frame and hacking cough; but in that soul lay deeper death than that. He found a chapel in New York,—the church of his father; he labored for it in poverty and starvation, scorned by his fellow priests. Half in despair, he wandered across the sea, a beggar with outstretched hands. Englishmen clasped them,—Wilberforce and Stanley, Thirwell and Ingles, and even Froude and Macaulay; Sir Benjamin Brodie bade him rest awhile at Queen's College in Cambridge, and there he lingered, struggling for health of body and mind, until he took his degree in '53. Restless still and unsatisfied, he turned toward Africa, and for long years, amid the spawn of the slave-smugglers, sought a new heaven and a new earth.

So the man groped for light; all this was not Life,—it was the world-wandering of a soul in search of itself, the striving of one who vainly sought his place in the world, ever haunted by the shadow of a death that is more than death,—the passing of a soul that has missed its duty. Twenty years he wandered,—twenty years and more; and yet the hard rasping question kept gnawing within him, "What, in God's name, am I on earth for?" In the narrow New York parish his soul seemed cramped and smothered. In the fine old air of the English University he heard the millions wailing over the sea. In the wild fever-cursed swamps of West Africa he stood helpless and alone.

You will not wonder at his weird pilgrimage,—you who in the swift whirl of living, amid its cold paradox and marvellous vision, have fronted life and asked its riddle face to face. And if you find that riddle hard to read, remember that yonder black boy finds it just a little harder; if it is difficult for you to find and face your duty, it is a shade more difficult for him; if your heart sickens in the blood and dust of battle, remember that to him the dust is thicker and the battle fiercer. No wonder the wanderers fall! No wonder we point to thief and murderer, and haunting prostitute, and the never-ending throng of unhearsed dead! The Valley of the Shadow of Death gives few of its pilgrims back to the world.

But Alexander Crummell it gave back. Out of the temptation of Hate, and burned by the fire of Despair, triumphant over Doubt, and steeled by Sacrifice against Humiliation, he turned at last home across the waters, humble and strong, gentle and determined. He bent to all the gibes and prejudices, to all hatred and discrimination, with that rare courtesy which is the armor of pure souls. He fought among his own, the low, the grasping, and the wicked, with that unbending righteousness which is the sword of the just. He never faltered, he seldom complained; he simply worked, inspiring the young, rebuking the old, helping the weak, guiding the strong.

So he grew, and brought within his wide influence all that was best of those who walk within the Veil. They who live without knew not nor dreamed of that full power within, that mighty inspiration which the dull gauze of caste decreed that most men should not know. And now that he is gone, I sweep the Veil away and cry, Lo! the soul to whose dear memory I bring this little tribute. I can see his face still, dark and heavy-lined beneath his snowy hair; lighting and shading, now with inspiration for the future, now in innocent pain at some human wickedness, now with sorrow at some hard memory from the past. The more I met Alexander Crummell, the more I felt how much that world was losing which knew so little of him. In another age he might have sat among the elders of the land in purple-bordered toga; in another country mothers might have sung him to the cradles.

He did his work,—he did it nobly and well; and yet I sorrow that here he worked alone, with so little human sympathy. His name today, in this broad land, means little, and comes to fifty million ears laden with no incense of memory or emulation. And herein lies the tragedy of the age: not that men are poor,—all men know something of poverty; not that men are wicked,—who is good? not that men are ignorant,—what is Truth? Nay, but that men know so little of men.

He sat one morning gazing toward the sea. He smiled and said, "The gate is rusty on the hinges." That night at star-rise a wind came moaning out of the west to blow the gate ajar, and then the soul I loved fled like a flame across the Seas, and in its seat sat Death.

I wonder where he is to-day? I wonder if in that dim world beyond, as he came gliding in, there rose on some wan throne a King,— a dark and pierced Jew, who knows the writhings of the earthly damned, saying, as he laid those heart-wrung talents down, "Well done!" while round about the morning stars sat singing.

CHAPTER **XIII**

Of the Coming of John

What bring they 'neath the midnight,
    Beside the River-sea?
They bring the human heart wherein
    No nightly calm can be;
That droppeth never with the wind,
    Nor drieth with the dew;
O calm it, God; thy calm is broad
    To cover spirits too.
    The river floweth on.

Mrs. Browning

Carlisle Street runs westward from the centre of Johnstown, across a great black bridge, down a hill and up again, by little shops and meat-markets, past single-storied homes, until suddenly it stops against a wide green lawn. It is a broad, restful place, with two large buildings outlined against the west. When at evening the winds come swelling from the east, and the great pall of the city's smoke hangs wearily above the valley, then the red west glows like a dream-land down Carlisle Street, and, at the tolling of the supper-bell, throws the passing forms of students in dark silhouette against the sky. Tall and black, they move slowly by, and seem in the sinister light to flit before the city like dim warning ghosts. Perhaps they are; for this is Wells Institute, and these black students have few dealings with the white city below.

And if you will notice, night after night, there is one dark form that ever hurries last and late toward the twinkling lights of Swain Hall,—for Jones is never on time. A long, straggling fellow he is, brown and hard-haired, who seems to be growing straight out of his clothes, and walks with a half-apologetic roll. He used perpetually to set the quiet dining-room into waves of merriment, as he stole to his place after the bell had tapped for prayers; he seemed so perfectly awkward. And yet one glance at his face made one forgive him much,— that broad, good-natured smile in which lay no bit of art or artifice, but seemed just bubbling good-nature and genuine satisfaction with the world.

He came to us from Altamaha, away down there beneath the gnarled oaks of Southeastern Georgia, where the sea croons to the sands and the sands listen till they sink half drowned beneath the waters, rising only here and there in long, low islands. The white folk of Altamaha voted John a good boy,—fine plough-hand, good in the rice-fields, handy everywhere, and always good-natured and respectful. But they shook their heads when his mother wanted to send him off to school. "It'll spoil him,—ruin him," they said; and they talked as though they knew. But full half the black folk followed him proudly to the station, and carried his queer little trunk and many bundles. And there they shook and shook hands, and the girls kissed him shyly and the boys clapped him on the back. So the train came, and he pinched his little sister lovingly, and put his great arms about his mother's neck, and then was away with a puff and a roar into the great yellow world that flamed and flared about the doubtful pilgrim. Up the coast they hurried, past the squares and palmettos of Savannah, through the cotton-fields and through the weary night, to Millville, and came with the morning to the noise and bustle of Johnstown.

And they that stood behind, that morning in Altamaha, and watched the train as it noisily bore playmate and brother and son away to the world, had thereafter one ever-recurring word,—"When John comes." Then what parties were to be, and what speakings in the churches; what new furniture in the front room,—perhaps even a new front room; and there would be a new schoolhouse, with John as teacher; and then perhaps a big wedding; all this and more—when John comes. But the white people shook their heads.

At first he was coming at Christmas-time,—but the vacation proved too short; and then, the next summer,—but times were hard and schooling costly, and so, instead, he worked in Johnstown. And so it drifted to the next summer, and the next,—till playmates scattered, and mother grew gray, and sister went up to the Judge's kitchen to work. And still the legend lingered,—"When John comes."

Up at the Judge's they rather liked this refrain; for they too had a John—a fair-haired, smooth-faced boy, who had played many a long summer's day to its close with his darker namesake. "Yes, sir! John is at Princeton, sir," said the broad-shouldered gray-haired Judge every morning as he marched down to the post-office. "Showing the Yankees what a Southern gentleman can do," he added; and strode home again with his letters and papers. Up at the great pillared house they lingered long over the Princeton letter,—the Judge and his frail wife, his sister and growing daughters. "It'll make a man of him," said the Judge, "college is the place." And then he asked the shy little waitress, "Well, Jennie, how's your John?" and added reflectively, "Too bad, too bad your mother sent him off,—it will spoil him." And the waitress wondered.

Thus in the far-away Southern village the world lay waiting, half consciously, the coming of two young men, and dreamed in an inarticulate way of new things that would be done and new thoughts that all would think. And yet it was singular that few thought of two Johns,—for the black folk thought of one John, and he was black; and the white folk thought of another John, and he was white. And neither world thought the other world's thought, save with a vague unrest.

Up in Johnstown, at the Institute, we were long puzzled at the case of John Jones. For a long time the clay seemed unfit for any sort of moulding. He was loud and boisterous, always laughing and singing, and never able to work consecutively at anything. He did not know how to study; he had no idea of thoroughness; and with his tardiness, carelessness, and appalling good-humor, we were sore perplexed. One night we sat in faculty-meeting, worried and serious; for Jones was in trouble again. This last escapade was too much, and so we solemnly voted "that Jones, on account of repeated disorder and inattention to work, be suspended for the rest of the term."

It seemed to us that the first time life ever struck Jones as a really serious thing was when the Dean told him he must leave school. He stared at the gray-haired man blankly, with great eyes. "Why,—why," he faltered, "but—I haven't graduated!" Then the Dean slowly and clearly explained, reminding him of the tardiness and the carelessness, of the poor lessons and neglected work, of the noise and disorder, until the fellow hung his head in confusion. Then he said quickly, "But you won't tell mammy and sister,—you won't write mammy, now will you? For if you won't I'll go out into the city and work, and come back next term and show you something." So the Dean promised faithfully, and John shouldered his little trunk, giving neither word nor look to the giggling boys, and walked down Carlisle Street to the great city, with sober eyes and a set and serious face.

Perhaps we imagined it, but someway it seemed to us that the serious look that crept over his boyish face that afternoon never left it again. When he came back to us he went to work with all his rugged strength. It was a hard struggle, for things did not come easily to him,—few crowding memories of early life and teaching came to help him on his new way; but all the world toward which he strove was of his own building, and he builded slow and hard. As the light dawned lingeringly on his new creations, he sat rapt and silent before the vision, or wandered alone over the green campus peering through and beyond the world of men into a world of thought. And the thoughts at times puzzled him sorely; he could not see just why the circle was not square, and carried it out fifty-six decimal places one midnight,—would have gone further, indeed, had not the matron rapped for lights out. He caught terrible colds lying on his back in the meadows of nights, trying to think out the solar system; he had grave doubts as to the ethics of the Fall of Rome, and strongly suspected the Germans of being thieves and rascals, despite his text-books; he pondered long over every new Greek word, and wondered why this meant that and why it couldn't mean something else, and how it must have felt to think all things in Greek. So he thought and puzzled along for himself,—pausing perplexed where others skipped merrily, and walking steadily through the difficulties where the rest stopped and surrendered.

Thus he grew in body and soul, and with him his clothes seemed to grow and arrange themselves; coat sleeves got longer, cuffs appeared, and collars got less soiled. Now and then his boots shone, and a new dignity crept into his walk. And we who saw daily a new thoughtfulness growing in his eyes began to expect something of this plodding boy. Thus he passed out of the preparatory school into college, and we who watched him felt four more years of change, which almost transformed the tall, grave man who bowed to us commencement morning. He had left his queer thought-world and come back to a world of motion and of men. He looked now for the first time sharply about him, and wondered he had seen so little before. He grew slowly to feel almost for the first time the Veil that lay between him and the white world; he first noticed now the oppression that had not seemed oppression before, differences that erstwhile seemed natural, restraints and slights that in his boyhood days had gone unnoticed or been greeted with a laugh. He felt angry now when men did not call him "Mister," he clenched his hands at the "Jim Crow" cars, and chafed at the color-line that hemmed in him and his. A tinge of sarcasm crept into his speech, and a vague bitterness into his life; and he sat long hours wondering and planning a way around these crooked things. Daily he found himself shrinking from the choked and narrow life of his native town. And yet he always planned to go back to Altamaha,—always planned to work there. Still, more and more as the day approached he hesitated with a nameless dread; and even the day after graduation he seized with eagerness the offer of the Dean to send him North with the quartette during the summer vacation, to sing for the Institute. A breath of air before the plunge, he said to himself in half apology.

It was a bright September afternoon, and the streets of New York were brilliant with moving men. They reminded John of the sea, as he sat in the square and watched them, so changelessly changing, so bright and dark, so grave and gay. He scanned their rich and faultless clothes, the way they carried their hands, the shape of their hats; he peered into the hurrying carriages. Then, leaning back with a sigh, he said, "This is the World." The notion suddenly seized him to see where the world was going; since many of the richer and brighter seemed hurrying all one way. So when a tall, light-haired young man and a little talkative lady came by, he rose half hesitatingly and followed them. Up the street they went, past stores and gay shops, across a broad square, until with a hundred others they entered the high portal of a great building.

He was pushed toward the ticket-office with the others, and felt in his pocket for the new five-dollar bill he had hoarded. There seemed really no time for hesitation, so he drew it bravely out, passed it to the busy clerk, and received simply a ticket but no change. When at last he realized that he had paid five dollars to enter he knew not what, he stood stock-still amazed. "Be careful," said a low voice behind him; "you must not lynch the colored gentlemen simply because he's in your way," and a girl looked up roguishly into the eyes of her fair-haired escort. A shade of annoyance passed over the escort's face. "You *will* not understand us at the South," he said half impatiently as if continuing an argument. "With all your professions, one never sees in the North so cordial and intimate relations between white and black as are everyday occurrences with us. Why, I remember my closest playfellow in boyhood was a little Negro named after me, and surely no two,—*well!*" The man stopped short and flushed to the roots of his hair, for there directly beside his reserved orchestra chairs sat the Negro he had stumbled over in the hallway. He hesitated and grew pale with anger, called the usher and gave him his card, with a few peremptory words, and slowly sat down. The lady deftly changed the subject.

All this John did not see, for he sat in a half-maze minding the scene about him; the delicate beauty of the hall, the faint perfume, the moving myriad of men, the rich clothing and low hum of talking seemed all a part of a world so different from his, so strangely more beautiful than anything he had known, that he sat in dreamland, and started when, after a hush, rose high and clear the music of Lohengrin's swan. The infinite beauty of the wail lingered and swept through every muscle of his frame, and put it all a-tune. He closed his eyes and grasped the elbows of the chair, touching unwittingly the lady's arm. And the lady drew away. A deep longing swelled in all his heart to rise with that clear music out of the dirt and dust of that low life that held him prisoned and befouled. If he would only live up in the free air where birds sang and setting suns had no touch of blood! Who had called him to be the slave and butt of all? And if he had called, what right had he to call when a world like this lay open before men?

Then the movement changed, and fuller, mightier harmony swelled away. He looked thoughtfully across the hall, and wondered why the beautiful gray-haired woman looked so listless, and what the little man could be whispering about. He would not like to be listless and idle, he thought, for he felt with the music the movement of power within him. If he but had some master-work, some life-service, hard,— aye, bitter hard, but without the cringing and sickening servility, without the cruel hurt that hardened his heart and soul. When at last a soft sorrow crept across the violins, there came to him the vision of a far-off home,—the great eyes of his sister, and the dark drawn face of his mother. And his heart sank below the waters, even as the sea-sand sinks by the shores of Altamaha, only to be lifted aloft again with that last ethereal wail of the swan that quivered and faded away into the sky.

It left John sitting so silent and rapt that he did not for some time notice the usher tapping him lightly on the shoulder and saying politely, "Will you step this way, please, sir?" A little surprised, he arose quickly at the last tap, and, turning to leave his seat, looked full into the face of the fair-haired young man. For the first time the young man recognized his dark boyhood playmate, and John knew that it was the Judge's son. The white John started, lifted his hand, and then froze into his chair; the black John smiled lightly, then grimly, and followed the usher down the isle. The manager was sorry, very, very sorry,— but he explained that some mistake had been made in selling the gentleman a seat already disposed of; he would refund the money, of course,—and indeed felt the matter keenly, and so forth, and—before he had finished John was gone, wallking hurriedly across the square and down the broad streets, and as he passed the park he buttoned his coat and said, "John Jones, you're a natural-born fool." Then he went to his lodgings and wrote a letter, and tore it up; he wrote another, and threw it in the fire. Then he seized a scrap of paper and wrote: "Dear Mother and Sister—I am coming—John."

"Perhaps," said John, as he settled himself on the train, "perhaps I am to blame myself in struggling against my manifest destiny simply because it looks hard and unpleasant. Here is my duty to Altamaha plain before me; perhaps they'll let me help settle the Negro problems there,—perhaps they won't. 'I will go in to the King, which is not according to the law; and if I perish, I perish.' " And then he mused and dreamed, and planned a life-work; and the train flew south.

Down in Altamaha, after seven long years, all the world knew John was coming. The homes were scrubbed and scoured,—above all, one; the gardens and yards had an unwonted trimness, and Jennie bought a new gingham. With some finesse and negotiation, all the dark Methodists and Presbyterians were induced to join in a monster welcome at the Baptist Church; and as the day drew near, warm discussions arose on every corner as to the exact extent and nature of John's accomplishments. It was noontide on a gray and cloudy day when he came. The black town flocked to the depot, with a little of the white at the edges,—a happy throng, with "Good-mawnings" and "Howdys" and laughing and joking and jostling. Mother sat yonder in the window watching; but sister Jennie stood on the platform, nervously fingering her dress,—tall and lithe, with soft brown skin and loving eyes peering from out a tangled wilderness of hair. John rose gloomily as the train stopped, for he was thinking of the "Jim Crow" car; he stepped to the platform, and paused: a little dingy station, a black crowd gaudy and dirty, a half-mile of dilapidated shanties along a straggling ditch of mud. An overwhelming sense of the sordidness and narrowness of it all seized him; he look in vain for his mother, kissed coldly the tall, strange girl who called him brother, spoke a short, dry word here and there; then, lingering neither for hand-shaking nor gossip, started silently up the street, raising his hat merely to the least eager old aunty, to her open-mouthed astonishment. The people were distinctly bewildered. This silent, cold man,—was this John? Where was his smile and hearty hand-grasp? " 'Peared kind o' down in the mouf," said the Methodist preacher thoughtfully. "Seemed monstus stuck up," complained a Baptist sister. But the white postmaster from the edge of the crowd expressed the opinion of his folks plainly. "That damn Nigger," said he, as he shouldered the mail and arranged his tobacco, "has gone North and got plum full o' fool notions; but they won't work in Altamaha." And the crowd melted away.

The meeting of welcome at the Baptist Church was a failure. Rain spoiled the barbecue, and thunder turned the milk in the ice-cream. When the speaking came at night, the house was crowded to overflowing. The three preachers had especially prepared themselves, but somehow John's manner seemed to throw a blanket over everything,— he seemed so cold and preoccupied, and had so strange an air of restraint that the Methodist brother could not warm up to his theme and elicited not a single "Amen"; the Presbyterian prayer was but feebly responded to, and even the Baptist preacher, though he wakened faint enthusiasm, got so mixed up in his favorite sentence that he had to close it by stopping fully fifteen minutes sooner than he meant. The people moved uneasily in their seats as John rose to reply. He spoke slowly and methodically. The age, he said, demanded new ideas; we were far different from those men of the seventeenth and eighteenth centuries,—with broader ideas of human brotherhood and destiny. Then he spoke of the rise of charity and popular education, and particularly of the spread of wealth and work. The question was, then, he added reflectively, looking at the low discolored ceiling, what part the Negroes of this land would take in the striving of the new century. He sketched in vague outline the new Industrial School that might rise among these pines, he spoke in detail of the charitable and philanthropic work that might be organized, of money that might be saved for banks and business. Finally he urged unity, and deprecated especially religious and denominational bickering. "To-day," he said, with a smile, "the world cares little whether a man be Baptist or Methodist, or indeed a churchman at all, so long as he is good and true. What difference does it make whether a man be baptized in river or wash-bowl, or not at all? Let's leave all that littleness, and look higher." Then, thinking of nothing else, he slowly sat down. A painful hush seized that crowded mass. Little had they understood of what he said, for he spoke an unknown tongue, save the last word about baptism; that they knew, and they sat very still while the clock ticked. Then at last a low suppressed snarl came from the Amen corner, and an old bent man arose, walked over the seats, and climbed straight up into the pulpit. He was wrinkled and black, with scant gray and tufted hair; his voice and hands shook as with palsy; but on his face lay the intense rapt look of the religious fanatic. He seized the Bible with his rough, huge hands; twice he raised it inarticulate, and then fairly burst into the words, with rude and awful eloquence. He quivered, swayed, and bent; then rose aloft in perfect majesty, till the people moaned and wept, wailed and shouted, and a wild shrieking arose from the corners where all the pent-up feeling of the hour gathered itself and rushed into the air. John never knew clearly what the old man said; he only felt himself held up to scorn and scathing denunciation for trampling on the true Religion, and he realized with amazement that all unknow-ingly he had put rough, rude hands on something this little world held sacred. He arose silently, and passed out into the right. Down toward the sea he went, in the fitful starlight, half conscious of the girl who followed timidly after him. When at last he stood upon the bluff, he turned to his little sister and looked upon her sorrowfully, remember-ing with sudden pain how little thought he had given her. He put his arm about her and let her passion of tears spend itself on his shoulder.

Long they stood together, peering over the gray unresting water.

"John," she said, "does it make every one—unhappy when they study and learn lots of things?"

He paused and smiled. "I am afraid it does," he said.

"And, John, are you glad you studied?"

"Yes," came the answer, slowly but positively.

She watched the flickering lights upon the sea, and said thought-fully, "I wish I was unhappy,—and—and," putting both arms about his neck, "I think I am, a little, John."

It was several days later that John walked up to the Judge's house to ask for the privilege of teaching the Negro school. The Judge himself met him at the front door, stared a little hard at him, and said brusquely, "Go 'round to the kitchen door, John, and wait." Sitting on the kitchen steps, John stared at the corn, thoroughly perplexed. What on earth had come over him? Every step he made offended some one. He had come to save his people, and before he left the depot he had hurt them. He sought to teach them at the church, and had outraged their deepest feelings. He had schooled himself to be respectful to the Judge, and then blundered into his front door. And all the time he had meant right,—and yet, and yet, somehow he found it so hard and strange to fit his old surroundings again, to find his place in the world about him. He could not remember that he used to have any difficulty in the past, when life was glad and gay. The world seemed smooth and easy then. Perhaps,—but his sister came to the kitchen door just then and said the Judge awaited him.

The Judge sat in the dining-room amid his morning's mail, and he did not ask John to sit down. He plunged squarely into the business. "You've come for the school, I suppose. Well, John, I want to speak to you plainly. You know I'm a friend to your people. I've helped you and your family, and would have done more if you hadn't got the notion of going off. Now I like the colored people, and sympathize with all their reasonable aspirations; but you and I both know, John, that in this country the Negro must remain subordinate, and can never expect to be the equal of white men. In their place, your people can be honest and respectful; and God knows, I'll do what I can to help them. But when they want to reverse nature, and rule white men, and marry white women, and sit in my parlor, then, by God! we'll hold them under if we have to lynch every Nigger in the land. Now, John, the question is, are you, with your education and Northern notions, going to accept the situation and teach the darkies to be faithful servants and laborers as your fathers were,—I knew your father, John, he belonged to my brother, and he was a good Nigger. Well—well, are you going to be like him, or are you going to try to put fool ideas of rising and equality into these folks' heads, and make then discontented and unhappy?"

"I am going to accept the situation, Judge Henderson," answered John, with a brevity that did not escape the keen old man. He hesitated a moment, and then said shortly, "Very well,—we'll try you awhile. Good-morning."

It was a full month after the opening of the Negro school that the other John came home, tall, gay, and headstrong. The mother wept, the sisters sang. The whole white town was glad. A proud man was the Judge, and it was a goodly sight to see the two swinging down Main Street together. And yet all did not go smoothly between them, for the younger man could not and did not veil his contempt for the little town, and plainly had his heart set on New York. Now the one cherished ambition of the Judge was to see his son mayor of Altamaha, representative to the legislature, and—who could say?—governor of Georgia. So the argument often waxed hot between them. "Good heavens, father," the younger man would say after dinner, as he lighted a cigar and stood by the fireplace, "you surely don't expect a young fellow like me to settle down permanently in this—this God-forgotten town with nothing but mud and Negroes?" "*I did,*" the Judge would answer laconically; and on this particular day it seemed from the gathering scowl that he was about to add something more emphatic, but neighbors had already begun to drop in to admire his son, and the conversation drifted.

"Heah that John is livenin' things up at the darky school," volunteered the postmaster, after a pause.

"What now?" asked the Judge, sharply.

"Oh, nothin' in particulah,—just his almighty air and uppish ways. B'lieve I did heah somethin' about his givin' talks on the French Revolution, equality, and such like. He's what I call a dangerous Nigger."

"Have you heard him say anything out of the way?"

"Why, no,—but Sally, our girl, told my wife a lot of rot. Then, too, I don't need to heah: a Nigger what won't say 'sir' to a white man, or—"

"Who is this John?" interrupted the son.

"Why, it's little black John, Peggy's son,—your old playfellow."

The young man's face flushed angrily, and then he laughed.

"Oh," said he, "it's the darky that tried to force himself into a seat beside the lady I was escorting—"

But Judge Henderson waited to hear no more. He had been nettled all day, and now at this he rose with a half-smothered oath, took his hat and cane, and walked straight to the schoolhouse.

For John, it had been a long, hard pull to get things started in the rickety old shanty that sheltered his school. The Negroes were rent into factions for and against him, the parents were careless, the children irregular and dirty, and books, pencils, and slates largely missing. Nevertheless, he struggled hopefully on, and seemed to see at last some glimmering of dawn. The attendance was larger and the children were a shade cleaner this week. Even the booby class in reading showed a little comforting progress. So John settled himself with renewed patience this afternoon.

"Now, Mandy," he said cheerfully, "that's better; but you mustn't chop your words up so: 'If—the—man—goes.' Why, your little brother even wouldn't tell a story that way, now would he?"

"Naw, suh, he cain't talk."

"All right; now let's try again: 'If the man—' "

"John!"

The whole school started in surprise, and the teacher half arose, as the red, angry face of the Judge appeared in the open doorway.

"John, this school is closed. You children can go home and get to work. The white people of Altamaha are not spending their money on black folks to have their heads crammed with impudence and lies. Clear out! I'll lock the door myself."

Up at the great pillared house the tall young son wandered aimlessly about after his father's abrupt departure. In the house there was little to interest him; the books were old and stale, the local newspaper flat, and the women had retired with headaches and sewing. He tried a nap, but it was too warm. So he sauntered out into the fields, complaining disconsolately, "Good Lord! how long will this imprisonment last!" He was not a bad fellow,—just a little spoiled and self-indulgent, and as headstrong as his proud father. He seemed a young man pleasant to look upon, as he sat on the great black stump at the edge of the pines idly swinging his legs and smoking. "Why, there isn't even a girl worth getting up a respectable flirtation with," he growled. Just then his eye caught a tall, willowy figure hurrying toward him on the narrow path. He looked with interest at first, and then burst into a laugh as he said, "Well, I declare, if it isn't Jennie, the little brown kitchen-maid! Why, I never noticed before what a trim little body she is. Hello, Jennie! Why, you haven't kissed me since I came home," he said gaily. The young girl stared at him in surprise and confusion,—faltered something inarticulate, and attempted to pass. But a wilful mood had seized the young idler, and he caught at her arm. Frightened, she slipped by; and half mischievously he turned and ran after her through the tall pines.

Yonder, toward the sea, at the end of the path, came John slowly, with his head down. He had turned wearily homeward from the schoolhouse; then, thinking to shield his mother from the blow, started to meet his sister as she came from work and break the news of his dismissal to her. "I'll go away," he said slowly; "I'll go away and find work, and send for them. I cannot live here longer." And then the fierce, buried anger surged up into his throat. He waved his arms and hurried wildly up the path.

The great brown sea lay silent. The air scarce breathed. The dying day bathed the twisted oaks and mighty pines in black and gold. There came from the wind no warning, not a whisper from the cloudless sky. There was only a black man hurrying on with an ache in his heart, seeing neither sun nor sea, but starting as from a dream at the frightened cry that woke the pines, to see his dark sister struggling in the arms of a tall and fair-haired man.

He said not a word, but, seizing a fallen limb, struck him with all the pent-up hatred of his great black arm; and the body lay white and still beneath the pines, all bathed in sunshine and in blood. John looked at it dreamily, then walked back to the house briskly, and said in a soft voice, "Mammy, I'm going away,—I'm going to be free."

She gazed at him dimly and faltered, "No'th, honey, is yo' gwine No'th agin?"

He looked out where the North Star glistened pale above the waters, and said, "Yes, mammy, I'm going—North."

Then, without another word, he went out into the narrow lane, up by the straight pines, to the same winding path, and seated himself on the great black stump, looking at the blood where the body had lain. Yonder in the gray past he had played with that dead boy, romping together under the solemn trees. The night deepened; he thought of the boys at Johnstown. He wondered how Brown had turned out, and Carey? And Jones,—Jones? Why, *he* was Jones, and he wondered what they would all say when they knew, when they knew, in that great long dining-room with its hundreds of merry eyes. Then as the sheen of the starlight stole over him, he thought of the gilded ceiling of that vast concert hall, and heard stealing toward him the faint sweet music of the swan. Hark! was it music, or the hurry and shouting of men? Yes, surely! Clear and high the faint sweet melody rose and fluttered like a living thing, so that the very earth trembled as with the tramp of horses and murmur of angry men.

He leaned back and smiled toward the sea, whence rose the strange melody, away from the dark shadows where lay the noise of horses galloping, galloping on. With an effort he roused himself, bent forward, and looked steadily down the pathway, softly humming the "Song of the Bride,"—

"Freudig geführt, ziehet dahin."

Amid the trees in the dim morning twilight he watched their shadows dancing and heard their horses thundering toward him, until at last they came sweeping like a storm, and he saw in front that haggard white-haired man, whose eyes flashed red with fury. Oh, how he pitied him,—pitied him,—and wondered if he had the coiling twisted rope. Then, as the storm burst round him, he rose slowly to his feet and turned his closed eyes toward the Sea.

And the world whistled in his ears.

CHAPTER **XIV**

The Sorrow Songs

I walk through the churchyard
To lay this body down;
I know moon-rise, I know star-rise;
I walk in the moonlight, I walk in the starlight;
I'll lie in the grave and stretch out my arms,
I'll go to judgment in the evening of the day,
And my soul and thy soul shall meet that day,
When I lay this body down.

Negro Song

They that walked in darkness sang songs in the olden days—Sorrow Songs—for they were weary at heart. And so before each thought that I have written in this book I have set a phrase, a haunting echo of these weird old songs in which the soul of the black slave spoke to men. Ever since I was a child these songs have stirred me strangely. They came out of the South unknown to me, one by one, and yet at once I knew them as of me and of mine. Then in after years when I came to Nashville I saw the great temple builded of these songs towering over the pale city. To me Jubilee Hall seemed ever made of the songs themselves, and its bricks were red with the blood and dust of toil. Out of them rose for me morning, noon, and night, bursts of wonderful melody, full of the voices of my brothers and sisters, full of the voices of the past.

Little of beauty has America given the world save the rude grandeur God himself stamped on her bosom; the human spirit in this new world has expressed itself in vigor and ingenuity rather than in beauty. And so by fateful chance the Negro folk-song—the rhythmic cry of the slave—stands to-day not simply as the sole American music, but as the most beautiful expression of human experience born this side the seas. It has been neglected, it has been, and is, half despised, and above all it has been persistently mistaken and misunderstood; but notwithstanding, it still remains as the singular spiritual heritage of the nation and the greatest gift of the Negro people.

Away back in the thirties the melody of these slave songs stirred the nation, but the songs were soon half forgotten. Some, like "Near the lake where drooped the willow," passed into current airs and their source was forgotten; others were caricatured on the "minstrel" stage and their memory died away. Then in war-time came the singular Port Royal experiment after the capture of Hilton Head, and perhaps for the first time the North met the Southern slave face to face and heart to heart with no third witness. The Sea Islands of the Carolinas, where they met, were filled with a black folk of primitive type, touched and moulded less by the world about them than any others outside the Black Belt. Their appearance was uncouth, their language funny, but their hearts were human and their singing stirred men with a mighty power. Thomas Wentworth Higginson hastened to tell of these songs, and Miss McKim and others urged upon the world their rare beauty. But the world listened only half credulously until the Fisk Jubilee Singers sang the slave songs so deeply into the world's heart that it can never wholly forget them again.

There was once a blacksmith's son born at Cadiz, New York, who in the changes of time taught school in Ohio and helped defend Cincinnati from Kirby Smith. Then he fought at Chancellorsville and Gettysburg and finally served in the Freedman's Bureau at Nashville. Here he formed a Sunday school class of black children in 1866, and sang with them and taught them to sing. And then they taught him to sing, and when once the glory of the Jubilee songs passed into the soul of George L. White, he knew his life-work was to let those Negroes sing to the world as they had sung to him. So in 1871 the pilgrimage of the Fisk Jubilee Singers began. North to Cincinnati they rode,—four half-clothed black boys and five girl-women,—led by a man with a cause and a purpose. They stopped at Wilberforce, the oldest of Negro schools, where a black bishop blessed them. Then they went, fighting cold and starvation, shut out of hotels, and cheerfully sneered at, ever northward; and ever the magic of their song kept thrilling hearts, until a burst of applause in the Congregational Council at Oberlin revealed them to the world. They came to New York and Henry Ward Beecher dared to welcome them, even though the metropolitan dailies sneered at his "Nigger Minstrels." So their songs conquered till they sang across the land and across the sea, before Queen and Kaiser, in Scotland and Ireland, Holland and Switzerland. Seven years they sang, and brought back a hundred and fifty thousand dollars to found Fisk University.

Since their day they have been imitated—sometimes well, by the singers of Hampton and Atlanta, sometimes ill, by straggling quartettes. Caricature has sought again to spoil the quaint beauty of the music, and has filled the air with many debased melodies which vulgar ears scarce know from the real. But the true Negro folk-song still lives in the hearts of those who have heard them truly sung and in the hearts of the Negro people.

What are these songs, and what do they mean? I know little of music and can say nothing in technical phrase, but I know something of men, and knowing them, I know that these songs are the articulate message of the slave to the world. They tell us in these eager days that life was joyous to the black slave, careless and happy. I can easily believe this of some, of many. But not all the past South, though it rose from the dead, can gainsay the heart-touching witnesss of these songs. They are the music of an unhappy people, of the children of disappointment; they tell of death and suffering and unvoiced longing toward a truer world, of misty wanderings and hidden ways.

The songs are indeed the siftings of centuries; the music is far more ancient than the words, and in it we can trace here and there signs of development. My grandfather's grandmother was seized by an evil Dutch trader two centuries ago; and coming to the valleys of the Hudson and Housatonic, black, little, and lithe, she shivered and shrank in the harsh north winds, looking longingly at the hills, and often crooned a heathen melody to the child between her knees, thus:

Do   ba - na   co - ba, ge - ne   me,   ge - ne   me!

Do   ba - na   co - ba, ge - ne   me,   ge - ne   me!

Ben d' nu - li, nu - li, nu - li, nu - li, ben   d'   le.

The child sang it to his children and they to their children's children, and so two hundred years it has travelled down to us and we sing it to our children, knowing as little as our fathers what its words may mean, but knowing well the meaning of its music.

This was primitive African music; it may be seen in larger form in the strange chant which heralds "The Coming of John":

> "You may bury me in the East,
> You may bury me in the West,
> But I'll hear the trumpet sound in that morning,"

—the voice of exile.

Ten master songs, more or less, one may pluck from this forest of melody—songs of undoubted Negro origin and wide popular currency, and songs peculiarly characteristic of the slave. One of these I have just mentioned. Another whose strains begin this book is "Nobody knows the trouble I've seen." When, struck with a sudden poverty, the United States refused to fulfill its promises of land to the freedmen, a brigadier-general went down to the Sea Islands to carry the news. An old woman on the outskirts of the throng began singing this song; all the mass joined with her, swaying. And the soldier wept.

The third song is the cradle-song of death which all men know,—

"Swing low, sweet chariot,"—whose bars begin the life story of "Alexander Crummell." Then there is the song of many waters, "Roll, Jordan, roll," a mighty chorus with minor cadences. There were many songs of the fugitive like that which opens "The Wings of Atalanta," and the more familiar "Been a-listening." The seventh is the song of the End and the Beginning—"My Lord, what a mourning! when the stars begin to fall"; a strain of this is placed before "The Dawn of Freedom." The song of groping—"My way's cloudy"—begins "The Meaning of Progress"; the ninth is the song of this chapter—"Wrestlin' Jacob, the day is a-breaking,"—a pæan of hopeful strife. The last master song is the song of songs—"Steal away,"—sprung from "The Faith of the Fathers."

There are many others of the Negro folk-songs as striking and characteristic as these, as, for instance, the three strains in the third, eighth, and ninth chapters; and others I am sure could easily make a selection on more scientific principles. There are, too, songs that seem to me a step removed from the more primitive types: there is the maze-like medley, "Bright sparkles," one phrase of which heads "The Black Belt"; the Easter carol, "Dust, dust and ashes"; the dirge, "My mother's took her flight and gone home"; and that burst of melody hovering over "The Passing of the First-Born"—"I hope my mother will be there in that beautiful world on high."

These represent a third step in the development of the slave song, of which "You may bury me in the East" is the first, and songs like "March on" (chapter six) and "Steal away" are the second. The first is African music, the second Afro-American, while the third is a blending of Negro music with the music heard in the foster land. The result is still distinctively Negro and the method of blending original, but the elements are both Negro and Caucasian. One might go further and find a fourth step in this development, where the songs of white America have been distinctively influenced by the slave songs or have incorporated whole phrases of Negro melody, as "Swanee River" and "Old Black Joe." Side by side, too, with the growth has gone the debasements and imitations—the Negro "minstrel" songs, many of the "gospel" hymns, and some of the contemporary "coon" songs,—a mass of music in which the novice may easily lose himself and never find the real Negro melodies.

In these songs, I have said, the slave spoke to the world. Such a message is naturally veiled and half articulate. Words and music have lost each other and new and cant phrases of a dimly understood theology have displaced the older sentiment. Once in a while we catch a strange world of an unknown tongue, as the "Mighty Myo," which figures as a river of death; more often slight words or mere doggerel are joined to music of singular sweetness. Purely secular songs are few in number, partly because many of them were turned into hymns by a change of words, partly because the frolics were seldom heard by the stranger, and the music less often caught. Of nearly all the songs, however, the music is distinctly sorrowful. The ten master songs I have mentioned tell in word and music of trouble and exile, of strife and hiding; they grope toward some unseen power and sigh for rest in the End.

The words that are left to us are not without interest, and, cleared of evident dross, they conceal much of real poetry and meaning beneath conventional theology and unmeaning rhapsody. Like all primitive folk, the slave stood near to Nature's heart. Life was a "rough and rolling sea" like the brown Atlantic of the Sea Islands; the "Wilderness" was the home of God, and the "lonesome valley" led to the way of life. "Winter'll soon be over," was the picture of life and death to a tropical imagination. The sudden wild thunderstorms of the South awed and impressed the Negroes,—at times the rumbling seemed to them "mournful," at times imperious:

> "My Lord calls me,
> He calls me by the thunder,
> The trumpet sounds it in my soul."

The monotonous toil and exposure is painted in many words. One sees the ploughmen in the hot, moist furrow, singing:

> "Dere's no rain to wet you,
> Dere's no sun to burn you,
> Oh, push along, believer,
> I want to go home."

The bowed and bent old man cries, with thrice-repeated wail:

> "O Lord, keep me from sinking down,"

and he rebukes the devil of doubt who can whisper:

> "Jesus is dead and God's gone away."

Yet the soul-hunger is there, the restlessness of the savage, the wail of the wanderer, and the plaint is put in one little phrase:

My soul wants some thing that's new, that's new

Over the inner thoughts of the slaves and their relations one with another the shadow of fear ever hung, so that we get but glimpses here and there, and also with them, eloquent omissions and silences. Mother and child are sung, but seldom father; fugitive and weary wanderer call for pity and affection, but there is little of wooing and wedding; the rocks and the mountains are well known, but home is unknown. Strange blending of love and helplessness sings through the refrain:

> "Yonder's my ole mudder,
> Been waggin' at de hill so long;
> 'Bout time she cross over,
> Git home bime-by."

Elsewhere comes the cry of the "motherless" and the "Farewell, farewell, my only child."

Love-songs are scarce and fall into two categories—the frivolous and light, and the sad. Of deep successful love there is ominous silence, and in one of the oldest of these songs there is a depth of history and meaning:

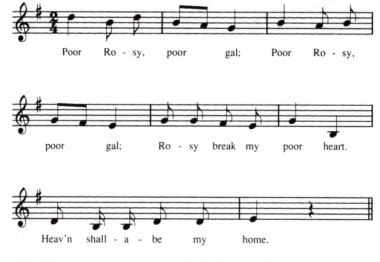

A black woman said of the song, "It can't be sung without a full heart and a troubled sperrit." The same voice sings here that sings in the German folk-song:

> "Jetz Geh i' an's brunele, trink' aber net."

Of death the Negro showed little fear, but talked of it familiarly and even fondly as simply a crossing of the waters, perhaps—who knows?—back to his ancient forests again. Later days transfigured his fatalism, and amid the dust and dirt the toiler sang:

> "Dust, dust and ashes, fly over my grave,
> But the Lord shall bear my spirit home."

The things evidently borrowed from the surrounding world undergo characteristic change when they enter the mouth of the slave. Especially is this true of Bible phrases. "Weep, O captive daughter of Zion," is quaintly turned into "Zion, weep-a-low," and the wheels of Ezekiel are turned every way in the mystic dreaming of the slave, till he says:

> "There's a little wheel a-turnin' in-a-my heart."

As in olden time, the words of these hymns were improvised by some leading minstrel of the religious band. The circumstances of the gathering, however, the rhythm of the songs, and the limitations of allowable thought, confined the poetry for the most part to single or double lines, and they seldom were expanded to quatrains or longer tales, although there are some few examples of sustained efforts, chiefly paraphrases of the Bible. Three short series of verses have always attracted me,—the one that heads this chapter, of one line of which Thomas Wentworth Higginson has fittingly said, "Never, it seems to me, since man first lived and suffered was his infinite longing for peace uttered more plaintively." The second and third are descriptions of the Last Judgment,—the one a late improvisation, with some traces of outside influence:

> "Oh, the stars in the elements are falling,
> And the moon drips away into blood,
> And the ransomed of the Lord are returning unto God,
> Blessed be the name of the Lord."

And the other earlier and homelier picture from the low coast lands:

> "Michael, haul the boat ashore,
> Then you'll hear the horn they blow,
> Then you'll hear the trumpet sound,
> Trumpet sound the world around,
> Trumpet sound for rich and poor,
> Trumpet sound the Jubilee,
> Trumpet sound for you and me."

Through all the sorrow of the Sorrow Songs there breathes a hope—a faith in the ultimate justice of things. The minor cadences of despair change often to triumph and calm confidence. Sometimes it is faith in life, sometimes a faith in death, sometimes assurance of boundless justice in some fair world beyond. But whichever it is, the meaning is always clear: that sometime, somewhere, men will judge men by their souls and not by their skins. Is such a hope justified? Do the Sorrow Songs sing true?

The silently growing assumption of this age is that the probation of races is past, and that the backward races of today are of proven inefficiency and not worth the saving. Such an assumption is the arrogance of peoples irreverent toward Time and ignorant of the deeds of men. A thousand years ago such an assumption, easily possible, would have made it difficult for the Teuton to prove his right to life. Two thousand years ago such dogmatism, readily welcome, would have scouted the idea of blond races ever leading civilization. So wofully unorganized is sociological knowledge that the meaning of progress, the meaning of "swift" and "slow" in human doing, and the limits of human perfectability, are veiled, unanswered sphinxes on the shores of science. Why should Æschylus have sung two thousand years before Shakespeare was born? Why has civilization flourished in Europe, and flickered, flamed, and died in Africa? So long as the world stands meekly dumb before such questions, shall this nation proclaim its ignorance and unhallowed prejudices by denying freedom of opportunity to those who brought the Sorrow Songs to the Seats of the Mighty?

Your country? How came it yours? Before the Pilgrims landed we were here. Here we have brought our three gifts and mingled them with yours: a gift of story and song—soft, stirring melody in an ill-harmonized and unmelodious land; the gift of sweat and brawn to beat back the wilderness, conquer the soil, and lay the foundations of this vast economic empire two hundred years earlier than your weak hands could have done it; the third, a gift of the Spirit. Around us the history of the land has centered for thrice a hundred years; out of the nation's heart we have called all that was best to throttle and subdue all that was worst; fire and blood, prayer and sacrifice, have billowed over this people, and they have found peace only in the altars of the God of Right. Nor has our gift of the Spirit been merely passive. Actively we have woven ourselves with the very warp and woof of this nation,— we fought their battles, shared their sorrow, mingled our blood with theirs, and generation after generation have pleaded with a headstrong, careless people to despise not Justice, Mercy, and Truth, lest the nation be smitten with a curse. Our song, our toil, our cheer, and warning have been given to this nation in blood-brotherhood. Are not these gifts worth the giving? Is not this work and striving? Would America have been America without her Negro people?

Even so is the hope that sang in the songs of my father well sung.
If somewhere in this whirl and chaos of things there dwells Eternal
Good, pitiful yet masterful, then anon in His good time America shall
rend the Veil and the prisoned shall go free. Free, free as the sunshine
trickling down the morning into these high windows of mine, free as
yonder fresh young voices welling up to me from the caverns of brick
and mortar below—swelling with song, instinct with life, tremulous
treble and darkening bass. My children, my little children, are singing
to the sunshine, and thus they sing:

Let us cheer the wea - ry trav - el - ler,_____

Cheer the wea - ry trav - el - er, Let us

cheer the wea - ry trav - el - er A -

long the heav - en - ly way.

And the traveller girds himself, and sets his face toward the Morning, and goes his way.

The Afterthought

Hear my cry, O God the Reader; vouchsafe that this my book fall not still-born into the world-wilderness. Let there spring, Gentle One, from out its leaves vigor of thought and thoughtful deed to reap the harvest wonderful. (Let the ears of a guilty people tingle with truth, and seventy millions sigh for the righteousness which exalteth nations, in this drear day when human brotherhood is mockery and a snare.) Thus in Thy good time may infinite reason turn the tangle straight, and these crooked marks on a fragile leaf be not indeed

THE END

CHAPTER 3

Representative Men

O ne could construct a revealing study of Du Bois's intellect and the transfiguration of his ideas over time from only his periodic speeches and essays on famous individuals. Although Du Bois was an ardent supporter of women's rights, these portraits of influential figures were almost exclusively devoted to men. Like Ralph Waldo Emerson, whose *Representative Men* recounted the key ideas and powerful personal traits of figures such as Shakespeare, Goethe, and Napoleon, or like Thomas Carlyle, whose *Heroes and Hero Worship* was another index of the nineteenth-century fascination with history as the drama of great men on the world stage, Du Bois was enamoured of the lives and ideas of those men who had had a profound impact on the issues and events of their day. His Fisk University graduation speech on German Chancellor Otto von Bismarck, whose political acumen Du Bois took as a model for organizing African Americans behind strong leaders, was a premonition of the more complex argument he would make about Jefferson Davis in a student commencement address given at Harvard in 1890. In much of his writing about these and other great men, one finds explicit or at least implicit self-portraits, admiring and sometimes prophetic pictures of the kind of leader Du Bois himself wished to become.

Although Du Bois would build his own career on a public argument with Booker T. Washington, stated most famously in a chapter of *The Souls of Black Folk*, his review of *Up From Slavery* in 1901 was much more attuned to Washington's achievements. In various short pieces and editorials written while he was editor of *The Crisis*, Du Bois paid tribute to important black figures such as Charles Young (1922), a World War I hero, but he also used the same forum to ridicule other American heroes such as Robert E. Lee (1928). Far more complex was Du Bois's attitude toward his rival, Marcus Garvey, for whom he initially expressed grudging admiration when Garvey brought the UNIA to Harlem and successfully rallied urban African Americans around his philosophy of black pride and Afrocentrism. Garvey's antipathy to the NAACP and his verbal assaults on Du

Bois alienated the two men, however, and Du Bois responded forcefully in an essay whose original title, "Back to Africa" (1923), mocked Garvey's doomed scheme to repatriate African Americans.

In an essay based on a lecture given at Hull House in 1907, Du Bois expressed his appreciation of Abraham Lincoln not simply as the president who brought about emancipation but also as proof that in the United States equal opportunity might truly be spread across all races and classes. The radical abolitionist John Brown, in contrast, became the subject of an entire 1909 book in which Du Bois collated existing biographical accounts of Brown into the portrait of a messianic, revolutionary hero caught up in the battle against slavery launched by Toussaint L'Ouverture in Haiti at the turn of the century. (Du Bois missed the chance to take Frederick Douglass as his subject in this book, part of a series of American biographies, when a confusion in correspondence ended with Douglass being assigned to Booker T. Washington. After Du Bois proposed Nat Turner, he settled on John Brown at the editor's request.) Du Bois cited Toussaint L'Ouverture as a great black hero on many occasions throughout his career. Turning back to a point he had made briefly in his first major work, *The Suppression of the African Slave-Trade to the United States* (1896), Du Bois featured Toussaint in some detail in a late essay on the impact of the French Revolution on New World history entitled "Africa and the French Revolution" (1961).

Following a period during the 1930s and 1940s when Du Bois wrote less often about the achievements of individuals (perhaps because his maturing Marxism prompted him to place more weight on the united action of the masses, as in *Black Reconstruction*), he produced a series of important sketches of world figures that appeared in a variety of forums but recalled his previous uses of representative men as the magnets of historical forces. His description of Ghanian president Kwame Nkrumah (who would be responsible for Du Bois's ultimate choice to settle in Ghana in 1961) comes from Du Bois's review of the African leader's 1957 autobiography; his tribute to the educator Carter Woodson is a eulogy written on the occasion of his death in 1950; in his polemical 1950 defense of the famous black singer and actor Paul Robeson against charges that his communism made him a traitor to the United States, Du Bois joined the voices of many on the left who sought to resist the constricted political atmosphere of the cold war; his 1953 essay on Stalin is one of several instances wherein Du Bois excused Soviet state repression and terror in order to laud the potential of communism; and in his 1957 essay on the lessons of Gandhi for the American civil rights movement, one finds an example of Du Bois's different attempts during this period to place the activism of the American civil rights movement, under the leadership of Martin Luther King, Jr., in the context of his long-held theory of Pan-Colored global cooperation.

❖

JEFFERSON DAVIS AS A REPRESENTATIVE OF CIVILIZATION

Jefferson Davis was a typical Teutonic Hero; the history of civilization during the last millenium has been the development of the idea of the Strong Man of which he was the embodiment. The Anglo-Saxon loves a soldier—Jefferson Davis was an Anglo-Saxon, Jefferson Davis was a soldier. There was not a phase in that familiarly strange life that would not have graced a mediaeval romance: from the fiery and impetuous young lieutenant who stole as his bride the daughter of a ruler-elect of the land, to the cool and ambitious politician in the Senate hall. So boldly and surely did that cadaverous figure with the thin nervous lips and flashing eye, write the first line of the new page of American history, that the historian of the future must ever see back of the war of Secession, the strong arm of one imperious man, who defied disease, trampled on precedent, would not be defeated, and never surrendered. A soldier and a lover, a statesman and a ruler; passionate, ambitious and indomitable; bold reckless guardian of a peoples' All—judged by the whole standard of Teutonic civilization, there is something noble in the figure of Jefferson Davis; and judged by every canon of human justice, there is something fundamentally incomplete about that standard.

I wish to consider not the man, but the type of civilization which his life represented: its foundation is the idea of the strong man—Individualism coupled with the rule of might—and it is this idea that has made the logic of even modern history, the cool logic of the Club. It made a naturally brave and generous man, Jefferson Davis—now advancing civilization by murdering Indians, now hero of a national disgrace called by courtesy, the Mexican War; and finally, as the crowning absurdity, the peculiar champion of a people fighting to be free in order that another people should not be free. Whenever this idea has for a moment, escaped from the individual realm, it has found an even more secure foothold in the policy and philosophy of the State. The Strong Man and his mighty Right Arm has become the Strong Nation with its armies. Under whatever guise, however, a Jefferson Davis may appear as man, as race, or as nation, his life can only logically mean this: the advance of a part of the world at the expense of the whole; the overweening sense of the I, and the consequent forgetting of the Thou. It has thus happened, that advance in civilization has always been handicapped by shortsighted national selfishness. The vital principle of division of labor has been stifled not only in industry, but also in civilization; so as to render it well nigh impossible for a new race to introduce a new idea into the world except by means of the cudgel. To say that a nation is in the way of civilization is a contradiction in terms, and a system of human culture whose principle is the rise of one race on the ruins of another is a farce and a lie. Yet this is the type of civilization which Jefferson Davis represented: it represents a field for stalwart manhood and heroic character, and at the same time for moral obtuseness and refined brutality. These striking contradictions of character always arise when a people seemingly become convinced that the object of the world is not civilization, but Teutonic civilization. Such a type is not wholly evil or fruitless: the world has needed and will need its Jefferson Davises; but such a type is incomplete and never can serve its best purpose until checked by its complementary ideas. Whence shall these come?

To the most casual observer, it must have occurred that the Rod of Empire has in these days, turned towards the South. In every Southern country, however destined to play a future part in the world—in Southern North America, South America, Australia, and Africa—a new nation has a more or less firm foothold. This circumstance, has, however, attracted but incidental notice, hitherto; for wherever the Negro people have touched civilization their rise has been singularly unromantic and unscientific. Through the glamour of history, the rise of a nation has ever been typified by the Strong Man crushing out an effete civilization. That brutality buried aught else beside Rome when it descended golden haired and drunk from the blue north has scarcely entered human imagination. Not as the muscular warrior came the Negro, but as the cringing slave. The Teutonic met civilization and crushed it—the Negro met civilization and was crushed by it. The one was the hero the world has ever worshipped, who gained unthought of triumphs and made unthought of mistakes; the other was the personification of dogged patience bending to the inevitable, and waiting. In the history of this people, we seek in vain the elements of Teutonic deification of Self, and Roman brute force, but we do find an idea of submission apart from cowardice, laziness or stupidity, such as the world never saw before. This is the race which by its very presence must play a part in the world of tomorrow; and this is the race whose rise, I contend, has practically illustrated an idea which is at once the check and complement of the Teutonic Strong Man. It is the doctrine of the Submissive Man—given to the world by strange coincidence, by the race of whose rights, Jefferson Davis had not heard.

What then is the change made in the conception of civilization, by adding to the idea of the Strong Man, that of the Submissive Man? It is this: the submission of the strength of the Strong to the advance of all—not in mere aimless sacrifice, but recognizing the fact that, "To no one type of mind is it given to discern the totality of Truth," that civilization cannot afford to lose the contribution of the very least of nations for its full development: that not only the assertion of the I, but also the submission to the Thou is the highest individualism.

The Teuton stands today as the champion of the idea of Personal Assertion: the Negro as the peculiar embodiment of the idea of Personal Submission: either, alone, tends to an abnormal development—towards Despotism on the one hand which the world has just cause to fear, and yet covertly admires, or towards slavery on the other which the world despises and which yet is not wholly despicable. No matter how great and striking the Teutonic type of impetuous manhood may be, it must receive the cool purposeful "Ich Dien" of the African for its round and full development. In the rise of Negro people and development of this idea, you whose nation was founded on the loftiest ideals, and who many times forgot those ideals with a strange forgetfulness, have more than a sentimental interest, more than a sentimental duty. You owe a debt to humanity for this Ethiopia of the Outstretched Arm, who has made her beauty, patience, and her grandeur, law.

BOOKER T. WASHINGTON

In every generation of our national life, from Phillis Wheatley to Booker Washington, the Negro race in America has succeeded in bringing forth men whom the country, at times spontaneously, at times in spite of itself, has been impelled to honor and respect. Mr. Washington is one of the most striking of these cases, and his autobiography is a partial history of the steps which made him a group leader, and the one man who in the eyes of the nation typifies at present more nearly than all others the work and worth of his nine million fellows.

The way in which groups of human beings are led to choose certain of their number as their spokesmen and leaders is at once the most elementary and the nicest problem of social growth. History is but the record of this group leadership; and yet how infinitely changeful is its type and history! And of all types and kinds, what can be more instructive than the leadership of a group within a group—that curious double movement where real progress may be negative and actual advance be relative retrogression? All this is the social student's inspiration and despair.

When sticks and stones and beasts form the sole environment of a people, their attitude is ever one of determined opposition to, and conquest of, natural forces. But when to earth and brute is added an environment of men and ideas, then the attitude of the imprisoned group may take three main forms: a feeling of revolt and revenge; an attempt to adjust all thought and action to the will of the greater group; or, finally, a determined attempt at self-development, self-realization, in spite of environing discouragements and prejudice. The influence of all three of these attitudes is plainly to be traced in the evolution of race leaders among American Negroes. Before 1750 there was but the one motive of revolt and revenge which animated the terrible Maroons and veiled all the Americas in fear of insurrection. But the liberalizing tendencies of the latter half of the eighteenth century brought the first thought of adjustment and assimilation in the crude and earnest songs of Phillis and the martyrdom of Attucks and Salem.

The cotton-gin changed all this, and men then, as the Lyman Abbotts of to-day, found a new meaning in human blackness. A season of hesitation and stress settled on the black world as the hope of emancipation receded. Forten and the free Negroes of the North still hoped for eventual assimilation with the nation; Allen, the founder of the great African Methodist Church, strove for unbending self-development, and the Southern freedmen followed him; while among the black slaves at the South arose the avenging Nat Turner, fired by the memory of Toussaint the Savior. So far, Negro leadership had been local and spasmodic; but now, about 1840, arose a national leadership—a dynasty not to be broken. Frederick Douglass and the moral revolt against slavery dominated Negro thought and effort until after the war. Then, with the sole weapon of self-defense in perilous times, the ballot, which the nation gave the freedmen, men like Langston and Bruce sought to guide the political fortunes of the blacks, while Payne and Price still clung to the old ideal of self-development.

Then came the reaction. War memories and ideals rapidly passed, and a period of astonishing commercial development and expansion ensued. A time of doubt and hesitation, of storm and stress, overtook the freedmen's sons; and then it was that Booker Washington's leadership began. Mr. Washington came with a clear simple program, at the psychological moment; at a time when the nation was a little ashamed of having bestowed so much sentiment on Negroes and was concentrating its energies on Dollars. The industrial training of Negro youth was not an idea originating with Mr. Washington, nor was the policy of conciliating the white South wholly his. But he first put life, unlimited energy, and perfect faith into this program; he changed it from an article of belief into a whole creed; he broadened it from a by-path into a veritable Way of Life. And the method by which he accomplished this is an interesting study of human life.

Mr. Washington's narrative gives but glimpses of the real struggle which he has had for leadership. First of all, he strove to gain the sympathy and cooperation of the white South, and gained it after that epoch-making sentence spoken at Atlanta: "In all things that are purely social we can be as separate as the fingers, yet one as the hand in all things essential to mutual progress." This conquest of the South is by all odds the most notable thing in Mr. Washington's career. Next to this comes his achievement in gaining place and consideration in the North. Many others less shrewd and tactful would have fallen between these two stools; but as Mr. Washington knew the heart of the South from birth and training, so by singular insight he intuitively grasped the spirit of the age that was dominating the North. He learned so thoroughly the speech and thought of triumphant commercialism and the ideals of material prosperity that he pictures as the height of absurdity a black boy studying a French grammar in the midst of weeds and dirt. One wonders how Socrates or St. Francis of Assisi would receive this!

And yet this very singleness of vision and thorough oneness with his age is a mark of the successful man. It is as though Nature must needs make men a little narrow to give them force. At the same time, Mr. Washington's success, North and South, with his gospel of Work and Money, raised opposition to him from widely divergent sources. The spiritual sons of the Abolitionists were not prepared to acknowledge that the schools founded before Tuskegee, by men of broad ideals and self-sacrificing souls, were wholly failures, or worthy of ridicule. On the other hand, among his own people Mr. Washington found deep suspicion and dislike for a man on such good terms with Southern whites.

Such opposition has only been silenced by Mr. Washington's very evident sincerity of purpose. We forgive much to honest purpose which is accomplishing something. We may not agree with the man at all points, but we admire him and cooperate with him so far as we conscientiously can. It is no ordinary tribute to this man's tact and power, that, steering as he must amid so many diverse interests and opinions, he to-day commands not simply the applause of those who believe in his theories, but also the respect of those who do not.

Among the Negroes, Mr. Washington is still far from a popular leader. Educated and thoughtful Negroes everywhere are glad to honor him and aid him, but all cannot agree with him. He represents in Negro thought the old attitude of adjustment to environment, emphasizing the economic phase; but the two other strong currents of feeling, descended from the past, still oppose him. One is the thought of a small but not unimportant group, unfortunate in their choice of spokesman, but nevertheless of much weight, who represent the old ideas of revolt and revenge, and see in migration alone an outlet for the Negro people. The second attitude is that of the large and important group represented by Dunbar, Tanner, Chesnutt, Miller, and the Grimkés, who, without any single definite program, and with complex aims, seek nevertheless that self-development and self-realization in all lines of human endeavor which they believe will eventually place the Negro beside the other races. While these men respect the Hampton-Tuskegee idea to a degree, they believe it falls far short of a complete program. They believe, therefore, also in the higher education of Fisk and Atlanta Universities; they believe in self-assertion and ambition; and they believe in the right of suffrage for blacks on the same terms with whites.

Such is the complicated world of thought and action in which Mr. Booker Washington has been called of God and man to lead, and in which he has gained so rare a meed of success.

ABRAHAM LINCOLN

It is to be my pleasure to speak to you about Abraham Lincoln. I do not want simply to recall to your minds the facts of his life, but rather to make you realize that broader fact of his character, and of the meaning of that character for our good in America today. For after all the thing that interests human beings and ought to interest them is not the place of a man's birth and death, and the little every day things he did, but rather his whole attitude towards life—what life meant to him and what he made out of life: because in the whirl and mystery of this world we ever strain our eyes for and seek an interpreter, some one who will tell us truly what living really is. You all know that Abraham Lincoln was a great American, that he was born 98 years ago today in the state of Kentucky—the son of a woman whose father had never married her mother and that he came in shame and frailty an illegitimate into the world. And this woman's boy worked with his hands, studied at night and became a lawyer with a little country practice. He went into politics, became known throughout this state and then in a crisis was suddenly called to be chief magistrate of the nation at the time of its greatest and most fearful need; there he became the man who preserved the American union, swept slavery from the United States and is looked upon as Lowell has said even today, as "the First American."

When now a man has accomplished so much and has woven himself so boldly and wonderfully into the history of a great land, you and I who sit and look at life and try to interpret its meaning must ask first of all, What sort of man was he? And when we ask that we have an answer, in this case, which does not coincide with many of our preconceived ideas. When we think of greatness, we think unconsciously of greatness in every thing, of lofty bearing, of wonderful training, of high position, of great respect. But if we think of Abraham Lincoln we have few or none of these things. He was to be sure a tall man, but he was not a man of particularly impressive bearing; he was on the contrary, a homely man. We like to use that adjective in speaking of him; a face hard and heavily carven, without refining lines, with blunt, even harsh speech—a man unpolished in his ways, whose clothes did not fit, whose personal appearance did not suggest neatness nor refinement—a man who had in many ways something of vulgarity; a man who was always telling jokes, many of which would not always pass muster in good society. Not only that, but he was not what the world calls a pushing man. He was a slow man—a dreamer—a man who liked to loaf around country stores, looking for the unexpected thing. He was not a man that saved much. He was always poor—poor when he began, poor during his life, poor when he died. And then, climax of all, he was not a happy man. Sorrow was written across his face, a sort of curious never absent melancholy. Jovial he was to be sure, at times, but never lighthearted or glowing with the thought or experience of the happy life.

Now when we think and know a character of this sort, it cuts across many of our most favored preconceptions. Here is a great man, one of the world's greatest men, who did not for instance belong to the best society—who did not have the higher training—who did not pursue the busy life—who did not become wealthy and happy. On the other hand there is no doubt of his greatness and that this consisted of a few simple things. The first was his clear sightedness—the way that he could brush aside cobwebs of convention and of difficulty and see with perfect clearness the right and justice and logic of life. But he did not always see the right at first, and in that very fact lies his second claim to greatness and that is his capacity for growth. He was not a man that could boast that he had held his opinions for twenty and thirty and forty years. There are some men that can boast of this; and woe to them and woe to the world that holds them! If in the lapse of ten or twenty years a man has not capacity for growth and has not received enough of knowledge to make him change the most of his opinions, then he is indeed a hopeless case. But Abraham Lincoln not only had this capacity for growth, this capacity to receive the new knowledge as it came, but had it in so wonderful a degree that he became a leader of men.

He was not for instance an abolitionist when he became president. He disliked slavery, but like most of us in the case of disagreeable things he was willing, if not eager, to let it severely alone. Once, however, it dawned on him that this land could not exist half slave and half free and once he realized that his was the power to break the paradox, then he turned suddenly and led the very leaders into freedom; and finally, not only did he have this peculiar clearness of vision at critical times, so that the truth grew and blossomed in his soul, but he had too a certain simple greatness of energy and decision that enabled him to put his whole life and soul into realizing the truth when he once saw it, a perfect capacity for sacrifice.

Now when we have enumerated these things as characteristic of the greatness of Abraham Lincoln, then every one feels like asking, What do we care if he did not belong to the best society? So much the worse for the best if it could not receive and recognize this greatest American; What do we care if his clothes did not fit him, if he was awkward always and vulgar sometimes, if after all he had that great soul that ruled above all awkwardness of body, and that perfect purity, that clearness of mind, to which the little vulgarities of his manners hung loosely as evidence that they did not belong there? What do we care if he was poor, so long as he was rich in the capacity for gaining knowledge? And if he had not what the world called an education, then the pity of it is that the world has not revised its attempts at human training. Thus our first thought is on seeing and hearing and learning of a man like Abraham Lincoln to have rather a mean contempt for a world that does not seem altogether responsible for him, which did not know him nor recognize him until he had become great and indeed until he was dead. And yet we must not pass too hurried judgment on the world; we must remember that the world is groping, painfully groping, after certain great ideals and that when the ideal itself suddenly flashes across the sky it may not recognize it because of the very pain of its own struggle. But one thing it must do, watching the ideal when it comes to know it and watching its own struggle it must realize how far behind we are in our struggles toward the best and what it is that is wrong with our ideals. Therefore as I have said, I want to consider the character of Abraham Lincoln and to consider the ideals that we have here in America and ask what it is in Lincoln's life and character that may teach us to have better and greater and more successful ideals. That brings me to say that, after all, the things for which we strive and upon which we pour a certain contempt now and then because our striving seems so vain, are the things toward which every human society must strive.

I have said that Abraham Lincoln never belonged to the best society. Why the impatient ones ask insistently: What kind of a world is it whose best reject the best—who receive King Leopold of Belgium and reject Abraham Lincoln? The reply is: If the best society does this the fault is not solely with them; it lies heavily on you and on me. When the social elect pour contempt upon your effort and upon my effort, upon the greatness of Socrates and Jesus Christ, upon the greatness of Frederick Douglass and Abraham Lincoln for *that very reason* we must not pour contempt upon the ideal of a *best* in society. We must simply say that we have not yet found the right criterion, we have not yet risen to that great view which enables us to make in our social world a real aristocracy.

But notwithstanding that, we need an aristocracy. We need to bring together and exalt and put in power and to thrust into leadership the real thought and best feeling of the world. We need to do this, not only for the sake of the best itself, but for the sake of the worst—not only for your sake, but for my sake, and so, however the world has failed upon its quest of the real aristocracy, it must still search for this Holy Grail. Now it is manifest that many of the criteria, of the ways of judging what is best among men in the world have been in the past absurd and inadequate, so that we have often rushed to the fore-front men and ideas and ways of thought which we ourselves refuse afterward to consider the best. For instance, we have said if a man has reached pre-eminence, we must show our respect for him not simply in himself but in his children; and there is something of right and truth in this. A man with education and virtue makes a good grandfather. Given a good grandfather, there is a chance better than most chances of having a good father. Having a good father is a wonderful way to start in the world with hopes of success. But if once we have begun this respect for fathers and grandfathers, how easily it could be turned into ancestor worship; and few ideas have been more perverted than this. Judged by his ancestors Abraham Lincoln had a chance in the world, only in the 19th century. If he had lived probably in any century before that, the Door of Opportunity would have been miserably closed in his face; not because of lack of desert on his part, but simply because his father and his mother, his grandfather and grandmother were not people of distinction or indeed of any great worth. In this respect, therefore, today we live in a new century and in a new land. We need to congratulate ourselves that through pain and through blood and terrible striving, the world has at last come to a time when it is willing to accept a man upon his merit even though he did not have a distinguished father or grandfather—even though his mother was nameless! This seems so simple a thing: Why on earth should not a world receive a man on his own merit? If not on his own merit on whose merit can he possibly be received? And yet, we must realize the terrific stress of that aristocratic idea that made the family and the descent every thing, and the individual almost nothing. But if we have reached this vantage ground where we can say: "Look to the man and his deeds and not to somebody else, in judging him," how necessary it is that we should fight to keep this advantage open to the world, to our brothers and to our sisters. And yet there are tendencies against which I warn you; there are times coming even here in the Twentieth century, when if an Abraham Lincoln should rise in the United States and if he should be a Jew in race or a Japanese in color, or a Negro in descent, that he would be judged not by the greatness of his soul or the clearness of his vision or the saneness of his judgments, but that his soul would be pressed and shut out of the republic of the civilized, simply because of his race or his color or the previous life of his ancestors. So that today we are fighting to leave the path open, the Door of Opportunity wide for men who come of humble birth and humble beginning. But this is not all. The choice of the chosen is ours. If we were today then choosing those persons who should represent our best society, we think we would choose at least in theory men like Abraham Lincoln and Benjamin Franklin and Alexander Hamilton. But if as a matter of fact we take up our daily newspapers and look for the news of the best society we find the names of no such people as these, but rather today we find the names of those who by accident and extravagance, by their show and influence, by their wealth and impudence have come by general consent to be regarded as forming the best society of Chicago or New York or the United States. Now whose fault is this? Is it theirs? By no means. You could hardly ask any man of that stamp, to refuse that which you and I and the common judgment of his fellows thrust upon him. The real difficulty then lies with us. If we really believe men of the type of Abraham Lincoln to be the best sort of men for this world, then our best society would by our own vote and judgment hold such men. But it is because in our heart of hearts we never have reached the height of even appreciating a character like Lincoln's that we give this form of aristocracy to those persons who represent in their lives that which we really worship. What today do we worship? We worship *show;* we worship, *wealth;* we worship *self-assertion;* we worship *brute power* and so long as we worship these things, these are the things that become the mark of our aristocracy. Therefore again we who are by our silent forceful public opinion really choosing the leaders and the leading classes of men, it behooves us really to get in our own minds the right idea, the right thought as to what is greatness and what is best and worth while in this life of ours.

In the second place the thing that is perhaps the most striking about Abraham Lincoln and the thing which puzzles us most is the fact that while he was an uneducated man he was yet a man of wonderful training. If there is one thing upon which the modern world has spent time and thought and money and great anxiety of soul it is upon the matter of training men. We know that the world is continually lapsing back into its former barbarism; we know that only by thought and striving and deed we can so train children as to let them start in the twentieth century instead of the tenth. And so we have an elaborate system of public schools sorts to train human beings into a realization of what life really is and their relation to life. And yet in spite of this, now and then there comes a man who has had little of this training of the schools, who knows nothing of formal education and yet he has a most wonderful vision of soul which simply sweeps far beyond the vision of any of these men whom we have striven so faithfully to educate. There again our first thought is to pour contempt upon education and systems of education and to say that Abraham Lincoln stands as a living proof of the futility of trying to do in schools what schools cannot do. Abraham Lincoln got his education, where? He got it in his work; he got it in his dreaming; he got it in his reading. He was not a college man; he was not a high school graduate; he was, as I have said, not what you call today an educated man. Yet we study some of his wonderful speeches as specimens of the most exquisite English. We follow his foresight as giving us examples of the best thinking and we look upon his character as one of the simplest and purest which the world has known. Now this matter of training is of especial interest to us. Many of you here are waiting for the finishing of your life's training; others are hesitating as to how to train boys and girls; are wanting so far as possible to give them the correct vision of life and they wonder how it shall be done. On the other hand we must of course recognize at once that simply because our schools do not turn out men of peculiar facility of mind and balance of training which Abraham Lincoln had, that that does not necessarily mean that they are a failure. But on the other hand we must ask ourselves are our schools conducted to give to the world such kind of minds in any degree as Lincoln possessed. Young men and women who are able to see clearly the truth of life because in the first place they have had experience in clearness of thought and because in the second place they know something of what the world has thought.

Here again the teaching of Lincoln's life ought to impress us with the fact that it is thinking itself and not methods of thought—it is the souls of children and not the bricks of school houses that make the true measure of education. And the more we consider this, the more we remember that boys and girls who come through our schools too often face the world befuddled and bewildered with anything but clear thinking, with anything but accurate knowledge. Why? Some would have us think that our methods are bad or our teachers unlearned, and often there is some thing of truth in this. But the main difficulty—a difficulty against which Lincoln warns us in words and deed is our own hurry and rush. We seek to turn out the finished article in fully-trained boys as we turn out so much cloth. America today stands for hurrying and rush and work. We call ourselves a hustling nation. We do or we try to do a great deal more in a day than the average person in other lands, in other ages have done. But when we look at the life of this first American we see something that gives us pause. Why was it that Lincoln thought so clearly? It was first of all, because he *thought* and because he gave himself leisure to think. Many are the stories that they tell of him stretched out doing nothing, loafing here and there, whittling a stick, looking leisurely at the world. He *thought*. And that is one thing that the average American today does not do. That is one thing we do not do in our schools. The poor, hurried, worried children get no time to think, get no time to get acquainted with themselves. We then, as Americans, must take pattern of Lincoln and remember that before all, we must get acquainted with ourselves. We must get acquainted with this country of ours and not take the image or hearsay for the reality. This is in many respects a wonderful country, but it is not wonderful in the sense that it will not have to go through the same birth pains and have the same troubles of growth, find the same great difficulties of living, the same evils, the same great shadow of Death that all nations have found; and the quicker it realizes this the more carefully will it pause and think and plan. Abraham Lincoln's life gives us little sense of hurry. And yet Lincoln, as the world has known him, has been one of the world's great workers. And the reason is clear; if the human soul gets time to think and expand how much better it can work. Not that it always will work; many a man of the Lincoln type has loafed and dreamed his life away without ever putting it to the test of deeds. Many a nation has had the leisure that America lacks and squandered it.

Who had more leisure than the aristocratic leaders of other days? Who have more leisure today than the idle rich of this land? When we want leisure then, when we ask America for leisure, we are asking not for idleness, but we are asking for pause in the rush and worry of doing so that we can have time to think and plan and grow. The United States ought to pause in her rush to get rich in order that she may have time to get wisdom. We ought to rest so that the balance of work and rest would make full rounded men about her and give this world of ours a chance really to find itself. Not simply hurry, not simply wealth, but the leisure in the midst of work to know what work means.

Now it is often said that if things were balanced in this world and were as they ought to be, that there would be greatly increased happiness. And yet I do not doubt that many men looking upon that sorrow-carven face of Abraham Lincoln and remembering how hard he toiled to be a man and how great a man he made, will say, If such a man had such a life of grief and sorrow, what is the use of trying? Of the sorrows that Abraham Lincoln reaped there is no doubt. First there was the sorrow of his narrow and sordid youthful surroundings; then there was the sorrow of political defeat; after that came the sorrow of misapprehension; of being half buried, of being patronized by men whose superior he was and knew he was. Then there was the sorrow of responsibility; if anything went wrong during those fearful years of war and turmoil, Abraham Lincoln was responsible for it; if anything went right, somebody else reaped the laurels and the praise. And then above all, there was the lonely sorrow of the lonely soul sitting above the world without companionship, little understood, who must suffer and be silent. He did not even have the solace of a wife who knew and sympathized with his great soul. His family life was not what we like to picture as ideal family life. He was alone, peculiarly alone. Is this then the rightful reward of the life of a man who came up in spite of adversity, who worked his way through the turmoil of life and did his duty? There are people who say, Yes, we ought to be glad to suffer for the good; but it seems to me that that is the wrong interpretation to put upon a life of this sort. It is right that the world should be a happy place. It is wrong in so far as it is not a happy place. The life of every man ought to make the world happier and it should also make the man himself happier. But this is certain; that sometime and often there comes the call that one man utterly sacrifice his happiness in order that all men may be made happy, and the peculiarity of that call is, that viewed in the light of reason there is no *must* to it. The only *must* that is felt is felt in the soul that sees the need.

> Tho Love repine and Reason chafe,
>   There came a voice without reply,
> 'Tis Man's perdition to be safe
>   When for the truth he ought to die.

To Abraham Lincoln the voice came. He was a martyr not so much in his death as in his life. It was in his life that he was crucified for the good.

We have then learned in the life of Abraham Lincoln the finer ideals of what is best in society, a clearer knowledge of the need of time in education, and a realization of the fact that life cannot be all hurry and work. We must have the leisure to know and feel, to realize our own selves. We have learned that wealth does not necessarily give leisure nor work happiness, but that while out of wealth and work must come happiness to the mass, it is often at the sacrifice of the life and the well-being of single great individuals who are willing to offer themselves for the good of the world. If this is the meaning of the life of Abraham Lincoln what particular duty lies before us today? Here we are representing many lands and many nations coming from all the ends of the earth, showing forth in our faces, our life and thought the history of all that mass of men what make up human life today. We have come to a land of ideals, and we are here because of these ideals, and those ideals had their finest fruition and greatest presentation in the life and character of Abraham Lincoln. And if therefore, we have seen and known in America something to love and live for, then we must try and see that the ideals which Abraham Lincoln typified, the ideals on which America was founded be not be lowered on account of us, suffer in no way because of our neglect, but by our coming and our being here, by our joint heritage in this vast and wonderful country, these ideals must grow greater and purer and better. Perhaps few of you realize that today the things for which Abraham Lincoln stood are as I have said in danger. In the first place the very type of man that he was, the simple, poorly bred, vulgar, but honest and great-hearted man is passing from the American stage. We have in his stead a man far better in looks, nicer, sleeker, shrewder, richer. Not only that, but we have growing up in this country, slowly, surely the idea that the world is not for everybody; that the world and its opportunities belong to a certain class of favorite individuals and while the class of the claimants today in America is still recognized as being much larger than the people of the Middle Age thought or the people of some European lands think, yet nevertheless it is a restricted class to which all human beings are not permitted. Then too, there is growing up in America the idea that we must be careful how we train children, that if their heritage is to be narrow and not the full, free, broad heritage toward which Abraham Lincoln looked they must be trained for their narrow heritage; that it is the business of most people to work and not to think and therefore we must make little provision for their thinking, and that above all, we must go on accumulating and heaping up wealth because the greatness of America lies in its richness. Now unless you and I are very careful we will find ourselves carried away by this philosophy and in being carried away we shall lose our appreciation for a man like Abraham Lincoln. Let us, therefore, set our faces like flint against the new old growing but dangerous philosophy. Let us insist that "All men are created free and equal." Let us say that the best society of America, no matter what the daily newspapers may tell us, consists of that company of the educated and the thoughtful and the true who are trying to make the world better. That unto all human souls the door of training must be opened just as far as the toil for bread and butter will allow, and that the accumulation of wealth in America and the deterioration of soul that goes with it, far from measuring our greatness, measures our shame. It is the most sinister thing that is happening today. I would leave with you then this thought: Thinking of the great man who nearly a century ago was born in circumstances as humble as any of ours, let us emulate his example, so far as we may with our narrow gifts, let us keep his ideals and let us make America still a land where men like Abraham Lincoln may flourish and be recognized—a land of opportunity and of opportunity not simply to the rich, but to the poor, not simply to the Gentile, but to the Jew, not simply to the white, but to the black, a land of opportunity for *all men*, and for all women, too.

JOHN BROWN

"That it might be fulfilled which was spoken of the Lord by the prophet saying, Out of Egypt have I called My son."

[Matthew 2:15]

The mystic spell of Africa is and ever was over all America. It has guided her hardest work, inspired her finest literature, and sung her sweetest songs. Her greatest destiny—unsensed and despised though it be,—is to give back to the first of continents the gifts which Africa of old gave to America's fathers' fathers.

Of all inspiration which America owes to Africa, however; the greatest by far is the score of heroic men whom the sorrows of these dark children called to unselfish devotion and heroic self-realization: Benezet, Garrison, and Harriet Stowe; Sumner, Douglass and Lincoln—these and others, but above all, John Brown.

John Brown was a stalwart, rough-hewn man, mightily yet tenderly carven. To his making went the stern justice of a Cromwellian "Ironside," the freedom-loving fire of a Welsh Celt, and the thrift of a Dutch housewife. And these very things it was—thrift, freedom, and justice—that early crossed the unknown seas to find asylum in America. Yet they came late, for before them came greed, and greed brought black slaves from Africa.

The Negroes came on the heels, if not on the very ships of Columbus. They followed De Soto to the Mississippi; saw Virginia with D'Ayllon, Mexico with Cortez, Peru with Pizarro; and led the western wanderings of Coronado in his search for the Seven Cities of Cibola. Something more than a decade after the Cavaliers, and a year before the Pilgrims, they set lasting foot on the North American continent.

These black men came not of their own willing, but because the hasty greed of new America selfishly and half-thoughtlessly sought to revive in the New World the dying but unforgotten custom of enslaving the world's workers. So with the birth of wealth and liberty west of the seas, came slavery, and a slavery all the more cruel and hideous because it gradually built itself on a caste of race and color, thus breaking the common bonds of human fellowship and weaving artificial barriers of birth and appearance.

The result was evil, as all injustice must be. At first the black men writhed and struggled and died in their bonds, and their blood reddened the paths across the Atlantic and around the beautiful isles of the Western Indies. Then as the bonds gripped them closer and closer, they succumbed to sullen indifference or happy ignorance, with only here and there flashes of wild red vengeance.

For, after all, these black men were but men, neither more nor less wonderful than other men. In build and stature, they were for the most part among the taller nations and sturdily made. In their mental equipment and moral poise, they showed themselves full brothers to all men—"intensely human"; and this too in their very modifications and peculiarities—their warm brown and bronzed color and crisp curled hair under the heat and wet of Africa; their sensuous enjoyment of the music and color of life; their instinct for barter and trade; their strong family life and government. Yet these characteristics were bruised and spoiled and misinterpreted in the rude uprooting of the slave trade and the sudden transplantation of this race to other climes, among other peoples. Their color became a badge of servitude, their tropical habit was deemed laziness, their worship was thought heathenish, their family customs and government were ruthlessly overturned and debauched; many of their virtues became vices, and much of their vice, virtue.

The price of repression is greater than the cost of liberty. The degradation of men costs something both to the degraded and those who degrade. While the Negro slaves sank to listless docility and vacant ignorance, their masters found themselves whirled in the eddies of mighty movements: their system of slavery was twisting them backwards toward darker ages of force and caste and cruelty, while forward swirled swift currents of liberty and uplift.

They still felt the impulse of the wonderful awakening of culture from its barbaric sleep of centuries which men call the Renaissance; they were own children of the mighty stirring of Europe's conscience which we call the Reformation; and they and their children were to be prime actors in laying the foundations of human liberty in a new century and a new land. Already the birth pains of the new freedom were felt in that land. Old Europe was begetting in the new continent a vast longing for spiritual space. So there was builded into America the thrift of the searchers of wealth, the freedom of the Renaissance and the stern morality of the Reformation.

Three lands typified these three things which time planted in the New World: England sent Puritanism, the last white flower of the Lutheran revolt; Holland sent the new vigor and thrift of the Renaissance; while Celtic lands and bits of lands like France and Ireland and Wales, sent the passionate desire for personal freedom. These three elements came, and came more often than not in the guise of humble men—an English carpenter on the *Mayflower*, an Amsterdam tailor seeking a new ancestral city, and a Welsh wanderer. From three such men sprang in the marriage of years, John Brown. . . .

There was hell in Hayti in the red waning of the eighteenth century, in the days when John Brown was born. The dark wave of the French Revolution had raised the brilliant sinister Napoleon to its crest. Already he had stretched greedy arms toward American empire in the rich vale of the Mississippi, when in a flash, out of the dirt and sloth and slavery of the West Indies, the black inert and heavy cloud of African degradation writhed to sudden life and lifted up the dark figure of Toussaint. Ten thousand Frenchmen gasped and died in the fever-haunted hills, while the black men in sudden frenzy fought like devils for their freedom and won it. Napoleon saw his gateway to the Mississippi closed; armed Europe was at his back. What was this wild and empty America to him, anyway? So he sold Louisiana for a song and turned to the shame of Trafalgar and the glory of Austerlitz.

John Brown was born just as the shudder of Hayti was running through all the Americas, and from his earliest boyhood he saw and felt the price of repression—the fearful cost that the western world was paying for slavery. From his earliest boyhood he had dimly conceived, and the conception grew with his growing, that the cost of liberty was less than the price of repression. Perhaps he was so near the humanistic enthusiasm of the French Revolution that he undervalued the cost of liberty. But yet he was right, for it was scarce possible to overrate the price of repression. True, in these latter days men and women of the South, and honest ones, too, have striven feverishly to pain Negro slavery in bright alluring colors. They have told of childlike devotion, faithful service and light-hearted irresponsibility, in the fine old aristocracy of the plantation. Much they have said is true. But when all is said and granted, the awful fact remains congealed in law and indisputable record that American slavery was the foulest and filthiest blot on nineteenth century civilization. As a school of brutality and human suffering, of female prostitution and male debauchery; as a mockery of marriage and defilement of family life; as a darkening of reason, and spiritual death, it had no parallel in its day. It took millions upon millions of men—human men and lovable, light and liberty-loving children of the sun, and threw them with no sparing of brutality into one rigid mold: humble, servile, dog-like devotion, surrender of body, mind and soul, and unaspiring animal content—toward this ideal the slave might strive, and did. Wonderful, even beautiful examples of humble service he brought forth and made the eternal heritage of men. But beyond this there was nothing. All were crushed to this mold and of them that did not fit, the sullen were cowed, the careless brutalized and the rebellious killed. Four things make life worthy to most men: to move, to know, to love, to aspire. None of these was for Negro slaves. A white child could halt a black man on the highway and send him slinking to his kennel. No black slave could legally learn to read. And love? If a black slave loved a lass, there was not a white man from the Potomac to the Rio Grande that could not prostitute her to his lust. Did the proud sons of Virginia and Carolina stoop to such bestial tyranny? Ask the grandmothers of the two million mulattoes that dot the states to-day. Ask the suffering and humiliated wives of the master caste. If a Negro married a wife, there was not a master in the land that could not take her from him. . . .

. . . The great black mass of Southern slaves were cowed, but they were not conquered. Stretched as they were over wide miles of land, and isolated; guarded in speech and religion; peaceful and light-hearted as was their nature, still the fire of liberty burned in them. In Louisiana and Tennessee and twice in Virginia they raised the night cry of revolt, and once slew fifty Virginians, holding the state for weeks at bay there in those same Alleghanies which John Brown loved and listened to. On the ships of the sea they rebelled and murdered; to Florida they fled and turned like beasts on their pursuers till whole armies dislodged them and did them to death in the everglades; and again and again over them and through them surged and quivered a vast unrest which only the eternal vigilance of the masters kept down. Yet the fear of that great bound beast was ever there—a nameless, haunting dread that never left the South and never ceased, but ever nerved the remorseless cruelty of the master's arm.

One thing saved the South from the blood-sacrifice of Hayti—not, to be sure, from so successful a revolt, for the disproportion of races was less, but from a desperate and bloody effort—and that was the escape of the fugitive.

Along the Great Black Way stretched swamps and rivers, and the forests and crests of the Alleghanies. A widening, hurrying stream of fugitives swept to the havens of refuge, taking the restless, the criminal and the unconquered—the natural leaders of the more timid mass. These men saved slavery and killed it. They saved it by leaving it to a false seductive dream of peace and the eternal subjugation of the laboring class. They destroyed it by presenting themselves before the eyes of the North and the world as living specimens of the real meaning of slavery. What was the system that could enslave a Frederick Douglass? They saved it too by joining the free Negroes of the North, and with them organizing themselves into a great black phalanx that worked and schemed and paid and finally fought for the freedom of black men in America.

Thus it was that John Brown, even as a child, saw the puzzling anomalies and contradictions in human right and liberty all about him. Ever and again he saw this in the North, leading to concerted action among the free Negroes, especially in cities where they were brought in contact with one another, and had some chance of asserting their nominal freedom. Just at the close of the eighteenth century, first in Philadelphia and then in New York, small groups of them withdrew from the white churches to escape disgraceful discrimination and established churches of their own, which still live with millions of adherents. In the year of John Brown's birth, 1800, Gabriel planned his formidable uprising in Virginia, and the year after his marriage, 1821, Denmark Vesey of South Carolina went grimly to the scaffold, after one of the shrewdest Negro plots that ever frightened the South into hysterics. Of all this John Brown, the boy and young man, knew little. In after years he learned of Gabriel and Vesey and Turner, and told of their exploits and studied their plans; but at the time he was far off from the world, carrying on his tannery and marrying a wife. Perhaps as a lad he heard some of the oratory that celebrated the act of 1808, stopping the slave trade, as the beginning of the end of slavery. Perhaps not, for the act did little good until it was reënforced in 1820. All the time, however, John Brown's keen eyes were searching for the way of life and his tender heart was sensitive to injustice and wrong everywhere. Indeed, it is not unlikely that the first black folk to gain his aid and sympathies and direct his thoughts to what afterward became his life-work, were the fugitive slaves from the South. . . .

. . . Has John Brown no message—no legacy, then, to the twentieth century? He has and it is this great word: the cost of liberty is less than the price of repression. The price of repressing the world's darker races is shown in a moral retrogression and an economic waste unparalleled since the age of the African slave-trade. What would be the cost of liberty? what would be the cost of giving the great stocks of mankind every reasonable help and incentive to self-development—opening the avenues of opportunity freely, spreading knowledge, suppressing war and cheating, and treating men and women as equals the world over whenever and wherever they attain equality? It would cost something. It would cost something in pride and prejudice, for eventually many a white man would be blacking black men's boots; but this cost we may ignore—its greatest cost would be the new problems of racial intercourse and intermarriage which would come to the front. Freedom and equal opportunity in this respect would inevitably bring some intermarriage of whites and yellows and browns and blacks. This might be a good thing and it might not be. We do not know. Our belief on the matter may be strong and even frantic, but it has no adequate scientific foundation. If such marriages are proven inadvisable, how could they be stopped? Easily. We associate with cats and cows, but we do not fear intermarriage with them, even though they be given all freedom of development. So, too, intelligent human beings can be trained to breed intelligently without the degradation of such of their fellows as they may not wish to breed with. In the Southern United States, on the contrary, it is assumed that unwise marriages can be stopped only by the degradation of the blacks—the classing of all darker women with prostitutes, the loading of a whole race with every badge of public isolation, degradation and contempt, and by burning offenders at the stake. Is this civilization? No. The civilized method of preventing ill-advised marriage lies in the training of mankind in the ethics of sex and child-bearing. We cannot ensure the survival of the best blood by the public murder and degradation of unworthy suitors, but we can substitute a civilized human selection of husbands and wives which shall ensure the survival of the fittest. Not the methods of the jungle, not even the careless choices of the drawing-room, but the thoughtful selection of the schools and laboratory is the ideal of future marriage. This will cost something in ingenuity, self-control and toleration, but it will cost less than forcible repression.

Not only is the cost of repression to-day large—it is a continually increasing cost: the procuring of coolie labor, the ruling of India, the exploitation of Africa, the problem of the unemployed, and the curbing of the corporations, are a tremendous drain on modern society with no near end in sight. The cost is not merely in wealth but in social progress and spiritual strength, and it tends ever to explosion, murder, and war. All these things but increase the difficulty of beginning a régime of freedom in human growth and development—they raise the cost of liberty. Not only that but the very explosions, like the Russo-Japanese War, which bring partial freedom, tend in the complacent current philosophy to prove the wisdom of repression. "Blood will tell," men say. "The fit will survive; stop up the tea-kettle and eventually the steam will burst the iron," and therefore only the steam that bursts is worth the generating; only organized murder proves the fitness of a people for liberty. This is a fearful and dangerous doctrine. It encourages wrong leadership and perverted ideals at the very time when loftiest and most unselfish striving is called for—as witness Japan after her emancipation, or America after the Civil War. Conversely, it leads the shallow and unthinking to brand as demagogue and radical every group leader who in the day of slavery and struggle cries out for freedom.

For such reasons it is that the memory of John Brown stands to-day as a mighty warning to his country. He saw, he felt in his soul the wrong and danger of that most daring and insolent system of human repression known as American slavery. He knew that in 1700 it would have cost something to overthrow slavery and establish liberty; and that by reason of cowardice and blindness the cost in 1800 was vastly larger but still not unpayable. He felt that by 1900 no human hand could pluck the vampire from the body of the land without doing the nation to death. He said, in 1859, "Now is the accepted time." Now is the day to strike for a free nation. It will cost something—even blood and suffering, but it will not cost as much as waiting. And he was right. Repression bred repression—serfdom bred slavery until in 1861 the South was farther from freedom than in 1800.

The edict of 1863 was the first step in emancipation and its cost in blood and treasure was staggering. But that was not all—it was only a first step. There were other bills to pay of material reconstruction, social regeneration, mental training and moral uplift. These the nation started to meet in the Fifteenth Amendment, the Freedman's Bureau, the crusade of school-teachers and the Civil Rights Bill. But the effort was great and the determination of the South to pay no single cent or deed for past error save by force, led in the revolution of 1876 to the triumph of reaction. Reaction meant and means a policy of state, society and individual, whereby no American of Negro blood shall ever come into the full freedom of modern culture. In the carrying out of this program by certain groups and sections, no pains have been spared—no expenditure of money, ingenuity, physical or moral strength. The building of barriers around these black men has been pushed with an energy so desperate and unflagging that it has seriously checked the great outpouring of benevolence and sympathy that greeted the freedman in 1863. It has come so swathed and gowned in graciousness as to disarm philanthropy and chill enthusiasm. It has used double-tongued argument with deadly effect. Has the Negro advanced? Beware his further strides. Has the Negro retrograded? It is his fate, why seek to help him? Thus has the spirit of repression gained attention, complacent acquiescence, and even coöperation. To be sure, there still stand staunch souls who cannot yet believe the doctrine of human repression, and who pour out their wealth for Negro training and freedom in the face of the common cry. But the majority of Americans seem to have forgotten the foundation principles of their government and the recklessly destructive effect of the blows meant to bind and tether their fellows. We have come to see a day here in America when one citizen can deprive another of his vote at his discretion; can restrict the education of his neighbors' children as he sees fit; can with impunity load his neighbor with public insult on the king's highway; can deprive him of his property without due process of law; can deny him the right of trial by his peers, or of any trial whatsoever if he can get a large enough group of men to join him; can refuse to protect or safeguard the integrity of the family of some men whom he dislikes; finally, can not only close the door of opportunity in commercial and social lines in a fully competent neighbor's face, but can actually count on the national and state governments to help and make effective this discrimination.

Such a state of affairs is not simply disgraceful; it is deeply and increasingly dangerous. Not only does the whole nation feel already the loosening of joints which these vicious blows on human liberty have caused—lynching, lawlessness, lying and stealing, bribery and divorce—but it can look for darker deeds to come.

And this not merely because of the positive harm of this upbuilding of barriers, but above all because within these bursting barriers are men—human forces which no human hand can hold. It is human force and aspiration and endeavor which are moving there amid the creaking of timbers and writhing of souls. It is human force that has already done in a generation the work of many centuries. It has saved over a half-billion dollars in property, bought and paid for landed estate half the size of all England, and put homes thereon as good and as pure as the homes of any corresponding economic class the world around; it has crowded eager children through a wretched and half-furnished school system until from an illiteracy of seventy per cent., two-thirds of the living adults can read and write. These proscribed millions have 50,000 professional men, 200,000 men in trade and transportation, 275,000 artisans and mechanics, 1,250,000 servants and 2,000,000 farmers working with the nation to earn its daily bread. These farmers raise yearly on their own and hired farms over 4,000,000 bales of cotton, 25,000,000 pounds of rice, 10,000,000 bushels of potatoes, 90,000,000 pounds of tobacco and 100,000,000 bushels of corn, besides that for which they labor on the farms of others. They have given America music inspired art and literature, made its bread, dug its ditches, fought its battles, and suffered in its misfortunes. The great mass of these men is becoming daily more thoroughly organized, more deeply self-critical, more conscious of its power. Threatened though it has been naturally, as a proletariat, with degeneration and disease, it is to-day reducing its death-rate and beginning organized rescue of its delinquents and defectives. The mass can still to-day be called ignorant, poor and but moderately efficient, but it is daily growing better trained, richer and more intelligent. And as it grows it is sensing more and more the vantage-ground which it holds as a defender of the right of the freedom of human development for black men in the midst of a centre of modern culture. It sees its brothers in yellow, black and brown held physically at arms' length from civilization lest they become civilized and less liable to conquest and exploitation. It sees the world-wide effort to build an aristocracy of races and nations on a foundation of darker half-enslaved and tributary peoples. It knows that the last great battle of the West is to vindicate the right of any man of any nation, race, or color to share in the world's goods and thoughts and efforts to the extent of his effort and ability. . . .

CHARLES YOUNG

The life of Charles Young was a triumph of tragedy. No one ever knew the truth about the Hell he went through at West Point. He seldom even mentioned it. The pain was too great. Few knew what faced him always in his army life. It was not enough for him to do well—he must always do better; and so much and so conspicuously better, as to disarm the scoundrels that ever trailed him. He lived in the army surrounded by insult and intrigue and yet he set his teeth and kept his soul serene and triumphed.

He was one of the few men I know who literally turned the other cheek with Jesus Christ. He was laughed at for it and his own people chided him bitterly, yet he persisted. When a white Southern pigmy at West Point protested at taking food from a dish passed first to Young, Young passed it to him first and afterward to himself. When officers of inferior rank refused to salute a "nigger," he saluted them. Seldom did he lose his temper, seldom complain.

With his own people he was always the genial, hearty, half-boyish friend. He kissed the girls, slapped the boys on the back, threw his arms about his friends, scattered his money in charity; only now and then behind the Veil did his nearest comrades see the Hurt and Pain graven on his heart; and when it appeared he promptly drowned it in his music—his beloved music, which always poured from his quick, nervous fingers, to caress and bathe his soul.

Steadily, unswervingly he did his duty. And Duty to him, as to few modern men, was spelled in capitals. It was his lodestar, his soul; and neither force nor reason swerved him from it. His second going to Africa, after a terrible attack of black water fever, was suicide. He knew it. His wife knew it. His friends knew it. He had been sent to *Africa* because the Army considered his blood pressure too high to let him go to *Europe!* They sent him there to die. They sent him there because he was one of the very best officers in the service and if he had gone to Europe he could not have been denied the stars of a General. They could not stand a black American General. Therefore they sent him to the fever coast of Africa. They ordered him to make roads back in the haunted jungle. He knew what they wanted and intended. He could have escaped it by accepting his retirement from active service, refusing his call to active duty and then he could have lounged and lived at leisure on his retirement pay. But Africa needed him. He did not yell and collect money and advertise great schemes and parade in crimson—he just went quietly, ignoring appeal and protest.

He is dead. But the heart of the Great Black Race, the Ancient of Days—the Undying and Eternal—rises and salutes his shining memory: Well done! Charles Young, Soldier and Man and unswerving Friend.

MARCUS GARVEY

It was upon the tenth of August, in High Harlem of Manhattan Island, where a hundred thousand Negroes live. There was a long, low, unfinished church basement, roofed over. A little, fat black man, ugly, but with intelligent eyes and big head, was seated on a plank platform beside a "throne," dressed in a military uniform of the gayest mid-Victorian type, heavy with gold lace, epaulets, plume, and sword. Beside him were "potentates," and before him knelt a succession of several colored gentlemen. These in the presence of a thousand or more applauding dark spectators were duly "knighted" and raised to the "peerage" as knight-commanders and dukes of Uganda and the Niger. Among the lucky recipients of titles was the former private secretary of Booker T. Washington!

What did it all mean? A casual observer might have mistaken it for the dress-rehearsal of a new comic opera, and looked instinctively for Bert Williams and Miller and Lyle. But it was not; it was a serious occasion, done on the whole soberly and solemnly. Another might have found it simply silly. All ceremonies are more or less silly. Some Negroes would have said that this ceremony had something symbolic, like the coronation, because it was part of a great "back-to-Africa" movement and represented self-determination for the Negro race and a relieving of America of her most difficult race problem by a voluntary operation.

On the other hand, many American Negroes and some others were scandalized by something which they could but regard as simply child's play. It seemed to them sinister, this enthroning of a demagogue, a blatant boaster, who with monkey-shines was deluding the people and taking their hard-earned dollars; and in High Harlem there rose an insistent cry, "Garvey must go!"

Knowledge of all this seeped through to the greater world because it was sensational and made good copy for the reporters. The great world now and then becomes aware of certain currents within itself,—tragedies and comedies, movements of mind, gossip, personalities,—in some inner whirlpool of which it had been scarcely aware before. Usually these things are of little interest or influence for the main current of events; and yet is not this same main current made up of the impinging of these smaller swirlings of little groups? No matter how segregated and silent the smaller whirlpool is, if it is American, at some time it strikes and influences the American world. What, then, is the latest news from this area of Negrodom spiritually so foreign to most of white America?

2

The sensation that Garvey created was due not so much to his program as to his processes of reasoning, his proposed methods of work, and the width of the stage upon which he essayed to play his part.

His reasoning was at first new and inexplicable to Americans because he brought to the United States a new Negro problem. We think of our problem here as *the* Negro problem, but we know more or less clearly that the problem of the American Negro is very different from the problem of the South African Negro or the problem of the Nigerian Negro or the problem of the South American Negro. We have not hitherto been so clear as to the way in which the problem of the Negro in the United States differs from the problem of the Negro in the West Indies. For a long time we have been told, and we have believed, that the race problem in the West Indies, and particularly in Jamaica, has virtually been settled.

Let us note the facts. Marcus Garvey was born on the northern coast of Jamaica in 1887. He was a poor black boy, his father dying later in the almshouse. He received a little training in the Church of England grammer-school, and then learned the trade of printing, working for years as foreman of a printing plant. Then he went to Europe, and wandered about England and France, working and observing until he finally returned to Jamaica. He found himself facing a stone wall. He was poor, he was black, he had no chance for a university education, he had no likely chance for preferment in any line, but could work as an artisan at small wage for the rest of his life.

Moreover, he knew that the so-called settlement of the race problem in Jamaica was not complete; that as a matter of fact throughout the West Indies the development has been like this: most white masters had cohabited with Negro women, and some had actually married them; their children were free by law in most cases, but were not the recognized equals of the whites either socially, politically, or economically. Because of the numbers of the free Negroes as compared with the masters, and because of their continued growth in wealth and intelligence, they began to get political power, and they finally either expelled the whites by uniting with the blacks, as in Haiti, or forced the whites to receive the mulattoes, or at least the lighter-hued ones, as equals.

This is the West Indian solution of the Negro problem. The mulattoes are virtually regarded and treated as whites, with the assumption that they will, by continued white intermarriage, bleach out their color as soon as possible. There survive, therefore, few white colonials, save new-comers, who are not of Negro descent in some more or less remote ancestor. Mulattoes intermarry, then, largely with the whites, and the so-called disappearance of the color-line is the disappearance of the line between the whites and mulattoes, and not between the whites and the blacks or even between the mulattoes and the blacks.

Thus the privileged and exploiting group in the West Indies is composed of whites and mulattoes, while the poorly paid and ignorant proletariats are the blacks, forming a peasantry vastly in the majority, but socially, politically, and economically helpless and nearly voiceless. This peasantry, moreover, has been systematically deprived of its natural leadership because the black boy who showed initiative or who accidentally gained wealth and education soon gained the recognition of the white-mulatto group and might be incorporated with them, particularly if he married one of them. Thus his interests and efforts were identified with the mulatto-white group.

There must naturally arise a more or less insistent demand among the black peasants for self-expression and for an exposition of their grievances by one of their own group. Such leaders have indeed arisen from time to time, and Marcus Garvey was one. His notoriety comes not from his ability and accomplishment, but from the Great War. Not that he was without ability. He was a facile speaker, able to express himself in grammatical and forceful English; he had spent enough time in world cities like London to get an idea of world movements, and he honestly believed that the backwardness of the blacks was simply the result of oppression and lack of opportunity.

On the other hand, Garvey had no thorough education and a very hazy idea of the technic of civilization. He fell easily into the common error of assuming that because oppression has retarded a group, the mere removal of the injustice will at a bound restore the group to full power. Then, too, he personally had his drawbacks: he was inordinately vain and egotistic, jealous of his power, impatient of details, a poor judge of human nature, and he had the common weakness of untrained devotees that no dependence could be put upon his statements of fact. Not that he was a conscious liar, but dream, fact, fancy, wish, were all so blurred in his thinking that neither he himself nor his hearers could clearly or easily extricate them.

Then came the new economic demand for Negro peasant labor on the Panama Canal, and finally the Great War. Black West-Indians began to make something like decent wages, they began to travel, and they began to talk and think. Garvey talked and thought with them. In conjunction with white and colored sympathizers he planned a small Jamaican Tuskegee. This failed, and he conceived the idea of a purely Negro organization to establish independent Negro states and link them with commerce and industry. His "Universal Negro Improvement Association," launched August 1, 1914, in Jamaica, was soon in financial difficulties. The war was beginning to change the world, and as white American laborers began to be drawn into war work there was an opening in many lines not only for Southern American Negroes as laborers and mechanics, but also for West Indians as servants and laborers. They began to migrate in larger numbers. With this new migration came Marcus Garvey.

He established a little group of his own Jamaica countrymen in Harlem and launched his program. He took no account of the American Negro problem; he knew nothing about it. What he was trying to do was to settle the Jamaican problem in the United States. On the other hand, American Negroes knew nothing about the Jamaican problem, and they were excited and indignant at being brought face to face with a man who was full of wild talk about Africa and the West Indies and steamship lines and "race pride," but who said nothing and apparently knew nothing about the right to vote, the horrors of lynching and mob law, and the problem of racial equality.

Moreover, they were especially incensed at the new West Indian conception of the color-line. Color-lines had naturally often appeared in colored America, but the development had early taken a far different direction from that in the West Indies. Migration by whites had numerically overwhelmed both masters and mulattoes, and compelled most American masters to sell their own children into slavery. Freedom, therefore, rather than color, became the first line of social distinction in the American Negro world despite the near-white aristocracies of cities like Charleston and New Orleans, and despite the fact that the proportion of mulattoes who were free and who gained some wealth and education was greater than that of blacks because of the favor of their white parents.

After emancipation, color caste tended to arise again, but the darker group was quickly welded into one despite color by caste legislation, which applied to a white man with one Negro great-grandfather as well as to a full-blooded Bantu. There were still obvious advantages to the Negro American of lighter hue in passing for white or posing as Spanish or Portuguese, but the pressing demand for ability and efficiency and honesty within this fighting, advancing group continually drove the color-line back before reason and necessity, and it came to be generally regarded as the poorest possible taste for a Negro even to refer to differences of color. Colored folk as white as the whitest came to describe themselves as Negroes. Imagine, then, the surprise and disgust of these Americans when Garvey launched his Jamaican color scheme.

He did this, of course, ignorantly and with no idea of his mistake and no wit to read the signs. He meant well. He saw what seemed to him the same color-lines which he hated in Jamaica, and he sought here as there to oppose white supremacy and the white ideal by a crude and equally brutal black supremacy and black ideal. His mistake did not lie in the utter impossibility of this program,—greater upheavals in ideal have shaken the world before,—but rather in its spiritual bankruptcy and futility; for what shall this poor world gain if it exchange one race supremacy for another?

Garvey soon sensed that somewhere he was making a mistake, and he began to protest that he was not excluding mulattoes from his organization. Indeed, he has men of all colors and bloods in his organization, but his propaganda still remains "all-black," because this brings cash from the Jamaica peasants. Once he was actually haled to court and made to apologize for calling a disgruntled former colleague "white"! His tirades and twistings have landed him in strange contradictions. Thus with one voice he denounced Booker T. Washington and Frederick Douglass as bastards, and with the next named his boarding-house and first steamship after these same men!

3

Aside from his color-lines, Garvey soon developed in America a definite and in many respects original and alluring program. He proposed to establish the "Black Star Line" of steamships, under Negro ownership and with Negro money, to trade between the United States, the West Indies, and Africa. He proposed to establish a factories corporation which was going to build factories and manufacture goods both for local consumption of Negroes and for export. He was going eventually to take possession of Africa and establish independent Negro governments there.

The statement of this program, with tremendous head-lines, wild eloquence, and great insistence and repetition, caught the attention of all America, white and black. When Mr. Garvey brought his cohorts to Madison Square Garden, clad in fancy costumes and with new songs and ceremonies, and when, ducking his dark head at the audience, he yelled, "We are going to Africa to tell England, France, and Belgium to get out of there," America sat up, listened, laughed, and said here at least is something new.

Negroes, especially West Indians, flocked to his movement and poured money into it. About three years ago he had some 80,000 members in his organization, and perhaps 20,000 or 30,000 were paying regularly thirty-five cents a month into his chest. These numbers grew in his imagination until he was claiming 4,500,000 followers, and speaking for "Four hundred million Negroes"! He did not, however, stop with dreams and promises. If he had been simply a calculating scoundrel, he would carefully have skirted the narrow line between promise and performance and avoided as long as possible the inevitable catastrophe. But he believed in his program and he had a childish ignorance of the stern facts of the world into whose face he was flying.

Being an islander, and born in a little realm where half a day's journey takes one from ocean to ocean, the world always seemed small to him, and it was perhaps excusable for this black peasant of Jamaica to think of Africa as a similar, but slightly larger, island which could easily be taken possession of.

His first practical step toward this was to establish the Black Star Line, and here he literally left his critics and opponents breathless by suddenly announcing in 1919 that the *Frederick Douglass,* a steamship, had been bought by his line, was on exhibition at a wharf in New York, and was about to sail to the West Indies with freight and passengers. The announcement was electrical even for those who did not believe in Garvey. With a splendid, audacious faith, this poor black leader, with his storming tongue, compelled a word of admiration from all. But the seeds of failure were in his very first efforts. This first boat, the *Yarmouth* (never renamed the Frederick Douglass probably because of financial difficulties), was built in the year Garvey was born, and was an old sea-scarred hulk. He was cheated in buying it, and paid $140,000 for it—at least twice as much as the boat was worth. She made three trips to the West Indies in three years, and then was docked for repairs, attached for debt, and finally, in December, 1921, sold at auction for $1625!

The second boat that Garvey bought was a steam yacht originally built for a Standard Oil magnate. It, too, was old and of doubtful value, but Garvey paid $60,000 for it, and sent it down to do a small carrying trade between the West Indies Islands. The boat broke down, and it cost $70,000 or $80,000 more to repair it than Garvey paid for it. Finally it was wrecked or seized in Cuba, and the crew was transported to the United States at government expense.

The third boat was a Hudson River ferry-boat that Garvey bought for $35,000. With this he carried excursionists up and down the Hudson during one summer and used it as a vivid advertisement to collect more money. The boat, however, ran only that summer, and then had to be abandoned as beyond repair.

Finally, Garvey tried to buy of the United States Shipping Board the steamship *Orion* for $250,000. This boat was to be renamed the *Phyllis Wheatley,* and its sailings were advertised in Garvey's weekly paper for several months, and some passages were sold; but the boat never was delivered because sufficient payments were not made.

Thus the Black Star Line arose and disappeared, and with it went some $800,000 of the savings of West Indians and a few American Negroes. With this enterprise the initial step and greatest test of Mr. Garvey's movement failed utterly. His factories corporation never really got started. In its place he has established a number of local grocery stores in Harlem and one or two shops, including a laundry and a printing-press, which may or may not survive.

His African program was made impossible by his own pigheadedness. He proposed to make a start in Liberia with industrial enterprises. From this center he would penetrate all Africa and gradually subdue it. Instead of keeping this plan hidden and working cautiously and intelligently toward it, he yelled and shouted and telegraphed it all over the world. Without consulting the Liberians, he apparently was ready to assume partial charge of their state. He appointed officials with high-sounding titles, and announced that the headquarters of his organization was to be removed to Liberia in January, 1922. Such announcements, together with his talk about conquest and "driving Europe out," aroused European governments to inquire about Garvey and his backing. Diplomatic representations were made to Liberia, asking it how far it intended to coöperate in this program. Liberia was naturally compelled to repudiate Garveyism, root and branch. The officials told Garvey that he or any one else was welcome to migrate to Liberia and develop industry within legal lines, but that they could recognize only one authority in Liberia and that was the authority of the Liberian Government, and that Liberia could not be the seat of any intrigue against her peaceful neighbors. They made it impossible for Garvey to establish any headquarters in Africa unless it was done by the consent of the very nations whom he was threatening to drive out of Africa!

This ended his African program and reduced him to the curious alternative of sending a delegate to the third assembly of the League of Nations to ask them to hand over as a gift to his organization a German colony in order that he might begin his work.

4

Thus the bubble of Garveyism burst; but its significance, its meaning, remains. After all, one has to get within Garvey to know him, to understand him. He is not simply a liar and blatant fool. Something of both, to be sure, is there; but that is not all. He is the type of dark man whom the white world is making daily, molding, marring, tossing to the air. All his life whites have laughed and sneered at him and torn his soul. All his life he has hated the half-whites who, rejecting their darker blood, have gloried in their pale shame. He has stormed and fought within, and then at last it all burst out. He had to guard himself before the powers and be careful of law and libel and hunger, but where he could be free, he snarled and cursed at the whites, insulted the mullatoes with unpardonable epithets, and bitterly reviled the blacks for their cowardice.

Suppose, now, for a moment that Garvey had been a man of first-rate ability, canny, shrewd, patient, dogged? He might have brought a world war of races a generation nearer, he might have deprived civilization of that precious generation of respite where we have yet time to sit and consider if difference of human color must necessarily mean blows and blood. As a matter of fact, Garvey did not know how to approach his self-appointed task; he had not the genius to wait and laboriously learn, yet he pompously seized the pose; he kept extremely busy, rushed hither and thither. He collected and squandered thousands, almost millions. He would, he must, succeed. He appeared in the uniforms of his dream triumphs, in 1921 with an academic cap and gown, weird in colors; in 1922 with cocked hat, gold lace, and sword— the commander-in-chief of the African Legion! He did not quite dare call himself King Marcus I, but he sunned himself awhile in the address of "your Majesty." He held court and made knights, lords, and dukes; and yet, as he feverishly worked, he knew he had failed; he knew he had missed the key to some dark arcanum. He grew suspicious, morose, complaining, furious at the "fools" and "scoundrels" who were "plotting" his ruin and the overthrow of his cause. With all the provincial backwoods love of courts and judges, he rushed into and reveled in litigation, figuring in at least fifty suits, suing for libel, breach of contract, slander, divorce, assault—everything and anything; while in turn his personal enemies sued him, rioted against him, and one shot him, so that to-day he dares not stir without a sturdy bodyguard.

Beaten and overwhelmed with loss and disappointment, he will not yet surrender, and seeks by surrounding himself with new officials and by announcing new enterprises—a daily paper, a new line of steamships, and the like—to re-form his lines. So he sits to-day. He is a world figure in minute microcosm. On a larger field, with fairer opportunity, he might have been great, certainly notorious. He is to-day a little puppet, serio-comic, funny, yet swept with a great veil of tragedy; meaning in himself little more than a passing agitation, moving darkly and uncertainly from a little island of the sea to the panting, half-submerged millions of the first world state. And yet he means something to the world. He is type of a mighty coming thing. He voices a vague, formless, but growing, integrating human mind which some day will arrest the world.

Just what it has cost the Negro race in money to support Garvey it is hard to say, but certainly not less than a million dollars. And yet with all this there are certain peculiar satisfactions. Here has come a test to the American Negro which he has not had before. A demagogue has appeared, not the worst kind of demagogue, but, on the contrary, a man who had much which was attractive and understandable in his personality and his program; nevertheless, a man whose program anybody with common sense knew was impossible. With all the arts of the demagogue, Garvey appealed to crowds of people with persuasive eloquence, with the ringing of all possible charges of race loyalty and the bastardy of the mulatto and the persons ashamed of their race, and the implacable enmity of the whites. It was the sort of appeal that easily throws ignorant and inexperienced people into orgies of response and generosity. Yet with all this, coming at a critical time, when the Negro was hurt at his war experience and his post-war treatment, when lynching was still a national institution and mob-law a ready resort; when the rank and file of ignorant West-Indian Negroes were going wild over Garvey, the American Negroes sat cool and calm, and were neither betrayed into wild and unjust attacks upon Garvey nor into uncritical acceptance.

His following has ebbed and flowed. Its main and moving nucleus has been a knot of black Jamaica peasants resident in America as laborers and servants, mostly unlettered, poor, and ignorant, who worship Garvey as their ideal incarnate. Garvey is bold. Garvey lashes the white folk. Garvey downs the mulattoes. Garvey forever! no matter what he does. Does he steal? Better let him steal than let white folk. Does he squander? It's our money; let him waste. Does he fail? Others have failed.

It is this blind and dangerous nucleus that explains Garvey's success in holding his power. Around these are a mass of West Indians, resident in the islands and in the United States, who have honestly supported Garvey in the hope that this new leader would direct them out of the West Indian *impasse* of low wages, little educational opportunity, no industrial openings, and caste. Especially they seized upon the Black Star Line, as isolated islanders would, as a plan of real practical hope. This group reached sixty or seventy thousand in number during Garvey's heyday, but with the failure of his enterprises it is rapidly falling away.

With these groups have always been a number of American Negroes: the ignorant, drawn by eloquence and sound; the grafters who saw a chance of sharing spoils; and with these some honest, thinking folk who paused and inquired, "Who is Garvey, and what is his program?" This American following, though always small, grew here and there, and in centers like Norfolk, Chicago, and Pittsburgh reached for a time into the thousands. But, on the whole, American Negroes stood the test well.

Garvey's proposal of such a new, autonomous, and hostile black world in league with the brown and yellow peoples brought from American Negroes a simple Missouri "Show us." They asked: "What are you doing, and how? What are your concrete and practical proposals?" They did not follow the more impatient counsels of "Garvey must go." They did not slander or silence or ignore him. The two hundred Negro weeklies treated him fairly, and audiences listened to his words and read his literature. And right here lay his undoing, for the more his flamboyant promises were carefully compared with his results, the sooner the utter futility of his program was revealed.

Here is a world that for a thousand years, from the First Crusade to the Great War, had been breaking down the barriers between nations and races in order to build a world-wide economic unity and cultural solidarity. The process has involved slavery, peonage, rape, theft, and extermination, but it is slowly uniting humanity. It is now proposed to turn back and cut out of this world its black eighth or its colored two thirds. Not only is this virtually impossible, but its attempt to-day would certainly involve the white and colored worlds in a death-struggle whose issue none can surely foretell. The power of the yellow, black, and brown worlds to-day is the economic dependence of the white world on them, and the power of the white world is its economic technic and organization. The super-diplomacy of race politics to-morrow is to transmute this interdependence into cultural sympathy, spiritual tolerance, and human freedom. Not in segregation, but in closer, larger unity lies interracial peace.

Not with entire clearness and yet with a certain fundamental and tremendously significant clarity the American Negro realizes this, and as yet no demagoguery or pipe dreams have been able to divorce him from the facts. The present generation of Negroes has survived two grave temptations, the greater one, fathered by Booker T. Washington, which said, "Let politics alone, keep in your place, work hard, and do not complain," and which meant perpetual color caste for colored folk by their own cooperation and consent, and the consequent inevitable debauchery of the white world; and the lesser, fathered by Marcus Garvey, which said: "Give up! Surrender! The struggle is useless; back to Africa and fight the white world."

It is no ordinary tribute to American Negro poise and common sense, and ability to choose and reject leadership, that neither of these programs has been able to hold them. One of the most singular proofs of this is that the latest support of Garveyism is from the notorious Ku Klux Klan. When Garvey saw his Black Star Line disappear, his West Indian membership fall off, and his American listeners grow increasingly critical, he flew South to consult the Grand Cyclops of the Invisible Empire. Whether the initiative came from him or from the Klan is not known, but probably the Klan invited him. They were indeed birds of a feather, believing in titles, flummery, and mumbo-jumbo, and handling much gullible money.

Garvey's motives were clear. The triumph of the Klan would drive Negroes to his program in despair, while the Klan's sympathy would enable him to enter the South, where he has not dared to work and exploit the ignorant black millions. The Klan's object was to encourage anything that would induce Negroes to believe that their fight for freedom in America was vain. Garvey's secretary said that the Klan would probably finance the Black Star Line, and Garvey invited the Grand Cyclops to speak at his convention. But Garvey reckoned without his host. A storm of criticism rose among Negroes and kept Garvey explaining, contradicting, and repudiating the unholy alliance, and finally drove it under cover, although Garvey openly advertised the

Klan's program as showing the impossibility of the Negro's remaining in America, and the Klan sent out circulars defending Garvey and declaring that the opposition to him was from the Catholic Church!

Again it is High Harlem, with its music and laughter, its conversations shouted aloft, its brown and black and cream-like faces, its crisp and curling hair. As the setting sun sends its last crimson light from the heights that hold the Hudson from the Harlem, it floods 138th Street and lights three blocks. One is a block of homes built by the Equitable Life Assurance Society, but now sold to Negroes, some crowded, some carelessly kept, but most of them beautiful, even luxurious, perhaps as handsome a block as middle-class America, white or black, affords. Next the sun softens the newness of a brick block on Seventh Avenue, stretching low and beautiful from the Y.W.C.A., with a moving-picture house of the better class and a colored five-and-ten cent store built and owned by black folk. Down beyond, on 138th Street, the sun burns the raising spire of Abyssinian Church, a vast and striking structure built by Negroes who for a hundred years have supported one organization and are now moving to their newest and luxurious home of soft carpets, stained windows, and swelling organ. Finally, the dying rays hit a low, rambling basement of brick and rough stone. It was designed as the beginning of a church long ago, but abandoned. Marcus Garvey roofed it over, and out of this squat and dirty old "Liberty Hall" he screams his propaganda. As compared with the homes, the business, the church, Garvey's basement represents nothing in accomplishment and only waste in attempt.

Yet it has a right to be. It represents something spiritual, however poor and futile today. Deep in the black man's heart he knows that he needs more than homes and stores and churches. He needs manhood—liberty, brotherhood, equality. The call of the spirit urges him restlessly to and fro with all men of the despised and forgotten, seeking, seeking. Misled they often are, and again and again they play in microcosm the same tragic drama that other worlds and other groups have played. Here is Garvey yelling to life, from the black side, a race consciousness which leaps to meet Madison Grant and Lothrop Stoddard and other worshipers of the great white race. It is symptomatic and portentous. If with a greater and more gifted and efficient Garvey it sometime blazes to real flame, it means world war and eternal hate and blood. It means the setting of the world clock back a thousand years. And yet the world's Garvey's are not solely to blame, but rather every worshiper of race superiority and human inequality. On the other hand, back of all this lurks the quieter, more successful, more insistent, and hopeful fact. Races are living together. They are buying and selling, marrying and rearing children, laughing and crying. They are fighting mobs and lynchers and those that enslave and despise, and they have not yet failed in that fight. Their faith in their ultimate and complete triumph are these homes, this business block, this church, duplicated a hundred thousand times in a nation of twelve million. Here, then, are the two future paths, outlined with a certain sullen dimness in the world's blood-crimson twilight, and yet to be descried easily by those with the seeing hearts. Which path will America choose?

ROBERT E. LEE

Each year on the 19th of January there is renewed effort to canonize Robert E. Lee, the great confederate general. His personal comeliness, his aristocratic birth and his military prowess all call for the verdict of greatness and genius. But one thing—one terrible fact—militates against this and that is the inescapable truth that Robert E. Lee led a bloody war to perpetuate human slavery. Copperheads like the New York *Times* may magisterially declare: "of course, he never fought for slavery." Well, for what did he fight? State rights? Nonsense. The South cared only for State Rights as a weapon to defend slavery. If nationalism had been a stronger defense of the slave system than particularism, the South would have been as nationalist in 1861 as it had been in 1812.

No. People do not go to war for abstract theories of government. They fight for property and privilege and that was what Virginia fought for in the Civil War. And Lee followed Virginia. He followed Virginia not because he particularly loved slavery (although he certainly did not hate it), but because he did not have the moral courage to stand against his family and his clan. Lee hesitated and hung his head in shame because he was asked to lead armies against human progress and Christian decency and did not dare refuse. He surrendered not to Grant, but to Negro Emancipation.

Today we can best perpetuate his memory and his nobler traits, not by falsifying his moral débacle, but by explaining it to the young white South. What Lee did in 1861, other Lees are doing in 1928. They lack the moral courage to stand up for justice to the Negro because of the overwhelming public opinion of their social environment. Their fathers in the past have condoned lynching and mob violence, just as today they acquiesce in the disfranchisement of educated and worthy black citizens, provide wretchedly inadequate public schools for Negro children and endorse a public treatment of sickness, poverty and crime which disgraces civilization.

It is the punishment of the South that its Robert Lees and Jefferson Davises will always be tall, handsome and well-born. That their courage will be physical and not moral. That their leadership will be weak compliance with public opinion and never costly and unswerving revolt for justice and right. It is ridiculous to seek to excuse Robert Lee as the most formidable agency this nation ever raised to make 4 million human beings goods instead of men. Either he knew what slavery meant when he helped maim and murder thousands in its defense, or he did not. If he did not he was a fool. If he did, Robert Lee was a traitor and a rebel—not indeed to his country, but to humanity and humanity's God.

A PORTRAIT OF CARTER G. WOODSON

Carter Godwin Woodson, who died in Washington on April 3 at the age of seventy-one, illustrates what race prejudice can do to a human soul and also what it is powerless to prevent. Of course, race prejudice is only one particular form of the oppression which human beings have used toward each other throughout the ages. Oppression cramps thought and development, individuality and freedom. Woodson was naturally a big strong man with a good mind; not brilliant, not a genius, but steady, sound and logical in his thinking processes, and capable of great application and concentration in his work. He was a man of normal appetites, who despite extraordinary circumstances carved out a good valuable career. As it happened, he did not have the chance for normal development; he spent his childhood working in a mine and did not get education enough to enter high school until he was twenty; he never married, and one could say almost that he never played; he could laugh and joke on occasion but those occasions did not often arise.

I knew him for forty years and more, and have often wondered what he did for recreation, if anything. He had very little outdoor life, he had few close friends. He cared nothing for baseball or football and did not play cards, smoke or drink. In later years his only indulgence was over-eating so that after fifty he was considerably overweight.

All this arose, in the first place, because like most people on earth he was born poor. But his poverty was the special case of being one of nine children of poor American Negroes who had been born slaves. This meant that from the beginning he was handicapped; it was difficult for him to go regularly to the very poor country school in his neighborhood, and for six years during his youth, when he ought to have been in school, he was working in a coal mine; so that he was grown before he entered high school in Huntington, West Virginia. Once started, however, he went to college at Berea, Kentucky, then to the University of Chicago. He alternated with public school teaching, travel and study in Europe and finally taught ten years, from 1908 to 1918, in the public schools of Washington, D.C.

In 1912, Woodson took his doctorate of philosophy at Harvard in history. It is quite possible that had he been a white man he might have entered a university career, as instructor and eventually as a professor with small but adequate salary; enough for marriage, home and children. But of course, at the time he got his doctorate, there was not the slightest thought that a black man could ever be on the faculty of Harvard or of any other great school. In Washington, he got his main experience of regular teaching work. It was hard and not inspiring. The "Jim Crow" school system of the District of Columbia is perhaps the best of its kind in the United States; but it had the shortcomings of all segregated schools, with special arrangements and peculiar difficulties; they are not the kind of schools which would inspire most men to further study or to an academic career.

After that experience Woodson turned to college work. He served as dean for a year at Howard University and for four years at West Virginia College. He might have ended his career in this way as president of a small Southern colored college. His duties would have been collecting funds and superintending discipline among teachers and students; or if it had been in a state school, he would have cajoled and played up to a set of half-educated Southern whites as trustees, so as to get for Negroes a third or a half of the funds they were legally entitled to. It would have been the kind of executive job which has killed many a man, white and black, either physically or mentally or both; and it was the sort of thing that Woodson was determined not to do.

He had by this time made up his mind that he was going to devote himself to the history of the Negro people as a permanent career. In doing that he knew the difficulties which he would have to face. Study and publication, if at all successful, call for money, and money for any scientific effort for or by a Negro means abject begging; and at begging Woodson was not adept.

It was a time, moreover, when all Negro education was largely charity, not only college education, but elementary and high school training. Groups of Negro and white teachers in Southern schools made regular pilgrimages to the North to collect money from churches and philanthropists in order to support their schools. But the job which Woodson had carved out for himself was not a school; it was a matter of a periodical, with research and publication, and it was to be done in a field not only unpopular but practically unrecognized. Most people, even historians, would have doubted if there was enough of distinctly Negro history in America to call for publication. For thirteen years at Atlanta University we had tried to raise money for research and publication of studies in Negro sociology; five thousand a year, outside my salary. We had to give up the attempt in 1910. But one thing that Woodson's career had done for him was to make him stubborn and single-minded. He had no ties, family or social; he had chosen this life work and he never wavered from it after 1922.

His efforts at raising money for the work had some initial success; for ten years or more Julius Rosenwald, the Jewish philanthropist of Chicago, gave him $400 a year. Woodson organized the Association for the Study of Negro Life and History and already as early as January,

1916, while still teaching, he began publication of *The Journal of Negro History*, a quarterly which is now in its thirty-fourth year of continuous publication.

The Journal was an excellent piece of work and received commendation from high sources. The Carnegie Foundation and afterwards the Spelman Memorial Fund of the Rockefellers gave him $50,000 in installments of $5,000 a year beginning in 1921. But Woodson did not prove the ideal recipient of philanthropy.

He was not a follower of the school of Booker T. Washington and had neither the humility nor the finesse of social uplifters. His independence of thought and action was exaggerated; he went out to meet opposition before it arose, and he was fiercely determined to be master of his own enterprises and final judge of what he wanted to do and say. He pretty soon got the reputation of not being the kind of "trustworthy" Negro to whom help should be given. It was not for a moment intimated that the philanthropists wanted to curb his work or guide it, but if Woodson had anticipated their wishes and conformed to their attitudes, money would have poured in. Only those persons who followed the Washington philosophy and whose attitude toward the South was in accord with the new orientation of the North, could be sure to have encouragement and continued help. After a while it became the settled policy of philanthropic foundations and of academic circles to intimate that Carter Woodson was altogether too self-centered and self-assertive to receive any great encouragement. His work was individual with no guarantee of permanence.

There was just enough truth in this accusation to make the criticism stick. Even his colored friends and admirers encountered refusal to co-operate or take counsel. Twice, alarmed because of his meager income, and his overwork, I ventured to propose alliance and help; I offered to incorporate *The Journal* into the Department of Publications and Research of the N.A.A.C.P., with promise of as much autonomy as was allowed me. He considered, but refused, unless an entirely separate department was set up for him. This the Board refused to consider as I knew it would. Then I suggested incorporation of his work into that of Howard University; but after trial, this also fell through, and his friends concluded that he must be left to carry on his great work without interference in any way from others. Several times he took in assistants and helpers, but never gave them authority or permanent tenure. He was always the lone pioneer and remained this until his death.

It was this very attitude, however, that brought out the iron in Woodson's soul. He was forty-four in 1922 when he began this independent career. He therefore gradually buckled up his belt, gave up most of the things which a man of his age would be looking forward to and put the whole of his energy into his work. As I have said, he never married, he never had a home; he lived in lodgings as a boarder, or ate in restaurants; he schooled himself to small and uncertain income; it is probable that he lived many years on not more than $1000 and probably never as much as $5000.

Deliberately he cut down his wants and that was not difficult in Washington. Washington had no theatre for Negroes; its music was limited; there were art galleries, but they were not particularly attractive until recent years and never catered to black folk. In many cases they refused to exhibit the work of Negro artists. Parks and public recreation had many restrictions; there was little chance at club life or opportunity to meet men of standing, either American or passing foreigners. Woodson did not have enough money to spend much time in New York or abroad. He therefore concentrated his time, his energy, and his little money in building up his enterprise, and especially in organizing a constituency among American Negroes to support his work. That was the most astonishing result of his career.

From subscriptions to his quarterly, from donations made by small groups and organizations, from sale of books, he not only continued to publish his magazine, but he also went into the publishing business and issued a score of books written by himself and by others; and then as the crowning achievement, he established Negro History Week. He literally made this country, which has only the slightest respect for people of color, recognize and celebrate each year, a week in which it studied the effect which the American Negro has upon life, thought and action in the United States. I know of no one man who in a lifetime has, unaided, built up such a national celebration.

Every year in practically every state of the United States, Negro History Week is celebrated; and its celebration was almost forced upon school authorities, on churches and other organizations by the influence of the groups of people who had banded themselves together to help Carter Woodson's Association for the Study of Negro Life and History. His chief work, *The Negro in Our History*, went through eight editions, with its nearly eight hundred pages and wealth of illustration, and was used in the Negro public schools of the nation. More lately his monthly *Bulletin* of news had wide circulation and use.

It is a unique and marvelous monument which Carter Woodson has thus left to the people of the United States. But in this and in all his life, he was, and had to be, a cramped soul. There was in him no geniality and very little humor. To him life was hard and cynically logical; his writing was mechanical and unemotional. He never had the opportunity to develop warm sympathy with other human beings; and he did develop a deep-seated dislike, if not hatred, for the white people of the United States and of the world. He never believed in their generosity or good faith. He did not attack them; he did not complain about them, he simply ignored them so far as possible and went on with his work without expecting help or sympathetic cooperation from them.

He did not usually attend meetings of scientists in history; he was not often asked to read papers on such occasions; for the most part so far as the professors in history of this country were concerned he was forgotten and passed over; and yet few men have made so deep an imprint as Carter Woodson on thousands of scholars in historical study and research.

In his death he does not leave many very warm friends; there were few tears shed at his grave. But on the other hand, among American Negroes, and among those whites who knew about his work, and among those who in after years must learn about it, there will be vast respect and thankfulness for the life of this man. He was one who under the hardest conditions of environment kept himself to one great goal, worked at it stubbornly and with unwavering application and died knowing that he had accomplished much if not all that he had planned.

He left unfinished an *Encyclopedia Africana;* it was an idea which I had toyed with in 1909, securing as collaborators Sir Harry Johnston, Flinders-Petrie, Guiseppi Sergi, Albert Hart and Franz Boas. But my project never got beyond the name stage and was forgotten. Later Woodson took up the idea as a by-product of his *Journal;* but few knew of this project at the time. Finally in 1931, the Phelps-Stokes Fund projected an *Encyclopedia of the Negro,* but invited neither Woodson nor me to participate.

However, the group called together, including Moton of Tuskegee and Hope of Atlanta, protested and finally we were both invited. I attended the subsequent meetings but Woodson refused. I and many others talked to him and begged him to come in; but no; there were two reasons: this was, he considered, a white enterprise forced on Negroes; and secondly, he had himself already collected enough data eventually to make an encyclopedia. We demurred, not because we were unwilling to have him work on the encyclopedia; indeed we were eager; but because we knew that one man and especially one man with a rather narrow outlook which had been forced upon him, could not write a scientific encyclopedia of sufficient breadth to satisfy the world. Eventually this Phelps-Stokes project was unable to collect sufficient funds chiefly, I am sure, because I had been named Editor-in-Chief. So this project closed its effort with the publication of only one thin preliminary volume. But Woodson left the kernel of a great work. It would be a magnificent monument to his memory, if this were to be made the basis of broad rewriting and extension and published as a memorial to his life work.

As a historian, Woodson left something to be desired. He was indefatigable in research: for instance, his collection of photographs of Negroes and abolitionists is invaluable; his *Negro in American History* deserved the wide use which it has had. Some of his works like his *Education of the Negro prior to 1861, A Century of Negro Migration, Negro Orators and their Orations, Free Negro Owners of Slaves in the United States in 1830, Free Negro Heads of Families in the United States, The Mind of the Negro as Reflected in Letters Written During the Crisis, 1800–60,* are solid works of historical research. Others of his books were not of so great value.

Indeed his service to history was not so much his books as his editorship of the *Journal,* which brought into print some of the best scholars in this branch of history. On the other hand, Woodson himself lacked background for broad historical writing; he was almost contemptuous of emotion; he had limited human contacts and sympathies; he had no conception of the place of woman in creation. His book reviews were often pedantic and opinionated. Much of his otherwise excellent research will have to be reinterpreted by scholars of wider reading and better understanding of the social sciences, especially in economics and psychology; for Woodson never read Karl Marx.

The passing of Carter Woodson leaves a vacuum hard to fill. His memory leaves a lesson of determination and sacrifice which all men, young and old, black and white, may emulate to the glory of man and the uplift of his world.

PAUL ROBESON

It was in Paris, on Wednesday, April 20, 1949. The Salle Pleyel was packed to the high, many-balconied ceiling with delegates from 60 countries representing practically all the world. Paul Robeson entered and the whole audience rose and cheered with 2500 voices and in all human tongues. I doubt if any other person on earth could have elicited such spontaneous tribute. It was a many-sided outburst to a magnificent voice; to a recent visitor in every country of Europe—England, Denmark, Sweden, the Soviet Union, Poland, Czechoslovakia and Austria, whence he had flown to Paris; to a son of black slaves, a coworker not with wealthy and titled snobs but with laborers of all climes and colors. We had men of stature and renown at that gathering: Joliot-Curie and Aragon, Nenni and Picasso, Bernal, Zilliacus and Fadeev; none of these received so tumultuous a tribute. The program was interrupted and Robeson ascended the podium. His great voice rose in song—song of black slaves, song of white slaves, songs of Russia and France. Then among the few words of a short speech, Robeson said: "The black folk of America will never fight against the Soviet Union!" The applause swept up to the skies.

That was what happened. What was Robeson in reality saying? He knew better than most men, because he had long experience in both the Soviet Union and the United States, that of all countries, Russia alone has made race prejudice a crime; of all great imperialisms, Russia alone owns no colonies of dark serfs or white and what is more important has no investments in colonies and is lifting no blood-soaked profits from cheap labor in Asia and Africa. Robeson believed that facing the possibility of war with such a country, no black American of intelligence would for a moment take up arms. In a rare case a Britisher might fight Britain an Italian war against Italy or a German against the Fatherland; but that would be because of principle and not against fundamental conviction. For a man or a people to fight against his own conscience, against the very foundation of all he believed made life worth living, Robeson could not conceive that any people would do that and live and look men in the face. And so he declared that American Negro victims of color prejudice, serfdom, slavery and race hate, if in their right minds, would never fight a country which alone among nations opposes these crimes against civilization.

It was the natural conclusion of a clear-headed, straight-thinking artist and idealist which Robeson has always been. Robeson was wrong but wrong not in his logic, much less in his lofty ideals; he was wrong only in having too great faith in human beings. What then he really was saying was: *From my nature and beliefs, it is to me inconceivable that 15,000,000 descendants of Negro slaves who know from bitter and continuing experience what race prejudice and the enslavement of Africa and Asia has done not only to my people, but to civilization and Christianity and human decency for 500 years—it is inconceivable that these people would in any single case willingly join in war against the one great modern country which has opposed prejudice in a land once riddled by it, and the conquest and subjection of colonies in a world where colonial imperialism has murdered millions and which is suffering today in the eyes of Britain, France and America, mainly for this stand.*

Immediately this word of Robeson's, so dangerous to those who make money out of war and get huge income out of the gold and diamonds of South Africa, the rubber of Indo-China and tin of Indonesia, was spoken, the bought press agencies lifted this out of all which this greatest of peace congresses was saying—and it was saying brave and indisputable things—and featured Paul Robeson's voice in America as treason; and treason in truth it was to all who want war at any price and who are more than willing to use "niggers" to gain their ends. Moreover, certain Negro leaders hastened to "beat the gun" in denouncing Robeson before they even knew with certainty what he said or meant. This was the old plantation technique which hastened to outdo "Ole Massa" himself in denouncing any slave who dared lift his head for a minute out of the dirt of slavery.

I wrote at that time, a short word to express my feeling and sent it to the New York Times, the Herald-Tribune and the colored press. I said:

> "I agree with Paul Robeson absolutely, that Negroes should never willingly fight in an unjust war. I do not share his honest hope that all will not. A certain sheep-like disposition, inevitably born of slavery, will, I am afraid, lead many of them to join America in any enterprise, provided the whites will grant them equal right to do wrong."

The white press ignored this. Some Negro papers printed it. Why is all this important? Why should we worry if the white race is set on dragging down in one maelstrom the remnants of human culture and decency which two wars of unexampled cost, cruelty and destruction both physical and moral have begun? As people who now for two generations have been striving desperately to be recognized as American citizens, is it not only our duty but our strategy to agree with the United States in everything she wants or thinks she needs, going along eagerly with the current majority toward any goals they envision? This is a common belief of American Negroes. It is smart, they argue; it brings popularity and pays dividends in jobs and gifts to our schools and churches. Moreover, argue these statesmen out of the sides of their mouths, what business is it of ours if the White World is bent on suicide and the sabotage of all they have done to make this a decent world?

I submit that this selfish and self-centered philosophy is worse than idiotic; it spells self-destruction and the collapse of a civilization which is the property of black folk as well as white; and the ruin of a nation which our blood has fertilized and in whose future we have more than a stake. Are we trying to prove that those opponents of Negro suffrage were right when they declared that giving freedmen votes would add nothing to our strength or wise judgment? That at best Negroes would herd like tame sheep with those who offered them the most food or bought their vote at the highest price? There were others, black and white who declared and still aver that democracy is a contribution and reservoir and not merely a privilege; that we Negroes are Americans, not simply to follow, but to lead in fields where our experience makes us experts. And on war we are expert. The American Civil War was not fought to free the slaves and if it accomplished this partially, a wiser nation could have done more by peace than by murder and destruction. We gained nothing in the First nor Second World War which was not neutralized by the plunging of this country into the grip of a Plutocracy ruled increasingly for the benefit of the rich and the ruthless all over the world.

A Third World War would destroy the very culture which today we are beginning to share and enlarge. Our interest is not in destruction and revenge; not even in gloating over the disaster of the boastful white rulers of the universe; but far more in rescuing from imminent destruction that culture to which we have given song and rhythm, hard work and creative patience and a capacity for spiritual life unequalled by any similar group on earth. Peace on earth today is a must for us. We need it for survival, for accomplishment, for equality with the best of earth's peoples.

Instead of realizing this, we are being led like the Gadarene swine down to the depths of murder, destruction and hate; by spending our hard-earned dollars for atom bombs instead of houses and bread. And remember it is OUR money that is financing war; the nine hundred millions which today we are gaily sending to Europe does not come from the rich of America—they easily escape their just share of taxation; but from the poor, the laborers, the scrubwomen, the shop-girls, the small merchants and teachers who must pay on the nail or go to jail.

What would $900,000,000 dollars do for Negro education? It would insure the utter disappearance of illiteracy in a generation; the college training of Negroes of ability; the professional training of enough Negro physicians to do away with preventable disease; the ridding of jails of Negro sick and insane, now classed with criminals; the building of decent Negro homes where marriage could flourish; all this and easily. Small wonder that so many Americans prefer to spend this fortune on murderous explosions and goose-stepping.

Moreover the case is so clear; the arguments for peace so overwhelming; the lie of the threat of Russia and Communism so phony, that every effort is taken to stop the public from hearing the truth or discussing it. The press is so monopolized that the truth is suppressed or half-told or deliberately lied about all over the land. The chief magazines are owned by banking syndicates. Any man who dares to talk peace or Russia is not only in danger of personal violence as at Peekskill, but what is frightening, may lose his job or find himself in jail, on accusations which often he cannot know because of "security."

Less than a year ago, a prominent member of the Negro College Fund, said openly that advocacy of the FEPC and civil rights was "subversive." Negro postal clerks have been threatened with dismissal for attending a NAACP meeting; and the effort of American Negroes to cooperate with the emancipation of Africa has been officially called dangerous by an Attorney-General of the United States, who now graces the Supreme Court to poison the sources of constitutional law from that high vantage ground.

I freely admit that in the present hysteria and witch-hunting, there are Negroes whose responsibility to home and family closes their mouths. But my dear friend, Henry Hunt used to say, "I can keep still in seven languages!" When he did talk he told the truth. I can understand the lockjaw which is affecting most of our college presidents, teachers and civil servants. The President of Morgan College invited me to deliver the Commencement Address last June. Then he begged me frantically not to come because I had "been present" when Robeson spoke in Paris! I commend his staunch courage to his students.

I am unable to understand why our professional men, our preachers, and business men; our artisans and housewives should join the hounds of American reaction to stop free speech; to hamper thought and the search for truth, just because this happens to be the popular sport today. Paul Robeson is a great American and an honest man. Every Negro should defend his right to think and speak whether he agrees with him or not. To sneer at him and help gag him is beneath contempt.

We are selling our birthright in a great nation not for a mess—and a pretty nasty mess—of pottage, but only for the promise of such a mess; when the pay-off is due, the happy President of the United States is fishing and the Republican Copperhead from Michigan does the dirty work in the Senate, feeling that he has the Negro vote of Michigan in his pious pockets.

Promises sweetened with appointments judiciously scattered are supposed to keep Negroes' mouths shut. State appropriations for Negro schools will close the mouths of many college presidents. But all this will not keep Paul Robeson quiet and it ought not to. What we want, what the world wants, is not agreement, not unanimity, but "Light, more Light"; argument, facts, persuasion, appeal. It does not answer Robeson's demand for opposition to war with Russia to call him "silly" or declare pontifically that Robeson does not speak for the American Negro. Neither for that matter does Phillip Randolph although at times one might think so. But Robeson does speak for Paul Robeson and more Negroes agree with his thought than with many other American Negroes; and many more would agree if they had a chance to hear the truth from his mouth or from others. That is the reason and none other that Robeson concerts are opposed by mobs of the American Legion.

This is the crisis of modern civilization. The Negroes of the United States more than any Negroid group in the world and as much as any underprivileged group have the legal right to influence and help to decide the issue in these perilous times. We can save civilization if we have the sense and courage. But today we, in common with the majority of our white fellow-citizens, are scared. We are deathly afraid to act or talk or even think in any way which is in opposition or can be interpreted as opposing the current hysteria. Those who have brains and use them, know perfectly well that propaganda about Russia and her threat of war is in part an elaborately concocted lie, and in part groundless fear.

All men know the Soviet Union has never started a war but has been the repeated victim of invasion, aggression, spying and betrayal; they know that her overtures for peace and comity with the West were spurned until her co-operation was absolutely indispensable for stopping Nazi conquest of the world; they know that Russia laid down fifteen million lives to save Europe and America, while we and Britain fiddled about to await her destruction; we know when, to our astonishment, she conquered Hitler, we have been trying to welch on our bargain until finally we have made Russia our enemy and Nazi Germany our future ally.

All intelligent men know that Socialism is growing in every civilized country on earth; that our New Deal was socialism pure and simple, and must be restored or continued war expenditure will end in worse disaster than the Great Depression. We ought to know that Communism is Socialism with more extreme methods and more immediate goals, but that the Russia of the Czars could have been rescued from utter collapse by no other method. If America and other lands can reform their industry and social ills by methods other than Communism, Russia has never tried to force them to do otherwise. The only area where Russia has actively supported Communism is in the countries on her border where western Europe repeatedly and by elaborate spying and intrigue, tried to make Poland, Esthonia, Latvia, Lithuania, Czechoslovakia, Finland and the Balkans, jumping off places to re-conquer Russia and East Europe, for the cause of high profits based on ignorance and cheap labor. This is the reason that certain powerful elements in America do not want Socialism or Communism even discussed, and will call any Progressive Party or movement "subversive." Paul Robeson stands for Peace and Free Speech to fight War and Poverty.

JOSEPH STALIN

Joseph Stalin was a great man; few other men of the 20th century approach his stature. He was simple, calm and courageous. He seldom lost his poise; pondered his problems slowly, made his decisions clearly and firmly; never yielded to ostentation nor coyly refrained from holding his rightful place with dignity. He was the son of a serf, but stood calmly before the great without hesitation or nerves. But also—and this was the highest proof of his greatness—he knew the common man, felt his problems, followed his fate.

Stalin was not a man of conventional learning; he was much more than that: he was a man who thought deeply, read understandingly and listened to wisdom, no matter whence it came. He was attacked and slandered as few men of power have been; yet he seldom lost his courtesy and balance; nor did he let attack drive him from his convictions nor induce him to surrender positions which he knew were correct. As one of the despised minorities of man, he first set Russia on the road to conquer race prejudice and make one nation out of its 140 groups without destroying their individuality.

His judgment of men was profound. He early saw through the flamboyance and exhibitionism of Trotsky, who fooled the world, and especially America. The whole ill-bred and insulting attitude of Liberals in the U.S. today began with our naive acceptance of Trotsky's magnificent lying propaganda, which he carried around the world. Against it, Stalin stood like a rock and moved neither right nor left, as he continued to advance toward a real socialism instead of the sham Trotsky offered.

Three great decisions faced Stalin in power and he met them magnificently: first, the problem of the peasants, then the West European attack, and last the Second World War. The poor Russian peasant was the lowest victim of tsarism, capitalism and the Orthodox Church. He surrendered the Little White Father easily; he turned less readily but perceptibly from his ikons; but his kulaks clung tenaciously to capitalism and were near wrecking the revolution when Stalin risked a second revolution and drove out the rural bloodsuckers.

Then came intervention, the continuing threat of attack by all nations, halted by the Depression, only to be re-opened by Hitlerism. It was Stalin who steered the Soviet Union between Scylla and Charybdis: Western Europe and the U.S. were willing to betray her to fascism, and then had to beg her aid in the Second World War. A lesser man than Stalin would have demanded vengeance for Munich, but he had the wisdom to ask only justice for his fatherland. This Roosevelt granted but Churchill held back. The British Empire proposed first to save itself in Africa and southern Europe, while Hitler smashed the Soviets.

The Second Front dawdled, but Stalin pressed unfalteringly ahead. He risked the utter ruin of socialism in order to smash the dictatorship of Hitler and Mussolini. After Stalingrad the Western World did not know whether to weep or applaud. The cost of victory to the Soviet Union was frightful. To this day the outside world has no dream of the hurt, the loss and the sacrifices. For his calm, stern leadership here, if nowhere else, arises the deep worship of Stalin by the people of all the Russias.

Then came the problem of Peace. Hard as this was to Europe and America, it was far harder to Stalin and the Soviets. The conventional rulers of the world hated and feared them and would have been only too willing to see the utter failure of this attempt at socialism. At the same time the fear of Japan and Asia was also real. Diplomacy therefore took hold and Stalin was picked as the victim. He was called in conference with British Imperialism represented by its trained and well-fed aristocracy; and with the vast wealth and potential power of America represented by its most liberal leader in half a century.

Here Stalin showed his real greatness. He neither cringed nor strutted. He never presumed, he never surrendered. He gained the friendship of Roosevelt and the respect of Churchill. He asked neither adulation nor vengeance. He was reasonable and conciliatory. But on what he deemed essential, he was inflexible. He was willing to resurrect the League of Nations, which had insulted the Soviets. He was willing to fight Japan, even though Japan was then no menace to the Soviet Union, and might be death to the British Empire and to American trade. But on two points Stalin was adamant: Clemenceau's "Cordon Sanitaire" must be returned to the Soviets, whence it had been stolen as a threat. The Balkans were not to be left helpless before Western exploitation for the benefit of land monopoly. The workers and peasants there must have their say.

Such was the man who lies dead, still the butt of noisy jackals and of the illbred men of some parts of the distempered West. In life he suffered under continuous and studied insult; he was forced to make bitter decisions on his own lone responsibility. His reward comes as the common man stands in solemn acclaim.

KWAME NKRUMAH

When one remembers the contempt and insult which for four hundred years white civilization, in literature, church and school has visited on people with black skins, not to mention slavery, caste and lynching, it is extraordinary to read the calm story of a man who lived through some of the worst features of this disgraceful era, and now heads a state with the nations of the world paying homage.

Ghana is not a large nation, just as England was never outstanding for size. But the nine million folk of Ghana have an economic significance, a cultural unity and a *joie de vivre* which makes it remarkable. It has experienced oppression since that British scoundrel, John Hawkins ranged its coast in the ship "Jesus" and stole slaves which secured him knighthood from Queen Elizabeth; to the day, when after six wars ranging over 90 years, England not only conquered the great state of Ashanti but humiliated the king by demanding that he kiss the white governor's feet. When in 1871, the Fanti, who had helped Britain against the Ashanti, drew up a constitution for self-government under the British, their leaders were thrown into jail.

After this history comes Nkrumah. He is from a humble family. He was educated in missionary schools and at the government college at Achimota where he studied under Kwegyir Aggrey, a West African educated in the United States. This determined Nkrumah to seek an education in America. Through letters of introduction from a Negro leader who, following the First Pan-African Congress had called a similar congress in Nigeria, Nkrumah entered Lincoln University, a Negro college near Philadelphia. He stayed ten years in America and learned what it means to be black in the "land of the free." He had very little money and on vacations tried to find work. He sold fish in Harlem, but could make no profit. He got a job in a soap factory and learned that black folk in America usually get the hard and dirty jobs:

"It turned out to be by far the filthiest and most unsavory job that I ever had. All the rotting entrails and lumps of fat of animals were dumped by lorries into a yard. Armed with a fork I had to load as much as I could of this reeking and utterly repulsive cargo into a wheelbarrow and then transport it, load after load, to the processing plant. As the days went by, instead of being steadily toughened, I had the greatest difficulty in trying not to vomit the whole time."

Nkrumah tried waiting on table and dish-washing; he slept out-doors and in parks; he got cheap food in Father Divine's restaurants. Once in Baltimore he asked a white waiter for a drink of water. The waiter pointed to a spittoon.

By work outside his studies and desperate application he was grad-uated from Lincoln University in 1939 and voted the "most interesting" of his classmates. He wanted to study journalism at Columbia but he had no money and as usual the "missionaries" tried to force him into the ministry. He studied at the Lincoln School of Theology but also took courses at the University of Pennsylvania, 50 miles away; so that in 1942 he became Bachelor of Theology at Lincoln and Master of Sci-ence in Education at the University of Pennsylvania. The next year he received his Master of Arts in Philosophy at Pennsylvania and lacked only a thesis to secure his doctorate. During this study he became in-terested in the future of West Africa and formulated many of the plans which he is now carrying out. He met and talked with African fellow students and did some teaching and lecturing.

For support he took a job in a ship building yard in Chester: "I worked in all weathers from twelve midnight until eight the following morning. It froze so hard on several occasions that my hands almost stuck to the steel and although I put on all the clothes that I possessed, I was chilled to the marrow. At 8 A.M. I used to return to my lodgings, have breakfast, sleep for a few hours and then begin research for the writing of my thesis." Naturally there came an attack of pneumonia. After recovery, in May 1945, Nkrumah left New York for London.

In October of that year I saw Kwame Nkrumah for the first time in Manchester, England, where we were holding the Fifth Pan-African Congress. There were some 200 delegates and he was one of a number of young West Africans many of whom had just attended a trade union meeting in Paris. I did not really get acquainted with Kwame. He was busy with organization work, a bit shabby and not talkative. He was in earnest and intelligent and I never forgot him. We had a mutual friend in George Padmore who had sparked this meeting.

Nkrumah stayed in London two years as Secretary of the West African National Secretariat and to edit a magazine. He tried to organize the colored workers and kept in touch with leaders of the Labor Party. He attended meetings of the Communist Party. But he lost faith in British Labor and in any attempt to lead Africa from Europe. In November 1947, Nkrumah left Liverpool for the Gold Coast after being held up by the authorities because of his political activities while in Britain.

Nkrumah arrived on the West Coast when the long advertised system of "indirect rule" of British officials through African chiefs was beginning to break up. The chiefs had become paid agents of Britain and after the two world wars the people of the Gold Coast were beginning to repudiate the chiefs and to demand self-rule. They felt on the one hand the weakness of poverty, ignorance and disease and on the other, their strength as producers of cocoa and other products which were making white Europe rich. The black folk, however, were divided by age-old tribal jealousies and disputes over the power of chiefs, many of whom traced their aristocratic descent back hundreds of years.

Nkrumah went over the heads of the chiefs and under the authority of British overlords and appealed to the mass of people who never before had had effective leadership. The United Gold Coast Convention was organized as a group of non-partisan leaders. But Nkrumah soon decided that a regular political alignment was needed and he organized the Convention People's Party, a group demanding immediate self-government. He declared himself a socialist and repeats this statement in this book. His plan of organization as stated in "The Circle," reprinted as an appendix, forecasts the creation of a "revolutionary vanguard for the struggle of West African unity and national independence." The Convention People's Party was organized in every hamlet all over the Gold Coast. Social bodies interested in all kinds of welfare work were integrated, a central office opened, newspapers were started and mass meetings held.

Then came an incident which Nkrumah had hoped to avoid but which British officials must have prayed for: ex-service men called a boycott on high prices and the police shot at a peaceful demonstration. The whole town of Accra was soon rioting, with looting of stores and assault of Europeans. The police immediately arrested Nkrumah and his associates although they were not the instigators of the riot and would have strongly advised against it. The uprising was in fact spontaneous and quite beyond control. But it was just the excuse which the government needed. They found on Nkrumah his "Circle" for socialization of the country and they faced him with his London activities. He was accused of being a "Communist" and kept in jail for eight weeks. Many of his associates deserted him. He was finally tried and sentenced to three years imprisonment. In jail he was treated as a criminal, confined with 11 persons in one cell, with a bucket in one corner as a latrine. The food was poor and scanty. They were deprived of writing material and newspapers.

But outside, Nkrumah's party stood firm. After he had been 15 months in jail, the election was held and Nkrumah, as candidate for parliamentary leader received 22,780 votes out of 23,122 cast. He was released and carried on the shoulders of a vast crowd to party headquarters. He now became Leader of Government Business in Parliament and began reform. He worked on the civil service and began to integrate Negro officials. He reorganized the selling of cocoa by the government and the cutting out of diseased cocoa trees. He began to look into foreign investment and industrial expansion.

It was a hard job; there was opposition from the British officeholders, from Negro leaders and from cocoa farmers, especially from those who defended the traditional authority of the chiefs. Nkrumah pressed Britain to set a definite date for Ghana independence; the British tried to sidetrack and sabotage the demand. At last they asked for a new election before the terms of the Parliament then sitting had ended. They were assured by malcontents that Nkrumah would be overwhelmingly defeated. Nkrumah, contrary to expectations, assented to the test. His party won 72 of the 104 members of Parliament. Nkrumah became Prime Minister and on March 6th Ghana became an independent nation.

What next? A small new nation of nine millions is usually of little significance in the modern world save as the loot of empires. But Ghana is exceptional. It supplies the world with most of its cocoa and chocolate. In the last decade it has raised an average of 228,000 tons of cocoa annually on 300,000 peasant-owned farms. Each year Ghana raises three millions tons of food. The fight on animal diseases has brought herds of cattle and sheep. It has 8,000 square miles in valuable hardwoods under government control; it catches 20,000 tons of fish a year and plans to motorize its fishing crafts. It has vast deposits of bauxite, the raw material of aluminum; it has gold, manganese and diamonds. It has a rapidly growing system of popular education and a native college, and it has a leader of integrity, courage and ideas, who knows the modern world.

Nkrumah is faced by three pressing problems: First, the unity of Ghana, with integration of the chiefs and northern Moslems into the social body of the nation; with development of socialism rather than of a bourgeois democracy with exploited workers, and with private profit. This will be no easy task, but Nkrumah is experienced and fully aware of the difficulties. He has seen private capitalism in Europe and America.

Second, Nkrumah must industrialize Ghana so that it will not remain the exploited victim of foreign investors. Already he faces long-established mining companies who have made vast profits on low rents and wages and inadequate taxation; if such corporations were exterminated forthwith as they deserve to be, where would Ghana get the new capital to mine bauxite and manufacture aluminum? Where would she get the funds for power development of the Volta river? One reason that the inauguration of Ghana attracted the cormorants of private capital from all the world was this chance for tremendous profit, provided the rulers of Ghana will play the game as it is being played in the Middle East. Nkrumah has been non-committal, but reasonable. He is not scaring private investment away; neither is he inviting it with promise of unlimited profit. If he can get capital on reasonable terms he will welcome and protect it. Already he is curbing the greed of the mines and the cocoa crop has been socialized in sales, transport and care of growing trees. Industrialization under government control has begun in small industries like soap, matches, cigarettes and timber sawing. Suppose Ghana should begin to process its cocoa?

Third and beyond all these weighty matters, Nkrumah proposes to attack frankly and head-on the whole question of the status and treatment of black Africans in modern civilization. He proposes to continue the program of Pan-Africa which began in 1919 on the initiative of American Negroes. For this Ghana occupies a strategic position. Liberia was surrounded by Britain and France who systematically choked it and invited Germany in, while America stood aside until it saw a chance of unusual exploitation of land and labor. Ghana is surrounded by 23 million French Africans who are beginning to demand autonomy; not far away is Nigeria, a British colony of 32 million blacks who are already started toward independence. Across the Sahara is the Sudan, once dominated by Britain and Egypt but now free with nine million black folk seated at the head waters of the Nile. East of the Sudan is the long independent Kingdom of Ethiopia with 20 million blacks and mulattoes. Below it is Kenya seething with hate and hurt toward Britain; and Uganda starting toward independence. Here dwell 11 million blacks. Further on is Somaliland to be free from Italy in 1960 and, below, Tanganyika, a mandate set for freedom in the near future; the vast Congo which has just voiced an extraordinary demand for government partnership with Belgium. Then come Portuguese Africa, Bechuanaland, the Rhodesias, Nyassaland and South Africa.

Nkrumah proposes, as one of his first acts of state to invite the rulers of all these lands in addition to Egypt and North Africa to meet and consider the conditions and future of Africa. He says in the last chapter of his book, independence will not be confined to Ghana:

"From now on it must be Pan-African nationalism, and the ideology of African political consciousness and African political emancipation must spread throughout the whole continent, into every nook and corner of it. I have never regarded the struggle for the Independence of the Gold Coast as an isolated objective but always as a part of the general world historical pattern. The African in every territory of this vast continent has been awakened and the struggle for freedom will go on. It is our duty as the vanguard force to offer what assistance we can to those now engaged in the battle that we ourselves have fought and won. Our task is not done and our own safety is not assured until the last vestiges of colonialism have been swept from Africa."

GANDHI AND THE AMERICAN NEGROES

Mohandas Gandhi was born nineteen months after my birth. As a school-boy in a small town in the northeastern part of the United States, I knew little of Asia and the schools taught less. The one tenuous link which bound me to India was skin color. That was important in America and even in my town, although little was said about it. But I was conscious of being the only brown face in my school and although my dark family had lived in this valley for two hundred years or more, I was early cognizant of a status different from that of my white schoolmates.

As I grew up there seemed to be no future for me in the place of my birth, and at seventeen I went South, where formerly colored people had been slaves, so that I could be trained to work among them. There at Fisk University I first became aware of a world of colored folk and I learned not only of the condition of American Negroes but began to read of China and India; and to make Africa the special object of my study. I published my first book in 1896 while Gandhi was in South Africa, and my subject was the African slave trade. We did not at the time have much direct news from Africa in the American newspapers, but I did have several black students from South Africa and began to sense the tragedy of that awful land. It was not until after the First World War that I came to realize Gandhi's work for Africa and the world.

I was torn by the problem of peace. As a youth I was certain that freedom for the colored peoples of the earth would come only by war; by doing to white Europe and America what they had done to black Africa and colored Asia. This seemed the natural conclusion from the fairy tales called history on which I had been nourished. Then in the last decades of the 19th century, as I came to manhood, I caught the vision of world peace and signed the pledge never to take part in war.

With the First World War came my first knowledge of Gandhi. I came to know Lajpat Rai and Madame Naidu. John Haynes Holmes was one of my co-workers in the National Association for the Advancement of Colored People, and he was a friend and admirer of Gandhi. Indeed the "Colored People" referred to in our name was not originally confined to America. I remember the discussion we had on inviting Gandhi to visit America and how we were forced to conclude that this land was not civilized enough to receive a colored man as an honored guest.

In 1929, as the Depression loomed, I asked Gandhi for a message to American Negroes, which I published in the *Crisis*. He said:

> Let not the 12 million Negroes be ashamed of the fact that they are the grandchildren of slaves. There is dishonor in being slave-owners. But let us not think of honor or dishonor in connection with the past. Let us realize that the future is with those who would be pure, truthful and loving. For as the old wise men have said: Truth ever is, untruth never was. Love alone binds and truth and love accrue only to the truly humble.

This was written on May Day, 1929. Through what phantasmagoria of hurt and evil the world has passed since then! We American Negroes have reeled and staggered from side to side and forward and back. In the First World War, we joined with American capital to keep Germany and Italy from sharing the spoils of colonial imperialism. In the Depression we sank beneath the burden of poverty, ignorance and disease due to discrimination, unemployment and crime. In the Second World War, we again joined Western capital against Fascism and failed to realize how the Soviet Union sacrificed her blood and savings to save the world.

But we did realize how out of war began to arise a new colored world free from the control of Europe and America. We began too to realize the role of Gandhi and to evaluate his work as a guide for the black people of the United States. As an integral part of this country, as workers, consumers and co-creators of its culture, we could not look forward to physical separation except as a change of masters. But what of Gandhi's program of peace and non-violence? Only in the last year have American Negroes begun to see the possibility of this program being applied to the Negro problems in the United States.

Personally I was long puzzled. After the World Depression, I sensed a recurring contradiction. I saw Gandhi's non-violence gain freedom for India, only to be followed by violence in all the world. I realized that the vaunted "hundred years of peace," from Waterloo to the Battle of the Marne, was not peace at all but war, of Europe and North America on Africa and Asia, with only troubled bits of peace between the colonial conquerors. I saw Britain, France, Belgium and North America trying to continue to force the world to sever them by monopoly of land, technique and machines, backed by physical force which has now culminated in the use of atomic power. Only the possession of this power by the Soviet Union prevents the restoration of colonial imperialism of the West over Asia and Africa, under the leadership of men like [John Foster] Dulles and [Anthony] Eden. Perhaps in this extraordinary impasse the teachings of Mahatma Gandhi may have a chance to prevail in the world. Recent events in the former slave territory of the United States throw a curious light on this possibility.

In Montgomery, Alabama, the former capital of the Confederate States which fought for years to make America a slave nation, the black workers last year refused any longer to use the public buses on which their seats had long been segregated from those of the white passengers, paying the same fare. In addition to separation, there was abuse and insult by the white conductors. This custom had continued for 75 years. Then last year a colored seamstress got tired of insult and refused to give her seat to a white man. The black workers led by young, educated ministers began a strike which stopped the discrimination, aroused the state and the nation and presented an unbending front of non-violence to the murderous mob which hitherto has ruled the South. The occurrence was extraordinary. It was not based on any first-hand knowledge of Gandhi and his work. Their leaders like Martin Luther King knew of non-resistance in India; many of the educated teachers, business and professional men had heard of Gandhi. But the rise and spread of this movement was due to the truth of its underlying principles and not to direct teaching or propaganda. In this aspect it is a most interesting proof of the truth of the Gandhian philosophy.

The American Negro is not yet free. He is still discriminated against, oppressed and exploited. The recent court decisions in his favor are excellent but are as yet only partially enforced. It may well be that the enforcement of these laws and real human equality and brotherhood in the United States will come only under the leadership of another Gandhi.

TOUSSAINT L'OUVERTURE

If you should penetrate the campus of an American Ivy League college and challenging a Senior, ask what, in his opinion, was the influence of Africa on the French Revolution, he would answer in surprise if not pity, "None." If, after due apology, you should venture to approach his teacher of "historiography," provided such sacrilege were possible, you would be told that between African slavery in America and the greatest revolution of Europe, there was of course some connection, since they both took place on the same earth; but nothing causal, nothing of real importance, since Africans have no history.

Nevertheless, it is a perfectly defensible thesis of scientific history that Africans and African slavery in the West Indies were the main causes and influences of the American Revolution and of the French Revolution. And when, after long controversy and civil war, Negro slavery and serfdom were not suppressed, the United States turned from democracy to plutocracy and opened the path to colonial imperialism and made wide the way for the final world Revolutions in the twentieth century. . . .

. . . When the revolution broke out in France in 1787 San Domingo was the source of the greatest accumulation of wealth. San Domingo had more than three-quarter million slaves, the cities of France were flourishing with the slave trade. The French who were gaining equality with the former aristocrats were basing this equality on the profits of the slave trade and on crops grown by black slaves. From the very beginning two parties appeared in France: the moral philosophers and the social theorists, demanding freedom of the slaves. On the other hand, the planters demanded recognition as citizens and the exclusion of the poor whites and mulattoes.

The planters supported the monarchy against the revolution. The poor whites supported the revolution against the King but opposed the mulattoes. The mulattoes sought alliance with either or both groups of whites. In 1789 the mulattoes sent Raymond and Oge to Paris with 6 million pounds in gold and a promise of this and one-fifth of the property which the mulattoes owned in San Domingo to pay the French public debt. The delegates were received by the Constituent Assembly, and the Assembly thus recognized the citizenship of free Negroes. The planters were opposed as were also the manufacturers and merchants of the great French cities. The Constituent Assembly voted by [a] large majority not to interfere with the internal government of the colonies and refused to abolish the slave trade. But on March 18, 1790, the Amis des Noirs secured a vote declaring free Negroes citizens. Planters in Martinique, Guadaloupe and San Domingo all decreed that the law recognizing the right to vote applied only to white persons. The planters and poor whites fought each other, but both were against the Negroes.

The planters of San Domingo by secret manipulation placed six of their number in the Constituent Assembly. When representatives of the free Negroes and mulattoes appeared in Paris to demand hearing they were received and backed by the organization called the Friends of Negroes. The Declaration of the Rights of Man was adopted.

Oge returned to America with British money, landing secretly in north San Domingo. He collected 300 men. He was attacked and took refuge in the Spanish part of the island; the governor surrendered him. Oge and Chavannes were sentenced while alive to have their arms, legs and spines broken and then be exposed to the sun. This was done in the presence of the northern provincial assembly gathered in state.

War started between the planters and the free Negroes. The planters, reinforced by poor whites from France pouring in to make money from slavery, numbered 40,000. The free Negroes and mulattoes were about 26,000. And, despite the supporting votes of the National Convention, the war was going against them.

Then the unexpected happened. The bolder slaves had formed bands of Maroons in the mountains and before 1700 became dangerous. Over 1,000 Maroons are reported in 1720, 3,000 in 1751. By 1750 their greatest chief was Macandel. He planned a rebellion but was captured and burned alive. The planters were determined that nothing would interfere with their methods and the slave system. A half-million black Africans long self-trained in the mountains of Haiti on August 22, 1791, in a midnight thunderstorm, attacked. Theirs tells us: "In an instant twelve hundred coffee and two hundred sugar plantations were in flames; the buildings, the machinery, the farmhouses, were reduced to ashes; and unfortunate proprietors were hunted down, murdered or thrown into the flames, by the infuriated Negroes. The horrors of a servile war universally appeared. The unchained African signalized his ingenuity by discovery of new methods and unheard-of modes of torture."

They killed, raped and murdered. They destroyed property. The smoke of the fires blotted out the sun for days. The richest colony of France lay in ruins. The world shuddered. The slave-holders were frightened to death. But only gradually on slow sailing ships, loaded with lies, did the truth about what was happening reach France. Only after months did it realize that the foundations of its wealth and prosperity had disappeared. It was this and not any demands from the masses of French workers or of European philanthropists that turned the reaction of Thermidor into a reality and in time brought the counter-revolution of the 18th Brumaire.

The Terror did not spread from France to Haiti in 1793. Already in 1791 it came to France from Haiti. It was Africa in America and Africans led by Toussaint L'Ouverture who struck the French Revolution after it had given freedom to property-holders, and faced it with chaos. They plunged into anarchy, tempered by murder, until the reaction of Thermidor restored property to power.

The revolt was all the more startling because while it had been in the fears and imagination of the colonists for two hundred years, it was always undreamed of as an actual occurrence. There had been numberless revolts, which had spread terror to whites all over the West Indies, Central America and the mainland of the United States; but once they were quickly suppressed, their details and facts minimized, the records destroyed and the memory forgotten.

In San Domingo itself the dangers of slave revolts were not unknown. For years runaway slaves had hidden in the mountains, especially in the northeastern part of the island. There were serious slave revolts in 1679, 1691 and 1718, and in the middle of the eighteenth century a Negro, Macandel, carried out systematic poisoning which created a panic.

In Europe the organization of the lowest classes of workers and servants, peasants and laborers to gain political power and property was rare and cannot be compared to the corresponding organizations of African slaves in the West Indies and South America. Many European revolts which are pictured as risings of the masses are nothing of the sort. The Protest revolution had no sympathy with the peasants and Martin Luther kicked them in the teeth when they revolted. There were revolts of the suffering masses in Hungary, France and England but they were small compared with the concerted, long-continued rebellion of the black Maroons. While the blacks of San Domingo were in wild rebellion France faced two paths: one was that of Babeuf who came up from the bottom of modern class organization, the servant class; he saw the masses starving, he felt their misery and he sang the dirge of the dying. He struggled for a commune of the workers; equality not of property owners but of those who gave property its value. He prayed and struggled for his Paris commune, but the mounting power of the property owners pushed and beat him back until he died. He died on the scaffold in 1796 but he rose from the dead in 1848 and again in 1871; in 1917 in Russia; in 1939 in China and in 1961 in Cuba.

France repudiating Babeuf, in its unconscious frenzy, took refuge in the reaction of Thermidor, after abolishing monarchy, killing the King and murdering their leaders. Thermidor was the rule of the property-holders displacing the aristocrats. But in San Domingo horror faced Toussaint and his rebels. Toussaint revered the King, his Chieftain; he believed in discipline and authority. He deserted impious France and led his legions to the service of Charles IV of Spain. Slowly he and his successors in after years developed his ancient tribal communalism in San Domingo. Beyond these political provisions, he turned attention toward the economic; the island was divided into districts with inspectors who were to see that the freedmen returned to their work. A fifth part of the produce of each estate was to go to the workers. Commercial arrangements were made with the United States and England. He immediately issued a manifesto to all Negroes and mulattoes. "I am Toussaint L'Ouverture; my name is perhaps known to you. I have undertaken to avenge your wrongs. It is my desire that liberty and equality shall reign in San Domingo! I am striving to this end. Come and unite with us, brothers, and fight with us for the same cause."

Through the prowess of Toussaint, the Spanish pushed the French farther and farther back and in a short time secured possession of nearly the whole north of the island and part of the south. The French commission found itself in a tight place and tried to extricate itself in June, 1793, by offering to free all slaves who would enroll in the army. In August they went even further and proclaimed universal emancipation in San Domingo, and this action was confirmed by the French National Convention, February 4, 1794.

The first proclamation had no influence upon Toussaint. As a Spanish general, he refused to recognize the authority of the French. But when the English invaded San Domingo, the aspect of things changed. They landed in September and soon had captured that city with its heavy artillery and two million dollars' worth of shipping in its harbor. Toussaint knew the British as slave traders, and he now suspected that Spain wanted vengeance on France rather than freedom for the slaves. When, therefore, the French government affirmed universal emancipation early in 1794, he returned to French allegiance to the open delight of the commission. They said, "Remember that distinctions of color are no more!"

The blacks under Toussaint now proceeded to restore San Domingo to France. The mere magic of his name did much without fighting. In April Toussaint left the Spanish army; in May the French Flag was flying at Gonaives. From now on Toussaint was known as L'Ouverture, the Savior. Gradually the whole northern part of the island was in his possession. As Sonthonax wrote in his diary, "These Negroes perform miracles of bravery."

In after years, the successors of Toussaint, Dessalines and Christophe developed communalism and made the Haitian state independent and owner of its land and crops; but the surrounding world whirled away: it monopolized wealth in private hands, organized military power in their hand and France, the United States and Britain forced Haiti to become the victim of their stooge who rules Haiti today. Still high in its mountains roll the tom-toms of ancient Africa and its dreams. . . .

On October 1, 1798, Toussaint entered Mole St. Nicholas as conqueror. The white troops saluted him. He was dined in the public square, on a silver service which was afterwards presented to him in the name of the King of England. A treaty was signed by which the English gave up the island, recognized Haiti as independent, and entered into a commercial agreement. Then they tried secretly to induce Toussaint to declare himself King, but he refused. . . .

The Directory which ruled from 1794 to 1799 turned to Napoleon who hated blacks. Nevertheless, he married the granddaughter of a Negro, Josephine, who was a leader of current French society. On the other hand, he dismissed General Dumas from his army solely because of his color. Napoleon was rising to prominence. He conducted a brilliant campaign in Italy and then from the foot of the Pyramids looked toward India, but the British blocked him until unemployment in England brought the Peace of Amiens.

The French planters appealed to Napoleon. He took their side, saying: "the liberty of the blacks is an insult to Europe." But Toussaint was powerful. Napoleon had to flatter and cajole him. After consultation with French bankers, Napoleon planned an American empire based on African slavery. He lured Toussaint to France and killed him. He gathered a vast army under his brother-in-law, Leclerc, who sailed for San Domingo in 1801. He took five squadrons with 80 vessels and

21,000 troops. The Africans and the fever conquered this army and left Dessalines and Christophe, successors of Toussaint, masters of Haiti.

Napoleon was unable to start colonial imperialism in America. That was accomplished in later years when American democracy restored African slavery in the cotton kingdom.

But the world hailed Toussaint, he was one of the great men of his time. He made an extraordinary impression upon those who knew him personally or studied his life, whether they were friends or enemies. Auguste Comte included him with Washington, Plato, Buddha and Charlemagne as worthy to replace all the calendar saints. Morvins, biographer of Napoleon, calls him "a man of genius." Beauchamp refers to him as "one of the most extraordinary men of a period when so many extraordinary men appeared on the scene." Lamartine wrote a drama with Toussaint as his hero. Harriet Martineau wrote a novel on his life. Whittier wrote about him. Sir Spencer St. John, consular agent in Haiti, called him "one grand figure of a cruel war." Rainsford, a British officer, refers to him as "that only great man." Chateaubriand charges that Bonaparte not only murdered, but imitated him.

A French planter said, "God in his terrestrial Globe did not commune with a purer spirit." Wendell Phillips said, "You think me a fanatic, for you read history, not with your eyes, but with your prejudices. But fifty years hence, when Truth gets a hearing, the Muse of history will put Phocion for the Greek, Brutus for the Roman, Hampden for England, LaFayette for France; choose Washington as the bright consummate flower of our earliest civilization; and then, dipping her pen in the sunlight, will write in the clear blue, above them all, the name of the soldier, the statesman, the martyr, Toussaint L'Ouverture." Wordsworth sang:

> There's not a breathing of the common wind
> That will forget thee: thou hast great allies;
> Thy friends are exultations, agonies,
> And love, and Man's unconquerable mind.

In 1802 and 1803 nearly forty thousand French soldiers died of war and fever. Leclerc himself died in November, 1803. Rochambeau succeeded to his command and was promised soldiers by Napoleon; but already in May, 1803, Great Britain started new war with France and communication between France and San Domingo was impossible. The black insurgents held the land; the British held the sea. In November, 1803, Rochambeau surrendered and white authority died in San Domingo forever.

The effect of all this was far-reaching. Napoleon gave up his dream of American empire and sold Louisiana for a song. As DeWit Talmadge said: "Thus, all of Montana and the Dakotas, and most of Colorado and Minnesota, all of Washington and Oregon States, came to us as the indirect work of a despised Negro. Praise, if you will, the work of a Robert Livingstone or a Jefferson, but today let us not forget our debt to Toussaint L'Ouverture, who was indirectly the means of America's expansion by the Louisiana Purchase of 1803."

CHAPTER 4

Literature and Art

A s in his essays on representative men, so in his book reviews one can follow the course of Du Bois's ideas in some detail. Usually brief, Du Bois's opinions about works of fiction, philosophy, political science, history, anthropology, and miscellaneous other topics, most collected in Herbert Aptheker's edition of Du Bois's *Book Reviews,* demonstrate nevertheless his constant engagement with current events and arguments. Among his reviews are short pieces promoting the work of writers such as Jessie Fausset and Nella Larsen, for example, or another attacking Claude McKay's *Home to Harlem* for its supposed immorality. Had he not written so extensively in so many other fields, it seems likely that Du Bois might have grown to be one of the most important literary critics of his day. Most unusual among his reviews is Du Bois's own short interpretation of *The Souls of Black Folk,* which expresses his doubts about the book's structure but also reveals some key elements of his racial self-conception at the time.

Du Bois frequently reviewed theatrical productions as well as books, and he did not hesitate to praise white playwrights such as Eugene O'Neill or Ridgely Torrence for work that he thought advanced the cause of African Americans. In "Negro Art" (1921), he defended such productions while distinguishing them from the prevailing stereotypes of white racism. As his own writings make abundantly clear, moreover, Du Bois was quite taken with dramatic form as a means of argument, and one finds stage- or pageant-like scenes in *Darkwater, Dark Princess, The Quest for the Silver Fleece,* and *Dusk of Dawn,* to name just a few of his works where a kind of metaphysical lifting of the veil, as though on a stage, is in operation. *The Star of Ethiopia* was a short dramatic pageant first staged in New York as part of the National Emancipation Exposition in October 1913, with later presentations in Philadelphia, Washington, D.C., and Los Angeles. Entitled "The People of Peoples and Their Gifts to Men" in *The Crisis,* Du Bois's prose version of the pageant gives some flavor of the potentially grand stage effects achieved in his retelling of the story of blacks in Africa and the New World. The moral dimension of African American art is implicit in Du Bois's pageant, just as it is in much of his fiction. Likewise, in "Criteria of Negro Art" (1926), an address to the Chicago NAACP in which Du Bois announced his notorious and usually misunderstood view that "all art is propaganda," one finds that this aphorism refers, first of all, to Du Bois's deeply held belief in the ethical and political responsibility of art and literature. A different aspect of culture's moral dimension was treated by Du Bois in a short piece for the *Mark Twain Quarterly* entitled "The Humor of Negroes" (1942), a topic that has been taken up by many black writers and studied extensively in more recent works on African American culture such as Lawrence Levine's *Black Culture and Black Consciousness* (1977) and Mel Watkins' *On the Real Side: Laughing, Lying, and Signifying* (1994).

Du Bois's penchant for dramatic form appears also in his unorthodox essay on Phillis Wheatley, first presented as a 1941 lecture at Fisk University under the title "The Vision of Phillis the Blessed (An Allegory of Negro American Literature in the Eighteenth and Nineteenth Centuries)." Beginning with a rehearsal of Wheatley's career, Du Bois makes her the foundation for a tradition that includes the slave spirituals, early New Orleans African American poets, William Wells Brown, Alberry Whitman, Charles Chesnutt, and Paul Laurence Dunbar. To write the history of African American culture had been a concern of Du Bois from the outset of his career. His attention to the spirituals in *The Souls of Black Folk* is the most obvious and lasting example. But the straightforward exposition of black literary and artistic history was also something to which Du Bois returned on several occasions. Like other turn-of-the-century black writers such as George Washington Williams and William Ferris, Du Bois frequently anchored his accounts of African American art and literature in the prehistory of African culture. A good instance is "Negro Art and Literature," a chapter from *The Gift of Black Folks* (1924), which displays a lingering racialism in Du Bois's interpretation of the varying "gifts" of different racial cultures. As a part of the whole volume, however, the chapter places its subjects in a broad Afrocentric context and offers a fine, detailed evocation of the history of African American literature, music, and art through the early twentieth century.

ON *THE SOULS OF BLACK FOLK*

One who is born with a cause is predestined to a certain narrowness of view, and at the same time to some clearness of vision within his limits with which the world often finds it well to reckon. My book has many of the defects and some of the advantages of this situation. Because I am a Negro I lose something of that breadth of view which the more cosmopolitan races have, and with this goes an intensity of feeling and conviction which both wins and repels sympathy, and now enlightens, now puzzles.

The Souls of Black Folk is a series of fourteen essays written under various circumstances and for different purposes during a period of seven years. It has, therefore, considerable, perhaps too great, diversity. There are bits of history and biography, some description of scenes and persons, something of controversy and criticism, some statistics and a bit of story-telling. All this leads to rather abrupt transitions of style, tone and viewpoint and, too, without doubt, to a distinct sense of incompleteness and sketchiness.

On the other hand, there is a unity in the book, not simply the general unity of the larger topic, but a unity of purpose in the distinctively subjective note that runs in each essay. Through all the book runs a personal and intimate tone of self-revelation. In each essay I sought to speak from within—to depict a world as we see it who dwell therein. In thus giving up the usual impersonal and judicial attitude of the traditional author I have lost in authority but gained in vividness. The reader will, I am sure, feel in reading my words peculiar warrant for setting his judgment against mine, but at the same time some revelation of how the world looks to me cannot easily escape him.

This is not saying that the style and workmanship of the book make its meaning altogether clear. A clear central message it has conveyed to most readers, I think, but around this center there has lain a penumbra of vagueness and half-veiled allusion which has made these and others especially impatient. How far this fault is in me and how far it is in the nature of the message I am not sure. It is difficult, strangely difficult, to translate the finer feelings of men into words. The Thing itself sits clear before you; but when you have dressed it out in periods it seems fearfully uncouth and inchoate. Nevertheless, as the feeling is deep the greater the impelling force to seek to express it. And here the feeling was deep.

In its larger aspects the style is tropical—African. This needs no apology. The blood of my fathers spoke through me and cast off the English restraint of my training and surroundings. The resulting accomplishment is a matter of taste. Sometimes I think very well of it and sometimes I do not.

THE STAR OF ETHIOPIA

Prelude

The lights of the Court of Freedom blaze. A trumpet blast is heard and four heralds, black and of gigantic stature, appear with silver trumpets and standing at the four corners of the temple of beauty cry:

"Hear ye, hear ye! Men of all the Americas, and listen to the tale of the eldest and strongest of the races of mankind, whose faces be black. Hear ye, hear ye, of the gifts of black men to this world, the Iron Gift and Gift of Faith, the Pain of Humility and the Sorrow Song of Pain, the Gift of Freedom and of Laughter, and the undying Gift of Hope. Men of the world, keep silence and hear ye this!"

Four banner bearers come forward and stand along the four walls of the temple. On their banners is written:

"The First Gift of the Negro to the world, being the Gift of Iron. This picture shall tell how, in the deep and beast-bred forests of Africa, mankind first learned the welding of iron, and thus defense against the living and the dead."

What the banners tell the heralds solemnly proclaim.

Whereat comes the

First Episode. The Gift of Iron:

The lights grow dim. The roar of beasts is heard and the crash of the storm. Lightnings flash. The dark figure of an African savage hurries across the foreground, frightened and cowering and dancing. Another follows defying the lightning and is struck down; others come until the space is filled with 100 huddling, crowding savages. Some brave the storm, some pray to their Gods with incantation and imploring dance. Mothers shield their children, and husbands their wives. At last, dimly enhaloed in mysterious light, the Veiled Woman appears, commanding in stature and splendid in garment, her dark face faintly visible, and in her right hand Fire, and Iron in her left. As she passes slowly round the Court the rhythmic roll of tomtoms begins. Then music is heard; anvils ring at the four corners. The arts flourish, huts arise, beasts are brought in and there is joy, feasting and dancing.

A trumpet blast calls silence and the heralds proclaim

The Second Episode, saying:

"Hear ye, hear ye! All them that come to know the Truth, and listen to the tale of the wisest and gentlest of the races of men whose faces be black. Hear ye, hear ye, of the Second Gift of black men to this world, the Gift of Civilization in the dark and splendid valley of the Nile. Men of the world, keep silence and hear ye this." The banners of the banner bearers change and read:

"The Second Gift of the Negro to the world, being the Gift of the Nile. This picture tells how the meeting of Negro and Semite in ancient days made the civilization of Egypt the first in the world."

There comes a strain of mighty music, dim in the distance and drawing nearer. The 100 savages thronged round the whole Court rise and stand listening. Slowly there come fifty veiled figures and with them come the Sphinx, Pyramid, the Obelisk and the empty Throne of the Pharoah drawn by oxen. As the cavalcade passes, the savages, wondering, threatening, inquiring, file by it. Suddenly a black chieftain appears in the entrance, with the Uraeus in one hand and the winged Beetle in the other. The Egyptians unveil and display Negroes and mulattoes clothed in the splendor of the Egyptian Court. The savages salaam; all greet him as Ra, the Negro. He mounts the throne and the cavalcade, led by posturing dancers and Ra, and followed by Egyptians and savages, pass in procession around to the right to the thunder of music and tomtoms. As they pass, Ra is crowned as Priest and King. While the Queen of Sheba and Candace of Ethiopia join the procession at intervals.

Slowly all pass out save fifty savages, who linger examining their gifts. The lights grow dim as Egyptian culture dies and the fifty savages compose themselves to sleep. As they sleep the light returns and the heralds proclaim

The Third Episode, saying:
"Hear ye, hear ye! All them that come to see the light and listen to the tale of the bravest and truest of the races of men, whose faces be black. Hear ye, hear ye, of the Third Gift of black men to this world—a Gift of Faith in Righteousness hoped for but unknown; men of the world, keep silence and hear ye this!" The banners change and read:

"The Third Gift of the Negro to the world, being a Gift of Faith. This episode tells how the Negro race spread the faith of Mohammed over half the world and built a new culture thereon."

There is a sound of battle. The savages leap to their feet. Mohammed and fifty followers whirl in and rushing to the right beat the savages back. Fifty Songhay enter and attack the Mohammedans. Fifty other Mohammedans enter and attack the Songhay. Turning, the Songhay bear the last group of Mohammedans back to the left where they clash with the savages. Mohammedan priests strive and exhort among the warriors. At each of the four corners of the temple a priest falls on his face and cries: "God is God! God is God! There is no God but God, and Mohammed is his prophet!" Four more join, others join until gradually all is changed from battle to the one universal cry: "God is God! God is God! There is no God but God, and Mohammed is his prophet!" In each corner, however, some Mohammedans hold slaves in shackles, secretly.

Mansa Musa appears at the entrance with entourage on horseback, followed by black Mohammedan priests and scholars. The procession passes around to the right with music and dancing, and passes out with Mohammedans and Songhay, leaving some Mohammedans and their slaves on the stage.

The herald proclaims

307

The Fourth Episode, saying:

"Hear ye, hear ye! All them that know the sorrow of the world. Hear ye, hear ye, and listen to the tale of the humblest and the mightiest of the races of men whose faces be black. Hear ye, hear ye, and learn how this race did suffer of Pain, of Death and Slavery and yet of this Humiliation did not die. Men of the world, keep silence and hear ye this!" The banners change again and say:

"The Fourth Gift of the Negro to the world, being a Gift of Humiliation. This gift shows how men can bear even the Hell of Christian slavery and live."

The Mohammedans force their slaves forward as European traders enter. Other Negroes, with captives, enter. The Mohammedans take gold in barter. The Negroes refuse gold, but are seduced by beads and drink. Chains rattle. Christian missionaries enter, but the slave trade increases. The wail of the missionary grows fainter and fainter until all is a scene of carnage and captivity with whip and chain and only a frantic priest, staggering beneath a cross and crowned with bloody thorns, wanders to and fro in dumb despair.

There is silence. Then a confused moaning. Out of the moaning comes the slave song, "Nobody Knows the Trouble I've Seen," and with it and through the chained and bowed forms of the slaves as they pass out is done the Dance of Death and Pain.

The stage is cleared of all its folk. There is a pause, in which comes the Dance of the Ocean, showing the transplantation of the Negro race over seas.

Then the heralds proclaim

The Fifth Episode, saying:

"Hear ye, hear ye! All them that strive and struggle. Hear ye, hear ye, and listen to the tale of the stoutest and the sturdiest of the races of men whose faces be black. Hear ye, hear ye, and learn how this race did rise out of slavery and the valley of the shadow of death. Men of the world, keep silence and hear ye this!" The banners change again and read:

"The Fifth Gift of the Negro to the world, being a Gift of Struggle Toward Freedom. This picture tells of Alonzo, the Negro pilot of Columbus, of Stephen Dorantes who discovered New Mexico, of the brave Maroons and valiant Haytians, of Crispus Attucks, George Lisle and Nat Turner."

Twenty-five Indians enter, circling the Court right and left, stealthily and watchfully. As they sense the coming of the whites, they gather to one side of the temple, watching.

Alonzo, the Negro, enters and after him Columbus and Spaniards, in mail, and one monk. They halt the other side of the temple and look about searchingly, pointing at the Indians. Slaves follow. One of the slaves, Stephen Dorantes, and the monk seek the Indians. The monk is killed and Stephen returns, circling the Court, tells his tale and dies. The Spaniards march on the Indians. Their slaves—the Maroons—revolt and march to the left and meet the Indians on the opposite side. The French, some of the mulattoes and Negroes, enter with more slaves. They march after the Spanish. Their slaves, helped by mulattoes and Toussaint, revolt and start back. The French follow the Spaniards, but the returning Haytians meet oncoming British. The Haytians fight their way through and take their place next to the Maroons. Still more slaves and white Americans follow the British. The British and Americans dispute. Attucks leads the Americans and the British are put to flight. Spanish, French and British, separated by dancing Indians, file around the Court and out, while Maroons, Haytians and slaves file around in the opposite direction and meet the Americans. As they pass the French, by guile induce Toussaint to go with them. There is a period of hesitation. Some slaves are freed, some Haytians resist aggression. George Lisle, a freed Negro, preaches the true religion as the masters listen. Peace ensues and the slaves sing at their tasks. Suddenly King Cotton arrives, followed by Greed, Vice, Luxury and Cruelty. The slave-holders are seduced. The old whips and chains appear. Nat Turner rebels and is killed. The slaves drop into despair and work silently and sullenly. The faint roll of tomtoms is heard.

The hearalds proclaim

The Sixth Episode, saying:
"Hear ye, hear ye! Citizens of New York, and learn of the deeds of eldest and strongest of the races of men whose faces be black. Hear ye, hear ye, of the Sixth and Greatest Gift of black men to the world, the Gift of Freedom for the workers. Men of New York, keep silence and hear ye this." The banners change and say:
"The sixth and last episode, showing how the freedom of black slaves meant freedom for the world. In this episode shall be seen the work of Garrison and John Brown; of Abraham Lincoln and Frederick Douglass, the marching of black soldiers to war and the hope that lies in little children."

The slaves work more and more dejectedly and drivers force them. Slave music comes. The tomtoms grow louder. The Veiled Woman appears with fire and iron. The slaves arise and begin to escape, passing through each other to and fro, confusedly. Benezet, Walker and Garrison enter, scattering their writings, and pass slowly to the right, threatened by slave drivers. John Brown enters, gesticulating. A knot of Negroes follow him. The planters seize him and erect a gallows, but the slaves seize his body and begin singing "John Brown's Body."

Frederick Douglass enters and passes to the right. Sojourner Truth enters and passes to the left. Sojourner Truth cries "Frederick, is God dead?" Voices take up the cry, repeating: "Frederick, is God dead?" Douglass answers: "No, and therefore slavery must end in blood." The heralds repeat: "Slavery must end in blood."

The roll of drums is heard and the soldiers enter. First, a company in blue with Colonel Shaw on horseback.

A single voice sings "O Freedom." A soprano chorus takes it up.

The Boy Scouts march in.

Full brasses take up "O Freedom."

Little children enter, and among them symbolic figures of the Laborer, the Artisan, the Servant of Men, the Merchant, the Inventor, the Musician, the Actor, the Teacher, Law, Medicine and Ministry, the All-Mother, formerly the Veiled Woman, now unveiled in her chariot with her dancing brood, and the bust of Lincoln at her side.

With burst of music and blast of trumpets, the pageant ends and the heralds sing:

"Hear ye, hear ye, men of all the Americas, ye who have listened to the tale of the eldest and strongest of the races of mankind, whose faces be black. Hear ye, hear ye, and forget not the gift of black men to this world—the Iron Gift and Gift of Faith, the Pain of Humility and Sorrow Song of Pain, the Gift of Freedom and Laughter and the undying Gift of Hope. Men of America, break silence, for the play is done."

Then shall the banners announce:

"The play is done!"

NEGRO ART

Negro art is today plowing a difficult row, chiefly because we shrink at the portrayal of the truth about ourselves. We are so used to seeing the truth distorted to our despite, that whenever we are portrayed on canvas, in story or on the stage, as simply human with human frailities, we rebel. We want everything that is said about us to tell of the best and highest and noblest in us. We insist that our Art and Propaganda be one.

This is wrong and in the end it is harmful. We have a right, in our effort to get just treatment, to insist that we produce something of the best in human character and that it is unfair to judge us by our criminals and prostitutes. This is justifiable propaganda.

On the other hand we face the Truth of Art. We have criminals and prostitutes, ignorant and debased elements just as all folk have. When the artist paints us he has a right to paint us whole and not ignore everything which is not as perfect as we would wish it to be. The black Shakespeare must portray his black Iagos as well as his white Othellos.

We shrink from this. We fear that evil in us will be called racial, while in others it is viewed as individual. We fear that our shortcomings are not merely human but foreshadowings and threatenings of disaster and failure. The more highly trained we become the less can we laugh at Negro comedy—we will have it all tragedy and the triumph of dark Right over pale Villainy.

The results are not merely negative—they are positively bad. With a vast wealth of human material about us, our own writers and artists fear to paint the truth lest they criticize their own and be in turn criticized for it. They fail to see the Eternal Beauty that shines through all Truth, and try to portray a world of stilted artificial black folk such as never were on land or sea.

Thus the white artist looking in on the colored world, if he be wise and discerning, may often see the beauty, tragedy and comedy more truly than we dare. Of course if he be simply a shyster like Tom Dixon, he will see only exaggerated evil, and fail as utterly in the other extreme as we in ours. But if, like Sheldon, he writes a fine true work of art like "The Nigger"; or like Ridgely Torrence, a beautiful comedy like "The Rider of Dreams"; or like Eugene O'Neill, a splendid tragedy like "The Emperor Jones"—he finds to his own consternation the Negroes and even educated Negroes, shrinking or openly condemning.

Sheldon's play has repeatedly been driven from the stage by ill-advised Negroes who objected to its name; Torrence's plays were received by educated blacks with no great enthusiasm; and only yesterday a protest of colored folk in a western city declared that

" 'The Emperor Jones' is the kind of play that should never be staged under any circumstances, regardless of theories, because it portrays the worst traits of the bad element of both races."

No more complete misunderstanding of this play or of the aim of Art could well be written, although the editors of the *Century* and *Current Opinion* showed almost equal obtuseness.

Nonsense. We stand today secure enough in our accomplishment and self-confidence to lend the whole stern human truth about ourselves to the transforming hand and seeing eye of the Artist, white and black, and Sheldon. Torrence and O'Neill are our great benefactors—forerunners of artists who will yet arise in Ethiopia of the Outstretched Arm.

NEGRO ART AND LITERATURE

The Negro is primarily an artist. The usual way of putting this is to speak disdainfully of his "sensuous" nature. This means that the only race which has held at bay the life destroying forces of the tropics, has gained therefrom in some slight compensation a sense of beauty, particularly for sound and color, which characterizes the race. The Negro blood which flowed in the veins of many of the mightiest of the Pharaohs accounts for much of Egyptian art, and indeed Egyptian civilization owes much in its origin to the development of the large strain of Negro blood which manifested itself in every grade of Egyptian society.

Semitic civilization also had its Negroid influences, and these continually turn toward art as in the case of black Nosseyeb, one of the five great poets of Damascus under the Ommiades, and the black Arabian hero, Antar. It was therefore not to be wondered at that in modern days one of the greatest of modern literatures, the Russian, should have been founded by Pushkin, the grandson of a full blooded Negro, and that among the painters of Spain was the mulatto slave, Gomez. Back of all this development by way of contact, come the artistic sense of the indigenous Negro as shown in the stone figures of Sherbro, the bronzes of Benin, the marvelous hand work in iron and other metals which has characterized the Negro race so long that archaeologists today, with less and less hesitation, are ascribing the discovery of the welding of iron to the Negro race.

Beyond the specific ways in which the Negro has contributed to American art stands undoubtedly his spirit of gayety and the exotic charm which his presence has loaned the parts of America which were spiritually free enough to enjoy it. In New Orleans, for instance, after the war of 1812 and among the free people of color there was a beautiful blossoming of artistic life which the sordid background of slavery had to work hard to kill. The "people of color" grew in number and waxed wealthy. Famous streets even today bear testimony of their old importance. Congo Square in the old Creole quarter where Negroes danced the weird "Bamboula" long before colored Coleridge-Taylor made it immortal and Gottschalk wrote his Negro dance. Camp street and Julia street took their names from the old Negro field and from the woman who owned land along the Canal. Americans and Spanish both tried to get the support and sympathy of the free Negroes. The followers of Aaron Burr courted them.

"Writers describing the New Orleans of this period agree in presenting a picture of a continental city, most picturesque, most un-American, and as varied in color as a street of Cairo. There they saw French, Spaniards, English, Bohemians, Negroes, mulattoes, varied clothes, picturesque white dresses of the fairer women, brilliant cottons of the darker ones. The streets, banquettes, we should say, were bright with color, the nights filled with song and laughter. Through the scene, the people of color add the spice of color; in the life, they add the zest of romance."

Music is always back of this gay Negro spirit and the folk song which the Negro brought to America was developed not simply by white men but by the Negro himself. Musicians and artists sprung from the Louisiana group. There was Eugene Warburg who distinguished himself as a sculptor in Italy. There was Victor Sejour who became a poet and composer in France, Dubuclet became a musician in Bordeaux and the seven Lamberts taught and composed in America, France and Brazil. One of the brothers Sydney was decorated for his work by the King of Portugal. Edmund Dèdè became a director of a leading orchestra in France.

Among other early colored composers of music are J. Hemmenway who lived in Philadelphia in the twenties; A. J. Conner of Philadelphia between 1846–57 published numbers of compositions; in the seventies Justin Holland was well known as a composer in Cleveland, Ohio; Samuel Milady, known by his stage name as Sam Lucas, was born in 1846 and died in 1916. He wrote many popular ballads, among them "Grandfather's Clock Was Too Tall For The Shelf." George Melbourne, a Negro street minstrel, composed "Listen to the Mocking-Bird," although a white man got the credit. James Bland wrote "Carry me Back to Ole Virginny"; Gussie L. Davis composed popular music at Cincinnati.

Coming to our day we remember that the Anglo-African Samuel Coleridge-Taylor received much of his inspiration from his visits to the American Negro group; then comes Harry T. Burleigh, perhaps the greatest living song writer in America. Among his works are "Five Songs" by Laurence Hope; "The Young Warrior," which became one of the greatest of the war songs; "The Grey Wolf" and "Ethiopia Saluting the Colors." His adaptations of Negro folk-songs are widely known and he assisted Dvorak in his "New World Symphony." R. Nathaniel Dett has written "Listen to the Lambs," a carol widely known, and "The Magnolia Suite." Rosamond Johnson wrote "Under the Bamboo Tree" and a dozen popular favorites beside choruses and marches. Clarence Cameron White has composed and adapted and Maud Cuney Hare has revived and explained Creole music. Edmund T. Jenkins has won medals at the Royal Academy in London. Among the colored performers on the piano are R. Augustus Lawson, who has often been soloist at the concerts of the Hartford Philharmonic Orchestra; Hazel Harrison, a pupil of Busoni; and Helen Hagen who took the Sanford scholarship at Yale. Carl Diton is a pianist who has transcribed many Negro melodies. Melville Charlton has done excellent work on the organ.

Then we must remember the Negro singers, the "Black Swan" of the early 19th century whose voice compared with Jenny Lind's; the Hyer sisters, Flora Batson, Florence Cole Talbert, and Roland W. Hayes, the tenor whose fine voice has charmed London, Paris and Vienna and who is now one of the leading soloists of the Boston Symphony Orchestra.

The Negro has been one of the greatest originators of dancing in the United States and in the world. He created the "cake walk" and most of the steps in the "clog" dance which has so enthralled theatre audiences. The modern dances which have swept over the world like the "Tango" and "Turkey Trot" originated among the Negroes of the

West Indies. The Vernon Castles always told their audiences that their dances were of Negro origin.

We turn now to other forms of art and more particularly literature. Here the subjects naturally divides itself into three parts: *first*, the influence which the Negro has had on American literature,—and *secondly*, the development of a literature for and by Negroes. And lastly the number of Negroes who have gained a place in National American literature.

From the earliest times the presence of the black man in America has inspired American writers. Among the early Colonial writers the Negro was a subject as, for instance, in Samuel Sewall's "Selling of Joseph," the first American anti-slavery tract published in 1700. But we especially see in the influence of the Negro's condition in the work of the masters of the 19th century, like Ralph Waldo Emerson, John Greenleaf Whittier, James Russell Lowell, Walt Whitman, Julia Ward Howe, Harriet Beecher Stowe and Lydia Maria Child. With these must be named the orators Wendell Phillips, Charles Sumner, John C. Calhoun, Henry Ward Beecher. In our own day, we have had the writers of fiction, George W. Cable, Thomas Nelson Page, Thomas Dixson, Ruth McEnery Stewart, William Dean Howells, Thomas Wentworth Higginson.

It may be said that the influence of the Negro here is a passive influence and yet one must remember that it would be inconceivable to have an American literature, even that written by white men, and not have the Negro as a subject. He has been the lay figure, but after all, the figure has been alive, it has moved, it has talked, felt and influenced.

In the minds of these and other writers how has the Negro been portrayed? It is a fascinating subject which I can but barely touch: in the days of Shakespeare and Southerne the black man of fiction was a man, a brave, fine, if withal overtrustful and impulsive, hero. In science he was different but equal, cunning in unusual but mighty possibilities. Then with the slave trade he suddenly became a clown and dropped from sight. He emerged slowly beginning about 1830 as a dull stupid but contented slave, capable of doglike devotion, superstitious and incapable of education. Then, in the abolition controversy he became a victim, a man of sorrows, a fugitive chased by bloodhounds, a beautiful raped octoroon, a crucified Uncle Tom, but a lay figure, objectively pitiable but seldom subjectively conceived. Suddenly a change came after Reconstruction. The black man was either a faithful old "Befoh de wah" darky worshipping lordly white folk, or a frolicking ape, or a villain, a sullen scoundrel, a violator of womanhood, a low thief and misbirthed monster. He was sub-normal and congenitally incapable. He was represented as an unfit survival of Darwinian natural selection. Philanthropy and religion stood powerless before his pigmy brain and undeveloped morals. In a "thousands years"? Perhaps. But at present, an upper beast. Out of this today he is slowly but tentatively, almost apologetically rising—a somewhat deserving, often poignant, but hopeless figure; a man whose only proper end is dramatic suicide physically or morally. His trouble is natural and inborn inferiority, slight by scientific measurement but sufficient to make absolute limits to his possibilities, save in exceptional cases.

And here we stand today. As a normal human being reacting humanly to human problems the Negro has never appeared in the fiction or the science of white writers, with a bare half dozen exceptions; while to the white southerner who "knows him best" he is always an idiot or a monster, and he sees him as such, no matter what is before his very eyes. And yet, with all this, the Negro has held the stage. In the South he is everything. You cannot discuss religion, morals, politics, social life, science, earth or sky, God or devil without touching the Negro. It is a perennial and continuous and continual subject of books, editorials, sermons, lectures and smoking car confabs. In the north and west while seldom in the center, the Negro is always in the wings waiting to appear or screaming shrill lines off stage. What would intellectual America do if she woke some fine morning to find no "Negro" Problem?

Coming now to the slowly swelling stream of a distinct group literature, by and primarily for the Negro, we enter a realm only partially known to white Americans. First, there come the rich mass of Negro folk lore transplanted from Africa and developed in America. A white writer, Joel Chandler Harris, first popularized "Uncle Remus" and "Brer Rabbit" for white America; but he was simply the deft and singularly successful translator—the material was Negroid and appears repeatedly among the black peasants and various forms and versions. Take for instance the versions of the celebrated tar-baby story of Joel Chandler Harris. C. C. Jones took down a striking version apparently direct from Negro lips early in the 19th century:

" 'Do Buh Wolf, bun me: broke me neck, but don't trow me in de brier patch. Lemme dead one time. Don't tarrify me no mo.' Buh Wolf yet bin know wuh Buh Rabbit up teh. Eh tink eh bin guine tare Bur Rabbit hide off. So, wuh eh do? Eh loose Buh Rabbit from de spakleberry bush, an eh tek um by de hine leg, an eh swing um roun', en eh trow um way in de tick brier patch fuh tare eh hide and cratch eh yeye out. De minnit Buh Rabbit drap in de brier patch, eh cock up eh tail, eh jump, an holler back to Buh Wolf: 'Good bye, Budder! Dis de place me mammy fotch me up,—dis de place me mammy fotch me up.' An eh gone before Buh Wolf kin ketch um. Buh Rabbit too scheemy."

The Harris version shows the literary touch added by the white man. But the Negro version told by Jones has all the meat of the primitive tale.

Next we note the folk rhymes and poetry of Negroes, sometimes accompanying their music and sometimes not. A white instructor in English literature at the University of Virgina says:

"Of all the builders of the nation the Negro alone has created a species of lyric verse that all the world may recognize as a distinctly American production."

T. W. Talley, a Negro, has recently published an exhaustive collection of these rhymes. They form an interesting collection of poetry often crude and commonplace but with here and there touches of real poetry and quaint humor.

The literary expression of Negroes themselves has had continuous development in America since the eighteenth century. It may however be looked upon from two different points of view: We may think of the writing of Negroes as self-expression and as principally for themselves. Here we have a continuous line of writers. Only a few of these, however would we think of as contributing to American literature as such and yet this inner, smaller stream of Negro literature overflows faintly at first and now evidently more and more into the wider stream of American literature; on the other hand there have been figures in American literature who happen to be of Negro descent and who are but vaguely to be identified with the group stream as such. Both these points of view are interesting but let us first take up the succession of authors who form a group literature by and for Negroes.

As early as the eighteenth century, and even before the Revolutionary War the first voices of Negro authors were heard in the United States. Phillis Wheatley, the black poetess, was easily the pioneer, her first poems appearing in 1773, and other editions in 1774 and 1793. Her earliest poem was in memory of George Whitefield. She was honored by Washington and leading Englishmen and was as a writer above the level of her American white contemporaries.

She was followed by Richard Allen, first Bishop of the African Methodist Church whose autobiography, published in 1793 was the beginning of that long series of personal appears and narratives of which Booker T. Washington's "Up From Slavery" was the latest. Benjamin Banneker's almanacs represented the first scientific work of American Negroes, and began to be issued in 1792.

Coming now to the first decades of the nineteenth century we find some essays on freedom by the African Society of Boston, and an apology for the new Negro church formed in Philadelphia. Paul Cuffe, disgusted with America, wrote an early account of Sierra Leone, while the celebrated Lemuel Haynes, ignoring the race question, dipped deeply into the New England theological controversy about 1815. In 1829 came the first full-voiced, almost hysterical, protest against slavery and the color line in David Walker's Appeal which aroused Southern legislatures to action. This was followed by the earliest Negro conventions which issued interesting minutes; two appeals against disfranchisement in Pennsylvania appeared in this decade, one written by Robert Purvis, who also wrote a biography of his father-in-law, Mr. James Forten, and the other appeal written by John Bowers and others. The life of Gustavus Vassa, also known by his African name of Olaudah Equiana, was published in America in 1837 continuing the interesting personal narratives.

In 1840 some strong writers began to appear. Henry Highland Garnet and J. W. C. Pennington preached powerful sermons and gave some attention to Negro history in their pamphlets: R. B. Lewis made a more elaborate attempt at Negro history. Whitfield's poems appeared in 1846, and William Wells Brown began a career of writing which lasted from 1847 until after the Civil War. He began his literary career by the publication of his "Narrative of a Fugitive Slave" in 1847. This was followed by a novel in 1853, "Sketches" from abroad in 1855, a play in 1858, "The Black Man" in 1863, "The Negro in the American Rebellion" in 1867, and "The Rising Son" in 1874. The Colored Convention in Cincinnati and Cleveland published reports in this decade and Bishop Loguen wrote his life history. In 1845 Douglass' autobiography made its first appearance, destined to run through endless editions until the last in 1893. Moreover it was in 1841 that the first Negro magazine appeared in America, edited by George Hogarth and published by the A. M. E. Church.

In the fifties James Whitfield published further poems, and a new poet arose in the person of Frances E. W. Harper, a woman of no little ability who died lately; Martin R. Delany and William Cooper Nell wrote further of Negro history, Nell especially making valuable contributions of the history of the Negro soldiers. Three interesting biographies were added in this decade to the growing number; Josiah Henson, Samuel C. Ward and Samuel Northrop; while Catto, leaving general history came down to the better known history of the Negro church.

In the sixties slave narratives multiplied, like that of Linda Brent, while two studies of Africa based on actual visits were made by Robert Campbell and Dr. Alexander Crummell; William Douglass and Bishop Daniel Payne continued the history of the Negro church, and William Wells Brown carried forward his work in general Negro history. In this decade, too, Bishop Tanner began his work in Negro theology.

Most of the Negro talent in the seventies was taken up in politics; the older men like Bishop Wayman wrote of their experiences; Sojourner Truth added her story to the slave narratives. A new poet arose in the person of A. A. Whitman, while James Monroe Trotter was the first to take literary note of the musical ability of his race. Robert Brown Elliott stirred the nation by his eloquence in Congress. The Fisk edition of the Songs of the Jubilee Singers appeared.

In the eighties there are signs of unrest and conflicting streams of thought. On the one hand the rapid growth of the Negro church is shown by the writers on church subjects like Moore and Wayman. The historical spirit was especially strong. Still wrote of the Underground Railroad; Simmons issued his interesting biographical dictionary, and the greatest historian of the race appeared when George W. Williams issued his two-volume history of the Negro Race in America. The political turmoil was reflected in Langston's Freedom and Citizenship, Fortune's Black and White, and Straker's New South, and found its bitterest arraignment in Turner's pamphlets; but with all this went other new thought: Scarborough published "First Greek Lessons"; Bishop Payne issued his Treatise on Domestic Education, and Stewart studied Liberia.

In the nineties came histories, essays, novels and poems, together with biographies and social studies. The history was represented by Payne's History of the A. M. E. Church, Hood's "One Hundred Years of the A. M. E. Zion Church, Anderson's sketch of Negro Presbyterianism and Hagood's Colored Man in the M. E. Church; general history of the older type was represented by R. L. Perry's Cushite and of the newer type in E. A. Johnson's histories, while one of the secret societies found their historian in Brooks; Crogman's essays appeared and Archibald Grimke's biographies. The race question was discussed in Frank Grimke's published sermons, social studies were made by Penn, Wright, Mossell, Crummell, Majors and others. Most notable, however, was the rise of the Negro novelist and poet with national recognition: Frances Harper was still writing and Griggs began his racial novels, but both of these spoke primarily to the Negro race; on the other hand, Chesnutt's six novels and Dunbar's inimitable works spoke of the whole nation. J. T. Wilson's "Black Phalanx," the most complete study of the Negro soldier, came in these years.

Booker T. Washington's work began with his address at Atlanta in 1895, "Up From Slavery" in 1901, "Working with the Hands" in 1904, and "The Man Farthest Down" in 1912. The American Negro Academy, a small group, began the publication of occasional papers in 1897 and has published a dozen or more numbers including a "Symposium on the Negro and the Elective Franchise" in 1905, a "Comparative Study of the Negro Problem" in 1899, Love's "Disfranchisement of the Negro" in 1899, Grimke's Study of Denmark Vesey in 1901 and Steward's "Black St. Domingo Legion" in 1899. Since 1900 the stream of Negro writing has continued. Dunbar has found a successor in the critic and compiler of anthologies, W. S. Braithwaite; Booker T. Washington has given us his biography and Story of the Negro; Kelly Miller's trenchant essays have appeared in book form and he has issued numbers of critical monographs on the Negro problem with wide circulation. Scientific historians have appeared in Benjamin Brawley and Carter Woodson and George W. Mitchell. Sinclair's Aftermath of Slavery has attracted attention, as have the studies made by Atlanta University. The Negro in American Sculpture has been studied by H. F. M. Murray.

The development in poetry has been significant, beginning with Phillis Wheatley. Jupiter Hammon came in the 18th century, George M. Horton in the early part of the 19th century followed by Frances Harper who began publishing in 1854 and A. A. Whitman whose first attempts at epic poetry were published in the seventies. In 1890 came the first thin volume of Paul Lawrence Dunbar, the undoubted laureate of the race, who published poems and one or two novels up until the beginning of the 20th century. He was succeeded by William Stanley Braithwaite whose fame rests chiefly upon his poetic criticism and his anthologies, and finally by James Weldon Johnson, Claude McKay who came out of the West Indies with a new and sincere gift, Fenton Johnson, Georgia Johnson and Jessie Fauset. Joseph S. Cotter, Jr., Langston Hughes, Roscoe C. Jamison and Countée Cullen have done notable work in verse. Campbell, Davis and others have continued the poetic tradition of Negro dialect.

On the whole, the literary output of the American Negro has been both large and creditable, although, of course, comparatively little known; few great names have appeared and only here and there work that could be called first class, but this is not a peculiarity of Negro literature.

The time has not yet come for the great development of American Negro literature. The economic stress is too great and the racial persecution too bitter to allow the leisure and the poise for which literature calls. "The Negro in the United States is consuming all his intellectual energy in this gruelling race-struggle. And the same statement may be made in a general way about the white South. Why does not the white South produce literature and art? The white South, too, is consuming all of its intellectual energy in this lamentable conflict. Nearly all of the mental efforts of the white South run through one narrow channel. The life of every southern white man and all of his activities are impassably limited by the ever present Negro problem. And that is why, as Mr. H. L. Mencken puts it, in all that vast region, with its thirty or forty million people and its territory as large as half a dozen Frances or Germanys, "there is not a single poet, not a serious historian, not a creditable composer, not a critic good or bad, not a dramatist dead or alive."

On the other hand, never in the world has a richer mass of material been accumulated by a people than that which the Negroes possess today and are becoming increasingly conscious of. Slowly but surely they are developing artists of technic who will be able to use this material. The nation does not notice this for everything touching the Negro has hitherto been banned by magazines and publishers unless it took the form of caricature or bitter attack, or was so thoroughly innocuous as to have no literary flavor. This attitude shows signs of change at last.

Most of the names in this considerable list except those toward the last would be unknown to the student of American literature. Nevertheless they form a fairly continuous tradition and a most valuable group expression. From them several have arisen, as I have said, to become figures in the main stream of American literature. Phillis Wheatley was an American writer of Negro descent just as Dumas was a French writer of Negro descent. She was the peer of her best American contemporaries but she represented no conscious Negro group. Lemuel Haynes wrote for Americans rather than for Negroes.

Dunbar occupies a unique place in American literature. He raised a dialect and a theme from the minstrel stage to literature and became and remains a national figure. Charles W. Chesnutt followed him as a novelist, and many white people read in form of fiction a subject which they did not want to read or hearken to. He gained his way unaided and by sheer merit and is a recognized American novelist. Braithwaite is a critic whose Negro descent is not generally known and has but slightly influenced his work. His place in American literature is due more to his work as a critic and anthologist than to his work as a poet. "There is still another role he has played, that of friend of poetry and poets. It is a recognized fact that in the work which preceded the present revival of poetry in the United States, no one rendered more unremitting and valuable service than Mr. Braithwaite. And it can be said that no future study of American poetry of this age can be made without reference to Braithwaite."

Of McKay's poems, Max Eastman writes that it "should be illuminating to observe that while these poems are characteristic of that race as we most admire it—they are gentle, simple, candid, brave and friendly, quick of laughter and of tears—yet they are still more characteristic of what is deep and universal in mankind. There is no special or exotic kind of merit in them, no quality that demands a transmutation of our own natures to perceive. Just as the sculptures and wood and ivory carvings of the vast forgotten African Empires of Ife and Benin, although so wistful in their tranquility, are tranquil in the possession of the qualities of all classic and great art, so these poems, the purest of them, move with a sovereignty that is never new to the lovers of the high music of human utterance."

The later writers like Jean Toomer, Claude McKay, Jessie Fauset and others have come on the stage when the stream of Negro literature has grown to be of such importance and gained so much of technique and merit that it tends to merge into the broad flood of American literature and any notable Negro writer became *ipso facto* a national writer.

One must not forget the Negro orator. While in the white world the human voice as a vehicle of information and persuasion has waned in importance until the average man is somewhat suspicious of "eloquence," in the Negro world the spoken word is still dominant and Negro orators have wielded great influence upon both white and black from the time of Frederick Douglass and Samuel Ward down to the day of J. C. Price and Booker T. Washington. There is here, undoubtedly, something of unusual gift and personal magnetism.

One must note in this connection the rise and spread of a Negro press—magazines and weeklies which are voicing to the world with increasing power the thought of American Negroes. The influence of this new force in America is being recognized and the circulation of these papers aggregate more than a million copies.

On the stage the Negro has naturally had a most difficult chance to be recognized. He has been portrayed by white dramatists and actors, and for a time it seemed but natural for a character like Othello to be drawn, or for Southerne's Oroonoko to be presented in 1696 in England with a black Angola prince as its hero. Beginning, however, with the latter part of the 18th century the stage began to make fun of the Negro and the drunken character Mungo was introduced at Drury Lane.

In the United States this tradition was continued by the "Negro Minstrels" which began with Thomas D. Rice's imitation of a Negro cripple, Jim Crow. Rice began his work in Louisville in 1828 and had great success. Minstrel companies imitating Negro songs and dances and blackening their faces gained a great vogue until long after the Civil War. Negroes themselves began to appear as principals in minstrel companies after a time and indeed as early as 1820 there was an "African company" playing in New York. No sooner had the Negro become the principal in the minstrel shows than he began to develop and uplift the art. This took a long time but eventually there appeared Cole and Johnson, Ernest Hogan and Williams and Walker. Their development of a new light comedy marked an epoch and Bert Williams was at his recent death without doubt the leading comedian on the American stage.

In the legitimate drama there was at first no chance for the Negro in the United States. Ira Aldridge, born in Maryland, had to go to Europe for opportunity. There he became associated with leading actors like Edmund Keene and was regarded in the fifties as one of the two or three greatest actors in the world. He was honored and decorated by the King of Sweden, the King of Prussia, the Emperor of Austria and the Czar of Russia. He had practically no successor until Charles Gilpin triumphed in "The Emperor Jones" in New York during the season 1920–21.

Efforts to develop a new distinctly racial drama and portray the dramatic struggle of the Negro in America and elsewhere have rapidly been made. Mrs. Emily Hapgood made determined effort to initiate a Negro theatre. She chose the plays of Ridgeley Torrence, a white playwright, who wrote for the Negro players "Granny Maumee" and "The Rider of Dreams," pieces singularly true to Negro genius. The plays were given with unusual merit and gained the highest praise.

This movement, interrupted by the war, has been started again by the Ethiopian Players of Chicago and especially by the workers at Howard University where a Negro drama with Negro instructors, Negro themes and Negro players is being developed. One of the most interesting pageants given in America was written, staged and performed by Negroes in New York, Philadelphia and Washington.

Charles Gilpin had been trained with Williams and Walker and other colored companies. He got his first chance on the legitimate stage by playing the part of Curtis in Drinkwater's "Abraham Lincoln." Then he became the principal in O'Neill's wonderful play and was nominated by the Drama League in 1921 as one of the ten persons who had contributed most to the American theatre during the year. Paul Robeson and Evelyn Preer are following Gilpin's footsteps.

There is no doubt of the Negro's dramatic genius. Stephen Graham writes:

"I visited one evening a Negro theatre where a musical comedy was going on—words and music both by Negroes. It opened with the usual singing and dancing chorus of Negro girls. They were clad in yellow and crimson and mauve combinations with white tapes on one side from the lace edge of the knicker to their dusky arms. They danced from the thigh rather than from the knee, moving waist and bosom in unrestrained undulation, girls with large, startled seeming eyes and uncontrollable masses of dark hair. A dance of physical joy and abandon, with no restraint in the toes or the knees, no veiling of the eyes, no half shutting of the lips, no holding in of the hair. Accustomed to the very aesthetic presentment of the Bacchanalia in the Russian ballet, it might be difficult to call one of those Negro dancers a Bacchante, and yet there was one whom I remarked again and again, a Queen of Sheba in her looks, a face like starry night, and she was clad slightly in mauve, and went into such ecstacies during the many encores that her hair fell down about her bare shoulders, and her cheeks and knees, glistening with perspiration, outshone her eyes. . . . I had seen nothing so pretty or so amusing, so bewilderingly full of life and color, since Sanine's production of the 'Fair of Sorochinsky' in Moscow."

Turning now to painting, we note a young African painter contemporary with Phillis Wheatley who had gained some little renown. Then a half century ago came E. M. Banister, the center of a group of artists forming the Rhode Island Art Club, and one of whose pictures took a medal at the Centennial Exposition in 1876.

William A. Harper died in 1910. His "Avenue of Poplars" took a prize of $100 at the Chicago Art Institute. William Edward Scott studied in Paris under Tanner. His picture "La Pauvre Voisine" was hung in the salon in 1910 and bought by the government of the Argentine Republic. Another picture was hung in Paris and took first prize at the

Indiana State Fair, and a third picture was exhibited in the Royal Academy in London. Lately Mr. Scott has specialized in mural painting. His work is found in ten public schools in Chicago, in four in Indianapolis and in the latter city he decorated two units in the City Hospital with 300 life sized pictures. In many of these pictures he has especially emphasized the Negro type.

Richard Brown, Edwin Harleston, Albert A. Smith, Laura Wheeler and a number of rising young painters have shown the ability of the Negro in this line of art; but their dean is, of course, Henry Ossawa Tanner. Tanner is today one of the leading painters of the world and universally is so recognized. He was born an American Negro in Pittsburgh in 1859, the son of an African Methodist minister; he studied at the Academy of Fine Arts in Philadelphia and became a photographer in Atlanta. Afterward he taught at Clark University in Atlanta. In all this time he had sold less than $200 worth of pictures; but finally he got to Paris and was encouraged by Benjamin Constant. He soon turned toward his greatest forte, religious pictures. His "Daniel in the Lion's Den" was hung in the salon in 1896 and the next year the "Raising of Lazarus" was bought by the French government and hung in the Luxembourg. Since then he has won medals in all the greatest expositions, and his works are sought by connoisseurs. He has recently received knighthood in the French Legion of Honor.

In sculpture we may again think of two points of view,—first, there is the way in which the Negro type has figured in American sculpture as, for instance, the libyan Sybil of W. A. Story, Bissell's Emancipation group in Scotland, the Negro woman on the military monument in Detroit, Ball's Negro in the various emancipation groups, Ward's colored woman on the Beecher monument, the panel on the Cleveland monument of Scofield, Africa in D. C. French's group in front of the Custom's House in New York City, Calder's black boy in the Nations of the West group in the Panama-Pacific exhibition and, of course, the celebrated Shaw monument in Boston. On the other hand, there have been a few Negro sculptors, three of whom merit mention: Edmonia Lewis, who worked during the Civil War, Meta Warrick Fuller, a pupil of Rodin, and May Howard Jackson, who has done some wonderful work in the portraying of the mulatto type.

To appraise rightly this body of art one must remember that it represents mainly the work of those artists whom accident set free; if the artist had a white face his Negro blood did not militate against him in the fight for recognition; if his Negro blood was visible white relatives may have helped him; in a few cases ability was united to indomitable will. But the shrinking, modest, black artist without special encouragement had little or no chance in a world determined to make him a menial. Today the situation is changing. The Negro world is demanding expression in art and beginning to pay for it. The white world is able to see dimly beyond the color line. This sum of accomplishment then is but a beginning and an imperfect indication of what the Negro race is capable of in America and in the world. . . .

CRITERIA OF NEGRO ART

I do not doubt but there are some in this audience who are a little disturbed at the subject of this meeting, and particularly at the subject I have chosen. Such people are thinking something like this: "How is it that an organization like this, a group of radicals trying to bring new things into the world, a fighting organization which has come up out of the blood and dust of battle, struggling for the right of black men to be ordinary human beings—how is it that an organization of this kind can turn aside to talk about Art? After all, what have we who are slaves and black to do with Art?"

Or perhaps there are others who feel a certain relief and are saying, "After all it is rather satisfactory after all this talk about rights and fighting to sit and dream of something which leaves a nice taste in the mouth."

Let me tell you that neither of these groups is right. The thing we are talking about tonight is part of the great fight we are carrying on and it represents a forward and an upward look—a pushing onward. You and I have been breasting hills; we have been climbing upward; there has been progress and we can see it day by day looking back along blood-filled paths. But as you go through the valleys and over the foothills, so long as you are climbing, the direction,—north, south, east or west,—is of less importance. But when gradually the vista widens and you begin to see the world at your feet and the far horizon, then it is time to know more precisely whither you are going and what you really want.

What do we want? What is the thing we are after? As it was phrased last night it had a certain truth: We want to be Americans, full-fledged Americans, with all the rights of other American citizens. But is that all? Do we want simply to be Americans? Once in a while through all of us there flashes some clairvoyance, some clear idea, of what America really is. We who are dark can see America in a way that white Americans can not. And seeing our country thus, are we satisfied with its present goals and ideals?

In the high school where I studied we learned most of Scott's "Lady of the Lake" by heart. In after life once it was my privilege to see the lake. It was Sunday. It was quiet. You could glimpse the deer wandering in unbroken forests; you could hear the soft ripple of romance on the waters. Around me fell the cadence of that poetry of my youth. I fell asleep full of the enchantment of the Scottish border. A new day broke and with it came a sudden rush of excursionists. They were mostly Americans and they were loud and strident. They poured upon the little pleasure boat,—men with their hats a little on one side and drooping cigars in the wet corners of their mouths; women who shared their conversation with the world. They all tried to get everywhere first. They pushed other people out of the way. They made all sorts of incoherent noises and gestures so that the quiet home folk and the visitors from other lands silently and half-wonderingly gave way before them. They struck a note not evil but wrong. They carried, perhaps, a sense of strength and accomplishment, but their hearts had no conception of the beauty which pervaded this holy place.

If you tonight suddenly should become full-fledged Americans; if your color faded, or the color line here in Chicago was miraculously forgotten; suppose, too, you became at the same time rich and powerful;—what is it that you would want? What would you immediately seek? Would you buy the most powerful of motor cars and outrace Cook County? Would you buy the most elaborate estate on the North Shore? Would you be a Rotarian or a Lion or a What-not of the very last degree? Would you wear the most striking clothes, give the richest dinners and buy the longest press notices?

Even as you visualize such ideals you know in your hearts that these are not the things you really want. You realize this sooner than the average white American because, pushed aside as we have been in America, there has come to us not only a certain distaste for the tawdry and flamboyant but a vision of what the world could be if it were really a beautiful world; if we had the true spirit; if we had the Seeing Eye, the Cunning Hand, the Feeling Heart; if we had, to be sure, not perfect happiness, but plenty of good hard work, the inevitable suffering that always comes with life; sacrifice and waiting, all that—but, nevertheless, lived in a world where men know, where men create, where they realize themselves and where they enjoy life. It is that sort of a world we want to create for ourselves and for all America.

After all, who shall describe Beauty? What is it? I remember tonight four beautiful things: The Cathedral at Cologne, a forest in stone, set in light and changing shadow, echoing with sunlight and solemn song; a village of the Veys in West Africa, a little thing of mauve and purple, quiet, lying content and shining in the sun; a black and velvet room where on a throne rests, in old and yellowing marble, the broken curves of the Venus of Milo; a single phrase of music in the Southern South—utter melody, haunting and appealing, suddenly arising out of night and eternity, beneath the moon.

Such is Beauty. Its variety is infinite, its possibility is endless. In normal life all may have it and have it yet again. The world is full of it; and yet today the mass of human beings are choked away from it, and their lives distorted and made ugly. This is not only wrong, it is silly. Who shall right this well-nigh universal failing? Who shall let this world be beautiful? Who shall restore to men the glory of sunsets and the peace of quiet sleep?

We black folk may help for we have within us as a race new stirrings; stirrings of the beginning of a new appreciation of joy, of a new desire to create, of a new will to be; as though in this morning of group life we had awakened from some sleep that at once dimly mourns the past and dreams a splendid future; and there has come the conviction that the Youth that is here today, the Negro Youth, is a different kind of Youth, because in some new way it bears this mighty prophecy on its breast, with a new realization of itself, with new determination for all mankind.

What has this Beauty to do with the world? What has Beauty to do with Truth and Goodness—with the facts of the world and the right actions of men? "Nothing", the artists rush to answer. They may be right. I am but an humble disciple of art and cannot presume to say. I am one who tells the truth and exposes evil and seeks with Beauty and for Beauty to set the world right. That somehow, somewhere eternal and perfect Beauty sits above Truth and Right I can conceive, but here and now and in the world in which I work they are for me unseparated and inseparable.

This is brought to us peculiarly when as artists we face our own past as a people. There has come to us . . . a realization of that past, of which for long years we have been ashamed, for which we have apologized. We thought nothing could come out of that past which we wanted to remember; which we wanted to hand down to our children. Suddenly, this same past is taking on form, color and reality, and in a half shamefaced way we are beginning to be proud of it. We are remembering that the romance of the world did not die and lie forgotten in the Middle Age; that if you want romance to deal with you must have it here and now and in your own hands.

I once knew a man and woman. They had two children, a daughter who was white and a daughter who was brown; the daughter who was white married a white man; and when her wedding was preparing the daughter who was brown prepared to go and celebrate. But the mother said, "No!" and the brown daughter went into her room and turned on the gas and died. Do you want Greek tragedy swifter than that?

Or again, here is a little Southern Town and you are in the public square. On one side of the square is the office of a colored lawyer and on all the other sides are men who do not like colored lawyers. A white woman goes into the black man's office and points to the white-filled square and says, "I want five hundred dollars now and if I do not get it I am going to scream." . . .

. . . Suppose the only Negro who survived some centuries hence was the Negro painted by white Americans in the novels and essays they have written. What would people in a hundred years say of black Americans? Now turn it around. Suppose you were to write a story and put in it the kind of people you know and like and imagine. You might get it published and you might not. And the "might not" is still far bigger than the "might." The white publishers catering to white folk would say, "It is not interesting"—to white folk, naturally not. They want Uncle Toms, Topsies, good "darkies" and clowns. I have in my office a story with all the earmarks of truth. A young man says that he started out to write and had his stories accepted. Then he began to write about the things he knew best about, that is, about his own people. He submitted a story to a magazine which said, "We are sorry, but we cannot take it." "I sat down and revised my story, changing the color of the characters and the locale and sent it under an assumed name with a change of address and it was accepted by the same magazine that had refused it, the editor promising to take anything else I might send in providing it was good enough."

We have, to be sure, a few recognized and successful Negro artists; but they are not all those fit to survive or even a good minority. They are but the remnants of that ability and genius among us whom the accidents of education and opportunity have raised on the tidal waves of chance. We black folk are not altogether peculiar in this. After all, in the world at large, it is only the accident, the remnant, that gets the chance to make the most of itself; but if this is true of the white world it is infinitely more true of the colored world. It is not simply the great clear tenor of Roland Hayes that opened the ears of America. We have had many voices of all kinds as fine as his and America was and is as deaf as she was for years to him. Then a foreign land heard Hayes and put its imprint on him and immediately America with all its imitative snobbery woke up. We approved Hayes because London, Paris and Berlin approved him and not simply because he was a great singer.

Thus it is the bounden duty of black America to begin this great work of the creation of Beauty, of the preservation of Beauty, of the realization of Beauty, and we must use in this work all the methods that men have used before. And what have been the tools of the artist in times gone by? First of all, he has used the Truth—not for the sake of truth, not as a scientist seeking truth, but as one upon whom Truth eternally thrusts itself as the highest handmaid of imagination, as the one great vehicle of universal understanding. Again artists have used Goodness—goodness in all its aspects of justice, honor and right—not for sake of an ethical sanction but as the one true method of gaining sympathy and human interest.

The apostle of Beauty thus becomes the apostle of Truth and Right not by choice but by inner and outer compulsion. Free he is but his freedom is ever bounded by Truth and Justice; and slavery only dogs him when he is denied the right to tell the Truth or recognize an ideal of Justice.

Thus all Art is propaganda and ever must be, despite the wailing of the purists. I stand in utter shamelessness and say that whatever art I have for writing has been used always for propaganda for gaining the right of black folk to love and enjoy. I do not care a damn for any art that is not used for propaganda. But I do care when propaganda is confined to one side while the other is stripped and silent. . . .

PHILLIS WHEATLEY AND AFRICAN AMERICAN CULTURE

> The blessed Damozel leaned out
> From the gold bar of Heaven:
> Her eyes were deeper than the depth
> Of waters stilled at even;
> She had three lilies in her hand
> And the stars in her hair were seven.

I find in these well-known verses of Rossetti, a text upon which to build a brief review of the literature of American Negroes before the twentieth century. In 1754 there was born in West Africa a little black girl who was miraculously lifted across the wide Atlantic and set down as a servant to a pious well-read New England woman.

"I was a poor little outcast and a stranger when she took me in, not only into her house, but I presently became a sharer in her most tender affections. I was treated by her more like her child than her servant."

Phillis was a child of seven when she landed in Boston; old enough to know the beginnings of life; the first patterns of her ancestral culture; she remembered her mother pouring libations before the rising sun; she sensed the contrast between tropical Africa and bleak New England. From portrait and description we know her as frail and slight, with little hands and feet, thin lips, small nose and wide temples. Her skin was darkly brown, velvet and glossy. Her hair, tight-curled, grasped her high round head like a close woven cap of tendrils. Her eyes were large and black—

> Her eyes were deeper than the depth,
> Of waters stilled at even.

Her gift of verse in a foreign tongue and a stilted repressed culture was not great and yet it was there. She sang to the Earl of Dartmouth when the Stamp Act was repealed—

Should you, my lord, while you peruse my song,
Wonder from whence my love of freedom sprung;
Whence flow those wishes for the common good,
By feeling hearts alone best understood—
I, young in life, by seeming cruel fate,
Was snatched from Afric's fancied happy seat.
What pangs excruciating must molest,
What sorrows labour in my parents' breast!
Steeled was that soul, and by no misery moved,
That from a father seized his babe beloved:
Such, such my case.

She made a strange and lonesome figure in the America of the day just before the Revolution—calm and correct without, silent. Her deep sense of religion and evangelical patois veiled her more human soul to us as it did to Thomas Jefferson. Yet within must have bloomed and sung a world of Phantasy. It is these imagined visions of Phillis, in the long days of her childhood wonder, her first happiness of young womanhood and the hard long martyrdom of her after years that made her Phillis the Blessed. There was in Phillis just the suggestion—not more—of something fey, wild and elemental, sternly repressed, confined so that the inner soul never burst through, only the transmuted echo—refined (she loved the word), not crude, not brash:

Before my mortal eyes,
The lightnings blaze across the vaulted skies,
And, as the thunder shakes the heav'nly plains,
A deep felt horror thrills through all my veins.
When gentler strains demand thy graceful song,
The length'ning lines moves languishing along.

Was Phillis blessed? Yes! with security and affection, with education beyond her status, by contact with cultured folk. Surely this is the beginning of blessing; and then with sorrow and bereavement, with poverty and hunger, with death and pain. Only Love was lacking—love and its loss. Reverence, affection, friendship—all these were hers; but she was a loveless child, woman and wife. Lacking this miracle, she could never be a Saint—but she was Phillis the Blessed.

Always a certain sense of mystery lurked in the furtherest reaches of Phillis' consciousness—the miracle of her sudden transport to this far land; the hoarse voice of the Visions, the dire deep Visions, thus floated and drifted, loomed and died in her thoughts and dreams. In the only home she knew—and the only friends she had, she was always partly a stranger. Only her phantasy was real, only her dreams were true. She could not help but have visions—prophetic visions—she who in a single childhood had encompassed the ends of earth.

She loved flowers and saw but few: buttercups and daisies, arbutus and violets; less often, a rose. She dimly remembered riots of blooms; purple wisteria, flowering bougainvillea, orange poinciana and crimson poinsettas; but she shrank from these—thither lay riot and revolt and wild desire and hate; and she shrunk within herself—peace, quiet, silence was her way; only she yearned for quiet lilies; and the stars in her hair were seven.

The stars were her friends, her old and trusted friends. They alone knew her tall ghost mother, and sisters;—Were there sisters and brothers? She thought so, but they were dim and vague. But her tall straight mother, she was real. So were the stars. Some stars were gone—a little jeweled cross from the south was lost as she was; others were misplaced. But she knew them and loved them. They were hers. Mornings they sang together.

Looking out from her own singular and narrow corner of the world, Phillis must have had visions of the souls and voices, who, coming after her, continued and fulfilled her promise and tradition— David Walker and his bitter cry; the lilt of love that sang in Armand Lanusse; the busy chronicle of George Williams; the labored tales of Wells Brown; Alberry Whitman trying desperately to sing; and finally the grown and finished figures of Charles Waddell Chesnutt, master of fiction; and Paul Laurence Dunbar, the Song of Songs.

I seem to see her there then one hundred sixty-five years ago, with hands holding the three lilies of her thought; the tall, white lily of her faith—faith despite the world's paradox, which she saw all too well; the tiger lily, gold and black and typifying her inward frightened revolt; and finally the little purple flower of her sorrow.

She leaned out and then as now Heaven was barred with gold. Without lay poverty, darkness and dirt; without crawled crime and disease, while within the angels sang; and far above and beyond gleamed the morning stars; they sang together, and slowly seven came down and nestled in her hair—her stiff and crinkly close-curled hair; so the stars in her hair were seven. And Phillis yearned down from heaven to earth, striving to lift the soul of a people.

The singing of stars and the odor of lilies typified strange new happenings in America. For in the new born nation, a new folk-song was being born in the throats of slaves and the words set to it made a new folk poetry—unformed, unset, peering out here and there amid dross, in sudden beauty, and halting phrase. These words of the Negro Folk song have been seldom studied, but must not be forgot. Phillis did not hear them, save as vague prophecy of unremembered things. I set their voices down at hazard with a few dozen phrases. They are songs which Phillis never knew but always sensed:

Swing Low Sweet Chariot,
Roll, Jordan, roll!

Steal Away, Steal Away Home!
Nobody Knows the Trouble I See,
Dark Midnight Was My Cry;
I Been Listening All the Night Long,
I Couldn't Hear Nobody Pray.
I'm So Glad Trouble Don't Last Always—

Good News, the Chariot's Coming!
I'm Going to Lay Down My Burden!
Go Down Moses Way Down in Egypt Land!
Stand the Storm, It Won't Be Long,
O the Rocks and the Mountains Shall All Flee Away;
The Moon Runs Down in a Purple Stream,
Deep River, I Want to Cross Over Into Camp Ground!
'Tis Me, 'Tis Me, O Lord Standing in the Need of Prayer!

My God! What a Morning When the Stars Begin to Fall;
O the Stars of the Elements Are Falling and the Moon Drips
    Away Into Blood,
I Hope to Shout Glory When the World's On Fire,
Rise and Shine and Give God the Glory,
Ride On, King Jesus!
Listen to the Lambs All A-Crying;
Children We All Shall Be Free!
O the Land I Am Bound For;
I've Heard of a City Called Heaven
I'm Tramping, Tramping, Trying to Make Heaven My
    Home.

You may bury me in the east,
    You may bury me in the west,
I'll lie in the grave and stretch out my arms;
Dust, dust and ashes, fly over my grave;
I got a rainbow round my shoulder!

Sometimes, not often, and more rarely as time flew, Phillis remembered echoes of African fairy legend. They glided ghostly behind her thought, bringing thrills of happiness, which were almost memories, but never quite. One little tale kept up its mystic, vanishing dance:

The rabbit raced by; the elephant, waiting for his dinner beside the anthill asked
"Who are you?"
"I am a hare."
"Where are you going?"
"Blind one, haven't you seen all my comrades passing?"
And the rabbit, circling secretly, ran by again and again. The elephant became uneasy, imagining hundreds of rabbits; so at last as the rabbit again ran by, he saw only the far-off wagging of the elephant's tail.

331

"There he is! There he is!" cried the rabbit, as the elephant rushed out of sight and left the ant-hill for the rabbit's dinner.

From such vague, half-remembered folk-lore, Phillis never knew how the African rabbit came into American literature.

Continuing my allegory, I see the seven stars in Phillis' hair, set like rare jewels in the dense and clinging mass that crowned her womanhood, as points of utter light, upward towards which strove little unborn souls for whom the soul of Phillis strove and yearned. One by one, over years and centuries, they leapt heavenward like thin flames; and over the birth of each, Phillis shivered with appeal and longing; and before her eyes the Visions passed. Men they were, who for one hundred fifty years, in stress and striving, continued the vision of Phillis the Blessed. They not only mirrored her soul but illumined the ages. What they became in later years, she in a very real sense, foreshadowed and fore-knew.

With her careful training, her yearning for peace, her obedience to authority and conformity with life, she shared the culture of old New England, and was at home in a world into which her natural disposition fitted. Yet withal she saw its incongruities and contradictions. She was painfully aware that her color set her singularly apart, but she seldom mentioned it. She was aware of slavery but said little about it. She came to know poverty and hardship and in seeking love found death and saw her starving children waste away.

The heaven where she stood as a girl, became transformed in her womanhood. Its golden bar was lowered; happiness poured out, poverty and pain rushed in. Yet she never wavered in the high price she placed on her own womanhood or in her conception of the destiny of her people. Ever she yearned downward to her folk, calling to the skies, the thin flames within their souls.

The reason for this lay deeper than timidity or fear. The world of Phillis Wheatley lay around the American Revolution and the beginnings of a new United States. Black folk of that day were full of hope. The national holiday was the day of dark Crispus Attucks' death. After rebuff, black soldiers had been welcomed into the American armies. Slavery practically disappeared in Massachusetts before Phillis died and the wave of manumission swept south. Soon it seemed, all men would be free and equal.

There came change. There came the death of Phillis Wheatley in 1784, pitiful in her desertion, squalor and poverty; and her dying breath almost swept the face of David Walker even as he was born. He must have been a vision of Phillis the Blessed as she died; the nightmare of that bleak winter of tragedy. Walker never saw Phillis; but he heard of her after he came from North Carolina and conducted his second-hand clothing shop on Brattle Street. He knew that between 1784 when Phillis died and he was born, and 1830 the date of his death, the situation of black folk in the United States changed. It was indeed almost revolutionized. Slavery was no longer dying. It was increasingly excused and defended. For black slaves had become the founding stone of the Cotton Kingdom. The culture of America grew harsher and more vulgar; Southern greed and Yankee thrift on wide rich acres of land and with rich natural resources were beginning to assert themselves and dominate the land. America was no longer Sanctuary; it was becoming Wealth and Power. Restriction and discrimination increasingly surrounded the Negro and the iron entered his soul.

Out of this rose a harsh voice and the voice was David Walker. He shrieked rather than spoke; he stuttered and never sang; yet his reaction to the new-rooted slavery and the growing degradation of the Negro race was so human and natural a reaction, that he must be set down among men who make literature because he so fiercely voiced his day. The thin flame of the soul of Phillis the Blessed became red revolt in David Walker, he whose stilted, hard-born bitterness cried first in the night of the nineteenth-century slavery. David Walker, six feet in height, dark with flying hair, was the voice of revolt; and before Garrison spoke or Douglass pled, he damned slavery to hell in sharp, angry staccato phrase, with italics and capitals, set down in one thin book which scared a whole nation and brought him death. He had neither English nor manners. He had no grace nor comeliness, but he flamed. He said in 1829, "We (coloured people of these United States) are the most degraded, wretched and abject set of beings, that ever lived since the world began, and I pray God, that none like us ever may live until time shall be no more."

He threw the Declaration of Independence in the nation's face. "See your declaration, Americans!!! Do you understand your own language? Hear your language, proclaimed to the world, July 4, 1776, 'We hold these truths to be self evident—that ALL men are CREATED EQUAL!! that they are endowed by their Creator with certain unalienable rights; that among these are life, liberty, and the pursuit of happiness'!!! compare your own language above, extracted from your Declaration of Independence, with your cruelties and murders inflicted . . . on our fathers and on us!"

The South stormed protest and offered rich reward for Walker's silence. But Walker's *Appeal* ran to three editions in seven months. Suddenly he died.

If David Walker was the bitter vision of Phillis' dying breath, it was not the typical vision of her life. That we shall find in the springtime of 1769. She was then a girl of fifteen, timidly straining at her chrysalis; she had begun to study astronomy and Latin. She was essaying poetry and writing of "the happy dead." She dreamed her dream lying on the newborn grass and bashful flowers of a New England spring. Birds sang in the dark branches of the great trees. The song murmured to melody and dance; far away there was gayety and love; the day dream of Phillis became a Vision. She saw New Orleans and heard it as it lived seventy-five years later, in 1769.

It is rather singular that the same movements and forces which were crushing the mass of Negroes, were in one part of the United States far removed from New England, bringing to Negroes and mulattoes the first flowering of literature; and not simply to black America but to white. The free Negroes of Louisiana profited by the slave system despite the pall it laid upon them; they owned slaves and land; some were wealthy land holders; others, well-to-do in professions and as artisans, easily passed into art and literature. They fought bitterly a caste system which bracketed with slaves those who were not slaves, and with Negroes, those who were only in part of Negro descent.

Education and wealth united their tongues to voice both joy and sorrow. They led singing and dancing in Louisiana, France and Spain. In 1840 a group of young Negro writers in New Orleans, secure in income, if not in wealth, and some of them trained in Europe, began to publish their writings, as well as compose music. First came their lovely folk songs like "Pov' piti Lolotte"; and then in 1843 the *Literary Album*, a journal of young folk, amateurs in literature, appeared, written in French. Finally in 1845, under the leadership of Armand Lanusse, there was published the first anthology of Negro verse, and the second of any verse, in America. It was on a literary level far higher than anything produced contemporaneously anywhere else in the land. It was French in language, culture and fashion; and yet, American in content and American Negro. Scrupulously avoiding propaganda and racial consciousness, nevertheless the under-current of its language had to be the American color line and the slave system.

Some of the young men who produced *Les Cenelles*, that is, "The Holly-Berries," as the anthology was called—rank high in French literature; particularly Camille Thierry; but the leader of the group, Lanusse, was born and educated in Louisiana and was the moving spirit of this literary blossoming. He dedicated the beautifully printed volume "to the fair sex of Louisiana," and said:

> Receive these Holly-Berries,
> From our devoted hearts;
> A modest glance from eyes cast down
> Will pay us more than wide renown.

In the introduction he explained: "One begins to understand that in the position that fate has placed us, a sound education is the shield to blunt the arrows of scorn and calumny aimed at us. It is then with a feeling of pride that we see increasing daily the number of those among us who pursue with firm step, the difficult path of those arts and sciences toward which they are attracted."

Seventeen colored poets contributed to "The Holly-Berries" which contained eighty-two poems and covered two hundred fifteen pages. Nothing in American Negro literature would have as completely answered the dreams and aspirations of Phillis' soul and the rare pattern of her culture, as *Les Cenelles* published fifty-eight years after her death.

In the summer of 1763 Phillis was nineteen, and already the cold New England climate had affected her lungs. Her thoughtful mistress took her to England where almost literally she stood before kings. Phillis became a center of aristocratic flattery and attention and published her first book of poems under high patronage. She was there the first of a series of Negro American visitors and must have been stirred by ambition. Standing in the sumptuous drawing-room of the Countess of Huntingdon, surrounded by well-bred and well-dressed people, she would certainly dream of a day when some of these skins would be black—when it would be natural to see folk of all races mingling in a democracy of culture. Standing thus and dreaming, if Phillis could have looked forward eighty years, she would have seen another visitor of England—a young and handsome, curly-haired brown man.

He was William Wells Brown. Born in 1815, and dying in 1884, he became one of the most prolific of colored writers, pouring forth essays, novels and histories. None of his writings were great but many of them were widely read. His novel *Clotelle* was a bold venture and had for its heroine the mulatto daughter of a president of the United States. There is a charming passage in his *Black Man* where he tells of seeing Alexandre Dumas at the opera:

> I had been in Paris a week without seeing Dumas, for my letter of introduction from Louis Blanc, who was then in exile in England, and to M. Eugene Sue, had availed me nothing as regarded a sight of the great colored author. . . . In a double box nearly opposite me, containing a party of six or eight, I noticed a light complexioned mulatto, apparently about fifty years of age—curly hair, full-face, dressed in a black coat, white vest, white kids—who seemed to be the centre of attraction, not only in his own circle, but in others. Those in the pit looked up, those in the gallery looked down, while curtains were drawn aside at other boxes and stalls to get a sight of the colored man. So recently from America, where caste was so injurious to my race, I began to think that it was his wooly head that attracted attention, when I was informed that the mulatto before me was no less a person than Alexandre Dumas. Every move, look and gesture of the celebrated romancer were watched in the closest manner by the audience. Even Mario appeared to feel that his part on the stage was of less importance than that of the colored man in the royal box.

There is a passage in another book, when as a delegate to the great Peace Congress of 1849 held in Paris, Brown was invited to the home of De Tocqueville, Minister of Foreign Affairs, and seated on the sofa by Madame De Tocqueville's side: "I recognised among many of my countrymen, who were gazing at me, the American Consul, Mr. Walsh. My position did not improve his looks."

But I quote from *Clotell*:

> The child, however, watched the chaise, and startled her mother by screaming out at the top of her voice, "Papa! papa!" and clapped her little hands for joy. The mother turned in haste to look at the strangers, and her eyes encountered those of Henry's pale and dejected countenance. Gertrude's eyes were on the child. The swiftness with which Henry drove by could not hide from his wife the striking resemblance of the child to himself. The young wife had heard the child exclaim "Papa! papa!" and she immediately saw by the quivering of his lips and the agitation depicted in his countenance, that all was not right.
>
> "Who is the woman? And why did the child call you papa?" she inquired, with a trembling voice.

Once in a dim and stately Boston library, I can imagine Phillis Wheatley, shrinking from curious eyes, might find herself in an alcove and scanning the volumes she would be startled to see two, strangely almost impossibly, lettered—gold on green. She took a volume down reverently. She saw a steel engraving of the close-cropped hair and strong mulatto face of George Washington Williams. She remembered George Washington. She saw him again with all his aides in military glory as he bent above her dark little hand. She had written to him:

> Where high unfurl'd the ensign waves in air.
> Shall I to Washington their praise recite?
> Enough thou knowest them in the field of fight.
> Thee first in place and honours—we demand
> The grace and glory of thy martial band.
> Fam'd for thy valour, for thy virtues more,
> Hear every tongue thy guardian aid implore!

Washington replied, "However undeserving I may be of such encomium and panegyric, the style and manner exhibit a striking proof of your poetical talents." That was in 1776; but this book, *History of the Negro Race*, was begun in 1876, one hundred years later! Phillis started as she saw its date of publication, one hundred years after her own death. The darkness of sleep fell about her.

George Washington Williams, the first of American Negro historians, was different in thought and kind from Phillis Wheatley. Any vision which Phillis had of him would have been blurred and uncertain. He was a quick, positive, systematic American. I remember seeing him once at the home of a cousin; a rather short man, light brown, with an air of tireless efficiency. This was shown by his monumental history of the Negro race in America. He tells the story of its inception:

> I was requested to deliver an oration on the Fourth of July, 1876, at Avondale, Ohio. It being the one hundredth birthday of the American Republic, I determined to prepare an oration on the American Negro. I at once began an investigation of the records of the nation to secure material for the oration. I was surprised and delighted to find that the historical memorials of the Negro were so abundant and so creditable to him. . . . I became convinced that a history of the Colored people in America was required because of the amply historically trustworthy material at hand; because the Colored people themselves had been the most vexatious problem in North America, from the time of its discovery down to the present day. . . . The single reason that there was no history of the Negro race would have been sufficient reason for writing one. . . . In the preparation of this work I have consulted over twelve thousand volumes—about one thousand of which are referred to in the footnotes—and thousands of pamphlets.

All the while, in these days of Phillis' dreaming, there were ever prophetic whisperings that were hardly voices—never Visions, yet discernible; Jupiter Hammond and George Horton, who put down earnest broken words; Frances Harper, who almost sang; William Nell, who foreran George Williams; and Gustavus Vassa, who started the stream of slave narratives which rose to a flood of protest, plea and threat. The trumpet calls of Douglass and Ringold Ward and the sermons of Crummell rolled back across the years; but they were tuned above the ears of Phillis; they were not literature, they were Life.

From 1774 to 1780, waves of disaster overwhelmed Phillis Wheatley. From the height of favor and restored health at the British Court, she heard of sickness at home and refusing to wait for presentation to George III in person, she hurried back to the death of both kind foster parents. Homeless and aghast, she lived a space alone and with members of the Wheatley family, and then married.

While Phillis never saw among British aristocracy anyone resembling William Wells Brown, when she came back to America, she did become acquainted with the rather unusual figure of John Peters. Little is known of him, and he has been variously and usually rather disparagingly judged. Yet from the scattered facts, the picture of this man is clear. He was one of those atypical men who in the face of public opinion rose above his station and stubbornly clung there in the face of the winds of adversity, perhaps despite his own shortcomings. He was a free colored man who opened a grocery store in Court Street, who dabbled both in medicine and in law, and made a fair living, almost a fortune, for his day. He carried himself as a gentleman of his time: he was handsome and well set-up; he wore a wig and carried a cane; he spoke and wrote with fluency. But when misfortune came, when with dozens of his whiter neighbors he sank beneath the ruin of war and lost his business and his income, he did not surrender; he would not become a servant nor a day laborer. He clung desperately to his role of gentleman and went to jail for debt rather than dig ditches. The world, white and black, snarled and jibed at him.

Coming back from England with the picture of English gentleman in her mind's eye, with the far off vision of what black folk might become even in a white world, Phillis met and was dazzled by John Peters. They were married in 1778 and with his encouragement she planned to publish another volume of poems dedicated to Benjamin Franklin. But before it appeared, misfortune overtook them. The war ruined Peters. They moved out into the country. Two children were born and died. In 1784, Peters was in jail and Phillis laboring as a servant. A third child and Phillis herself died that year.

The brooding of Phillis in those awful days brought out all the contradiction, the clash of religious submission against the self-assertion of revolt. She sang:

> But here I sit, and mourn a grov'ling mind,
> That fain would mount, and ride upon the wind.
> Not you, my friend, these plaintive strains become,
> Not you, whose bosom is the Muses home;
> When they from tow'ring Helicon retire,
> They fan in you the bright immortal fire,
> But I less happy, cannot raise the song,
> The fault'ring music dies upon my tongue.

This friend of poets to whom she sang, sang in turn to a soul not yet born; he was not yet alive; he was not yet struggling with the uprush of song within him. He came to earth seventy-five years later than the day when Phillis, sitting beside the sea, heard it crash and roar against New England rock. Even so the hills and skies of Kentucky struggled in the childhood and youth of Alberry Whitman. This unhappy singer saw poverty like that of Phillis. He became a poor preacher, but above all a poet. He sang because he must; because the repressed flood of song born in Phillis and living again in Lanusse, now raged in him for utterance.

The scene had vastly changed since the day of David Walker. Negroes had begun to find themselves and to act in their own defense. They had fought the good fight of employment, from the decades when Irish mobs of competing laborers beat them to death in Cincinnati and New York, to the reign of the celebrated guild of Philadelphia caterers who founded and introduced a new vocation and a new source of income between 1840 and 1870. Negroes had met in convention, they had published newspapers, they had produced public advocates like Frederick Douglass. They had produced in Whitman, a preacher in the African Methodist Church, an agent seeking to raise funds for the new colored university at Wilberforce, a young man who tried desperately to rise above a limited training, amid the examples of mediocre expression current in America, and enter the stream of real literature.

Perhaps he did not quite succeed. Certainly he never became popular. He died prematurely at the age of fifty in Atlanta, and only through his daughters on the vaudeville stage could his family make a living.

But Alberry Whitman had a real gift of song and his long narrative poems still deserve attention. Stanzas like this, live:

> The tall forests swim in a crimson sea,
> Out of whose bright depths rising silently,
> Great Golden spires shoot into the skies,
> Among the isles of cloudland high, that rise,
> Float, scatter, burst, drift off, and slowly fade,
> Deep in the twilight, shade succeeding shade.

Out of winters of war and disaster, rolled the spring of 1784, the last Spring of Phillis Wheatley. Boston lay still freezing beneath a blanket of soiled snow. Phillis looked out of her attic window on black and staggering buildings, through broken panes and fog. Within was cold and hunger. On a pallet her last child lay dying, moaning and rolling her little head. All others were gone—family, husband, friends. Phillis leaned against the wall back of the bed, fronting the window. Her body was wracked with pain, the child became a gasp. The falling snow without grew whiter and thicker, until it seemed to take the form of Death, Phillis whispered

> O happy Death!

The child died. And it was as if Death took Phillis up into his mighty arms where she lay black and frail with star-shine in her uncurbed hair, with crimson drops on her lips. Her great black eyes were straining upwards:

> Her eyes were deeper than the depth
> Of waters stilled at even.

They grew softer as she glimpsed the starlit heavens above the storm. She saw the white heat of Sirius and remembered her vision of the Bitter Cry; she heard again the Songs of the Lilt of Love, which were the blue stars of Orion's belt; her vision of the Labored Tale came back in red Arcturus, and she read again the Annals in the multi-colored Swan. Crimson Antares was surely the song that broke in Whitman's throat. She sighed and closed her weary eyes, but felt the lightening of the world. Morning was breaking in the east and above it blazed the morning star.

"Am I dead?" she asked.
Death murmured "You shall never die."
"Whose are these stars" she asked.
"They are your children; they are seven."
She shook her head with infinite weariness.
"My children and my dreams are dead."
"The stars are your children; your dreams are immortal."
"What is this last light of morning?"

There loomed behind the fading wraith of Death, the vast black figure of Time, earth-wide and heaven-high. And Death and Time together said:

"In very truth, Charles Chesnutt is child of the tradition and aspiration of Phillis the Blessed. What matter if they lived a century apart?"

Charles Waddell Chesnutt was a white man with Negro blood; a lawyer and court stenographer, born in North Carolina and living most of his life as a distinguished citizen of Cleveland, Ohio. He was born one hundred years after the birth of Phillis. He was first among us to sense the dramatic possibilities of the life of Negroes and mulattoes in America since the Civil War. Chesnutt knew the American public from close social intermingling and intercourse with them, and finally he was master of a clear, trained English style. The result was that his venture in romance, first published in the *Atlantic Monthly*, soon became a series of volumes, treating nearly every phase of current interracial relations. I need not bring notice of these books to your attention. Surely you know them: *The House Behind the Cedars*, *The Conjure Woman*, *The Wife of His Youth*, *The Colonel's Dream*. Perhaps I might pause for a moment to recall one thrilling picture in *The Marrow of Tradition*.

The colored Janet is facing her white sister, who hitherto has ignored her but now begs Janet's husband, a skilled physician, to save her child, speaks:

"Listen!" she cried, dashing her tears aside. "I have but one word for you—one last word—and then I hope never to see your face again! My mother died of want, and I was brought up by the hand of charity. Now, when I have married a man who can supply my needs, you offer me back the money which you and your friends have robbed me of! You imagined

that the shame of being a Negro swallowed up every other ignominy—
and in your eyes I am a Negro, though I am your sister, and you are
white, and people have taken me for you on the streets—and you, therefore, left me nameless all my life! Now, when an honest man has given
me a name of which I can be proud, you offer me the one of which you
robbed me, and of which I can make no use. For twenty-five years I, poor,
despicable fool, would have kissed your feet for a word, a nod, a smile.
Now, when this tardy recognition comes, for which I have waited so long,
it is tainted with fraud and crime and blood, and I must pay for it with
my child's life!"

"And I must forfeit that of mine, it seems, for withholding it so long,"
sobbed the other, as, tottering, she turned to go. "It is but just."

"Stay—do not go yet!" commanded Janet imperiously, her pride still
keeping back her tears. "I have not done. I throw you back your father's
name, your father's wealth, your sisterly recognition. I want none of
them—they are bought too dear! ah, God, they are bought too dear! But
that you may know that a woman may be foully wronged, and yet may
have a heart to feel, even for one who has injured her, you may have your
child's life, if my husband can save it! Will," she said, throwing open the
door into the next room, "go with her!"

So Phillis died in the thirtieth year of her youth, and never saw the
seventh star which was the Song of Songs. She lay stark and stiff, thin
as a skeleton, worn to a shadow, her little dark hands crossed on her
flat chest, clasping three lilies. Her crinkled hair formed a dim halo
about her head. Yet it was even as the crone said, who shrouded her
in white: she did not die; she rose again and lived incarnate in Paul
Laurence Dunbar. Again that soul of song lived in a thin, black body
and behind eyes

> Deeper than the depth
> Of waters stilled at even.

Again there was the same timid sensitiveness, the same restraint;
the same inborn culture. Both souls vainly sought love—she silently
and sorrow-bound, he whipt of the furies; Phillis died choking to sing;
in Dunbar the gift of song was surer, stronger, deeper.

Paul Laurence Dunbar, one hundred years after Phillis' death, became one of the great American poets. As William Dean Howells said
in an oft quoted passage,

Paul Dunbar was the only man of pure African blood and of American
civilization to feel the Negro life aesthetically and express it lyrically. It
seemed to me that this had come to its most modern consciousness in
him, and that his brilliant and unique achievement was to have studied
the American Negro objectively, and to have presented him as he found

him to be, with humor, with sympathy, and yet with what the reader must instinctively feel to be entire truthfulness. I said that a race which had come to this effect in any member of it, had attained civilization in him, and I permitted myself the imaginative prophecy that the hostilities and the prejudices which had so long constrained his race were destined to vanish in the arts; that these were to be the final proof God had made of one blood all nations of men.

Dunbar poems are household words in America: "li'l gal," "Little Brown Baby," "When de Co'n pone's hot," "O Mother Race," and "When Malindy sings":

> She jes' spread huh mouf and hollahs,
> "Come to Jesus," twell you hyeah
> Sinnahs' tremblin' steps and voices,
> Timid-lak a-drawin' neah;
> Den she tu'ns to "Rock of Ages,"
> Simply to de cross she clings,
> An' you fin' yo' teahs a-drappin;
> When Malindy sings.

In one stanza he wrote his own epitaph

> O Earth, O Sky, O Ocean, both surpassing,
> O heart of mine, O soul that dreads the dark!
> Is there no hope for me: Is there no way
> That I may sight and check that speeding bark
> Which out of sight and sound is passing, passing?

And so the story ends and the phantasy is finished. The seven stars have lived and died, if stars ever die; while the tradition of Phillis the Blessed sinks with odor of lilies below the horizon, as her memory rises; Last night and each night:

> The blessed Damozel leaned out
>   From the gold bar of Heaven:
> Her eyes were deeper than the depth
>   Of waters stilled at even;
> She had three lilies in her hand
>   And the stars in her hair were seven.

THE HUMOR OF NEGROES

There is a feeling among most Americans that the Negro is quite naturally and incurably humorous. One has only to see Africa to be cured of this. There is nothing more dignified nor serious than the African in his natural tribal relations. I shall never forget the sight of a Mandingran Mohammedan striding along in his beautiful white cloak and embroidered boots, tall, black and with perfect dignity; or the way in which Black West Africa went to its knees at sunset and bowed toward Mecca. Further down the coast the chiefs of the villages I visited, the porters, the children had nothing of what we associate with Negro humor.

On the other hand in the United States and the West Indies, the Negroes are humorous; they are filled with laughter and delicious chuckling. They enjoy themselves; they enjoy jokes; they perpetrate them on each other and on white folk. In part that is a defense mechanism; reaction from tragedy; oppositions set out in the face of the hurt and insult. In part it supplies those inner pleasures and gratifications which are denied in broad outline to a caste ridden and restricted people. Of course this is not universally so. There is an undercurrent of resentment, of anger and vengeance which lies not far beneath the surface and which sometimes exhibits itself at the most unexpected times and under unawaited circumstances.

In general it would be impossible to classify, without such careful study as has not been possible in my case, the kinds of humor, the variety of jokes which characterize the American Negro. I imagine that in large they would fall in the same general categories with those of people the world over. Certain sorts of humor have been exaggerated and emphasized among Negroes; for instance, the dry mockery of the pretensions of white folk. I remember when a celebrated Texan politician was shouting a fervent oration, two undistinguished Negroes listened to him from a distance: "Who is dat man?" said one. The other looked on, without smiling: "I dunno, but he sutin'ly do recommen' hisself mos' high." Many is the time that a truculent white man has been wholly disarmed before the apparently innocent and really sophisticated joke of the Negro, whom he meant to berate.

Then among themselves Negroes have developed a variety of their own humor. The use of the word "nigger," which no white man must use, is coupled with innuendo and suggestion which brings irresistable gales of laughter. They imitate the striver, the nouveau riche, the partially educated man of large words and the entirely untrained. [Bert] Williams and [George] Walker in their celebrated team work brought this to a high and delicious point of efficiency. Probably the new anthropology will have something to tell us of Negro humor in the future, which will be illuminating and instructive. As it is, one can only say, that to the oppressed and unfortunate, to those who suffer, God mercifully grants the divine gift of laughter. These folk are not all black nor all white, but with inborn humor, men of all colors and races face the tragedy of life and make it endurable.

CHAPTER 5

Politics, Economics, and Education

T he great bulk of Du Bois's writing, especially his many editorials and unsigned short essays for *The Crisis,* is devoted to politics, economics, and education, for these topics were central parts of his every argument for African American civil rights, no matter what the occasion. At the same time, however, many of these writings are also concerned with racial theory, with the cultural continuum between Africa and America, and with human rights more broadly understood. Du Bois wrote alternately and equally well as a sociologist, an economist, a political scientist, an educator, an artist, and a civil rights advocate, and more often than not, several of these intellectual roles were combined in any given speech or essay. That is to say, just as all of Du Bois's work might be called "political," almost all of his political writings have significant other dimensions as well.

Drawn from Du Bois's landmark sociological study *The Philadelphia Negro* (1899), "What Is the Negro Problem?" replies to the late-nineteenth-century white preoccupation with the supposed liabilities of the "Negro problem" by focusing on the economic and political causes of African American impoverishment, unemployment, and broken families. In Du Bois's view, both whites and blacks have parts to play in improving opportunities for African Americans in the urban North, the focus of his study. As a forerunner of the NAACP, the Niagara Movement, founded in 1906 at Harper's Ferry, West Virginia, (the site of John Brown's attack on slavery in 1859), provided an occasion for Du Bois's early statement of principles that were to remain generally unchanged throughout his life. Like the NAACP, the Niagara Movement stood for voting rights, equal protection under the law, social equality, economic rights, and opportunities for equal education. Du Bois's lifelong brief for these conjoined rights took many forms.

"The Training of Negroes for Social Power" was first printed as an Atlanta University pamphlet entitled *The Training of Negroes for Social Reform,* but Du Bois changed the concluding phrase when the essay was published in 1903. Here, as in other essays such as "The Future of the Negro Race in America" (1904) and "The Social Equality of Whites and Blacks" (1920), Du Bois disputed prevailing theories of racial hierarchy and argued that equality had to be achieved through simultaneous activism and education. "Cultural Equality" records Du Bois's side of a 1929 debate in Chicago against Lothrop Stoddard, white supremacist author of the best-selling *The Rising Tide of Color,* who argued that blacks were inferior and should not be granted rights leading to social or cultural equality.

World War I was a great disappointment to Du Bois and other African Americans who had hoped that it would bring about the sorts of reform listed in "Awake America" (1917). In another famous editorial entitled "Close Ranks," Du Bois advocated acceptance of segregated armed forces as a means to achieve the commissioning of black officers. When black soldiers encountered racism in service and violence and job discrimination at home after the war, Du Bois adopted the more militant response that appears in "Returning Soldiers" (1919). Many of Du Bois's most angry writings in *The Crisis* and other magazines were sparked by his reaction to racial violence and the lynching of African Americans. "Triumph" (1911) is characteristic of this work, whereas "The Shape of Fear" (1926) is a more studied exposé of the Ku Klux Klan. Du Bois's anticipation of late-twentieth-century retorts to the dominance of Anglo-European culture in the United States is evident in the brief endorsement of pluralism entitled "Americanization" (1922). "Woman Suffrage" (1915) is one of the several essays Du Bois devoted to the topic of women's voting rights, and one should read it in the context of "The Damnation of Women" and "The Burden of Black Women," those parts of *Darkwater* that constitute Du Bois's most passionate defense of women's social and sexual rights in America and Africa alike.

As Du Bois responded to the Depression's impact on black Americans during the 1930s by turning increasingly toward Marxism, he made voluntary segregation and racial separatism a way to advance civil rights. Although he would ultimately renounce the United States and join the Communist Party when he moved to Ghana in 1961, during the 1930s Du Bois remained skeptical of the solutions offered to African Americans by the Communist Party, a view spelled out in "The Negro and Communism" (1931) and other essays of the period. Separatism he considered to be not an end in itself but a step toward successful integration, a means to strengthen African Americans economically and politically. His reasons for promoting a separatist ideology are detailed in "A Negro Nation within the Nation" (1935), "The Field and Function of the American Negro College" (1933), and "Does the Negro Need Separate Schools?" (1935), the last two essays especially notable for the arguments they make in favor of black colleges and an Afrocentric education. From the 1920s on, Du Bois took an increasingly polemical stance toward the historical and social theories promoted by leading white scholars of the day, and his monumental revisionist text *Black Reconstruction* (1935) included "The Propaganda of History," a scathing attack on the misrepresentation of black life in early-twentieth-century histories of Reconstruction.

The last two decades of Du Bois's life were marked by his increasing participation in questions of world human rights, accompanied by his increasing alienation from his own country and his persecution by the U.S. government for his political activities. In "The Case for the Jews" (1948) and "The Negro and the Warsaw Ghetto" (1952), Du Bois supported the creation of the State of Israel and reflected on the significance of the Holocaust in relation to minority rights. "An Appeal to the World" is Du Bois's introduction to a 1947 document prepared by various scholars that asked the Commission on Human Rights of the United Nations to consider the denial of civil rights to African Americans as an issue of direct concern to the newly formed United Nations. Du Bois's political activities on behalf of the Cultural and Scientific Conference for World Peace and the Stockholm Appeal, the latter a petition to ban atomic weapons, resulted in his indictment by the federal government (the charge of failing to register as the agent of a foreign power, the Soviet Union, was eventually dropped) and led at length to his decision to emigrate to Ghana. Du Bois's frequently expressed opposition to the cold war appears in a much-publicized essay entitled "I Take My Stand for Peace" (1951), and his fervent defense of the totalitarian regimes of the Soviet Union and Communist China, both of which he considered the victims of the United States's cold war ideology, is well represented by his view of China, written soon after a trip to that country in 1959 and later published in his posthumous *Autobiography* (1968).

WHAT IS THE NEGRO PROBLEM?

. . . Two sorts of answers are usually returned to the bewildered American who asks seriously: What is the Negro problem? The one is straightforward and clear: it is simply this, or simply that, and one simple remedy long enough applied will in time cause it to disappear. The other answer is apt to be hopelessly involved and complex—to indicate no simple panacea, and to end in a somewhat hopeless— There it is; what can we do? Both of these sorts of answers have something of truth in them: the Negro problem looked at in one way is but the old world questions of ignorance, poverty, crime, and the dislike of the stranger. On the other hand it is a mistake to think that attacking each of these questions single-handed without reference to the others will settle the matter: a combination of social problems is far more than a matter of mere addition,—the combination itself is a problem. Nevertheless the Negro problems are not more hopelessly complex than many others have been. Their elements despite their bewildering complication can be kept clearly in view: they are after all the same difficulties over which the world has grown gray: the question as to how far human intelligence can be trusted and trained; as to whether we must always have the poor with us; as to whether it is possible for the mass of men to attain righteousness on earth; and then to this is added that question of questions: after all who are Men? Is every featherless biped to be counted a man and brother? Are all races and types to be joint heirs of the new earth that men have striven to raise in thirty centuries and more? Shall we not swamp civilization in barbarism and drown genius in indulgence if we seek a mythical Humanity which shall shadow all men? The answer of the early centuries to this puzzle was clear: those of any nation who can be called Men and endowed with rights are few: they are the privileged classes—the well-born and the accidents of low-birth called up by the King. The rest, the mass of the nation, the *pöbel,* the mob, are fit to follow, to obey, to dig and delve, but not to think or rule or play the gentleman. We who were born to another philosophy hardly realize how deep-seated and plausible this view of human capabilities and powers once was; how utterly incomprehensible this republic would have been to Charlemagne or Charles V. or Charles I. We rather hasten to forget that once the courtiers of English kings looked upon the ancestors of most Americans with far greater contempt than these Americans look upon Negroes—and perhaps, indeed, had more cause. We forget that once French peasants were the "Niggers" of France, and that German princelings once discussed with doubt the brains and humanity of the *bauer.*

Much of this—or at least some of it—has passed and the world has glided by blood and iron into a wider humanity, a wider respect for simple manhood unadorned by ancestors or privilege. Not that we have discovered, as some hoped and some feared, that all men were created free and equal, but rather that the differences in men are not so vast as we had assumed. We still yield the well-born the advantages of birth, we still see that each nation has its dangerous flock of fools and rascals; but we also find most men have brains to be cultivated and souls to be saved.

And still this widening of the idea of common Humanity is of slow growth and to-day but dimly realized. We grant full citizenship in the World-Commonwealth to the "Anglo-Saxon" (whatever that may mean), the Teuton and the Latin; then with just a shade of reluctance we extend it to the Celt and Slav. We half deny it to the yellow races of Asia, admit the brown Indians to an ante-room only on the strength of an undeniable past; but with the Negroes of Africa we come to a full stop, and in its heart the civilized world with one accord denies that these come within the pale of nineteenth century Humanity. This feeling, widespread and deep-seated, is, in America, the vastest of the Negro problems; we have, to be sure, a threatening problem of ignorance but the ancestors of most Americans were far more ignorant than the freedmen's sons; these ex-slaves are poor but not as poor as the Irish peasants used to be; crime is rampant but not more so, if as much, as in Italy; but the difference is that the ancestors of the English and the Irish and the Italians were felt to be worth educating, helping and guiding because they were men and brothers, while in America a census which gives a slight indication of the utter disappearance of the American Negro from the earth is greeted with ill-concealed delight.

Other centuries looking back upon the culture of the nineteenth would have a right to suppose that if, in a land of freemen, eight millions of human beings were found to be dying of disease, the nation would cry with one voice, "Heal them!" If they were staggering on in ignorance, it would cry, "Train them!" If they were harming themselves and others by crime, it would cry, "Guide them!" And such cries are heard and have been heard in the land; but it was not one voice and its volume has been ever broken by counter-cries and echoes, "Let them die!" "Train them like slaves!" "Let them stagger downward!"

This the spirit that enters in and complicates all Negro social problems and this is a problem which only civilization and humanity can successfully solve. Meantime we have the other problems before us— we have the problems arising from the uniting of so many social questions about one centre. In such a situation we need only to avoid underestimating the difficulties on the one hand and overestimating them on the other. The problems are difficult, extremely difficult, but they are such as the world has conquered before and can conquer again. Moreover the battle involves more than a mere altruistic interest in an alien people. It is a battle for humanity and human culture. If in the hey-day of the greatest of the world's civilizations, it is possible for one people ruthlessly to steal another, drag them helpless across the water, enslave them, debauch them, and then slowly murder them by economic and social exclusion until they disappear from the face of the earth—if the consummation of such a crime be possible in the twentieth century, then our civilization is vain and the republic is a mockery and a farce.

But this will not be; first, even with the terribly adverse circumstances under which Negroes live, there is not the slightest likelihood of their dying out; a nation that has endured the slave-trade, slavery, reconstruction, and present prejudice three hundred years, and under it increased in numbers and efficiency, is not in any immediate danger of extinction. Nor is the thought of voluntary or involuntary emigration more than a dream of men who forget that there are half as many Negroes in the United States as Spaniards in Spain. If this be so then a few plain propositions may be laid down as axiomatic:

1. The Negro is here to stay.
2. It is to the advantage of all, both black and white, that every Negro should make the best of himself.
3. It is the duty of the Negro to raise himself by every effort to the

standards of modern civilization and not to lower those standards in any degree.

4. It is the duty of the white people to guard their civilization against debauchment by themselves or others; but in order to do this it is not necessary to hinder and retard the efforts of an earnest people to rise, simply because they lack faith in the ability of that people.

5. With these duties in mind and with a spirit of self-help, mutual aid and co-operation, the two races should strive side by side to realize the ideals of the republic and make this truly a land: of equal opportunity for all men.

The Duty of the Negroes.—That the Negro race has an appalling work of social reform before it need hardly be said. Simply because the ancestors of the present white inhabitants of America went out of their way barbarously to mistreat and enslave the ancestors of the present black inhabitants, gives those blacks no right to ask that the civilization and morality of the land be seriously menaced for their benefit. Men have a right to demand that the members of a civilized community be civilized; that the fabric of human culture, so laboriously woven, be not wantonly or ignorantly destroyed. Consequently a nation may rightly demand, even of a people it has consciously and intentionally wronged, not indeed complete civilization in thirty or one hundred years, but at least every effort and sacrifice possible on their part toward making themselves fit members of the community within a reasonable length of time; that thus they may early become a source of strength and help instead of a national burden. Modern society has too many problems of its own, too much proper anxiety as to its own ability to survive under its present organization, for it lightly to shoulder all the burdens of a less advanced people, and it can rightly demand that as far as possible and as rapidly as possible the Negro bend his energy to the solving of his own social problems—contributing to his poor, paying his share of the taxes and supporting the schools and public administration. For the accomplishment of this the Negro has a right to demand freedom for self-development, and no more aid from without than is really helpful for furthering that development. Such aid must of necessity be considerable: it must furnish schools and reformatories, and relief and preventive agencies; but the bulk of the work of raising the Negro must be done by the Negro himself, and the greatest help for him will be not to hinder and curtail and discourage his efforts. Against prejudice, injustice and wrong the Negro ought to protest energetically and continuously, but he must never forget that he protests because those things hinder his own efforts, and that those efforts are the key to his future.

And those efforts must be mighty and comprehensive, persistent, well-aimed and tireless; satisfied with no partial success, lulled to sleep by no colorless victories; and, above all, guided by no low selfish ideals; at the same time they must be tempered by common sense and rational expectation. In Philadelphia those efforts should first be directed toward a lessening of Negro crime; no doubt the amount of crime imputed to the race is exaggerated, no doubt features of the Negro's environment over which he has no control, excuse much that is committed; but beyond all this the amount of crime that can without doubt rightly be laid at the door of the Philadelphia Negro is large and is a menace to a civilized people. Efforts to stop this crime must commence in the Negro homes; they must cease to be, as they often are, breeders of idleness and extravagance and complaint. Work, continuous and intensive; work, although it be menial and poorly rewarded; work, though done in travail of soul and sweat of brow, must be so impressed upon Negro children as the road to salvation, that a child would feel it a greater disgrace to be idle than to do the humblest labor. The homely virtues of honesty, truth and chastity must be instilled in the cradle, and although it is hard to teach self-respect to a people whose million fellow-citizens half-despise them, yet it must be taught as the surest road to gain the respect of others.

It is right and proper that Negro boys and girls should desire to rise as high in the world as their ability and just desert entitle them. They should be ever encouraged and urged to do so, although they should be taught also that idleness and crime are beneath and not above the lowest work. It should be the continual object of Negroes to open up better industrial chances for their sons and daughters. Their success here must of course rest largely with the white people, but not entirely. Proper co-operation among forty or fifty thousand colored people ought to open many chances of employment for their sons and daughters in trades, stores and shops, associations and industrial enterprises.

Further, some rational means of amusement should be furnished young folks. Prayers meetings and church socials have their place, but they cannot compete in attractiveness with the dance halls and gambling dens of the city. There is a legitimate demand for amusement on the part of the young which may be made a means of education, improvement and recreation. A harmless and beautiful amusement like dancing might with proper effort be rescued from its low and unhealthful associations and made a means of health and recreation. The billiard table is no more wedded to the saloon than to the church if good people did not drive it there. If the Negro homes and churches cannot amuse their young people, and if no other efforts are made to satisfy this want, then we cannot complain if the saloons and clubs and bawdy-houses send these children to crime, disease and death.

There is a vast amount of preventive and rescue work which the Negroes themselves might do: keeping little girls off the street at night, stopping the escorting of unchaperoned young ladies to church and elsewhere, showing the dangers of the lodging system, urging the buying of homes and removal from crowded and tainted neighborhoods, giving lectures and tracts on health and habits, exposing the dangers of gambling and policy-playing, and inculcating respect for women. Day-nurseries and sewing-schools, mothers' meetings, the parks and airing places, all these things are little known or appreciated among the masses of Negroes, and their attention should be directed to them.

The spending of money is a matter to which Negroes need to give especial attention. Money is wasted to-day in dress, furniture, elaborate entertainments, costly church edifices, and "insurance" schemes, which ought to go toward buying homes, educating children, giving simple healthful amusement to the young, and accumulating something in the savings bank as against the "insurance" society ought to be started in the Seventh Ward without delay.

Although directly after the war there was great and remarkable enthusiasm for education, there is no doubt but that this enthusiasm has fallen off, and there is to-day much neglect of children among the Negroes, and failure to send them regularly to school. This should be looked into by the Negroes themselves and every effort made to induce full regular attendance.

Above all, the better classes of the Negroes should recognize their duty toward the masses. They should not forget that the spirit of the twentieth century is to be the turning of the high toward the lowly, the bending of Humanity to all that is human; the recognition that in the slums of modern society lie the answers to most of our puzzling problems of organization and life, and that only as we solve those problems is our culture assured and our progress certain. This the Negro is far from recognizing for himself; his social evolution in cities like Philadelphia is approaching a mediæval stage when the centrifugal forces of repulsion between social classes are becoming more powerful than those of attraction. So hard has been the rise of the better class of Negroes that they fear to fall if now they stoop to lend a hand to their fellows. This feeling is intensified by the blindness of those outsiders who persist even now in confounding the good and bad, the risen and fallen in one mass. Nevertheless the Negro must learn the lesson that other nations learned so laboriously and imperfectly, that his better classes have their chief excuse for being in the work they may do toward lifting the rabble. This is especially true in a city like Philadelphia which has so distinct and creditable a Negro aristocracy; that they do something already to grapple with these social problems of their race is true, but they do not yet do nearly as much as they must, nor do they clearly recognize their responsibility.

Finally, the Negroes must cultivate a spirit of calm, patient persistence in their attitude toward their fellow citizens rather than of loud and intemperate complaint. A man may be wrong, and know he is wrong, and yet some finesse must be used in telling him of it. The white people of Philadelphia are perfectly conscious that their Negro citizens are not treated fairly in all respects, but it will not improve matters to call names or impute unworthy motives to all men. Social reforms move slowly and yet when Right is reinforced by calm but persistent Progress we somehow all feel that in the end it must triumph.

The Duty of the Whites.—There is a tendency on the part of many white people to approach the Negro question from the side which just now is of least pressing importance, namely, that of the social inter-mingling of races. The old query: Would you want your sister to marry a Nigger? still stands as a grim sentinel to stop much rational discussion. And yet few white women have been pained by the addresses of black suitors, and those who have, easily got rid of them. The whole discussion is little less than foolish; perhaps a century from to-day we may find ourselves seriously discussing such questions of social policy, but it is certain that just as long as one group deems it a serious *mésalliance* to marry with another just so long few marriages will take place, and it will need neither law nor argument to guide human choice in such a matter. Certainly the masses of whites would hardly acknowledge that an active propaganda of repression was necessary to ward off intermarriage. Natural pride of race, strong on one side and growing on the other, may be trusted to ward off such mingling as might in this stage of development prove disastrous to both races. All this therefore is a question of the far-off future.

To-day, however, we must face the fact that a natural repugnance to close intermingling with unfortunate ex-slaves has descended to a discrimination that very seriously hinders them from being anything better. It is right and proper to object to ignorance and consequently to ignorant men; but if by our actions we have been responsible for their ignorance and are still actively engaged in keeping them ignorant, the argument loses its moral force. So with the Negroes: men have a right to object to a race so poor and ignorant and inefficient as the mass of the Negroes; but if their policy in the past is parent of much of this condition, and if to-day by shutting black boys and girls out of most avenues of decent employment they are increasing pauperism and vice, then they must hold themselves largely responsible for the deplorable results.

There is no doubt that in Philadelphia the centre and kernel of the Negro problem so far as the white people are concerned is the narrow opportunities afforded Negroes for earning a decent living. Such discrimination is morally wrong, politically dangerous, industrially wasteful, and socially silly. It is the duty of the whites to stop it, and to do so primarily for their own sakes. Industrial freedom of opportunity has by long experience been proven to be generally best for all. Moreover the cost of crime and pauperism, the growth of slums, and the pernicious influences of idleness and lewdness, cost the public far more than would the hurt to the feelings of a carpenter to work beside a black man, or a shop-girl to stand beside a darker mate. This does not contemplate the wholesale replacing of white workmen for Negroes out of sympathy or philanthropy; it does mean that talent should be rewarded, and aptness used in commerce and industry whether its owner be black or white; that the same incentive to good, honest, effective work be placed before a black office boy as before a white one—before a black porter as before a white one; and that unless this is done the city has no right to complain that black boys lose interest in work and drift into idleness and crime. Probably a change in public opinion on this point to-morrow would not make very much difference in the positions occupied by Negroes in the city: some few would be promoted, some few would get new places—the mass would remain as they are; but it would make one vast difference: it would inspire the young to try harder, it would stimulate the idle and discouraged and it would take away from this race the omnipresent excuse for failure: prejudice. Such a moral change would work a revolution in the criminal rate during the next ten years. Even a Negro bootblack could black boots better if he knew he was a menial not because he was a Negro but because he was best fitted for that work.

We need then a radical change in public opinion on this point; it will not and ought not to come suddenly, but instead of thoughtless acquiescence in the continual and steadily encroaching exclusion of Negroes from work in the city, the leaders of industry and opinion ought to be trying here and there to open up new opportunities and give new chances to bright colored boys. The policy of the city to-day simply drives out the best class of young people whom its schools have educated and social opportunities trained, and fills their places with idle and vicious immigrants. It is a paradox of the times that young men and women from some of the best Negro families of the city—families born and reared here and schooled in the best traditions of this municipality have actually had to go to the South to get work, if they wished to be aught but chambermaids and bootblacks. Not that such work may not be honorable and useful, but that is as wrong to make scullions of engineers as it is to make engineers of scullions. Such a situation is a disgrace to the city—a disgrace to its Christianity, to its spirit of justice, to its common sense; what can be the end of such a policy but increased crime and increased excuse for crime? Increased poverty and more reason to be poor? Increased political serfdom of the mass of black voters to the bosses and rascals who divide the spoils? Surely here lies the first duty of a civilized city.

Secondly, in their efforts for the uplifting of the Negro the people of Philadelphia must recognize the existence of the better class of Negroes and must gain their active aid and co-operation by generous and polite conduct. Social sympathy must exist between what is best in both races and there must no longer be the feeling that the Negro who makes the best of himself is of least account to the city of Philadelphia, while the vagabond is to be helped and pitied. This better class of Negro does not want help or pity, but it does want a generous recognition of its difficulties, and a broad sympathy with the problem of life as it presents itself to them. It is composed of men and women educated and in many cases cultured; with proper co-operation they could be a vast power in the city, and the only power that could successfully cope with many phases of the Negro problems. But their active aid cannot be gained for purely selfish motives, or kept by churlish and ungentle manners; and above all they object to being patronized.

Again, the white people of the city must remember that much of the sorrow and bitterness that surrounds the life of the American Negro comes from the unconscious prejudice and half-conscious actions of men and women who do not intend to wound or annoy. One is not compelled to discuss the Negro question with every Negro one meets or to tell him of a father who was connected with the Underground Railroad; one is not compelled to stare at the solitary black face in the audience as though it were not human; it is not necessary to sneer, or be unkind or boorish, if the Negroes in the room or on the street are not all the best behaved or have not the most elegant manners; it is hardly necessary to strike from the dwindling list of one's boyhood and girlhood acquaintances or school-day friends all those who happen to have Negro blood, simply because one has not the courage now to greet them on the street. The little decencies of daily intercourse can go on, the courtesies of life be exchanged even across the color line without any danger to the supremacy of the Anglo-Saxon or the social ambition of the Negro. Without doubt social differences are facts not fancies and cannot lightly be swept aside; but they hardly need to be looked upon as excuses for downright meanness and incivility.

A polite and sympathetic attitude toward these striving thousands; a delicate avoidance of that which wounds and embitters them; a generous granting of opportunity to them; a seconding of their efforts, and a desire to reward honest success—all this, added to proper striving on their part, will go far even in our day toward making all men, white and black, realize what the great founder of the city meant, when he named it the City of Brotherly Love.

THE TRAINING OF NEGROES FOR SOCIAL POWER

The responsibility for their own social regeneration ought to be placed largely upon the shoulders of the Negro people. But such responsibility must carry with it a grant of power; responsibility without power is a mockery and a farce. If, therefore, the American people are sincerely anxious that the Negro shall put forth his best efforts to help himself, they must see to it that he is not deprived of the freedom and power to strive. The responsibility for dispelling their own ignorance implies that the power to overcome ignorance is to be placed in black men's hands; the lessening of poverty calls for the power of effective work; and the responsibility for lessening crime calls for control over social forces which produce crime.

Such social power means, assuredly, the growth of initiative among Negroes, the spread of independent thought, the expanding consciousness of manhood; and these things to-day are looked upon by many with apprehension and distrust, and there is systematic and determined effort to avoid this inevitable corollary of the fixing of social responsibility. Men openly declare their design to train these millions as a subject caste, as men to be thought for, but not to think; to be led, but not to lead themselves.

Those who advocate these things forget that such a solution flings them squarely on the other horn of the dilemma: such a subject child-race could never be held accountable for its own misdeeds and short-comings; its ignorance would be part of the Nation's design, its poverty would arise partly from the direct oppression of the strong and partly from thriftlessness which such oppression breeds; and, above all, its crime would be the legitimate child of that lack of self-respect which caste systems engender. Such a solution of the Negro problem is not one which the saner sense of the Nation for a moment contemplates; it is utterly foreign to American institutions, and is unthinkable as a future for any self-respecting race of men. The sound afterthought of the American people must come to realize that the responsibility for dispelling ignorance and poverty and uprooting crime among Negroes cannot be put upon their own shoulders unless they are given such independent leadership in intelligence, skill, and morality as will inevitably lead to an independent manhood which cannot and will not rest in bonds.

Let me illustrate my meaning particularly in the matter of educating Negro youth.

The Negro problem, it has often been said, is largely a problem of ignorance—not simply of illiteracy, but a deeper ignorance of the world and its ways, of the thought and experience of men; an ignorance of self and possibilities of human souls. This can be gotten rid of only by training; and primarily such training must take the form of that sort of social leadership which we call education. To apply such leadership to themselves, and to profit by it, means that Negroes would have among themselves men of careful training and broad culture, as teachers and teachers of teachers. There are always periods of educational evolution when it is deemed quite proper for pupils in the fourth reader to teach those in the third. But such a method, wasteful and ineffective at all times, is peculiarly dangerous when ignorance is widespread and when there are few homes and public institutions to supplement the work of the school. It is, therefore, of crying necessity among Negroes that the heads of their educational system—the teachers in the normal schools, the heads of high schools, the principals of public systems, should be unusually well trained men; men trained not simply in common-school branches, not simply in the technique of school management and normal methods, but trained beyond this, broadly and carefully, into the meaning of the age whose civilization it is their peculiar duty to interpret to the youth of a new race, to the minds of untrained people. Such educational leaders should be prepared by long and rigorous courses of study similar to those which the world over have been designed to strengthen the intellectual powers, fortify character, and facilitate the transmission from age to age of the stores of the world's knowledge.

Not all men—indeed, not the majority of men, only the exceptional few among American Negroes or among any other people—are adapted to this higher training, as, indeed, only the exceptional few are adapted to higher training in any line; but the significance of such men is not to be measured by their numbers, but rather by the numbers of their pupils and followers who are destined to see the world through their eyes, hear it through their trained ears, and speak to it through the music of their words.

Such men, teachers of teachers and leaders of the untaught. Atlanta University and similar colleges seek to train. We seek to do our work thoroughly and carefully. We have no predilections or prejudices as to particular studies or methods, but we do cling to those time-honored sorts of discipline which the experience of the world has long since proven to be of especial value. We sift as carefully as possible the student material which offers itself, and we try by every conscientious method to give to students who have character and ability such years of discipline as shall make them stronger, keener, and better for their peculiar mission. The history of civilization seems to prove that no group or nation which seeks advancement and true development can despise or neglect the power of well-trained minds; and this power of intellectual leadership must be given to the talented tenth among American Negroes before this race can seriously be asked to assume the responsibility of dispelling its own ignorance. Upon the foundation-stone of a few well equipped Negro colleges of high and honest standards can be built a proper system of free common schools in the South for the masses of the Negro people; any attempt to found a system of public schools on anything less than this—on narrow ideals, limited or merely technical training—is to call blind leaders for the blind.

The very first step toward the settlement of the Negro problem is the spread of intelligence. The first step toward wider intelligence is a free public-school system; and the first and most important step toward a public-school system is the equipment and adequate support of a sufficient number of Negro colleges. These are first steps, and they involve great movements; first, the best of the existent colleges must not be abandoned to slow atrophy and death, as the tendency is to-day; secondly, systematic attempt must be made to organize secondary education. Below the colleges and connected with them must come the normal and high schools, judiciously distributed and carefully manned. In no essential particular should this system of common and secondary schools differ from educational systems the world over. Their chief function is the quickening and training of human intelligence; they can do much in the teaching of morals and manners incidentally, but they cannot and ought not to replace the home as the chief moral teacher; they can teach valuable lessons as to the meaning of work in the world, but they cannot replace technical schools and apprenticeship in actual life, which are the real schools of work. Manual training can and ought to be used in these schools, but as a means and not as an end—to quicken intelligence and self-knowledge and not to teach carpentry; just as arithmetic is used to train minds and not skilled accountants.

Whence, now, is the money coming for this educational system? For the common schools the support should come from local communities, the State governments, and the United States Government; for secondary education, support should come from local and State governments and private philanthropy; for the colleges, from private philanthropy and the United States Government. I make no apology for bringing the United States Government in thus conspicuously. The General Government must give aid to Southern education if illiteracy and ignorance are to cease threatening the very foundations of civilization within any reasonable time. Aid to common-school education could be appropriated to the different States on the basis of illiteracy. The fund could be administered by State officials, and the results and needs reported upon by United States educational inspectors under the Bureau of Education. The States could easily distribute the funds so as to encourage local taxation and enterprise and not result in pauperizing the communities. As to higher training, it must be remembered that the cost of a single battle-ship like the *Massachusetts* would endow all the distinctively college work necessary for Negroes during the next half-century; and it is without doubt true that the unpaid balance from bounties withheld from Negroes in the Civil War would, with interest, easily supply this sum.

But spread of intelligence alone will not solve the Negro problem. If this problem is largely a question of ignorance, it is also scarcely less a problem of poverty. If Negroes are to assume the responsibility of raising the standards of living among themselves, the power of intelligent work and leadership toward proper industrial ideals must be placed in their hands. Economic efficiency depends on intelligence, skill, and thrift. The public-school system is designed to furnish the necessary intelligence for the ordinary worker, the secondary school for the more gifted workers, and the college for the exceptional few.

Technical knowledge and manual dexterity in learning branches of the world's work are taught by industrial and trade schools, and such schools are of prime importance in the training of colored children. Trade-teaching cannot be effectively combined with the work of the common schools because the primary curriculum is already too crowded, and thorough common-school training should precede trade-teaching. It is, however, quite possible to combine some of the work of the secondary schools with purely technical training, the necessary limitations being matters of time and cost: the question whether the boy can afford to stay in school long enough to add parts of a high-school course to the trade course, and particularly the question whether the school can afford or ought to afford to give trade-training to high-school students who do not intend to become artisans. A system of trade-schools, therefore, supported by State and private aid, should be added to the secondary school system.

An industrial school, however, does not merely teach technique. It is also a school—a center of moral influence and of mental discipline. As such it has peculiar problems in securing the proper teaching force. It demands broadly trained men: the teacher of carpentry must be more than a carpenter, and the teacher of the domestic arts more than a cook; for such teachers must instruct, not simply in manual dexterity, but in mental quickness and moral habits. In other words, they must be teachers as well as artisans. It thus happens that college-bred men and men from other higher schools have always been in demand in technical schools, and it has been the high privilege of Atlanta University to furnish during the thirty-six years of its existence a part of the teaching force of nearly every Negro industrial school in the United States, and to-day our graduates are teaching in more than twenty such institutions. The same might be said of Fisk University and other higher schools. If the college graduates were to-day withdrawn from the teaching force of the chief Negro industrial schools, nearly every one of them would have to close its doors. These facts are forgotten by such advocates of industrial training as oppose the higher schools. Strong as the argument for industrial schools is—and its strength is undeniable—its cogency simply increases the urgency of the plea for higher training-schools and colleges to furnish broadly educated teachers.

But intelligence and skill alone will not solve the Southern problem of poverty. With these must go that combination of homely habits and virtues which we may loosely call thrift. Something of thrift may be taught in school, more must be taught at home; but both these agencies are helpless when organized economic society denies to workers the just rewards of thrift and efficiency. And this has been true of black laborers in the South from the time of slavery down through the scandal of the Freedmen's Bank to the peonage and crop-lien system of to-day. If the Southern Negro is shiftless, it is primarily because over large areas a shiftless Negro can get on in the world about as well as an industrious black man. This is not universally true in the South, but it is true to so large an extent as to discourage striving in precisely that class of Negroes who most need encouragement. What is the remedy? Intelligence—not simply the ability to read and write or to sew—but the intelligence of a society permeated by that larger vision of life and broader tolerance which are fostered by the college and university. Not that all men must be college-bred, but that some men, black and white, must be, to leaven the ideals of the lump. Can any serious student of the economic South doubt that this to-day is her crying need?

Ignorance and poverty are the vastest of the Negro problems. But to these later years have added a third—the problem of Negro crime. That a great problem of social morality must have become eventually the central problem of emancipation is as clear as day to any student of history. In its grosser form as a problem of serious crime it is already upon us. Of course it is false and silly to represent that white women in the South are in daily danger of black assaulters. On the contrary, white womanhood in the South is absolutely safe in the hands of ninety-five per cent of the black men—ten times safer than black womanhood is in the hands of white men. Nevertheless, there is a large and dangerous class of Negro criminals, paupers, and outcasts. The existence and growth of such a class, far from causing surprise, should be recognized as the natural result of that social disease called the Negro problem; nearly every untoward circumstance known to human experience has united to increase Negro crime: the slavery of the past, the sudden emancipation, the narrowing of economic opportunity, the lawless environment of wide regions, the stifling of natural ambition, the curtailment of political privilege, the disregard of the sanctity of black men's homes, and, above all, a system of treatment for criminals calculated to breed crime far faster than all other available agencies could repress it. Such a combination of circumstances is as sure to increase the numbers of the vicious and outcast as the rain is to wet the earth. The phenomenon calls for no delicately drawn theories of race differences; it is a plain case of cause and effect.

But, plain as the causes may be, the results are just as deplorable, and repeatedly to-day the criticism is made that Negroes do not recognize sufficiently their responsibility in this matter. Such critics forget how little power to-day Negroes have over their own lower classes. Before the black murderer who strikes his victim to-day, the average black man stands far more helpless than the average white, and too, suffers ten times more from the effects of the deed. The white man has political power, accumulated wealth, and knowledge of social forces; the black man is practically disfranchised, poor, and unable to discriminate between the criminal and the martyr. The Negro needs the defense of the ballot, the conserving power of property, and, above all, the ability to cope intelligently with such vast questions of social regeneration and moral reform as confront him. If social reform among Negroes be without organization or trained leadership from within, if the administration of law is always for the avenging of the white victim and seldom for the reformation of the black criminal, if ignorant black men misunderstand the functions of government because they have had no decent instruction, and intelligent black men are denied a voiced in government because they are black—under such circumstances to hold Negroes responsible for the suppression of crime among themselves is the cruelest of mockeries.

On the other hand, a sincere desire among the American people to help the Negroes undertake their own social regeneration means, first, that the Negro be given the ballot on the same terms as other men, to protect him against injustice and to safeguard his interests in the administration of law; secondly, that through education and social organization he be trained to work, and save, and earn a decent living. But these are not all: wealth is not the only thing worth accumulating; experience and knowledge can be accumulated and handed down, and no people can be truly rich without them. Can the Negro do without these? Can this training in work and thrift be truly effective without the guidance of trained intelligence and deep knowledge—without that same efficiency which has enabled modern peoples to grapple so successfully with the problems of the Submerged Tenth? There must surely be among Negro leaders the philanthropic impulse, the uprightness of character and strength of purpose, but there must be more than these; philanthropy and purpose among blacks as well as among whites must be guided and curbed by knowledge and mental discipline—knowledge of the forces of civilization that make for survival, ability to organize and guide those forces, and realization of the true meaning of those broader ideals of human betterment which may in time bring heaven and earth a little nearer. This is social power—it is gotten in many ways by experience, by social contact, by what we loosely call the chances of life. But the systematic method of acquiring and imparting it is by the training of youth to thought, power, and knowledge in the school and college. And that group of people whose mental grasp is by heredity weakest, and whose knowledge of the past is for historic reasons most imperfect, that group is the very one which needs above all, for the talented of its youth, this severe and careful course of training; especially if they are expected to take immediate part in modern competitive life, if they are to hasten the slower courses of human development, and if the responsibility for this is to be in their own hands.

Three things American slavery gave the Negro—the habit of work, the English language, and the Christian religion; but one priceless thing is debauched, destroyed, and took from him, and that was the organized home. For the sake of intelligence and thrift, for the sake of work and morality, this home-life must be restored and generated with newer ideals. How? The normal method would be by actual contact with a higher home-life among his neighbors, but this method the social separation of white and black precludes. A proposed method is by schools of domestic arts, but, valuable as these are, they are but subsidiary aids to the establishment of homes; for real homes are primarily centers of ideals and teaching and only incidentally centers of cooking. The restoration and raising of home ideals must, then, come from social life among Negroes themselves; and does that social life need no leadership? It needs the best possible leadership of pure hearts and trained heads, the highest leadership of carefully trained men.

Such are the arguments for the Negro college, and such is the work that Atlanta University and a few similar institutions seek to do. We believe that a rationally arranged college course of study for men and women able to pursue it is the best and only method of putting into the world Negroes with the ability to use the social forces of their race so as to stamp out crime, strengthen the home, eliminate degenerates, and inspire and encourage the higher tendencies of the race not only in thought and aspiration but in every-day toil. And we believe this, not simply because we have argued that such training ought to have these effects, or merely because we hope for such results in some dim future, but because already for years we have seen in the work of our graduates precisely such results as I have mentioned; successful teachers of teachers, intelligent and upright ministers, skilled physicians, principals of industrial schools, business men, and, above all, makers of model homes and leaders of social groups, out from which radiate subtle but tangible forces of uplift and inspiration. The proof of this lies scattered in every State of the South, and, above all, in the half-unwilling testimony of men disposed to decry our work.

Between the Negro college and industrial school there are the strongest grounds for co-operation and unity. It is not a matter of mere emphasis, for we would be glad to see ten industrial schools to every college. It is not a fact that there are to-day too few Negro colleges, but rather that there are too many institutions attempting to do college work. But the danger lies in the fact that the best of the Negro colleges are poorly equipped and are to-day losing support and countenance, and that, unless the Nation awakens to its duty, ten years will see the annihilation of higher Negro training in the South. We need a few strong, well-equipped Negro colleges, and we need them now, not to-morrow; unless we can have them and have them decently supported. Negro education in the South, both common-school and industrial, is doomed to failure, and the forces of social regeneration will be fatally weakened, for the college to-day among Negroes is, just as truly as it was yesterday among whites, the beginning and not the end of human training, the foundation and not the capstone of popular education.

Strange, is it not, my brothers, how often in America those great watchwords of human energy—"Be strong!" "Know thyself!" "Hitch your wagon to a star!"—how often these die away into dim whispers when we face these seething millions of black men? And yet do they not belong to them? Are they not their heritage as well as yours? Can they bear burdens without strength, know without learning, and aspire without ideals? Are you afraid to let them try? Fear rather, in this our common fatherland, lest we live to lose those great watchwords of Liberty and Opportunity which yonder in the eternal hills their fathers fought with your fathers to preserve.

THE FUTURE OF THE NEGRO RACE IN AMERICA

There are, as it seems to me, four ways in which the American Negro may develop: first, his present condition of serfdom may be perpetuated; secondly, his race may die out and become extinct in this land; thirdly, he may migrate to some foreign land; and fourthly, he may become an American citizen.

In all history slavery has usually been succeeded by a period of semi-slavery or serfdom. Just how far this is necessary, and how far it is the result of imperfect emancipation, it is difficult to determine. There was a disposition in the United States, for a few years following the Civil War, to insure the complete emancipation of the Negro slave. This was a tremendously difficult undertaking, but not necessarily impossible. The nation, however, quickly tired of the task, and the present state of serfdom ensued. Throughout the United States the mass of the Negro population is curtailed in personal liberty, is insecure in life and property, has peculiar difficulty in earning a decent living, has almost no voice in its own government, does not enjoy adequate educational facilities, and suffers, no matter what its ability or desert, discount, impertinence and contempt, by reason of race and color. To be more specific, it is clear that Negroes are usually unable to enjoy fully the ordinary rights of domicile or of travel, the use of public conveniences, and of many facilities for instruction and entertainment. The black man is in continual danger of mob violence in New York as in New Orleans, in the West as in the South; his economic condition is especially unfortunate; he was emancipated suddenly, without land, capital, or tools, or skill, and generously bidden to go to work, be sober, and save money. And yet his most frantic efforts, under the circumstances, could not save him from sinking into an economic serfdom which, at its best, is organized and systematic pauperism. To turn astray in modern competitive industry a mass of ignorant, unguided working-men, whose employers despise them, and for whom the rest of the nation evinces only spasmodic concern, is to invite oppression. The result is oppression. On the plantation of the southern backwoods the Negro is a peon bound to the soil without wages or rights; throughout the rural South cunningly devised labor laws—laws as to contract and lien, vagrancy, and employer and servant—are so applied to black men as to reduce them to the level of fourteenth-century serfs. In the cities of the South and in the North the color line is so drawn as to increase competition against the Negro, restrict his chances of employment, and lower his labor price, and while agencies for his degradation welcome and invite him, those for his uplifting are closed or coldly tolerant.

In a day when political power is, for weal or woe, so intimately bound up with economic success and efficiency, the Negro is being systematically and quickly disfranchised. Taxation without representation is the rule of his life. In the South he is taxed for libraries which he may not use, for public high schools and colleges which he may not attend, and for public parks where he cannot sit. The fear of political consequences or of labor strikes never deters an employer from discharging his Negro hands or reducing their wages, while that same fear may keep out Negro laborers or lead to the substitution of whites even at an economic disadvantage.

In regard to the present educational facilities of the land only one Negro child in three receives regular instruction, and that for only a few months in the year, under teachers often poorly equipped and sometimes not equipped at all. It is fair to say that less than 20 per cent of the Negro children in the United States to-day are getting good elementary school training. There are a number of poorly furnished high schools for training teachers, and a few institutions doing college work. The only branch of education that to-day can command large and ungrudging support is manual and industrial training, the importance of which, great as it certainly is, is being obviously exaggerated and unduly emphasized at present. If those at the higher schools for Negroes' training should turn their class-rooms into blacksmiths' shops and make wagons instead of making men, they would get far more enthusiastic support. They have not all seen fit to do this—not that for a moment they fail to recognize the importance of wagons or fail to honor the artisan. They simply maintain that there is a place in the world for training men as such, and until the public comes to agree with them they must close their doors.

In this plain statement I am not seeking to minimize the vast efforts put forth for Negro education in the United States; I am simply pointing out that, great as those efforts have been, they are strikingly inadequate, and that under present conditions the majority of Negro children are growing up in ignorance, and without the proper moral and intellectual leadership of adequately trained teachers, ministers, and heads of families.

And finally the whole social atmosphere in which the Negro lives and works, the intangible and powerful spiritual environment of the race, is such as to foster more and more either a false humility or hypocrisy, or an unreasoning radicalism and despair.

This is a condition of serfdom. Its symptoms vary, of course, in time and place; localities might easily be found where certain phases of the condition are better then I have indicated, and others where they are worse. The picture I have painted is perhaps an average one.

Now, I have said that *the first possible future of the American Negro* is the perpetuation and perfection of this present serfdom. This would involve the strengthening of present proscriptive laws, the further disfranchisement of black men, and the legal recognition of customary caste distinctions. This has been the distinct tendency of the South in the last decade, and this program has gained respectful hearing and acquiescence in influential parts of the North.

The question then is: What does such a policy involve so far as the Negro is concerned? If along with the repression and proscription there could be expected cheerful acquiescence in inferiority and faithful work, then this solution would have much in its favor. It is, however, difficult to see how under the long continuance of the present system anything but degeneration into hopelessness, immorality, and crime could ensue. Under modern conditions of life and social and economic organization, a permanent and successful caste system is impossible. The essence of modern democracy is the placing in the hand of the individual the power and responsibility for maintaining his right and liberty; and even in the larger social democracy which we see in the future the corner-stone must be that no social group is to be placed at the mercy of, or in entire dependence upon, the sense of justice of another group. To-day and to-morrow the reduction of a mass of men to permanent or long-continued economic and political inferiority means the deliberate reduction of their chances of survival, and the deliberate encouragement of degeneration among them.

In any social group, however prosperous, degenerative tendencies may always be disclosed. The situation becomes critical and fatal when such tendencies are more manifest than those of upbuilding and progress. Among American Negroes the tendencies to degeneration, while not yet in the ascendency, have undoubtedly been encouraged and fostered by the history of the last two decades. To-day men criticize American Negroes and say that they are not trustworthy—they cannot bear responsibility; they seem lacking in self-respect and personal dignity and in courage; and they have even lost something of the tact and courtesy of their fathers. Now a careful consideration of these defects will clearly show that they are the children, and the legitimate children, of a caste system. What is it that slavery and serfdom have been most assiduous in teaching the Negro if it be not timidity, lack of a sense of personal worth, and inability to bear responsibility, and must not such teaching eventually engender carelessness and lack of courtesy? These men must be ever hesitant as to their rights and duties; in the face of continued disappointment their courage must waver; it is hard to maintain one's self-respect when all the world, even to the urchins on the street, regard you with evident contempt; and self-reliance and persistency must be fed by reasonable hope of success if it is to become characteristic of a people.

On the other hand, those qualities of character which, by four hundred years of persistent artificial selection, have been partially educated out of the Negro are the very qualities upon which the civilized world is putting an exaggerated emphasis to-day. A people without pluck that borders on brazenness and courage akin to brutality is ruthlessly thrust aside, euphoniously designated as "lesser breeds without the law," and is robbed, routed, and raped by every civilized agency from the battleship to the Christian Church.

From such considerations it seems inevitable that the present policy of the nation toward the Negro must eventually result in increasing hopelessness, immorality, and crime. Indeed, it is one of the most curious developments of the present to witness the widespread and touching surprise of the people of the United States at the spread of crime among Negroes. Men shake their heads and say, "How surprising! And such a docile and sweet-tempered race!" And yet is it surprising? If you enslave and oppress a people, ravish and degrade their women, emancipate them into poverty, helplessness, and ignorance, systematically teach them humility in a braggart age—would you expect to develop angels or devils? The Negro criminal has appeared, and Negro crime is spreading. Is this phenomenon a new and peculiar race characteristic, or simply the logical effect of known causes?

Suppose, now, that these tendencies to degenerate among the Negroes gain the ascendency over the persistent struggles of the Negro to rise; suppose that crime and immorality gain such a headway as to check and choke the accumulation of wealth and the education of children—what then?

There seems to be a fatuous and curious notion among some Americans that such a consummation is devoutly to be wished; they discover with evident glee any indication that a wholesale process of degeneration has finally mastered the Negro. But has America no interest—no merely selfish interest—in such an outcome? If men fear with a mighty fear an epidemic of smallpox, or are urged to extraordinary exertions to stamp out yellow fever, can they look with equanimity and lack-lustre eye upon the infection of ten million neighbors with a far more deadly virus? Can anyone but a fool think it is to his interest to make every ninth man in his country a pauper and a criminal, in addition to the growing load of his own degenerates? Not even a rich and healthy land like America could, without imminent and lasting peril, stand the moral and physical shock, the frightful contagion which must accompany the slow degradation and social murder of ten million human souls. Every selfish interest of this land—and I hesitate to appeal to higher motives—every selfish interest of this land demands that if the Negro is to remain there he be raised rapidly to the level of the best culture of the day.

The second possible future of the American Negro arises from the possibility hinted at that the Negro is not destined to remain long in this land. It is the expectation of many Americans, and Americans too of honesty and integrity, that gradually but inevitably the Negro will die out before degeneration sets in to such an extent as to make him a menace to the land. These are the portion of Americans who cannot conceive how the Negro can ever become an integral part of this republic; for the sake of the land, therefore, and the interests of the many, and from no especial dislike or prejudice against the Negro, they hope that the race will either die out or migrate from the land. This is the practical and unemotional way in which the Darwinian doctrine of survival is applied in America to the Negro problem. And I presume it is fair to say that a very large proportion, if not the majority, of the thinking people of America have adopted this attitude.

The question of race and survival which is thus touched upon is of so deep a significance to-day, when European civilization is coming in contact with nearly all the world's great races, that it is of the utmost importance that sane and corrects ideas on the subject should be current among the mass of citizens. To-day this is not the case. On the contrary, there is unfortunately widespread ignorance of the doctrines of race survival and human efficiency current even among people who ought to think more clearly. And this ignorance is helped on by the marvellous ignorance of human history permissible among people called intelligent, among Jingo writers, and the readers of Kipling's doggerel.

In such a way we have come to a more or less clearly conceived public opinion which considers the present civilization of Europe and America as by far the greatest the world has seen; which gives the credit of this culture to the white Germanic peoples, and considers that these races have a divine right to rule the world in such way as they think best. This, I take it, is the creed of most Englishmen and Americans to-day. That such a creed is dangerous and needs the most careful scrutiny and revision is clear from the extraordinary deeds that have been committed under its guidance. The red-handed crimes that to-day may be laid at the door of men who have honestly and sincerely sought to work in accordance with this scheme of survival are enough to cause heart-searching among decent people, not to mention Christians and Christian Churches.

I need cite here but a single case. There lies to the westward of America, in the summer seas, a cluster of islands bursting with beauty and fragrance, with men and women and children neither better nor worse than the average of primitive folk. Some of the grandfathers and grandmothers of present Americans wandered over there with the Bible in their hands and the golden rule of Christ on their lips. They told these children of the sea of Christian civilization founded on Justice and Truth and Right, and then they invited their fellow-citizens to come over and finish the tale. And they came, and with them came land-grabbers, swindlers, and whoremongers, who began the work of robbery and debauchery until finally they suddenly discovered that the God of the Americans never intended islands so sweet and rich for weak-minded immoral Hawaiians, so they stole the soil from beneath the converts' feet, sent their queen wandering on the face of the earth, and gave the booty to America, and America took it. You may dress this tale of Hawaii in the most gracious clothing you can command. You may emphasize the degradation of the nation, the guileless altru-ism of the Americans, and the present prosperity of the sugar-planters; and yet if there sits beyond the stars a God of Justice who metes out to men their reward for murder and theft and adultery, then the blood of this helpless people will rest on America and on its children's children.

This is but one of the many tales of nineteenth-century enterprise in civilizing the heathen, and arranging for the survival of the fittest: West Africa, South Africa, Uganda, the Congo Free State, China, Cuba, and the Philippines are similar chapters. Making all due allow-ance for different ways of interpreting facts, it must be confessed by all honest men that a theory of human civilization which stands sponsor for the enormities committed by European civilization on native races is an outrage and a lie.

But do the theories of Darwin and Spencer, properly interpreted, support any crude views of justice and right and the spread of civiliza-tion as those current to-day? It may be safely answered they do not. Ignorant and selfish interpretation of great sociological laws must not any longer be allowed to obscure and degrade those laws.

First of all, the man of true learning and breadth of views is less sanguine of the overmastering completeness of our present culture, of its incomparable superiority over civilizations of the past. He sees its strength and its weaknesses, and above all he realizes that the one conspicuous triumph of modern culture—namely, the diffusion of its benefits among the lower strata of society—is an accomplishment which is, logically, a flat contradiction to the theory of the natural aris-tocracy of races. He knows that the world has staggered and struggled up to the idea that national welfare is not simply the welfare of a privi-leged few, and he consequently has serious doubts of a theory of races which assumes that white-faced men must inherit the earth simply be-cause they have bigger guns and looser morals, and which forestalls the writhings of other races by branding them as inferior and then sitting on them.

Such a course is not simply arrogant, it is at once dangerous and unreasonable. Why is it that, while European races are at present leading civilization, most African races are in barbarism? This is a question that cannot be satisfactorily and definitely answered. A Greek of the age of Pericles might have put just as puzzling and unanswerable a query to the ancestors of the present Europeans who were crawling about the forests of Germany half-naked and periodically drunk. And the ancient Egyptians in the day of their glory might have put equally uncomfortable queries to the ancestors of the Greeks. Why at certain times in the world's history civilizations have flashed up here and there, have smoldered and died, smoldered and burned anew, while the rest of the world lay still in common darkness, is a mystery which true intelligence frankly acknowledges to be such.

But the failure of complete knowledge here is not denial or disparagement of the great light thrown upon race development by the theories of evolution and by sociological research. It has become clearer to us that races and nations as well as men may be healthy and vigorous, may contract diseases and waste away, may commit sin and pay the penalty. It may easily happen too that circumstances and surroundings which favor one race may be fatal to another. And it is here that those who look for the extinction of the Negro in America may legitimately take their stand. If, for instance, under conditions of civilized life as favorable as ordinary justice can make them, a race of people have not the sheer physical stamina to survive, then, however pitiable the spectacle, there is little that surrounding civilization can do. And it certainly cannot jeopardize the lives and prospects of the great mass of people by efforts to save a doomed remnant. While this is certainly true, it is by no means certain that such a case often occurs. Nearly all the instances of native races fading away on the advent of civilization have been instances where the fading away was easily explicable. If all authority is stripped from a people, their customs interfered with, their religion laughed at, their children corrupted, and ruin, gambling, and prostitution forced upon them—such a proceeding will undoubtedly kill them off, and kill them quickly. But that is not the survival of the fittest—it is plain murder.

Turning, then, to the second possible future of the Negro in America—namely, that he may die out—it must be candidly acknowledged that this is quite possible. If the Negro is given no voice in his own government and welfare, if he continues increasingly to be shut out of employment, if his wages become lower and lower, and his chances of justice and consideration less; if, in consequence of this, he loses hope and lets himself sink deeper and deeper into carelessness, incompetence and crime; if, instead of educating his brains, we get increasing pleasure and profit in making him simply a useful instrument of labor—a mere hand—if his common school system continues to be neglected, if his family life has no respect in custom and little in law, it is quite possible—I might say probable—that the American Negro will dwindle away and die from starvation and excess. This will simply add a few million more murders to the account of civilization. But it would, of course, prove nothing as to the stamina and capabilities of the Negro race.

Such a course of action is to-day impossible, however. The chances are that, along with the repressive, discouraging, and debauching influences, philanthropic and educational agencies will continue their work, and in some degree counteract them. In such event everything depends on the ability of the Negroes to keep up their courage and hope. If they succeed in this, the chances of their dying out are exceedingly small. A people that have withstood the horrors of the African slave trade, American slavery, reconstruction, disfranchisement, the disruption of the family, unhealthy homes, famine, pestilence, and disease, and, above all, the studied, ingenious, and bitter prejudice and contempt of their fellow-citizens, and yet, in a single century, with practically no additions from without, have increased from one to ten million souls, are, to say the least, in no immediate danger of extinction. If extinction comes, it will be a long and tedious process covering many decades, accompanied by widespread crime and disease, and caused by unusual race bitterness and proscription. And during such a process we must always face the possibility of revolt and insurrection on the part of the oppressed.

I was sitting in the Philadelphia depot not long ago with the editor of an influential paper. We spoke of a late riot against Negroes, and he turned to me after several minutes of general talk and said point-blank, "Why didn't the Negroes fight?" I answered, "Because they are hopeful." The Negro knows that in a trial of brute strength the odds are infinitely against him. He still believes, however, that he can in other ways gain success at some time. So long as that hope remains general, there is little chance of widespread degeneration or extinction. But when that hope goes, and in its place comes blank despair, when the desperation of disappointed striving and the mockery of effort seize the millions of black people in this land, no man can answer for the consequences. That seventy-two millions can eventually overpower nine millions goes without saying. But it will cost something.

Suppose, then, that we acknowledge that present conditions cannot continue, that the doctrine of the survival of the fit races is incapable of advancement, or likely with an ordinary chance of living to become extinct in America, there are then left two possible alternatives—the migration of the Negro or his raising himself to full citizenship.

It is the irony of fate that the solution of the Negro problem which would seem in some respects most simple is made complex and improbable by the very theory that most warmly supports it—viz., the theory of race compatibility and relative inferiority. I mean this, the present tendency among civilized nations towards land-grabbing and overawing weaker nations and races makes the possibility of any permanent settlement by American Negroes being left in peace extremely small. Nay, more, the absorption has already gone so far that nowhere is there left in the world a foothold for a new nation; certainly not in Africa, where every inch of soil is claimed, and where the Negro immigrant would only exchange the tyranny of America for the tyranny of Europe, with the additional disadvantage of being further from the ear of the sovereign power.

Moreover, modern methods make it impossible to hold a rich or even moderately rich country without capital to exploit it. Yet the Negro immigrants from the United States must be comparatively poor. Let a gold mine appear in their midst, or an iron mine, or even good crops of potatoes, and immediately some one would hear the voice of God calling him to rescue this beautiful land from the lazy blacks—at a profit of seventy per cent.

If there were a land where Negro immigrants would be welcomed, and reasonably secure of their rights and liberties and of a chance to earn a living, it might and undoubtedly would attract a large proportion of American Negroes. It would, however, attract the very class that America could best afford to keep—the intelligent, the thrifty, those who had some capital and those who had self-respect. In other words, you would skim the cream from the mass, and leave perhaps a worse problem than before.

The hope that an asylum beyond the sea would attract all the Negro population, or that they could be under any circumstances removed *en masse*, is, of course, chimerical. Five hundred Negro children are being born every twenty-four hours in America. To carry these alone out of the country would call for a fleet of a dozen or score of ships plying constantly between America and the African coast. No such stupendous transplanting of a nation has ever been successfully attempted in human history. Six million Negroes were brought to Brazil, but it took three hundred years and cost perhaps ten million human lives. Unless the transportation is to be sheer butchery, the property of Negroes must be bought from them, and those with no property must be furnished with tools and food; transportation across the United States must be given and subsistence while in transport; indeed, it is safe to say that the cost of such an enterprise would exceed the cost of the Civil War, even taking it for granted that the Negro wished to go—and he does not wish to do so. He has sense enough not to jump from the frying pan into the fire, not to give up a fighting chance in America for a hopeless struggle against the combined civilized world. A helpless child may be ill-treated and abused in its own home, but that is little excuse for midnight wandering amid the marauders of the street.

There is left the last alternative—the raising of the Negro in America to full rights and citizenship. And I mean by this no half-way measures; I mean full and fair equality. That is, the chance to obtain work regardless of color, to aspire to position and preferment on the basis of desert alone, to have the right to use public conveniences to enter public places of amusement on the same terms as other people, and to be received socially by such persons as might wish to receive them. These are not extravagant demands, and yet their granting means the abolition of the color line. The question is: Can American Negroes hope to attain to this result? The answer to this is by no means simple. To use mathematical terms, the problem is a dynamic one, with two dependent and two independent variables. Let us consider first the dependent variables; they are the social condition of the Negro on the one hand, and public opinion or social environment on the other. These are dependent variables in the sense that, as the social condition of the Negro improves, public opinion toward him is more tolerant, and *vice versa*, as public opinion is more sympathetic, it is easier for him to improve his social condition. Now, thinkers unacquainted with the problem often see here an easy solution. One says: "Let the Negroes improve in morality, gain wealth and education, and the battle is won." The other says: "Let public opinion change toward the Negro, give him work and encouragement, treat him fairly and justly, and he will rapidly rise in the world." Here are two propositions which contain a subtle logical contradiction, and yet practically all of the solutions of the Negro problem outside the radical ones I have mentioned have been based on the emphasis of *one* of these propositions. From 1860–1880 the United States insisted on the duty of liberalizing the public conscience; from 1880 to 1900 they have insisted on social progress among the Negroes. The difficulty with these propositions is that each one is a half-truth which may under certain circumstances become a flat mockery. I saw once in the Black Belt a tall sad-faced young fellow with a new wife and baby; he had married in the spring and started up in the world with a mule and cabin furniture. But the season was bad, cotton fell in price, and at harvest time the landlord took the cotton and took the mule, and stripped the cabin of bed and chairs and bureau, and left the little family naked to the world. Shall I tell that man that the way to gain the world's respect and help is to rise in the world and become wealthier and wiser? On the other hand, a New York merchant hires a Negro servant; he finds her incompetent, untrustworthy and slovenly; his meals are late and not worth eating when they come; his servant is unaccommodating and sour-faced, and leaves without notice. Is there anything to be gained in telling this man that a more liberal attitude and broader appreciation towards the colored race will make them more careful and deserving? And yet, while taken apart these phrases are half true, if not at times untrue, yet taken together they certainly express a truth—viz., that, given a continuous improvement in social conditions, there will follow increased respect and consideration, and given liberal intelligent public interest, there will be stimulated in any class a desire to be richer, truer, and better. The difficulty is, with the problem stated thus dynamically, to get the double movement started; social condition may greatly improve before public opinion realizes it. Public opinion may grow liberal before men are aware of the new chances opening. And, above all, the continual tendency in such dynamic problems is to a stable equilibrium—where public opinion becomes fixed and immovable, and social condition merely holds its own. That has been the continual tendency with the Negro problem; for a few brief years after the war a whirling revolution of public opinion was accompanied by a phenomenal rush and striving upward. Then the public conscience grew cold, the cement of the new nation hardened, and while in a few brief years we had turned slaves into serfs, we left them mainly serfs, nothing more. In fine there is a great and important truth in the often-spoken-of interdependence of condition and environment in the rise of a social group; but it is no simple thing—it is rather a matter of peculiar subtlety and complexity.

There is a further point: when I said that public opinion and social condition were dependent variables, and varied inversely to each other, it must have occurred to many that sometimes this variable failed to respond proportionately; that an improving people, sometimes far from reaping approbation, reap additional hate and difficulty, and increasing liberality in the national conscience is sometimes repaid by degradation and degeneration. In plainer terms, there is, without doubt, an independent element in these variable social quantities which is above all rule and reason. And in the matter of social condition and the independent variable is the question of the real capability of the Negro race; and deep down beyond all questions of public prejudice. Radical partisans usually place themselves upon these arguments. The radical American Southerner says that back of all questions of social condition lies the ineradicable question of race, and that varieties of the human species so utterly different as the white and black races can never live together on a basis of equality; either subordination or extermination must ensue when they come in contact. The radical Negro, on the other hand, resents warmly any intimation that the Negro race is deficient in ability and capacity compared with other races; he points out that for such differences as exist to-day good and sufficient cause may be found in the slave trade and slavery reconstruction; he insists that every generation in this land has seen Negroes of more than ordinary ability from Phillis Wheatley and [Benjamin] Banneker to Douglass and Dunbar. He thinks that in the history of the modern world Negro genius has shown itself in Pushkin, Toussaint L'Ouverture, and Alexander Dumas, not to mention men whose Negro blood was seldom acknowledged from the time of the Pharaohs to that of Robert Browning.

There are a good many exaggerations and contradictions in the statements made in regard to the accomplishments of the Negro race since emancipation, but it is clear beyond dispute that the Negro has done five things. He has (1) restored the home, (2) earned a living, (3) learned to read and write, (4) saved money and bought some twelve million acres of land, (5) begun to furnish his own group leaders.

There is no way of denying that these comparatively simple things are really extraordinary accomplishments. The Negro home is not thoroughly pure or self-protecting or comfortable, but it is a home created by main strength out of a system of concubinage and amid discouragement and mockery. The living earned has been a poor one, and yet without hesitation, lawlessness, or wholesale pauperism the Negroes have changed themselves from dumb driven cattle to laborers bearing the responsibility of their own support.

From enforced ignorance so great that over 90 per cent of the colored people could not read and write at the close of the war, they have brought themselves to the place where 56 per cent can read and write. Starting a generation ago, without a cent or the ownership of their own bodies, they have saved property to the value of not less than 300,000,000 dollars, besides supporting themselves; and finally they have begun to evolve among themselves men who know their situation and needs.

All this does not prove that the future is bright and clear, or that there is no question of race antipathy or Negro capacity; but it is distinctly and emphatically hopeful, and in the light of history and human development it puts the burden of proof rather on those who deny the capabilities of the Negro than on those who assume that they are not essentially different from those of other members of the great human family.

If such a hopeful attitude toward the race problem in America is to prevail, then the attitude of the cultured classes of England and Europe can do much to aid its triumph. Hitherto English sympathy and opinion has been largely cast on the side of slavery and retrogression. Can we not hope for a change? Better than that, may we not look for an example of large-hearted tolerance and far-seeing philanthropy in the treatment of our brothers in South Africa that may shame the sons of Englishmen in the United States?

THE NIAGARA MOVEMENT

The men of the Niagara movement coming from the toil of the year's hard work and pausing a moment from the earning of their daily bread turn toward the nation and again ask in the name of ten million the privilege of a hearing. In the past year the work of the Negro hater has flourished in the land. Step by step the defenders of the rights of American citizens have retreated. The work of stealing the black man's ballot has progressed and the fifty and more representatives of stolen votes still sit in the nation's capital. Discrimination in travel and public

373

accommodation has so spread that some of our weaker brethren are actually afraid to thunder against color discrimination as such and are simply whispering for ordinary decencies.

Against this the Niagara Movement eternally protests. We will not be satisfied to take one jot or tittle less than our full manhood rights. We claim for ourselves every single right that belongs to a freeborn American, political, civil and social; and until we get these rights we will never cease to protest and assail the ears of America. The battle we wage is not for ourselves alone but for all true Americans. It is a fight for ideals, lest this, our common fatherland, false to its founding, become in truth the land of the thief and the home of the Slave—a by-word and a hissing among the nations for its sounding pretentions and pitiful accomplishment.

Never before in the modern age has a great and civilized folk threatened to adopt so cowardly a creed in the treatment of its fellow-citizens born and bred on its soil. Stripped of verbiage and subterfuge and in its naked nastiness the new American creed says: Fear to let black men even try to rise lest they become the equals of the white. And this is the land that professes to follow Jesus Christ. The blasphemy of such a course is only matched by its cowardice.

In detail our demands are clear and unequivocal. First, we would vote; with the right to vote goes everything: Freedom, manhood, the honor of your wives, the chastity of your daughters, the right to work, and the chance to rise, and let no man listen to those who deny this.

We want full manhood suffrage, and we want it now, henceforth and forever.

Second. We want discrimination in public accommodation to cease. Separation in railway and street cars, based simply on race and color, is un-American, undemocratic, and silly. We protest against all such discrimination.

Third. We claim the right of freemen to walk, talk, and be with them that wish to be with us. No man has a right to choose another man's friends, and to attempt to do so is an impudent interference with the most fundamental human privilege.

Fourth. We want the laws enforced against rich as well as poor; against Capitalist as well as Laborer; against white as well as black. We are not more lawless than the white race, we are more often arrested, convicted and mobbed. We want justice even for criminals and outlaws. We want the Constitution of the country enforced. We want Congress to take charge of Congressional elections. We want the Fourteenth amendment carried out to the letter and every State disfranchised in Congress which attempts to disfranchise its rightful voters. We want the Fifteenth amendment enforced and No State allowed to base its franchise simply on color.

The failure of the Republican Party in Congress at the session just closed to redeem its pledge of 1904 with reference to suffrage condi-

th seems a plain, deliberate, and premeditated breach
stamps that party as guilty of obtaining votes under

\t our children educated. The school system in the
the South is a disgrace and in few towns and cities
ols what they ought to be. We want the national
in and wipe out illiteracy in the South. Either the
'estroy ignorance or ignorance will destroy the

for education we mean real education. We be-
\elves are workers, but work is not necessarily
the development of power and ideal. We want
intelligent human beings should be, and we
inst any proposal to educate black boys and
\d underlings, or simply for the use of other
'o know, to think, to aspire.
:hief things which we want. How shall we
ve may vote, by persistent, unceasing agi-
'ruth, by sacrifice and work.
ence, neither in the despised violence of
:e of the soldier, nor the barbarous vio-
elieve in John Brown, in that incarnate
lie, that willingness to sacrifice money,
altar of right. And here on the scene
econsecrate ourselves, our honor, our
' of the race which John Brown died

\e present, are fighting the stars in
must prevail. We live to tell these
ounsel, wavering and weak—that
omise of wealth or fame, is worth
r the loss of a man's self-respect.
o of this race to cowards and
\ted as men. On this rock we
give up, though the trump of

d it, the present foretells it.
for Garrison and Douglass!
rt Gould Shaw, and all the
: God for all those to-day,
gotten the divine brother-
\or, fortunate and unfor-

of this nation, to those
\d snobbery and racial
\elves worthy of your

All
ght,
ning
and,
rning
rink.

st tradi-
lders of
citizens
t superi-
not that
\ at mere
most folk.
\d act of a
ck.
crimes, as
ly proven.
y. A black
ecessary, as
opportunity
the pretext
crime, made
s, mere mur-
must do.
American cul-
public to read
reat and glori-
mers, toilworn
chforks in their
\pers. Splendid!
its deacons and
? Did they not
Prince of Peace.
\ flames beat and
ed. The scorched

heritage and whether born north or south dare to treat men as me
Cannot the nation that has absorbed ten million foreigners into its p
litical life without catastrophe absorb ten million Negro Americans ir
that same political life at less cost than their unjust and illegal exclus
will involve?

Courage brothers! The battle for humanity is not lost or losing.
across the skies sit signs of promise. The Slav is raising in his mi
the yellow millions are tasting liberty, the black Africans are writ
toward the light, and everywhere the laborer, with ballot in his h
is voting open the gates of Opportunity and Peace. The mo
breaks over blood-stained hills. We must not falter, we may not sl
Above are the everlasting stars.

TRIUMPH

Let the eagle scream! Again the burden of upholding the be
tions of Anglo-Saxon civilization has fallen on the sturdy shou
the American republic. Once more a howling mob of the best
in a foremost State of the Union has vindicated the self-eviden
ority of the white race. The case was perfectly clear; it was
murder had been done, for we Americans are not squeamisl
murder. Off and on we do more of that kind of thing than
Moreover, there was not much of a murder—only the craze
drunken man quite unpremeditated. The point is he was bla

Blackness must be punished. Blackness is the crime of
the opera-bouffe senator-elect from Mississippi has amp
Why is it a crime? Because it threatens white supremac
might—why, civilization might be black! It is therefore n
every white scoundrel in the nation knows, to let slip no
of punishing this crime of crimes. Of course, if possible
should be great and overwhelming—some awful stunning
even more horrible by reporters' imaginations. Failing th
der, arson, barn burning or impudence may do; indeed,

Once the pretext given, then let loose the majesty of
ture. It must warm the hearts of every true son of the re
how the brawn and sinew of Coatesville rallied to the g
ous deed. It deserves a poem; think of the hoary far
with the light of a holy purpose in their eyes and pit
hands. "The churches were nearly deserted," say the p
Was it not fitting that Coatesville religion should lend
Sunday-school superintendents to the holy crusade
choose a noble day? Sunday, the festival of the risen

Ah, the splendor of that Sunday night dance. The
curled against the moonlit sky. The church bells chim

and crooked thing, self-wounded and chained to his cot, crawled to the edge of the ash with a stifled groan, but the brave and sturdy farmers pricked him back with the bloody pitchforks until the deed was done.

Let the eagle scream!

Civilization is again safe.

"Oh, say, can you see by the dawn's early light" that soap box of blackened bones and dust, standing in the dew and sunlight on the King's highway to the City of Brotherly Love, while, as the press reports, "all day long, not only from Coatesville, but from all Chester County, and even from Philadelphia, people walked and drove out to the scene of the burning. Men and women poked the ashes and a shout of glee would signalize the finding of a blackened tooth or mere portions of unrecognizable bones. By noon the black heap had been leveled and only the scorched ground was left to tell what had happened there."

Some foolish people talk of punishing the heroic mob, and the Governor of Pennsylvania seems to be real provoked. We hasten to assure our readers that nothing will be done. There may be a few formal arrests, but the men will be promptly released by the mob sitting as jury—perhaps even as judge.

America knows her true heroes.

Again, let the eagle scream!

But let every black American gird up his loins. The great day is coming. We have crawled and pleaded for justice and we have been cheerfully spit upon and murdered and burned. We will not endure it forever. If we are to die, in God's name let us perish like men and not like bales of hay.

WOMAN SUFFRAGE

This month 200,000 Negro voters will be called upon to vote on the question of giving the right of suffrage to women. *The Crisis* sincerely trusts that everyone of them will vote *Yes*. But *The Crisis* would not have them go to the polls without having considered every side of the question. Intelligence in voting is the only real support of democracy. For this reason we publish with pleasure Dean Kelly Miller's article against woman suffrage. We trust that our readers will give it careful attention and that they will compare it with that marvelous symposium which we had the pleasure to publish in our August number. Meantime, Dean Miller will pardon us for a word in answer to his argument.

Briefly put, Mr. Miller believes that the bearing and rearing of the young is a function which makes it practically impossible for women to take any large part in general, industrial and public affairs; that women are weaker than men; that women are adequately protected under man's suffrage; that no adequate results have appeared from woman suffrage and that office-holding by women is "risky."

All these arguments sound today ancient. If we turn to easily available statistics we find that instead of the women of this country or of any other country being confined chiefly to child-bearing they are as a matter of fact engaged and engaged successfully in practically every pursuit in which men are engaged. The actual work of the world today depends more largely upon women than upon men. Consequently this man-ruled world faces an astonishing dilemma: either Woman the Worker is doing the world's work successfully or not. If she is not doing it well why do we not take from her the necessity of working? If she is doing it well why not treat her as a worker with a voice in the direction of work?

The statement that woman is weaker than man is sheer rot: It is the same sort of thing that we hear about "darker races" and "lower classes." Difference, either physical or spiritual, does not argue weakness or inferiority. That the average woman is spiritually different from the average man is undoubtedly just as true as the fact that the average white man differs from the average Negro; but this is no reason for disfranchising the Negro or lynching him. It is inconceivable that any person looking upon the accomplishments of women today in every field of endeavor, realizing their humiliating handicap and the astonishing prejudices which they face and yet seeing despite this that in government, in the professions, in sciences, art and literature and the industries they are leading and dominating forces and growing in power as their emancipation grows,—it is inconceivable that any fair-minded person could for a moment talk about a "weaker" sex. The sex of Judith, Candace, Queen Elizabeth, Sojourner Truth and Jane Addams was the merest incident of human function and not a mark of weakness and inferiority.

To say that men protect women with their votes is to overlook the flat testimony of the facts. In the first place there are millions of women who have no natural men protectors: the unmarried, the widowed, the deserted and those who have married failures. To put this whole army incontinently out of court and leave them unprotected and without voice in political life is more than unjust, it is a crime.

There was a day in the world when it was considered that by marriage a woman lost all her individuality as a human soul and simply became a machine for making men. We have outgrown that idea. A woman is just as much a thinking, feeling, acting person after marriage as before. She has opinions and she has a right to have them and she has a right to express them. It is conceivable, of course, for a country to decide that its unit of representation should be the family and that one person in that family should express its will. But by what possible process of rational thought can it be decided that the person to express that will should always be the male, whether he be genius or drunkard, imbecile or captain of industry? The meaning of the twentieth century is the freeing of the individual soul; the soul longest in slavery and still in the most disgusting and indefensible slavery is the soul of womanhood. . . .

AWAKE AMERICA

Let us enter this war for Liberty with clean hands. May no blood-smeared garments bind our feet when we rise to make the world safe for Democracy. The New Freedom cannot survive if it means Waco, Memphis and East St. Louis. We cannot lynch 2,867 untried black men and women in thirty-one years and pose successfully as leaders of civilization. Rather let us bow our shamed heads and in sack cloth and ashes declare that when in awful war we raise our weapons against the enemies of mankind, so, too, and in that same hour here at home we raise our hands to Heaven and pledge our sacred honor to make our own America a real land of the free:

To stop lynching and mob violence.

To stop disfranchisement for race and sex.

To abolish Jim Crow cars.

To resist the attempt to establish an American ghetto.

To stop race discrimination in Trade Unions, in Civil Service, in places of public accommodation, and in the Public School.

To secure Justice for all men in the courts.

To insist that individual desert and ability shall be the test of real American manhood and not adventitious differences of race or color or descent.

Awake! Put on they strength, America—put on thy beautiful robes. Become not a bye word and jest among the nations by the hypocrisy of your word and contradiction of your deeds. Russia has abolished the ghetto—shall we restore it? India is overthrowing caste—shall we upbuild it? China is establishing democracy—shall we strengthen our Southern oligarchy?

In five wars and now the sixth we black men have fought for your freedom and honor. Wherever the American flag floats today, black hands have helped to plant it. American Religion, American Industry, American Literature, American Music and American Art are as much the gift of the American Negro as of the American white man. This is as much our country as yours, and as much the world's as ours. We Americans, black and white, are the servants of all mankind and ministering to a greater, fairer heaven. Let us be true to our mission. No land that loves to lynch "niggers" can lead the hosts of Almighty God.

RETURNING SOLDIERS

We are returning from war! THE CRISIS and tens of thousands of black men were drafted into a great struggle. For bleeding France and what she means and has meant and will mean to us and humanity and against the threat of German race arrogance, we fought gladly and to the last drop of blood: for America and her highest ideals, we fought in far-off hope: for the dominant southern oligarchy entrenched in Washington, we fought in bitter resignation. For the America that represents and gloats in lynching, disfranchisement, caste, brutality and devilish insult—for this, in the hateful upturning and mixing of things, we were forced by vindictive fate to fight, also.

But today we return! We return from the slavery of uniform which the world's madness demanded us to don to the freedom of civil garb. We stand again to look America squarely in the face and call a spade a spade. We sing: This country of ours, despite all its better souls have done and dreamed, is yet a shameful land.

It *lynches*.

And lynching is barbarism of a degree of contemptible nastiness unparalleled in human history. Yet for fifty years we have lynched two Negroes a week, and we have kept this up right through the war.

It *disfranchises* its own citizens.

Disfranchisement is the deliberate theft and robbery of the only protection of poor against rich and black against white. The land that disfranchises its citizens and calls itself a democracy lies and knows it lies.

It encourages *ignorance*.

It has never really tried to educate the Negro. A dominant minority does not want Negroes educated. It wants servants, dogs, whores and monkeys. And when this land allows a reactionary group by its stolen political power to force as many black folk into these categories as it possibly can, it cries in contemptible hypocrisy: "They threaten us with degeneracy; they cannot be educated."

It *steals* from us.

It organizes industry to cheat us. It cheats us out of our land; it cheats us out of our labor. It confiscates our savings. It reduces our wages. It raises our rent. It steals our profit. It taxes us without representation. It keeps us consistently and universally poor, and then feeds us on charity and derides our poverty.

It *insults* us.

It has organized a nation-wide and latterly a world-wide propaganda of deliberate and continuous insult and defamation of black blood wherever found. It decrees that it shall not be possible in travel nor residence, work nor play, education nor instruction for a black man to exist without tacit or open acknowledgement of his inferiority to the dirtiest white dog. And it looks upon any attempt to question or even discuss this dogma as arrogance, unwarranted assumption and treason.

This is the country to which we Soldiers of Democracy return. This is the fatherland for which we fought! But it is *our* fatherland. It was right for us to fight. The faults of *our* country are *our* faults. Under similar circumstances, we would fight again. But by the God of Heaven, we are cowards and jackasses if now that that war is over, we do not marshal every ounce of our brain and brawn to fight a sterner, longer, more unbending battle against the forces of hell in our own land.

We *return*.

We *return from fighting*.

We *return fighting*.

Make way for Democracy! We saved it in France, and by the Great Jehovah, we will save it in the United States of America, or know the reason why.

THE SOCIAL EQUALITY OF WHITES AND BLACKS

When The National Association for the Advancement of Colored People was organized it seemed to us that the subject of "social equality" between races was not one that we need touch officially whatever our private opinions might be. We announced clearly our object as being the political and civil rights of Negroes and this seemed to us a sufficiently clear explanation of our work.

We soon found, however, certain difficulties: Was the right to attend a theatre a civil or a social right? Is a hotel a private or a public institution? What should be our stand as to public travel or public celebrations or public dinners to discuss social uplift? And above all, should we be silent when laws were proposed taking away from a white father all legal responsibility for his colored child?

Moreover, no matter what our attitude, acts and clear statements have been, we were continually being "accused" of advocating "social equality" and back of the accusations were implied the most astonishing assumptions: our secretary was assaulted in Texas for "advocating social equality" when in fact he was present to prove that we were a legal organization under Texas law. Attempts were made in North Carolina to forbid a state school from advertising in our organ THE CRISIS on the ground that "now and then it injects a note of social equality" and in general we have seen theft, injustice, lynchings, riot and murder based on "accusations" or attempts at "social equality."

The time has, therefore, evidently come for THE CRISIS to take a public stand on this question in the interest of Justice and clear thinking. Let us openly define our terms and beliefs and let there be no further unjustifiable reticence on our part or underground skulking by enemies of the Negro race. This statement does not imply any change of attitude on our part; it simply means a clear and formal expression on matters which hitherto we have mistakenly assumed were unimportant in their relation to our main work.

We make this statement, too, the more willingly because recent events lead us to realize that there lurks in the use and the misuse of the phrase "social equality" much of the same virus that for thousands of years has separated and insulted and injured men of many races and groups and social classes.

We believe that social equality, by a reasonable interpretation of the words, means moral, mental and physical fitness to associate with one's fellowmen. In this sense THE CRISIS believes absolutely in the Social Equality of the Black and White and Yellow races and it believes too that any attempt to deny this equality by law or custom is a blow at Humanity, Religion and Democracy.

No sooner is this incontestable statement made, however, than many minds immediately adduce further implications: they say that such a statement and belief implies the right of black folk to force themselves into the private social life of whites and to intermarry with them.

This is a forced and illogical definition of social equality. Social equals, even in the narrowest sense of the term, do not have the *right* to be invited to, or attend private receptions, or to marry persons who do not wish to marry them. Such a right would imply not mere equality—it would mean superiority. Such rights inhere in reigning monarchs in certain times and countries, but no man, black or white, ever dreamed of claiming a right to invade the private social life of any man.

On the other hand, every self-respecting person does claim the right to mingle with his fellows *if he is invited* and to be free from insult or hindrance because of his presence. When, therefore, the public is invited, or when he is privately invited to social gatherings, the Negro has a right to accept and no other guest has a right to complain: they have only the right to absent themselves. The late Booker T. Washington could hardly be called an advocate of "social equality" in any sense and yet he repeatedly accepted invitations to private and public functions and certainly had the right to.

To the question of intermarriage there are three aspects:

1. The individual right
2. The social expediency
3. The physical result

As to the individual right of any two sane grown individuals of any race to marry there can be no denial in any civilized land. The moral results of any attempt to deny this right are too terrible and of this the southern United States is an awful and abiding example. Either white people and black people want to mingle sexually or they do not. If they do, no law will stop them and attempted laws are cruel, inhuman and immoral. If they do not, no laws are necessary.

But above the individual problem lies the question of the social expediency of the intermarriage of whites and blacks today in America. The answer to this is perfectly clear: it is not socially expedient today for such marriages to take place; the reasons are evident: where there are great differences of ideal, culture, taste and public esteem, the intermarriage of groups is unwise because it involves too great a strain to evolve a compatible, agreeable family life and to train up proper children. On this point there is almost complete agreement among colored and white people and the strong opinion here is not only that of the whites—it is the growing determination of the blacks to accept no alliances so long as there is any shadow of condescension; and to build a great black race tradition of which the Negro and the world will be as proud in the future as it has been in the ancient world.

THE CRISIS, therefore, most emphatically advises against race intermarriage in America but it does so while maintaining the moral and legal right of individuals who may think otherwise and it most emphatically refuses to base its opposition on other than social grounds.

THE CRISIS does not believe, for instance, that the intermarriage of races is physically criminal or deleterious. The overwhelming weight of scientific opinion and human experience is against this assumption and it is a cruel insult to seek to transmute a perfectly permissible social taste or thoughtful social advice into a confession or accusation of physical inferiority and contamination.

To sum up then: THE CRISIS advises strongly against interracial marriage in the United States today because of social conditions and prejudice and not for physical reasons; at the same time it maintains absolute legal right of such marriage for such as will, for the simple reason that any other solution is immoral and dangerous.

THE CRISIS does not for a moment believe that any man has a right to force his company on others in their private lives but it maintains just as strongly that the right of any man to associate privately with those who wish to associate with him and publicly with anybody so long as he conducts himself gently, is the most fundamental right of a Human Being.

AMERICANIZATION

We are far from forgetting the gift of New England to America and in particular the gift of New England to the American Negro, but we

cannot fail to foresee that today the same dry rot of aristocracy is entering New England and Harvard that has ruined in other days the aristocracies of the world. What we think we mean by Americanization is
the making of this country one great homogeneous whole working for
the same ideals, defending its integrity, preserving its hard found liberty. As a matter of fact what the powerful and the privileged mean by
Americanization is the determination to make the English New England stock dominant in the United States, and to make it dominate
not only in its fine language and democratic ideals and freedom of
thought, but in any modern narrowing and contradiction and denial of
these older ideals which newer and lesser men may bring. It is but a
renewal of the Anglo-Saxon cult; the worship of the Nordic totem, the
disfranchisement of Negro, Jew, Irishman, Italian, Hungarian, Asiatic
and South Sea islander—the world rule of Nordic white through brute
force.

Others may come in but only as dumb laborers or silent witnesses
or as those willing to surrender their will and deeds to the glory of the
"Anglo-Saxon"! And yet, the majority of people in the United States
are not of English descent. They admire much that England has done,
they criticise and hate other things. They propose that America shall
be a land for American development and that into that development
shall grow many different roots. They do not propose that New England thought, past or present, shall dominate American future. They
do not propose that America shall be a colony of England. They see
England today, despite her splendid past, as one of the great foes of
human liberty, and they do not propose that this power shall be felt
this side the water.

It is this feeling that is making in the vast empire of the Middle
West, centers of thought and effort diametrically opposed politically,
economically, socially, to New England and the Atlantic coast. It is the
fight against this new strong development of Americanism of the Middle West that is slowly, but surely uniting New England with the
South; because, after all, the white South is "pure" Anglo-Saxon, despite the fact that it is so widely degraded, reactionary, and without
art, literature or humanitarian impulse. Neither side in this vast developing controversy loves Jew or Negro or Irishman as such. But the
West has a vision of Democracy that reaches beyond Englishmen or
New Englander. Moreover the West is not blind. The same forces
south and east that are fighting democracy in the United States are
fighting black men and fighting Jews. The great alliance then between
the darker people the world over, between disadvantaged groups like
the Irish and the Jew and between the working classes everywhere is
the one alliance that is going to keep down privilege as represented by
New England and old England.

THE SHAPE OF FEAR

Faced by the fact of the Ku Klux Klan, the United States has tried to get rid of it by laughing it off. We have talked of masquerading "in sheets and pillow cases"; we have caricatured the Klan upon the stage; we have exposed its silly methods, the dishonesty of some of its leaders, and the like. But we have not succeeded in scaring it away by ridicule. It is there. It is a fact, and those who do not wish to believe the sinister meaning of its existence should go to the nearest movie and see that Washington parade, that tremendous outpouring of hosts, white-gowned and hooded if not masked.

It is quite beside the point to compare the present Ku Klux Klan with the Ku Klux Klan of Reconstruction days. They have nothing in common except their birthplace and their methods. The present Klan is a different movement from the older Klan. It has simply made the older movement's name its present starting point.

Until last year I was of those mildly amused at the K. K. K. It seemed to me incredible that in 1925 such a movement could attract any number of people or become really serious. And then at first hand and at second I saw the Klan and its workings in widely different places. I was lecturing in Akron, Ohio. Now Ohio is one of those States upon whose essential Americanism and devotion to the finer ideals of democracy I have long banked. There in the Middle West that finer flower of democracy, born in New England, and later choked by the industrialism of the East, had, to my mind, gone for replanting and renewal. I looked for sanity in the United States to come from a democratic appeal to the Middle West. And yet, there in Akron, in the land of Joshua R. Giddings, in the Western Reserve, I found the Klan calmly and openly in the saddle. The leader of the local Klan was president of the Board of Education and had just been tremendously busied in driving a Jew out of the public schools. The Mayor, the secretary of the Y.M.C.A., prominent men in many walks of life, were either open Klansmen or secret sympathizers. I was too astonished to talk. Throughout parts of Ohio, Illinois and Indiana I found a similar state of affairs.

I am not saying that the Klan was triumphant everywhere, but it was there; it was influential; it was recognized; it was important. Again, and further west, the work of the Klan has been manifest. To-day there are under arrest at Detroit, Michigan, a young colored physician, well-trained and successful; his wife, torn from her infant child, and nine of his friends; and they are on trial for murder in the first degree because they shot at the mob that tried to drive them out of their own homes and that had a few months before driven out another Negro physician and destroyed his furniture; and that mob was there because the Ku Klux Klan aroused it and sent it; and the Ku Klux Klan is so tremendous a power in that city which is, in some ways, the most significant of American cities, that the Mayor is openly appealing against its activities.

Or again: the National Association for the Advancement of Colored People held its annual meeting in May, 1925, in Denver, and there appeared before it two speakers: one, a little man, nervous with energy and shrill of speech. He was, without doubt, one of the dozen notable figures which America has given to the world, Ben Lindsay, the maker of the Children's Court. The other had been one of the most successful and enlightened Governors in America. And yet they stood speaking in self-defense; defending themselves against this city and this State; and the great, dark, menacing thing that turned them from social uplift and political reform was the Ku Klux Klan.

In the East, New England and New Jersey, the Klan has been mobilized; and need one mention the South?

What is the cause of all this? There can be little doubt but that the Klan in its present form is a legacy of the World War. Whatever there was of it before that great catastrophe was negligible and of little moment. The wages of War is Hate; and the End, and indeed the Beginning, of Hate is Fear. The civilized world today and the world half-civilized and uncivilized are desperately afraid. The Shape of Fear looms over them. Germany fears the Jew, England fears the Indian; America fears the Negro, the Christian fears the Moslem, Europe fears Asia, Protestant fears Catholic, Religion fears Science. Above all, Wealth fears Democracy. These fears and others are ancient or at least long-standing fears. But they are renewed and revivified today because the world has at present a severe case of nerves; it feels it necessary to be nervous because the Unexpected has happened.

For years we talked of the possibility of European War with bated breath; then we talked of it jauntily; and then we almost joked about it. While here was a Fear, it was one so far away that it did not seem possible for it ever to materialize, at least not in our day. And then suddenly it became a terrible fact, horrible beyond the dream of men. So that all our other fears today have become portentous. Abd-el Krim may be the vanguard of the launching of Asia against Europe; Gandhi and Das may be at the point of destroying the British Empire; the American Negro, despite all precautions, may force himself into a place where he will enter Congress, storm Wall Street and marry white women.

Now against such fears as these there are three possible attitudes. One is the attitude of reason and examination. What does the ferment in the colored world mean and how far is our fear of it but a reflex of its fear of us? What do colored folk really want, and do their wants interfere with and oppose the just desires of the white world? How far is free, scientific inquiry going to undermine religious sanction? What is there in the objects of the Bolsheviki which should not appear in the objects of American social reformers? These questions indicate one attitude, mental, moral and practical, toward great pending questions; but it is not the attitude which we are disposed to take today in the world.

On the contrary so imminent does our danger seem to some people that they turn to one of two other methods. They are both forms of Force; one an open appeal to force; Fascismo, either in its bold, physical form as it is appearing in Italy and Spain or in its more spiritual form as it appears in American Fundamentalism; in the determination to drive out of the Church every person who will not honestly or by perjury subscribe to a certain, narrow, outworn and partially false creed.

The other method is the method of Force which hides itself in secrecy, and that is the method of the Ku Klux Klan. It is a method as old as humanity. The kind of thing which men are afraid or ashamed to do openly and by day, they accomplish secretly, masked and at night. The method has certain advantages. It uses Fear to cast out Fear; it dares things at which open methods hesitate; it may with a certain impunity attack the high and the low; it need hesitate at no outrage of maiming or murder; it shields itself in the mob mind and then throws over all a veil of darkness which becomes glamor. It attracts people who otherwise could not be reached. It harnesses the mob.

How is it that men who want certain things done by brute force can so often depend upon the mob? Total depravity, human hate and *schadenfreude*, do not explain fully the mob spirit in this land. Before the wide eyes of the mob is ever the Shape of Fear. Back of the writhing, yelling, cruel-eyed demons who break, destroy, maim and lynch and burn at the stake is a knot, large or small, of normal human beings and these human beings at heart are desperately afraid of something. Of what? of many things but usually of losing their jobs, of being declassed, degraded or actually disgraced; of losing their hopes, their savings, their plans for their children; of the actual pangs of hunger; of dirt, of crime. And of all this, most ubiquitous in modern industrial society is that fear of unemployment.

It is this nucleus of ordinary men that continually gives the mob its initial and awful impetus. Around this nucleus, to be sure, gather snowball-wise all manner of flotsam, filth and human garbage and every inhibition of alcohol and current fashion. But all this is the horrible covering of this inner nucleus of Fear.

How then is the mob to be met and quelled? If it represents public opinion, even passing, passionate public opinion, it cannot permanently be put down by the police which public opinion appoints and pays. Three methods of quelling the mob are at hand, analogous to the three attitudes noted above: the first, by proving to its human, honest nucleus that the Fear is false, ill-grounded, unnecessary; or secondly, if its Fear is true or apparently or partially true, by attacking the fearful thing openly either by the organized police power or by frank civil war as did Mussolini and George Washington; or thirdly, by secret, hidden and underground ways, the method of the Ku Klux Klan.

Why do we not take the first way? Because this is a world that believes in War and Ignorance and has no hope in our day of realizing an intelligent majority of men and Peace on Earth. There are many, many exceptions but in general it is true that there is scarcely a Bishop in Christiandom, a priest in New York, a President, Governor, mayor or legislator in the United States, a college professor or public school teacher who does not in the end stand by War and Ignorance as the main method for the settlement of our pressing human problems. And this despite the fact that they may deny it with their mouths every day.

But here again open civil war like Italy's is difficult, costly and hard to guide. The Right toward which it aims must be made obvious even if it is Wrong. In 1918 in order to win the war we *had* to make Germans into Huns and rapists. Today we *have* to make Negroes into rapists and idiots. Tomorrow we *must* make Latins, South-Eastern Europeans, Turks and other Asiatics into actual "lesser breeds without the law." Some seem to see today anti-Christ in Catholicism, and in Jews, international plotters of the Protocol. Even if these things be true it is difficult to bring the truth clearly before the ignorant mob and guide it toward the overthrow of evil. But if these be half true or wholly false, the mob can only be stirred by wholesale lying, and this is costly; or by secret underground whispering, the methods of night and mask, the psychology of vague and unknown ill, the innuendo that cannot be answered.

Now there are two things that stand out in this explanation of the mob and the Klan. First, the double tongues of our leaders in religion and social uplift; and secondly, this fear of losing jobs. Dayton, Tennessee brought the first vividly to our minds. We heard of a sudden, people talking a religious *patois* which educated folk had well nigh forgotten: Biblical Truth; the Plan of Salvation; the Blood of Christ. And suddenly we began to see what results widespread ignorance of modern science not only had brought but could bring under the leadership of the demagogue. It sent a thrill of amazement through us.

But whom had we to blame? Manifestly, not the farmers and shopkeepers of Tennessee, but those intellectual leaders of the United States who have been willing to subscribe to a religious dogma that they did not honestly believe and yet which they were willing that the mass of people should think they were believing. Was there any surer way of destroying the ability of the Man of the Street to think straight and argue logically? And to stop even his endeavor to think, comes the Fundamentalist; and his answer to Science is Dogma; and his reason for bringing it forward is again, not perverse hatred of the Truth, but the Shape of Fear. The religionist of today sees the sanctions of moral conduct being swept and battered away, laughed at and caricatured.

How shall he meet this wicked thing? He can do it by intelligence and argument and persuasion or he can do it by dogma which is spiritual mob-violence; today he is choosing the mob.

Or again; why is it that in a rich country like the United States, in many respects the richest and most prosperous organization of men in the world, we continually have mobs fighting and doing unutterable things because at bottom men are afraid of being unable to earn a respectable living? The answer is that our post-war prosperity is built more on gambling than on honest productive industry. Gambling was the result of war, born in war-time and coming from the sudden demand for technique machinery and goods, which paid those who happened to hold them enormous marginal rents. The chance to the gambler, the promoter and the manipulator of industry has come during the reconstruction since the war, in the monopoly of land and homes, in the manipulation of industrial power, in the use of new inventions and discoveries, in the reorganization of corporate ownership.

We have today in the United States, cheek by jowl, Prosperity and Depression. Depression among those who are selling their services, raising raw material and manufacturing goods; prosperity among those who are manipulating prices, monopolizing land and mortgaging ability and output.

How shall we meet this situation? Again we revert to the three paths: first and foremost by the spread of wider and deeper understanding among the masses of men of the modern industrial process and the method of distributing income, so that intelligently we may attack Production and Distribution and re-make industrial society. Or, a second method, by hue and cry and propaganda to stop all criticism and desire for change by dubbing every reformer "Bolshevik" and by frightening the wage earner with loss of the very foundation of his wage. And this is the kind of attack that again easily sinks to the whispering courses underground and attempts to save modern industry through mobs engineered by the secret Ku Klux Klan.

I can no better illustrate my meaning than by an actual case. The world has forgotten Mer Rouge—the Red Sea of Louisiana where a few years ago a terrible series of murders was laid at the doors of the Ku Klux Klan. It was so horrible a tale that we hastened to forget it before we really understood it. But it deserved thought and intelligent comprehension.

The cotton and sugar soil of the Mississippi and Red River valleys form a junction in Louisiana. It is a section bounded on the south by the scene of Uncle Tom's Cabin, on the north by the Helena riots, and on the east by that bit of hell which is sometimes called the Mississippi Delta. In the center of this district, in northeastern Louisiana, is Morehouse Parish and in the midst of Morehouse Parish is Mer Rouge. Mer Rouge has the peculiar problems of a little town in the Black Belt. It is ruled by the whites, and since the whites must stand united as rulers there is amongst them a rather extreme sense of social equality which even wealth and education cannot wholly break down. They go to the same churches and there their social life centers. They send their children to the same schools except the few that go away to boarding school. All this works out fairly well as long as the character of the ruling class of whites is essentially homologous. But today a change is taking place in Morehouse Parish. There are about 20,000 inhabitants there. The white population has increased from five to six thousand in the last ten years while the Negro population has decreased from fourteen to thirteen thousand. This is because of the migration of Negro laborers to the city and north; so that instead of being a county three-fourths black it is today about two-thirds black. To replace these migrating Negroes the poor whites from the neighborhood have been pressing in. They stream in especially from one poor county directly toward the east where there is a majority of poor whites and these new comers bring problems, problems of unrest, of drink, of gambling, of wayward women.

Now Mer Rouge has traditions of the time when its white folk were great landowners protecting their women in elaborate homes and having a pretentious social code. These newer and poorer whites coming in not only brought a lower moral tone but a new economic condition. They have become tenant farmers, so that between 1900 and 1920 there was an increase of nearly one third in the number of tenants. But the great landowners are still in the ascendancy, two hundred and fifty of them with farms of one hundred to more than a thousand acres, with crops valued at two and one half million dollars a year, chiefly cotton, corn and sugar cane. In addition to this the value of the land is rapidly increasing. It has doubled every ten years since 1900. Then too, to complicate the situation further there are a number of small Negro farmers who own their own land, some two hundred and thirty-one in all as compared with the two hundred and fifty large white landowners and one hundred and nineteen small white owners. One can easily scent here tremendous and bitter rivalry between the rich and poor white owners, and crushed under all of it lie the mass of black tenants. These tenants are ignorant, forty per cent of them acknowledge that they cannot read or write, and in truth this number should probably be sixty or seventy per cent. There is no modern wage system, but nearly all is barter and debt peonage. The county reported only one hundred dollars a year in wages for each worker, and this included the white workers as well as the colored.

Here then we have the setting. Here is the little town of Mer Rouge, which proposes to stop the growing lawlessness among the whites and the breaking down of social conventions. Shall it openly appeal to the ballot? Certainly not. There are 6,524 Negroes of voting age and only 3,000 whites; but of course there is no question in Mer Rouge of the black man's voting. A thousand or more Negroes are landowners able to read and write, but they cannot vote. The white women, too, are disfranchised despite the law, so that the voting population consists of about 1,500 white men, and among these the new white tenants, shopkeepers, artisans and small landowners, or in other words the lawless and easy-going new comers, could outvote the whole aristocracy.

Mer Rouge, therefore, turned to the Ku Klux Klan, and when afterward the matter came out it defended itself and claimed with undoubted truth that the Ku Klux Klan was an organization of the best elements in the community and that they were trying to put down the worst, believing that they could do by secrecy and force what they could not do openly at the polls. It was natural for them to come to this conclusion. Secrecy, force and murder have been part of the Black Belt social economy for fifty years. The landlords lived with their hands on the trigger. Formerly this was because of the fear of servile revolt or the hint of it. That fear is still there; but in addition to that there is another fear and these men did not hesitate. They were used to taking the law in their hands. They face baffling social problems. A white face is no longer a badge of aristocracy. A white woman may be rival to a black concubine. Formerly the relations of white men and colored women were open and complacent. The sheriff's son recently was killed in a colored woman's cabin. Then too the sex distribution is illuminating: More colored women than colored men and eleven per cent more white men than white women. To this are added the bootleggers and the loose white women. There is no place, no treatment for them. Colored women, however decent, can always be treated like prostitutes; but unless white prostitutes are treated like ladies the whole scheme of white supremacy fails.

All this led logically, as Mer Rouge thought, to one solution: bootleggers, gamblers and bad women were to be driven out by the Ku Klux Klan. But they miscalculated. The new whites fought back. They were not scared by hoods and nightgowns. The result was appalling. Kidnapping, whipping, murder almost wholesale, torture that would shame the Middle Ages, an atmosphere of terror, hatred and feud that attracted the attention of the world. And in the midst of it all the black, driven cattle who form sixty-eight per cent of the population were dumb.

Here were white men afraid of degradation; here were white men afraid of hunger; here were black men afraid of hunger and black men afraid of death. And here were secret midnight oath and murder seeking to right it all.

Such were the elements that make for secret mob law: economic rivalry, race hatred, class hatred, sex rivalry, religious dogmatism and before all the Shape of Fear. For years and centuries this method of organized secrecy, sworn to unlimited and ruthless action, has been used to accomplish certain things. Strong arguments have been brought to defend it and it may be admitted that one can easily see circumstances when the only way to make the survival of certain ideas and ideals certain, would be to force them through by secrecy and stealth.

But are we ready to say that this is the case in the first half of the twentieth century? Can we for a moment admit this? Is not the very thought a monstrous attack upon all that civilization and religion have accomplished?

What is there after all, of truth back of what the Klan attacks? And perhaps first, what does the Klan attack? I will not stop to argue this. I simply quote from their own blank application for membership seven of their twenty questions: "7.—Were your parents born in the United States of America?" "8.—Are you a Gentile or Jew?" "9.—Are you of the white race or of a colored race?" "13.—Do you believe in White Supremacy?" "15.—What is your religious faith?" "17.—Of what religious faith are your parents?" "20.—Do you owe ANY KIND of allegiance to any foreign nation, government, institution, sect, people, ruler or person?"

Here then is clearly the groundwork for opposition to the foreign-born, the Jew, the colored races and the Catholic Church. I am not the one to defend Catholic or Jew. The Catholic Church and modern European civilization are largely synonymous and to attack the one is to accuse the other. For the alleged followers of Jesus Christ and worshipers of the Old Testament to revile Hebrew culture is too impudent for words. But in this crazy combination of hates fathered by the Ku Klux Klan (and so illogical that in any intelligent country it would be laughed out of court), is included the American Negro. What is the indictment against him? He was a slave. He is ignorant. He is poor. He has the stigmata of poverty and ignorance—that is crime. He laughs and sings and dances. He is black. He isn't all black. The very statement of such a bill of indictment is like accusing ashes of fire. The real arraignment of the Negro is the fear that white America with its present machinery is not going to be able to keep black folk down. They are achieving equality with startling swiftness. Neither caricature nor contempt, rape of women or insult of children, murder or burning at the stake, have succeeded in daunting this extraordinary group.

Against it open reasoning and argument has been employed but it has failed to convince even those who employed it. This was followed by propaganda; and the propaganda of emphasizing "race," "racial" characteristics, "racial" inferiority, is a propaganda which according to all modern scientific dicta is unreliable and untrue. Yet these terms flourish and these things are taught in school and college; they appear in books and lectures and they are used because of what men want them to accomplish, namely, the continual fear and hate of black folk instead of that natural rebound of sympathy and admiration which their work in a half century deserves.

But as I have said, even this propaganda has not been successful. What next then? Next comes the Ku Klux Klan. Next comes the leadership of mob and perpetration of outrage by forces, secret, hidden and underground. And the danger and shame are not in the movement itself, so much as in the wide tolerance and sympathy which its methods evoke among educated and decent Americans. These people see in the Ku Klux Klan a way of doing and saying that which they themselves are ashamed to do and say. Go into any western town from Pittsburgh to Kansas City: "The Klan? Silly—*but!*—You see these Catholics, rich, powerful, silent, organized. Got all the foreigners corraled—I don't *know*. And Jews—the Jews own the country. They are trying to rule the world. They are too smart, pushing, impudent. And *niggers!* And that isn't all. Dagoes, Japs; and then *Russia!* I tell you we gotta *do* something. The Klan?—silly, of course—*but*—."

Thus the Ku Klux Klan is doing a job which the American people, or certainly a considerable portion of them, want done; and they want it done because as a nation they have fear of the Jews, the immigrant, the Negro. They realize that the American of English descent is not holding his own physically or spiritually in this country; that America survives and flourishes because of the alien immigrant with his strong arm, his simply life, his faith and hope, his song, his art, his religion. They realize that no group in the United States is working harder to push themselves forward and upward than the Negroes; and over all this rises the Shape of Fear.

The worst aspect of all this is that when we resort to the underground method it involves a conscious surrender of Truth. It must base itself upon lies. One of the greatest difficulties in estimating the power and spread of the Ku Klux Klan is that its members are evidently sworn to lie. They are ordered to deny their membership in the Klan; they are ordered to deny their participation in certain of its deeds; they are ordered above all to keep at least partially secret its real objects and desires. Now the lie has often been used to advance human culture, but it is an extremely dangerous weapon, and surely we have lived beyond the need of it today.

Consequently the greatest thing that we have to fear in any such underground movement as the Ku Klux Klan, a thing that makes it much more fearful than anything that has been alleged of Bolshevism or Fascism, is the danger and ease of its being used for exactly the opposite of the things for which it is established or which the thoughts or ideals which its leaders profess. If it is possible to establish a widespread underground movement against Jews, Negroes and Catholics, why isn't it just as easy to establish similar movements against millionaires, machinery and foreign commerce, or against "Anglo-Saxons," Protestants and Germans, or against any set of people or set of ideas which any particular group of people dislike, hate or fear? It may be said that at present it is possible to mobilize larger numbers of people in a common hatred against the Hebrew race, the black race, and the Catholic Church than against any similar things; but this is not necessarily true and it certainly is not true in all places and will not be true at all times.

Without doubt, of all the dangerous weapons that civilized man has attempted to use in order to advance human culture the secret mass lie is the most dangerous and the most apt to prove a boomerang. This is the real thing that we are to fear in the Ku Klux Klan. We need not fear its logic. It has no logic. Whatever there is of truth in its hatred of three groups of Americans can be discussed openly and fearlessly by civilized men. If Negroes are ignorant underbidders of labor, unhealthy and lazy aspirants to undeserved equality there are plain and well-known social restraints and remedies. First, to improve the condition of Negroes so far as it is improvable; secondly, to teach them the reason behind the objections to their rise so far as there are reasons; and above all to examine thoroughly and honestly what the real questions at issue are. If the hierarchy of the Catholic church is in any way threatening democracy in American there is a chance for perfectly open and honest investigation and conference between this young democracy and that old and honorable government of the spirit of men. If the Jew in self-defense against age-long persecution has closed his fist against the world there is more than a chance to clasp that human hand. In fine, unless we are willing to give up human civilization in order to preserve civilization we cannot for a moment contemplate turning to secret, underground methods as a cure for anything; and the appearance of such a movement is not a case where we stop to ask whether the movement in itself has at present laudable objects or not. It does not make any difference what the Ku Klux Klan is fighting for or against. Its method is wrong and dangerous and uncivilized, and those who oppose it, whether they be its victims like the Jews, Catholics and Negroes, or those who are lauded as its moral sponsors like the white Southerners, the American Legion and the "Anglo-Saxons," it is the duty of all these people to join together in solemn phalanx against the method which is an eternal menace to human culture.

CULTURAL EQUALITY

We may well ask in the beginning: just what does one mean by "equality"? And what is "cultural" equality? We might even ask, just what are "Negroes"?—and, how are you going to "encourage" anyone to seek this sort of equality?

I am going to take the broad commonsense view of what these words mean. By equality, I do not mean absolute identity or similarity of gift, but gifts of essentially equal values to human culture. By culture, I mean that organized tide which men call civilization. And persons are encouraged to seek cultural equality by the taking down of bars and doing away with discriminations—by abolishing all efforts that directly or indirectly impede people in attaining a certain goal.

If you were not familiar with the race problem in the United States or in the modern world, you would ask: Why should you not encourage Negroes or anybody else in the wide world to seek cultural equality? Is not this the aim of civilization? Is it not the ideal for which all men yearn? What could you conceive as better than a world in which all citizens were not only encouraged to cultural equality but accomplished their aim? Would not this be the best conceivable sort of world?

And yet you who know America, know perfectly well that large numbers of people have always denied to the Negro even the chance to try to reach such a goal. This denial has taken two forms or perhaps two degrees of emphasis on the same thesis. In early days Americans said frankly: the Negro should not be encouraged to seek cultural equality because he cannot reach it; he is not really human in the sense that other people are human. One does not encourage dogs to do the things that men do, not because one has anything against dogs, but because dogs are not men and cannot act like men. And the same way (although perhaps the analogy is overdrawn), Americans do not encourage Negroes to share modern culture because they cannot share it; we would simply make them unhappy if we let them try to reach to things which they can never reach.

Some years ago that was a logical statement and a statement difficult to answer. But in the last generation things have happened, and they have happened fast. We have had since emancipation a bounding forward of these millions of dark people in America. It does not make any difference how far you may wish to minimize what Negroes have done or what judgment you have as to its lasting value, there is no doubt about the work that has been done by these millions of emancipated slaves and their descendants in America. It is one of the wonderful accomplishments of this generation. It has few parallels in human history.

Some people might assume that this rise of the American Negro from slavery to freedom, from squalor, poverty, and ignorance to thrift and intelligence and the beginnings of wealth, would bring unstinted applause. Negroes themselves expected this. They looked eagerly forward to this day when you cannot write a history or statement of American civilization and leave the black man out, as proof of their equality and manhood and they expected their advance, incomplete or imperfect though it remains, nevertheless, to be greeted with applause.

On the contrary, all Negroes know that with all the generous praise given us there has been no phase of the advance that has not been looked on with a strong undercurrent of apprehension. America has feared the coming forward of these black men; it has looked upon it as a sort of threat—and if you should ask just why that is so, white

Americans would state the thesis which they have stated before but with some modification; they would say that the coming forward of these people does not prove that they can make as great a gift to culture as the white people have made; but whether they can or not, they must not be allowed to come forward because it threatens civilization! If you ask how this can possibly be—how the advance of one-tenth of a nation can be a threat to the rest—you have various kinds of answers.

In the first place some seem to regard culture as a quantitative sort of thing; there is a certain amount of culture in the world; if you divide it up among all people you have that much less for other people. Of course everybody knows that the quantitative theory of civilization does not hold, that the analogy is not perfect, and yet the reason we use it is because we do regard civilization today in terms of the number of our physical possessions. We are buried beneath our material wealth, and if we think, say, of motor cars, we conclude that if black people have motor cars, there are so many less for the white people to occupy. And so on. We go through the whole catalog of what a material age calls civilization, and think that if it is distributed to certain people, other people are not going to have as much.

Discarding this quantitative analogy we fall back to the other argument. After all, it is not the things which people have that makes the major part of civilization—the real civilization; real culture depends on quality and not quantity; it is not, therefore, so much a matter of distribution of goods—of distribution of quantity as of contamination of quality in goods and deeds.

And there we have brought back into the modern world the theory which the world has held and heard again and again—a few people have the chance to get unusual advancement; they have the chance to learn; they have leisure to think; they have food and shelter and encouragement; they push forward in the world, and then, after they have reached certain heights, suddenly they are overcome with admiration for themselves; suddenly it is suggested to them that they are wonderful and unusual people; that the universe was made particularly and especially for them; that never before have human beings attained such height and mastery—and finally we have the theory of the Chosen People!

The theory is as old as human culture is old, and yet today it comes back to us in the new dress of the belief that everything that has been done in modern times has been done by the Nordic people; that they are the people who are the salt of the earth; that if anything is done to change their type of civilization, then civilization fails and falls; that what we have got to be afraid of is the coming forward of a mass of black people without real gift, without real knowledge of what culture is, who are going to spoil the divine gifts of the Nordics.

To a theory of this sort, the world—the overwhelming majority of human beings who are not Nordic—have a right to two replies:

First, your theory is unproven. There is no scientific proof that modern culture is of Nordic origin or that Nordic brains and physique are of better intrinsic quality than Mediterranean, Indian, Chinese or Negro. In fact, the proofs of essential human equality of gift are overwhelming.

But, if Nordics believe in their own superiority; if they wish voluntarily to work by themselves and for the development and encouragement of their own gifts; if they prefer not to mingle their blood with other races, or contaminate their culture with foreign strains, nothing is to hinder them from carrying out this program except themselves.

Nobody is going to make Nordics marry outside of their group unless they want to marry outside. They can keep their group closed if they wish. Of course, civilization is by the definition of the term, civilization for all mankind; but nobody is going to withhold applause if you make your contribution to the world.

Of course, civilization is the rightful heritage of all and cannot be monopolized and confined to one group. A group organization to increase and forward culture is legitimate and will bring its reward in universal recognition and applause.

But this has never been the Nordic program. Their program is the subjection and rulership of the world for the benefit of the Nordics. They have overrun the earth and brought not simply modern civilization and technique, but with it exploitation, slavery and degradation to the majority of men. They have broken down native family life, desecrated homes of weaker peoples and spread their bastards over every corner of land and sea. They have been responsible for more intermixture of races than any other people, ancient or modern, and they have inflicted this miscegenation on helpless, unwilling slaves by force, fraud and insult; and this is the folk that today has the impudence to turn on the darker races when they demand a share of civilization, and cry: "You shall not marry our daughters!"

The blunt, crude reply is: Who in hell asked to marry your daughters? If this race problem must be reduced to a matter of sex, what we demand is the right to protect the decency of our own daughters.

But the insistent demand of the Darker World is far wider and deeper than this. The black and brown and yellow men demand the right to be men. They demand the right to have the artificial barriers placed in their path torn down and destroyed; they demand a voice in their own government; the organization of industry for the benefit of colored workers and not merely for white owners and masters; they demand education on the broadest and highest lines and they demand as human beings social contact with other human beings on a basis of perfect equality.

That is what they call civilization. That is what we American Negroes demand and the demand is so reasonable and logical that to deny it is not simply to hurt and hinder them, it is to fly in the face of your own white civilization.

Think of what has been done in the name of "white supremacy" right here in the United States; the Middle West today is politically helpless because in order to deprive black Americans of the right to vote, they allowed the South to cast two votes—the vote of the white man and of the disfranchised Negro. The double political power of these rotten boroughs of the South makes democratic government in the United States a farce.

You decry lawlessness. Where do you get the lawlessness of Chicago and of the United States? You began it when as a nation you disregarded the Thirteenth, Fourteenth and Fifteenth Amendments and then are vastly surprised when you cannot enforce the Eighteenth. You have organized your life so as not to carry out the laws which you yourselves made and you have the heritage of lawlessness to pay for it.

You have created here in the United States, which today pretends to the moral leadership of the world, a situation where on the last night of the old year you can slowly and publicly burn a human being alive for the amusement of Americans who represent some of the purest strains of Nordic blood in that great place, Mississippi, which has done so much for the civilization of the world!

Not simply in these things have you attacked your own civilization. You have made it almost impossible for America to think logically.

I said to you a while ago that I might ask you what Negroes were. I come back to that question. I stand here gladly as the representative of the Negro race, and yet I know and you know that I can equally stand here as a representative of the Nordic race. Wherever it seems necessary to deny me any privilege, then I am a Negro, and whenever I do anything that is worth doing, suddenly I become preponderately white. The United States measured soldiers in the great war and came to wonderful conclusions concerning their intelligence, but the conclusions they came to were conclusions for the Negro race, and they knew perfectly well the men they were measuring were not Negroes, but that perhaps 70 percent of them had white blood. It is impossible by any scientific measurement to divide men into races, and even to prove there are separate races, and yet we talk about races, and prescribe races and measure races; and because we are not talking logically when we talk about races, so we cannot talk logically about anything else— the tariff, farm relief, unemployment, credit, wages or capital.

The matter of our logic is not merely so important as that of our ethics and religion. Here you are, a great white nation with a magnificent Plan of Salvation. You have an ethical code far beyond anything the world ever knew—if you do not believe it, listen to what you preach to the darker peoples. You are followers of the Golden Rule and of the meek and lowly Jesus. Yet you do not try to follow out your own religion because you know when your religion comes up against the race problem that religion has nothing absolutely to do with your attitude toward Negroes. The attacks that white people themselves have made upon their own moral structure are worse for civilization than anything that any body of Negroes could ever do.

Therefore, you stand today before the Great Alternative. Are you going to allow the colored people in the United States and the colored races in the world to go forward toward the goals of civilization free and unhampered, or are you going to organize to see that these people are kept in the places where you think they ought to stay? Here is a great decision, a decision which the white world has got to face.

The temptation to hold these colored people back is tremendous, because it is not merely a matter of academic wish or of wanton prejudice, but it is the kernel of the organization of modern life. You have got the colored people working for you all through the world. You have got your investments so made that they depend upon colored labor in Asia, Africa, in the southern states of the United States, and in the islands of the sea. Your income and your power depends upon that organization being kept intact. If it is overthrown, if these black laborers get higher wages, if they begin to understand what life may be, if they increase in knowledge, self-assertion and power, it means the overthrow of the whole system of exploitation which is at the bottom of modern white civilization. What now is your decision?

Suppose you turn to the other side. Suppose you say, despite anything that the darker races, including the Negroes in the United States may ask, we are going to sit tight and keep them where they belong. Then the question is, can you do it?

In the first place, have you the ability to do it? It is going to call for ability. It is going to call for brains and genius of the highest order, and looking back upon the history of what you have done with the colored world, you have no right to preen yourselves on what you are going to do in the future. A few years ago you fell out among yourselves, not because of any quarrel you had with each other, but on the question as to how you are going to divide among yourselves territory and raw materials belonging to colored people. The World War was a matter of jealousy in the division of the spoils of Asia and Africa, and by it you nearly ruined civilization. Have you the genius and the brains to carry out further an organization of men by which the white people of the world are going to sit on top of it, using it mainly for their own advantage and make the rest of the world serve?

If you have the ability to do this, there then comes the next question: have you the force? Have you the physical force and the machines to do it? Oh, you can do it in the United States. You outnumber us ten to one. You can sweep us off the face of the earth. You can starve us to death or make us wish we had starved to death in the face of your insults. But, remember, you are standing before the whole world, with hundreds of darker millions watching. No matter what happens to us, these colored people of the world are not going to take forever the kind of treatment they have been taking. They have got beyond that. They have come to the place where they know what civilization is, and if you are going to keep them in their place, you are going to do it by brute force. Have you got the force, and is it likely that you are going to get it?

THE NEGRO AND COMMUNISM

The Scottsboro, Alabama, cases have brought squarely before the American Negro the question of his attitude toward Communism.

The importance of the Russian Revolution can not be gainsaid. It is easily the greatest event in the world since the French Revolution and possibly since the fall of Rome. The experiment is increasingly successful. Russia occupies the center of the world's attention today and as a state it is recognized by every civilized nation, except the United States, Spain, Portugal and some countries of South America.

The challenge to the capitalistic form of industry and to the governments which this form dominates, is more and more tremendous because of the present depression. If Socialism as a form of government and industry is on trial in Russia, capitalism as a form of industry and government is just as surely on trial throughout the world and is more and more clearly recognizing the fact.

The American Worker

It has always been felt that the United States was an example of the extraordinary success of capitalistic industry, and that this was proven by the high wage paid labor and the high standard of intelligence and comfort prevalent in this country. Moreover, for many years, democratic political control of our government by the masses of the people made it possible to envisage without violence any kind of reform in government or industry which appeared to the people. Recently, however, the people of the United States have begun to recognize that their political power is curtailed by organized capital in industry and that in this industry, democracy does not prevail; and that until wider democracy does prevail in industry, democracy in government is seriously curtailed and often quite ineffective. Also, because of recurring depressions the high wage is in part illusory.

The American Negro

Moreover, there is in the United States one class of people who more than any other suffer under present conditions. Because of wholesale disfranchisement and a system of color caste, discriminatory legislation and widespread propaganda, 12,000,000 American Negroes have only a minimum of that curtailed freedom which the right to vote and influence on public opinion gives to white Americans. And in industry Negroes are for historic and social reasons upon the lowest round.

Proposed Reform

The proposals to remedy the economic and political situation in America range from new legislation, better administration and government aid, offered by the Republican and Democratic parties, on to liberal movements fathered by Progressives, the Farmer-Labor movement and the Socialists, and finally to the revolutionary proposals of the Communists. The Progressives and Socialists propose in general increased government ownership of land and natural resources, state control of the larger public services and such progressive taxation of incomes and inheritance as shall decrease the number and power of the rich. The Communists, on the other hand, propose an entire sweeping away of the present organization of industry; the ownership of land, resources, machines and tools by the state, the conducting of business by the state under incomes which the state limits. And in order to introduce this complete Socialistic regime, Communists propose a revolutionary dictatorship by the working class, as the only sure, quick and effective path.

Advice to Negroes

With these appeals in his ears, what shall the American Negro do? In the letters from United States Senators published in this issue of THE CRISIS, we find, with all the sympathy and good-will expressed, a prevailing helplessness when it comes to advice on specific action. Reactionaries like Fess, Conservatives like Bulkley and Capper, Progressives like Borah and Norris, all can only say: "You have done as well as could be expected; you suffer many present disadvantages; there is nothing that we can do to help you, and your salvation lies in patience and further effort on your own part." The Socialist, as represented by Norman Thomas in the February CRISIS, invites the Negro as a worker to vote for the Socialist Party as the party of workers. He offers the Negro no panacea for prejudice and caste but assumes that the uplift of the white worker will automatically emancipate the yellow, brown and black.

The Scottsboro Cases

Finally, the Scottsboro cases come and put new emphasis on the appeal of the Communists. Advocating the defense of the eight Alabama black boys, who without a shadow of doubt have been wrongly accused of crime, the Communists not only asked to take charge of the defense of these victims, but they proceeded to build on this case an appeal to the American Negro to join the Communist movement as the only solution of their problem.

Immediately, these two objects bring two important problems; first, can the Negroes with their present philosophy and leadership defend the Scottsboro cases successfully? Secondly, even if they can, will such defense help them to solve their problem of poverty and caste?

If the Communistic leadership in the United States had been broad-minded and far-sighted, it would have acknowledged frankly that the honesty, earnestness and intelligence of the N.A.A.C.P. during twenty years of desperate struggle proved this organization under present circumstances to be the only one, and its methods the only methods available, to defend these boys and it would have joined capitalists and laborers north and south, black and white in every endeavor to win freedom for victims threatened with judicial murder. Then beyond that and with Scottsboro as a crimson and terrible text, Communists could have proceeded to point out that legal defense alone, even if successful, will never solve the larger Negro problem but that further and more radical steps are needed.

Communist Strategy

Unfortunately, American Communists are neither wise nor intelligent. They sought to accomplish too much at one stroke. They tried to prove at once that the N.A.A.C.P. did not wish to defend the victims at Scottsboro and that the reason for this was that Negro leadership in the N.A.A.C.P. was allied with the capitalists. The first of these two efforts was silly and the Communists tried to accomplish it by deliberate lying and deception. They accused the N.A.A.C.P. of stealing, misuse of funds, lack of interest in the Scottsboro cases, cowardly surrender to malign forces, inefficiency and a policy of do-nothing.

Now whatever the N.A.A.C.P. has lacked, it is neither dishonest nor cowardly, and already events are proving clearly that the only effective defense of the Scottsboro boys must follow that which has been carefully organized, engineered and paid for by the N.A.A.C.P., and that the success of this defense is helped so far as the Communists cooperate by hiring bourgeois lawyers and appealing to bourgeois judges; but is hindered and made doubtful by ill-considered and foolish tactics against the powers in whose hands the fate of the Scottsboro victims lies.

If the Communists want these lads murdered, then their tactics of threatening judges and yelling for mass action on the part of white southern workers is calculated to insure this.

And, on the other hand, lying and deliberate misrepresentation of friends who are fighting for the same ideals as the Communists, are old capitalistic, bourgeois weapons of which the Communists ought to be ashamed. The final exploit at Camp Hill is worthy of the Russian Black Hundreds, whoever promoted it: black sharecroppers, half-starved and desperate were organized into a "Society for the Advancement of Colored People" and then induced to meet and protest against Scottsboro. Sheriff and white mob killed one and imprisoned 34. If this was instigated by Communists, it is too despicable for words; not because the plight of the black peons does not shriek for remedy but because this is no time to bedevil a delicate situation by drawing a red herring across the trail of eight innocent children.

Nevertheless, the N.A.A.C.P. will defend these 34 victims of Southern fear and communist irresponsibility.

The ultimate object of the Communists, was naturally not merely nor chiefly to save the boys accused at Scottsboro; it was to make this case a center of agitation to expose the helpless condition of Negroes, and to prove that anything less than the radical Communist program could not emancipate them.

The Negro Bourgeoisie

The question of the honesty and efficiency of the N.A.A.C.P. in the defense of the Scottsboro boys, just as in a dozen other cases over the length and breadth of the United States, is entirely separate from the question as to whether or not Negro leadership is tending toward socialism and communism or toward capitalism.

The charge of the Communists that the present set-up of Negro America is that of the petit bourgeois minority dominating a helpless black proletariat, and surrendering to white profiteers is simply a fantastic falsehood. The attempt to dominate Negro Americans by purely capitalistic ideas died with Booker T. Washington. The battle against it was begun by the Niagara Movement and out of the Niagara Movement arose the N.A.A.C.P. Since that time there has never been a moment when the dominating leadership of the American Negro has been mainly or even largely dominated by wealth or capital or by capitalistic ideals.

There are naturally some Negro capitalists: some large landowners, some landlords, some industrial leaders and some investors; but the great mass of Negro capital is not owned or controlled by this group. Negro capital consists mainly of small individual savings invested in homes, and in insurance, in lands for direct cultivation and individually used tools and machines. Even the automobiles owned by Negroes represent to a considerable extent personal investments, designed to counteract the insult of the "Jim Crow" car. The Insurance business, which represents a large amount of Negro capital is for mutual cooperation rather than exploitation. Its profit is limited and its methods directed by the State. Much of the retail business is done in small stores with small stocks of goods, where the owner works side by side with one or two helpers, and makes a personal profit less than a normal American wage. Negro professional men—lawyers, physicians, nurses and teachers—represent capital invested in their education and in their office equipment, and not in commercial exploitation. There are few colored manufacturers of material who speculate on the products of hired labor. Nine-tenths of the hired Negro labor is under the control of white capitalists. There is probably no group of 12 million persons in the modern world which exhibits smaller contrasts in personal income than the American Negro group. Their emancipation will not come, as among the Jews, from an internal readjustment and ousting of exploiters; rather it will come from a wholesale emancipation from the grip of the white exploiters without.

It is, of course, always possible, with the ideals of America, that a full fledged capitalistic system may develop in the Negro group; but the dominant leadership of the Negro today, and particularly the leadership represented by the N.A.A.C.P. represents no such tendency. For two generations the social leaders of the American Negro with very few exceptions have been poor men, depending for support on their salaries, owning little or no real property; few have been business men, none have been exploiters, and while there have been wide differences of ultimate ideal these leaders on the whole, have worked unselfishly for the uplift of the masses of Negro folk.

There is no group of leaders on earth who have so largely made common cause with the lowest of their race as educated American Negroes, and it is their foresight and sacrifice and theirs alone that has saved the American freedman from annihilation and degradation.

This is the class of leaders who have directed and organized and defended black folk in America and whatever their shortcomings and mistakes—and they are legion—their one great proof of success is the survival of the American Negro as the most intelligent and effective group of colored people fighting white civilization face to face and on its own ground, on the face of the earth.

The quintessence and final expression of this leadership is the N.A.A.C.P. For twenty years it has fought a battle more desperate than any other race conflict of modern times and it has fought with honesty and courage. It deserves from Russia something better than a kick in the back from the young jackasses who are leading Communism in America today.

What Is the N.A.A.C.P.?

The N.A.A.C.P. years ago laid down a clear and distinct program. Its object was to make 12 million Americans:

Physically free from peonage.

Mentally free from ignorance.

Politically free from disfranchisement.

Socially free from insult.

Limited as this platform may seem to perfectionists, it is so far in advance of anything ever attempted before in America, that it has gained an extraordinary following. On this platform we have succeeded in uniting white and black, employers and laborers, capitalists and communists, socialists and reformers, rich and poor. The funds which support this work come mainly from poor colored people, but on the other hand, we have in 20 years of struggle, enlisted the sympathy and co-operation of the rich, the white and the powerful; and so long as this co-operation is given upon the basis of the platform we have laid down, we seek and welcome it. On the other hand, we know perfectly well that the platform of the N.A.A.C.P. is no complete program of social reform. It is a pragmatic union of certain definite problems, while far beyond its program lies the whole question of the future of the darker races and the economic emancipation of the working classes.

White Labor

Beyond the Scottsboro cases and the slurs on Negro leadership, there still remains for Negroes and Communists, the pressing major question: How shall American Negroes be emancipated from economic slavery? In answer to this both Socialists and Communists attempted to show the Negro that his interest lies with that of white labor. That kind of talk to the American Negro is like a red rag to a bull. Throughout the history of the Negro in America, white labor has been the black man's enemy, his oppressor, his red murderer. Mobs, riots and the discrimination of trade unions have been used to kill, harass and starve black men. White labor disfranchised Negro labor in the South, is keeping them out of jobs and decent living quarters in the North, and is curtailing their education and civil and social privileges throughout the nation. White laborers have formed the backbone of the Ku Klux Klan and have furnished hands and ropes to lynch 3,560 Negroes since 1882.

Since the death of Terence Powderly not a single great white labor leader in the United States has wholeheartedly and honestly espoused the cause of justice to black workers.

Socialists and Communists explain this easily: white labor in its ignorance and poverty has been misled by the propaganda of white capital, whose policy is to divide labor into classes, races and unions and pit one against the other. There is an immense amount of truth in this explanation: Newspapers, social standards, race pride, competition for jobs, all work to set white against black. But white American Laborers are not fools. And with few exceptions the more intelligent they are, the higher they rise, the more efficient they become, the more determined they are to keep Negroes under their heels. It is no mere coincidence that Labor's present representative in the President's cabinet belongs to a union that will not admit a Negro, and himself was for years active in West Virginia in driving Negroes out of decent jobs. It is intelligent white labor that today keeps Negroes out of the trades, refuses them decent homes to live in and helps nullify their vote. Whatever ideals white labor today strives for in America, it would surrender nearly every one before it would recognize a Negro as a man.

Communists and the Color Line

The American Communists have made a courageous fight against the color line among the workers. They have solicited and admitted Negro members. They have insisted in their strikes and agitation to let Negroes fight with them and that the object of their fighting is for black workers as well as white workers. But in this they have gone dead against the thought and desire of the overwhelming mass of white workers, and face today a dead blank wall even in their own school in Arkansas. Thereupon instead of acknowledging defeat in their effort to make white labor abolish the color line, they turn and accuse Negroes of not sympathizing with the ideals of Labor!

Socialists have been franker. They learned that American labor would not carry the Negro and they very calmly unloaded him. They allude to him vaguely and as an afterthought in their books and platforms. The American Socialist party is out to emancipate the white worker and if this does not automatically free the colored man, he can continue in slavery. The only time that so fine a man and so logical a reasoner as Norman Thomas becomes vague and incoherent is when he touches the black man, and consequently he touches him as seldom as possible.

When, therefore, Negro leaders refuse to lay down arms and surrender their brains and action to "Nigger"-hating white workers, liberals and socialists understand exactly the reasons for this and spend what energy they can spare in pointing out to white workers the necessity of recognizing Negroes. But the Communists, younger and newer, largely of foreign extraction, and thus discounting the hell of American prejudice, easily are led to blame the Negroes and to try to explain the intolerable American situation on the basis of an imported Marxist pattern, which does not at all fit the situation.

For instance, from Moscow comes this statement to explain Scottsboro and Camp Hill:

"Again, as in the case of Sacco and Vanzetti, the American Bourgeoisie is attempting to go against proletarian social opinion. It is attempting to carry through its criminal provocation to the very end."

This is a ludicrous misapprehension of local conditions and illustrates the error into which long distance interpretation, unsupported by real knowledge, may fall. The Sacco-Vanzetti cases in Massachusetts represented the fight of prejudiced, entrenched capital against racial propaganda; but in Jackson County, northeastern Alabama, where Scottsboro is situated, there are over 33,000 Native whites and less than 3,000 Negroes. The vast majority of these whites belong to the laboring class and they formed the white proletarian mob which is determined to kill the eight Negro boys. Such mobs of white workers demand the right to kill "niggers" whenever their passions, especially in sexual matters, are inflamed by propaganda. The capitalists are willing to curb this blood lust when it interferes with their profits. They know that the murder of 8 innocent black boys will hurt organized industry and government in Alabama; but as long as 10,000 armed white workers demand these victims they do not dare move. Into this delicate and contradictory situation, the Communists hurl themselves and pretend to speak for the workers. They not only do not speak for the white workers but they even intensify the blind prejudices of these lynchers and leave the Negro workers helpless on the one hand and the white capitalists scared to death on the other.

The persons who are killing blacks in Northern Alabama and demanding blood sacrifice are the white workers—sharecroppers, trade unionists and artisans. The capitalists are against mob-law and violence and would listen to reason and justice in the long run because industrial peace increases their profits. On the other hand, the white workers want to kill the competition of "Niggers." Thereupon, the Communists, seizing leadership of the poorest and most ignorant blacks head them toward inevitable slaughter and jail-slavery, while they hide safely in Chattanooga and Harlem.

American Negroes do not propose to be the shock troops of the Communist Revolution, driven out in front to death, cruelty and humiliation in order to win victories for white workers. They are picking no chestnuts from the fire, neither for capital nor white labor.

Negroes know perfectly well that whenever they try to lead revolution in America, the nation will unite as one fist to crush them and them alone. There is no conceivable idea that seems to the present overwhelming majority of Americans higher than keeping Negroes "in their place."

Negroes perceive clearly that the real interests of the white worker are identical with the interests of the black worker; but until the white worker recognizes this, the black worker is compelled in sheer self-defense to refuse to be made the sacrificial goat.

The Negro and the Rich

The remaining grain of truth in the Communist attack on Negro leadership is the well-known fact that American wealth has helped the American Negro and that without this help the Negro could not have attained his present advancement. American courts from the Supreme Court down are dominated by wealth and Big Business, yet they are today the Negro's only protection against complete disfranchisement, segregation and the abolition of his public schools. Higher education for Negroes is the gift of the Standard Oil, the Power Trust, the Steel Trust and the Mail Order Chain Stores, together with the aristocratic Christian Church; but these have given Negroes 40,000 black leaders to fight white folk on their own level and in their own language. Big industry in the last 10 years has opened occupations for a million Negro workers, without which we would have starved in jails and gutters.

Socialists and Communists may sneer and say that the capitalists sought in all this profit, cheap labor, strike-breakers and the training of conservative, reactionary leaders. They did. But Negroes sought food, clothes, shelter and knowledge to stave off death and slavery and only damned fools would have refused the gift.

Moreover, we who receive education as the dole of the rich have not all become slaves of wealth.

Meanwhile, what have white workers and radical reformers done for Negroes? By strikes and agitation, by self-denial and sacrifice, they have raised wages and bettered working conditions; but they did this for themselves and only shared their gains with Negroes when they had to. They have preached freedom, political power, manhood rights and social uplift for everybody, when nobody objected; but for "white people only" when anybody demanded it. White labor segregated Dr. Sweet in Detroit; white laborers chased the Arkansas peons; white laborers steal the black children's school funds in South Carolina, white laborers lynch Negroes in Alabama. Negroes owe much to white labor but it is not all, or mostly, on the credit side of the ledger.

The Next Step

Where does this leave the Negro? As a practical program, it leaves him just where he was before the Russian Revolution; sympathetic with Russia and hopeful for its ultimate success in establishing a Socialistic state; sympathetic with the efforts of the American workingman to establish democratic control of industry in this land; absolutely certain that as a laborer his interests are the interests of all labor; but nevertheless fighting doggedly on the old battleground, led by the N.A.A.C.P. to make the Negro laborer a laborer on equal social footing with the white laborer; to maintain the Negro's right to a political vote, notwithstanding the fact that this vote means increasingly less and less to all voters; to vindicate in the courts the Negro's civil rights and American citizenship, even though he knows how the courts are prostituted to the power of wealth; and above all, determined by plain talk and agitation to show the intolerable injustice with which America and the world treats the colored peoples and to continue to insist that in this injustice, the white workers of Europe and America are just as culpable as the white owners of capital; and that these workers can gain black men as allies only and insofar as they frankly, fairly and completely abolish the Color Line.

Present organization of industry for private profit and control of government by concentrated wealth is doomed to disaster. It must change and fall if civilization survives. The foundation of its present world-wide power is the slavery and semi-slavery of the colored world including the American Negroes. Until the colored man, yellow, red, brown, and black, becomes free, articulate, intelligent and the receiver of a decent income, white capital will use the profit derived from his degradation to keep white labor in chains.

There is no doubt, then, as to the future, or as to where the true interests of American Negroes lie. There is no doubt, too, but that the first step toward the emancipation of colored labor must come from white labor.

THE FIELD AND FUNCTION OF THE AMERICAN NEGRO COLLEGE

Once upon a time some four thousand miles east of this place, I saw the functioning of a perfect system of education. It was in West Africa, beside a broad river; and beneath the palms, bronze girls were

dancing before the President of Liberia and the native chiefs, to celebrate the end of the Bush Retreat and their arrival at marriageable age.

There under the Yorubas and other Sudanese and Bantu tribes, the
education of the child began almost before it could walk. It went about
with mother and father in their daily tasks; it learned the art of sowing
and reaping and hunting; it absorbed the wisdom and folk lore of the
tribe; it knew the lay of land and river. Then at the age of puberty it
went into the Bush and there for a season the boys were taught the
secrets of sex and the girls in another school learned of motherhood
and marriage. They came out of the Bush with a ceremony of graduation, and immediately were given and taken in marriage.

Even after that, their education went on. They sat in council with
their elders and learned the history and science and art of the tribe and
practiced all in their daily life. Thus education was completely integrated with life. There could be no uneducated people. There could be
no education that was not at once for use in earning a living and for
use in living a life. Out of this education and out of the life it typified
came, as perfect expressions, song and dance and saga, ethics and religion.

Nothing more perfect has been invented than this system of training youth among primitive African tribes. And one sees it in the beautiful courtesy of black children; in the modesty and frankness of womanhood, and in the dignity and courage of manhood; and too, in
African music and art with its world-wide influence.

If a group has a stable culture which moves, if we could so conceive it, on one general level, here would be the ideal of our school
and university. But, of course, this can never be achieved by human
beings on any wide stage.

First and most disconcerting, men progress, which means that they
change their home, their work, their division of wealth, their philosophy. And how shall men teach children that which they themselves do
not know or transmit a philosophy or religion that is already partly
disbelieved and partly untrue? This is a primal and baffling problem of
education and we have never wholly solved it. Or in other words, education of youth in a changing world is a puzzling problem with every
temptation for lying and propaganda. But this is but the beginning of
trouble. Within the group and nation significant differentiations and
dislocations appear, so that education of youth becomes a preparation
not for one common national life but for the life of a particular class or
group; and yet the tendency is to regard as real national education only
the training for this group which assumes to represent the nation because of its power and privilege, and despite the fact that it is usually
a small numerical minority in the nation. Manifestly in such case if a
member of one of the suppressed groups receives the national education in such a land, he must become a member of the privileged aristoc-

racy or be educated for a life which he cannot follow and be compelled to live a life which he does not like or which he deeply despises.

This is the problem of education with which the world is most familiar and it tends to two ends: It makes the mass of men dissatisfied with life and it makes the university a system of culture for the cultured.

With this kind of university, we are most familiar. It reached in our day perhaps its greatest development in England in the Victorian era. Eton and Harrow, Oxford and Cambridge, were for the education of gentlemen—those people who inherited wealth and who by contact and early training acquired a body of manners and a knowledge of life and even an accent of English which placed them among the well-bred; these were taken up and further trained for the particular sort of life which they were to live; a life which pre-supposed a large income, travel, cultivated society; and activity in politics, art, and imperial industry.

This type of university training has deeply impressed the world. It is foundation for a tenacious legend preserved in fiction, poetry, and essay. There are still many people who quite instinctively turn to this sort of thing when they speak of a university. And out of this ideal arose one even more exotic and apart. Instead of the university growing down and seeking to comprehend in its curriculum the life and experience, the thought and expression, of lower classes; it almost invariably tended to grow up and narrow itself to a sublimated elite of mankind.

It conceived of culture, exquisite and fragile, as a thing in itself, disembodied from flesh and action; and this culture as existing for its own sake. It was a sort of earthly heaven into which the elect of wealth and privilege and courtly address, with a few chance neophytes from the common run of men, entered and lived in a region above and apart. One gets from this that ideal of cloistered ease for Science and Beauty, partaken of by those who sit far from the noise and fury, clamor and dust of the world, as the world's aristocrats, artists and scholars.

And yet, the argument against such an ideal of a university is more an argument of fact than logic. For just as soon as such a system of training is established or as men seek to establish it, it dies. It dies like a plant without room, withering into fantastic forms, that bring ridicule or hate. Or it becomes so completely disassociated from the main currents of real life that men forget it and the world passes on as though it was not for it and had not been. Thus the university cut off from its natural roots and from the mass of men becomes a university of the air and does not establish and does not hold the ideal of universal culture which it sought, in its earlier days, to make its great guiding end.

How is it now that failure to reach this, often if not always, kills the university? The reasons to me seem clear. Human culture in its broadest and finest sense can never be wholly the product of the few. There is no natural aristocracy of man, either within a nation or among the races of the world, which unless fed copiously from without can build up and maintain and diversify a broad human culture. A system, therefore, of national education which tries to confine its benefits to preparing the few for the life of the few, dies of starvation. And this every aristocracy which the world has ever seen can prove a thousand times. There are two ways in which this can be remedied: The aristocracy may be recruited from the masses, still leaving the aim of education as the preparation of men for the life of this privileged class. This has been the desperate effort of England and in this way English aristocracy has kept its privilege and its wealth more successfully than any modern or ancient land. But even here the method fails because the life of the English aristocrat is after all not the broadest and fullest life.

It is only, therefore, as the university lives up to its name and reaches down to the mass of universal men and makes the life of normal men the object of its training, it is only in this way that the marvelous talent and diversity and emotion of all mankind pours up through this method of human training and establishes a national culture and a national art. Herein lies the eternal logic of democracy.

Thus in the progress of human culture you have not simply a development that produces different classes of men, because classes may harmonize more or less and above the peasant, the artisan and the merchant may exist a leisured class; a class culture may be built, which may flourish long and wide. But the difficulty goes further than the narrowness and ultimate sterility of this plan. Dislocations come within these classes. Their relations to each other may change and break and the foundations upon which the cultured class has been built may crumble. In this case your system of human training becomes not only a system for the supposed benefit of the privileged few, but cannot, indeed, carry out its function even for them. Its system of learning does not fit the mass of men nor the relations of its constituents to that mass.

One can see examples of this the world over. In Kenya, which used to be German East Africa, there are millions of black natives and a few thousand white Englishmen who have seized and monopolized the best land, leaving the natives scarcely enough poor land for subsistence. By physical slavery, economic compulsion or legal sanction, the natives work the land of the whites. On the recent discovery of gold, the natives were dispossessed of their own land in favor of white miners.

What kind of education will suit Kenya? The minority of landed aristocracy will be taught by tutors in Africa and then go to the great English schools and universities. The middle class of immigrant Indian merchants will learn to read and write and count at home or in elementary schools. The great mass of the black millions will be taught something of the art of agriculture, something of the work of artisans, perhaps some ability to read and write, although whether this should be in English or merely in the native tongue is the question. But on this foundation there can grow in Kenya no national university of education, because there are no national ideals. No culture, either African or European, can be built on any such economic foundation. Education in Kenya is a misnomer.

Thus the university, if it is to be firm, must hark back to the original ideal of the Bush School. It must train the children of a nation for life and for making a living. And if it does that, and insofar as it does it, it becomes the perfect expression of the life and the center of the intellectual and cultural expression of its age.

I have seen in my life three expressions of such an ideal; all of them imperfect, all of them partial, and yet each tending toward a broad and singularly beautiful expression of universal education. My first sight of it was here at Fisk University in the fall of 1885 when I arrived as a boy of seventeen. The buildings were few, the cost of tuition, board, room and clothes was less than $200 a year; and the college numbered less than twenty-five. And yet the scheme of education as it existed in our minds, in the class room, in the teaching of professors, in the attitude of students, was a thing of breadth and enthusiasm with an unusual unity of aim. We were a small group of young men and women who were going to transform the world by giving proof of our own ability, by teaching our less fortunate fellows so that they could follow the same path, by proclaiming to the world our belief in American democracy, and the place which Negroes would surely take in it. In none of these propositions did there exist in our minds any hesitation or doubt. There was no question as to employment and perfectly proper employment for graduates, for the ends which we had in view. There was no question of our remaining in school for no good or earnest student ever left.

Above all, to our unblinking gaze, the gates of the World would open—were opening. We never for a moment contemplated the possibility that seven millions of Americans who proved their physical and mental worth could be excluded from the national democracy of a common American culture. We came already bringing gifts. The song we sang was fresh from the lips that threw it round the world. We saw and heard the voices that charmed an emperor and a queen. We believed in the supreme power of the ballot in the hands of the masses to transform the world. Already the North was breaking the Color Line and for the South we were willing to wait.

I saw the same thing a few years later in Harvard University at the end of the nineteenth century. Harvard had broadened its earlier ideals. It was no longer simply a place where rich and learned New England gave the accolade to the social elite. It had broken its shell and stretched out to the West and to the South, to yellow students and to black. I had for the mere asking been granted a fellowship of $300.00— a sum so vast to my experience that I was surprised when it did not pay my first year's expenses. Men sought to make Harvard an expression of the United States, and to do this by means of leaders unshackled in thought and custom who were beating back bars of ignorance and particularism and prejudice. There were William James and Josiah Royce; Nathaniel Shaler and Charles Eliot Norton; George Santayana; Albert Bushnell Hart, and President Eliot himself. There were at least a dozen men—rebels against convention, unorthodox in religion, poor in money, who for a moment held in their hands the culture of the United States, typified it, expressed it, and pushed it a vast step forward. Harvard was not in 1888 a perfect expression of the American soul, or the place where the average American would have found adequate training for his life work. But perhaps it came nearer that high eminence than any other American institution had before or has since.

Again a few years later, I saw the University of Berlin. It represented in 1892 a definite and unified ideal. It did not comprehend at once the culture of all Germany, but I do not believe that ever in modern days and certainly not at Fisk or Harvard did a great university come so near expressing a national ideal. It was as though I had been stepping up from a little group college with a national outlook to a national institution which came near gathering to itself the thought and culture of forty million human beings. Every great professor of Germany, with few exceptions, had the life ambition to be called to a Chair in the Friedrich Wilhelm's Universitaet zu Berlin. I sat beneath the voice of a man who perhaps more than any single individual embodied the German ideal and welded German youth into that great aggressive fist which literally put Deutschland ueber Alles! I remember well Heinrich von Treitschke. With swift flying words that hid a painfully stuttering tongue, he hammered into the young men who sat motionless and breathless beneath his voice, the doctrine of the inborn superiority of the German race. He told us few foreigners to our faces, that we felt and acknowledged our inferiority. And out and around that university for a thousand miles, millions of people shared in its ideal teaching, and did this in spite of caste of birth and poverty, jostling wealth because they believe in an ultimate unity which Bismarkian state socialism promised. They sang their national songs and joined in national festivals with enthusiasm that brought tears to the onlooker. And it made you realize the ideal of a single united nation and what it could express in matchless poetry, daring science and undying music.

Yet in each of these cases, the ultimate ideal of a national much less a universal university was a vision never wholly attained, and in the very nature of the case it could not be. Fisk had to be a Negro university because it was teaching Negroes and they were a caste with their own history and problems. Harvard was still a New England provincial institution and Berlin was sharply and determinedly German. Their common characteristic was that starting where they did and must, they aimed and moved toward universal culture.

Now with these things in mind, let us turn back to America and to the American Negro. It has been said many times that a Negro university is nothing more and nothing less than a university. Quite recently one of the great leaders of education in the United States, Abraham Flexner, said something of that sort concerning Howard University. As President of the Board of Trustees, he said he was seeking to build not a Negro university but a University. And by those words he brought again before our eyes the ideal of a great institution of learning which becomes a center of universal culture. With all good will toward them that speak such words it is the object of this paper to insist that there can be no college for Negroes which is not a Negro college and that while an American Negro university, just like a German or a Swiss university may rightly aspire to a universal culture unhampered by limitations of race and culture, yet it must start on the earth where we sit and not in the skies whither we aspire. May I develop this thought?

In the first place, we have got to remember that here in America, in the year 1933, we have a situation which cannot be ignored. There was a time when it seemed as though we might best attack the Negro problem by ignoring its most unpleasant features. It was not and is not yet in good taste to speak generally about certain facts which characterize our situation in America. We are politically hamstrung. We have the greatest difficulty in getting suitable and remunerative work. Our education is more and more not only being confined to our own schools but to a segregated public school system far below the average of the nation with one-third of our children continuously out of school. And above all, and this we like least to mention, we suffer a social ostracism which is so deadening and discouraging that we are compelled either to lie about it or to turn our faces toward the red flag of revolution. It consists of the kind of studied and repeated and emphasized public insult of the sort which during all the long history of the world has led men to kill or be killed. And in the full face of any effort which any black man may make to escape this ostracism for himself, stands this flaming word of racial doctrine which will distract his effort and energy if it does not lead him to spiritual suicide.

We boast and have a right to boast of our accomplishment between the days that I studied here and this Forty-fifth Anniversary of my graduation. It is a calm appraisal of fact to say that the history of modern civilization cannot surpass if it can parallel the advance of American Negroes in every essential line of culture in these years. And yet when we have said this we must have the common courage honestly to admit that every step we have made forward has been greeted by a backward step on the part of the American public in caste intoleration, mob law, and racial hatred.

I need but remind you that when I graduated from Fisk there was no "Jim Crow" car in Tennessee and I saw Hunter of '89 once sweep a brakeman aside at the Union Station and escort a crowd of Fisk students into the first-class seats for which they had paid. There was no legal disfranchisement and a black Fiskite sat in the Legislature; and while the Chancellor of Vanderbilt University had annually to be reintroduced to the President of Fisk, yet no white Southern group presumed to dictate the internal social life of this institution.

Manifestly with all that can be said, pro and con, and in extenuation, and by way of excuse and hope, this is the situation and we know it. There is no human way by which these facts can be ignored. We cannot do our daily work, sing a song, or write a book or carry on a university and act as though these things were not.

If this is true, then no matter how much we may dislike the statement, the American Negro problem is and must be the center of the Negro American university. It has got to be. You are teaching Negroes. There is no use pretending that you are teaching white Americans or that you are teaching citizens of the world. You are teaching American Negroes in 1933, and they are the subjects of a caste system in the Republic of the United States of America and their life problem is primarily this problem of caste.

Upon these foundations, therefore, your university must start and build. Nor is the thing so entirely unusual or unheard of as it sounds. A university in Spain is not simply a university. It is a Spanish university. It is a university located in Spain. It uses the Spanish language. It starts with Spanish history and makes conditions in Spain the starting point of its teaching. Its education is for Spaniards, not for them as they may be or ought to be, but as they are with their present problems and disadvantages and opportunities.

In other words, the Spanish university is founded and grounded in Spain, just as surely as a French university is French. There are some people who have difficulty in apprehending this very clear truth. They assume, for instance, that the French university is in a singular sense universal, and is based on a comprehension and inclusion of all mankind and of their problem. But it is not, and the assumption that it arises simply because so much of French culture has been built into universal civilization. A French university is founded in France; it uses the French language and assumes a knowledge of French history. The present problems of the French people are its major problems and it becomes universal only so far as other peoples of the world comprehend and are at one with France in its mighty and beautiful history.

In the same way, a Negro university in the United States of America begins with Negroes. It uses that variety of the English idiom which they understand; and above all, it is founded, or it should be founded on a knowledge of the history of their people in Africa and in the United States, and their present condition. Without white-washing or translating wish into facts, it begins with that; and then it asks how shall these young men and women be trained to earn a living and live a life under the circumstances in which they find themselves or with such changing of those circumstances as time and work and determination will permit.

Is this statement of the field of a Negro university a denial of aspiration or a change from older ideals? I do not think it is, although I admit in my own mind some change of thought and modification of method.

The system of learning which bases itself upon the actual condition of certain classes and groups of human beings is tempted to suppress a minor premise of fatal menace. It proposes that the knowledge given and the methods pursued in such institutions of learning shall be for the definite object of perpetuating present conditions or of leaving their amelioration in the hands of and at the initiative of other forces and other folk. This was the great criticism that those of us who fought for higher education of Negroes thirty years ago brought against the industrial school.

The industrial school founded itself and rightly upon the actual situation of American Negroes and said: "What can be done to change this situation?" And its answer was: A training in technique and method such as would incorporate the disadvantaged group into the industrial organization of the country, and in that organization the leaders of the Negro had perfect faith. Since that day the industrial machine has cracked and groaned. Its technique has changed faster than any school could teach; the relations of capital and labor have increased in complication and it has become so clear that Negro poverty is not primarily caused by ignorance of technical knowledge that the industrial school has almost surrendered its program.

In opposition to that, the proponents of college training in those earlier years said: "What black men need is the broader and more universal training so that they can apply the general principles of knowledge to the particular circumstances of their condition."

Here again was indubitable truth but incomplete truth. The technical problem lay in the method of teaching this broader and more universal truth and here just as in the industrial program, we must start where we are and not where we wish to be.

As I said a few years ago at Howard University both these positions had thus something of truth and right. Because of the peculiar economic situation in our country the program of the industrial school came to grief first and has practically been given up. Starting even though we may with the actual condition of the Negro peasant and artisan, we cannot ameliorate his condition simply by his learning a trade which is the transient technique of a passing era. More vision and knowledge is needed than that. But on the other hand, while the Negro college of a generation ago set down a defensible and true program of applying knowledge to facts, it unfortunately could not completely carry it out and it did not carry it out because the one thing that the industrial philosophy gave to education, the Negro college did not take and that was that the university education of black men in the United States must be grounded in the condition and work of those black men!

On the other hand, it would be of course idiotic to say, as the former industrial philosophy almost said, that so far as most black men are concerned education must stop with this. No, starting with present conditions and using the facts and the knowledge of the present situation of American Negroes, the Negro university expands toward the possession and the conquest of all knowledge. It seeks from a beginning of the history of the Negro in America and in Africa to interpret all history; from a beginning of social development among Negro slaves and freedmen in America and Negro tribes and kingdoms in Africa, to interpret and understand the social development of all mankind in all ages. It seeks to reach modern science of matter and life from the surroundings and habits and aptitudes of American Negroes and thus lead up to understanding of life and matter in the universe.

And this is a different program than a similar function would be in a white university or in a Russian university or in an English university, because it starts from a different point. It is a matter of beginnings and integrations of one group which sweep instinctive knowledge and inheritance and current reactions into a universal world of science, sociology, and art. In no other way can the American Negro college function. It cannot begin with history and lead to Negro history. It cannot start with sociology and end with Negro sociology.

Why was it that the Renaissance of literature which began among Negroes ten years ago has never taken real and lasting root? It was because it was a transplanted and exotic thing. It was a literature written for the benefit of white people and at the behest of white readers, and starting out primarily from the white point of view. It never had a real Negro constituency and it did not grow out of the inmost heart and frank experience of Negroes; on such an artificial basis no real literature can grow.

On the other hand, if starting in a great Negro university you have knowledge, beginning with the particular, and going out to universal comprehension and unhampered expression, you are going to begin to realize for the American Negro the full life which is denied him now. And then after that comes a realization of the older object of our college—to bring this universal culture down and apply it to the individual life and individual condition of living Negroes.

The university must become not simply a center of knowledge but a center of applied knowledge and guide of action. And this is all the more necessary now since we easily see that planned action especially in economic life is going to be the watchword of civilization.

If the college does not thus root itself in the group life and afterward apply its knowledge and culture to actual living, other social organs must replace the college in this function. A strong, intelligent family life may adjust the student to higher culture; and, too, a social clan may receive the graduate and induct him into life. This has happened and is happening among a minority of privileged people. But it costs society a fatal price. It tends to hinder progress and hamper change—it makes education propaganda for things as they are. It leaves the mass of those without family training and without social standing—misfits and rebels who despite their education are uneducated in its meaning and application. The only college which stands for the progress of all—mass as well as aristocracy—functions in root and blossom as well as in the overshadowing and heaven filling tree. No system of learning—no university—can be universal before it is German, French, Negro. Grounded in inexorable fact and condition, in Poland or Italy, it may seek the universal and haply it may find it— and finding it bring it down to earth and to us.

We have imbibed from the surrounding white world a childish idea of progress. Progress means bigger and better results always and forever. But there is no such rule of life. In six thousand years of human culture, the losses and retrogressions have been enormous. We have no assurance that twentieth century civilization will survive. We do not know that American Negroes will survive. There are sinister signs about us, antecedent to and unconnected with the great depression. The organized might of industry north and south is relegating the Negro to the edge of survival and using him as a labor reservoir on starvation wage. No secure professional class, no science, literature nor art can live on such sub-soil. It is an insistent deep-throated cry for rescue, guidance, and organized advance that greets the black leader today and the college that trains him has got to let him know at least as much about the great black miners strike in Alabama as about the age of Pericles. By singular accident—almost by compelling fate—I drove by as I came here yesterday—the region where I taught a country school over forty years ago. There is no progress there. There is only space, disillusion, and death beside the same eternal hills. There where I first heard the Sorrow Songs are the graves of men and women and children who had the making of a fine intelligent upstanding yeomanry. There remains but the half-starved farmer, the casual laborer, the unpaid servant. Why in a land rich with wealth, muscle, and colleges?

To the New Englander of wealth and family Harvard and Yale are parts and only parts of a broad training which the New England home begins and a State Street or Wall Street business ends. How fine and yet how fatal! There lies root and reason for the World War and the

Great Depression. To the American Negro, culture must adjust itself to a different family history and apply itself to a new system of social caste and in this adjustment comes new opportunity of making education and progress possible and not antagonistic.

We are on the threshold of a new era. Let us not deceive ourselves with outworn ideals of wealth and servants and luxuries, reared on a foundation of ignorance, starvation and want. Instinctively, we have absorbed these ideals from our twisted white American environment. This new economic planning is not for us unless we do it. Unless the American Negro today, led by trained university men of broad vision, sits down to work out by economics and mathematics, by physics and chemistry, by history and sociology, exactly how and where he is to earn a living and how he is to establish a reasonable life in the United States or elsewhere, unless this is done the university has missed its field and function and the American Negro is doomed to be a suppressed and inferior caste in the United States for incalculable time.

Here, then, is a job for the American Negro university. It cannot be successfully ignored or dodged without the growing menace of disaster. I lay the problem before you as one which you must not ignore.

To carry out this plan, two things and only two things are necessary—teachers and students. Buildings and endowments may help, but they are not indispensable. It is necessary first to have teachers who comprehend this program and know how to make it live among their students. This is calling for a good deal, because it asks that teachers teach that which they have learned in no American school and which they never will learn until we have a Negro university of the sort that I am visioning. No teacher, black or white, who comes to a university like Fisk, filled simply with general ideas of human culture or general knowledge of disembodied science, is going to make a university of this school. Because a university is made of human beings, learning of the things they do not know from things they do know in their own lives.

And secondly, we must have students. They must be chosen for ability to learn. There is always the temptation to assume that the children of privileged classes, the rich, the noble, the white, are those who can best take education. One has but to express this to realize its utter futility. But perhaps the most dangerous thing among us is for us, without thought, to imitate the white world and assume that we can choose students at Fisk because of the amount of money of which their parents have happened to get hold of. That basis of selection is going to give us an extraordinary aggregation. We want by the nicest methods possible, to seek out the talented and the gifted among our constituency, quite regardless of their wealth or position, and to fill this university and similar institutions with persons who have got brains enough to take fullest advantage of what the university offers. There is no other way. With teachers who know what they are teaching and whom they are teaching and the life that surrounds both the knowledge and the knower, and with students who have the capacity and the will to absorb this knowledge, we can build the sort of Negro university which will emancipate not simply the black folk of the United States, but those white folk who in their effort to suppress Negroes have killed their own culture—men who in their desperate effort to replace equality with caste and to build inordinate wealth on a foundation of abject poverty have succeeded in killing democracy, art, and religion.

Only a universal system of learning, rooted in the will and condition of the masses and blossoming from that manure up toward the stars, is worth the name. Once builded it can only grow as it brings down sunlight and star shine and impregnates the mud. The chief obstacle in this rich land endowed with every national resource and with the abilities of a hundred different peoples—the chief and only obstacle to the coming of that kingdom of economic equality which is the only logical end of work, is the determination of the white world to keep the black world poor and make themselves rich. The disaster which this selfish and short-sighted policy has brought lies at the bottom of this present depression, and too, its cure lies beside it. Your clear vision of a world without wealth, of capital without profit, of income based on work alone, is the path cut not only for you but for all men.

Is not this a program of segregation, emphasis of race and particularism as against national unity and universal humanity? It is and it is not by choice but for force; you do not get humanity by wishing it nor do you become American citizens simply because you want to. A Negro university from its high ground of unfaltering facing of the Truth, from its unblinking stare at hard facts does not advocate segregation, apart, hammered into a separate unity by spiritual intolerance and legal sanction backed by mob law, and that this separation is growing in strength and fixation; that it is worse today than a half century ago and that no character, address, culture or desert is going to change it, in our day or for centuries to come. Recognizing this brute fact, groups of cultured, trained, and devoted men gathering in great institutions of learning proceed to ask: What are we going to do about it? It is silly to ignore and gloss the truth; it is idiotic to proceed as though we were white or yellow, English or Russian. Here we stand. We are American Negroes. It is beside the point to ask whether we form a real race. Biologically we are mingled of all conceivable elements, but race is psychology, not biology; and psychologically we are a unified race with one history, one red memory, and one revolt. It is not ours to argue whether we will be segregated or whether we ought to be a caste. We are segregated; we are a caste. This is our given and at present unalterable fact. Our problem is: How far and in what way can we consciously and scientifically guide our future so as to insure our physical survival, our spiritual freedom and our social growth? Either we do this or we die. There is no alternative. If America proposes the murder of this group, its moral descent into imbecility and crime and its utter loss of manhood, self-assertion, and courage, the sooner we realize this the better. By that great line of McKay: "If we must die, let it not be like hogs." But the alternative of not dying like hogs is not that of dying or killing like snarling dogs. It is rather conquering the world by thought and brain and plan; by expression and organized cultural ideals. Therefore, let us not beat futile wings in impotent frenzy, but carefully plan and guide our segregated life, organize in industry and politics to protect it and expand it, and above all to give it unhampered spiritual expression in art and literature. It is the council of fear and cowardice to say this cannot be done. What must be can be and it is only a question of Science and Sacrifice to bring the great consummation.

What that will be, none knows. It may be a great physical segregation of the world along the Color Line; it may be an economic rebirth which insures spiritual and group integrity amid physical diversity. It may be utter annihilation of class and race and color barriers in one ultimate mankind, differentiated by talent, susceptibility and gift—but any of these ends are matters of long centuries and not years. We live in years, swift flying, transient years. We hold the possible future in our hands but not by wish and will, only by thought, plan, knowledge, and organization. If the college can pour into the coming age an American Negro who knows himself and his plight and how to protect himself and fight race prejudice, then the world of our dream will come and not otherwise.

> The golden days are gone. Why do we wait
> So long upon the marble steps, blood
> Falling from our open wounds? and why
> Do our black faces search the empty sky?
> Is there something we have forgotten?
> Some precious thing we have lost,
> Wandering in strange lands?

What we have lost is the courage of independent self-assertion. We have had as our goal—American full citizenship, nationally recognized. This has failed—flatly and decisively failed. Very well. We're not dead yet. We are not going to die. If we use our brains and strength there is no way to stop our ultimate triumph as creators of modern culture—if we use our strength and brains.

And what pray stops us but our dumb caution—our fear, our very sanity? Let us then be insane with courage.

> Like a mad man's dream, there came
> One fair, swift flash to me

Of distances, of streets aflame,
With joy and agony;
And further yet, a moonlit sea
Foaming across its bars
And further yet, the infinity
Of wheeling suns and stars.

DOES THE NEGRO NEED SEPARATE SCHOOLS?

There are in the United States some four million Negroes of school age, of whom two million are in school, and of these, four-fifths are taught by forty-eight thousand Negro teachers in separate schools. Less than a half million are in mixed schools in the North, where they are taught almost exclusively by white teachers. Beside this, there are seventy-nine Negro universities and colleges with one thousand colored teachers, beside a number of private secondary schools.

The question which I am discussing is: Are these separate schools and institutions needed? And the answer, to my mind, is perfectly clear. They are needed just so far as they are necessary for the proper education of the Negro race. The proper education of any people includes sympathetic touch between teacher and pupil; knowledge on the part of the teacher, not simply of the individual taught, but of his surroundings and background, and the history of his class and group; such contact between pupils, and between teacher and pupil, on the basis of perfect social equality, as will increase this sympathy and knowledge; facilities for education in equipment and housing, and the promotion of such extra-curricular activities as will tend to induct the child into life.

If this is true, and if we recognize the present attitude of white America toward black America, then the Negro not only needs the vast majority of these schools, but it is a grave question if, in the near future, he will not need more such schools, both to take care of his natural increase, and to defend him against the growing animosity of the whites. It is of course fashionable and popular to deny this; to try to deceive ourselves into thinking that race prejudice in the United States across the Color Line is gradually softening and that slowly but surely we are coming to the time when racial animosities and class lines will be so obliterated that separate schools will be anachronisms.

Certainly, I shall welcome such a time. Just as long as Negroes are taught in Negro schools and whites in white schools; the poor in the slums, and the rich in private schools; just as long as it is impracticable to welcome Negro students to Harvard, Yale and Princeton; just as long as colleges like Williams, Amherst and Wellesley tend to become the property of certain wealthy families, where Jews are not solicited;

just so long we shall lack in America that sort of public education which will create the intelligent basis of a real democracy.

Much as I would like this, and hard as I have striven and shall strive to help realize it, I am no fool; and I know that race prejudice in the United States today is such that most Negroes cannot receive proper education in white institutions. If the public schools of Atlanta, Nashville, New Orleans and Jacksonville were thrown open to all races tomorrow, the education that colored children would get in them would be worse than pitiable. It would not be education. And in the same way, there are many public school systems in the North where Negroes are admitted and tolerated, but they are not educated; they are crucified. There are certain Northern universities where Negro students, no matter what their ability, desert, or accomplishment, cannot get fair recognition, either in classroom or on the campus, in dining halls and student activities, or in common human courtesy. It is well-known that in certain faculties of the University of Chicago, no Negro has yet received the doctorate and seldom can achieve the mastership in arts; at Harvard, Yale and Columbia, Negroes are admitted but not welcomed; while in other institutions, like Princeton, they cannot even enroll.

Under such circumstances, there is no room for argument as to whether the Negro needs separate schools or not. The plain fact faces us, that either he will have separate schools or he will not be educated. There may be, and there is, considerable difference of opinion as to how far this separation in schools is today necessary. There can be argument as to what our attitude toward further separation should be Suppose, for instance, that in Montclair, New Jersey, a city of wealth and culture, the Board of Education is determined to establish separate schools for Negroes; suppose that, despite the law, separate Negro schools are already established in Philadelphia, and pressure is being steadily brought to extend this separation at least to the junior high school; what must be our attitude toward this?

Manifestly, no general and inflexible rule can be laid down. If public opinion is such in Montclair that Negro children can not receive decent and sympathetic education in the white schools, and no Negro teachers can be employed, there is for us no choice. We have got to accept Negro schools. Any agitation and action aimed at compelling a rich and powerful majority of the citizens to do what they will not do, is useless. On the other hand, we have a right and a duty to assure ourselves of the truth concerning this attitude; by careful conferences, by public meetings and by petitions, we should convince ourselves whether this demand for separate schools is merely the agitation of a prejudiced minority, or the considered and final judgement of the town.

There are undoubtedly cases where a minority of leaders force their opinions upon the majority, and induce a community to establish separate schools, when as a matter of fact, there is no general demand for it; there has been no friction in the schools; and Negro children have been decently treated. In that case, a firm and intelligent appeal to public opinion would eventually settle the matter. But the futile attempt to compel even by law a group to do what it is determined not to do, is a silly waste of money, time, and temper.

On the other hand, there are also cases where there has been no separation in schools and no movement toward it. And yet the treatment of Negro children in the schools, the kind of teaching and the kind of advice they get, is such that they ought to demand either a thorough-going revolution in the official attitude toward Negro students, or absolute separation in educational facilities. To endure bad schools and wrong education because the schools are "mixed" is a costly if not fatal mistake. I have long been convinced, for instance that the Negroes in the public schools of Harlem are not getting an education that is in any sense comparable in efficiency, discipline, and human development with that which Negroes are getting in the separate public schools in Washington, D.C. And yet on its school situation, black Harlem is dumb and complacent, if not actually laudatory.

Recognizing the fact that for the vast majority of colored students in elementary, secondary, and collegiate education, there must be today separate educational institutions because of an attitude on the part of the white people which is not going materially to change in our time, our customary attitude toward these separate schools must be absolutely and definitely changed. As it is today, American Negroes almost universally disparage their own schools. They look down upon them; they often treat the Negro teachers in them with contempt; they refuse to work for their adequate support; and they refuse to join public movements to increase their efficiency.

The reason for this is quite clear, and may be divided into two parts: (1) the fear that any movement which implies segregation even as a temporary, much less as a relatively permanent institution, in the United States, is a fatal surrender of principle which in the end will rebound and bring more evils on the Negro than he suffers today. (2) The other reason is at bottom an utter lack of faith on the part of Negroes that their race can do anything really well. If Negroes could conceive that Negroes could establish schools quite as good as or even superior to white schools; if Negro colleges were of equal grade in accomplishment and in scientific work with white colleges; then separation would be a passing incident and not a permanent evil; but as long as American Negroes believe that their race is constitutionally and permanently inferior to white people, they necessarily disbelieve in every possible Negro Institution.

The first argument is more or less metaphysical and cannot be decided *a priori* for every case. There are times when one must stand up for principle at the cost of discomfort, harm, and death. But in the case of the education of the young, you must consider not simply yourself but the children and the relation of children to life. It is difficult to think of anything more important for the development of a people than proper training for their children; and yet I have repeatedly seen wise and loving colored parents take infinite pains to force their children into schools where the white children, white teachers, and white parents despise and resented the dark child, made mock of it, neglected or bullied it, and literally rendered its life a living hell. Such parents want their child to "fight" this thing out,—but, dear God, at what a cost! Sometimes, to be sure, the child triumphs and teaches the school community a lesson; but even in such cases, the cost may be high, and the child's whole life turned into an effort to win cheap applause at the expense of healthy individuality. In other cases, the result of the experiment may be complete ruin of character, gift, and ability and ingrained hatred of schools and men. For the kind of battle thus indicated, most children are under no circumstances suited. It is the refinement of cruelty to require it of them. Therefore, in evaluating the advantage and disadvantage of accepting race hatred as a brutal but real fact, or of using a little child as a battering ram upon which its nastiness can be thrust, we must give greater value and greater emphasis to the rights of the child's own soul. We shall get a finer, better balance of spirit; an infinitely more capable and rounded personality by putting children in schools where they are wanted, and where they are happy and inspired, than in thrusting them into hells where they are ridiculed and hated.

Beyond this, lies the deeper, broader fact. If the American Negro really believed in himself; if he believe that Negro teachers can educate children according to the best standards of modern training; if he believed that Negro colleges transmit and add to science, as well as or better than other colleges, then he would bend his energies, not to escaping inescapable association with his own group, but to seeing that his group had every opportunity for its best and highest development. He would insist that his teachers be decently paid; that his schools were properly housed and equipped; that his colleges be supplied with scholarship and research funds; and he would be far more interested in the efficiency of these institutions of learning, than in forcing himself into other institutions where he is not wanted.

As long as the Negro student wishes to graduate from Columbia, not because Columbia is an institution of learning, but because it is attended by white students; as long as a Negro student is ashamed to attend Fisk or Howard because these institutions are largely run by black folk, just so long the main problem of Negro education will not be segregation but self-knowledge and self-respect.

There are not many teachers in Negro schools who would not esteem it an unparalleled honor and boast of it to their dying day, if instead of teaching black folk, they could get a chance to teach poor-whites, Irishmen, Italians or Chinese in a "white" institution. This is not unnatural. This is to them a sort of acid test of their worth. It is but the logical result of the "white" propaganda which has swept civilization for the last thousand years, and which is now bolstered and defended by brave words, high wages, and monopoly of opportunities. But this state of mind is suicidal and must be fought, and fought doggedly and bitterly: first, by giving Negro teachers decent wages, decent schoolhouses and equipment, and reasonable chances for advancement; and then by kicking out and leaving to the mercy of the white world those who do not and cannot believe in their own.

Lack of faith in Negro enterprise leads to singular results: Negroes will fight frenziedly to prevent segregated schools; but if segregation is forced upon them by dominant white public opinion, they will suddenly lose interest and scarcely raise a finger to see that the resultant Negro schools get a fair share of the public funds so as to have adequate equipment and housing; to see that real teachers are appointed, and that they are paid as much as white teachers doing the same work. Today, when the Negro public schools system gets from half to one-tenth of the amount of money spent on white schools, and is often consequently poorly run and poorly taught, colored people tacitly if not openly join with white people in assuming that Negroes cannot run Negro enterprises, and cannot educate themselves, and that the very establishment of a Negro school means starting an inferior school.

The N.A.A.C.P. and other Negro organizations have spent thousands of dollars to prevent the establishment of segregated Negro schools, but scarcely a single cent to see that the division of funds between white and Negro schools, North and South, is carried out with some faint approximation of justice. There can be no doubt that if the Supreme Court were overwhelmed with cases where the blatant and impudent discrimination against Negro education is openly acknowledged, it would be compelled to hand down decisions which would make this discrimination impossible. We Negroes do not dare to press this point and force these decisions because, forsooth, it would acknowledge the fact of separate schools, a fact that does not need to be acknowledged, and will not need to be for two centuries.

Howard, Fisk, and Atlanta are naturally unable to do the type and grade of graduate work which is done at Columbia, Chicago, and Harvard; but why attribute this to a defect in the Negro race, and not to the fact that the large white colleges have from one hundred to one thousand times the funds for equipment and research that Negro colleges can command? To this, it may logically be answered, all the more reason that Negroes should try to get into better equipped schools, and who pray denies this? But the opportunity for such entrance is becoming more and more difficult, and the training offered less and less suited to the American Negro of today. Conceive a Negro teaching in a Southern school the economics which he learned at the Harvard Business School! Conceive a Negro teacher of history retailing to his black students the sort of history that is taught at the University of Chicago! Imagine the history of Reconstruction being handed by a colored professor from the lips of Columbia professors to the ears of the black belt! The results of this kind of thing are often fantastic, and call for Negro history and sociology, and even physical science taught by men who understand their audience, and are not afraid of the truth.

There was a time when the ability of Negro brains to do first-class work had to be proven by facts and figures, and I was a part of the movement that sought to set the accomplishments of Negro ability before the world. But the world before which I was setting this proof was a disbelieving white world. I did not need the proof for myself. I did not dream that my fellow Negroes needed it; but in the last few years, I have become curiously convinced that until American Negroes believe in their own power and ability, they are going to be helpless before the white world, and the white world, realizing this inner paralysis and lack of self-confidence, is going to persist in its insane determination to rule the universe for its own selfish advantage.

Does the Negro need separate schools? God knows he does. But what he needs more than separate schools is a firm and unshakable belief that twelve million American Negroes have the inborn capacity to accomplish just as much as any nation of twelve million anywhere in the world ever accomplished, and that this is not because they are Negroes but because they are human.

So far, I have noted chiefly negative arguments for separate Negro institutions of learning based on the fact that in the majority of cases Negroes are not welcomed in public schools and universities nor treated as fellow human beings. But beyond this, there are certain positive reasons due to the fact that American Negroes have, because of their history, group experiences and memories, a distinct entity, whose spirit and reactions demand a certain type of education for its development.

In the past, this fact has been noted and misused for selfish purposes. On the ground that Negroes needed a type of education "suited" to them, we have an attempt to train them as menials and dependents; or in the case of West Indians, an attempt to perpetuate their use as low-paid laborers by limiting their knowledge; or in the case of African natives, efforts to deprive them of modern languages and modern science in order to seal their subordination to out-worn mores, reactionary native rulers, industrialization.

What I have in mind is nothing like this. It is rather an honest development of the premises from which this plea for special education starts. It is illustrated by these facts: Negroes must know the history of the Negro race in America, and this they will seldom get in white institutions. Their children ought to study textbooks like Brawley's "Short History," the first edition of Woodson's "Negro in Our History," and Cromwell, Turner and Dykes' "Readings from Negro Authors." Negroes who celebrate the birthdays of Washington and Lincoln, and the worthy, but colorless and relatively unimportant "founders" of various Negro colleges, ought not to forget the 5th of March,—that first national holiday of this country, which commemorates the martyrdom of Crispus Attucks. They ought to celebrate Negro Health Week and Negro History Week. They ought to study intelligently and from their own point of view, the slave trade, slavery, emancipation, Reconstruction, and present economic development.

Beyond this, Negro colleges ought to be studying anthropology, psychology, and the social sciences, from the point of view of the colored races. Today, the anthropology that is being taught, and the expeditions financed for archeological and ethnographical explorations, are for the most part straining every nerve to erase the history of black folk from the record. One has only to remember that the majority of anthropologists have peopled the continent of Africa itself with almost no Negroes, while men like Sayce and Reisner have even declared that the Ethiopians have no Negro blood. All this has been done by the legardemain and metaphysics of nomenclature, and in the face of the great and important history of black blood in the world.

Recently, something has been done by colored scholars to correct the extraordinary propaganda of post-war psychology which sent men like Brigham and McDougall rushing into scientific proof of Negro congenital inferiority. But much more is necessary and demanded of Negro scholarship. In history and the social sciences the Negro school and college have an unusual opportunity and role. It does not consist simply in trying to parallel the history of white folk with similar boasting about black and brown folk, but rather an honest evaluation of human effort and accomplishment, without color blindness, and without transforming history into a record of dynasties and prodigies.

Here, we have in America, a working class which in our day has achieved physical freedom, and mental clarity. An economic battle has just begun. It can be studied and guided; it can teach consumers' cooperation, democracy, and socialism, and be made not simply a record and pattern for the Negro race, but a guide for the rise of the working classes throughout the world, just at the critical time when these classes are about to assume their just political domination which is destined to become the redemption of mankind.

Much has been said of the special esthetic ability of the Negro race. Naturally, it has been exaggerated. Naturally, it is not a racial characteristic in the sense of hereditary, inborn, and heritable difference; but there is no doubt but what the tremendous psychic history of the American and West Indian groups has made it possible for the present generation to accumulate a wealth of material which, with encouragement and training, could find expression in the drama, in color and form, and in music. And where could this training better be pursued than in separate Negro schools under competent and intelligent teachers? What little has already been done in this line is scarcely a beginning of what is possible, provided the object is not simple entertainment or bizarre efforts at money raising.

In biology, the pioneering work of Carolyn Bond Day could be extended indefinitely in Negro laboratories; and in the purely physical and chemical sciences, the need of Negroes familiar with the intricate technical basis of modern civilization would not only help them to find their place in the industrial scene for their own organization, but also enable them to help Abyssinia, India, China, and the colored world, to maintain their racial integrity, and their economic independence. It could easily be the mission and duty of American Negroes to master this scientific basis of modern invention, and give it to all mankind.

Thus, instead of our schools being simply separate schools, forced on us by grim necessity, they can become centers of a new and beautiful effort at human education, which may easily lead and guide the world in many important and valuable aspects. It is for this reason that when our schools are separate, the control of the teaching force, the expenditure of money, the choice of textbooks, the discipline and other administrative matters of this sort ought, also, to come into our hands, and be incessantly demanded and guarded.

I remember once, in Texas, reading in a high-school textbook for colored students, the one anecdote given concerning Abraham Lincoln: he was pictured as chasing Negro thieves all night through the woods from his Mississippi flatboat! Children could read that history in vain to learn any word of what had been accomplished in American history by Benjamin Bannekar, Jan Matzeliger, Elijah McCoy, Frederick Douglass, or James Dunn. In fact, one of the peculiar tragedies of the smaller Southern colleges is that they hire as teachers of history, economics and sociology, colored men trained in Northern institutions where not a word of any information concerning these disciplines, so far as Negroes are concerned, has ever been imparted to them. I speak from experience, because I came to Atlanta University to teach history in 1897, without the slightest idea from my Harvard tuition, that Negroes ever had any history!

I know that this article will forthwith be interpreted by certain illiterate "nitwits" as a plea for segregated Negro schools and colleges. It is not. It is simply calling a spade a spade. It is saying in plain English: that a separate Negro school, where children are treated like human beings, trained by teachers of their own race, who know what it means to be black in the year of salvation 1935, is infinitely better than making our boys and girls doormats to be spit and trampled upon and lied to by ignorant social climbers, whose sole claim to superiority is ability to kick "niggers" when they are down. I say, too, that certain studies and discipline necessary to Negroes can seldom be found in white schools.

It means this, and nothing more.

To sum up this: theoretically, the Negro needs neither segregated schools nor mixed schools. What he needs is Education. What he must remember is that there is no magic, either in mixed schools or in segregated schools. A mixed school with poor and unsympathetic teachers, with hostile public opinion, and no teaching of truth concerning black folk, is bad. A segregated school with ignorant placeholders, inadequate equipment, poor salaries, and wretched housing, is equally bad. Other things being equal, the mixed school is the broader, more natural basis for the education of all youth. It gives wider contacts; it inspires greater self-confidence; and suppresses the inferiority complex. But other things seldom are equal, and in that case, Sympathy, Knowledge, and the Truth, outweigh all that the mixed school can offer.

A NEGRO NATION WITHIN THE NATION

No more critical situation ever faced the Negroes of America than that of today—not in 1830, nor in 1861, nor in 1867. More than ever the appeal of the Negro for elementary justice falls on deaf ears.

Three-fourths of us are disfranchised; yet no writer on democratic reform, no third-party movement says a word about Negroes. The Bull Moose crusade in 1912 refused to notice them; the La Follette uprising in 1924 was hardly aware of them; the Socialists still keep them in the background. Negro children are systematically denied education; when the National Educational Association asks for federal aid to education it permits discrimination to be perpetuated by the present local authorities. Once or twice a month Negroes convicted of no crime are openly and publicly lynched, and even burned; yet a National Crime Convention is brought to perfunctory and unwilling notice of this only by mass picketing and all but illegal agitation. When a man with every qualification is refused a position simply because his great-grandfather was black there is not a ripple of comment or protest.

Long before the depression Negroes in the South were losing "Negro" jobs, those assigned them by common custom—poorly paid and largely undesirable toil, but nevertheless life-supporting. New techniques, new enterprises, mass production, impersonal ownership and control have been largely displacing the skilled white and Negro worker in tobacco manufacturing, in iron and steel, in lumbering and mining, and in transportation. Negroes are now restricted more and more to common labor and domestic service of the lowest paid and worst kind. In textile, chemical and other manufactures Negroes were from the first nearly excluded, and just as slavery kept the poor white out of profitable agriculture, so freedom prevents the poor Negro from finding a place in manufacturing. The worldwide decline in agriculture has moreover carried the mass of black farmers, despite heroic endeavor among the few, down to the level of landless tenants and peons.

The World War and its wild aftermath seemed for a moment to open a new door; two million black workers rushed North to work in iron and steel, make automobiles and pack meat, build houses and do the heavy toil in factories. They met first the closed trade union which excluded them from the best-paid jobs and pushed them into the low-wage gutter, denied them homes and mobbed them. Then they met the depression.

Since 1929 Negro workers, like white workers, have lost their jobs, have had mortgages foreclosed on their farms and homes, have used up their small savings. But, in the case of the Negro worker, everything has been worse in larger or smaller degree; the loss has been greater and more permanent. Technological displacement, which began before the depression, has been accelerated, while unemployment and falling wages struck black men sooner, went to lower levels and will last longer.

Negro public schools in the rural South have often disappeared, while southern city schools are crowded to suffocation. The Booker Washington High School in Atlanta, built for 1,000 pupils, has 3,000 attending in double daily sessions. Above all, federal and state relief holds out little promise for the Negro. It is but human that the unemployed white man and the starving white child should be relieved first by local authorities who regard them as fellowmen, but often regard Negroes as subhuman. While the white worker has sometimes been given more than relief and been helped to his feet, the black worker has often been pauperized by being just kept from starvation. There are some plans for national rehabilitation and the rebuilding of the whole industrial system. Such plans should provide for the Negro's future relations to American industry and culture, but those provisions the country is not only unprepared to make but refuses to consider.

In the Tennessee Valley beneath the Norris Dam, where do Negroes come in? And what shall be their industrial place? In the attempt to rebuild agriculture the southern landholder will in all probability be put on his feet, but the black tenant has been pushed to the edge of despair. In the matter of housing, no comprehensive scheme for Negro homes has been thought out and only two or three local projects planned. Nor can broad plans be made until the nation or the community decides where it wants or will permit Negroes to live. Negroes are largely excluded from subsistence homesteads because Negroes protested against segregation, and whites, anxious for cheap local labor, also protested.

The colored people of America are coming to face the fact quite calmly that most white Americans do not like them, and are planning neither for their survival, nor for their definite future if it involves free, self-assertive modern manhood. This does not mean all Americans. A saving few are worried about the Negro problem; a still larger group are not ill-disposed, but they fear prevailing public opinion. The great mass of Americans are, however, merely representatives of average humanity. They muddle along with their own affairs and scarcely can be expected to take seriously the affairs of strangers or people whom they partly fear and partly despise.

For many years it was the theory of most Negro leaders that this attitude was the insensibility of ignorance and inexperience, that white America did not know of or realize the continuing plight of the Negro. Accordingly, for the last two decades, we have striven by book and periodical, by speech and appeal, by various dramatic methods of agitation, to put the essential facts before the American people. Today there can be no doubt that Americans know the facts; and yet they remain for the most part indifferent and unmoved.

The main weakness of the Negro's position is that since emancipation he has never had an adequate economic foundation. Thaddeus Stevens recognized this and sought to transform the emancipated freedmen into peasant proprietors. If he had succeeded, he would have changed the economic history of the United States and perhaps saved the American farmer from his present plight. But to furnish 50,000,000 acres of good land to the Negroes would have cost more money than the North was willing to pay, and was regarded by the South as highway robbery.

The whole attempt to furnish land and capital for the freedmen fell through, and no comprehensive economic plan was advanced until the advent of Booker T. Washington. He had a vision of building a new economic foundation for Negroes by incorporating them into white industry. He wanted to make them skilled workers by industrial education and expected small capitalists to rise out of their ranks. Unfortunately, he assumed that the economic development of America in the twentieth century would resemble that of the nineteenth century, with free industrial opportunity, cheap land and unlimited resources under the control of small competitive capitalists. He lived to see industry more and more concentrated, land monopoly extended and industrial technique changed by wide introduction of machinery.

As a result, technology advanced more rapidly than Hampton or Tuskegee could adjust their curricula. The chance of an artisan's becoming a capitalist grew slimmer, even for white Americans, while the whole relation of labor to capital became less a matter of technical skill than of basic organization and aim.

Those of us who in that day opposed Booker Washington's plans did not foresee exactly the kind of change that was coming, but we were convinced that the Negro could succeed in industry and in life only if he had intelligent leadership and far-reaching ideals. The object of education, we declared, was not "to make men artisans but to make artisans men." The Negroes in America needed leadership so that, when change and crisis came, they could guide themselves to safety.

The educated group among American Negroes is still small, but it is large enough to begin planning for preservation through economic advancement. The first definite movement of this younger group was toward direct alliance of the Negro with the labor movement. But white labor today as in the past refuses to respond to these overtures.

For a hundred years, beginning in the thirties and forties of the nineteenth century, the white laborers of Ohio, Pennsylvania and New York beat, murdered and drove away fellow workers because they were black and had to work for what they could get. Seventy years ago in New York, the center of the new American labor movement, white laborers hanged black ones to lamp posts instead of helping to free them from the worst of modern slavery. In Chicago and St. Louis, New Orleans and San Francisco, black men still carry the scars of the bitter hatred of white laborers for them. Today it is white labor that keeps Negroes out of decent low-cost housing, that confines the protection of the best unions to "white" men, that often will not sit in the same hall with black folk who already have joined the labor movement. White labor has to hate scabs; but it hates black scabs not because they are scabs but because they are black. It mobs white scabs to force them into labor fellowship. It mobs black scabs to starve and kill them. In the present fight of the American Federation of Labor against company unions it is attacking the only unions that Negroes can join.

Thus the Negro's fight to enter organized industry has made little headway. No Negro, no matter what his ability, can be a member of any of the railway unions. He cannot be an engineer, fireman, conductor, switchman, brakeman or yardman. If he organizes separately, he may, as in the case of the Negro Firemen's Union, be assaulted and even killed by white firemen. As in the case of the Pullman Porters' Union, he may receive empty recognition without any voice or collective help. The older group of Negro leaders recognize this and simply say it is a matter of continued striving to break down these barriers.

Such facts are, however, slowly forcing Negro thought into new channels. The interests of labor are considered rather than those of capital. No greater welcome is expected from the labor monopolist who mans armies and navies to keep Chinese, Japanese and Negroes in their places than from the captains of industry who spend large sums of money to make laborers think that the most worthless white man is better than any colored man. The Negro must prove his necessity to the labor movement and that it is a disastrous error to leave him out of the foundation of the new industrial state. He must settle beyond cavil the question of his economic efficiency as a worker, a manager and controller of capital.

The dilemma of these younger thinkers gives men like James Weldon Johnson a chance to insist that the older methods are still the best; that we can survive only by being integrated into the nation, and that we must consequently fight segregation now and always and force our way by appeal, agitation and law. This group, however, does not seem to recognize the fundamental economic bases of social growth and the changes that face American industry. Greater democratic control of production and distribution is bound to replace existing autocratic and monopolistic methods.

In this broader and more intelligent democracy we can hope for progressive softening of the asperities and anomalies of race prejudice, but we cannot hope for its early and complete disappearance. Above all, the doubt, deep-planted in the American mind, as to the Negro's ability and efficiency as worker, artisan and administrator will fade but slowly. Thus, with increased democratic control of industry and capital, the place of the Negro will be increasingly a matter of human choice, of willingness to recognize ability across the barriers of race, of putting fit Negroes in places of power and authority by public opinion. At present, on the railroads, in manufacturing, in the telephone, telegraph and radio business, and in the larger divisions of trade, it is only under exceptional circumstances that any Negro no matter what his ability, gets an opportunity for position and power. Only in those lines where individual enterprise still counts, as in some of the professions, in a few of the trades, in a few branches of retail business and in artistic careers, can the Negro expect a narrow opening.

Negroes and other colored folk nevertheless, exist in larger and growing numbers. Slavery, prostitution to white men, theft of their labor and goods have not killed them and cannot kill them. They are growing in intelligence and dissatisfaction. They occupy strategic positions, within nations and beside nations, amid valuable raw material and on the highways of future expansion. They will survive, but on what terms and conditions? On this point a new school of Negro thought is arising. It believes in the ultimate uniting of mankind and in a unified American nation, with economic classes and racial barriers leveled, but it believes this is an ideal and is to be realized only by such intensified class and race consciousness as will bring irresistible force rather than mere humanitarian appeals to bear on the motives and actions of men.

The peculiar position of Negroes in America offers an opportunity. Negroes today cast probably 2,000,000 votes in a total of 40,000,000, and their vote will increase. This gives them, particularly in northern cities, and at critical times, a chance to hold a very considerable balance of power, and the mere threat of this being used intelligently and with determination may often mean much. The consuming power of 2,800,000 Negro families has recently been estimated at $166,000,000 a month—a tremendous power when intelligently directed. Their manpower as laborers probably equals that of Mexico or Yugoslavia. Their illiteracy is much lower than that of Spain or Italy. Their estimated per capita wealth about equals that of Japan.

For a nation with this start in culture and efficiency to sit down and await the salvation of a white God is idiotic. With the use of their political power, their power as consumers, and their brainpower, added to that chance of personal appeal which proximity and neighborhood always give to human beings, Negroes can develop in the United States an economic nation within a nation, able to work through inner cooperation, to found its own institutions, to educate its genius, and at the same time, without mob violence or extremes of race hatred, to keep in helpful touch and cooperate with the mass of the nation. This has happened more often than most people realize, in the case of groups not so obviously separated from the mass of people as are American Negroes. It must happen in our case, or there is no hope for the Negro in America.

Any movement toward such a program is today hindered by the absurd Negro philosophy of Scatter, Suppress, Wait, Escape. There are even many of our educated young leaders who think that because the Negro problem is not in evidence where there are few or no Negroes, this indicates a way out! They think that the problem of race can be settled by ignoring it and suppressing all reference to it. They think that we have only to wait in silence for the white people to settle the problem for us; and finally and predominantly, they think that the problem of twelve million Negro people, mostly poor, ignorant workers, is going to be settled by having their more educated and wealthy classes gradually and continually escape from their race into the mass of the American people, leaving the rest to sink, suffer and die.

Proponents of this program claim, with much reason, that the plight of the masses is not the fault of the emerging classes. For the slavery and exploitation that reduced Negroes to their present level or at any rate hindered them from rising, the white world is to blame. Since the age-long process of raising a group is through the escape of its upper class into welcome fellowship with risen peoples, the Negro intelligentsia would submerge itself if it bent its back to the task of lifting the mass of people. There is logic in this answer, but futile logic.

If the leading Negro classes cannot assume and bear the uplift of their own proletariat, they are doomed for all time. It is not a case of ethics; it is a plain case of necessity. The method by which this may be done is, first, for the American Negro to achieve a new economic solidarity.

There exists today a chance for the Negroes to organize a cooperative state within their own group. By letting Negro farmers feed Negro artisans, and Negro technicians guide Negro home industries, and Negro thinkers plan this integration of cooperation, while Negro artists dramatize and beautify the struggle, economic independence can be achieved. To doubt that this is possible is to doubt the essential humanity and the quality of brains of the American Negro.

No sooner is this proposed than a great fear sweeps over older Negroes. They cry "No segregation"—no further yielding to prejudice and race separation. Yet any planning for the benefit of American Negroes on the part of a Negro intelligentsia is going to involve organized and deliberate self-segregation. There are plenty of people in the United States who would be only too willing to use such a plan as a way to increase existing legal and customary segregation between the races. This threat which many Negroes see is no mere mirage. What of it? It must be faced.

If the economic and cultural salvation of the American Negro calls for an increase in segregation and prejudice, then that must come. American Negroes must plan for their economic future and the social survival of their fellows in the firm belief that this means in a real sense the survival of colored folk in the world and the building of a full humanity instead of a petty white tyranny. Control of their own education, which is the logical and inevitable end of separate schools, would not be an unmixed ill; it might prove a supreme good. Negro schools once meant poor schools. They need not today; they must not tomorrow. Separate Negro sections will increase race antagonism, but they will also increase economic cooperation, organized self-defense and necessary self-confidence.

The immediate reaction of most white and colored people to this suggestion will be that the thing cannot be done without extreme results. Negro thinkers have from time to time emphasized the fact that no nation within a nation can be built because of the attitude of the dominant majority, and because all legal and police power is out of Negro hands, and because large-scale industries, like steel and utilities, are organized on a national basis. White folk, on the other hand, simply say that, granting certain obvious exceptions, the American Negro has not the ability to engineer so delicate a social operation calling for such self-restraint, careful organization and sagacious leadership.

In reply, it may be said that this matter of a nation within a nation has already been partially accomplished in the organization of the Negro church, the Negro school and the Negro retail business, and, despite all the justly due criticism, the result has been astonishing. The great majority of American Negroes are divided not only for religious but for a large number of social purposes into self-supporting economic units, self-governed, self-directed. The greatest difficulty is that these organizations have no logical and reasonable standards and do not attract the finest, most vigorous and best educated Negroes . When all these things are taken into consideration it becomes clearer to more and more American Negroes that, through voluntary and increased segregation, by careful autonomy and planned economic organization, they may build so strong and efficient a unit that twelve million men can no longer be refused fellowship and equality in the United States.

THE PROPAGANDA OF HISTORY

What are American children taught today about Reconstruction? Helen Boardman has made a study of current textbooks and notes these three dominant theses:

I. *All Negroes were ignorant.*

"All were ignorant of public business." (Woodburn and Moran, "Elementary American History and Government")

"Although the Negroes were now free, they were also ignorant and unfit to govern themselves." (Everett Barnes, "American History for Grammar Grades")

"The Negroes got control of these states. They had been slaves all their lives, and were so ignorant they did not even know the letters of the alphabet. Yet they now sat in the state legislatures and made the laws." (D. H. Montgomery, "The Leading Facts of American History")

"In the South, the Negroes who had so suddenly gained their freedom did not know what to do with it." (Hubert Cornish and Thomas Hughes, "History of the United States for Schools")

"In the legislatures, the Negroes were so ignorant that they could only watch their white leaders—carpetbaggers, and vote aye or no as they were told." (S. E. Forman, "Advanced American History," Revised Edition)

"Some legislatures were made up of a few dishonest white men and several Negroes, many too ignorant to know anything about lawmaking." (Hubert Cornish and Thomas Hughes, "History of the United States for Schools")

2. *All Negroes were lazy, dishonest and extravagant.*

"These men knew not only nothing about the government, but also cared for nothing except what they could gain for themselves." (Helen F. Giles, "How the United States Became a World Power")

"Legislatures were often at the mercy of Negroes, childishly ignorant, who sold their votes openly, and whose 'loyalty' was gained by allowing them to eat, drink and clothe themselves at the state's expense." (William J. Long, "America—A History of Our Country")

"Some Negroes spent their money foolishly, and were worse off than they had been before." (Carl Russell Fish, "History of America")

"This assistance led many freed men to believe that they need no longer work. They also ignorantly believed that the lands of their former masters were to be turned over by Congress to them, and that every Negro was to have as his allotment 'forty acres and a mule.' " (W. F. Gordy, "History of the United States")

"Thinking that slavery meant toil and that freedom meant only idleness, the slave after he was set free was disposed to try out his freedom by refusing to work." (S. E. Forman, "Advanced American History")

"They began to wander about, stealing and plundering. In one week, in a Georgia town, 150 Negroes were arrested for thieving." (Helen F. Giles, "How the United States Became a World Power")

3. *Negroes were responsible for bad government during Reconstruction:*

"Foolish laws were passed by the black law-makers, the public money was wasted terribly and thousands of dollars were stolen straight. Self-respecting Southerners chafed under the horrible régime." (Emerson David Fite, "These United States")

"In the exhausted states already amply 'punished' by the desolation of war, the rule of the Negro and his unscrupulous carpetbagger and scalawag patrons, was an orgy of extravagance, fraud and disgusting incompetency." (David Saville Muzzey, "History of the American People")

"The picture of Reconstruction which the average pupil in these sixteen States receives is limited to the South. The South found it necessary to pass Black Codes for the control of the shiftless and sometimes vicious freedmen. The Freedmen's Bureau caused the Negroes to look to the North rather than to the South for support and by giving them a false sense of equality did more harm than good. With the scalawags, the ignorant and non-propertyholding Negroes under the leadership of the carpetbaggers, engaged in a wild orgy of spending in the legislatures. The humiliation and distress of the Southern whites was in part relieved by the Ku Klux Klan, a secret organization which frightened the superstitious blacks."

Grounded in such elementary and high school teaching, an American youth attending college today would learn from current textbooks of history that the Constitution recognized slavery; that the chance of getting rid of slavery by peaceful methods was ruined by the Abolitionists; that after the period of Andrew Jackson, the two sections of the United States "had become fully conscious of their conflicting interests. Two irreconcilable forms of civilization . . . in the North, the democratic . . . in the South, a more stationary and aristocratic civilization." He would read that Harriet Beecher Stowe brought on the Civil War; that the assault on Charles Sumner was due to his "coarse invective" against a South Carolina Senator; and that Negroes were the only people to achieve emancipation with no effort on their part. That Reconstruction was a disgraceful attempt to subject white people to ignorant Negro rule; and that, according to a Harvard professor of history (the italics are ours), "Legislative expenses were grotesquely extravagant; the *colored members in some states engaging in a saturnalia of corrupt expenditure*" (Encyclopaedia Britannica, 14th Edition, by Frederick Jackson Turner).

In other words, he would in all probability complete his education without any idea of the part which the black race has played in America; of the tremendous moral problem of abolition; of the cause and meaning of the Civil War and the relation which Reconstruction had to democratic government and the labor movement today.

Herein lies more than mere omission and difference of emphasis. The treatment of the period of Reconstruction reflects small credit upon American historians as scientists. We have too often a deliberate attempt so to change the facts of history that the story will make pleasant reading for Americans. The editors of the fourteenth edition of the Encyclopaedia Britannica asked me for an article on the history of the American Negro. From my manuscript they cut out all my references to Reconstruction. I insisted on including the following statement:

"White historians have ascribed the faults and failures of Reconstruction to Negro ignorance and corruption. But the Negro insists that it was Negro loyalty and the Negro vote alone that restored the South to the Union; established the new democracy, both for white and black, and instituted the public schools."

This the editor refused to print, although he said that the article otherwise was "in my judgment, and in the judgment of others in the office, an excellent one, and one with which it seems to me we may all be well satisfied." I was not satisfied and refused to allow the article to appear.

War and especially civil strife leave terrible wounds. It is the duty of humanity to heal them. It was therefore soon conceived as neither wise nor patriotic to speak of all the causes of strife and the terrible results to which sectional differences in the United States had led. And so, first of all, we minimized the slavery controversy which convulsed the nation from the Missouri Compromise down to the Civil War. On top of that, we passed by Reconstruction with a phrase of regret or disgust.

But are these reasons of courtesy and philanthropy sufficient for denying Truth? If history is going to be scientific, if the record of human action is going to be set down with that accuracy and faithfulness of detail which will allow its use as a measuring rod and guidepost for the future of nations, there must be set some standards of ethics in research and interpretation.

If, on the other hand, we are going to use history for our pleasure and amusement, for inflating our national ego, and giving us a false but pleasurable sense of accomplishment, then we must give up the idea of history either as a science or as an art using the results of science, and admit frankly that we are using a version of historic fact in order to influence and educate the new generation along the way we wish.

It is propaganda like this that has led men in the past to insist that history is "lies agreed upon"; and to point out the danger in such misinformation. It is indeed extremely doubtful if any permanent benefit comes to the world through such action. Nations reel and stagger on their way; they make hideous mistakes; they commit frightful wrongs; they do great and beautiful things. And shall we not best guide humanity by telling the truth about all this, so far as the truth is ascertainable?

Here in the United States we have a clear example. It was morally wrong and economically retrogressive to build human slavery in the United States in the eighteenth century. We know that now, perfectly well; and there were many Americans North and South who knew this and said it in the eighteenth century. Today, in the face of new slavery established elsewhere in the world under other names and guises, we ought to emphasize this lesson of the past. Moreover, it is not well to be reticent in describing that past. Our histories tend to discuss American slavery so impartially, that in the end nobody seems to have done wrong and everybody was right. Slavery appears to have been thrust upon unwilling helpless America, while the South was blameless in becoming its center. The difference of development, North and South, is explained as a sort of working out of cosmic social and economic law.

One reads, for instance, Charles and Mary Beard's "Rise of American Civilization," with a comfortable feeling that nothing right or wrong is involved. Manufacturing and industry develop in the North; agrarian feudalism develops in the South. They clash, as winds and waters strive, and the stronger forces develop the tremendous industrial machine that governs us so magnificently and selfishly today.

Yet in this sweeping mechanistic interpretation, there is no room for the real plot of the story, for the clear mistake and guilt of rebuilding a new slavery of the working class in the midst of a fateful experiment in democracy; for the triumph of sheer moral courage and sacrifice in the abolition crusade; and for the hurt and struggle of degraded black millions in their fight for freedom and their attempt to enter democracy. Can all this be omitted or half suppressed in a treatise that calls itself scientific?

Or, to come nearer the center and climax of this fascinating history: What was slavery in the United States? Just what did it mean to the owner and the owned? Shall we accept the conventional story of the old slave plantation and its owner's fine, aristocratic life of cultured leisure? Or shall we note slave biographies, like those of Charles Ball, Sojourner Truth, Harriet Tubman and Frederick Douglass; the careful observations of Olmsted and the indictment of Hinton Helper?

No one can read that first thin autobiography of Frederick Douglass and have left many illusions about slavery. And if truth is our object, no amount of flowery romance and the personal reminiscences of its protected beneficiaries can keep the world from knowing that slavery was a cruel, dirty, costly and inexcusable anachronism, which nearly ruined the world's greatest experiment in democracy. No serious and unbiased student can be deceived by the fairy tale of a beautiful Southern slave civilization. If those who really had opportunity to know the South before the war wrote the truth, it was a center of widespread ignorance, undeveloped resources, suppressed humanity and unrestrained passions, with whatever veneer of manners and culture that could lie above these depths.

Coming now to the Civil War, how for a moment can anyone who reads the *Congressional Globe* from 1850 to 1860, the lives of contemporary statesmen and public characters, North and South, the discourses in the newspapers and accounts of meetings and speeches, doubt that Negro slavery was the cause of the Civil War? What do we gain by evading this clear fact, and talking in vague ways about "Union" and "State Rights" and differences in civilization as the cause of that catastrophe?

Of all historic facts there can be none clearer than that for four long and fearful years the South fought to perpetuate human slavery; and that the nation which "rose so bright and fair and died so pure of stain" was one that had a perfect right to be ashamed of its birth and glad of its death. Yet one monument in North Carolina achieves the impossible by recording of Confederate soldiers: "They died fighting for liberty!"

On the other hand, consider the North and the Civil War. Why should we be deliberately false, like Woodward, in "Meet General Grant," and represent the North as magnanimously freeing the slave without any effort on his part?

"The American Negroes are the only people in the history of the world, so far as I know, that ever became free without any effort of their own. . . .

"They had not started the war nor ended it. They twanged banjos around the railroad stations, sang melodious spirituals, and believed that some Yankee would soon come along and give each of them forty acres of land and a mule."

The North went to war without the slightest idea of freeing the slave. The great majority of Northerners from Lincoln down pledged themselves to protect slavery, and they hated and harried Abolitionists. But on the other hand, the thesis which Beale tends to support that the whole North during and after the war was chiefly interested in making money, is only half true; it was abolition and belief in democracy that gained for a time the upper hand after the war and led the North in Reconstruction; business followed abolition in order to maintain the tariff, pay the bonds and defend the banks. To call this business program "the program of the North" and ignore abolition is unhistorical. In growing ascendancy for a calculable time was a great moral movement which turned the North from its economic defense of slavery and led it to Emancipation. Abolitionists attacked slavery because it was wrong and their moral battle cannot be truthfully minimized or forgotten. Nor does this fact deny that the majority of Northerners before the war were not abolitionists, that they attacked slavery only in order to win the war and enfranchised the Negro to secure this result.

One has but to read the debates in Congress and state papers from Abraham Lincoln down to know that the decisive action which ended the Civil War was the emancipation and arming of the black slave; that, as Lincoln said: "Without the military help of black freedmen, the war against the South could not have been won." The freedmen, far from being the inert recipients of freedom at the hands of philanthropists, furnished 200,000 soldiers in the Civil War who took part in nearly 200 battles and skirmishes, and in addition perhaps 300,000 others as effective laborers and helpers. In proportion to population, more Negroes than whites fought in the Civil War. These people, withdrawn from the support of the Confederacy, with threat of the withdrawal of millions more, made the opposition of the slaveholder useless, unless they themselves freed and armed their own slaves. This was exactly what they started to do; they were only restrained by realizing that such action removed the very cause for which they began fighting. Yet one would search current American histories almost in vain to find a clear statement or even faint recognition of these perfectly well-authenticated facts.

All this is but preliminary to the kernel of the historic problem with which this book deals, and that is Reconstruction. The chorus of agreement concerning the attempt to reconstruct and organize the South after the Civil War and emancipation is overwhelming. There is scarce a child in the street that cannot tell you that the whole effort was a hideous mistake and an unfortunate incident, based on ignorance, revenge and the perverse determination to attempt the impossible; that the history of the United States from 1866 to 1876 is something of which the nation ought to be ashamed and which did more to retard and set back the American Negro than anything that has happened to him; while at the same time it grievously and wantonly wounded again a part of the nation already hurt to death.

True it is that the Northern historians writing just after the war had scant sympathy for the South, and wrote ruthlessly of "rebels" and "slave-drivers." They had at least the excuse of a war psychosis.

As a young labor leader, Will Herberg, writes: "The great traditions of this period and especially of Reconstruction are shamelessly repudiated by the official heirs of Stevens and Sumner. In the last quarter of a century hardly a single book has appeared consistently championing or sympathetically interpreting the great ideals of the crusade against slavery, whereas scores and hundreds have dropped from the presses in ignoble 'extenuation' of the North, in open apology for the Confederacy, in measureless abuse of the Radical figures of Reconstruction. The Reconstruction period as the logical culmination of decades of previous development, has borne the brunt of the reaction."

First of all, we have James Ford Rhodes' history of the United States. Rhodes was trained not as an historian but as an Ohio business man. He had no broad formal education. When he had accumulated a fortune, he surrounded himself with a retinue of clerks and proceeded to manufacture a history of the United States by mass production. His method was simple. He gathered a vast number of authorities; he selected from these authorities those whose testimony supported his thesis, and he discarded the others. The majority report of the great Ku Klux investigation, for instance, he laid aside in favor of the minority report, simply because the latter supported his sincere belief. In the report and testimony of the Reconstruction Committee of Fifteen, he did practically the same thing.

Above all, he begins his inquiry convinced, without admitting any necessity of investigation, that Negroes are an inferior race:

"No large policy in our country has ever been so conspicuous a failure as that of forcing universal Negro suffrage upon the South. The Negroes who simply acted out their nature, were not to blame. How indeed could they acquire political honesty? What idea could barbarism thrust into slavery obtain of the rights of property? . . .

"From the Republican policy came no real good to the Negroes. Most of them developed no political capacity, and the few who raised themselves above the mass, did not reach a high order of intelligence."

Rhodes was primarily the historian of property; of economic history and the labor movement, he knew nothing; of democratic government, he was contemptuous. He was trained to make profits. He used his profits to write history. He speaks again and again of the rulership of "intelligence and property" and he makes a plea that intelligent use of the ballot for the benefit of property is the only real foundation of democracy.

The real frontal attack on Reconstruction, as interpreted by the leaders of national thought in 1870 and for some time thereafter, came from the universities and particularly from Columbia and Johns Hopkins.

The movement began with Columbia University and with the advent of John W. Burgess of Tennessee and William A. Dunning of New Jersey as professors of political science and history.

Burgess was an ex-Confederate soldier who started to a little Southern college with a box of books, a box of tallow candles and a Negro boy; and his attitude toward the Negro race in after years was subtly colored by this early conception of Negroes as essentially property like books and candles. Dunning was a kindly and impressive professor who was deeply influenced by a growing group of young Southern students and began with them to re-write the history of the nation from 1860 to 1880, in more or less conscious opposition to the classic interpretations of New England.

Burgess was frank and determined in his anti-Negro thought. He expounded his theory of Nordic supremacy which colored all his political theories:

"The claim that there is nothing in the color of the skin from the point of view of political ethics is a great sophism. A black skin means membership in a race of men which has never of itself succeeded in subjecting passion to reason, has never, therefore, created any civilization of any kind. To put such a race of men in possession of a 'state' government in a system of federal government is to trust them with the development of political and legal civilization upon the most important subjects of human life, and to do this in communities with a large white population is simply to establish barbarism in power over civilization."

Burgess is a Tory and open apostle of reaction. He tells us that the nation now believes "that it is the white man's mission, his duty and his right, to hold the reins of political power in his own hands for the civilization of the world and the welfare of mankind."

For this reason America is following "the European idea of the duty of civilized races to impose their political sovereignty upon civilized, or half civilized, or not fully civilized, races anywhere and everywhere in the world."

He complacently believes that "There is something natural in the subordination of an inferior race to a superior race, even to the point of the enslavement of the inferior race; but there is nothing natural in the opposite." He therefore denominates Reconstruction as the rule "of the uncivilized Negroes over the whites of the South." This has been the teaching of one of our greatest universities for nearly fifty years.

Dunning was less dogmatic as a writer, and his own statements are often judicious. But even Dunning can declare that "all the forces [in the South] that made for civilization were dominated by a mass of barbarous freedmen"; and that "the antithesis and antipathy of race and color were crucial and ineradicable." The work of most of the students whom he taught and encouraged has been one-sided and partisan to the last degree. Johns Hopkins University has issued a series of studies similar to Columbia's; Southern teachers have been welcomed to many Northern universities, where often Negro students have been systematically discouraged, and thus a nation-wide university attitude has arisen by which propaganda against the Negro has been carried on unquestioned.

The Columbia school of historians and social investigators have issued between 1895 and the present time sixteen studies of Reconstruction in the Southern States, all based on the same thesis and all done according to the same method: first, endless sympathy with the white South; second, ridicule, contempt or silence for the Negro; third, a judicial attitude towards the North, which concludes that the North under great misapprehension did a grievous wrong, but eventually saw its mistake and retreated.

These studies vary, of course, in their methods. Dunning's own work is usually silent so far as the Negro is concerned. Burgess is more than fair in law but reactionary in matters of race and property, regarding the treatment of a Negro as a man as nothing less than a crime, and admitting that "the mainstay of property is the courts."

In the books on Reconstruction written by graduates of these universities and others, the studies of Texas, North Carolina, Florida, Virginia and Louisiana are thoroughly bad, giving no complete picture of what happened during Reconstruction, written for the most part by men and women without broad historical or social background, and all designed not to seek the truth but to prove a thesis. Hamilton reaches the climax of this school when he characterizes the black codes, which even Burgess condemned, as "not only . . . on the whole reasonable, temperate and kindly, but, in the main, necessary."

Thompson's "Georgia" is another case in point. It seeks to be fair, but silly stories about Negroes indicating utter lack of even common sense are included, and every noble sentiment from white people. When two Negro workers, William and Jim, put a straightforward advertisement in a local paper, the author says that it was "evidently written by a white friend." There is not the slightest historical evidence to prove this, and there were plenty of educated Negroes in Augusta at the time who might have written this. Lonn's "Louisiana" puts Sheridan's words in Sherman's mouth to prove a petty point.

There are certain of these studies which, though influenced by the same general attitude, nevertheless have more of scientific poise and cultural background. Garner's "Reconstruction in Mississippi" conceives the Negro as an integral part of the scene and treats him as a human being. With this should be bracketed the recent study of "Reconstruction in South Carolina" by Simkins and Woody. This is not as fair as Garner's, but in the midst of conventional judgment and conclusion, and reproductions of all available caricatures of Negroes, it does not hesitate to give a fair account of the Negroes and of some of their work. It gives the impression of combining in one book two antagonistic points of view, but in the clash much truth emerges.

Ficklen's "Louisiana" and the works of Fleming are anti-Negro in spirit, but, nevertheless, they have a certain fairness and sense of historic honesty. Fleming's "Documentary History of Reconstruction" is done by a man who has a thesis to support, and his selection of documents supports the thesis. His study of Alabama is pure propaganda.

Next come a number of books which are openly and blatantly propaganda, like Herbert's "Solid South," and the books by Pike and Reynolds on South Carolina, the works by Pollard and Carpenter, and especially those by Ulrich Phillips. One of the latest and most popular of this series is "The Tragic Era" by Claude Bowers, which is an excellent and readable piece of current newspaper reporting, absolutely devoid of historical judgment or sociological knowledge. It is a classic example of historical propaganda of the cheaper sort.

We have books like Milton's "Age of Hate" and Winston's "Andrew Johnson" which attempt to re-write the character of Andrew Johnson. They certainly add to our knowledge of the man and our sympathy for his weakness. But they cannot, for students, change the calm testimony of unshaken historical facts. Fuess' "Carl Schurz" paints the picture of this fine liberal, and yet goes out of its way to show that he was quite wrong in what he said he saw in the South.

The chief witness in Reconstruction, the emancipated slave himself, has been almost barred from court. His written Reconstruction record has been largely destroyed and nearly always neglected. Only three or four states have preserved the debates in the Reconstruction conventions; there are few biographies of black leaders. The Negro is refused a hearing because he was poor and ignorant. It is therefore assumed that all Negroes in Reconstruction were ignorant and silly and that therefore a history of Reconstruction in any state can quite ignore him. The result is that most unfair caricatures of Negroes have been carefully preserved; but serious speeches, successful administration and upright character are almost universally ignored and forgotten. Wherever a black head rises to historic view, it is promptly slain by an adjective—"shrewd," "notorious," "cunning"—or pilloried by a sneer; or put out of view by some quite unproven charge of bad moral character. In other words, every effort has been made to treat the Negro's part in Reconstruction with silence and contempt.

When recently a student tried to write on education in Florida, he found that the official records of the excellent administration of the colored Superintendent of Education, Gibbs, who virtually established the Florida public school, had been destroyed. Alabama has tried to obliterate all printed records of Reconstruction.

Especially noticeable is the fact that little attempt has been made to trace carefully the rise and economic development of the poor whites and their relation to the planters and to Negro labor after the war. There were five million or more non-slaveholding whites in the South in 1860 and less than two million in the families of all slaveholders. Yet one might almost gather from contemporary history that the five million left no history and had no descendants. The extraordinary history of the rise and triumph of the poor whites has been largely neglected, even by Southern white students.

The whole development of Reconstruction was primarily an economic development, but no economic history or proper material for it has been written. It has been regarded as a purely political matter, and of politics most naturally divorced from industry.

All this is reflected in the textbooks of the day and in the encyclopedias, until we have got to the place where we cannot use our experiences during and after the Civil War for the uplift and enlightenment of mankind. We have spoiled and misconceived the position of the historian. If we are going, in the future, not simply with regard to this one question, but with regard to all social problems, to be able to use human experience for the guidance of mankind, we have got clearly to distinguish between fact and desire.

In the first place, somebody in each era must make clear the facts with utter disregard to his own wish and desire and belief. What we have got to know, so far as possible, are the things that actually happened in the world. Then with that much clear and open to every reader, the philosopher and prophet has a chance to interpret these facts; but the historian has no right, posing as scientist, to conceal or distort facts; and until we distinguish between these two functions of the chronicler of human action, we are going to render it easy for a muddled world out of sheer ignorance to make the same mistake ten times over.

One is astonished in the study of history at the recurrence of the idea that evil must be forgotten, distorted, skimmed over. We must not remember that Daniel Webster got drunk but only remember that he was a splendid constitutional lawyer. We must forget that George Washington was a slave owner, or that Thomas Jefferson had mulatto children, or that Alexander Hamilton had Negro blood, and simply remember the things we regard as creditable and inspiring. The difficulty, of course, with this philosophy is that history loses its value as an incentive and example; it paints perfect men and noble nations, but it does not tell the truth.

No one reading the history of the United States during 1850–1860 can have the slightest doubt left in his mind that Negro slavery was the cause of the Civil War, and yet during and since we learn that a great nation murdered thousands and destroyed millions on account of abstract doctrines concerning the nature of the Federal Union. Since the attitude of the nation concerning state rights has been revolutionized by the development of the central government since the war, the whole argument becomes an astonishing *reductio ad absurdum*, leaving us apparently with no cause for the Civil War except the recent reiteration of statements which make the great public men on one side narrow, hypocritical fanatics and liars, while the leaders on the other side were extraordinary and unexampled for their beauty, unselfishness and fairness.

Not a single great leader of the nation during the Civil War and Reconstruction has escaped attack and libel. The magnificent figures of Charles Sumner and Thaddeus Stevens have been besmirched almost beyond recognition. We have been cajoling and flattering the South and slurring the North, because the South is determined to re-write the history of slavery and the North is not interested in history but in wealth.

This, then, is the book basis upon which today we judge Reconstruction. In order to paint the South as a martyr to inescapable fate, to make the North the magnanimous emancipator, and to ridicule the Negro as the impossible joke in the whole development, we have in fifty years, by libel, innuendo and silence, so completely misstated and obliterated the history of the Negro in America and his relation to its work and government that today it is almost unknown. This may be fine romance, but it is not science. It may be inspiring, but it is certainly not the truth. And beyond this it is dangerous. It is not only part foundation of our present lawlessness and loss of democratic ideals; it has, more than that, led the world to embrace and worship the color bar as social salvation and it is helping to range mankind in ranks of mutual hatred and contempt, at the summons of a cheap and false myth.

Nearly all recent books on Reconstruction agree with each other in discarding the government reports and substituting selected diaries, letters, and gossip. Yet it happens that the government records are an historic source of wide and unrivaled authenticity. There is the report of the select Committee of Fifteen, which delved painstakingly into the situation all over the South and called all kinds and conditions of men to testify; there are the report of Carl Schurz and the twelve volumes of reports made on the Ku Klux conspiracy; and above all, the *Congressional Globe*. None who has not read page by page the *Congressional Globe*, especially the sessions of the 39th Congress, can possibly have any idea of what the problems of Reconstruction facing the United States were in 1865–1866. Then there were the reports of the Freedmen's Bureau and the executive and other documentary reports of government officials, especially in the war and treasury departments, which give the historian the only groundwork upon which he can build a real and truthful picture. There are certain historians who have not tried deliberately to falsify the picture: Southern whites like Frances Butler Leigh and Susan Smedes; Northern historians, like McPherson, Oberholtzer, and Nicolay and Hay. There are foreign travelers like Sir George Campbell, Georges Clemenceau and Robert Somers. There are the personal reminiscences of Augustus Beard, George Julian, George F. Hoar, Carl Schurz and John Sherman. There are the invaluable work of Edward McPherson and the more recent studies by Paul Haworth, A. A. Taylor, and Charles Wesley. Beale simply does not take Negroes into account in the critical year of 1866.

Certain monographs deserve all praise, like those of Hendricks and Pierce. The work of Flack is prejudiced but built on study. The defense of the carpetbag régime by Tourgée and Allen, Powell Clayton, Holden and Warmoth are worthy antidotes to the certain writers.

The lives of Stevens and Sumner are revealing even when slightly apologetic because of the Negro; while Andrew Johnson is beginning to suffer from writers who are trying to prove how seldom he got drunk, and think that important.

It will be noted that for my authority in this work I have depended very largely upon secondary material; upon state histories of Reconstruction, written in the main by those who were convinced before they began to write that the Negro was incapable of government, or of becoming a constituent part of a civilized state. The fairest of these histories have not tried to conceal facts; in other cases, the black man has been largely ignored; while in still others, he has been traduced and ridiculed. If I had had time and money and opportunity to go back to the original sources in all cases, there can be no doubt that the weight of this work would have been vastly strengthened, and as I firmly believe, the case of the Negro more convincingly set forth.

Various volumes of papers in the great libraries like the Johnson papers in the Library of Congress, the Sumner manuscripts at Harvard, the Schurz correspondence, the Wells papers, the Chase papers, the Fessenden and Greeley collections, the McCulloch, McPherson, Sherman, Stevens and Trumbull papers, all must have much of great interest to the historians of the American Negro. I have not had time nor opportunity to examine these, and most of those who have examined them had little interest in black folk.

Negroes have done some excellent work on their own history and defense. It suffers of course from natural partisanship and a desire to prove a case in the face of a chorus of unfair attacks. Its best work also suffers from the fact that Negroes with difficulty reach an audience. But this is also true of such white writers as Skaggs and Bancroft who could not get first-class publishers because they were saying something that the nation did not like.

The Negro historians began with autobiographies and reminiscences. The older historians were George W. Williams and Joseph T. Wilson; the new school of historians is led by Carter G. Woodson; and I have been greatly helped by the unpublished theses of four of the youngest Negro students. It is most unfortunate that while many young white Southerners can get funds to attack and ridicule the Negro and his friends, it is almost impossible for first-class Negro students to get a chance for research or to get finished work in print.

I write then in a field devastated by passion and belief. Naturally, as a Negro, I cannot do this writing without believing in the essential humanity of Negroes, in their ability to be educated, to do the work of the modern world, to take their place as equal citizens with others. I cannot for a moment subscribe to that bizarre doctrine of race that makes most men inferior to the few. But, too, as a student of science, I want to be fair, objective and judicial; to let no searing of the memory by intolerable insult and cruelty make me fail to sympathize with human frailties and contradiction, in the eternal paradox of good and evil. But armed and warned by all this, and fortified by long study of the facts, I stand at the end of this writing, literally aghast at what American historians have done to this field.

What is the object of writing the history of Reconstruction? Is it to wipe out the disgrace of a people which fought to make slaves of Negroes? Is it to show that the North had higher motives than freeing black men? Is it to prove that Negroes were black angels? No, it is simply to establish the Truth, on which Right in the future may be built. We shall never have a science of history until we have in our colleges men who regard the truth as more important than the defense of the white race, and who will not deliberately encourage students to gather thesis material in order to support a prejudice or buttress a lie.

Three-fourths of the testimony against the Negro in Reconstruction is on the unsupported evidence of men who hated and despised Negroes and regarded it as loyalty to blood, patriotism to country, and filial tribute to the fathers to lie, steal or kill in order to discredit these black folk. This may be a natural result when a people have been humbled and impoverished and degraded in their own life; but what is inconceivable is that another generation and another group should regard this testimony as scientific truth, when it is contradicted by logic and by fact. This chapter, therefore, which in logic should be a survey of books and sources, becomes of sheer necessity an arraignment of American historians and an indictment of their ideals. With a determination unparalleled in science, the mass of American writers have started out so to distort the facts of the greatest critical period of American history as to prove right wrong and wrong right. I am not familiar enough with the vast field of human history to pronounce on the relative guilt of these and historians of other times and fields; but I do say that if history of the past has been written in the same fashion, it is useless as science and misleading as ethics. It simply shows that with sufficient general agreement and determination among the dominant classes, the truth of history may be utterly distorted and contradicted and changed to any convenient fairy tale that the masters of men wish.

I cannot believe that any unbiased mind, with an ideal of truth and of scientific judgment, can read the plain, authentic facts of our history, during 1860–1880, and come to conclusions essentially different from mine; and yet I stand virtually alone in this interpretation. So much so that the very cogency of my facts would make me hesitate, did I not seem to see plain reasons. Subtract from Burgess his belief that only white people can rule, and he is in essential agreement with me. Remember that Rhodes was an uneducated money-maker who hired clerks to find the facts which he needed to support his thesis, and one is convinced that the same labor and expense could easily produce quite opposite results.

One fact and one alone explains the attitude of most recent writers

451

toward Reconstruction; they cannot conceive Negroes as men; in their minds the word "Negro" connotes "inferiority" and "stupidity" lightened only by unreasoning gayety and humor. Suppose the slaves of 1860 had been white folk. Stevens would have been a great statesman, Sumner a great democrat, and Schurz a keen prophet, in a mighty revolution of rising humanity. Ignorance and poverty would easily have been explained by history, and the demand for land and the franchise would have been justified as the birthright of natural freemen.

But Burgess was a slaveholder, Dunning a Copperhead and Rhodes an exploiter of wage labor. Not one of them apparently ever met an educated Negro of force and ability. Around such impressive thinkers gathered the young post-war students from the South. They had been born and reared in the bitterest period of Southern race hatred, fear and contempt. Their instinctive reactions were confirmed and encouraged in the best of American universities. Their scholarship, when it regarded black men, became deaf, dumb and blind. The clearest evidence of Negro ability, work, honesty, patience, learning and efficiency became distorted into cunning, brute toil, shrewd evasion, cowardice and imitation—a stupid effort to transcend nature's law.

For those seven mystic years between Johnson's "swing 'round the circle" and the panic of 1873, a majority of thinking Americans in the North believed in the equal manhood of black folk. They acted accordingly with a clear-cut decisiveness and thorough logic, utterly incomprehensible to a day like ours which does not share this human faith; and to Southern whites this period can only be explained by deliberate vengeance and hate.

The panic of 1873 brought sudden disillusion in business enterprise, economic organization, religious belief and political standards. A flood of appeal from the white South reënforced this reaction—appeal with no longer the arrogant bluster of slave oligarchy, but the simple moving annals of the plight of a conquered people. The resulting emotional and intellectual rebound of the nation made it nearly inconceivable in 1876 that ten years earlier most men had believed in human equality.

Assuming, therefore, as axiomatic the endless inferiority of the Negro race, these newer historians, mostly Southerners, some Northerners who deeply sympathized with the South, misinterpreted, distorted, even deliberately ignored any fact that challenged or contradicted this assumption. If the Negro was admittedly sub-human, what need to waste time delving into his Reconstruction history? Consequently historians of Reconstruction with a few exceptions ignore the Negro as completely as possible, leaving the reader wondering why an element apparently so insignificant filled the whole Southern picture at the time. The only real excuse for this attitude is loyalty to a lost cause, reverence for brave fathers and suffering mothers and sisters, and fidelity to the ideals of a clan and class. But in propaganda against the

Negro since emancipation in this land, we face one of the most stupendous efforts the world ever saw to discredit human beings, an effort involving universities, history, science, social life and religion.

The most magnificent drama in the last thousand years of human history is the transportation of ten million human beings out of the dark beauty of their mother continent into the new-found Eldorado of the West. They descended into Hell; and in the third century they arose from the dead, in the finest effort to achieve democracy for the working millions which this world had ever seen. It was a tragedy that beggared the Greek; it was an upheaval of humanity like the Reformation and the French Revolution. Yet we are blind and led by the blind. We discern in it no part of our labor movement; no part of our industrial triumph; no part of our religious experience. Before the dumb eyes of ten generations of ten million children, it is made mockery of and spit upon; a degradation of the eternal mother; a sneer at human effort; with aspiration and art deliberately and elaborately distorted. And why? Because in a day when the human mind aspired to a science of human action, a history and psychology of the mighty effort of the mightiest century, we fell under the leadership of those who would compromise with truth in the past in order to make peace in the present and guide policy in the future.

One reads the truer deeper facts of Reconstruction with a great despair. It is at once so simple and human, and yet so futile. There is no villain, no idiot, no saint. There are just men; men who crave ease and power, men who know want and hunger, men who have crawled. They all dream and strive with ecstasy of fear and strain of effort, balked of hope and hate. Yet the rich world is wide enough for all, wants all, needs all. So slight a gesture, a word, might set the strife in order, not with full content, but with growing dawn of fulfillment. Instead roars the crash of hell; and after its whirlwind a teacher sits in academic halls, learned in the tradition of its elms and its elders. He looks into the upturned face of youth and in him youth sees the gowned shape of wisdom and hears the voice of God. Cynically he sneers at "chinks" and "niggers." He says that the nation "has changed its views in regard to the political relation of races and has at last virtually accepted the ideas of the South upon that subject. The white men of the South need now have no further fear that the Republican party, or Republican Administrations, will ever again give themselves over to the vain imagination of the political equality of man."

Immediately in Africa, a black back runs red with the blood of the lash; in India, a brown girl is raped; in China, a coolie starves; in Alabama, seven darkies are more than lynched; while in London, the white limbs of a prostitute are hung with jewels and silk. Flames of jealous murder sweep the earth, while brains of little children smear the hills.

This is education in the Nineteen Hundred and Thirty-fifth year of the Christ; this is modern and exact social science; this is the university course in "History 12" set down by the Senatus academicus; ad quos hae literae pervenerint: Salutem in Domino, sempeternam! . . .

AN APPEAL TO THE WORLD

There were in the United States of America, 1940, 12,865,518 citizens and residents, something less than a tenth of the nation, who form largely a segregated caste, with restricted legal rights, and many illegal disabilities. They are descendants of the Africans brought to America during the sixteenth, seventeenth, eighteenth and nineteenth centuries and reduced to slave labor. This group has no complete biological unity, but varies in color from white to black, and comprises a great variety of physical characteristics, since many are the offspring of white European-Americans as well as of Africans and American Indians. There are a large number of white Americans who also descend from Negroes but who are not counted in the colored group nor subjected to caste restrictions because the preponderance of white blood conceals their descent.

The so-called American Negro group, therefore, while it is in no sense absolutely set off physically from its fellow American, has nevertheless a strong, hereditary cultural unity, born of slavery, of common suffering, prolonged proscription and curtailment of political and civil rights; and especially because of economic and social disabilities. Largely from this fact, have arisen their cultural gifts to America—their rhythm, music and folk song; their religious faith and customs; their contribution to American art and literature; their defense of their country in every war, on land, sea and in the air; and especially the hard, continuous toil upon which the prosperity and wealth of this continent has largely been built.

The group has long been internally divided by dilemma as to whether its striving upward should be aimed at strengthening its inner cultural and group bonds, both for intrinsic progress and for offensive power against caste; or whether it should seek escape wherever and however possible into the surrounding American culture. Decision in this matter has been largely determined by outer compulsion rather than inner plan; for prolonged policies of segregation and discrimination have involuntarily welded the mass almost into a nation within a nation with its own schools, churches, hospitals, newspapers and many business enterprises.

The result has been to make American Negroes to a wide extent provincial, introvertive, self-conscious and narrowly race-loyal; but it has also inspired them to frantic and often successful effort to achieve, to deserve, to show the world their capacity to share modern civilization. As a result there is almost no area of American civilization in which the Negro has not made creditable showing in the face of all his handicaps.

If, however, the effect of the color caste system on the North American Negro has been both good and bad, its effect on white America has been disastrous. It has repeatedly led the greatest modern attempt at democratic government to deny its political ideals, to falsify its philanthropic assertions and to make its religion to a great extent hypocritical. A nation which boldly declared "That all men are created equal," proceeded to build its economy on chattel slavery; masters who declared race mixture impossible, sold their own children into slavery and left a mulatto progeny which neither law nor science can today disentangle; churches which excused slavery as calling the heathen to God, refused to recognize the freedom of converts or admit them to equal communion. Sectional strife over the profits of slave labor and conscientious revolt against making human beings real estate led to bloody civil war, and to a partial emancipation of slaves which nevertheless even to this day is not complete. Poverty, ignorance, disease and crime have been forced on these unfortunate victims of greed to an extent far beyond any social necessity; and a great nation, which today ought to be in the forefront of the march toward peace and democracy, finds itself continuously making common cause with race hate, prejudiced exploitation and oppression of the common man. Its high and noble words are turned against it, because they are contradicted in every syllable by the treatment of the American Negro for three hundred and twenty-eight years. . . .

. . . The United States has always professed to be a democracy. She has never wholly attained her ideal, but slowly she has approached it. The privilege of voting has in time been widened by abolishing limitations of birth, religion and lack of property. After the Civil War, which abolished slavery, the nation in gratitude to the black soldiers and laborers who helped win that war, sought to admit to the suffrage all persons without distinction of "race, color or previous condition of servitude." They were warned by the great leaders of abolition, like Sumner, Stevens and Douglass, that this could only be effective, if the freedmen were given schools, land and some minimum of capital. A Freedmen's Bureau to furnish these prerequisites to effective citizenship was planned and put into partial operation. But Congress and the nation, weary of the costs of war and eager to get back to profitable industry, refused the necessary funds. The effort died, but in order to restore friendly civil government in the South the enfranchised freedmen, seventy-five percent illiterate, without land or tools, were thrown into competitive industry with a ballot in their hands. By herculean effort, helped by philanthropy and their own hard work, Negroes built a school system, bought land and cooperated in starting a new economic order in the South. In a generation they had reduced their illiteracy by half and had become wage-earning laborers and sharecroppers. They still were handicapped by poverty, disease and crime, but nevertheless the rise of American Negroes from slavery in 1860 to freedom in 1880 has few parallels in modern history.

However, opposition to any democracy which included the Negro race on any terms was so strong in the former slaveholding South, and found so much sympathy in large parts of the rest of the nation, that despite notable improvement in the condition of the Negro by every standard of social measurement, the effort to deprive him of the right to vote succeeded. At first he was driven from the polls in the South by mobs and violenced; then he was openly cheated; finally by a "gentlemen's agreement" with the North, the Negro was disfranchised in the South by a series of laws, methods of administration, court decisions and general public policy, so that today three-fourths of the Negro population of the nation is deprived of the right to vote by open and declared policy.

Most persons seem to regard this as simply unfortunate for Negroes, as depriving a modern working class of the minimum rights for self-protection and opportunity for progress. This is true as has been shown in poor educational opportunities, discrimination in work, health and protection and in the courts. But the situation is far more serious than this: the disfranchisement of the American Negro makes the functioning of all democracy in the nation difficult; and as democracy fails to function in the leading democracy in the world, it fails in the world.

Let us face the facts: the representation of the people in the Congress of the United States is based on population; members of the House of Representatives are elected by groups of approximately 275,000 to 300,000 persons living in 435 Congressional Districts. Naturally difficulties of division within state boundaries, unequal growth of population, migration from year to year, and slow adjustment of these and other changes, make equal population of these districts only approximate; but unless by and large, and in the long run, essential equality is maintained, the whole basis of democratic representation is marred and as in the celebrated "rotten borough" cases in England in the nineteenth century, representation must be eventually equalized or democracy relapses into oligarchy or even fascism.

This is exactly what threatens the United States today because of the unjust disfranchisement of the Negro and the use of his numerical presence to increase the political power of his enemies and of the enemies of democracy. The nation has not the courage to eliminate from citizenship all persons of Negro descent and thus try to restore slavery. It therefore makes its democracy unworkable by paradox and contradiction. . . .

. . . [Who] is interested in this disfranchisement and who gains power by it? It must be remembered that the South has the largest percentage of ignorance, of poverty, of disease in the nation. At the same time, and partly on account of this, it is the place where the labor movement has made the least progress; there are fewer unions and the unions are less effectively organized than in the North. Besides this, the fiercest and most successful fight against democracy in industry is centering in the South, in just that region where medieval caste conditions based mainly on color, and partly on poverty and ignorance, are more prevalent and most successful. And just because labor is so completely deprived of political and industrial power, investors and monopolists are today being attracted there in greater number and with more intensive organization than anywhere else in the United States.

Southern climate has made labor cheaper in the past. Slavery influenced and still influences the conditions under which southern labor works. There is in the South a reservoir of labor, more laborers than jobs, and competing groups eager for the jobs. Industry encourages the culture patterns which make these groups hate and fear each other. Company towns with control over education and religion are common. Machines displace many workers and increase the demand for jobs at any wage. The United States government economists declare that the dominant characteristics of the southern labor force are: (1) greater potential labor growth in the nation; (2) relatively larger number of non-white workers (which means cheaper workers); (3) predominance of rural workers (which means predominance of ignorant labor); (4) greater working year span (which means child labor and the labor of old people); (5) relatively fewer women in industrial employment. Whole industries are moving South toward this cheaper labor. The recent concentration of investment and monopoly in the South is tremendous.

If concentrated wealth wished to control congressmen or senators, it is far easier to influence voters in South Carolina, Mississippi or Georgia where it requires only from four thousand to sixteen thousand votes to elect a congressman, than to try this in Illinois, New York or Minnesota, where one hundred to one hundred and fifty thousand votes must be persuaded. This spells danger: danger to the American way of life, and danger not simply to the Negro, but to white folk all over the nation, and to the nations of the world.

The federal government has for these reasons continually cast its influence with imperial aggression throughout the world and withdrawn its sympathy from the colored peoples and from the small nations. It has become through private investment a part of the imperialistic bloc which is controlling the colonies of the world. When we tried to join the Allies in the First World War, our efforts were seriously interfered with by the assumed necessity of extending caste legislation into our armed forces. It was often alleged that American troops in France showed more animosity against Negro troops than against the Germans. During the Second World War, there was, in the Orient, in Great Britain, and on the battlefields of France and Italy, the same interference with military efficiency by the necessity of segregating and wherever possible subordinating the Negro personnel of the American army.

Now and then a strong political leader has been able to force back the power of monopoly and waste, and make some start toward preservation of natural resources and their restoration to the mass of the people. But such effort has never been able to last long. Threatened collapse and disaster gave the late President Roosevelt a chance to develop a New Deal of socialist planning for more just distribution of income under scientific guidance. But reaction intervened, and it was a reaction based on a South aptly called our "Number One Economic Problem": a region of poor, ignorant and diseased people, black and white, with exaggerated political power in the hands of a few resting on disfranchisement of voters, control of wealth and income, not simply by the South but by the investing North.

This paradox and contradiction enters into our actions, thoughts and plans. After the First World War, we were alienated from the proposed League of Nations because of sympathy for imperialism and because of race antipathy to Japan, and because we objected to the compulsory protection of minorities in Europe, which might lead to similar demands upon the United States. We joined Great Britain in determined refusal to recognize equality of races and nations; our tendency was toward isolation until we saw a chance to make inflated profits from the want which came upon the world. This effort of America to make profit out of the disaster in Europe was one of the causes of the depression of the thirties.

As the Second World War loomed, the federal government, despite the feelings of the mass of people, followed the captains of industry into attitudes of sympathy toward both fascism in Italy and Nazism in Germany. When the utter unreasonableness of fascist demands forced the United States in self-defense to enter the war, then at last the real feelings of the people were loosed and we again found ourselves in the forefront of democratic progress.

But today the paradox again looms after the Second World War. We have recrudescence of race hate and caste restrictions in the United States and of these dangerous tendencies not simply for the United States itself but for all nations. When will nations learn that their enemies are quite as often within their own country as without? It is not Russia that threatens the United States so much as Mississippi; not Stalin and Molotov but Bilbo and Rankin; internal injustice done to one's brothers is far more dangerous than the aggression of strangers from abroad.

Finally it must be stressed that the discrimination of which we complain is not simply discrimination against poverty and ignorance which the world by long custom is used to see: the discrimination practiced in the United States is practiced against American Negroes in spite of wealth, training and character. One of the contributors of this statement happens to be a white man, but the other three and the editor himself are subject to "Jim Crow" laws, and to denial of the right to vote, of an equal chance to earn a living, of the right to enter many places of public entertainment supported by their taxes. In other words, our complaint is mainly against a discrimination based mainly on color of skin, and it is that that we denounce as not only indefensible but barbaric.

It may be quite properly asked at this point to whom a petition and statement such as this should be addressed? Many persons say that this represents a domestic question which is purely a matter of internal concern; and that therefore it should be addressed to the people and government of the United States and the various states.

It must not be thought that this procedure has not already been taken. From the very beginning of this nation, in the late eighteenth century, and even before, in the colonies, decade by decade and indeed year by year, the Negroes of the United States have appealed for redress of grievances, and have given facts and figures to support their own contention.

It must also be admitted that this continuous hammering upon the gates of opportunity in the United States has had effect, and that because of this, and with the help of his white fellow citizens, the American Negro has emerged from slavery and attained emancipation from chattel slavery, considerable economic independence, social security and advance in culture.

But manifestly this is not enough; no large group of a nation can lag behind the average culture of that nation, as the American Negro still does, without suffering not only itself but becoming a menace to the nation.

In addition to this, in its international relations, the United States owes something to the world; to the United Nations of which it is a part, and to the ideals which it professes to advocate. Especially is this true since the United Nations has made its headquarters in New York. The United States is in honor bound not only to protect its own people and its own interests, but to guard and respect the various peoples of the world who are its guests and allies. Because of caste custom and legislation along the color line, the United States is today in danger of encroaching upon the rights and privileges of its fellow nations. Most people of the world are more or less colored in skin; their presence at the meetings of the United Nations as participants and as visitors renders them always liable to insult and to discrimination; because they may be mistaken for Americans of Negro descent.

Not very long ago the nephew of the ruler of a neighboring American state was killed by policemen in Florida, because he was mistaken for a Negro and thought to be demanding rights which a Negro in

Florida is not legally permitted to demand. Again and more recently in Illinois, the personal physician of Mahatma Gandhi, one of the great men of the world and an ardent supporter of the United Nations, was with his friends refused food in a restaurant, again because they were mistaken for Negroes. In a third case, a great insurance society in the United States in its development of a residential area, which would serve for housing the employees of the United Nations, is insisting and reserving the right to discriminate against the persons received as residents for reasons of race and color.

All these are but passing incidents, but they show clearly that a discrimination practiced in the United States against her own citizens and to a large extent a contravention of her own laws, cannot be persisted in, without infringing upon the rights of the peoples of the world and especially upon the ideals and the work of the United Nations.

This question then, which is without doubt primarily an internal and national question, becomes inevitably an international question and will in the future become more and more international, as the nations draw together. In this great attempt to find common ground and to maintain peace, it is therefore fitting and proper that the thirteen million American citizens of Negro descent should appeal to the United Nations and ask that organization in the proper way to take cognizance of a situation which deprives this group of their rights as men and citizens, and by so doing makes the function of the United Nations more difficult, if not in many cases impossible.

The United Nations surely will not forget that the population of this group makes it in size one of the considerable nations of the world. We number as many as the inhabitants of the Argentine or Czechoslovakia, or the whole of Scandinavia including Sweden, Norway and Denmark. We are very nearly the size of Egypt, Rumania and Yugoslavia. We are larger than Canada, Saudi Arabia, Ethiopia, Hungary or the Netherlands. We have twice as many persons as Australia or Switzerland, and more than the whole Union of South Africa. We have more people than Portugal or Peru; twice as many as Greece and nearly as many as Turkey. We have more people by far than Belgium and half as many as Spain. In sheer numbers then we are a group which has a right to be heard; and while we rejoice that other smaller nations can stand and make their wants known in the United Nations, we maintain equally that our voice should not be suppressed or ignored.

We are not to be regarded as completely ignorant, poverty-stricken, criminal or diseased people. In education our illiteracy is less than most of the peoples of Asia and South America, and less than many of the peoples of Europe. We are property holders, our health is improving rapidly and our crime rate is less than our social history and present disadvantages would justify. The census of 1940 showed that of American Negroes twenty-five years or over, one-fifth have had seven to eight years of training in grade schools; 4 percent have finished a four-year high-school course and nearly 2 percent are college graduates.

It is for this reason that American Negroes are appealing to the United Nations, and for the purposes of this appeal they have naturally turned toward the National Association for the Advancement of Colored People. This Association is not the only organization of American Negroes; there are other and worthy organizations. Some of these have already made similar appeal and others doubtless will in the future. But probably no organization has a better right to express the wishes of this vast group of people than the National Association for the Advancement of Colored People.

The National Association for the Advancement of Colored People, incorporated in 1910, is the oldest and largest organization among American Negroes designed to fight for their political, civil and social rights. It has grown from a small body of interested persons into an organization which had enrolled at the close of 1946, 452,289 members in 1,417 branches. At present it has over a half million members throughout the United States. The Board of Directors of this organization, composed of leading colored and white citizens of the United States, has ordered this statement to be made and presented to the Commission on Human Rights of the Economic and Social Council of the United Nations, and to the General Assembly of the United Nations.

THE CASE FOR THE JEWS

What is there right and wrong in the question of Palestine, which today faces not simply the Untied States but the whole world?

It is not a difficult question. There is something terribly simple about it.

Every child knows that ancient Jewish civilization and religion centered in Palestine. One has but to name its cities, rivers and places— Jerusalem, Bethlehem, Damascus, Jordan, Galilee and a hundred others.

Everyone knows the way in which the history of the Jewish religion is wound about Palestine and from there how the thread runs through all modern history.

INTO this land from 1700 B.C. to the 19th century, passed a succession of peoples and empires: Egypt, Assyria, Babylon, Persia, and Greece. About 1,000 B.C., the Hebrew monarchy arose and persisted with conquest and revival until the time of Alexander the Great. After his death began the world-wide dispersal of the Jews, their struggle with Rome and overthrow by Islam.

When, therefore, it comes a question of original possession and ownership there is no final answer for any people. After all, as Americans ought to know, the question of possession of a land is in the long run the question of the use to which the land is put.

PALESTINE is a land largely of plateaus, mountains, and deserts, sparsely inhabited, and could easily maintain millions more people than the two millions it has today. Among the million Arabs there is widespread ignorance, poverty and disease and fanatic belief in the Mohammedan religion, which makes these people suspicious of other peoples and other religions. Thier rulership is a family and clan despotism which makes effective use of democratic methods difficult.

Now it happens that the Jew wandering through Europe has for two thousand years been fighting for a place. He was not allowed in mediaeval Europe, because of his religion, to pursue the ordinary vocations of most people. He became, therefore, a peddler and a financier, beginning his work with the new capitalism that arose in the Middle Ages. Here he found his vocation and served in every country.

THERE is no question of the contribution which he made to modern civilization, not only in banking and finance, but in the arts, in the fineness of his family life, in the magnificent clearness of his intellect. But he was faced always by three alternatives: Should he lose himself in the surrounding population and through that give up his peculiar culture and religion; should he keep to himself, an integral unit; or finally, should he try to found a state of his own?

All three of these answers were made. Millions of Jews had lost themselves in the population of Europe and their blood mingles with that of other people's.

AT THE SAME time they have kept a curious and fruitful unity in their culture and in their religion. Finally, after a bitter fight, there arose with increasing voice, in the 19th century, a demand on the part of the Jews themselves that they should go back to Zion and refound the state which they had lost.

This Zionism met opposition from many thoughtful Jews. They said this would increase anti-Jewish attitudes rather than decrease them.

But the situation ceased to be academic. There began to be a growing feeling that certain of the Jews could only escape persecution by migration to a homeland.

THEN during the First World War, on November 2, 1917, came the great promise of the British Empire: "His Majesty's Government view with favour the establishment in Palestine of a national home for the Jewish people, and will use their best endeavours to facilitate the achievement of that object."

Moreover, this was no longer a mere question of religion and culture. It was a question of young and forward-thinking Jews bringing a new civilization into an old land and building up that land out of ignorance, disease, and poverty into which it had fallen; and by democratic methods erecting a new and peculiarly fateful modern state.

A start has been made in education, agriculture, water power, industry, and commerce.

ONE MAN furnished the catalysis for integration and that was Adolph Hitler. Rising on the backs of Jews because of the envy and jealousy which they had aroused in Germany, he built a new anti-Semitism in Europe which resulted in the murder of six million people and the dispersion of practically all of the Jews in Eastern Europe.

What had been a theoretical demand for a Zion, now became a necessity for more than a million displaced and homeless Jews. There was actually no other place on earth for them to go.

But at this time, because of the increased use of oil in industry and war, because of the fear of Russia, with her new plan for the emancipation of the mass of people, and the discovery of oil in Arabia, Great Britain opposed Zion.

ERNEST BEVIN, the Labor Party's Secretary of State for Foreign Affairs of Great Britain, building on some half-hidden dislike of Jews in his own mind, not only refused to carry out the British promise but used British troops against the Jews, trained Arab troops for use in the future against them, and used the Navy for keeping the displaced persons from migrating into Zion.

In the United States, President Truman, after having promised to stand by the founding of Zion, inexplicably went back upon his word, refused to permit arms to be given to the beleaguered Jews in Palestine and since then has been trying to straddle the fence and make any efforts of the United Nations ineffective and impossible.

This has precipitated a fatal test of the new effort to unite mankind. It was because the League of Nations refused to follow the lead of Russia into disarmament, and then refused to take any stand with regard to the rape of Ethiopia, that, primarily, the League of Nations died.

IN THE case of Palestine, the United Nations is now standing apparently helpless.

In the meantime, a million displaced Jews are begging to be allowed to migrate to Palestine, where there is room for them, where there is work for them to do, where what Jews have already done is for the advantage, not simply of the Jews, but of the Arabs. The British Navy is keeping the Jews out and when the British Navy ceases to act, the British-trained Arabian Army will walk in and begin war. This may be the beginning of third World War. If it is, the guilt of this final disaster of modern civilization lies upon the heads of Ernest Bevin and Harry Truman.

I TAKE MY STAND FOR PEACE

The world is astonished at recent developments in the United States. Our actions and attitudes are discussed with puzzled wonder on the streets of every city in the world. Reluctantly the world is coming to believe that we actually want war; that we must have war; that in no other way can we keep our workers employed and maintain huge profits save by spending seventy thousand million dollars a year for war preparation and adding to the vast debt of over 200 thousand millions which we already owe chiefly for war in the past.

Our present war expenditure must be increased yet we cannot tax the rich much more since the lawyers who make the tax laws can also break them and let the bulk of wealth go untaxed. We cannot raise the taxes on the poor much higher because rising prices leave less and less to tax. Citizens have borrowed 200 thousand million dollars on homes, farms, and furniture, and the poor and middle class have spent nearly all their savings. Yet we cannot stop; either we spend more and more on top of what we are spending or our whole industrial organization, with its billions of private profit monopoly, will face collapse.

On the other hand, the Soviet Union whom we are determined to destroy does not at present seem willing to fight. We have warned and dared it. We have publicly and privately insulted it. We have eagerly given currency to every charge which anyone at any time makes against the Soviet Union, its economy, its morals, its plans. We thought that at last in Korea we had them where they must fight and we prepared jauntily for World War III almost with shouts of joy.

We were sure the Russians had started the Korean uprising, were furnishing arms and ready to march to war. Henry Wallace actually saw them and ran backward so fast that he tripped over his own resolutions, and stepped in the faces of his friends. Still the Soviets did not fight and began instead to call for world peace; for union against the atom bomb; for peace congresses. But the United States was not misled; not they. They stopped the peace appeal. They picked up and jailed advocates of peace. They barred from our shores foreign advocates of peace, persons of the highest reputation.

Highly placed public officials and military men began openly to declare that if the Russians would not attack us, we would attack them to keep them from attacking us. Meantime, wave after wave of our young men are being trained for murder, and Congress is on the verge of calling every youth in the land for this purpose.

This is what Europe sees us set for, in contradiction to everything we once professed—liberty, free speech, truth and justice. To this our masters will lead us unless you intervene: unless right here and now you, the people of the United States, say No! Enough of this hysteria, this crazy foolishness!

Once . . . The Land of the Free

Our slow but steady descent into belief in complete and universal war and our determination to make all men agree with what some believe, rather than to let them exercise their free American heritage of choosing truth—this literal descent into Hell in our day, and in this our own country, has been so gradual and complete that many honest Americans cannot believe what they actually hear and see; and sit bewildered, rubbing their eyes in order to get some vague conception of what can have happened to the land which once declared "these truths to be self-evident, that all men are created equal, that they are endowed by their Creator with certain unalienable rights, that among these are life, liberty and the pursuit of happiness."

No American born before 1900 could possibly conceive that the United States would become a land approaching universal military service; with its armed forces in every continent and on every sea; pledged to conquer and control masses of mankind, order the thought and belief of the nations of the world, and ready to spend for these objects more money than it ever spent for religion, education or social uplift altogether.

When men arise and say this and try to prove its truth, every effort is made by secret police, organized spies and hired informers; by deliberate subversion of the fundamental principles of our law, to imprison, slander and silence such persons, and deprive them of earning an honest livelihood.

Avoiding all hysteria and exaggeration, all natural indignation and instinctive defense of the right of free speech and hatred of thought control, it is clear to all Americans who still dare to think, that my description of this America is true, and if true, frightening to all men who once thought of this land as the Land of the Free.

United States Alone Wants War . . .

My platform then, like the platform of every honest American who still dares believe in peace and freedom, takes its unalterable stand against war and slavery. There was a day when most men believed that progress depended on war; that by war, and mainly by war, had modern men gained freedom, religion and democracy. We believed this because we were taught this in our literature and science, in church and school, on platform and in newspaper. It was always a lie and as war has become universal and so horrible and destructive that everybody recognizes it as murder, crippling, insanity and stark death of human culture, we realize that there is scarce a victory formerly claimed by war which mankind might not have gained more cheaply and more decently and even more completely by methods of peace. If that was true in the past, it is so clear and indisputable today that no sane being denies it. And yet of all nations of earth today, the United States alone wants war, prepares for war, forces other nations to fight and asks you and me to impoverish ourselves, give up health and schools, sacrifice our sons and daughters to a Jim-Crow army, and commit suicide, for a world war that nobody wants but the rich Americans who profit by it.

If war were a matter of careful study and grave decision, of prayerful thought and solemn deliberation, we might take its fearful outbreak as at least no more than human error, soon to be stopped by decency and common sense. But when did you ever vote for war? You who have spent most of your lives in a fighting, murdering world? When did you ever have a chance to decide this matter of maiming and murder? Never! And you never will as long as an executive of his own initiative can start a "little police action" which costs the lives and health of over 60,000 American boys, in order that big business can interfere with the governments of Asia.

Of what are we in such deathly fear? Have we been invaded? Has anyone dropped an atom bomb on us? Have we been impoverished or enslaved by foreigners? Is our business failing, and are our millionaires disappearing? Has the rate of profit gone down, is our machinery less cunning, or our natural resources destroyed by strangers? Is there any sign that the United States of America is victim, or can be victim of any foreign country? No! Then of what are we afraid, and why are we trying to guard the earth from Pacific to Atlantic and from the North to the South Pole, unless it be from ourselves?

. . . Afraid of an Idea

Our rulers are afraid of an idea; tempted by a vision of power which this idea fights. The power they crave long misled and slaughtered the peoples of Europe and Asia, and now insidiously creeps into our own fever-mad heads; and that is Imperialism—world rule over the world. Once this was sought through black slavery: then it was made easy by yellow coolies: then by all "lesser breeds without the law," who could furnish a "white man's burden" and let him strut over the world, and lord it in Asia and Africa, and rule and rule without end, forever and forever. That was the vision of the nineteenth century. The fever of imperialism caught the United States as the nineteenth century died and we choked a few islands out of dying Spain. But these were but small change which whetted our appetite. With the first World War came the vision of an Imperial United States as successor of the empire on which the sun already sets. We rushed so madly at the spoils left by European empire that we brought down our whole industrial system about our own ears.

It would seem that the memory of the great depression of the Thirties would convince all thinking men that war is not the path to the millenium, and that what we need is reform of our own system of work and industrial organization, before we attempt to teach the world what to think or how to live.

But what the men of big business ignored was that the industrial system which they were seeking to re-install had already met a terrible and costly reverse; that modifications of imperialism and monopoly capitalism had already been suggested and tried. Such efforts comprehended loosely by the name "Socialism," were not invented by Russia nor first tried by Russia. On the contrary, Socialism is an English, French and German conception and was tried in Russia because that unhappy land was one of the last and worst victims of the capitalist system.

If tomorrow Russia disappeared from the face of the earth, the basic problem facing the modern world would remain: and that is, why is it, with the earth's abundance and our mastery of natural forces, and miraculous technique; with our commerce belting the earth, and goods and services pouring from our stores, factories, ships and warehouses—why is it that nevertheless, most human beings are starving to death, dying of preventable disease and too ignorant to know what is the matter, while a small minority are so rich that they cannot spend their income?

That is the problem which faces the world, and Russia was not the first to pose it, nor will she be the last to ask and demand answer. The nineteenth century said that this situation was inevitable and must always remain because of the natural inferiority of most men; the twentieth century knows better. It says that there can be food enough for all; that clothes and shelter for all can be provided; that most disease is preventable and that the overwhelming mass of human beings can be educated; that intelligence, health and decent comfort are not only possible, but should be demanded, by all men; planned by all states; and made increasingly effective by all voters in each election.

But the powerful who today own the earth and the fullness thereof; who monopolize its industry and own its press and screen its news, have another answer. They order us to fight an Idea, to "contain" and crush any dream of abolishing poverty, disease and ignorance; and to do this by organizing war, murder and destruction on any people who dare to try to plan plenty for all mankind. From the nineteenth century, they attempt to take over imperialism to bribe the workers and thinkers of the most powerful countries by high wage and privilege, in order to build a false and dishonest prosperity on the slavery and degradation, the low wage and disease, of Africa and Asia and the islands of the sea; and to pay the price for this, they demand that you, your sons and daughters, in endless stream, be murdered and crippled in endless wars.

This is why we are fighting or preparing to fight in Europe, Asia and Africa—not against an enemy, but against the Idea—against the rising demand of the working classes of the world for better wages, decent housing, regular employment, medical service and schools for all.

It does not answer this world-wide demand to say that we of America have these things in greater abundance than the rest of the world, if our prosperity is based on, or seeks to base itself on, the exploitation and degradation of the rest of mankind. Remember, it is American money that owns more and more of South African mines worked by slave labor; it is American enterprise that fattens off Rhodesian copper; it is American investors that seek to dominate China, India, Korea and Burma; who are throttling the starved workers of the Near East.

Yet is it not clear that such a program is sheer insanity? That no nation, however rich and smart, can conquer this world? Have not Egypt, Assyria, Greece, Rome, Britain and German taught us this? And also that no Idea based on truth and righteousness can ultimately be suppressed by force and murder?

What Can Be Done . . . ?

I never thought I would live to see the day that free speech and freedom of opinion would be so throttled in the United States as it is today. Today in this free country, no man can be sure of earning a living, of escaping slander and personal violence, or even of keeping out of jail unless publicly and repeatedly he proclaims:

—that he hates Russia.

—that he opposes Socialism and Communism.

—that he supports wholeheartedly the war in Korea.

—that he is ready to spend any amount for further war, anywhere or at anytime.

—that he is ready to fight the Soviet Union, China and any other country, or all countries together.

—that he believes in the use of the atom bomb or any other weapon of mass destruction, and regards anyone opposed as a traitor.

—that he not only believes in and consents to all these things, but is willing to spy on his neighbors and denounce them if they do not believe as he does.

The mere statement of this creed shows its absolute insanity. What can be done to bring this nation to its senses? Most people answer: nothing; just sit still; bend to the storm; if necessary, lie and join the witch-hunt, swear to God that never, never did you ever sympathize with the Russian peasants' fight to be free; that you never in your life belonged to a liberal organization, or had a friend who did; and if so, you were deceived, deluded and a damned fool.

I Take My Stand . . .

I want progress; I want education; I want social medicine; I want a living wage and old age security; I want employment for all and relief for the unemployed and sick; I want public works, public services and public improvements. I want freedom for my people. And because I know and you know that we cannot have these things, and at the same time fight, destroy and kill all around the world in order to make huge profit for big business; for that reason, I take my stand beside the millions in every nation and continent and cry *Peace—No More War!*

A new era of power, held and exercised by the working classes the world over, is dawning and while its eventual form is not yet clear, its progress cannot be held back by any power of man.

THE NEGRO AND THE WARSAW GHETTO

I have been to Poland three times. The first time was 59 years ago, when I was a student at the University of Berlin. I had been talking to my schoolmate, Stanislaus Ritter von Estreicher. I had been telling him of the race problem in America, which seemed to me at the time the only race problem and the greatest social problem of the world. He brushed it aside. He said, "You know nothing, really, about real race problems." Then he began to tell me about the problem of the Poles and particularly of that part of them who were included in the German empire; of their limited education; of the refusal to let them speak their own language; of the few careers that they were allowed to follow; of the continued insult to their culture and family life.

I was astonished; because race problems at the time were to me purely problems of color, and principally of slavery in the United States and near-slavery in Africa. I promised faithfully that when I went on my vacation that summer, I would stop to see him in his home at Krakow, Poland, where his father was librarian of the university.

Discovery of Jewish Question

I went down to South Germany through Switzerland to Italy, and then came back by Venice and Vienna and went out through Austria, Czechoslovakia and into German Poland and there, on the way, I had a new experience with a new race problem. I was travelling from Budapest through Hungary to a small town in Galicia, where I planned to spend the night. The cabman looked at me and asked if I wanted to stop *"unter die Juden."* I was a little puzzled, but told him "Yes." So we went to a little Jewish hotel on a small, out of the way street. There I realized another problem of race or religion, I did not know which, which had to do with the treatment and segregation of large numbers of human beings. I went on to Krakow, becoming more and more aware of two problems of human groups, and then came back to the university, not a little puzzled as to my own race problem and its place in the world.

Gradually I became aware of the Jewish problem of the modern world and something of its history. In Poland I learned little because the university and its teachers and students were hardly aware themselves of what this problem was, and how it influenced them, or what its meaning was in their life. In Germany I saw it continually obtruding, but being suppressed and seldom mentioned. I remember once visiting on a social occasion in a small German town. A German student was with me and when I became uneasily aware that all was not going well, he reassured me. He whispered, "They think I may be a Jew. It's not you they object to, it's me." I was astonished. It had never occurred to me until then that any exhibition of race prejudice could be anything but color prejudice. I knew that this young man was pure German, yet his dark hair and handsome face made our friends suspicious. Then I went further to investigate this new phenomenon in my experience.

Thirteen years after that I passed again through Poland and Warsaw. It was in the darkness, both physically and spiritually. Hitler was supreme in Germany where I had been visiting for five months and I sensed the oncoming storm. I passed through Warsaw into the Soviet Union just three years before the horror fell upon that city.

But in Berlin, before I left, I sensed something of the Jewish problem and its growth in the generation since my student days. I went to the Jewish quarter one day and entered a bookstore. It was quiet and empty. After a time a man came into the room and very quietly he asked me what I was looking for. I mentioned certain books and browsed among those he pointed out. He said nothing more nor did I. I felt his suspicion and at last I wandered out. I went that night to a teacher's home. There were a few Americans and several Germans present. The curtains were carefully drawn and then the teacher spoke. He defended the nazi program in the main—its employment, its housing and roads; but he frankly confessed that he was ashamed of the treatment of the Jews or at least some of them. He blamed some severely but he had friends among them and he was ashamed of their treatment.

Then, at midnight I entered Poland. It was dark—dark not only in the smoke, but in the soul of its people, who whispered in the night as we rode slowly through the murk of the railway yards.

Then finally, three years ago I was in Warsaw. I have seen something of human upheaval in this world: the scream and shots of a race riot in Atlanta; the marching of the Ku Klux Klan; the threat of courts and police; the neglect and destruction of human habitation; but nothing in my wildest imagination was equal to what I saw in Warsaw in 1949. I would have said before seeing it that it was impossible for a civilized nation with deep religious convictions and outstanding religious institutions; with literature and art; to treat fellow human beings as Warsaw had been treated. There had been complete, planned and utter destruction. Some streets had been so obliterated that only by using photographs of the past could they tell where the street was. And no one mentioned the total of the dead, the sum of destruction, the story of crippled and insane, the widows and orphans.

The astonishing thing, of course, was the way that in the midst of all these memories of war and destruction, the people were rebuilding the city with an enthusiasm that was simply unbelievable. A city and a nation was literally rising from the dead. Then, one afternoon, I was taken out to the former ghetto. I knew all too little of its story although I had visited ghettos in parts of Europe, particularly in Frankfort, Germany. Here there was not much to see. There was complete and total waste, and a monument. And the monument brought back again the problem of race and religion, which so long had been my own particular and separate problem. Gradually, from looking and reading, I rebuilt the story of this extraordinary resistance to oppression and wrong in a day of complete frustration, with enemies on every side: a resistance which involved death and destruction for hundreds and hundreds of human beings; a deliberate sacrifice in life for a great ideal in the face of the fact that the sacrifice might be completely in vain.

Enlarged View of Negro Question

The result of these three visits, and particularly of my view of the Warsaw ghetto, was not so much clearer understanding of the Jewish problem in the world as it was a real and more complete understanding of the Negro problem. In the first place, the problem of slavery, emancipation, and caste in the United States was no longer in my mind a separate and unique thing as I had so long conceived it. It was not even solely a matter of color and physical and racial characteristics, which was particularly a hard thing for me to learn, since for a lifetime the color line had been a real and efficient cause of misery. It was not merely a matter of religion. I had seen religions of many kinds—I had sat in the Shinto temples of Japan, in the Baptist churches of Georgia, in the Catholic cathedral of Cologne and in Westminster Abbey. No, the race problem in which I was interested cut across lines of color and physique and belief and status and was a matter of cultural patterns, perverted teaching and human hate and prejudice, which reached all sorts of people and caused endless evil to all men. So that the ghetto of Warsaw helped me to emerge from a certain social provincialism into a broader conception of what the fight against race segregation, religious discrimination and the oppression by wealth had to become if civilization was going to triumph and broaden in the world.

I remembered now my schoolmate, Stanislaus. He has long been dead and he died refusing to be a stoolpigeon for the nazis in conquered Poland. He gave his life for a great cause. How broad it eventually became! How much he realized that behind the Polish problem lay the Jewish problem and that all were one crime against civilization, I do not know.

I remember now one scene in Poland over a half century ago. It was of worship in a Catholic church. The peasants were crowded together and were grovelling on their knees. They were in utter subjection to a powerful hierarchy. And out of that, today, they have crawled and fought and struggled. They see the light.

Path to the Future

My friend, Gabriel D'Arboussier, an African, recently visited Warsaw and wrote: "At the entrance to the city rises an imposing mausoleum erected to the memory of the 40,000 soldiers of the Red Army who fell for the liberation of Warsaw and who are all buried there. This is no cemetery, cut off from the living, but the last resting place of these glorious dead, near whom the living come to sit and ponder the sacrifice of those to whom they owe life. Had I seen nothing else, that mausoleum alone would have taught me enough to understand the Polish people's will to peace and its attachment to the Soviet Union.

But there is more to tell and it cannot be too often told: of Poland's thirty-two million inhabitants six and a half million died. There is also Warsaw, 83 per cent destroyed and its population reduced from over a million to 22,000, and the poignant spectacle of the flattened ghetto."

But where are we going—whither are we drifting? We are facing war, taxation, hate and cowardice and particularly increasing division of aim and opinion within our own groups. Negroes are dividing by social classes, and selling their souls to those who want war and colonialism, in order to become part of the ruling plutarchy, and encourage their sons to kill "Gooks." Among Jews there is the same dichotomy and inner strife, which forgets the bravery of the Warsaw ghetto and the bones of the thousands of dead who still lie buried in that dust. All this should lead both these groups and others to reassess and reformulate the problems of our day, whose solution belongs to no one group: the stopping of war and preparation for war; increased expenditure for schools better than we have or are likely to have in our present neglect and suppression of education; the curbing of the freedom of industry for the public welfare; and amid all this, the right to think, talk, study, without fear of starvation or jail. This is a present problem of all Americans and becomes the pressing problem of the civilized world.

CHINA

I saw China first in 1936, on my trip from the Soviet Union to Japan. I was struck by its myriads of people. This amorphous mass of men, with age-old monuments of human power, beauty and glory; with its helpless, undefended welter of misery and toil, has an organization of life and impenetrable will to survive that neither imperial tyranny, nor industrial exploitation, nor famine, starvation and pestilence can kill—it is eternal life, facing disaster and triumphing imperturbably.

There passed a glory from the earth when Imperial China fell. Built as it was on skulls, it was bravely built and the remains are magnificent. In all essential respects they surpass the Stones of Europe. Where Europe counts its years in hundreds, Asia counts its in thousands. There is absent that all too apparent European effort to dramatize and exaggerate the past; to emphasize war and personal glory. China shows a finer effort to let the past stand silent, frank and unadorned; to tell the truth simply about men and fully; and to record the triumphs of education, family life and literature far more than murder.

I write this now as things were in 1936. I am standing on the Great Wall of China, with 23 centuries beneath my feet. The purple crags of Manchuria lie beyond the valley, while behind are the yellow and brown mountains of China. For 70 cents I have been carried up on the shoulders of four men and down again. And here I stand on what has been called the only work of man visible from Mars. It is no mud fence or pile of cobbles. It surpasses that mighty bastion of Constantinople, which for so many centuries saved Mediterranean civilization from German barbarism. This is a wall of carefully cut stone, fitted and laid with perfect matching and eternal mortar, from 20 to 50 feet high and 2,500 miles long; built by a million men, castellated with perfect brick, and standing mute and immutable for more than 2,000 years. Such is China.

Shanghai was an epitome of the racial strife, the economic struggle, the human paradox of modern life. Here was the greatest city of the most populous nation on earth, with the large part of it owned, governed and policed by foreign nations. With Europe largely controlling its capital, commerce, mines, rivers and manufactures; with a vast welter of the greatest working class in the world, paid less than an average of 25 cents a day; with a glittering modern life of skyscrapers, majestic hotels, theatres and night clubs. In this city of nations were 19,000 Japanese, 11,000 British, 10,000 Russians, 4,000 Americans, and 10,000 foreigners of other nationalities living in the midst of 3,000,000 Chinese. The city was divided openly by nations; black-bearded Sikhs under British orders policed its streets, foreign warships sat calmly at her wharfs; foreigners told this city what it may and may not do.

Even at that, matters were not as bad as they once had been. In 1936, foreigners acknowledged that Chinese had some rights in China. Chinese who could afford it might even visit the city race track from which they and dogs were long excluded. It was no longer common to kick a coolie or throw a rickshaw's driver on the ground. Yet, the afternoon before I saw a little English boy of perhaps four years order three Chinese children out of his imperial way on the sidewalk of the Bund; and they meekly obeyed and walked in the gutter. It looked quite like Mississippi. And, too, I met a "missionary" from Mississippi, teaching in the Baptist University of Shanghai!

I went by invitation to the American-supported University of Shanghai and I said to the president that I should like to talk to a group of Chinese and discuss frankly racial and social matters. He arranged a luncheon at the Chinese Banker's Club. There were present one of the editors of the China press, the secretary-general of the Bank of China, the general manager of the China Publishing Company, the director of the Chinese Schools for Shanghai, and the executive secretary of the China Institute of International Relations.

We talked nearly three hours. I plunged in recklessly. I told them of my slave ancestors, of my education and travels; of the Negro problem. Then I turned on them and said, "How far do you think Europe can continue to dominate the world, or how far do you envisage a world whose spiritual center is Asia and the colored races? You have escaped from the domination of Europe politically since the World

War—at least in part; but how do you propose to escape from the domination of European capital? How are your working classes progressing? Why is it that you hate Japan more than Europe when you have suffered more from England, France, and Germany than from Japan?"

There ensued a considerable silence, in which I joined. Then we talked. They said, "Asia is still under the spell of Europe, although not as completely as a while back. It is not our ideal simply to ape Europe. We know little of India or Africa, or Africa in America. We see the danger of European capital and are slowly extricating ourselves, by seeking to establish control of capital by the political power of taxation and regulation. We have stabilized our currency—no longer do English Hong Kong notes form our chief circulating medium. Our wages are too low but slowly rising; labor legislation is appearing; we have 16 million children in school with short terms and inadequate equipment, but a beginning of the fight against our 90 per cent illiteracy."

We talked three hours but it was nearly a quarter of a century before I realized how much we did not say. The Soviet Union was scarcely mentioned, although I knew how the Soviet Union was teaching the Chinese. Nothing was said of the Long March which had just ended its 6,000 miles from Kiangsi to Yenan, led by Mao Tse-tung and Chu Teh. We mentioned America only for its benefactions and scarcely for its exploitation. Of the Kuomintang and Chiang Kaishek, almost nothing was said, but hatred of Japan for its betrayal of Asia was amply pointed out.

In 1959 I came again to China. I wanted to re-visit China because it is a land of colored people; and again because in 1956 China had officially invited me to visit and lecture, but the United States had refused to permit me. My passport stated that it was "not good for travel to China." It was a fair conclusion that if I did not use this passport to secure entrance to China and made no claim on the United States for protection, the State Department had no legal right to forbid me to visit China. Certainly the United States could give me no less protection in China than it could in Mississippi. On the other hand by legal fiction, the United States was still "at war" with China, since the Korean War had never been legally finished. It was possible then if I went to China, to jail me for "trading with the enemy." This risk I thought it my duty to take, since my invitation to visit had been renewed by the cultural minister, Kuo Mo-jo and by Madame Soong Ching-ling.

I left Moscow February 9 and returned April 6. It was the most fascinating eight weeks of travel and sight-seeing I have ever experienced. We remember Peking; a city of six million; its hard workers, its building and re-building; that great avenue which passes the former forbidden city, and is as wide as Central Park; the bicycles and pedicycles, the carts and barrows. There was the university where I lectured on Africa, and a college of the 50 or more races of China. We looked out from our hotel window at the workers. They all wore rain-coats beneath the drizzle. We saw the planning of a nation and a system of work rising over the entrails of dead empire.

I have traveled widely on this earth since my first trip to Europe 67 years ago. Save South America and India, I have seen most of the civilized world and much of its backward regions. Many leading nations I have visited repeatedly. But I have never seen a nation which so amazed and touched me as China in 1959.

I traveled 5,000 miles, by railway, boat, plane and auto. I saw all the great cities: Peking, Shanghai, Hankow and its sisters; Canton, Chungking, Chengtu, Junming and Nanking. I rode its vast rivers, passed through its villages and sat in its communes. I visited its schools and colleges, lectured and broadcast to the world. I visited its minority groups. I spent four hours with Mao Tse-tung and dined twice with Chou En-lai, the tireless Prime Minister of this nation of 680 million souls.

We come to Chengtu. We ride about this farthest Western stopping place, close to the crowds and the workers and the homes, old and new. We visit a commune of 60,000 members. We climb the mountain to see irrigation being widened today, yet started 2,200 years ago. There is a glorious temple on its summit, and below a wide lake between winding roads. Four rivers roll down from the Himalayas, out of Tibet into the Yangtze.

Then we fly to Kunmin, the end of the American Burma Road. It is warm and quiet, and at the state school the minorities dance and sing welcome, and among them are Tibetans. There are more Tibetans in China than in Tibet. In Tibet while we were on its border in Szechuan, the landholders and slave drivers and the religious fanatics revolted against the Chinese, and failed as they deserved to. Tibet has belonged to China for centuries. The Communists linked the two by roads and began reforms in landholding, schools and trade, which now move quickly. At Kunmin we were at the end of the Burma Road and near the Great Mekong River. Below lay Vietnam, Laos, Cambodia and Thailand. The nest of grafters, whoremongers and gamblers at Saigon, helped by Americans, have broken the Geneva treaty which closed the French Indo-Chinese War, and are attacking the Communists. That is called "communist aggression." It is the attempt of American business and the American Navy to supplant France as colonial ruler in Southeast Asia.

There is at Canton a marble commercial building where the import and export exposition was recently opened. There are five floors of exhibits. I am convinced that America cannot make anything which is not today being made by China, or which cannot be made cheaper, and for the most part made quite as well; for out of the things that China makes come no profits for private exploiters. Most nations of the world are beginning to buy China's goods, except the United States. China sells increasingly to Europe, to Asia and South America; to India, Burma, Ceylon, Indonesia, and Malaya; to Africa and the West Indies; to Australia and New Zealand. And such goods: silk and woolen clothing, watches, clocks, radios and television sets; looms, machinery and lamps, shoes and hats, pottery and dishes. All Chinese seem to be at work, and not afraid of unemployment, and welcoming every suggestion that displaces muscle with machinery.

In every town and city we went to the opera, and can never forget the assault of the Monkey King on the hosts of Heaven, facing God and the angels. A night sleeping train took us over the 30-hour trip from Peking to Wuhan. There I saw the bridge that had been miraculously thrown across the Yangtze. We rested in a little hotel adorned with flowering cabbages. We visited the great steel mills and shook hands with welcoming workers. The colored American prisoner of war who stayed in China rather than return to America and is happy with his wife and baby, came to visit us.

My birthday was given national notice in China, and celebrated as never before; and we who all our lives have been liable to insult and discrimination on account of our race and color, in China have met universal goodwill and love, such as we never expected. As we leave may we thank them humbly for all they have done for us, and for teaching us what communism means.

The people of the land I saw: the workers, the factory hands, the farmers and laborers, scrubwomen and servants. I went to parks and restaurants, sat in the homes of the high and the low; and always I saw a happy people; people with faith that needs no church or priest, and who laugh gaily when the Monkey King overthrows the angels. In all my wandering, I never felt the touch or breath of insult or even dislike—I who for 90 years in America scarcely ever saw a day without some expression of hate for "niggers."

What is the secret of China in the second half of the 20th century? It is that the vast majority of a billion human beings have been convinced that human nature in some of its darkest recesses can be changed, if change is necessary. China knows, as no other people know, to what depths human meanness can go. I used to weep for American Negroes, as I saw what indignities and repressions and cruelties they had passed; but as I read Chinese history in these last months and had it explained to me stripped of Anglo-Saxon lies, I know that no depths of Negro slavery in America have plumbed such abysses as the Chinese have seen for 2,000 years and more. They have seen starvation and murder; rape and prostitution; sale and slavery of children; and religion cloaked in opium and gin, for converting the "heathen." This oppression and contempt came not only from Tartars, Mongolians, British, French, Germans and Americans, but from the

Chinese themselves: Mandarins and warlords, capitalists and murdering thieves like Chiang Kai-shek; Kuomintang socialists and intellectuals educated abroad.

Despite all this, China lives, and has been transformed and marches on. She is not ignored by the United States. She ignores the United States and leaps forward. What did it? What furnished the motive power and how was it applied? First it was the belief in himself and in his people by a man like Sun Yat-sen. He plunged on blind and unaided, repulsed by Britain and America, but welcomed by Russia. Then efforts toward socialism, which wobbled forward, erred and lost, and at last was bribed by America and Britain and betrayed by Chiang Kai-shek, with its leaders murdered and its aims misunderstood, when not deliberately lied about.

Then came the Long March from feudalism, past capitalism and socialism to communism in our day. Mao Tse-tung, Chou En-lai, Chu Teh and a half dozen others undertook to lead a nation by example, by starving and fighting; by infinite patience and above all by making a nation believe that the people and not merely the elite—that on the contrary the workers in factory, street and field—composed the real nation. Others have said this often, but no nation has tried it like the Soviet Union and China. And on the staggering and bitter effort of the Soviets, beleaguered by all Western civilization, and yet far-seeing enough to help weaker China even before a still weak Russia was safe—on this vast pyramid has arisen the saving nation of this stumbling, murdering, hating world.

In China the people—the laboring people, the people who in most lands are the doormats on which the reigning thieves and murdering rulers walk, leading their painted and jeweled prostitutes—the people walk and boast. These people of the slums and gutters and kitchens are the Chinese nation today. This the Chinese believe and on this belief they toil and sweat and cheer.

They believe this and for the last ten years their belief has been strengthened until today they follow their leaders because these leaders have never deceived them. Their officials are incorruptible, their merchants are honest, their artisans are reliable, their workers who dig and haul and lift do an honest day's work and even work overtime if their state asks it, for they are the state; they are China.

A kindergarten, meeting in the once Forbidden City, was shown the magnificence of this palace and told: "Your fathers built this, but did not enjoy it; but now it is yours; preserve it." And then, pointing across the Tien an Men Square to the vast building of the new Halls of Assembly, the speaker added: "Your fathers are building new palaces for you; enjoy them and guard them for yourselves and your children. They belong to you!"

China has no rank or classes; her universities grant no degrees; her government awards no medals. She has no blue book of "society." But she has leaders of learning and genius, scientists of renown, artisans of skill and millions who know and believe this and follow where these men lead. This is the joy of this nation, its high belief and its unfaltering hope.

China is no utopia. Fifth Avenue has better shops where the rich can buy and the whores parade. Detroit has more and better cars. The best American housing outstrips the Chinese, and Chinese women are not nearly as well-dressed as the guests of the Waldorf-Astoria. But the Chinese worker is happy. He has exorcised the Great Fear that haunts the West; the fear of losing his job; the fear of falling sick; the fear of accident; the fear of inability to educate his children; the fear of daring to take a vacation. To guard against such catastrophe Americans skimp and save, cheat and steal, gamble and arm for murder. The Soviet citizen, the Czech, the Pole, the Hungarian have kicked out the stooges of America and the hoodlums set to exploit the peasants. They and the East Germans no longer fear these disasters; and above all the Chinese sit high above these fears and laugh with joy. They will not be rich in old age, but they will eat. They will not enjoy sickness but they will be given care. They will not starve as thousands of Chinese did only a generation ago. They fear neither flood nor epidemic. They do not even fear war; as Mao Tse-tung told me, war for China is a "paper tiger." China can defend itself and back of China stands the unassailable might of the Soviet Union.

Envy and class hate are disappearing in China. Does your neighbor have better pay and higher position than you? He has this because of greater ability or better education, and more education is open to you and compulsory for your children. The young married couple do not fear children. The mother has pre-natal care. Her wage and job are safe. Nursery and kindergarten take care of the child and it is welcome, not to pampered luxury but to good food, constant medical care and education for his highest ability. All this is not yet perfect. Here and there it fails, falls short and falters; but it is so often and so widely true, that China believes, lives on realized hope, follows its leaders and sings: "O, Mourner, get up off your knees."

The women of China are becoming free. They wear pants so that they can walk, climb and dig; and climb and dig they do. They are not dressed simply for sex indulgence or beauty parades. They occupy positions from ministers of state to locomotive engineers, lawyers, doctors, clerks and laborers. They are escaping "household drudgery"; they are strong and healthy and beautiful not simply of leg and false bosom, but of brain, brawn, and rich emotion. In Wuhan I stood in one of the greatest steelworks of the world. A crane which moved a hundred tons loomed above. I said, "My God, Shirley, look up there!" Alone in the engine-room sat a girl with ribboned braids, running the vast machine.

You won't believe this, because you never saw anything like it; and if the State Department has its way, you never will. Let *Life* lie about communes; and the State Department shed crocodile tears over ancestral tombs. Let Hong Kong wire its lies abroad. Let "Divine Slavery" persist in Tibet until China kills it. The truth is there and I saw it.

Fifteen times I have crossed the Atlantic and once the Pacific. I have seen the world. But never so vast and glorious a miracle as China. This monster is a nation with a darktinted billion born at the beginning of time, and facing its end; this struggle from starved degradation and murder and suffering to the triumph of that Long March to world leadership. Oh beautiful, patient, self-sacrificing China, despised and unforgettable, victorious and forgiving, crucified and risen from the dead.

CHAPTER 6

Darkwater

ust as *The Souls of Black Folk* looked backward, summarizing the history of African America from slavery through the late nineteenth century, *Darkwater: Voices from Within the Veil* (1920) looked forward, anticipating as well as instigating modern Pan-Africanism and the culture of anticolonialism that has come to play such a prominent role in Western (or anti-Western) literature of the late twentieth century. If *The Souls of Black Folk* became the century's most important statement of African American resistance to segregation, *Darkwater* joined the battle for black civil rights in the United States to a broader campaign against European colonial rule abroad, especially in Africa.

Interpretation of *Darkwater* must begin with the fact that its meaning inheres in a collage of parts in several genres and several styles. In a far more pronounced fashion than *The Souls of Black Folk*, one must read the book by narrative juxtaposition in which rigorous economic logic and pungent analysis can suddenly give way to an intense lyric moment. For example, following "The Hands of Ethiopia" and preceding "Of Work and Wealth," a powerful quasi-socialist critique of the Jim Crow economics that resulted in the violent East St. Louis race riots of 1917, one finds "The Princess of the Hither Isles," an opaque anticolonial allegory that acts as an iconographic condensation of the analytic essays that surround it, crystallizing historical forces into a tragic figuration of the world conflict Du Bois saw being acted out through the agencies of labor and race.

The sharpened African American political consciousness set in motion by the New Negro Renaissance—a movement that may be traced to the decades before the flourishing of literary and artisitic activity better known as the Harlem Renaissance of the 1920s—was spurred on during World War I by the failure of black American veterans to win significant civil rights at home through their sacrifices abroad; by the continued migration of black southerners into the urban North, accompanied by increased labor violence; and by the ascendancy of white supremacist thought during the same period. The crisis of World War I gave Du Bois an arena in which to raise the pitch of his argument that the problem of the world color line was epitomized in Africa, which as the result of the imperial scramble of the nineteenth century had now become a key site in a world conflagration that would ultimately lead, as Du Bois forecast, to the collapse of colonial rule and its racial assumptions.

The Pan-African Conferences, especially those of 1919, 1921, and 1923, drew together a triangle of black intellectual ferment—African, American, and Caribbean—acted as a lightning rod for Du Bois's imagination, and provided a new forum for ideas about the centrality of Africa that had steadily grown more important in his thought up through *The Negro* in 1915. In the years surrounding the war, Du Bois joined world leaders of the African diaspora in demanding that Africa be ruled by Africans and that its resources not be harvested without the participation of Africans themselves, arguments central to a number of the essays, sketches, and poems of *Darkwater*. His best-known contribution to anticolonial writing during the war was the essay "The African Roots of the War," first published in the *Atlantic Monthly* in 1915. Du Bois's essay spawned a number of derivative studies, such as Benjamin Brawley's *Africa and the War* (1918) and A. Philip Randolph and Chandler Owen's *Terms of Peace and the Darker Races* (1917), before he incorporated it into *Darkwater* in 1920 under the title of "The Hands of Ethiopia."

Although *Darkwater* as a volume was sparked by the intersection of African anticolonialism and the American struggle for racial justice during the war, those concerns and several of Du Bois's original essays dated from earlier years. "Credo," a set of aphoristic pieties that came to exert power over popular black imagination comparable to Martin Luther King, Jr.'s, "I Have a Dream" speech (Lewis, 312), was first published in 1904, and "A Litany at Atlanta" emerged as a response to the bloody Atlanta race riot of 1906 that Du Bois witnessed while teaching at Atlanta University. "A Hymn to the Peoples" dated from the Universal Races Congress of 1911, where Du Bois first read it to the London gathering. "The Souls of White Folk," one of Du Bois's most bitter castigations of white racism, grew from one essay of the same name first published in 1910 and a second, "Of the Culture of White Folk," published in 1917. One of Du Bois's numerous parables in which the persecution of a Black Christ stands for racial violence, "Jesus Christ in Texas," originally appeared in *The Crisis* of 1911 as "Jesus Christ in Georgia," and the autobiographical essay "The Shadow of Years" appeared in that same magazine in 1918.

A central theme of *Darkwater* is the role of black women in the economy of racial oppression, and Du Bois here again drew on his own earlier writings as well as the work of others. "The Riddle of the Sphinx" first appeared in *The Horizon* in 1907 as "The Burden of Black Women." In its plea for the restitution of the family through the elevation of the black woman, "The Damnation of Women," written for *Darkwater*, borrows from previous work by Alexander Crummell and Anna Julia Cooper. Du Bois quotes extensively from Crummell's 1883 essay "The Black Woman of the South," and without naming her as the author, he cites a now famous passage from Cooper's *A Voice from the South* (1892): "Only the black woman can say 'when and where I enter, in the quiet, undisputed dignity of my womanhood, without violence and without suing or special patronage, then and there the whole Negro races enters with me.' " In his dramatization of the black woman superimposed on the American South and colonized Africa, a trope repeated in his novel *Dark Princess* (1928), Du Bois anticipated a good deal of late-twentieth-century criticism on the colonization of the body.

Granting its obvious difference from his rather prosaic novels and his best sustained work of autobiography and sociopolitical analysis, *Dusk of Dawn, Darkwater* is Du Bois's most successful sustained literary work after *The Souls of Black Folk*. Its radically experimental and visionary form makes it one of the most striking instances of black modernism, at once a work defined by its historical moment and a harbinger of later postcolonial ideology.

DARKWATER

VOICES FROM WITHIN THE VEIL

Postscript

These are the things of which men think, who live: of their own selves and the dwelling place of their fathers; of their neighbors; of work and service; of rule and reason and women and children; of Beauty and Death and War. To this thinking I have only to add a point of view: I have been in the world, but not of it. I have seen the human drama from a veiled corner, where all the outer tragedy and comedy have reproduced themselves in microcosm within. From this inner torment of souls the human scene without has interpreted itself to me in unusual and even illuminating ways. For this reason, and this alone, I venture to write again on themes on which great souls have already said greater words, in the hope that I may strike here and there a half-tone, newer even if slighter, up from the heart of my problem and the problems of my people.

Between the sterner flights of logic, I have sought to set some little alightings of what may be poetry. They are tributes to Beauty, unworthy to stand alone; yet perversely, in my mind, now at the end, I know not whether I mean the Thought for the Fancy—or the Fancy for the Thought, or why the book trails off to playing, rather than standing strong on unanswering fact. But this is alway—is it not?—the Riddle of Life.

Many of my words appear here transformed from other publications and

I thank the *Atlantic*, the *Independent*, the *Crisis*, and the *Journal of Race Development* for letting me use them again.

W. E. Burghardt Du Bois.

New York, 1919.

CONTENTS

Credo

    I believe in God, who made of one blood all nations that on earth do dwell. I believe that all men, black and brown and white, are brothers, varying through time and opportunity, in form and gift and feature, but differing in no essential particular, and alike in soul and the possibility of infinite development.

Especially do I believe in the Negro Race: in the beauty of its genius, the sweetness of its soul, and its strength in that meekness which shall yet inherit this turbulent earth.

I believe in Pride of race and lineage and self: in pride of self so deep as to scorn injustice to other selves; in pride of lineage so great as to despise no man's father; in pride of race so chivalrous as neither to offer bastardy to the weak nor beg wedlock of the strong, knowing that men may be brothers in Christ, even though they be not brothers-in-law.

I believe in Service—humble, reverent service, from the blackening of boots to the whitening of souls; for Work is Heaven, Idleness Hell, and Wage is the "Well done!" of the Master, who summoned all them that labor and are heavy laden, making no distinction between the black, sweating cotton hands of Georgia and the first families of Virginia, since all distinction not based on deed is devilish and not divine.

I believe in the Devil and his angels, who wantonly work to narrow the opportunity of struggling human beings, especially if they be black; who spit in the faces of the fallen, strike them that cannot strike again, believe the worst and work to prove it, hating the image which their Maker stamped on a brother's soul.

I believe in the Prince of Peace. I believe that War is Murder. I believe that armies and navies are at bottom the tinsel and braggadocio of oppression and wrong, and I believe that the wicked conquest of weaker and darker nations by nations whiter and stronger but foreshadows the death of that strength.

I believe in Liberty for all men: the space to stretch their arms and their souls, the right to breathe and the right to vote, the freedom to choose their friends, enjoy the sunshine, and ride on the railroads, uncursed by color; thinking, dreaming, working as they will in a kingdom of beauty and love.

I believe in the Training of Children, black even as white; the leading out of little souls into the green pastures and beside the still waters, not for pelf or peace, but for life lit by some large vision of beauty and goodness and truth; lest we forget, and the sons of the fathers, like Esau, for mere meat barter their birthright in a mighty nation.

Finally, I believe in Patience—patience with the weakness of the Weak and the strength of the Strong, the prejudice of the Ignorant and the ignorance of the Blind; patience with the tardy triumph of Joy and the mad chastening of Sorrow;—patience with God!

CHAPTER I

The Shadow of Years

I was born by a golden river and in the shadow of two great hills, five years after the Emancipation Proclamation. The house was quaint, with clapboards running up and down, neatly trimmed, and there were five rooms, a tiny porch, a rosy front yard, and unbelievably delicious strawberries in the rear. A South Carolinian, lately come to the Berkshire Hills, owned all this—tall, thin, and black, with golden earrings, and given to religious trances. We were his transient tenants for the time.

My own people were part of a great clan. Fully two hundred years before, Tom Burghardt had come through the western pass from the Hudson with his Dutch captor, "Coenraet Burghardt," sullen in his slavery and achieving his freedom by volunteering for the Revolution at a time of sudden alarm. His wife was a little, black, Bantu woman, who never became reconciled to this strange land; she clasped her knees and rocked and crooned:

> "Do bana coba—gene me, gene me!
> Ben d'nuli, ben d'le—"

Tom died about 1787, but of him came many sons, and one, Jack, who helped in the War of 1812. Of Jack and his wife, Violet, was born a mighty family, splendidly named: Harlow and Ira, Cloë, Lucinda, Maria, and Othello! I dimly remember my grandfather, Othello,—or "Uncle Tallow,"—a brown man, strong-voiced and redolent with tobacco, who sat stiffly in a great high chair because his hip was broken. He was probably a bit lazy and given to wassail. At any rate, grandmother had a shrewish tongue and often berated him. This grandmother was Sarah—"Aunt Sally"—a stern, tall, Dutch-African woman, beak-nosed, but beautiful-eyed and golden-skinned. Ten or more children were theirs, of whom the youngest was Mary, my mother.

Mother was dark shining bronze, with a tiny ripple in her black hair, black-eyed, with a heavy, kind face. She gave one the impression of infinite patience, but a curious determination was concealed in her softness. The family were small farmers on Egremont Plain, between Great Barrington and Sheffield, Massachusetts. The bits of land were too small to support the great families born on them and we were always poor. I never remember being cold or hungry, but I do remember that shoes and coal, and sometimes flour, caused mother moments of anxious thought in winter, and a new suit was an event!

At about the time of my birth economic pressure was transmuting the family generally from farmers to "hired" help. Some revolted and migrated westward, others went cityward as cooks and barbers. Mother worked for some years at house service in Great Barrington, and after a disappointed love episode with a cousin, who went to California, she met and married Alfred Du Bois and went to town to live by the golden river where I was born.

Alfred, my father, must have seemed a splendid vision in that little valley under the shelter of those mighty hills. He was small and beautiful of face and feature, just tinted with the sun, his curly hair chiefly revealing his kinship to Africa. In nature he was a dreamer,—romantic, indolent, kind, unreliable. He had in him the making of a poet, an adventurer, or a Beloved Vagabond, according to the life that closed round him; and that life gave him all too little. His father, Alexander Du Bois, cloaked under a stern, austere demeanor a passionate revolt against the world. He, too, was small, but squarish. I remember him as I saw him first, in his home in New Bedford,—white hair close-cropped; a seamed, hard face, but high in tone, with a gray eye that could twinkle or glare.

Long years before him Louis XIV drove two Huguenots, Jacques and Louis Du Bois, into wild Ulster County, New York. One of them in the third or fourth generation had a descendant, Dr. James Du Bois, a gay, rich bachelor, who made his money in the Bahamas, where he and the Gilberts had plantations. There he took a beautiful little mulatto slave as his mistress, and two sons were born: Alexander in 1803 and John, later. They were fine, straight, clear-eyed boys, white enough to "pass." He brought them to America and put Alexander in the celebrated Cheshire School, in Connecticut. Here he often visited him, but one last time, fell dead. He left no will, and his relations made short shrift of these sons. They gathered in the property, apprenticed grandfather to a shoemaker; then dropped him.

Grandfather took his bitter dose like a thoroughbred. Wild as was his inner revolt against this treatment, he uttered no word against the thieves and made no plea. He tried his fortunes here and in Haiti, where, during his short, restless sojourn, my own father was born. Eventually, grandfather became chief steward on the passenger boat between New York and New Haven; later he was a small merchant in Springfield; and finally he retired and ended his days at New Bedford. Always he held his head high, took no insults, made few friends. He was not a "Negro"; he was a man! Yet the current was too strong even for him. Then even more than now a colored man had colored friends or none at all, lived in a colored world or lived alone. A few fine, strong, black men gained the heart of this silent, bitter man in New York and New Haven. If he had scant sympathy with their social clannishness, he was with them in fighting discrimination. So, when the white Episcopalians of Trinity Parish, New Haven, showed plainly that they no longer wanted black folk as fellow Christians, he led the revolt which resulted in St. Luke's Parish, and was for years its senior warden. He lies dead in the Grove Street Cemetery, beside Jehudi Ashmun.

Beneath his sternness was a very human man. Slyly he wrote poetry,—stilted, pleading things from a soul astray. He loved women in his masterful way, marrying three beautiful wives in succession and clinging to each with a certain desperate, even if unsympathetic, affection. As a father he was, naturally, a failure,—hard, domineering, unyielding. His four children reacted characteristically: one was until past middle life a thin spinster, the mental image of her father; one died; one passed over into the white world and her children's children are now white, with no knowledge of their Negro blood; the fourth, my father, bent before grandfather, but did not break—better if he had. He yielded and flared back, asked forgiveness and forgot why, became the harshly-held favorite, who ran away and rioted and roamed and loved and married my brown mother.

So with some circumstance having finally gotten myself born, with a flood of Negro blood, a strain of French, a bit of Dutch, but, thank God! no "Anglo-Saxon," I come to the days of my childhood.

They were very happy. Early we moved back to Grandfather Burghardt's home,—I barely remember its stone fireplace, big kitchen, and delightful woodshed. Then this house passed to other branches of the clan and we moved to rented quarters in town,—to one delectable place "upstairs," with a wide yard full of shrubbery, and a brook; to another house abutting a railroad, with infinite interests and astonishing playmates; and finally back to the quiet street on which I was born,—down a long lane and in a homely, cozy cottage, with a living-room, a tiny sitting-room, a pantry, and two attic bedrooms. Here mother and I lived until she died, in 1884, for father early began his restless wanderings. I last remember urgent letters for us to come to New Milford, where he had started a barber shop. Later he became a preacher. But mother no longer trusted his dreams, and he soon faded out of our lives into silence.

From the age of five until I was sixteen I went to school on the same grounds,—down a lane, into a widened yard, with a big choke-cherry tree and two buildings, wood and brick. Here I got acquainted with my world, and soon had my criterions of judgment.

Wealth had no particular lure. On the other hand, the shadow of wealth was about us. That river of my birth was golden because of the woolen and paper waste that soiled it. The gold was theirs, not ours; but the gleam and glint was for all. To me it was all in order and I took it philosophically. I cordially despised the poor Irish and South Germans, who slaved in the mills, and annexed the rich and well-to-do as my natural companions. Of such is the kingdom of snobs!

Most of our townfolk were, naturally, the well-to-do, shading downward, but seldom reaching poverty. As playmate of the children I saw the homes of nearly every one, except a few immigrant New Yorkers, of whom none of us approved. The homes I saw impressed me, but did not overwhelm me. Many were bigger than mine, with newer and shinier things, but they did not seem to differ in kind. I think I probably surprised my hosts more than they me, for I was easily at home and perfectly happy and they looked to me just like ordinary people, while my brown face and frizzled hair must have seemed strange to them.

Yet I was very much one of them. I was a center and sometimes the leader of the town gang of boys. We were noisy, but never very bad,—and, indeed, my mother's quiet influence came in here, as I realize now. She did not try to make me perfect. To her I was already perfect. She simply warned me of a few things, especially saloons. In my town the saloon was the open door to hell. The best families had their drunkards and the worst had little else.

Very gradually,—I cannot now distinguish the steps, though here and there I remember a jump or a jolt—but very gradually I found myself assuming quite placidly that I was different from other children. At first I think I connected the difference with a manifest ability to get my lessons rather better than most and to recite with a certain happy, almost taunting, glibness, which brought frowns here and there. Then, slowly, I realized that some folks, a few, even several, actually considered my brown skin a misfortune; once or twice I became painfully aware that some human beings even thought it a crime. I was not for a moment daunted,—although, of course, there were some days of secret tears—rather I was spurred to tireless effort. If they beat me at anything, I was grimly determined to make them sweat for it! Once I remember challenging a great, hard farmer-boy to battle, when I knew he could whip me; and he did. But ever after, he was polite.

As time flew I felt not so much disowned and rejected as rather drawn up into higher spaces and made part of a mightier mission. At times I almost pitied my pale companions, who were not of the Lord's anointed and who saw in their dreams no splendid quests of golden fleeces.

Even in the matter of girls my peculiar phantasy asserted itself. Naturally, it was in our town voted bad form for boys of twelve and fourteen to show any evident weakness for girls. We tolerated them loftily, and now and then they played in our games, when I joined in quite as naturally as the rest. It was when strangers came, or summer boarders, or when the oldest girls grew up that my sharp senses noted little hesitancies in public and searchings for possible public opinion. Then I flamed! I lifted my chin and strode off to the mountains, where I viewed the world at my feet and strained my eyes across the shadow of the hills.

I was graduated from high school at sixteen, and I talked of "Wendell Phillips." This was my first sweet taste of the world's applause. There were flowers and upturned faces, music and marching, and there was my mother's smile. She was lame, then, and a bit drawn, but very happy. It was her great day and that very year she lay down with a sigh of content and has not yet awakened. I felt a certain gladness to see her, at last, at peace, for she had worried all her life. Of my own loss I had then little realization. That came only with the after-years. Now it was the choking gladness and solemn feel of wings! At last, I was going beyond the hills and into the world that beckoned steadily.

There came a little pause,—a singular pause. I was given to understand that I was almost too young for the world. Harvard was the goal of my dreams, but my white friends hesitated and my colored friends were silent. Harvard was a mighty conjure-word in that hill town, and even the mill owners' sons had aimed lower. Finally it was tactfully explained that the place for me was in the South among my people. A scholarship had been already arranged at Fisk, and my summer earnings would pay the fare. My relatives grumbled, but after a twinge I felt a strange delight! I forgot, or did not thoroughly realize, the curious irony by which I was not looked upon as a real citizen of my birth-town, with a future and a career, and instead was being sent to a far land among strangers who were regarded as (and in truth were) "mine own people."

Ah! the wonder of that journey, with its faint spice of adventure, as I entered the land of slaves; the never-to-be-forgotten marvel of that first supper at Fisk with the world "colored" and opposite two of the most beautiful beings God ever revealed to the eyes of seventeen. I promptly lost my appetite, but I was deliriously happy!

As I peer back through the shadow of my years, seeing not too clearly, but through the thickening veil of wish and after-thought, I seem to view my life divided into four distinct parts: the Age of Miracles, the Days of Disillusion, the Discipline of Work and Play, and the Second Miracle Age.

The Age of Miracles began with Fisk and ended with Germany. I was bursting with the joy of living. I seemed to ride in conquering might. I was captain of my soul and master of fate! I *willed* to do! It was done. I *wished!* The wish came true.

Now and then out of the void flashed the great sword of hate to remind me of the battle. I remember once, in Nashville, brushing by accident against a white woman on the street. Politely and eagerly I raised my hat to apologize. That was thirty-five years ago. From that day to this I have never knowingly raised my hat to a Southern white woman.

I suspect that beneath all of my seeming triumphs there were many failures and disappointments, but the realities loomed so large that they swept away even the memory of other dreams and wishes. Consider, for a moment, how miraculous it all was to a boy of seventeen, just escaped from a narrow valley: I willed and lo! my people came dancing about me,—riotous in color, gay in laughter, full of sympathy, need, and pleading; darkly delicious girls—"colored" girls—sat beside me and actually talked to me while I gazed in tongue-tied silence or babbled in boastful dreams. Boys with my own experiences and out of my own world, who knew and understood, wrought out with me great remedies. I studied eagerly under teachers who bent in subtle sympathy, feeling themselves some shadow of the Veil and lifting it gently that we darker souls might peer through to other worlds.

I willed and lo! I was walking beneath the elms of Harvard,—the name of allurement, the college of my youngest, wildest visions! I needed money; scholarships and prizes fell into my lap,—not all I wanted or strove for, but all I needed to keep in school. Commencement came and standing before governor, president, and grave, gowned men, I told them certain astonishing truths, waving my arms and breathing fast! They applauded with what now seems to me uncalled-for fervor, but then! I walked home on pink clouds of glory! I asked for a fellowship and got it. I announced my plan of studying in Germany, but Harvard had no more fellowships for me. A friend, however, told me of the Slater Fund and how the Board was looking for colored men worth educating. No thought of modest hesitation occurred to me. I rushed at the chance.

The trustees of the Slater Fund excused themselves politely. They acknowledged that they had in the past looked for colored boys of ability to educate, but, being unsuccessful, they had stopped searching. I went at them hammer and tongs! I plied them with testimonials and mid-year and final marks. I intimated plainly, impudently, that they were "stalling"! In vain did the chairman, Ex-President Hayes, explain and excuse. I took no excuses and brushed explanations aside. I wonder now that he did not brush me aside, too, as a conceited meddler, but instead he smiled and surrendered.

I crossed the ocean in a trance. Always I seemed to be saying, "It is not real; I must be dreaming!" I can live it again—the little, Dutch ship—the blue waters—the smell of new-mown hay—Holland and the Rhine. I saw the Wartburg and Berlin; I made the Harzreise and climbed the Brocken; I saw the Hansa towns and the cities and dorfs of South Germany; I saw the Alps at Berne, the Cathedral at Milan, Florence, Rome, Venice, Vienna, and Pesth; I looked on the boundaries of Russia; and I sat in Paris and London.

On mountain and valley, in home and school, I met men and women as I had never met them before. Slowly they became, not white folks, but folks. The unity beneath all life clutched me. I was not less fanatically a Negro, but "Negro" meant a greater, broader sense of humanity and world-fellowship. I felt myself standing, not against the world, but simply against American narrowness and color prejudice, with the greater, finer world at my back urging me on.

I built great castles in Spain and lived therein. I dreamed and loved and wandered and sang; then, after two long years, I dropped suddenly back into "nigger"-hating America!

My Days of Disillusion were not disappointing enough to discourage me. I was still upheld by that fund of infinite faith, although dimly about me I saw the shadow of disaster. I began to realize how much of what I had called Will and Ability was sheer Luck! *Suppose* my good mother had preferred a steady income from my child labor rather than bank on the precarious dividend of my higher training? *Suppose* that pompous old village judge, whose dignity we often ruffled and whose apples we stole, had had his way and sent me while a child to a "reform" school to learn a "trade"? *Suppose* Principal Hosmer had been born with no faith in "darkies," and instead of giving me Greek and Latin had taught me carpentry and the making of tin pans? *Suppose* I had missed a Harvard scholarship? *Suppose* the Slater Board had then, as now, distinct ideas as to where the education of Negroes should stop? Suppose *and* suppose! As I sat down calmly on flat earth and looked at my life a certain great fear seized me. Was I the masterful captain or the pawn of laughing sprites? Who was I to fight a world of color prejudice? I raise my hat to myself when I remember that, even with these thoughts, I did not hesitate or waver; but just went doggedly to work, and therein lay whatever salvation I have achieved.

First came the task of earning a living. I was not nice or hard to please. I just got down on my knees and begged for work, anything and anywhere. I wrote to Hampton, Tuskegee, and a dozen other places. They politely declined, with many regrets. The trustees of a backwoods Tennessee town considered me, but were eventually afraid. Then, suddenly, Wilberforce offered to let me teach Latin and Greek at $750 a year. I was overjoyed!

I did not know anything about Latin and Greek, but I did know of Wilberforce. The breath of that great name had swept the water and dropped into southern Ohio, where Southerners had taken their cure at Tawawa Springs and where white Methodists had planted a school; then came the little bishop, Daniel Payne, who made it a school of the African Methodists. This was the school that called me, and when reconsidered offers from Tuskegee and Jefferson City followed, I refused; I was so thankful for that first offer.

I went to Wilberforce with high ideals. I wanted to help to build a great university. I was willing to work night as well as day. I taught Latin, Greek, English, and German. I helped in the discipline, took part in the social life, begged to be allowed to lecture on sociology, and began to write books. But I found myself against a stone wall. Nothing stirred before my impatient pounding! Or if it stirred, it soon slept again.

Of course, I was too impatient! The snarl of years was not to be undone in days. I set at solving the problem before I knew it. Wilberforce was a colored church-school. In it were mingled the problems of poorly-prepared pupils, an inadequately-equipped plant, the natural politics of bishoprics, and the provincial reactions of a country town loaded with traditions. It was my first introduction to a Negro world, and I was at once marvelously inspired and deeply depressed. I was inspired with the children,—had I not rubbed against the children of the world and did I not find here the same eagerness, the same joy of life, the same brains as in New England, France, and Germany? But, on the other hand, the ropes and myths and knots and hindrances; the thundering waves of the white world beyond beating us back; the

scalding breakers of this inner world,—its currents and back eddies—
its meanness and smallness—its sorrow and tragedy—its screaming
farce!

In all this I was as one bound hand and foot. Struggle, work, fight
as I would, I seemed to get nowhere and accomplish nothing. I had all
the wild intolerance of youth, and no experience in human tangles. For
the first time in my life I realized that there were limits to my will to
do. The Day of Miracles was past, and a long, gray road of dogged
work lay ahead.

I had, naturally, my triumphs here and there. I defied the bishops
in the matter of public extemporaneous prayer and they yielded. I
bearded the poor, hunted president in his den, and yet was re-elected
to my position. I was slowly winning a way, but quickly losing faith in
the value of the way won. Was this the place to begin my life work?
Was this the work which I was best fitted to do? What business had I,
anyhow, to teach Greek when I had studied men? I grew sure that I
had made a mistake. So I determined to leave Wilberforce and try elsewhere. Thus, the third period of my life began.

First, in 1896, I married—a slip of a girl, beautifully dark-eyed and
thorough and good as a German housewife. Then I accepted a job to
make a study of Negroes in Philadelphia for the University of Pennsylvania,—one year at six hundred dollars. How did I dare these two
things? I do not know. Yet they spelled salvation. To remain at Wilberforce without doing my ideals meant spiritual death. Both my wife
and I were homeless. I dared a home and a temporary job. But it was
a different daring from the days of my first youth. I was ready to admit
that the best of men might fail. I meant still to be captain of my soul,
but I realized that even captains are not omnipotent in uncharted and
angry seas.

I essayed a thorough piece of work in Philadelphia. I labored morning, noon, and night. Nobody ever reads that fat volume on "The Philadelphia Negro," but they treat it with respect, and that consoles me.
The colored people of Philadelphia received me with no open arms.
They had a natural dislike to being studied like a strange species. I met
again and in different guise those curious cross-currents and inner social whirlings of my own people. They set me to groping. I concluded
that I did not know so much as I might about my own people, and
when President Bumstead invited me to Atlanta University the next
year to teach sociology and study the American Negro, I accepted
gladly, at a salary of twelve hundred dollars.

My real life work was done at Atlanta for thirteen years, from my
twenty-ninth to my forty-second birthday. They were years of great
spiritual upturning, of the making and unmaking of ideals, of hard
work and hard play. Here I found myself. I lost most of my manner-
isms. I grew more broadly human, made my closest and most holy
friendships, and studied human beings. I became widely-acquainted

with the real condition of my people. I realized the terrific odds which faced them. At Wilberforce I was their captious critic. In Philadelphia I was their cold and scientific investigator, with microscope and probe. It took but a few years of Atlanta to bring me to hot and indignant defense. I saw the race-hatred of the whites as I had never dreamed of it before,—naked and unashamed! The faint discrimination of my hopes and intangible dislikes paled into nothing before this great, red monster of cruel oppression. I held back with more difficulty each day my mounting indignation against injustice and misrepresentation.

With all this came the strengthening and hardening of my own character. The billows of birth, love, and death swept over me. I saw life through all its paradox and contradiction of streaming eyes and mad merriment. I emerged into full manhood, with the ruins of some ideals about me, but with others planted above the stars; scarred and a bit grim, but hugging to my soul the divine gift of laughter and withal determined, even unto stubbornness, to fight the good fight.

At last, forbear and waver as I would, I faced the great Decision. My life's last and greatest door stood ajar. What with all my dreaming, studying, and teaching was I going to *do* in this fierce fight? Despite all my youthful conceit and bumptiousness, I found developed beneath it all a reticence and new fear of forwardness, which sprang from searching criticisms of motive and high ideals of efficiency; but contrary to my dream of racial solidarity and notwithstanding my deep desire to serve and follow and think, rather than to lead and inspire and decide, I found myself suddenly the leader of a great wing of people fighting against another and greater wing.

Nor could any effort of mine keep this fight from sinking to the personal plane. Heaven knows I tried. That first meeting of a knot of enthusiasts, at Niagara Falls, had all the earnestness of self-devotion. At the second meeting, at Harper's Ferry, it arose to the solemnity of a holy crusade and yet without and to the cold, hard stare of the world it seemed merely the envy of fools against a great man, Booker Washington.

Of the movement I was willy-nilly leader. I hated the role. For the first time I faced criticism and *cared*. Every ideal and habit of my life was cruelly misjudged. I who had always overstriven to give credit for good work, who had never consciously stooped to envy was accused by honest colored people of every sort of small and petty jealousy, while white people said I was ashamed of my race and wanted to be white! And this of me, whose one life fanaticism had been belief in my Negro blood!

Away back in the little years of my boyhood I had sold the Springfield *Republican* and written for Mr. Fortune's *Globe*. I dreamed of being an editor myself some day. I am an editor. In the great, slashing days of college life I dreamed of a strong organization to fight the battles of the Negro race. The National Association for the Advancement of Colored People is such a body, and it grows daily. In the dark days at Wilberforce I planned a time when I could speak freely to my people and of them, interpreting between two worlds. I am speaking now. In the study at Atlanta I grew to fear lest my radical beliefs should so hurt the college that either my silence or the institution's ruin would result. Powers and principalities have not yet curbed my tongue and Atlanta still lives.

It all came—this new Age of Miracles—because a few persons in 1909 determined to celebrate Lincoln's Birthday properly by calling for the final emancipation of the American Negro. I came at their call. My salary even for a year was not assured, but it was the "Voice without reply." The result has been the National Association for the Advancement of Colored People and *The Crisis* and this book, which I am finishing on my Fiftieth Birthday.

Last year I looked death in the face and found its lineaments not unkind. But it was not my time. Yet in nature some time soon and in the fullness of days I shall die, quietly, I trust, with my face turned South and eastward; and, dreaming or dreamless, I shall, I am sure, enjoy death as I have enjoyed life.

A Litany at Atlanta

O Silent God, Thou whose voice afar in mist and mystery hath left our ears an-hungered in these fearful days—
Hear us, good Lord!
Listen to us, Thy children: our faces dark with doubt are made a mockery in Thy Sanctuary. With uplifted hands we front Thy Heaven, O God, crying:
We beseech Thee to hear us, good Lord!
We are not better than our fellows, Lord; we are but weak and human men. When our devils do deviltry, curse Thou the doer and the deed,—curse them as we curse them, do to them all and more than ever they have done to innocence and weakness, to womanhood and home.
Have mercy upon us, miserable sinners!
And yet, whose is the deeper guilt? Who made these devils? Who nursed them in crime and fed them on injustice? Who ravished and debauched their mothers and their grandmothers? Who bought and sold their crime and waxed fat and rich on public iniquity?
Thou knowest, good God!
Is this Thy Justice, O Father, that guile be easier than innocence and the innocent be crucified for the guilt of the untouched guilty?
Justice, O Judge of men!
Wherefore do we pray? Is not the God of the Fathers dead? Have not seers seen in Heaven's halls Thine hearsed and lifeless form stark amidst the black and rolling smoke of sin, where all along bow bitter forms of endless dead?
Awake, Thou that sleepest!
Thou art not dead, but flown afar, up hills of endless light, through blazing corridors of suns, where worlds do swing of good and gentle men, of

women strong and free—far from the cozenage, black hypocrisy, and chaste prostitution of this shameful speck of dust!

Turn again, O Lord; leave us not to perish in our sin!

From lust of body and lust of blood,—

Great God, deliver us!

From lust of power and lust of gold,—

Great God, deliver us!

From the leagued lying of despot and of brute,—

Great God, deliver us!

A city lay in travail, God our Lord, and from her loins sprang twin Murder and Black Hate. Red was the midnight; clang, crack, and cry of death and fury filled the air and trembled underneath the stars where church spires pointed silently to Thee. And all this was to sate the greed of greedy men who hide behind the veil of vengeance!

Bend us Thine ear, O Lord!

In the pale, still morning we looked upon the deed. We stopped our ears and held our leaping hands, but they—did they not wag their heads and leer and cry with bloody jaws: *Cease from Crime!* The word was mockery, for thus they train a hundred crimes while we do cure one.

Turn again our captivity, O Lord!

Behold this maimed and broken thing, dear God; it was an humble black man, who toiled and sweat to save a bit from the pittance paid him. They told him: *Work and Rise!* He worked. Did this man sin? Nay, but someone told how someone said another did—one whom he had never seen nor known. Yet for that man's crime this man lieth maimed and murdered, his wife naked to shame, his children to poverty and evil.

Hear us, O heavenly Father!

Doth not this justice of hell stink in Thy nostrils, O God? How long shall the mounting flood of innocent blood roar in Thine ears and pound in our hearts for vengeance? Pile the pale frenzy of blood-crazed brutes, who do such deeds, high on Thine Altar, Jehovah Jireh, and burn it in hell forever and forever!

Forgive us, good Lord; we know not what we say!

Bewildered we are and passion-tossed, mad with the madness of a mobbed and mocked and murdered people; straining at the armposts of Thy throne, we raise our shackled hands and charge Thee, God, by the bones of our stolen fathers, by the tears of our dead mothers, by the very blood of Thy crucified Christ: What meaneth this? Tell us the plan; give us the sign!

Keep not Thou silent, O God!

Sit not longer blind, Lord God, deaf to our prayer and dumb to our dumb suffering. Surely Thou, too, art not white, O Lord, a pale, bloodless, heartless thing!

Ah! Christ of all the Pities!

Forgive the thought! Forgive these wild, blasphemous words! Thou art still the God of our black fathers and in Thy Soul's Soul sit some soft darkenings of the evening, some shadowings of the velvet night.

But whisper—speak—call, great God, for Thy silence is white terror to our hearts! The way, O God, show us the way and point us the path!

Whither? North is greed and South is blood; within, the coward, and without, the liar. Whither? To death?

Amen! Welcome, dark sleep!

Whither? To life? But not this life, dear God, not this. Let the cup pass from us, tempt us not beyond our strength, for there is that clamoring and clawing within, to whose voice we would not listen, yet shudder lest we must,—and it is red. Ah! God! It is a red and awful shape.

Selah!

In yonder East trembles a star.

Vengeance is Mine; I will repay, saith the Lord!

Thy Will, O Lord, be done!

Kyrie Eleison!

Lord, we have done these pleading, wavering words.

We beseech Thee to hear us, good Lord!

We bow our heads and hearken soft to the sobbing of women and little children.

We beseech Thee to hear us, good Lord!

Our voices sink in silence and in night.

Hear us, good Lord!

In night, O God of a godless land!

Amen!

In silence, O Silent God.

Selah!

CHAPTER II

The Souls of White Folk

High in the tower, where I sit above the loud complaining of the human sea, I know many souls that toss and whirl and pass, but none there are that intrigue me more than the Souls of White Folk.

Of them I am singularly clairvoyant. I see in and through them. I view them from unusual points of vantage. Not as a foreigner do I come, for I am native, not foreign, bone of their thought and flesh of their language. Mine is not the knowledge of the traveler or the colonial composite of dear memories, words and wonder. Nor yet is my knowledge that which servants have of masters, or mass of class, or capitalist of artisan. Rather I see these souls undressed and from the back and side. I see the working of their entrails. I know their thoughts and they know that I know. This knowledge makes them now embarrassed, now furious. They deny my right to live and be and call me misbirth! My word is to them mere bitterness and my soul, pessimism. And yet as they preach and strut and shout and threaten, crouching as they clutch at rags of facts and fancies to hide their nakedness, they go twisting, flying by my tired eyes and I see them ever stripped,—ugly, human.

The discovery of personal whiteness among the world's peoples is a very modern thing,—a nineteenth and twentieth century matter, indeed. The ancient world would have laughed at such a distinction. The Middle Age regarded skin color with mild curiosity; and even up into the eighteenth century we were hammering our national manikins into one, great, Universal Man, with fine frenzy which ignored color and race even more than birth. Today we have changed all that, and the world in a sudden, emotional conversion has discovered that it is white and by that token, wonderful!

This assumption that of all the hues of God whiteness alone is inherently and obviously better than brownness or tan leads to curious acts; even the sweeter souls of the dominant world as they discourse with me on weather, weal, and woe are continually playing above their actual words an obligato of tune and tone, saying:

"My poor, un-white thing! Weep not nor rage. I know, too well, that the curse of God lies heavy on you. Why? That is not for me to say, but be brave! Do your work in your lowly sphere, praying the good Lord that into heaven above, where all is love, you may, one day, be born—white!"

I do not laugh. I am quite straight-faced as I ask soberly:

"But what on earth is whiteness that one should so desire it?" Then always, somehow, some way, silently but clearly, I am given to understand that whiteness is the ownership of the earth forever and ever, Amen!

Now what is the effect on a man or a nation when it comes passionately to believe such an extraordinary dictum as this? That nations are coming to believe it is manifest daily. Wave on wave, each with increasing virulence, is dashing this new religion of whiteness on the shores of our time. Its first effects are funny: the strut of the Southerner, the arrogance of the Englishman amuck, the whoop of the hoodlum who vicariously leads your mob. Next it appears dampening generous enthusiasm in what we once counted glorious; to free the slave is discovered to be tolerable only in so far as it freed his master! Do we sense somnolent writhings in black Africa or angry groans in India or triumphant banzais in Japan? "To your tents, O Israel!" These nations are not white!

After the more comic manifestations and the chilling of generous enthusiasm come subtler, darker deeds. Everything considered, the title to the universe claimed by White Folk is faulty. It ought, at least, to look plausible. How easy, then, by emphasis and omission to make children believe that every great soul the world ever saw was a white man's soul; that every great thought the world ever knew was a white man's thought; that every great deed the world ever did was a white man's deed; that every great dream the world ever sang was a white man's dream. In fine, that if from the world were dropped everything that could not fairly be attributed to White Folk, the world would, if anything, be even greater, truer, better than now. And if all this be a lie, is it not a lie in a great cause?

Here it is that the comedy verges to tragedy. The first minor note is struck, all unconsciously, by those worthy souls in whom consciousness of high descent brings burning desire to spread the gift abroad,—the obligation of nobility to the ignoble. Such sense of duty assumes two things: a real possession of the heritage and its frank appreciation by the humble-born. So long, then, as humble black folk, voluble with thanks, receive barrels of old clothes from lordly and generous whites, there is much mental peace and moral satisfaction. But when the black man begins to dispute the white man's title to certain alleged bequests of the Fathers in wage and position, authority and training; and when his attitude toward charity is sullen anger rather than humble jollity; when he insists on his human right to swagger and swear and waste,—then the spell is suddenly broken and the philanthropist is ready to believe that Negroes are impudent, that the South is right, and that Japan wants to fight America.

After this the descent to Hell is easy. On the pale, white faces which the great billows whirl upward to my tower I see again and again, often and still more often, a writing of human hatred, a deep and passionate hatred, vast by the very vagueness of its expressions. Down through the green waters, on the bottom of the world, where men move to and fro, I have seen a man—an educated gentleman—grow livid with anger because a little, silent, black woman was sitting by herself in a Pullman car. He was a white man. I have seen a great, grown man curse a little child, who had wandered into the wrong waiting-room, searching for its mother: "Here, you damned black————" He was white. In Central Park I have seen the upper lip of a quiet, peaceful man curl back in a tigerish snarl of rage because black folk rode by in a motor car. He was a white man. We have seen, you and I, city after city drunk and furious with ungovernable lust of blood; mad with murder, destroying, killing, and cursing; torturing human victims because somebody accused of crime happened to be of the same color as the mob's innocent victims and because that color was not white! We have seen,—Merciful God! in these wild days and in the name of Civilization, Justice, and Motherhood,—what have we not seen, right here in America, of orgy, cruelty, barbarism, and murder done to men and women of Negro descent.

Up through the foam of green and weltering waters wells this great mass of hatred, in wilder, fiercer violence, until I look down and know that today to the millions of my people no misfortune could happen,—of death and pestilence, failure and defeat—that would not make the hearts of millions of their fellows beat with fierce, vindictive joy! Do you doubt it? Ask your own soul what it would say if the next census were to report that half of black America was dead and the other half dying.

Unfortunate? Unfortunate. But where is the misfortune? Mine? Am I, in my blackness, the sole sufferer? I suffer. And yet, somehow, above the suffering, above the shackled anger that beats the bars, above the hurt that crazes there surges in me a vast pity,—pity for a people imprisoned and enthralled, hampered and made miserable for such a cause, for such a phantasy!

Conceive this nation, of all human peoples, engaged in a crusade to make the "World Safe for Democracy"! Can you imagine the United States protesting against Turkish atrocities in Armenia, while the Turks are silent about mobs in Chicago and St. Louis; what is Louvain compared with Memphis, Waco, Washington, Dyersburg, and Estill Springs? In short, what is the black man but America's Belgium, and how could America condemn in Germany that which she commits, just as brutally, within her own borders?

A true and worthy ideal frees and uplifts a people; a false ideal imprisons and lowers. Say to men, earnestly and repeatedly: "Honesty is best, knowledge is power; do unto others as you would be done by." Say this and act it and the nation must move toward it, if not to it. But say to a people: "The one virtue is to be white," and the people rush to the inevitable conclusion, "Kill the 'nigger'!"

Is not this the record of present America? Is not this its headlong progress? Are we not coming more and more, day by day, to making the statement "I am white," the one fundamental tenet of our practical morality? Only when this basic, iron rule is involved is our defense of right nation-wide and prompt. Murder may swagger, theft may rule and prostitution may flourish and the nation gives but spasmodic, intermittent and lukewarm attention. But let the murderer be black or the thief brown or the violator of womanhood have a drop of Negro blood, and the righteousness of the indignation sweeps the world. Nor would this fact make the indignation less justifiable did not we all know that it was blackness that was condemned and not crime.

In the awful cataclysm of World War, where from beating, slandering, and murdering us the white world turned temporarily aside to kill each other, we of the Darker Peoples looked on in mild amaze.

Among some of us, I doubt not, this sudden descent of Europe into hell brought unbounded surprise; to others, over wide area, it brought the *Schaden Freude* of the bitterly hurt; but most of us, I judge, looked on silently and sorrowfully, in sober thought, seeing sadly the prophecy of our own souls.

Here is a civilization that has boasted much. Neither Roman nor Arab, Greek nor Egyptian, Persian nor Mongol ever took himself and his own perfectness with such disconcerting seriousness as the modern white man. We whose shame, humiliation, and deep insult his aggrandizement so often involved were never deceived. We looked at him clearly, with world-old eyes, and saw simply a human thing, weak and pitiable and cruel, even as we are and were.

These super-men and world-mastering demi-gods listened, however, to no low tongues of ours, even when we pointed silently to their feet of clay. Perhaps we, as folk of simpler soul and more primitive type, have been most struck in the welter of recent years by the utter failure of white religion. We have curled our lips in something like contempt as we have witnessed glib apology and weary explanation. Nothing of the sort deceived us. A nation's religion is its life, and as such white Christianity is a miserable failure.

Nor would we be unfair in this criticism: We know that we, too, have failed, as you have, and have rejected many a Buddha, even as you have denied Christ; but we acknowledge our human frailty, while you, claiming super-humanity, scoff endlessly at our shortcomings.

The number of white individuals who are practising with even reasonable approximation the democracy and unselfishness of Jesus Christ is so small and unimportant as to be fit subject for jest in Sunday supplements and in *Punch, Life, Le Rire*, and *Fliegende Blätter*. In her foreign mission work the extraordinary self-deception of white religion is epitomized: solemnly the white world sends five million dollars worth of missionary propaganda to Africa each year and in the same twelve months adds twenty-five million dollars worth of the vilest gin manufactured. Peace to the augurs of Rome!

We may, however, grant without argument that religious ideals have always far outrun their very human devotees. Let us, then, turn to more mundane matters of honor and fairness. The world today is trade. The world has turned shopkeeper; history is economic history; living is earning a living. Is it necessary to ask how much of high emprise and honorable conduct has been found here? Something, to be sure. The establishment of world credit systems is built on splendid and realizable faith in fellow-men. But it is, after all, so low and elementary a step that sometimes it looks merely like honor among thieves, for the revelations of highway robbery and low cheating in the business world and in all its great modern centers have raised in the hearts of all true men in our day an exceeding great cry for revolution in our basic methods and conceptions of industry and commerce.

We do not, for a moment, forget the robbery of other times and races when trade was a most uncertain gamble; but was there not a certain honesty and frankness in the evil that argued a saner morality? There are more merchants today, surer deliveries, and wider well-being, but are there not, also, bigger thieves, deeper injustice, and more calloused selfishness in well-being? Be that as it may,—certainly the nicer sense of honor that has risen ever and again in groups of forword-thinking men has been curiously and broadly blunted. Consider our chiefest industry,—fighting. Laboriously the Middle Ages built its rules of fairness—equal armament, equal notice, equal conditions. What do we see today? Machine-guns against assegais; conquest sugared with religion; mutilation and rape masquerading as culture,— all this, with vast applause at the superiority of white over black soldiers!

War is horrible! This the dark world knows to its awful cost. But has it just become horrible, in these last days, when under essentially equal conditions, equal armament, and equal waste of wealth white men are fighting white men, with surgeons and nurses hovering near?

Think of the wars through which we have lived in the last decade: in German Africa, in British Nigeria, in French and Spanish Morocco, in China, in Persia, in the Balkans, in Tripoli, in Mexico, and in a dozen lesser places—were not these horrible, too? Mind you, there were for most of these wars no Red Cross funds.

Behold little Belgium and her pitiable plight, but has the world forgotten Congo? What Belgium now suffers is not half, not even a tenth, of what she has done to black Congo since Stanley's great dream of 1880. Down the dark forests of inmost Africa sailed this modern Sir Galahad, in the name of "the noble-minded men of several nations," to introduce commerce and civilization. What came of it? "Rubber and murder, slavery in its worst form," wrote Glave in 1895.

Harris declares that King Leopold's régime meant the death of twelve million natives, "but what we who were behind the scenes felt most keenly was the fact that the real catastrophe in the Congo was desolation and murder in the larger sense. The invasion of family life, the ruthless destruction of every social barrier, the shattering of every tribal law, the introduction of criminal practices which struck the chiefs of the people dumb with horror—in a word, a veritable avalanche of filth and immorality overwhelmed the Congo tribes."

Yet the fields of Belgium laughed, the cities were gay, art and science flourished; the groans that helped to nourish this civilization fell on deaf ears because the world round about was doing the same sort of thing elsewhere on its own account.

As we saw the dead dimly through rifts of battle-smoke and heard faintly the cursings and accusations of blood brothers, we darker men said: This is not Europe gone mad; this is not aberration nor insanity; this *is* Europe; this seeming Terrible is the real soul of white culture—back of all culture,—stripped and visible today. This is where the world has arrived,—these dark and awful depths and not the shining and ineffable heights of which it boasted. Here is whither the might and energy of modern humanity has really gone.

But may not the world cry back at us and ask: "What better thing have you to show? What have you done or would do better than this if you had today the world rule? Paint with all riot of hateful colors the thin skin of European culture,—is it not better than any culture that arose in Africa or Asia?"

It is. Of this there is no doubt and never has been; but why is it better? Is it better because Europeans are better, nobler, greater, and more gifted than other folk? It is not. Europe has never produced and never will in our day bring forth a single human soul who cannot be matched and over-matched in every line of human endeavor by Asia and Africa. Run the gamut, if you will, and let us have the Europeans who in sober truth over-match Nefertari, Mohammed, Rameses and Askia, Confucius, Buddha, and Jesus Christ. If we could scan the calendar of thousands of lesser men, in like comparison, the result would be the same; but we cannot do this because of the deliberately educated ignorance of white schools by which they remember Napoleon and forget Sonni Ali.

The greatness of Europe has lain in the width of the stage on which she has played her part, the strength of the foundations on which she has builded, and a natural, human ability no whit greater (if as great) than that of other days and races. In other words, the deeper reasons for the triumph of European civilization lie quite outside and beyond Europe,—back in the universal struggles of all mankind.

Why, then, is Europe great? Because of the foundations which the mighty past have furnished her to build upon: the iron trade of ancient, black Africa, the religion and empire-building of yellow Asia, the art and science of the "dago" Mediterranean shore, east, south, and west, as well as north. And where she has builded securely upon this great past and learned from it she has gone forward to greater and more splendid human triumph; but where she has ignored this past and forgotten and sneered at it, she has shown the cloven hoof of poor, crucified humanity,—she has played, like other empires gone, the world fool!

If, then, European triumphs in culture have been greater, so, too, may her failures have been greater. How great a failure and a failure in what does the World War betoken? Was it national jealousy of the sort of the seventeenth century? But Europe has done more to break down national barriers than any preceding culture. Was it fear of the balance of power in Europe? Hardly, save in the half-Asiatic problems of the Balkans. What, then, does Hauptmann mean when he says: "Our jealous enemies forged an iron ring about our breasts and we knew our breasts had to expand,—that we had to split asunder this ring or else we had to cease breathing. But Germany will not cease to breathe and so it came to pass that the iron ring was forced apart."

Whither is this expansion? What is that breath of life, thought to be so indispensable to a great European nation? Manifestly it is expansion overseas; it is colonial aggrandizement which explains, and alone adequately explains, the World War. How many of us today fully realize the current theory of colonial expansion, of the relation of Europe which is white, to the world which is black and brown and yellow? Bluntly put, that theory is this: It is the duty of white Europe to divide up the darker world and administer it for Europe's good.

This Europe has largely done. The European world is using black and brown men for all the uses which men know. Slowly but surely white culture is evolving the theory that "darkies" are born beasts of burden for white folk. It were silly to think otherwise, cries the cultured world, with stronger and shriller accord. The supporting arguments grow and twist themselves in the mouths of merchant, scientist, soldier, traveler, writer, and missionary: Darker peoples are dark in mind as well as in body; of dark, uncertain, and imperfect descent; of frailer, cheaper stuff; they are cowards in the face of mausers and maxims; they have no feelings, aspirations, and loves; they are fools, illogical idiots,—"half-devil and half-child."

Such as they are civilization must, naturally, raise them, but soberly and in limited ways. They are not simply dark white men. They are not "men" in the sense that Europeans are men. To the very limited extent of their shallow capacities lift them to be useful to whites, to raise cotton, gather rubber, fetch ivory, dig diamonds,—and let them be paid what men think they are worth—white men who know them to be well-nigh worthless.

Such degrading of men by men is as old as mankind and the invention of no one race or people. Ever have men striven to conceive of their victims as different from the victors, endlessly different, in soul and blood, strength and cunning, race and lineage. It has been left, however, to Europe and to modern days to discover the eternal world-wide mark of meanness,—color!

Such is the silent revolution that has gripped modern European culture in the later nineteenth and twentieth centuries. Its zenith came in Boxer times: White supremacy was all but world-wide, Africa was dead, India conquered, Japan isolated, and China prostrate, while white America whetted her sword for mongrel Mexico and mulatto South America, lynching her own Negroes the while. Temporary halt in this program was made by little Japan and the white world immediately sensed the peril of such "yellow" presumption! What sort of a world would this be if yellow men must be treated "white"? Immediately the eventual overthrow of Japan became a subject of deep thought and intrigue, from St. Petersburg to San Francisco, from the Key of Heaven to the Little Brother of the Poor.

The using of men for the benefit of masters is no new invention of modern Europe. It is quite as old as the world. But Europe proposed to apply it on a scale and with an elaborateness of detail of which no former world ever dreamed. The imperial width of the thing,—the heaven-defying audacity—makes its modern newness.

The scheme of Europe was no sudden invention, but a way out of long-pressing difficulties. It is plain to modern white civilization that the subjection of the white working classes cannot much longer be maintained. Education, political power, and increased knowledge of the technique and meaning of the industrial process are destined to make a more and more equitable distribution of wealth in the near future. The day of the very rich is drawing to a close, so far as individual white nations are concerned. But there is a loophole. There is a chance for exploitation on an immense scale for inordinate profit, not simply to the very rich, but to the middle class and to the laborers. This chance lies in the exploitation of darker peoples. It is here that the golden hand beckons. Here are no labor unions or votes or questioning onlookers or inconvenient consciences. These men may be used down to the very bone, and shot and maimed in "punitive" expeditions when they revolt. In these dark lands "industrial development" may repeat in exaggerated form every horror of the industrial history of Europe, from slavery and rape to disease and maiming, with only one test of success,—dividends!

This theory of human culture and its aims has worked itself through warp and woof of our daily thought with a thoroughness that few realize. Everything great, good, efficient, fair, and honorable is "white"; everything mean, bad, blundering, cheating, and dishonorable is "yellow"; a bad taste is "brown"; and the devil is "black." The changes of this theme are continually rung in picture and story, in newspaper heading and moving-picture, in sermon and school book, until, of course, the King can do no wrong,—a White Man is always right and a Black Man has no rights which a white man is bound to respect.

There must come the necessary despisings and hatreds of these savage half-men, this unclean *canaille* of the world—these dogs of men. All through the world this gospel is preaching. It has its literature, it has its priests, it has its secret propaganda and above all—it pays!

There's the rub,—it pays. Rubber, ivory, and palm-oil; tea, coffee, and cocoa; bananas, oranges, and other fruit; cotton, gold, and copper—they, and a hundred other things which dark and sweating bodies hand up to the white world from their pits of slime, pay and pay well, but of all that the world gets the black world gets only the pittance that the white world throws it disdainfully.

Small wonder, then, that in the practical world of things-that-be there is jealousy and strife for the possession of the labor of dark millions, for the right to bleed and exploit the colonies of the world where this golden stream may be had, not always for the asking, but surely for the whipping and shooting. It was this competition for the labor of yellow, brown, and black folks that was the cause of the World War. Other causes have been glibly given and other contributing causes there doubtless were, but they were subsidiary and subordinate to this vast quest of the dark world's wealth and toil.

Colonies, we call them, these places where "niggers" are cheap and the earth is rich; they are those outlands where like a swarm of hungry locusts white masters may settle to be served as kings, wield the lash of slave-drivers, rape girls and wives, grow as rich as Croesus and send homeward a golden stream. They belt the earth, these places, but they cluster in the tropics, with its darkened peoples: in Hong

Kong and Anam, in Borneo and Rhodesia, in Sierra Leone and Nigeria, in Panama and Havana—these are the El Dorados toward which the world powers stretch itching palms.

Germany, at last one and united and secure on land, looked across the seas and seeing England with sources of wealth insuring a luxury and power which Germany could not hope to rival by the slower processes of exploiting her own peasants and workingmen, especially with these workers half in revolt, immediately built her navy and entered into a desperate competition for possession of colonies of darker peoples. To South America, to China, to Africa, to Asia Minor, she turned like a hound quivering on the leash, impatient, suspicious, irritable, with blood-shot eyes and dripping fangs, ready for the awful word. England and France crouched watchfully over their bones, growling and wary, but gnawing industriously, while the blood of the dark world whetted their greedy appetites. In the background, shut out from the highway to the seven seas, sat Russia and Austria, snarling and snapping at each other and at the last Mediterranean gate to the El Dorado, where the Sick Man enjoyed bad health, and where millions of serfs in the Balkans, Russia, and Asia offered a feast to greed well-nigh as great as Africa.

The fateful day came. It had to come. The cause of war is preparation for war; and of all that Europe has done in a century there is nothing that has equaled in energy, thought, and time her preparation for wholesale murder. The only adequate cause of this preparation was conquest and conquest, not in Europe, but primarily among the darker peoples of Asia and Africa; conquest, not for assimilation and uplift, but for commerce and degradation. For this, and this mainly, did Europe gird herself at frightful cost for war.

The red day dawned when the tinder was lighted in the Balkans and Austro-Hungary seized a bit which brought her a step nearer to the world's highway; she seized one bit and poised herself for another. Then came that curious chorus of challenges, those leaping suspicions, raking all causes for distrust and rivalry and hatred, but saying little of the real and greatest cause.

Each nation felt its deep interests involved. But how? Not, surely, in the death of Ferdinand the Warlike; not, surely, in the old, half-forgotten *revanche* for Alsace-Lorraine; not even in the neutrality of Belgium. No! But in the possession of land overseas, in the right to colonies, the chance to levy endless tribute on the darker world,—on coolies in China, on starving peasants in India, on black savages in Africa, on dying South Sea Islanders, on Indians of the Amazon—all this and nothing more.

Even the broken reed on which we had rested high hopes of eternal peace,—the guild of the laborers—the front of that very important movement for human justice on which we had builded most, even this flew like a straw before the breath of king and kaiser. Indeed, the flying had been foreshadowed when in Germany and America "international" Socialists had all but read yellow and black men out of the kingdom of industrial justice. Subtly had they been bribed, but effectively: Were they not lordly whites and should they not share in the spoils of rape? High wages in the United States and England might be the skilfully manipulated result of slavery in Africa and of peonage in Asia.

With the dog-in-the-manger theory of trade, with the determination to reap inordinate profits and to exploit the weakest to the utmost there came a new imperialism,—the rage for one's own nation to own the earth or, at least, a large enough portion of it to insure as big profits as the next nation. Where sections could not be owned by one dominant nation there came a policy of "open door," but the "door" was open to "white people only." As to the darkest and weakest of peoples there was but one unanimity in Europe,—that which Herr Dernberg of the German Colonial Office called the agreement with England to maintain white "prestige" in Africa,—the doctrine of the divine right of white people to steal.

Thus the world market most wildly and desperately sought today is the market where labor is cheapest and most helpless and profit is most abundant. This labor is kept cheap and helpless because the white world despises "darkies." If one has the temerity to suggest that these workingmen may walk the way of white workingmen and climb by votes and self-assertion and education to the rank of men, he is howled out of court. They cannot do it and if they could, they shall not, for they are the enemies of the white race and the whites shall rule forever and forever and everywhere. Thus the hatred and despising of human beings from whom Europe wishes to extort her luxuries has led to such jealousy and bickering between European nations that they have fallen afoul of each other and have fought like crazed beasts. Such is the fruit of human hatred.

But what of the darker world that watches? Most men belong to this world. With Negro and Negroid, East Indian, Chinese, and Japanese they form two-thirds of the population of the world. A belief in humanity is a belief in colored men. If the uplift of mankind must be done by men, then the destinies of this world will rest ultimately in the hands of darker nations.

What, then, is this dark world thinking? It is thinking that as wild and awful as this shameful war was, *it is nothing to compare with that fight for freedom which black and brown and yellow men must and will make unless their oppression and humiliation and insult at the hands of the White World cease. The Dark World is going to submit to its present treatment just as long as it must and not one moment longer.*

Let me say this again and emphasize it and leave no room for mistaken meaning: The World War was primarily the jealous and avaricious struggle for the largest share in exploiting darker races. As such it is and must be but the prelude to the armed and indignant protest of these despised and raped peoples. Today Japan is hammering on the door of justice, China is raising her half-manacled hands to knock next, India is writhing for the freedom to knock, Egypt is sullenly muttering, the Negroes of South and West Africa, of the West Indies, and of the United States are just awakening to their shameful slavery. Is, then, this war the end of wars? Can it be the end, so long as sits enthroned, even in the souls of those who cry peace, the despising and robbing of darker peoples? If Europe hugs this delusion, then this is not the end of world war,—it is but the beginning!

We see Europe's greatest sin precisely where we found Africa's and Asia's,—in human hatred, the despising of men; with this difference, however: Europe has the awful lesson of the past before her, has the splendid results of widened areas of tolerance, sympathy, and love among men, and she faces a greater, an infinitely greater, world of men than any preceding civilization ever faced.

It is curious to see America, the United States, looking on herself, first, as a sort of natural peace-maker, then as a moral protagonist in this terrible time. No nation is less fitted for this rôle. For two or more centuries America has marched proudly in the van of human hatred,— making bonfires of human flesh and laughing at them hideously, and making the insulting of millions more than a matter of dislike,—rather a great religion, a world war-cry: Up white, down black; to your tents, O white folk, and world war with black and parti-colored mongrel beasts!

Instead of standing as a great example of the success of democracy and the possibility of human brotherhood America has taken her place as an awful example of its pitfalls and failures, so far as black and brown and yellow peoples are concerned. And this, too, in spite of the fact that there has been no actual failure; the Indian is not dying out, the Japanese and Chinese have not menaced the land, and the experiment of Negro suffrage has resulted in the uplift of twelve million people at a rate probably unparalleled in history. But what of this? America, Land of Democracy, wanted to believe in the failure of democracy so far as darker peoples were concerned. Absolutely without excuse she established a caste system, rushed into preparation for war, and conquered tropical colonies. She stands today shoulder to shoulder with Europe in Europe's worst sin against civilization. She aspires to sit among the great nations who arbitrate the fate of "lesser breeds without the law" and she is at times heartily ashamed even of the large number of "new" white people whom her democracy has admitted to place and power. Against this surging forward of Irish and German, of Russian Jew, Slav and "dago" her social bars have not availed, but against Negroes she can and does take her unflinching and immovable stand, backed by this new public policy of Europe. She trains her immigrants to this despising of "niggers" from the day of their landing, and they carry and send the news back to the submerged classes in the fatherlands.

All this I see and hear up in my tower, above the thunder of the seven seas. From my narrowed windows I stare into the night that looms beneath the cloud-swept stars. Eastward and westward storms are breaking,—great, ugly whirlwinds of hatred and blood and cruelty. I will not believe them inevitable. I will not believe that all that was must be, that all the shameful drama of the past must be done again today before the sunlight sweeps the silver seas.

If I cry amid this roar of elemental forces, must my cry be in vain, because it is but a cry,—a small and human cry amid Promethean gloom?

Back beyond the world and swept by these wild, white faces of the awful dead, why will this Soul of White Folk,—this modern Prometheus,—hang bound by his own binding, tethered by a fable of the past? I hear his mighty cry reverberating through the world, "I am white!" Well and good, O Prometheus, divine thief! Is not the world wide enough for two colors, for many little shinings of the sun? Why, then, devour your own vitals if I answer even as proudly, "I am black!"

The Riddle of the Sphinx

Dark daughter of the lotus leaves that watch the South-
    ern Sea!
Wan spirit of a prisoned soul a-panting to be free!
    The muttered music of thy streams, the whisper of
      the deep,
    Have kissed each other in God's name and kissed a
      world to sleep.

The will of the world is a whistling wind, sweeping a
    cloud-swept sky,
And not from the East and not from the West knelled
    that soul-waking cry,
    But out of the South,—the sad, black South—it
      screamed from the top of the sky,
    Crying: "Awake, O ancient race!" Wailing, "O
      woman, arise!"
And crying and sighing and crying again as a voice in
    the midnight cries,—
But the burden of white men bore her back and the
    white world stifled her sighs.

The white world's vermin and filth:
    All the dirt of London,

All the scum of New York;
Valiant spoilers of women
And conquerors of unarmed men;
Shameless breeders of bastards,
Drunk with the greed of gold,
Baiting their blood-stained hooks
With cant for the souls of the simple;
Bearing the white man's burden
Of liquor and lust and lies!
Unthankful we wince in the East,
Unthankful we wail from the westward,
Unthankfully thankful, we curse,
In the unworn wastes of the wild:
    I hate them, Oh!
    I hate them well,
    I hate them, Christ!
    As I hate hell!
    If I were God,
    I'd sound their knell
    This day!
Who raised the fools to their glory,
But black men of Egypt and Ind,
Ethiopia's sons of the evening,
Indians and yellow Chinese,
Arabian children of morning,
And mongrels of Rome and Greece?
    Ah, well!
And they that raised the boasters
Shall drag them down again,—
Down with the theft of their thieving
And murder and mocking of men;
Down with their barter of women
And laying and lying of creeds;
Down with their cheating of childhood
And drunken orgies of war,—
    down
      down
        deep down,
Till the devil's strength be shorn,
Till some dim, darker David, a-hoeing of his corn,
And married maiden, mother of God,
Bid the black Christ be born!
Then shall our burden be manhood,
Be it yellow or black or white;
And poverty and justice and sorrow,
The humble and simple and strong
Shall sing with the sons of morning
And daughters of even-song:
  Black mother of the iron hills that ward the
    blazing sea,

Wild spirit of a storm-swept soul, a-struggling
    to be free,
Where 'neath the bloody finger-marks thy
    riven bosom quakes,
Thicken the thunders of God's Voice and lo!
    a world awakes!

CHAPTER III

The Hands of Ethiopia

"Semper novi quid ex Africa," cried the Roman proconsul, and he voiced the verdict of forty centuries. Yet there are those who would write world history and leave out of account this most marvelous of continents. Particularly today most men assume that Africa is far afield from the center of our burning social problems and especially from our problem of world war.

Always Africa is giving us something new or some metempsychosis of a world-old thing. On its black bosom arose one of the earliest, if not the earliest, of self-protecting civilizations, which grew so mightily that it still furnishes superlatives to thinking and speaking men. Out of its darker and more remote forest fastnesses came, if we may credit many recent scientists, the first welding of iron, and we know that agriculture and trade flourished there when Europe was a wilderness.

Nearly every human empire that has arisen in the world, material and spiritual, has found some of its greatest crises on this continent of Africa, from Greece to Great Britain. As Mommsen says: "It was through Africa that Christianity became the religion of the world." In Africa the last flood of Germanic invasions spent itself within hearing of the last gasp of Byzantium, and it was through Africa that Islam came to play its great rôle of conqueror and civilizer.

With the Renaissance and the widened world of modern thought Africa came no less suddenly with her new-old gift. Shakespeare's "Ancient Pistol" cries:

A foutre for the world and worldlings base!
I speak of Africa and golden joys!

He echoes a legend of gold from the days of Punt and Ophir to those of Ghana, the Gold Coast, and the Rand. This thought had sent the world's greed scurrying down the hot, mysterious coasts of Africa to the Good Hope of gain, until for the first time a real world-commerce was born, albeit it started as a commerce mainly in the bodies and souls of men.

511

The present problem of problems is nothing more than democracy beating itself helplessly against the color bar,—purling, seeping, seething, foaming to burst through, ever and again overwhelming the emerging masses of white men in its rolling backwaters and held back by those who dream of future kingdoms of greed built on black and brown and yellow slavery.

The indictment of Africa against Europe is grave. For four hundred years white Europe was the chief support of that trade in human beings which first and last robbed black Africa of a hundred million human beings, transformed the face of her social life, overthrew organized government, distorted ancient industry, and snuffed out the lights of cultural development. Today instead of removing laborers from Africa to distant slavery, industry built on a new slavery approaches Africa to deprive the natives of their land, to force them to toil, and to reap all the profit for the white world.

It is scarcely necessary to remind the reader of the essential facts underlying these broad assertions. A recent law of the Union of South Africa assigns nearly two hundred and fifty million acres of the best of natives' land to a million and a half whites and leaves thirty-six million acres of swamp and marsh for four and a half-million blacks. In Rhodesia over ninety million acres have been practically confiscated. In the Belgian Congo all the land was declared the property of the state.

Slavery in all but name has been the foundation of the cocoa industry in St. Thome and St. Principe and in the mines of the Rand. Gin has been one of the greatest of European imports, having increased fifty per cent. in ten years and reaching a total of at least twenty-five million dollars a year today. Negroes of ability have been carefully gotten rid of, deposed from authority, kept out of positions of influence, and discredited in their people's eyes, while a caste of white overseers and governing officials has appeared everywhere.

Naturally, the picture is not all lurid. David Livingstone has had his successors and Europe has given Africa something of value in the beginning of education and industry. Yet the balance of iniquity is desperately large; but worse than that, it has aroused no world protest. A great Englishman, familiar with African problems for a generation, says frankly today: "There does not exist any real international conscience to which you can appeal."

Moreover, that treatment shows no certain signs of abatement. Today in England the Empire Resources Development Committee proposes to treat African colonies as "crown estates" and by intensive scientific exploitation of both land and labor to make these colonies pay the English national debt after the war! German thinkers, knowing the tremendous demand for raw material which would follow the war, had similar plans of exploitation. "It is the clear, common sense of the African situation," says H. G. Wells, "that while these precious regions of raw material remain divided up between a number of competitive European imperialisms, each resolutely set upon the exploitation of its 'possessions' to its own advantage and the disadvantage of the others, there can be no permanent peace in the world. It is impossible."

We, then, who fought the war against war; who in a hell of blood and suffering held hardly our souls in leash by the vision of a world organized for peace; who are looking for industrial democracy and for the organization of Europe so as to avoid incentives to war,—we, least of all, should be willing to leave the backward world as the greatest temptation, not only to wars based on international jealousies, but to the most horrible of wars,—which arise from the revolt of the maddened against those who hold them in common contempt.

Consider, my reader,—if you were today a man of some education and knowledge, but born a Japanese or a Chinaman, an East Indian or a Negro, what would you do and think? What would be in the present chaos your outlook and plan for the future? Manifestly, you would want freedom for your people,—freedom from insult, from segregation, from poverty, from physical slavery. If the attitude of the European and American worlds is in the future going to be based essentially upon the same policies as in the past, then there is but one thing for the trained man of darker blood to do and that is definitely and as openly as possible to organize his world for war against Europe. He may have to do it by secret, underground propaganda, as in Egypt and India and eventually in the United States; or by open increase of armament, as in Japan; or by desperate efforts at modernization, as in China; but he must do it. He represents the vast majority of mankind. To surrender would be far worse than physical death. There is no way out unless the white world opens the door. Either the white world gives up such insult as its modern use of the adjective "yellow" indicates, or its connotation of "chink" and "nigger" implies; either it gives up the plan of color serfdom which its use of the other adjective "white" implies, as indicating everything decent and every part of the world worth living in,—or trouble is written in the stars!

It is, therefore, of singular importance after disquieting delay to see the real Pacifist appear. Both England and Germany have recently been basing their claims to parts of black Africa on the wishes and interests of the black inhabitants. Lloyd George has declared "the general principle of national self-determination applicable at least to German Africa," while Chancellor Hertling once welcomed a discussion "on the reconstruction of the world's colonial possessions."

The demand that an Africa for Africans shall replace the present barbarous scramble for exploitation by individual states comes from singularly different sources. Colored America demands that "the conquered German colonies should not be returned to Germany, neither should they be held by the Allies. Here is the opportunity for the establishment of a nation that may never recur. Thousands of colored men, sick of white arrogance and hypocrisy, see in this their race's only salvation."

Sir Harry H. Johnston recently said: "If we are to talk, as we do, sentimentally but justly about restoring the nationhood of Poland, about giving satisfaction to the separatist feeling in Ireland, and about what is to be done for European nations who are oppressed, then we can hardly exclude from this feeling the countries of Africa."

Laborers, black laborers, on the Canal Zone write: "Out of this chaos may be the great awakening of our race. There is cause for rejoicing. If we fail to embrace this opportunity now, we fail to see how we will be ever able to solve the race question. It is for the British Negro, the French Negro, and the American Negro to rise to the occasion and start a national campaign, jointly and collectively, with this aim in view."

From British West Africa comes the bitter complaint "that the West Africans should have the right or opportunity to settle their future for themselves is a thing which hardly enters the mind of the European politician. That the Balkan States should be admitted to the Council of Peace and decide the government under which they are to live is taken as a matter of course because they are Europeans, but no extra-European is credited, even by the extremest advocates of human equality, with any right except to humbly accept the fate which Europe shall decide for him."

Here, then, is the danger and the demand; and the real Pacifist will seek to organize, not simply the masses in white nations, guarding against exploitation and profiteering, but will remember that no permanent relief can come but by including in this organization the lowest and the most exploited races in the world. World philanthropy, like national philanthropy, must come as uplift and prevention and not merely as alleviation and religious conversion. Reverence for humanity, as such, must be installed in the world, and Africa should be the talisman.

Black Africa, including British, French, Belgian, Portuguese, Italian, and Spanish possessions and the independent states of Abyssinia and Liberia and leaving out of account Egypt and North Africa, on the one hand, and South Africa, on the other, has an area of 8,200,000 square miles and a population well over one hundred millions of black men, with less than one hundred thousand whites.

Commercial exploitation in Africa has already larger results to show than most people realize. Annually $200,000,000 worth of goods was coming out of black Africa before the World War, including a third of the world's supply of rubber, a quarter of all of the world's cocoa, and practically all of the world's cloves, gum-arabic, and palm-oil. In exchange there was being returned to Africa one hundred millions in cotton cloth, twenty-five millions in iron and steel, and as much in foods, and probably twenty-five millions in liquors.

Here are the beginnings of a modern industrial system: iron and steel for permanent investment, bound to yield large dividends; cloth as the cheapest exchange for invaluable raw material; liquor to tickle the appetites of the natives and render the alienation of land and the break-down of customary law easier; eventually forced and contract labor under white drivers to increase and systematize the production of raw materials. These materials are capable of indefinite expansion: cotton may yet challenge the southern United States, fruits and vegetables, hides and skins, lumber and dye-stuffs, coffee and tea, grain and tobacco, and fibers of all sorts can easily follow organized and systematic toil.

Is it a paradise of industry we thus contemplate? It is much more likely to be a hell. Under present plans there will be no voice or law or custom to protect labor, no trades unions, no eight-hour laws, no factory legislation,—nothing of that great body of legislation built up in modern days to protect mankind from sinking to the level of beasts of burden. All the industrial deviltry, which civilization has been driving to the slums and the backwaters, will have a voiceless continent to conceal it. If the slave cannot be taken from Africa, slavery can be taken to Africa.

Who are the folk who live here? They are brown and black, curly and crisp-haired, short and tall, and longheaded. Out of them in days without date flowed the beginnings of Egypt; among them rose, later, centers of culture at Ghana, Melle, and Timbuktu. Kingdoms and empires flourished in Songhay and Zymbabwe, and art and industry in Yoruba and Benin. They have fought every human calamity in its most hideous form and yet today they hold some similar vestiges of a mighty past,—their work in iron, their weaving and carving, their music and singing, their tribal government, their town-meeting and marketplace, their desperate valor in war.

Missionaries and commerce have left some good with all their evil. In black Africa today there are more than a thousand government schools and some thirty thousand mission schools, with a more or less regular attendance of three-quarters of a million school children. In a few cases training of a higher order is given chiefs' sons and selected pupils. These beginnings of education are not much for so vast a land and there is no general standard or set plan of development, but, after all, the children of Africa are beginning to learn.

In black Africa today only one-seventeenth of the land and a ninth of the people in Liberia and Abyssinia are approximately independent, although menaced and policed by European capitalism. Half the land and the people are in domains under Portugal, France, and Belgium, held with the avowed idea of exploitation for the benefit of Europe under a system of caste and color serfdom. Out of this dangerous nadir of development stretch two paths: one is indicated by the condition of about three per cent of the people who in Sierra Leone, the Gold Coast, and French Senegal, are tending toward the path of modern development; the other path, followed by a fourth of the land and people, has local self-government and native customs and might evolve, if undisturbed, a native culture along their own peculiar lines. A tenth of the land, sparsely settled, is being monopolized and held for whites to make an African Australia. To these later folk must be added the four and one-half millions of the South African Union, who by every modern device are being forced into landless serfdom.

Before the World War tendencies were strongly toward the destruction of independent Africa, the industrial slavery of the mass of the blacks and the encouragement of white immigration, where possible, to hold the blacks in subjection.

Against this idea let us set the conception of a new African World State, a Black Africa, applying to these peoples the splendid pronouncements which have of late been so broadly and perhaps carelessly given the world: recognizing in Africa the declaration of the American Federation of Labor, that "no people must be forced under sovereignty under which it does not wish to live"; recognizing in President Wilson's message to the Russians, the "principle of the undictated development of all peoples"; recognizing the resolution of the recent conference of the Aborigines Protection Society of England, "that in any reconstruction of Africa, which may result from this war, the interests of the native inhabitants and also their wishes, in so far as those wishes can be clearly ascertained, should be recognized as among the principal factors upon which the decision of their destiny should be based." In other words, recognizing for the first time in the history of the modern world that black men are human.

It may not be possible to build this state at once. With the victory of the Entente Allies, the German colonies, with their million of square miles and one-half million black inhabitants, should form such a nucleus. It would give Black Africa its physical beginnings. Beginning with the German colonies two other sets of colonies could be added, for obvious reasons. Neither Portugal nor Belgium has shown any particular capacity for governing colonial peoples. Valid excuses may in both cases be advanced, but it would certainly be fair to Belgium to have her start her great task of reorganization after the World War with neither the burden nor the temptation of colonies; and in the same way Portugal has, in reality, the alternative of either giving up her colonies to an African State or to some other European State in the near future. These two sets of colonies would add 1,700,000 square miles and eighteen million inhabitants. It would not, however, be fair to despoil Germany, Belgium, and Portugal of their colonies unless, as Count Hertling once demanded, the whole question of colonies be opened.

How far shall the modern world recognize nations which are not nations, but combinations of a dominant caste and a suppressed horde of serfs? Will it not be possible to rebuild a world with compact nations, empires of self-governing elements, and colonies of backward peoples under benevolent international control?

The great test would be easy. Does England propose to erect in India and Nigeria nations brown and black which shall be eventually independent, self-governing entities, with a full voice in the British Imperial Government? If not, let these states either have independence at once or, if unfitted for that, be put under international tutelage and guardianship. It is possible that France, with her great heart, may welcome a Black France,—an enlarged Senegal in Africa; but it would seem that eventually all Africa south of twenty degrees north latitude and north of the Union of South Africa should be included in a new African State. Somaliland and Eritrea should be given to Abyssinia, and then with Liberia we would start with two small, independent African states and one large state under international control.

Does this sound like an impossible dream? No one could be blamed for so regarding it before 1914. I, myself, would have agreed with them. But since the nightmare of 1914–1918, since we have seen the impossible happen and the unspeakable become so common as to cease to stir us; in a day when Russia has dethroned her Czar, England has granted the suffrage to women and is in the act of giving Home Rule to Ireland; when Germany has adopted parliamentary government; when Jerusalem has been delivered from the Turks; and the United States has taken control of its railroads,—is it really so far-fetched to think of an Africa for the Africans, guided by organized civilization?

No one would expect this new state to be independent and self-governing from the start. Contrary, however, to present schemes for Africa the world would expect independence and self-government as the only possible end of the experiment. At first we can conceive of no better way of governing this state than through that same international control by which we hope to govern the world for peace. A curious and instructive parallel has been drawn by Simeon Strunsky: "Just as the common ownership of the northwest territory helped to weld the colonies into the United States, so could not joint and benevolent domination of Africa and of other backward parts of the world be a cornerstone upon which the future federation of the world could be built?"

From the British Labor Party comes this declaration: "With regard to the colonies of the several belligerents in tropical Africa, from sea to sea, the British Labor Movement disclaims all sympathy with the imperialist idea that these should form the booty of any nation, should be exploited for the profit of the capitalists, or should be used for the promotion of the militarists' aims of government. In view of the fact that it is impracticable here to leave the various peoples concerned to settle their own destinies it is suggested that the interests of humanity would be best served by the full and frank abandonment by all the belligerents of any dreams of an African Empire; the transfer of the present colonies of the European Powers in tropical Africa, however, and the limits of this area may be defined to the proposed Supernational Authority, or League of Nations."

Lloyd George himself has said in regard to the German colonies a word difficult to restrict merely to them: "I have repeatedly declared that they are held at the disposal of a conference, whose decision must have primary regard to the wishes and interests of the native inhabitants of such colonies. None of those territories is inhabited by Europeans. The governing consideration, therefore, must be that the inhabitants should be placed under the control of an administration acceptable to themselves, one of whose main purposes will be to prevent their exploitation for the benefit of European capitalists or governments."

The special commission for the government of this African State must, naturally, be chosen with great care and thought. It must represent, not simply governments, but civilization, science, commerce, social reform, religious philanthropy without sectarian propaganda. It must include, not simply white men, but educated and trained men of Negro blood. The guiding principles before such a commission should be clearly understood. In the first place, it ought by this time to be realized by the labor movement throughout the world that no industrial democracy can be built on industrial despotism, whether the two systems are in the same country or in different countries, since the world today so nearly approaches a common industrial unity. If, therefore, it is impossible in any single land to uplift permanently skilled labor without also raising common labor, so, too, there can be no permanent uplift of American or European labor as long as African laborers are slaves.

Secondly, this building of a new African State does not mean the segregation in it of all the world's black folk. It is too late in the history of the world to go back to the idea of absolute racial segregation. The new African State would not involve any idea of a vast transplantation of the twenty-seven million Negroids of the western world, of Africa, or of the gathering there of Negroid Asia. The Negroes in the United States and the other Americas have earned the right to fight out their problems where they are, but they could easily furnish from time to time technical experts, leaders of thought, and missionaries of culture for their backward brethren in the new Africa.

With these two principles, the practical policies to be followed out in the government of the new states should involve a thorough and complete system of modern education, built upon the present government, religion, and customary laws of the natives. There should be no violent tampering with the curiously efficient African institutions of local self-government through the family and the tribe; there should be no attempt at sudden "conversion" by religious propaganda. Obviously deleterious customs and unsanitary usages must gradually be abolished, but the general government, set up from without, must follow the example of the best colonial administrators and build on recognized, established foundations rather than from entirely new and theoretical plans.

The real effort to modernize Africa should be through schools rather than churches. Within ten years, twenty million black children ought to be in school. Within a generation young Africa should know the essential outlines of modern culture and groups of bright African students could be going to the world's great universities. From the beginning the actual general government should use both colored and white officials and later natives should be worked in. Taxation and industry could follow the newer ideals of industrial democracy, avoiding private land monopoly and poverty, and promoting co-operation in production and the socialization of income. Difficulties as to capital and revenue would be far less than many imagine. If a capable English administrator of British Nigeria could with $1,500 build up a cocoa industry of twenty million dollars annually, what might not be done in all Africa, without gin, thieves, and hypocrisy?

Capital could not only be accumulated in Africa, but attracted from the white world, with one great difference from present usage: no return so fabulous would be offered that civilized lands would be tempted to divert to colonial trade and invest materials and labor needed by the masses at home, but rather would receive the same modest profits as legitimate home industry offers.

There is no sense in asserting that the ideal of an African State, thus governed and directed toward independence and self-government, is impossible of realization. The first great essential is that the civilized world believe in its possibility. By reason of a crime (perhaps the greatest crime in human history) the modern world has been systematically taught to despise colored peoples. Men of education and decency ask, and ask seriously, if it is really possible to uplift Africa. Are Negroes human, or, if human, developed far enough to absorb, even under benevolent tutelage, any appreciable part of modern culture? Has not the experiment been tried in Haiti and Liberia, and failed?

One cannot ignore the extraordinary fact that a world campaign beginning with the slave-trade and ending with the refusal to capitalize the word "Negro," leading through a passionate defense of slavery by attributing every bestiality to blacks and finally culminating in the evident modern profit which lies in degrading blacks,—all this has unconsciously trained millions of honest, modern men into the belief that black folk are sub-human. This belief is not based on science, else it would be held as a postulate of the most tentative kind, ready at any time to be withdrawn in the face of facts; the belief is not based on history, for it is absolutely contradicted by Egyptian, Greek, Roman, Byzantine, and Arabian experience; nor is the belief based on any careful survey of the social development of men of Negro blood to-day in Africa and America. It is simply passionate, deep-seated heritage, and as such can be moved by neither argument nor fact. Only faith in humanity will lead the world to rise above its present color prejudice.

Those who do believe in men, who know what black men have done in human history, who have taken pains to follow even superficially the story of the rise of the Negro in Africa, the West Indies, and the Americas of our day know that our modern contempt of Negroes rests upon no scientific foundation worth a moment's attention. It is nothing more than a vicious habit of mind. It could as easily be overthrown as our belief in war, as our international hatreds, as our old conception of the status of women, as our fear of educating the masses, and as our belief in the necessity of poverty. We can, if we will, inaugurate on the Dark Continent a last great crusade for humanity. With Africa redeemed Asia would be safe and Europe indeed triumphant.

I have not mentioned North and South Africa, because my eye was centered on the main mass of the Negro race. Yet it is clear that for the development of Central Africa, Egypt should be free and independent, there along the highway to a free and independent India; while Morocco, Algeria, Tunis, and Tripoli must become a part of Europe, with modern development and home rule. South Africa, stripped of its black serfs and their lands, must admit the resident natives and colored folk to its body politic as equals.

The hands which Ethiopia shall soon stretch out unto God are not mere hands of helplessness and supplication, but rather are they hands of pain and promise; hard, gnarled, and muscled for the world's real work; they are hands of fellowship for the half-submerged masses of a distempered world; they are hands of helpfulness for an agonized God!

Twenty centuries before Christ a great cloud swept over seas and settled on Africa, darkening and wellnigh blotting out the culture of the land of Egypt. For half a thousand years it rested there, until a black woman, Queen Nefertari, "the most venerated figure in Egyptian history," rose to the throne of the Pharaohs and redeemed the world and her people. Twenty centuries after Christ, Black Africa,—prostrated, raped, and shamed, lies at the feet of the conquering Philistines of Europe. Beyond the awful sea a black woman is weeping and waiting, with her sons on her breast. What shall the end be? The world-old and fearful things,—war and wealth, murder and luxury? Or shall it be a new thing,—a new peace and a new democracy of all races,—a great humanity of equal men? *"Semper novi quid ex Africa!"*

The Princess of The Hither Isles

Her soul was beautiful, wherefore she kept it veiled in lightly-laced humility and fear, out of which peered anxiously and anon the white and blue and pale-gold of her face,—beautiful as daybreak or as the laughing of a child. She sat in the Hither Isles, well walled between the This and Now, upon a low and silver throne, and leaned upon its armposts, sadly looking upward toward the sun. Now the Hither Isles are flat and cold and swampy, with drear-drab light and all manner of slimy, creeping things, and piles of dirt and clouds of flying dust and sordid scraping and feeding and noise.

She hated them and ever as her hands and busy feet swept back the dust and slime her soul sat silver-throned, staring toward the great hill to the westward, which shone so brilliant-golden beneath the sunlight and above the sea.

The sea moaned and with it moaned the princess' soul, for she was lonely,—very, very lonely, and full weary of the monotone of life. So she was glad to see a moving in Yonder Kingdom on the mountainside, where the sun shone warm, and when the king of Yonder Kingdom, silken in robe and golden-crowned and warded by his hound, walked down along the restless waters and sat beside the armpost of her throne, she wondered why she could not love him and fly with him up the shining mountain's side, out of the dirt and dust that nested between the This and Now. She looked at him and tried to be glad, for he was bonny and good to look upon, this king of Yonder Kingdom,—tall and straight, thin-lipped and white and tawny. So, again, this last day, she strove to burn life into his singularly sodden clay,—to put his icy soul aflame wherewith to warm her own, to set his senses singing. Vacantly he heard her winged words, staring and curling his long mustaches with vast thoughtfulness. Then he said:

"We've found more gold in Yonder Kingdom."

"Hell seize your gold!" blurted the princess.

"No,—it's mine," he maintained stolidly.

She raised her eyes. "It belongs," she said, "to the Empire of the Sun."

"Nay,—the Sun belongs to us," said the king calmly as he glanced to where Yonder Kingdom blushed above the sea. She glanced, too, and a softness crept into her eyes.

"No, no," she murmured as with hesitating pause she raised her eyes above the sea, above the hill, up into the sky where the sun hung silent and splendid. Its robes were heaven's blue, lined and broidered in living flame, and its crown was one vast jewel, glistening in glittering glory that made the sun's own face a blackness,—the blackness of utter light. With blinded, tear-filled eyes she peered into that formless black and burning face and sensed in its soft, sad gleam unfathomed understanding. With sudden, wild abandon she stretched her arms toward it appealing, beseeching, entreating, and lo!

"Niggers and dagoes," said the king of Yonder Kingdom, glancing carelessly backward and lighting in his lips a carefully rolled wisp of fragrant tobacco. She looked back, too, but in half-wondering terror, for it seemed—

A beggar man was creeping across the swamp, shuffling through the dirt and slime. He was little and bald and black, rough-clothed, sodden with dirt, and bent with toil. Yet withal something she sensed about him and it seemed,—

521

The king of Yonder Kingdom lounged more comfortably beside the silver throne and let curl a tiny trail of light-blue smoke.

"I hate beggars," he said, "especially brown and black ones." And he then pointed at the beggar's retinue and laughed,—an unpleasant laugh, welded of contempt and amusement. The princess looked and shrank on her throne. He, the beggar man, was—was what? But his retinue,—that squalid, sordid, parti-colored band of vacant, dull-faced filth and viciousness—was writhing over the land, and he and they seemed almost crouching underneath the scorpion lash of one tall skeleton, that looked like Death, and the twisted woman whom men called Pain. Yet they all walked as one.

The king of Yonder Kingdom laughed, but the princess shrank on her throne, and the king on seeing her thus took a gold-piece from out of his purse and tossed it carelessly to the passing throng. She watched it with fascinated eyes,—how it rose and sailed and whirled and struggled in the air, then seemed to burst, and upward flew its light and sheen and downward dropped its dross. She glanced at the king, but he was lighting a match. She watched the dross wallow in the slime, but the sunlight fell on the back of the beggar's neck, and he turned his head.

The beggar passing afar turned his head and the princess straightened on her throne; he turned his head and she shivered forward on her silver seat; he looked upon her full and slow and suddenly she saw within that formless black and burning face the same soft, glad gleam of utter understanding, seen so many times before. She saw the suffering of endless years and endless love that softened it. She saw the burning passion of the sun and with it the cold, unbending duty-deeds of upper air. All she had seen and dreamed of seeing in the rising, blazing sun she saw now again and with it myriads more of human tenderness, of longing, and of love. So, then, she knew. She rose as to a dream come true, with solemn face and waiting eyes.

With her rose the king of Yonder Kingdom, almost eagerly.

"You'll come?" he cried. "You'll come and see my gold?" And then in sudden generosity, he added: "You'll have a golden throne,—up there—when we marry."

But she, looking up and on with radiant face, answered softly: "I come."

So down and up and on they mounted,—the black beggar man and his cavalcade of Death and Pain, and then a space; and then a lone, black hound that nosed and whimpered as he ran, and then a space; and then the king of Yonder Kingdom in his robes, and then a space; and last the princess of the Hither Isles, with face set sunward and lovelight in her eyes.

And so they marched and struggled on and up through endless years and spaces and ever the black beggar looked back past death and pain toward the maid and ever the maid strove forward with lovelit eyes, but ever the great and silken shoulders of the king of Yonder Kingdom arose between the princess and the sun like a cloud of storms.

Now, finally, they neared unto the hillside's topmost shoulder and there most eagerly the king bent to the bowels of the earth and bared its golden entrails,—all green and gray and rusted—while the princess strained her pitiful eyes aloft to where the beggar, set 'twixt Death and Pain, whirled his slim back against the glory of the setting sun and stood somber in his grave majesty, enhaloed and transfigured, outstretching his long arms, and around all heaven glittered jewels in a cloth of gold.

A while the princess stood and moaned in mad amaze, then with one wilful wrench she bared the white flowers of her breast and snatching forth her own red heart held it with one hand aloft while with the other she gathered close her robe and poised herself.

The king of Yonder Kingdom looked upward quickly, curiously, still fingering the earth, and saw the offer of her bleeding heart.

"It's a Negro!" he growled darkly; "it may not be."

The woman quivered.

"It's a nigger!" he repeated fiercely. "It's neither God nor man, but a nigger!"

The princess stepped forward.

The king grasped his sword and looked north and east; he raised his sword and looked south and west.

"I seek the sun," the princess sang, and started into the west.

"Never!" cried the king of Yonder Kingdom, "for such were blasphemy and defilement and the making of all evil."

So, raising his great sword he struck with all his might, and more. Down hissed the blow and it bit that little, white, heart-holding hand until it flew armless and disbodied up through the sunlit air. Down hissed the blow and it clove the whimpering hound until his last shriek shook the stars. Down hissed the blow and it rent the earth. It trembled, fell apart, and yawned to a chasm wide as earth from heaven, deep as hell, and empty, cold, and silent.

On yonder distant shore blazed the mighty Empire of the Sun in warm and blissful radiance, while on this side, in shadows cold and dark, gloomed the Hither Isles and the hill that once was golden, but now was green and slimy dross; all below was the sad and moaning sea, while between the Here and There flew the severed hand and dripped the bleeding heart.

Then up from the soul of the princess welled a cry of dark despair,—such a cry as only babe-raped mothers know and murdered loves. Poised on the crumbling edge of that great nothingness the princess hung, hungering with her eyes and straining her fainting ears against the awful splendor of the sky.

Out from the slime and shadows groped the king, thundering: "Back—don't be a fool!"

But down through the thin ether thrilled the still and throbbing warmth of heaven's sun, whispering "Leap!"

And the princess leapt.

CHAPTER IV

Of Work and Wealth

For fifteen years I was a teacher of youth. They were years out of the fullness and bloom of my younger manhood. They were years mingled of half breathless work, of anxious self-questionings, of planning and replanning, of disillusion, or mounting wonder.

The teacher's life is a double one. He stands in a certain fear. He tends to be stilted, almost dishonest, veiling himself before those awful eyes. Not the eyes of Almighty God are so straight, so penetrating, so all-seeing as the wonder-swept eyes of youth. You walk into a room: to the left is a tall window, bright with colors of crimson and gold and sunshine. Here are rows of books and there is a table. Somber black-boards clothe the walls to the right and beside your desk is the delicate ivory of a nobly cast head. But you see nothing of this: you see only a silence and eyes,—fringed, soft eyes; hard eyes; eyes great and small; eyes here so poignant with beauty that the sob struggles in your throat; eyes there so hard with sorrow that laughter wells up to meet and beat it back; eyes through which the mockery and ridicule of hell or some pulse of high heaven may suddenly flash. Ah! That mighty pause before the class,—that orison and benediction—how much of my life it has been and made.

I fought earnestly against posing before my class. I tried to be natural and honest and frank, but it was bitter hard. What would you say to a soft, brown face, aureoled in a thousand ripples of gray-black hair, which knells suddenly: "Do you trust white people?" You do not and you know that you do not, much as you want to; yet you rise and lie and say you do; you must say it for her salvation and the world's; you repeat that she must trust them, that most white folks are honest, and all the while you are lying and every level, silent eye there knows you are lying, and miserably you sit and lie on, to the greater glory of God.

I taught history and economics and something called "sociology" at Atlanta University, where, as our Mr. Webster used to say, we professors occupied settees and not mere chairs. I was fortunate with this teaching in having vivid in the minds of my pupils a concrete social problem of which we all were parts and which we desperately desired to solve. There was little danger, then, of my teaching or of their thinking becoming purely theoretical. Work and wage were thrilling realities to us all. What did we study? I can tell you best by taking a concrete human case, such as was continually leaping to our eyes and thought and demanding understanding and interpretation and what I could bring of prophecy.

St. Louis sprawls where mighty rivers meet,—as broad as Philadelphia, but three stories high instead of two, with wider streets and dirtier atmosphere, over the dull-brown of wide, calm rivers. The city overflows into the valleys of Illinois and lies there, writhing under its grimy cloud. The other city is dusty and hot beyond all dream,—a feverish Pittsburg in the Mississippi Valley—a great, ruthless, terrible thing! It is the sort that crushes man and invokes some living super-man,—a giant of things done, a clang of awful accomplishment.

Three men came wandering across this place. They were neither kings nor wise men, but they came with every significance—perhaps even greater—than that which the kings bore in the days of old. There was one who came from the North,—brawny and riotous with energy, a man of concentrated power, who held all the thunderbolts of modern capital in his great fists and made flour and meat, iron and steel, cunning chemicals, wood, paint and paper, transforming to endless tools a disemboweled earth. He was one who saw nothing, knew nothing, sought nothing but the making and buying of that which sells; who out from the magic of his hand rolled over miles of iron road, ton upon ton of food and metal and wood, of coal and oil and lumber, until the thronging of knotted ways in East and real St. Louis was like the red, festering ganglia of some mighty heart.

Then from the East and called by the crash of thunderbolts and forked-flame came the Unwise Man,—unwise by the theft of endless ages, but as human as anything God ever made. He was the slave for the miracle maker. It was he that the thunderbolts struck and electrified into gasping energy. The rasp of his hard breathing shook the midnights of all this endless valley and the pulse of his powerful arms set the great nation to trembling.

And then, at last, out of the South, like a still, small voice, came the third man,—black, with great eyes and greater memories; hesitantly eager and yet with the infinite softness and ancient calm which come from that eternal race whose history is not the history of a day, but of endless ages. Here, surely, was fit meeting-place for these curiously intent forces, for these epoch-making and age-twisting forces, for these human feet on their super-human errands.

Yesterday I rode in East St. Louis. It is the kind of place one quickly recognizes,—tireless and with no restful green of verdure; hard and uneven of street; crude, cold, and even hateful of aspect; conventional, of course, in its business quarter, but quickly beyond one sees the ruts and the hollows, the stench of ill-tamed sewerage, unguarded railroad crossings, saloons outnumbering churches and churches catering to saloons; homes impudently strait and new, prostitutes free and happy, gamblers in paradise, the town "wide open," shameless and frank; great factories pouring out stench, filth, and flame—these and all other things so familiar in the world market places, where industry triumphs over thought and products overwhelm men. May I tell, too, how yesterday I rode in this city past flame-swept walls and over gray ashes; in streets almost wet with blood and beside ruins, where the bones of dead men new-bleached peered out at me in sullen wonder?

Across the river, in the greater city, where bronze St. Louis,—that just and austere king—looks with angry, fear-swept eyes down from the rolling heights of Forest Park, which knows him not nor heeds him, there is something of the same thing, but this city is larger and older and the forces of evil have had some curbing from those who have seen the vision and panted for life; but eastward from St. Louis there is a land of no taxes for great industries; there is a land where you may buy grafting politicians at far less rate than you would pay for franchises or privileges in a modern town. There, too, you may escape the buying of indulgences from the great terminal fist, which squeezes industry out of St. Louis. In fact, East St. Louis is a paradise for high and frequent dividends and for the piling up of wealth to be spent in St. Louis and Chicago and New York and when the world is sane again, across the seas.

So the Unwise Men pouring out of the East,—falling, scrambling, rushing into America at the rate of a million a year,—ran, walked, and crawled to this maelstrom of the workers. They garnered higher wage than ever they had before, but not all of it came in cash. A part, and an insidious part, was given to them transmuted into whiskey, prostitutes, and games of chance. They laughed and disported themselves. God! Had not their mothers wept enough? It was a good town. There was no veil of hypocrisy here, but a wickedness, frank, ungilded, and open. To be sure, there were things sometimes to reveal the basic savagery and thin veneer. Once, for instance, a man was lynched for brawling on the public square of the county seat; once a mayor who sought to "clean up" was publicly assassinated; always there was theft and rumors of theft, until St. Clair County was a hissing in good men's ears; but always, too, there were good wages and jolly hoodlums and unchecked wassail of Saturday nights. Gamblers, big and little, rioted in East St. Louis. The little gamblers used cards and roulette wheels and filched the weekly wage of the workers. The greater gamblers used meat and iron and undid the foundations of the world. All the gods of chance flaunted their wild raiment here, above the brown flood of the Mississippi.

Then the world changed; then civilization, built for culture, rebuilt itself for wilful murder in Europe, Asia, America, and the Southern Seas. Hands that made food made powder, and iron for railways was iron for guns. The wants of common men were forgotten before the groan of giants. Streams of gold, lost from the world's workers, filtered and trickled into the hands of gamblers and put new power into the thunderbolts of East St. Louis.

Wages had been growing before the World War. Slowly but remorselessly the skilled and intelligent, banding themselves, had threatened the coffers of the mighty, and slowly the mighty had disgorged. Even the common workers, the poor and unlettered, had again and again gripped the sills of the city walls and pulled themselves to their chins; but, alas! there were so many hands and so many mouths and the feet of the Disinherited kept coming across the wet paths of the sea to this old El Dorado.

War brought subtle changes. Wages stood still while prices fattened. It was not that the white American worker was threatened with starvation, but it was what was, after all, a more important question,— whether or not he should lose his front-room and victrola and even the dream of a Ford car.

There came a whirling and scrambling among the workers,—they fought each other; they climbed on each others' backs. The skilled and intelligent, banding themselves even better than before, bargained with the men of might and held them by bitter threats; the less skilled and more ignorant seethed at the bottom and tried, as of old, to bring it about that the ignorant and unlettered should learn to stand together against both capital and skilled labor.

It was here that there came out of the East a beam of unearthly light,—a triumph of possible good in evil so strange that the workers hardly believed it. Slowly they saw the gates of Ellis Island closing, slowly the footsteps of the yearly million men became fainter and fainter, until the stream of immigrants overseas was stopped by the shadow of death at the very time when new murder opened new markets over all the world to American industry; and the giants with the thunderbolts stamped and raged and peered out across the world and called for men and evermore,—men!

The Unwise Men laughed and squeezed reluctant dollars out of the fists of the mighty and saw in their dream the vision of a day when labor, as they knew it, should come into its own; saw this day and saw it with justice and with right, save for one thing, and that was the sound of the moan of the Disinherited, who still lay without the walls. When they heard this moan and saw that it came not across the seas, they were at first amazed and said it was not true; and then they were mad and said it should not be. Quickly they turned and looked into the red blackness of the South and in their hearts were fear and hate!

What did they see? They saw something at which they had been taught to laugh and make sport; they saw that which the heading of every newspaper column, the lie of every cub reporter, the exaggeration of every press dispatch, and the distortion of every speech and book had taught them was a mass of despicable men, inhuman; at best, laughable; at worst, the meat of mobs and fury.

What did they see? They saw nine and one-half millions of human beings. They saw the spawn of slavery, ignorant by law and by deviltry, crushed by insult and debauched by systematic and criminal injustice. They saw a people whose helpless women have been raped by thousands and whose men lynched by hundreds in the face of a sneering world. They saw a people with heads bloody, but unbowed, working faithfully at wages fifty per cent. lower than the wages of the nation and under conditions which shame civilization, saving homes, training children, hoping against hope. They saw the greatest industrial miracle of modern days,—slaves transforming themselves to freemen and climbing out of perdition by their own efforts, despite the most contemptible opposition God ever saw,—they saw all this and what they saw the distraught employers of America saw, too.

The North called to the South. A scream of rage went up from the cotton monopolists and industrial barons of the new South. Who was this who dared to "interfere" with their labor? Who sought to own their black slaves but they? Who honored and loved "niggers" as they did?

They mobilized all the machinery of modern oppression: taxes, city ordinances, licenses, state laws, municipal regulations, wholesale police arrests and, of course, the peculiarly Southern method of the mob and the lyncher. They appealed frantically to the United States Government; they groveled on their knees and shed wild tears at the "suffering" of their poor, misguided black friends, and yet, despite this, the Northern employers simply had to offer two and three dollars a day and from one-quarter to one-half a million dark workers arose and poured themselves into the North. They went to the mines of West Virginia, because war needs coal; they went to the industries of New Jersey and Pennsylvania, because war needs ships and iron; they went to the automobiles of Detroit and the load-carrying of Chicago; and they went to East St. Louis.

Now there came fear in the hearts of the Unwise Men. It was not that their wages were lowered,—they went even higher. They received, not simply a living wage, but a wage that paid for some of the decencies, and, in East St. Louis, many of the indecencies of life. What they feared was not deprivation of the things they were used to and the shadow of poverty, but rather the definite death of their rising dreams. But if fear was new-born in the hearts of the Unwise Men, the black man was born in a house of fear; to him poverty of the ulgiest and straitest type was father, mother, and blood-brother. He was slipping stealthily northward to escape hunger and insult, the hand of oppression, and the shadow of death.

Here, then, in the wide valley which Father Marquette saw peaceful and golden, lazy with fruit and river, half-asleep beneath the nod of God,—here, then, was staged every element for human tragedy, every element of the modern economic paradox.

Ah! That hot, wide plain of East St. Louis is a gripping thing. The rivers are dirty with sweat and toil and lip, like lakes, along the low and burdened shores; flatboats ramble and thread among them, and above the steamers bridges swing on great arches of steel, striding with mighty grace from shore to shore. Everywhere are brick kennels,—tall, black and red chimneys, tongues of flame. The ground is littered with cars and iron, tracks and trucks, boxes and crates, metals and coal and rubber. Nature-defying cranes, grim elevators rise above pile on pile of black and grimy lumber. And ever below is the water,—wide and silent, gray-brown and yellow.

This is the stage for the tragedy: the armored might of the modern world urged by the bloody needs of the world wants, fevered today by a fabulous vision of gain and needing only hands, hands, hands! Fear of loss and greed of gain in the hearts of the giants; the clustered cunning of the modern workman, skilled as artificer and skilled in the rhythm of the habit of work, tasting the world's good and panting for more; fear of poverty and hate of "scabs" in the hearts of the workers; the dumb yearning in the hearts of the workers; the dumb yearning in the hearts of the oppressed; the echo of laughter heard at the foot of the Pyramids; the faithful, plodding slouch of the laborers; fear of the Shadow of Death in the hearts of black men.

We ask, and perhaps there is no answer, how far may the captain of the world's industry do his deeds, despite the grinding tragedy of its doing? How far may men fight for the beginning of comfort, out beyond the horrid shadow of poverty, at the cost of starving other and what the world calls lesser men? How far may those who reach up out of the slime that fills the pits of the world's damned compel men with loaves to divide with men who starve?

The answers to these questions are hard, but yet one answer looms above all,—justice lies with the lowest; the plight of the lowest man,—the plight of the black man—deserves the first answer, and the plight of the giants of industry, the last.

Little cared East St. Louis for all this bandying of human problems, so long as its grocers and saloon-keepers flourished and its industries steamed and screamed and smoked and its bankers grew rich. Stupidity, license, and graft sat enthroned in the City Hall. The new black folk were exploited as cheerfully as white Polacks and Italians; the rent of shacks mounted merrily, the street car lines counted gleeful gains, and the crimes of white men and black men flourished in the dark. The high and skilled and smart climbed on the bent backs of the ignorant; harder the mass of laborers strove to unionize their fellows and to bargain with employers.

Nor were the new blacks fools. They had no love for nothings in labor; they had no wish to make their fellows' wage envelopes smaller, but they were determined to make their own larger. They, too, were willing to join in the new union movement. But the unions did not want them. Just as employers monopolized meat and steel, so they sought to monopolize labor and beat a giant's bargain. In the higher trades they succeeded. The best electrician in the city was refused admittance to the union and driven from the town because he was black. No black builder, printer, or machinist could join a union or work in East St. Louis, no matter what his skill or character. But out of the stink of the stockyards and the dust of the aluminum works and the sweat of the lumber yards the willing blacks could not be kept.

They were invited to join unions of the laborers here and they joined. White workers and black workers struck at the aluminum works in the fall and won higher wages and better hours; then again in the spring they struck to make bargaining compulsory for the employer, but this time they fronted new things. The conflagration of war had spread to America; government and court stepped in and ordered no hesitation, no strikes; the work must go on.

Deeper was the call for workers. Black men poured in and red anger flamed in the hearts of the white workers. The anger was against the wielders of the thunderbolts, but here it was impotent because employers stood with the hand of the government before their faces; it was against entrenched union labor, which had risen on the backs of the unskilled and unintelligent and on the backs of those whom for any reason of race or prejudice or chicane they could beat beyond the bars of competition; and finally the anger of the mass of white workers was turned toward these new black interlopers, who seemed to come to spoil their last dream of a great monopoly of common labor.

These angers flamed and the union leaders, fearing their fury and knowing their own guilt, not only in the larger and subtler matter of bidding their way to power across the weakness of their less fortunate fellows, but also conscious of their part in making East St. Louis a miserable town of liquor and lust, leaped quickly to ward the gathering thunder from their own heads. The thing they wanted was even at their hands: here were black men, guilty not only of bidding for jobs which white men could have held at war prices, even if they could not fill, but also guilty of being black! It was at this blackness that the unions pointed the accusing finger. It was here that they committed the unpardonable crime. It was here that they entered the Shadow of Hell, where suddenly from a fight for wage and protection against industrial oppression East St. Louis became the center of the oldest and nastiest form of human oppression,—race hatred.

The whole situation lent itself to this terrible transformation. Everything in the history of the United States, from slavery to Sunday supplements, from disfranchisement to residence segregation, from "Jim-Crow" cars to a "Jim-Crow" army draft—all this history of discrimination and insult festered to make men think and willing to think that the venting of their unbridled anger against 12,000,000 humble, upstriving workers was a way of settling the industrial tangle of the ages. It was the logic of the broken plate, which, seared of old across its pattern, cracks never again, save along the old destruction.

So hell flamed in East St. Louis! The white men drove even black union men out of their unions and when the black men, beaten by night and assaulted, flew to arms and shot back at the marauders, five thousand rioters arose and surged like a crested storm-wave, from noonday until midnight; they killed and beat and murdered; they dashed out the brains of children and stripped off the clothes of women; they drove victims into the flames and hanged the helpless to the lighting poles. Fathers were killed before the faces of mothers; children were burned; heads were cut off with axes; pregnant women crawled and spawned in dark, wet fields; thieves went through houses and firebrands followed; bodies were thrown from bridges; and rocks and bricks flew through the air.

The Negroes fought. They grappled with the mob like beasts at bay. They drove them back from the thickest cluster of their homes and piled the white dead on the street, but the cunning mob caught the black men between the factories and their homes, where they knew they were armed only with their dinner pails. Firemen, policemen, and militiamen stood with hanging hands or even joined eagerly with the mob.

It was the old world horror come to life again: all that Jews suffered in Spain and Poland; all that peasants suffered in France, and Indians in Calcutta; all that aroused human deviltry had accomplished in ages past they did in East St. Louis, while the rags of six thousand half-naked black men and women fluttered across the bridges of the calm Mississippi.

The white South laughed,—it was infinitely funny—the "niggers" who had gone North to escape slavery and lynching had met the fury of the mob which they had fled. Delegations rushed North from Mississippi and Texas, with suspicious timeliness and with great-hearted offers to take these workers back to a lesser hell. The man from Greensville, Mississippi, who wanted a thousand got six, because, after all, the end was not so simple.

No, the end was not simple. On the contrary, the problem raised by East St. Louis was curiously complex. The ordinary American, tired of the persistence of "the Negro problem," sees only another anti-Negro mob and wonders, not when we shall settle this problem, but when we shall be well rid of it. The student of social things sees another mile-post in the triumphant march of union labor; he is sorry that blood and rapine should mark its march,—but, what will you? War is life!

Despite these smug reasonings the bare facts were these: East St. Louis, a great industrial center, lost 5,000 laborers,—good, honest, hard-working laborers. It was not the criminals, either black or white, who were driven from East St. Louis. They are still there. They will stay there. But half the honest black laborers were gone. The crippled ranks of industrial organization in the mid-Mississippi Valley cannot be recruited from Ellis Island, because in Europe men are dead and maimed, and restoration, when restoration comes, will raise a European demand for labor such as this age has never seen. The vision of industrial supremacy has come to the giants who lead American industry and finance. But it can never be realized unless the laborers are here to do the work,—the skilled laborers, the common laborers, the willing laborers, the well-paid laborers. The present forces, organized however cunningly, are not large enough to do what America wants; but there is another group of laborers, 12,000,000 strong, the natural heirs, by every logic of justice, to the fruits of America's industrial advance. They will be used simply because they must be used,—but their using means East St. Louis!

Eastward from St. Louis lie great centers, like Chicago, Indianapolis, Detroit, Cleveland, Pittsburg, Philadelphia, and New York; in every one of these and in lesser centers there is not only the industrial unrest of war and revolutionized work, but there is the call for workers, the coming of black folk, and the deliberate effort to divert the thoughts of men, and particularly of workingmen, into channels of race hatred against blacks. In every one of these centers what happened in East St. Louis has been attempted, with more or less success. Yet the American Negroes stand today as the greatest strategic group in the world. Their services are indispensable, their temper and character are fine, and their souls have seen a vision more beautiful than any other mass of workers. They may win back culture to the world if their strength can be used with the forces of the world that make for justice and not against the hidden hates that fight for barbarism. For fight they must and fight they will!

Rising on wings we cross again the rivers of St. Louis, winding and threading between the towers of industry that threaten and drown the towers of God. Far, far beyond, we sight the green of fields and hills; but ever below lies the river, blue,—brownish-gray, touched with the hint of hidden gold. Drifting through half-flooded lowlands, with shanties and crops and stunted trees, past struggling corn and straggling village, we rush toward the Battle of the Marne and the West, from this dread Battle of the East. Westward, dear God, the fire of Thy Mad World crimsons our Heaven. Our answering Hell rolls eastward from St. Louis.

Here, in microcosm, is the sort of economic snarl that arose continually for me and my pupils to solve. We could bring to its unraveling little of the scholarly aloofness and academic calm of most white universities. To us this thing was Life and Hope and Death!

How should we think such a problem through, not simply as Negroes, but as men and women of a new century, helping to build a new world? And first of all, here is no simple question of race antagonism. There are no races, in the sense of great, separate, pure breeds of men, differing in attainment, development, and capacity. There are great groups,—now with common history, now with common interests, now with common ancestry; more and more common experience and present interest drive back the common blood and the world today consists, not of races, but of the imperial commercial group of master capitalists, international and predominantly white; the national middle classes of the several nations, white, yellow, and brown, with strong blood bonds, common languages, and common history; the international laboring class of all colors; the backward, oppressed groups of nature-folk, predominantly yellow, brown, and black.

Two questions arise from the work and relations of these groups: how to furnish goods and services for the wants of men and how equitably and sufficiently to satisfy these wants. There can be no doubt that we have passed in our day from a world that could hardly satisfy the physical wants of the mass of men, by the greatest effort, to a world whose technique supplies enough for all, if all can claim their right. Our great ethical question today is, therefore, how may we justly distribute the world's goods to satisfy the necessary wants of the mass of men.

What hinders the answer to this question? Dislikes, jealousies, hatreds,—undoubtedly like the race hatred in East St. Louis; the jealousy of English and German; the dislike of the Jew and the Gentile. But these are, after all, surface disturbances, sprung from ancient habit more than from present reason. They persist and are encouraged because of deeper, mightier currents. If the white workingmen of East St. Louis felt sure that Negro workers would not and could not take the bread and cake from their mouths, their race hatred would never have been translated into murder. If the black workingmen of the South could earn a decent living under decent circumstances at home, they would not be compelled to underbid their white fellows.

Thus the shadow of hunger, in a world which never needs to be hungry, drives us to war and murder and hate. But why does hunger shadow so vast a mass of men? Manifestly because in the great organizing of men for work a few of the participants come out with more wealth than they can possibly use, while a vast number emerge with less than can decently support life. In earlier economic stages we defended this as the reward of Thrift and Sacrifice, and as the punishment of Ignorance and Crime. To this the answer is sharp: Sacrifice calls for no such reward and Ignorance deserves no such punishment. The chief meaning of our present thinking is that the disproportion between wealth and poverty today cannot be adequately accounted for by the thrift and ignorance of the rich and the poor.

Yesterday we righted one great mistake when we realized that the ownership of the laborer did not tend to increase production. The world at large had learned this long since, but black slavery arose again in America as an inexplicable anachronism, a wilful crime. The freeing of the black slaves freed America. Today we are challenging another ownership,—the ownership of materials which go to make the goods we need. Private ownership of land, tools, and raw materials may at one stage of economic development be a method of stimulating production and one which does not greatly interfere with equitable distribution. When, however, the intricacy and length of technical production increased, the ownership of these things becomes a monopoly, which easily makes the rich richer and the poor poorer. Today, therefore, we are challenging this ownership; we are demanding general consent as to what materials shall be privately owned and as to how materials shall be used. We are rapidly approaching the day when we shall repudiate all private property in raw materials and tools and demand that distribution hinge, not on the power of those who monopolize the materials, but on the needs of the mass of men.

Can we do this and still make sufficient goods, justly gauge the needs of men, and rightly decide who are to be considered "men"? How do we arrange to accomplish these things today? Somebody decides whose wants should be satisfied. Somebody organizes industry so as to satisfy these wants. What is to hinder the same ability and foresight from being used in the future as in the past? The amount and kind of human ability necessary need not be decreased,—it may even be vastly increased, with proper encouragement and rewards. Are we today evoking the necessary ability? On the contrary, it is not the Inventor, the Manager, and the Thinker who today are reaping the great rewards of industry, but rather the Gambler and the Highwayman. Rightly-organized industry might easily save the Gambler's Profit and the Monopolist's Interest and by paying a more discriminating reward in wealth and honor bring to the service of the state more ability and sacrifice than we can today command. If we do away with interest and profit, consider the savings that could be made; but above all, think how great the revolution would be when we ask the mysterious Somebody to decide in the light of public opinion whose wants should be satisfied. This is the great and real revolution that is coming in future industry.

But this is not the end of the revolution nor indeed, perhaps, its real beginning. What we must decide sometime is who are to be considered "men." Today, at the beginning of this industrial change, we are admitting that economic classes must give way. The laborers' hire must increase, the employers' profit must be curbed. But how far shall this change go? Must it apply to all human beings and to all work throughout the world?

Certainly not. We seek to apply it slowly and with some reluctance to white men and more slowly and with greater reserve to white women, but black folk and brown and for the most part yellow folk we have widely determined shall not be among those whose needs must justly be heard and whose wants must be ministered to in the great organization of world industry.

In the teaching of my classes I was not willing to stop with showing that this was unfair,—indeed I did not have to do this. They knew through bitter experience its rank injustice, because they were black. What I had to show was that no real reorganization of industry could be permanently made with the majority of mankind left out. These disinherited darker peoples must either share in the future industrial democracy or overturn the world.

Of course, the foundation of such a system must be a high, ethical ideal. We must really envisage the wants of humanity. We must want the wants of all men. We must get rid of the fascination for exclusiveness. Here, in a world full of folk, men are lonely. The rich are lonely. We are all frantic for fellow-souls, yet we shut souls out and bar the ways and bolster up the fiction of the Elect and the Superior when the great mass of men is capable of producing larger and larger numbers for every human height of attainment. To be sure, there are differences between men and groups and there will ever be, but they will be differences of beauty and genius and of interest and not necessarily of ugliness, imbecility, and hatred.

The meaning of America is the beginning of the discovery of the Crowd. The crowd is not so well-trained as a Versailles garden party of Louis XIV, but it is far better trained than the Sans-culottes and it has infinite possibilities. What a world this will be when human possibilities are freed, when we discover each other, when the stranger is no longer the potential criminal and the certain inferior!

What hinders our approach to the ideals outlined above? Our profit from degradation, our colonial exploitation, our American attitude toward the Negro. Think again of East St. Louis! Think back of that to slavery and Reconstruction! Do we want the wants of American Negroes satisfied? Most certainly not, and that negative is the greatest hindrance today to the reorganization of work and redistribution of wealth, not only in America, but in the world.

All humanity must share in the future industrial democracy of the world. For this it must be trained in intelligence and in appreciation of the good and the beautiful. Present Big Business,—that Science of Human Wants—must be perfected by eliminating the price paid for waste, which is Interest, and for Chance, which is Profit, and making all income a personal wage for service rendered by the recipient; by recognizing no possible human service as great enough to enable a person to designate another as an idler or as a worker at work which he cannot do. Above all, industry must minister to the wants of the many and not to the few, and the Negro, the Indian, the Mongolian, and the South Sea Islander must be among the many as well as Germans, Frenchmen, and Englishmen.

In this coming socialization of industry we must guard against that same tyranny of the majority that has marked democracy in the making of laws. There must, for instance, persist in this future economics a certain minimum of machine-like work and prompt obedience and submission. This necessity is a simple corollary from the hard facts of the physical world. It must be accepted with the comforting thought that its routine need not demand twelve hours a day or even eight. With Work for All and All at Work probably from three to six hours would suffice, and leave abundant time for leisure, exercise, study, and avocations.

But what shall we say of work where spiritual values and social distinctions enter? Who shall be Artists and who shall be Servants in the world to come? Or shall we all be artists and all serve?

The Second Coming

Three bishops sat in San Francisco, New Orleans, and New York, peering gloomily into three flickering fires, which cast and recast shuddering shadows on book-lined walls. Three letters lay in their laps, which said:

"And thou, Valdosta, in the land of Georgia, art not least among the princes of America, for out of thee shall come a governor who shall rule my people."

The white bishop of New York scowled and impatiently threw the letter into the fire. "Valdosta?" he thought,—"That's where I go to the governor's wedding of little Marguerite, my white flower,—" Then he forgot the writing in his musing, but the paper flared red in the fireplace.

"Valdosta?" said the black bishop of New Orleans, turning uneasily in his chair. "I must go down there. Those colored folk are acting strangely. I don't know where all this unrest and moving will lead to. Then, there's poor Lucy—" And he threw the letter into the fire, but eyed it suspiciously as it flamed green. "Stranger things than that have happened," he said slowly, " 'and ye shall hear of wars and rumors of wars . . . for nation shall rise against nation and kingdom against kingdom.' "

In San Francisco the priest of Japan, abroad to study strange lands, sat in his lacquer chair, with face like soft-yellow and wrinkled parchment. Slowly he wrote in a great and golden book: "I have been strangely bidden to the Val d' Osta, where one of those religious cults that swarm here will welcome a prophet. I shall go and report to Kioto."

So in the dim waning of the day before Christmas three bishops met in Valdosta and saw its mills and storehouses, its wide-throated and sandy streets, in the mellow glow of a crimson sun. The governor glared anxiously up the street as he helped the bishop of New York into his car and welcomed him graciously.

"I am troubled," said the governor, "about the niggers. They are acting queerly. I'm not certain but Fleming is back of it."

"Fleming?"

"Yes! He's running against me next term for governor; he's a fire-brand; wants niggers to vote and all that—pardon me a moment, there's a darky I know—" and he hurried to the black bishop, who had just descended from the "Jim-Crow" car, and clasped his hand cordially. They talked in whispers. "Search diligently," said the governor in parting, "and bring me word again." Then returning to his guest, "You will excuse me, won't you?" he asked, "but I am sorely troubled! I never saw niggers act so. They're leaving by the hundreds and those who stay are getting impudent! They seem to be expecting something. What's the crowd, Jim?"

The chauffeur said that there was some sort of Chinese official in town and everybody wanted to glimpse him. He drove around another way.

It all happened very suddenly. The bishop of New York, in full canonicals for the early wedding, stepped out on the rear balcony of his mansion, just as the dying sun lit crimson clouds of glory in the East and burned the West.

"Fire!" yelled a wag in the surging crowd that was gathering to celebrate a southern Christmas-eve; all laughed and ran.

The bishop of New York did not understand. He peered around. Was it that dark, little house in the far backyard that flamed? Forgetful of his robes he hurried down,—a brave, white figure in the sunset. He found himself before an old, black, rickety stable. He could hear the mules stamping within.

No. It was not fire. It was the sunset glowing through the cracks. Behind the hut its glory rose toward God like flaming wings of cherubim. He paused until he heard the faint wail of a child. Hastily he entered. A white girl crouched before him, down by the very mules' feet, with a baby in her arms,—a little mite of a baby that wailed weakly. Behind mother and child stood a shadow. The bishop of New York turned to the right, inquiringly, and saw a black man in bishop's robes that faintly re-echoed his own. He turned away to the left and saw a golden Japanese in golden garb. Then he heard the black man mutter behind him: "But He was to come the second time in clouds of glory, with the nations gathered around Him and angels—" at the word a shaft of glorious light fell full upon the child, while without came the tramping of unnumbered feet and the whirring of wings.

The bishop of New York bent quickly over the baby. *It was black!* He stepped back with a gesture of disgust, hardly listening to and yet hearing the black bishop, who spoke almost as if in apology:

"She's not really white; I know Lucy—you see, her mother worked for the governor—" The white bishop turned on his heel and nearly trod on the yellow priest, who knelt with bowed head before the pale mother and offered incense and a gift of gold.

Out into the night rushed the bishop of New York. The wings of the cherubim were folded black against the stars. As he hastened down the front staircase the governor came rushing up the street steps.

"We are late!" he cried nervously. "The bride awaits!" He hurried the bishop to the waiting limousine, asking him anxiously: "Did you hear anything? Do you hear that noise? The crowd is growing strangely on the streets and there seems to be a fire over toward the East. I never saw so many people here—I fear violence—a mob—a lynching—I fear—hark!"

What was that which he, too, heard beneath the rhythm of unnumbered feet? Deep in his heart a wonder grew. What was it? Ah, he knew! It was music,—some strong and mighty chord. It rose higher as the brilliantly-lighted church split the night, and swept radiantly toward them. So high and clear that music flew, it seemed above, around, behind them. The governor, ashen-faced, crouched in the car; but the bishop said softly as the ecstasy pulsed in his heart:

"Such music, such wedding music! What choir is it?"

CHAPTER V

"The Servant in the House"

The lady looked at me severely; I glanced away. I had addressed the little audience at some length on the disfranchisement of my people in society, politics, and industry and had studiously avoided the while her cold, green eye. I finished and shook weary hands, while she lay in wait. I knew what was coming and braced my soul.

"Do you know where I can get a good colored cook?" she asked.

I disclaimed all guilty concupiscence. She came nearer and spitefully shook a finger in my face.

"Why—won't—Negroes—work!" she panted. "I have given money for years to Hampton and Tuskegee and yet I can't get decent servants. They won't try. They're lazy! They're unreliable! They're impudent and they leave without notice. They all want to be lawyers and doctors and" (she spat the word in venom) "ladies!"

"God forbid!" I answered solemnly, and then being of gentle birth and unminded to strike a defenseless female of uncertain years, I ran; I ran home and wrote a chapter in my book and this is it.

I speak and speak bitterly as a servant and a servant's son, for my mother spent five or more years of her life as a menial; my father's family escaped, although grandfather as a boat steward had to fight hard to be a man and not a lackey. He fought and won. My mother's folk, however, during my childhood, sat poised on that thin edge between the farmer and the menial. The surrounding Irish had two chances, the factory and the kitchen, and most of them took the factory, with all its dirt and noise and low wage. The factory was closed to us. Our little lands were too small to feed most of us. A few clung almost sullenly to the old homes, low and red things crouching on a wide level; but the children stirred restlessly and walked often to town and saw its wonders. Slowly they dribbled off,—a waiter here, a cook there, help for a few weeks in Mrs. Blank's kitchen when she had summer boarders.

Instinctively I hated such work from my birth. I loathed it and shrank from it. Why? I could not have said. Had I been born in Carolina instead of Massachusetts I should hardly have escaped the taint of "service." Its temptations in wage and comfort would soon have answered my scruples; and yet I am sure I would have fought long even in Carolina, for I knew in my heart that thither lay Hell.

I mowed lawns on contract, did "chores" that left me my own man, sold papers, and peddled tea—anything to escape the shadow of the awful thing that lurked to grip my soul. Once, and once only, I felt the sting of its talons. I was twenty and had graduated from Fisk with a scholarship for Harvard; I needed, however, travel money and clothes and a bit to live on until the scholarship was due. Fortson was a fellow-student in winter and a waiter in summer. He proposed that the Glee Club Quartet of Fisk spend the summer at the hotel in Minnesota where he worked and that I go along as "Business Manager" to arrange for engagements on the journey back. We were all eager, but we knew nothing of table-waiting. "Never mind," said Fortson, "you can stand around the dining-room during meals and carry out the big wooden trays of dirty dishes. Thus you can pick up knowledge of waiting and earn good tips and get free board." I listened askance, but I went.

I entered that broad and blatant hotel at Lake Minnetonka with distinct forebodings. The flamboyant architecture, the great verandas, rich furniture, and richer dresses awed us mightily. The long loft reserved for us, with its clean little cots, was reassuring; the work was not difficult,—but the meals! There were no meals. At first, before the guests ate, a dirty table in the kitchen was hastily strewn with uneatable scraps. We novices were the only ones who came to eat, while the guests' dining-room, with its savors and sights, set our appetites on edge! After a while even the pretense of meals for us was dropped. We were sure we were going to starve when Dug, one of us, made a startling discovery: the waiters stole their food and they stole the best. We gulped and hesitated. Then we stole, too, (or, at least, they stole and I shared) and we all fattened, for the dainties were marvelous. You slipped a bit here and hid it there; you cut off extra portions and gave false orders; you dashed off into darkness and hid in corners and ate and ate! It was nasty business. I hated it. I was too cowardly to steal much myself, and not coward enough to refuse what others stole.

Our work was easy, but insipid. We stood about and watched overdressed people gorge. For the most part we were treated like furniture and were supposed to act the wooden part. I watched the waiters even more than the guests. I saw that it paid to amuse and to cringe. One particular black man set me crazy. He was intelligent and deft, but one day I caught sight of his face as he served a crowd of men; he was playing the clown,—crouching, grinning, assuming a broad dialect when he usually spoke good English—ah! it was a heartbreaking sight, and he made more money than any waiter in the dining-room.

I did not mind the actual work or the kind of work, but it was the dishonesty and deception, the flattery and cajolery, the unnatural assumption that worker and diner had no common humanity. It was uncanny. It was inherently and fundamentally wrong. I stood staring and thinking, while the other boys hustled about. Then I noticed one fat hog, feeding at a heavily gilded trough, who could not find his waiter. He beckoned me. It was not his voice, for his mouth was too full. It was his way, his air, his assumption. Thus Caesar ordered his legionaries or Cleopatra her slaves. Dogs recognized the gesture. I did not. He may be beckoning yet for all I know, for something froze within me. I did not look his way again. Then and there I disowned menial service for me and my people.

I would work my hands off for an honest wage, but for "tips" and "hand-me-outs," never! Fortson was a pious, honest fellow, who regarded "tips" as in the nature of things, being to the manner born; but the hotel that summer in other respects rather astonished even him. He came to us much flurried one night and got us to help him with a memorial to the absentee proprietor, telling of the wild and gay doings of midnights in the rooms and corridors among "tired" business men and their prostitutes. We listened wide-eyed and eager and wrote the filth out manfully. The proprietor did not thank Fortson. He did not even answer the letter.

When I finally walked out of that hotel and out of menial service forever, I felt as though, in a field of flowers, my nose had been held unpleasantly long to the worms and manure at their roots.

"Cursed be Canaan!" cried the Hebrew priests. "A servant of servants shall he be unto his brethren." With what characteristic complacency did the slaveholders assume that Canaanites were Negroes and their "brethren" white? Are not Negroes servants? *Ergo!* Upon such spiritual myths was the anachronism of American slavery built, and this was the degradation that once made menial servants the aristocrats among colored folk. House servants secured some decencies of food and clothing and shelter; they could more easily reach their master's ear; their personal abilities of character became known and bonds grew between slave and master which strengthened from friendship to love, from mutual service to mutual blood.

Naturally out of this the West Indian servant climbed out of slavery into citizenship, for few West Indian masters—fewer Spanish or Dutch—were callous enough to sell their own children into slavery. Not so with English and Americans. With a harshness and indecency seldom paralleled in the civilized world white masters on the mainland sold their mulatto children, half-brothers and half-sisters, and their own wives in all but name, into life-slavery by the hundreds and thousands. They originated a special branch of slave-trading for this trade and the white aristocrats of Virginia and the Carolinas made more money by this business during the eighteenth and nineteenth centuries than in any other way.

The clang of the door of opportunity thus knelled in the ears of the colored house servant whirled the whole face of Negro advancement as on some great pivot. The movement was slow, but vast. When emancipation came, before and after 1863, the house servant still held advantages. He had whatever education the race possessed and his white father, no longer able to sell him, often helped him with land and protection. Notwithstanding this the lure of house service for the Negro was gone. The path of salvation for the emancipated host of black folk lay no longer through the kitchen door, with its wide hall and pillared veranda and flowered yard beyond. It lay, as every Negro soon knew and knows, in escape from menial serfdom.

In 1860, 98 per cent of the Negroes were servants and serfs. In 1880, 30 per cent were servants and 65 per cent were serfs. The percentage of servants then rose slightly and fell again until 21 per cent were in service in 1910 and, doubtless, much less than 20 per cent today. This is the measure of our rise, but the Negro will not approach freedom until this hateful badge of slavery and mediaevalism has been reduced to less than 10 per cent.

Not only are less than a fifth of our workers servants today, but the character of their service has been changed. The million menial workers among us include 300,000 upper servants,—skilled men and women of character, like hotel waiters, Pullman porters, janitors, and cooks, who, had they been white, could have called on the great labor movement to lift their work out of slavery, to standardize their hours, to define their duties, and to substitute a living, regular wage for personal largess in the shape of tips, old clothes, and cold leavings of food. But the labor movement turned their backs on those black men when the white world dinned in their ears. *Negroes are servants; servants are Negroes.* They shut the door of escape to factory and trade in their fellows' faces and battened down the hatches, lest the 300,000 should be workers equal in pay and consideration with white men.

But, if the upper servants could not escape to modern, industrial conditions, how much the more did they press down on the bodies and souls of 700,000 washerwomen and household drudges,—ignorant, unskilled offal of a millionaire industrial system. Their pay was the lowest and their hours the longest of all workers. The personal degradation of their work is so great that any white man of decency would rather cut his daughter's throat than let her grow up to such a destiny. There is throughout the world and in all races no greater source of prostitution than this grade of menial service, and the Negro race in America has largely escaped this destiny simply because its innate decency leads black women to choose irregular and temporary sexual relations with men they like rather than to sell themselves to strangers. To such sexual morals is added (in the nature of self-defense) that revolt against unjust labor conditions which expresses itself in "soldiering," sullenness, petty pilfering, unreliability, and fast and fruitless changes of masters.

Indeed, here among American Negroes we have exemplified the last and worst refuge of industrial caste. Menial service is an anachronism,—the refuse of mediaeval barbarism. Why, then, does it linger? Why are we silent about it? Why in the minds of so many decent and up-seeing folks does the whole Negro problem resolve itself into the matter of their getting a cook or a maid?

No one knows better than I the capabilities of a system of domestic service at its best. I have seen children who were spiritual sons and daughters of their masters, girls who were friends of their mistresses, and old servants honored and revered. But in every such case the Servant had transcended the Menial, the Service had been exalted above the Wage. Now to accomplish this permanently and universally, calls for the same revolution in household help as in factory help and public service. While organized industry has been slowly making its help into self-respecting, well-paid men, and while public service is beginning to call for the highest types of educated and efficient thinkers, domestic service lags behind and insists upon seeking to evolve the best types of men from the worst conditions.

The cause of this perversity, to my mind, is twofold. First, the ancient high estate of Service, now pitifully fallen, yet gasping for breath; secondly, the present low estate of the outcasts of the world, peering with blood-shot eyes at the gates of the industrial heaven.

The Master spoke no greater word than that which said: "Whosoever will be great among you, let him be your servant!" What is greater than Personal Service! Surely no social service, no wholesale helping of masses of men can exist which does not find its effectiveness and beauty in the personal aid of man to man. It is the purest and holiest of duties. Some mighty glimmer of this truth survived in those who made the First Gentlemen of the Bedchamber, the Keepers of the Robes, and the Knights of the Bath, the highest nobility that hedged an anointed king. Nor does it differ today in what the mother does for the child or the daughter for the mother, in all the personal attentions in the old-fashioned home; this is Service! Think of what Friend has meant, not simply in spiritual sympathies, but in physical helpfulness. In the world today what calls for more of love, sympathy, learning, sacrifice, and long-suffering than the care of children, the preparation of food, the cleansing and ordering of the home, personal attendance and companionship, the care of bodies and their raiment—what greater, more intimate, more holy Services are there than these?

And yet we are degrading these services and loathing them and scoffing at them and spitting upon them, first, by turning them over to the lowest and least competent and worst trained classes in the world, and then by yelling like spoiled children if our babies are neglected, our biscuits sodden, our homes dirty, and our baths unpoured. Let one suggest that the only cure for such deeds is in the uplift of the doer and our rage is even worse and less explicable. We will call them by their first names, thus blaspheming a holy intimacy; we will confine them to back doors; we will insist that their meals be no gracious ceremony nor even a restful sprawl, but usually a hasty, heckled gulp amid garbage; we exact, not a natural, but a purchased deference, and we leave them naked to insult by our children and by our husbands.

I remember a girl,—how pretty she was, with the crimson flooding the old ivory of her cheeks and her gracious plumpness! She had come to the valley during the summer to "do housework." I met and walked home with her, in the thrilling shadows, to an old village home I knew well; then as I turned to leave I learned that she was there alone in that house for a week-end with only one young white man to represent the family. Oh, he was doubtless a "gentleman" and all that, but for the first time in my life I saw what a snare the fowler was spreading at the feet of the daughters of my people, baited by church and state.

Not alone is the hurt thus offered to the lowly,—Society and Science suffer. The unit which we seek to make the center of society,—the Home—is deprived of the help of scientific invention and suggestion. It is only slowly and by the utmost effort that some small foothold has been gained for the vacuum cleaner, the washing-machine, the power tool, and the chemical reagent. In our frantic effort to preserve the last vestiges of slavery and mediaevalism we not only set our faces against such improvements, but we seek to use education and the power of the state to train the servants who do not naturally appear.

Meantime the wild rush from house service, on the part of all who can scramble or run, continues. The rules of the labor union are designed, not simply to raise wages, but to guard against any likeness between artisan and servant. There is no essential difference in ability and training between a subway guard and a Pullman porter, but between their union cards lies a whole world.

Yet we are silent. Menial service is not a "social problem." It is not really discussed. There is no scientific program for its "reform." There is but one panacea: Escape! Get yourselves and your sons and daughters out of the shadow of this awful thing! Hire servants, but never be one. Indeed, subtly but surely the ability to hire at least "a maid" is still civilization's patent to respectability, while "a man" is the first word of aristocracy.

All this is because we still consciously and unconsciously hold to the "manure" theory of social organization. We believe that at the bottom of organized human life there are necessary duties and services which no real human being ought to be compelled to do. We push below this mudsill the derelicts and half-men, whom we hate and despise, and seek to build above it—Democracy! On such foundations is reared a Theory of Exclusiveness, a feeling that the world progresses by a process of excluding from the benefits of culture the majority of men, so that a gifted minority may blossom. Through this door the modern democrat arrives to the place where he is willing to allot two able-bodied men and two fine horses to the task of helping one wizened beldam to take the morning air.

Here the absurdity ends. Here all honest minds turn back and ask: Is menial service permanent or necessary? Can we not transfer cooking from the home to the scientific laboratory, along with the laundry? Cannot machinery, in the hands of self-respecting and well-paid artisans, do our cleaning, sewing, moving, and decorating? Cannot the training of children become an even greater profession than the attending of the sick? And cannot personal service and companionship be coupled with friendship and love where it belongs and whence it can never be divorced without degradation and pain?

In fine, can we not, black and white, rich and poor, look forward to a world of Service without Servants?

A miracle! you say? True. And only to be performed by the Immortal Child.

Jesus Christ in Texas

It was in Waco, Texas.

The convict guard laughed. "I don't know," he said, "I hadn't thought of that." He hesitated and looked at the stranger curiously. In the solemn twilight he got an impression of unusual height and soft, dark eyes. "Curious sort of acquaintance for the colonel," he thought; then he continued aloud: "But that nigger there is bad, a born thief, and ought to be sent up for life; got ten years last time—"

Here the voice of the promoter, talking within, broke in; he was bending over his figures, sitting by the colonel. He was slight, with a sharp nose.

"The convicts," he said, "would cost us $96 a year and board. Well, we can squeeze this so that it won't be over $125 apiece. Now if these fellows are driven, they can build this line within twelve months. It will be running by next April. Freights will fall fifty per cent. Why, man, you'll be a millionaire in less than ten years."

The colonel started. He was a thick, short man, with a clean-shaven face and a certain air of breeding about the lines of his countenance; the word millionaire sounded well to his ears. He thought—he thought a great deal; he almost heard the puff of the fearfully costly automobile that was coming up the road, and he said:

"I suppose we might as well hire them."

"Of course," answered the promoter.

The voice of the tall stranger in the corner broke in here:

"It will be a good thing for them?" he said, half in question.

The colonel moved. "The guard makes strange friends," he thought to himself. "What's this man doing here, anyway?" He looked at him, or rather looked at his eyes, and then somehow he felt a warming toward him. He said:

"Well, at least, it can't harm them; they're beyond that."

"It will do them good, then," said the stranger again.

The promoter shrugged his shoulders. "It will do us good," he said.

But the colonel shook his head impatiently. He felt a desire to justify himself before those eyes, and he answered: "Yes, it will do them good; or at any rate it won't make them any worse than they are." Then he started to say something else, but here sure enough the sound of the automobile breathing at the gate stopped him and they all arose.

"It is settled, then," said the promoter.

"Yes," said the colonel, turning toward the stranger again. "Are you going into town?" he asked with the Southern courtesy of white men to white men in a country town. The stranger said he was. "Then come along in my machine. I want to talk with you about this."

They went out to the car. The stranger as he went turned again to look back at the convict. He was a tall, powerfully built black fellow. His face was sullen, with a low forehead, thick, hanging lips, and bitter eyes. There was revolt written about his mouth despite the hangdog expression. He stood bending over his pile of stones, pounding listlessly. Beside him stood a boy of twelve,—yellow, with a hunted, crafty look. The convict raised his eyes and they met the eyes of the stranger. The hammer fell from his hands.

The stranger turned slowly toward the automobile and the colonel introduced him. He had not exactly caught his name, but he mumbled something as he presented him to his wife and little girl, who were waiting.

As they whirled away the colonel started to talk, but the stranger had taken the little girl into his lap and together they conversed in low tones all the way home.

In some way, they did not exactly know how, they got the impression that the man was a teacher and, of course, he must be a foreigner. The long, cloak-like coat told this. They rode in the twilight through the lighted town and at last drew up before the colonel's mansion, with its ghost-like pillars.

The lady in the back seat was thinking of the guests she had invited to dinner and was wondering if she ought not to ask this man to stay. He seemed cultured and she supposed he was some acquaintance of the colonel's. It would be rather interesting to have him there, with the judge's wife and daughter and the rector. She spoke almost before she thought:

"You will enter and rest awhile?"

The colonel and the little girl insisted. For a moment the stranger seemed about to refuse. He said he had some business for his father, about town. Then for the child's sake he consented.

Up the steps they went and into the dark parlor where they sat and talked a long time. It was a curious conversation. Afterwards they did not remember exactly what was said and yet they all remembered a certain strange satisfaction in that long, low talk.

Finally the nurse came for the reluctant child and the hostess bethought herself:

"We will have a cup of tea; you will be dry and tired."

She rang and switched on a blaze of light. With one accord they all looked at the stranger, for they had hardly seen him well in the glooming twilight. The woman started in amazement and the colonel half rose in anger. Why, the man was a mulatto, surely; even if he did not own the Negro blood, their practised eyes knew it. He was tall and straight and the coat looked like a Jewish gabardine. His hair hung in close curls far down the sides of his face and his face was olive, even yellow.

A peremptory order rose to the colonel's lips and froze there as he caught the stranger's eyes. Those eyes,—where had he seen those eyes before? He remembered them long years ago. The soft, tear-filled eyes of a brown girl. He remembered many things, and his face grew drawn and white. Those eyes kept burning into him, even when they were turned half away toward the staircase, where the white figure of the child hovered with her nurse and waved good-night. The lady sank into her chair and thought: "What will the judge's wife say? How did the colonel come to invite this man here? How shall we be rid of him?" She looked at the colonel in reproachful consternation.

Just then the door opened and the old butler came in. He was an ancient black man, with tufted white hair, and he held before him a large, silver tray filled with a china tea service. The stranger rose slowly and stretched forth his hands as if to bless the viands. The old man paused in bewilderment, tottered, and then with sudden gladness in his eyes dropped to his knees, and the tray crashed to the floor.

"My Lord and my God!" he whispered; but the woman screamed: "Mother's china!"

The doorbell rang.

"Heavens! here is the dinner party!" exclaimed the lady. She turned toward the door, but there in the hall, clad in her night clothes, was the little girl. She had stolen down the stairs to see the stranger again, and the nurse above was calling in vain. The woman felt hysterical and scolded at the nurse, but the stranger had stretched out his arms and with a glad cry the child nestled in them. They caught some words about the "Kingdom of Heaven" as he slowly mounted the stairs with his little, white burden.

The mother was glad of anything to get rid of the interloper, even for a moment. The bell rang again and she hastened toward the door, which the loitering black maid was just opening. She did not notice the shadow of the stranger as he came slowly down the stairs and paused by the newel post, dark and silent.

The judge's wife came in. She was an old woman, frilled and powdered into a semblance of youth, and gorgeously gowned. She came forward, smiling with extended hands, but when she was opposite the stranger, somewhere a chill seemed to strike her and she shuddered and cried:

"What a draft!" as she drew a silken shawl about her and shook hands cordially; she forgot to ask who the stranger was. The judge strode in unseeing, thinking of a puzzling case of theft.

"Eh? What? Oh—er—yes,—good evening," he said, "good evening." Behind them came a young woman in the glory of youth, and daintily silked, beautiful in face and form, with diamonds around her fair neck. She came in lightly, but stopped with a little gasp; then she laughed gaily and said:

"Why, I beg your pardon. Was it not curious? I thought I saw there behind your man"—she hesitated, but he must be a servant, she argued—"the shadow of great, white wings. It was but the light on the drapery. What a turn it gave me." And she smiled again. With her came a tall, handsome, young naval officer. Hearing his lady refer to the servant, he hardly looked at him, but held his gilded cap carelessly toward him, and the stranger placed it carefully on the rack.

Last came the rector, a man of forty, and well-clothed. He started to pass the stranger, stopped, and looked at him inquiringly.

"I beg your pardon," he said. "I beg your pardon,—I think I have met you?"

The stranger made no answer, and the hostess nervously hurried the guests on. But the rector lingered and looked perplexed.

"Surely, I know you. I have met you somewhere," he said, putting his hand vaguely to his head. "You—you remember me, do you not?"

The stranger quietly swept his cloak aside, and to the hostess' unspeakable relief passed out of the door.

"I never knew you," he said in low tones as he went.

The lady murmured some vain excuse about intruders, but the rector stood with annoyance written on his face.

"I beg a thousand pardons," he said to the hostess absently. "It is a great pleasure to be here,—somehow I thought I knew that man. I am sure I knew him once."

The stranger had passed down the steps, and as he passed, the nurse, lingering at the top of the staircase, flew down after him, caught his cloak, trembled, hesitated, and then kneeled in the dust.

He touched her lightly with his hand and said: "Go, and sin no more!"

With a glad cry the maid left the house, with its open door, and turned north, running. The stranger turned eastward into the night. As they parted a long, low howl rose tremulously and reverberated through the night. The colonel's wife within shuddered.

"The bloodhounds!" she said.

The rector answered carelessly:

"Another one of those convicts escaped, I suppose. Really, they need severer measures." Then he stopped. He was trying to remember that stranger's name.

The judge's wife looked about for the draft and arranged her shawl. The girl glanced at the white drapery in the hall, but the young officer was bending over her and the fires of life burned in her veins.

Howl after howl rose in the night, swelled, and died away. The stranger strode rapidly along the highway and out into the deep forest. There he paused and stood waiting, tall and still.

A mile up the road behind a man was running, tall and powerful and black, with crime-stained face and convicts' stripes upon him, and shackles on his legs. He ran and jumped, in little, short steps, and his chains rang. He fell and rose again, while the howl of the hounds rang louder behind him.

Into the forest he leapt and crept and jumped and ran, streaming with sweat; seeing the tall form rise before him, he stopped suddenly, dropped his hands in sullen impotence, and sank panting to the earth. A greyhound shot out of the woods behind him, howled, whined, and fawned before the stranger's feet. Hound after hound bayed, leapt, and lay there; then silently, one by one, and with bowed heads, they crept backward toward the town.

The stranger made a cup of his hands and gave the man water to drink, bathed his hot head, and gently took the chains and irons from his feet. By and by the convict stood up. Day was dawning above the treetops. He looked into the stranger's face, and for a moment a gladness swept over the stains of his face.

"Why, you are a nigger, too," he said.

Then the convict seemed anxious to justify himself.

"I never had no chance," he said furtively.

"Thou shalt not steal," said the stranger.

The man bridled.

"But how about them? Can they steal? Didn't they steal a whole year's work, and then when I stole to keep from starving—" He glanced at the stranger.

"No, I didn't steal just to keep from starving. I stole to be stealing. I can't seem to keep from stealing. Seems like when I see things, I just must—but, yes, I'll try!"

The convict looked down at his striped clothes, but the stranger had taken off his long coat; he had put it around him and the stripes disappeared.

In the opening morning the black man started toward the low, log farmhouse in the distance, while the stranger stood watching him. There was a new glory in the day. The black man's face cleared up, and the farmer was glad to get him. All day the black man worked as he had never worked before. The farmer gave him some cold food.

"You can sleep in the barn," he said, and turned away.

"How much do I git a day?" asked the black man.

The farmer scowled.

"Now see here," said he. "If you'll sign a contract for the season, I'll give you ten dollars a month."

"I won't sign no contract," said the black man doggedly.

"Yes, you will," said the farmer, threateningly, "or I'll call the convict guard." And he grinned.

The convict shrank and slouched to the barn. As night fell he looked out and saw the farmer leave the place. Slowly he crept out and sneaked toward the house. He looked through the kitchen door. No one was there, but the supper was spread as if the mistress had laid it and gone out. He ate ravenously. Then he looked into the front room and listened. He could hear low voices on the porch. On the table lay a gold watch. He gazed at it, and in a moment he was beside it,—his hands were on it! Quickly he slipped out of the house and slouched toward the field. He saw his employer coming along the highway. He fled back in terror and around to the front of the house, when suddenly he stopped. He felt the great, dark eyes of the stranger and saw the same dark, cloak-like coat where the stranger sat on the doorstep talking with the mistress of the house. Slowly, guiltily, he turned back, entered the kitchen, and laid the watch stealthily where he had found it; then he rushed wildly back toward the stranger, with arms outstretched.

The woman had laid supper for her husband, and going down from the house had walked out toward a neighbor's. She was gone but a little while, and when she came back she started to see a dark figure on the doorsteps under the tall, red oak. She thought it was the new Negro until he said in a soft voice:

"Will you give me bread?"

Reassured at the voice of a white man, she answered quickly in her soft, Southern tones:

"Why, certainly."

She was a little woman, and once had been pretty; but now her face was drawn with work and care. She was nervous and always thinking, wishing, wanting for something. She went in and got him some cornbread and a glass of cool, rich buttermilk; then she came out and sat down beside him. She began, quite unconsciously, to tell him about herself,—the things she had done and had not done and the things she had wished for. She told him of her husband and this new farm they were trying to buy. She said it was hard to get niggers to work. She said they ought all to be in the chain-gang and made to work. Even then some ran away. Only yesterday one had escaped, and another the day before.

At last she gossiped of her neighbors, how good they were and how bad.

"And do you like them all?" asked the stranger.

She hesitated.

"Most of them," she said; and then, looking up into his face and putting her hand into his, as though he were her father, she said:

"There are none I hate; no, none at all."

He looked away, holding her hand in his, and said dreamily:

"You love your neighbor as yourself?"

She hesitated.

"I try—"she began, and then looked the way he was looking; down under the hill where lay a little, half-ruined cabin.

"They are niggers," she said briefly.

He looked at her. Suddenly a confusion came over her and she insisted, she knew not why.

"But they are niggers!"

With a sudden impulse she arose and hurriedly lighted the lamp that stood just within the door, and held it above her head. She saw his dark face and curly hair. She shrieked in angry terror and rushed down the path, and just as she rushed down, the black convict came running up with hands outstretched. They met in midpath, and before he could stop he had run against her and she fell heavily to earth and lay white and still. Her husband came rushing around the house with a cry and an oath.

"I knew it," he said. "It's that runaway nigger." He held the black man struggling to the earth and raised his voice to a yell. Down the highway came the convict guard, with hound and mob and gun. They paused across the fields. The farmer motioned to them.

"He—attacked—my wife," he gasped.

The mob snarled and worked silently. Right to the limb of the red oak they hoisted the struggling, writhing black man, while others lifted the dazed woman. Right and left, as she tottered to the house, she searched for the stranger with a yearning, but the stranger was gone. And she told none of her guests.

"No—no, I want nothing," she insisted, until they left her, as they thought, asleep. For a time she lay still, listening to the departure of the mob. Then she rose. She shuddered as she heard the creaking of the limb where the body hung. But resolutely she crawled to the window and peered out into the moonlight; she saw the dead man writhe. He stretched his arms out like a cross, looking upward. She gasped and clung to the window sill. Behind the swaying body, and down where the little, half-ruined cabin lay, a single flame flashed up amid the far-off shout and cry of the mob. A fierce joy sobbed up through the terror in her soul and then sank abashed as she watched the flame rise. Suddenly whirling into one great crimson column it shot to the top of the sky and threw great arms athwart the gloom until above the world and behind the roped and swaying form below hung quivering and burning a great crimson cross.

She hid her dizzy, aching head in an agony of tears, and dared not look, for she knew. Her dry lips moved:

"Despised and rejected of men."

She knew, and the very horror of it lifted her dull and shrinking eyelids. There, heaven-tall, earth-wide, hung the stranger on the crimson cross, riven and blood-stained, with thorn-crowned head and pierced hands. She stretched her arms and shrieked.

He did not hear. He did not see. His calm dark eyes, all sorrowful, were fastened on the writhing, twisting body of the thief, and a voice came out of the winds of the night, saying:

"This day thou shalt be with me in Paradise!"

CHAPTER VI

Of the Ruling of Men

The ruling of men is the effort to direct the individual actions of many persons toward some end. This end theoretically should be the greatest good of all, but no human group has ever reached this ideal because of ignorance and selfishness. The simplest object would be rule for the Pleasure of One, namely the Ruler; or of the Few—his favorites; or of many—the Rich, the Privileged, the Powerful. Democratic movements inside groups and nations are always taking place and they are the efforts to increase the number of beneficiaries of the ruling. In 18th century Europe, the effort became so broad and sweeping that an attempt was made at universal expression and the philosophy of the movement said that if All ruled they would rule for All and thus Universal Good was sought through Universal Suffrage.

The unrealized difficulty of this program lay in the widespread ignorance. The mass of men, even of the more intelligent men, not only knew little about each other but less about the action of men in groups and the technique of industry in general. They could only apply universal suffrage, therefore, to the things they knew or knew partially: they knew personal and menial service, individual craftsmanship, agriculture and barter, taxes or the taking of private property for public ends and the rent of land. With these matters then they attempted to deal. Under the cry of "Freedom" they greatly relaxed the grip of selfish interests by restricting menial service, securing the right of property in handiwork and regulating public taxes; distributing land ownership and freeing trade and barter.

While they were doing this against stubborn resistance, a whole new organization of work suddenly appeared. The suddenness of this "Industrial Revolution" of the 19th century was partly fortuitous—in the case of Watt's teakettle—partly a natural development, as in the matter of spinning, but largely the determination of powerful and intelligent individuals to secure the benefits of privileged persons, as in the case of foreign slave trade.

The result was on the one hand a vast and unexampled development of industry. Life and civilization in the late 19th and early 20th century were Industry in its whole conception, language, and accomplishment: the object of life was to make goods. Now before this giant aspect of things, the new democracy stood aghast and impotent. It could not rule because it did not understand: an invincible kingdom of trade, business, and commerce ruled the world, and before its threshold stood the Freedom of 18th century philosophy warding the way. Some of the very ones who were freed from the tyranny of the Middle Age became the tyrants of the industrial age.

There came a reaction. Men sneered at "democracy" and politics, and brought forth Fate and Philanthropy to rule the world—Fate which gave divine right to rule to the Captains of Industry and their created Millionaires; Philanthropy which organized vast schemes of relief to stop at least the flow of blood in the vaster wounds which industry was making.

It was at this time that the lowest laborers, who worked hardest, got least and suffered most, began to mutter and rebel, and among these were the American Negroes. Lions have no historians, and therefore lion hunts are thrilling and satisfactory human reading. Negroes had no bards, and therefore it has been widely told how American philanthropy freed the slave. In truth the Negro revolted by armed rebellion, by sullen refusal to work, by poison and murder, by running away to the North and Canada, by giving point and powerful example to the agitation of the abolitionists and by furnishing 200,000 soldiers and many times as many civilian helpers in the Civil War. This war was not a war for Negro freedom, but a duel between two industrial systems, one of which was bound to fail because it was an anachronism, and the other bound to succeed because of the Industrial Revolution.

When now the Negro was freed the Philanthropists sought to apply to his situation the Philosophy of Democracy handed down from the 18th century.

There was a chance here to try democratic rule in a new way, that is, against the new industrial oppression with a mass of workers who were not yet in its control. With plenty of land widely distributed, staple products like cotton, rice, and sugar cane, and a thorough system of education, there was a unique chance to realize a new modern democracy in industry in the southern United States which would point the way to the world. This, too, if done by black folk, would have tended to a new unity of human beings and an obliteration of human hatreds festering along the color line.

Efforts were begun. The 14th and 15th amendments gave the right to vote to white and black laborers, and they immediately established a public school system and began to attack the land question. The United States government was seriously considering the distribution of land and capital—"40 acres and a mule"—and the price of cotton opened an easy way to economic independence. Co-operative movements began on a large scale.

But alas! Not only were the former slave-owners solidly arrayed against this experiment, but the owners of the industrial North saw disaster in any such beginnings of industrial democracy. The opposition based its objections on the color line, and Reconstruction became in history a great movement for the self-assertion of the white race against the impudent ambition of degraded blacks, instead of, in truth, the rise of a mass of black and white laborers.

The result was the disfranchisement of the blacks of the South and a world-wide attempt to restrict democratic development to white races and to distract them with race hatred against the darker races. This program, however, although it undoubtedly helped raise the scale of white labor, in much greater proportion put wealth and power in the hands of the great European Captains of Industry and made modern industrial imperialism possible.

This led to renewed efforts on the part of white European workers to understand and apply their political power to its reform through democratic control.

Whether known as Communism or Socialism or what not, these efforts are neither new nor strange nor terrible, but world-old and seeking an absolutely justifiable human ideal—the only ideal that can be sought: the direction of individual action in industry so as to secure the greatest good of all. Marxism was one method of accomplishing this, and its panacea was the doing away with private property in machines and materials. Two mighty attacks were made on this proposal. One was an attack on the fundamental democratic foundation: modern European white industry does not even theoretically seek the good of all, but simply of all Europeans. This attack was virtually unanswered—indeed some Socialists openly excluded Negroes and Asiatics from their scheme. From this it was easy to drift into that form of syndicalism which asks socialism for the skilled laborer only and leaves the common laborer in his bonds.

This throws us back on fundamentals. It compels us again to examine the roots of democracy.

Who may be excluded from a share in the ruling of men? Time and time again the world has answered:

The Ignorant
The Inexperienced
The Guarded
The Unwilling

That is, we have assumed that only the intelligent should vote, or those who know how to rule men, or those who are not under benevolent guardianship, or those who ardently desire the right.

These restrictions are not arguments for the wide distribution of the ballot—they are rather reasons for restriction addressed to the self-interest of the present real rulers. We say easily, for instance, "The ignorant ought not to vote." We would say, "No civilized state should have citizens too ignorant to participate in government," and this statement is but a step to the fact: that no state is civilized which has citizens too ignorant to help rule it. Or, in other words, education is not a prerequisite to political control—political control is the cause of popular education.

Again, to make experience a qualification for the franchise is absurd: it would stop the spread of democracy and make political power hereditary, a prerequisite of a class, caste, race, or sex. It has of course been soberly argued that only white folk or Englishmen, or men, are really capable of exercising sovereign power in a modern state. The statement proves too much: only yesterday it was Englishmen of high descent, or men of "blood," or sovereigns "by divine right" who could rule. Today the civilized world is being ruled by the descendants of persons who a century ago were pronounced incapable of ever developing a self-ruling people. In every modern state there must come to the polls every generation, and indeed every year, men who are inexperienced in the solutions of the political problems that confront them and who must experiment in methods of ruling men. Thus and thus only will civilization grow.

Again, what is this theory of benevolent guardianship for women, for the masses, for Negroes—for "lesser breeds without the law"? It is simply the old cry of privilege, the old assumption that there are those in the world who know better what is best for others than those others know themselves, and who can be trusted to do this best.

In fact no one knows himself but that self's own soul. The vast and wonderful knowledge of this marvelous universe is locked in the bosoms of its individual souls. To tap this mighty reservoir of experience, knowledge, beauty, love, and deed we must appeal not to the few, not to some souls, but to all. The narrower the appeal, the poorer the culture; the wider the appeal the more magnificent are the possibilities. Infinite is human nature. We make it finite by choking back the mass of men, by attempting to speak for others, to interpret and act for them, and we end by acting for ourselves and using the world as our private property. If this were all, it were crime enough—but it is not all: by our ignorance we make the creation of the greater world impossible; we beat back a world built of the playing of dogs and laughter of children, the song of Black Folk and worship of Yellow, the love of women and strength of men, and try to express by a group of doddering ancients the Will of the World.

There are people who insist upon regarding the franchise, not as a necessity for the many, but as a privilege for the few. They say of persons and classes: "They do not need the ballot." This is often said of women. It is argued that everything which women with the ballot might do for themselves can be done for them; that they have influence and friends "at court," and that their enfranchisement would simply double the number of ballots. So, too, we are told that American Negroes can have done for them by other voters all that they could possibly do for themselves with the ballot and much more because the white voters are more intelligent.

Further than this, it is argued that many of the disfranchised people recognize these facts. "Women do not want the ballot" has been a very effective counter war-cry, so much so that many men have taken refuge in the declaration: "When they want to vote, why, then—" So, too, we are continually told that the "best" Negroes stay out of politics.

Such arguments show so curious a misapprehension of the foundation of the argument for democracy that the argument must be continually restated and emphasized. We must remember that if the theory of democracy is correct, the right to vote is not merely a privilege, not simply a method of meeting the needs of a particular group, and least of all a matter of recognized want or desire. Democracy is a method of realizing the broadest measure of justice to all human beings. The world has, in the past, attempted various methods of attaining this end, most of which can be summed up in three categories:

The method of the benevolent tyrant.
The method of the select few.
The method of the excluded groups.

The method of intrusting the government of a people to a strong ruler has great advantages when the ruler combines strength with ability, unselfish devotion to the public good, and knowledge of what that good calls for. Such a combination is, however, rare and the selection of the right ruler is very difficult. To leave the selection to force is to put a premium on physical strength, chance, and intrigue; to make the selection a matter of birth simply transfers the real power from sovereign to minister. Inevitably the choice of rulers must fall on electors.

Then comes the problem, who shall elect. The earlier answer was: a select few, such as the wise, the best born, the able. Many people assume that it was corruption that made such aristocracies fail. By no means. The best and most effective aristocracy, like the best monarchy, suffered from lack of knowledge. The rulers did not know or understand the needs of the people and they could not find out, for in the last analysis only the man himself, however humble, knows his own condition. He may not know how to remedy it, he may not realize just what is the matter; but he knows when something hurts and he alone knows how that hurt feels. Or if sunk below feeling or comprehension or complaint, he does not even know that he is hurt, God help his country, for it not only lacks knowledge, but has destroyed the sources of knowledge.

So soon as a nation discovers that it holds in the heads and hearts of its individual citizens the vast mine of knowledge, out of which it may build a just government, then more and more it calls those citizens to select their rulers and to judge the justice of their acts.

Even here, however, the temptation is to ask only for the wisdom of citizens of a certain grade or those of recognized worth. Continually some classes are tacitly or expressly excluded. Thus women have been excluded from modern democracy because of the persistent theory of female subjection and because it was argued that their husbands or other male folks would look to their interests. Now, manifestly, most husbands, fathers, and brothers, will, so far as they know how or as they realize women's needs, look after them. But remember the foundation of the argument,—that in the last analysis only the sufferer knows his sufferings and that no state can be strong which excludes from its expressed wisdom the knowledge possessed by mothers, wives, and daughters. We have but to view the unsatisfactory relations of the sexes the world over and the problem of children to realize how desperately we need this excluded wisdom.

The same arguments apply to other excluded groups: if a race, like the Negro race, is excluded, then so far as that race is a part of the economic and social organization of the land, the feeling and the experience of that race are absolutely necessary to the realization of the broadest justice for all citizens. Or if the "submerged tenth" be excluded, then again, there is lost from the world an experience of untold value, and they must be raised rapidly to a place where they can speak for themselves. In the same way and for the same reason children must be educated, insanity prevented, and only those put under the guardianship of others who can in no way be trained to speak for themselves.

The real argument for democracy is, then, that in the people we have the source of that endless life and unbounded wisdom which the rulers of men must have. A given people today may not be intelligent, but through a democratic government that recognizes, not only the worth of the individual to himself, but the worth of his feelings and experiences to all, they can educate, not only the individual unit, but generation after generation, until they accumulate vast stores of wisdom. Democracy alone is the method of showing the whole experience of the race for the benefit of the future and if democracy tries to exclude women or Negroes or the poor or any class because of innate characteristics which do not interfere with intelligence, then that democracy cripples itself and belies its name.

From this point of view we can easily see the weakness and strength of current criticism of extension of the ballot. It is the business of a modern government to see to it, first, that the number of ignorant within its bounds is reduced to the very smallest number. Again, it is the duty of every such government to extend as quickly as possible the number of persons of mature age who can vote. Such possible voters must be regarded, not as sharers of a limited treasure, but as sources of new national wisdom and strength.

The addition of the new wisdom, the new points of view, and the new interests must, of course, be from time to time bewildering and confusing. Today those who have a voice in the body politic have expressed their wishes and sufferings. The result has been a smaller or greater balancing of their conflicting interests. The appearance of new interests and complaints means disarrangement and confusion to the older equilibrium. It is, of course, the inevitable preliminary step to that larger equilibrium in which the interests of no human soul will be neglected. These interests will not, surely, be all fully realized, but they will be recognized and given as full weight as the conflicting interests will allow. The problem of government thereafter would be to reduce the necessary conflict of human interests to the minimum.

From such a point of view one easily sees the strength of the demand for the ballot on the part of certain disfranchised classes. When women ask for the ballot, they are asking, not for a privilege, but for a necessity. You may not see the necessity, you may easily argue that women do not need to vote. Indeed, the women themselves in considerable numbers may agree with you. Nevertheless, women do need the ballot. They need it to right the balance of a world sadly awry because of its brutal neglect of the rights of women and children. With the best will and knowledge, no man can know women's wants as well as women themselves. To disfranchise women is deliberately to turn from knowledge and grope in ignorance.

So, too, with American Negroes: the South continually insists that a benevolent guardianship of whites over blacks is the ideal thing. They assume that white people not only know better what Negroes need than Negroes themselves, but that they are anxious to supply these needs. As a result they grope in ignorance and helplessness. They cannot "understand" the Negro; they cannot protect him from cheating and lynching; and, in general, instead of loving guardianship we see anarchy and exploitation. If the Negro could speak for himself in the South instead of being spoken for, if he could defend himself instead of having to depend on the chance sympathy of white citizens, how much healthier a growth of democracy the South would have.

So, too, with the darker races of the world. No federation of the world, no true inter-nation—can exclude the black and brown and yellow races from its counsels. They must equally and according to number act and be heard at the world's council.

It is not, for a moment, to be assumed that enfranchising women will not cost something. It will for many years confuse our politics. It may even change the present status of family life. It will admit to the ballot thousands of inexperienced persons, unable to vote intelligently. Above all, it will interfere with some of the present prerogatives of men and probably for some time to come annoy them considerably.

So, too, Negro enfranchisement meant reconstruction, with its theft and bribery and incompetency as well as its public schools and enlightened, social legislation. It would mean today that black men in the South would have to be treated with consideration, have their wishes respected and their manhood rights recognized. Every white Southerner, who wants peons beneath him, who believes in hereditary menials and a privileged aristocracy, or who hates certain races because of their characteristics, would resent this.

Notwithstanding this, if America is ever to become a government built on the broadest justice to every citizen, then every citizen must be enfranchised. There may be temporary exclusions, until the ignorant and their children are taught, or to avoid too sudden an influx of inexperienced voters. But such exclusions can be but temporary if justice is to prevail.

The principle of basing all government on the consent of the governed is undenied and undeniable. Moreover, the method of modern democracy has placed within reach of the modern state larger reserves of efficiency, ability, and even genius than the ancient or mediaeval state dreamed of. That this great work of the past can be carried further among all races and nations no one can reasonably doubt.

Great as are our human differences and capabilities there is not the slightest scientific reason for assuming that a given human being of any race or sex cannot reach normal, human development if he is granted a reasonable chance. This is, of course, denied. It is denied so volubly and so frequently and with such positive conviction that the majority of unthinking people seem to assume that most human beings are not human and have no right to human treatment or human opportunity. All this goes to prove that human beings are, and must be, woefully ignorant of each other. It always startles us to find folks thinking like ourselves. We do not really associate with each other, we associate with our ideas of each other, and few people have either the ability or courage to question their own ideas. None have more persistently and dogmatically insisted upon the inherent inferiority of women than the men with whom they come in closest contact. It is the husbands, brothers, and sons of women whom it has been most difficult to induce to consider women seriously or to acknowledge that women have rights which men are bound to respect. So, too, it is those people who live in closest contact with black folk who have most unhesitatingly asserted the utter impossibility of living beside Negroes who are not industrial or political slaves or social pariahs. All this proves that none are so blind as those nearest the thing seen, while, on the other hand, the history of the world is the history of the discovery of the common humanity of human beings among steadily-increasing circles of men.

If the foundations of democracy are thus seen to be sound, how are we going to make democracy effective where it now fails to function—

particularly in industry? The Marxists assert that industrial democracy will automatically follow public ownership of machines and materials. Their opponents object that nationalization of machines and materials would not suffice because the mass of people do not understand the industrial process. They do not know:

What to do

How to do it

Who could do it best

　　or

How to apportion the resulting goods.

There can be no doubt but that monopoly of machines and materials is a chief source of the power of industrial tyrants over the common worker and that monopoly today is due as much to chance and cheating as to thrift and intelligence. So far as it is due to chance and cheating, the argument for public ownership of capital is incontrovertible even though it involves some interference with long vested rights and inheritance. This is being widely recognized in the whole civilized world. But how about the accumulation of goods due to thrift and intelligence—would democracy in industry interfere here to such an extent as to discourage enterprise and make impossible the intelligent direction of the mighty and intricate industrial process of modern times?

The knowledge of what to do in industry and how to do it in order to attain the resulting goods rests in the hands and brains of the workers and managers, and the judges of the result are the public. Consequently it is not so much a question as to whether the world will admit democratic control here as how can such control be long avoided when the people once understand the fundamentals of industry. How can civilization persist in letting one person or a group of persons, by secret inherent power, determine what goods shall be made—whether bread or champagne, overcoats or silk socks? Can so vast a power be kept from the people?

But it may be opportunely asked: has our experience in electing public officials led us to think that we could run railways, cotton mills, and department stores by popular vote? The answer is clear: no, it has not, and the reason has been lack of interest in politics and the tyranny of the Majority. Politics have not touched the matters of daily life which are nearest the interests of the people—namely, work and wages; or if they have, they have touched it obscurely and indirectly. When voting touches the vital, everyday interests of all, nominations and elections will call for more intelligent activity. Consider too the vast unused and misused power of public rewards to obtain ability and genius for the service of the state. If millionaires can buy science and art, cannot the Democratic state outbid them not only with money but with the vast ideal of the common weal?

There still remains, however, the problem of the Majority.

What is the cause of the undoubted reaction and alarm that the citizens of democracy continually feel? It is, I am sure, the failure to feel the full significance of the change of rule from a privileged minority to that of an omnipotent majority, and the assumption that mere majority rule is the last word of government; that majorities have no responsibilities, that they rule by the grace of God. Granted that government should be based on the consent of the governed, does the consent of a majority at any particular time adequately express the consent of all? Has the minority, even though a small and unpopular and unfashionable minority, no right to respectful consideration?

I remember that excellent little high school text book, "Nordhoff's Politics," where I first read of government, saying this sentence at the beginning of its most important chapter: "The first duty of a minority is to become a majority." This is a statement which has its underlying truth, but it also has its dangerous falsehood; viz., any minority which cannot become a majority is not worthy of any consideration. But suppose that the out-voted minority is necessarily always a minority? Women, for instance, can seldom expect to be a majority; artists must always be the few; ability is always rare, and black folk in this land are but a tenth. Yet to tyrannize over such minorities, to browbeat and insult them, to call that government a democracy which makes majority votes an excuse for crushing ideas and individuality and self-development, is manifestly a peculiarly dangerous perversion of the real democratic ideal. It is right here, in its method and not in its object, that democracy in America and elsewhere has so often failed. We have attempted to enthrone any chance majority and make it rule by divine right. We have kicked and cursed minorities as upstarts and usurpers when their sole offense lay in not having ideas or hair like ours. Efficiency, ability, and genius found often no abiding place in such a soil as this. Small wonder that revolt has come and high-handed methods are rife, of pretending that policies which we favor or persons that we like have the anointment of a purely imaginary majority vote.

Are the methods of such a revolt wise, howsoever great the provocation and evil may be? If the absolute monarchy of majorities is galling and inefficient, is it any more inefficient than the absolute monarchy of individuals or privileged classes have been found to be in the past? Is the appeal from a numerous-minded despot to a smaller, privileged group or to one man likely to remedy matters permanently? Shall we step backward a thousand years because our present problem is baffling?

Surely not and surely, too, the remedy for absolutism lies in calling these same minorities to council. As the king-in-council succeeded the king by the grace of God, so in future democracies the toleration and encouragement of minorities and the willingness to consider as "men" the crankiest, humblest and poorest and blackest peoples, must be the real key to the consent of the governed. Peoples and governments will not in the future assume that because they have the brute power to enforce momentarily dominant ideas, it is best to do so without thoughtful conference with the ideas of smaller groups and individuals. Proportionate representation in physical and spiritual form must come.

That this method is virtually coming in vogue we can see by the minority groups of modern legislatures. Instead of the artificial attempts to divide all possible ideas and plans between two great parties, modern legislatures in advanced nations tend to develop smaller and smaller minority groups, while government is carried on by temporary coalitions. For a time we inveighed against this and sought to consider it a perversion of the only possible method of practical democracy. Today we are gradually coming to realize that government by temporary coalition of small and diverse groups may easily become the most efficient method of expressing the will of man and of setting the human soul free. The only hindrance to the faster development of this government by allied minorities is the fear of external war which is used again and again to melt these living, human, thinking groups into inhuman, thoughtless, and murdering machines.

The persons, then, who come forward in the dawn of the 20th century to help in the ruling of men must come with the firm conviction that no nation, race, or sex, has a monopoly of ability or ideas; that no human group is so small as to deserve to be ignored as a part, and as an integral and respected part, of the mass of men; that, above all, no group of twelve million black folk, even though they are at the physical mercy of a hundred million white majority, can be deprived of a voice in their government and of the right to self-development without a blow at the very foundations of all democracy and all human uplift; that the very criticism aimed today at universal suffrage is in reality a demand for power on the part of consciously efficient minorities,—but these minorities face a fatal blunder when they assume that less democracy will give them and their kind greater efficiency. However desperate the temptation, no modern nation can shut the gates of opportunity in the face of its women, its peasants, its laborers, or its socially damned. How astounded the future world-citizen will be to know that as late as 1918 great and civilized nations were making desperate endeavor to confine the development of ability and individuality to one sex,—that is, to one-half of the nation; and he will probably learn that similar effort to confine humanity to one race lasted a hundred years longer.

The doctrine of the divine right of majorities leads to almost humorous insistence on a dead level of mediocrity. It demands that all people be alike or that they be ostracized. At the same time its greatest accusation against rebels is this same desire to be alike: the suffragette is accused of wanting to be a man, the socialist is accused of envy of the rich, and the black man is accused of wanting to be white. That any one of these should simply want to be himself is to the average worshiper of the majority inconceivable, and yet of all worlds, may the good Lord deliver us from a world where everybody looks like his neighbor and thinks like his neighbor and is like his neighbor.

The world has long since awakened to a realization of the evil which a privileged few may exercise over the majority of a nation. So vividly has this truth been brought home to us that we have lightly assumed that a privileged and enfranchised majority cannot equally harm a nation. Insane, wicked, and wasteful as the tyranny of the few over the many may be, it is not more dangerous than the tyranny of the many over the few. Brutal physical revolution can, and usually does, end the tyranny of the few. But the spiritual losses from suppressed minorities may be vast and fatal and yet all unknown and unrealized because idea and dream and ability are paralyzed by brute force.

If, now, we have a democracy with no excluded groups, with all men and women enfranchised, what is such a democracy to do? How will it function? What will be its field of work?

The paradox which faces the civilized world today is that democratic control is everywhere limited in its control of human interests. Mankind is engaged in planting, forestry, and mining, preparing food and shelter, making clothes and machines, transporting goods and folk, disseminating news, distributing products, doing public and private personal service, teaching, advancing science, and creating art.

In this intricate whirl of activities, the theory of government has been hitherto to lay down only very general rules of conduct, marking the limits of extreme anti-social acts, like fraud, theft, and murder.

The theory was that within these bounds was Freedom—the Liberty to think and do and move as one wished. The real realm of freedom was found in experience to be much narrower than this in one direction and much broader in another. In matters of Truth and Faith and Beauty, the Ancient Law was inexcusably strait and modern law unforgivably stupid. It is here that the future and mighty fight for Freedom must and will be made. Here in the heavens and on the mountaintops, the air of Freedom is wide, almost limitless, for here, in the highest stretches, individual freedom harms no man, and, therefore, no man has the right to limit it.

On the other hand, in the valleys of the hard, unyielding laws of matter and the social necessities of time production, and human intercourse, the limits on our freedom are stern and unbending if we would exist and thrive. This does not say that everything here is governed by incontrovertible "natural" law which needs no human decision as to raw materials, machinery, prices, wages, news-dissemination, education of children, etc.; but it does mean that decisions here must be limited by brute facts and based on science and human wants.

Today the scientific and ethical boundaries of our industrial activities are not in the hands of scientists, teachers, and thinkers; nor is the intervening opportunity for decision left in the control of the public whose welfare such decisions guide. On the contrary, the control of industry is largely in the hands of a powerful few, who decide for their own good and regardless of the good of others. The making of the rules of Industry, then, is not in the hands of All, but in the hands of the Few. The Few who govern industry envisage, not the wants of mankind, but their own wants. They work quietly, often secretly, opposing Law, on the one hand, as interfering with the "freedom of industry"; opposing, on the other hand, free discussion and open determination of the rules of work and wealth and wages, on the ground that harsh natural law brooks no interference by Democracy.

These things today, then, are not matters of free discussion and determination. They are strictly controlled. Who controls them? Who makes these inner, but powerful, rules? Few people know. Others assert and believe these rules are "natural"—a part of our inescapable physical environment. Some of them doubtless are; but most of them are just as clearly the dictates of self-interest laid down by the powerful private persons who today control industry. Just here it is that modern men demand that Democracy supplant skilfully concealed, but all too evident, Monarchy.

In industry, monarchy and the aristocracy rule, and there are those who, calling themselves democratic, believe that democracy can never enter here. Industry, they maintain, is a matter of technical knowledge and ability, and, therefore, is the eternal heritage of the few. They point to the failure of attempts at democratic control in industry, just as we used to point to Spanish-American governments, and they expose, not simply the failures of Russian Soviets,—they fly to arms to prevent that greatest experiment in industrial democracy which the world has yet seen. These are the ones who say: We must control labor or civilization will fail; we must control white labor in Europe and America; above all, we must control yellow labor in Asia and black labor in Africa and the South, else we shall have no tea, or rubber, or cotton. And yet,—and yet is it so easy to give up the dream of democracy? Must industry rule men or may men rule even industry? And unless men rule industry, can they ever hope really to make laws or educate children or create beauty?

That the problem of the democratization of industry is tremendous, let no man deny. We must spread that sympathy and intelligence which tolerates the widest individual freedom despite the necessary public control; we must learn to select for public office ability rather than mere affability. We must stand ready to defer to knowledge and science and judge by result rather than by method; and finally we must face the fact that the final distribution of goods—the question of wages and income is an ethical and not a mere mechanical problem and calls for grave public human judgment and not secrecy and closed doors. All this means time and development. It comes not complete by instant revolution of a day, nor yet by the deferred evolution of a thousand years—it comes daily, bit by bit and step by step, as men and women learn and grow and as children are trained in Truth.

These steps are in many cases clear: the careful, steady increase of public democratic ownership of industry, beginning with the simplest type of public utilities and monopolies, and extending gradually as we learn the way; the use of taxation to limit inheritance and to take the unearned increment for public use beginning (but not ending) with a "single tax" on monopolized land values; the training of the public in business technique by co-operation in buying and selling, and in industrial technique by the shop committee and manufacturing guild.

But beyond all this must come the Spirit—the Will to Human Brotherhood of all Colors, Races, and Creeds; the Wanting of the Wants of All. Perhaps the finest contribution of current Socialism to the world is neither its light nor its dogma, but the idea back of its one mighty word—Comrade!

The Call

In the Land of the Heavy Laden came once a dreary day. And the King, who sat upon the Great White Throne, raised his eyes and saw afar off how the hills around were hot with hostile feet and the sound of the mocking of his enemies struck anxiously on the King's ears, for the King loved his enemies. So the King lifted up his hand in the glittering silence and spake softly, saying: "Call the Servants of the King." Then the herald stepped before the armpost of the throne, and cried: "Thus saith the High and Mighty One, who inhabiteth Eternity, whose name is Holy,—the Servants of the King!"

Now, of the servants of the king there were a hundred and forty-four thousand,—tried men and brave, brawny of arm and quick of wit; aye, too, and women of wisdom and women marvelous in beauty and grace. And yet on this drear day when the King called, their ears were thick with the dust of the enemy, their eyes were blinded with the flashing of his spears, and they hid their faces in dread silence and moved not, even at the King's behest. So the herald called again. And the servants cowered in very shame, but none came forth. But the third blast of the herald struck upon a woman's heart, afar. And the woman straightway left her baking and sweeping and the rattle of pans; and the woman straightway left her chatting and gossiping and the sewing of garments, and the woman stood before the King, saying: "The servant of thy servants, O Lord."

Then the King smiled,—smiled wondrously, so that the setting sun burst through the clouds, and the hearts of the King's men dried hard within them. And the low-voiced King said, so low that even they that listened heard not well: "Go, smite me mine enemies, that they cease to do evil in my sight." And the woman quailed and trembled. Three times she lifted her eyes unto the hills and saw the heathen whirling onward in their rage. And seeing, she shrank—three times she shrank and crept to the King's feet.

"O King," she cried, "I am but a woman."

And the King answered: "Go, then, Mother of Men."

And the woman said, "Nay, King, but I am still a maid." Whereat the King cried: "O maid, made Man, thou shalt be Bride of God."

And yet the third time the woman shrank at the thunder in her ears, and whispered: "Dear God, I am black!"

The King spake not, but swept the veiling of his face aside and lifted up the light of his countenance upon her and lo! it was black.

So the woman went forth on the hills of God to do battle for the King, on that drear day in the land of the Heavy Laden, when the heathen raged and imagined a vain thing.

CHAPTER **VII**

The Damnation of Women

I remember four women of my boyhood: my mother, cousin Inez, Emma, and Ide Fuller. They represented the problem of the widow, the wife, the maiden, and the outcast. They were, in color, brown and light-brown, yellow with brown freckles, and white. They existed not for themselves, but for men; they were named after the men to whom they were related and not after the fashion of their own souls.

They were not beings, they were relations and these relations were enfilmed with mystery and secrecy. We did not know the truth or believe it when we heard it. Motherhood! What was it? We did not know or greatly care. My mother and I were good chums. I liked her. After she was dead I loved her with a fierce sense of personal loss.

Inez was a pretty, brown cousin who married. What was marriage? We did not know, neither did she, poor thing! It came to mean for her a litter of children, poverty, a drunken, cruel companion, sickness, and death. Why?

There was no sweeter sight than Emma,—slim, straight, and dainty, darkly flushed with the passion of youth; but her life was a wild, awful struggle to crush her natural, fierce joy of love. She crushed it and became a cold, calculating mockery.

Last there was that awful outcast of the town, the white woman, Ide Fuller. What she was, we did not know. She stood to us as embodied filth and wrong,—but whose filth, whose wrong?

Grown up I see the problem of these women transfused; I hear all about me the unanswered call of youthful love, none the less glorious because of its clean, honest, physical passion. Why unanswered? Because the youth are too poor to marry or if they marry, too poor to have children. They turn aside, then, in three directions: to marry for support, to what men call shame, or to that which is more evil than nothing. It is an unendurable paradox; it must be changed or the bases of culture will totter and fall.

The world wants healthy babies and intelligent workers. Today we refuse to allow the combination and force thousands of intelligent workers to go childless at a horrible expenditure of moral force, or we damn them if they break our idiotic conventions. Only at the sacrifice of intelligence and the chance to do their best work can the majority of modern women bear children. This is the damnation of women.

All womanhood is hampered today because the world on which it is emerging is a world that tries to worship both virgins and mothers and in the end despises motherhood and despoils virgins.

The future woman must have a life work and economic independence. She must have knowledge. She must have the right of motherhood at her own discretion. The present mincing horror at free womanhood must pass if we are ever to be rid of the bestiality of free manhood; not by guarding the weak in weakness do we gain strength, but by making weakness free and strong.

The world must choose the free woman or the white wraith of the prostitute. Today it wavers between the prostitute and the nun. Civilization must show two things: the glory and beauty of creating life and the need and duty of power and intelligence. This and this only will make the perfect marriage of love and work.

> God is Love,
> Love is God;
> There is no God but Love
> And Work is His Prophet!

All this of woman,—but what of black women?

The world that wills to worship womankind studiously forgets its darker sisters. They seem in a sense to typify that veiled Melancholy:

> "Whose saintly visage is too bright
> To hit the sense of human sight,
> And, therefore, to our weaker view
> O'er-laid with black."

Yet the world must heed these daughters of sorrow, from the primal black All-Mother of men down through the ghostly throng of mighty womanhood, who walked in the mysterious dawn of Asia and

Africa; from Neith, the primal mother of all, whose feet rest on hell, and whose almighty hands uphold the heavens; all religion, from beauty to beast, lies on her eager breasts; her body bears the stars, while her shoulders are necklaced by the dragon; from black Neith down to

> "That starr'd Ethiop queen who strove
> To set her beauty's praise above
> The sea-nymphs,"

through dusky Cleopatras, dark Candaces, and darker, fiercer Zinghas, to our own day and our own land,—in gentle Phillis; Harriet, the crude Moses; the sybil, Sojourner Truth; and the martyr, Louise De Mortie.

The father and his worship is Asia; Europe is the precocious, self-centered, forward-striving child; but the land of the mother is and was Africa. In subtle and mysterious way, despite her curious history, her slavery, polygamy, and toil, the spell of the African mother pervades her land. Isis, the mother, is still titular goddess, in thought if not in name, of the dark continent. Nor does this all seem to be solely a survival of the historic matriarchate through which all nations pass,—it appears to be more than this,—as if the great black race in passing up the steps of human culture gave the world, not only the Iron Age, the cultivation of the soil, and the domestication of animals, but also, in peculiar emphasis, the mother-idea.

"No mother can love more tenderly and none is more tenderly loved than the Negro mother," writes Schneider. Robin tells of the slave who bought his mother's freedom instead of his own. Mungo Park writes: "Everywhere in Africa, I have noticed that no greater affront can be offered a Negro than insulting his mother. 'Strike me,' cries a Mandingo to his enemy, 'but revile not my mother!' " And the Krus and Fantis say the same. The peoples on the Zambezi and the great lakes cry in sudden fear or joy: "O, my mother!" And the Herero swears (endless oath) "By my mother's tears!" "As the mist in the swamps," cries the Angola Negro, "so lives the love of father and mother."

A student of the present Gold Coast life describes the work of the village headman, and adds: "It is a difficult task that he is set to, but in this matter he has all-powerful helpers in the female members of the family, who will be either the aunts or the sisters or the cousins or the nieces of the headman, and as their interests are identical with his in every particular, the good women spontaneously train up their children to implicit obedience to the headman, whose rule in the family thus becomes a simple and an easy matter. 'The hand that rocks the cradle rules the world.' What a power for good in the native state system would the mothers of the Gold Coast and Ashanti become by judicious training upon native lines!"

Schweinfurth declares of one tribe: "A bond between mother and child which lasts for life is the measure of affection shown among the Dyoor" and Ratzel adds:

"Agreeable to the natural relation the mother stands first among the chief influences affecting the children. From the Zulus to the Waganda, we find the mother the most influential counsellor at the court of ferocious sovereigns, like Chaka or Mtesa; sometimes sisters take her place. Thus even with chiefs who possess wives by hundreds the bonds of blood are the strongest and that the woman, though often heavily burdened, is in herself held in no small esteem among the Negroes is clear from the numerous Negro queens, from the medicine women, from the participation in public meetings permitted to women by many Negro peoples."

As I remember through memories of others, backward among my own family, it is the mother I ever recall,—the little, far-off mother of my grandmothers, who sobbed her life away in song, longing for her lost palm-trees and scented waters; the tall and bronzen grandmother, with beaked nose and shrewish eyes, who loved and scolded her black and laughing husband as he smoked lazily in his high oak chair; above all, my own mother, with all her soft brownness,—the brown velvet of her skin, the sorrowful black-brown of her eyes, and the tiny brown-capped waves of her midnight hair as it lay new parted on her forehead. All the way back in these dim distances it is mothers and mothers of mothers who seem to count, while fathers are shadowy memories.

Upon this African mother-idea, the westward slave trade and American slavery struck like doom. In the cruel exigencies of the traffic in men and in the sudden, unprepared emancipation the great pendulum of social equilibrium swung from a time, in 1800,—when America had but eight or less black women to every ten black men,—all too swiftly to a day, in 1870,—when there were nearly eleven women to ten men in our Negro population. This was but the outward numerical fact of social dislocation; within lay polygamy, polyandry, concubinage, and moral degradation, They fought against all this desperately, did these black slaves in the West Indies, especially among the half-free artisans; they set up their ancient household gods, and when Toussaint and Cristophe founded their kingdom in Haiti, it was based on old African tribal ties and beneath it was the mother-idea.

The crushing weight of slavery fell on black women. Under it there was no legal marriage, no legal family, no legal control over children. To be sure, custom and religion replaced here and there what the law denied, yet one has but to read advertisements like the following to see the hell beneath the system:

"One hundred dollars reward will be given for my two fellows, Abram and Frank. Abram has a wife at Colonel Stewart's, in Liberty County, and a mother at Thunderbolt, and a sister in Savannah.

"WILLIAM ROBERTS."

"Fifty dollars reward—Ran away from the subscriber a Negro girl named Maria. She is of a copper color, between thirteen and fourteen years of age—bareheaded and barefooted. She is small for her age—very sprightly and very likely. She stated she was going to see her mother at Maysville.

"SANFORD THOMSON."

"Fifty dollars reward—Ran away from the subscriber his Negro man Pauladore, commonly called Paul. I understand General R. Y. Hayne has purchased his wife and children from H. L. Pinckney, Esq., and has them now on his plantation at Goose Creek, where, no doubt, the fellow is frequently lurking.

"T. DAVIS."

The Presbyterian synod of Kentucky said to the churches under its care in 1835: "Brothers and sisters, parents and children, husbands and wives, are torn asunder and permitted to see each other no more. These acts are daily occurring in the midst of us. The shrieks and agony often witnessed on such occasions proclaim, with a trumpet tongue, the iniquity of our system. There is not a neighborhood where these heartrending scenes are not displayed. There is not a village or road that does not behold the sad procession of manacled outcasts whose mournful countenances tell that they are exiled by force from all that their hearts hold dear."

A sister of a president of the United States declared: "We Southern ladies are complimented with the names of wives, but we are only the mistresses of seraglios."

Out of this, what sort of black women could be born into the world of today? There are those who hasten to answer this query in scathing terms and who say lightly and repeatedly that out of black slavery came nothing decent in womanhood; that adultery and uncleanness were their heritage and are their continued portion.

Fortunately so exaggerated a charge is humanly impossible of truth. The half-million women of Negro descent who lived at the beginning of the 19th century had become the mothers of two and one-fourth million daughters at the time of the Civil War and five million granddaughters in 1910. Can all these women be vile and the hunted race continue to grow in wealth and character? Impossible. Yet to save from the past the shreds and vestiges of self-respect has been a terrible task. I most sincerely doubt if any other race of women could have brought its fineness up through so devilish a fire.

Alexander Crummell once said of his sister in the blood: "In her girlhood all the delicate tenderness of her sex has been rudely outraged. In the field, in the rude cabin, in the press-room, in the factory she was thrown into the companionship of coarse and ignorant men. No chance was given her for delicate reserve or tender modesty. From her childhood she was the doomed victim of the grossest passion. All the virtues of her sex were utterly ignored. If the instinct of chastity asserted itself, then she had to fight like a tiger for the ownership and possession of her own person and ofttimes had to suffer pain and lacerations for her virtuous self-assertion. When she reached maturity, all the tender instincts of her womanhood were ruthlessly violated. At the age of marriage,—always prematurely anticipated under slavery—she was mated as the stock of the plantation were mated, not to be the companion of a loved and chosen husband, but to be the breeder of human cattle for the field or the auction block."

Down in such mire has the black motherhood of this race struggled,—starving its own wailing offspring to nurse to the world their swaggering masters; welding for its children chains which affronted even the moral sense of an unmoral world. Many a man and woman in the South have lived in wedlock as holy as Adam and Eve and brought forth their brown and golden children, but because the darker woman was helpless, her chivalrous and whiter mate could cast her off at his pleasure and publicly sneer at the body he had privately blasphemed.

I shall forgive the white South much in its final judgment day: I shall forgive its slavery, for slavery is a world-old habit; I shall forgive its fighting for a well-lost cause, and for remembering that struggle with tender tears; I shall forgive its so-called "pride of race," the passion of its hot blood, and even its dear, old, laughable strutting and posing; but one thing I shall never forgive, neither in this world nor the world to come: its wanton and continued and persistent insulting of the black womanhood which it sought and seeks to prostitute to its lust. I cannot forget that it is such Southern gentlemen into whose hands smug Northern hypocrites of today are seeking to place our women's eternal destiny,—men who insist upon withholding from my mother and wife and daughter those signs and appellations of courtesy and respect which elsewhere he withholds only from bawds and courtesans.

The result of this history of insult and degradation has been both fearful and glorious. It has birthed the haunting prostitute, the brawler, and the beast of burden; but it has also given the world an efficient womanhood, whose strength lies in its freedom and whose chastity was won in the teeth of temptation and not in prison and swaddling clothes.

To no modern race does its women mean so much as to the Negro nor come so near to the fulfilment of its meaning. As one of our women writes: "Only the black woman can say 'when and where I enter, in the quiet, undisputed dignity of my womanhood, without violence and without suing or special patronage, then and there the whole Negro race enters with me.' "

They came first, in earlier days, like foam flashing on dark, silent waters,—bits of stern, dark womanhood here and there tossed almost carelessly aloft to the world's notice. First and naturally they assumed the panoply of the ancient African mother of men, strong and black, whose very nature beat back the wilderness of oppression and contempt. Such a one was that cousin of my grandmother, whom western Massachusetts remembers as "Mum Bett." Scarred for life by a blow received in defense of a sister, she ran away to Great Barrington and was the first slave, or one of the first, to be declared free under the Bill of Rights of 1780. The son of the judge who freed her, writes:

> "Even in her humble station, she had, when occasion required it, an air of command which conferred a degree of dignity and gave her an ascendancy over those of her rank, which is very unusual in persons of any rank or color. Her determined and resolute character, which enabled her to limit the ravages of Shay's mob, was manifested in her conduct and deportment during her whole life. She claimed no distinction, but it was yielded to her from her superior experience, energy, skill, and sagacity. Having known this woman as familiarly as I knew either of my parents, I cannot believe in the moral or physical inferiority of the race to which she belonged. The degradation of the African must have been otherwise caused than by natural inferiority."

It was such strong women that laid the foundations of the great Negro church of today, with its five million members and ninety millions of dollars in property. One of the early mothers of the church, Mary Still, writes thus quaintly, in the forties:

> "When we were as castouts and spurned from the large churches, driven from our knees, pointed at by the proud, neglected by the careless, without a place of worship, Allen, faithful to the heavenly calling, came forward and laid the foundation of this connection. The women, like the women at the sepulcher, were early to aid in laying the foundation of the temple and in helping to carry up the noble structure and in the name of their God set up their banner; most of our aged mothers are gone from this to a better state of things. Yet some linger still on their staves, watching with intense interest the ark as it moves over the tempestuous waves of opposition and ignorance. . . .
>
> "But the labors of these women stopped not here, for they knew well that they were subject to affliction and death. For the purpose of mutual aid, they banded themselves together in society capacity, that they might be better able to administer to each others' sufferings and to soften their own pillows. So we find the females in the early history of the church abounding in good works and in acts of true benevolence."

From such spiritual ancestry came two striking figures of war-time,—Harriet Tubman and Sojourner Truth.

For eight or ten years previous to the breaking out of the Civil War, Harriet Tubman was a constant attendant at anti-slavery conventions, lectures, and other meetings; she was a black woman of medium size, smiling countenance, with her upper front teeth gone, attired in coarse but neat clothes, and carrying always an old-fashioned reticule at her side. Usually as soon as she sat down she would drop off in sound sleep.

She was born a slave in Maryland, in 1820, bore the marks of the lash on her flesh; and had been made partially deaf, and perhaps to some degree mentally unbalanced by a blow on the head in childhood. Yet she was one of the most important agents of the Underground Railroad and a leader of fugitive slaves. She ran away in 1849 and went to Boston in 1854, where she was welcomed into the homes of the leading abolitionists and where every one listened with tense interest to her strange stories. She was absolutely illiterate, with no knowledge of geography, and yet year after year she penetrated the slave states and personally led North over three hundred fugitives without losing a single one. A standing reward of $10,000 was offered for her, but as she said: "The whites cannot catch us, for I was born with the charm, and the Lord has given me the power." She was one of John Brown's closest advisers and only severe sickness prevented her presence at Harper's Ferry.

When the war cloud broke, she hastened to the front, flitting down along her own mysterious paths, haunting the armies in the field, and serving as guide and nurse and spy. She followed Sherman in his great march to the sea and was with Grant at Petersburg, and always in the camps the Union officers silently saluted her.

The other woman belonged to a different type,—a tall, gaunt, black, unsmiling sybil, weighted with the woe of the world. She ran away from slavery and giving up her own name took the name of So-journer Truth. She says: "I can remember when I was a little, young girl, how my old mammy would sit out of doors in the evenings and look up at the stars and groan, and I would say, 'Mammy, what makes you groan so?' And she would say, 'I am groaning to think of my poor children; they do not know where I be and I don't know where they be. I look up at the stars and they look up at the stars!'"

Her determination was founded on unwavering faith in ultimate good. Wendell Phillips says that he was once in Faneuil Hall, when Frederick Douglass was one of the chief speakers. Douglass had been describing the wrongs of the Negro race and as he proceeded he grew more and more excited and finally ended by saying that they had no hope of justice from the whites, no possible hope except in their own right arms. It must come to blood! They must fight for themselves. Sojourner Truth was sitting, tall and dark, on the very front seat facing the platform, and in the hush of feeling when Douglass sat down she spoke out in her deep, peculiar voice, heard all over the hall:

"Frederick, is God dead?"

Such strong, primitive types of Negro womanhood in America seem to some to exhaust its capabilities. They know less of a not more worthy, but a finer type of black woman wherein trembles all of that delicate sense of beauty and striving for self-realization, which is as characteristic of the Negro soul as is its quaint strength and sweet laughter. George Washington wrote in grave and gentle courtesy to a Negro woman, in 1776, that he would "be happy to see" at his head-quarters at any time, a person "to whom nature has been so liberal and beneficial in her dispensations." This child, Phillis Wheatley, sang her trite and halting strain to a world that wondered and could not pro-duce her like. Measured today her muse was slight and yet, feeling her striving spirit, we call to her still in her own words:

"Through thickest glooms look back, immortal shade."

Perhaps even higher than strength and art loom human sympathy and sacrifice as characteristic of Negro womanhood. Long years ago, before the Declaration of Independence, Kate Ferguson was born in New York. Freed, widowed, and bereaved of her children before she was twenty, she took the children of the streets of New York, white and black, to her empty arms, taught them, found them homes, and with Dr. Mason of Murray Street Church established the first modern Sunday School in Manhattan.

Sixty years later came Mary Shadd up out of Delaware. She was tall and slim, of that ravishing dream-born beauty,—that twilight of the races which we call mulatto. Well-educated, vivacious, with determina-tion shining from her sharp eyes, she threw herself singlehanded into the great Canadian pilgrimage when thousands of hunted black men hurried northward and crept beneath the protection of the lion's paw. She became teacher, editor, and lecturer; tramping afoot through win-ter snows, pushing without blot or blemish through crowd and turmoil to conventions and meetings, and finally becoming recruiting agent for the United States government in gathering Negro soldiers in the West.

After the war the sacrifice of Negro women for freedom and uplift is one of the finest chapters in their history. Let one life typify all: Louise De Mortie, a free-born Virginia girl, had lived most of her life in Boston. Her high forehead, swelling lips, and dark eyes marked her for a woman of feeling and intellect. She began a successful career as a public reader. Then came the War and the Call. She went to the orphaned colored children of New Orleans,—out of freedom into insult and oppression and into the teeth of the yellow fever. She toiled and dreamed. In 1887 she had raised money and built an orphan home and that same year, in the thirty-fourth of her young life, she died, saying simply: "I belong to God."

As I look about me today in this veiled world of mine, despite the noisier and more spectacular advance of my brothers, I instinctively feel and know that it is the five million women of my race who really count. Black women (and women whose grandmothers were black) are today furnishing our teachers; they are the main pillars of those social settlements which we call churches; and they have with small doubt raised three-fourths of our church property. If we have today, as seems likely, over a billion dollars of accumulated goods, who shall say how much of it has been wrung from the hearts of servant girls and washer-women and women toilers in the fields? As makers of two million homes these women are today seeking in marvelous ways to show forth our strength and beauty and our conception of the truth.

In the United States in 1910 there were 4,931,882 women of Negro descent; over twelve hundred thousand of these were children, another million were girls and young women under twenty, and two and a half-million were adults. As a mass these women were unlettered,—a fourth of those from fifteen to twenty-five years of age were unable to write. These women are passing through, not only a moral, but an economic revolution. Their grandmothers married at twelve and fifteen, but twenty-seven per cent of these women today who have passed fifteen are still single.

Yet these black women toil and toil hard. There were in 1910 two and a half million Negro homes in the United States. Out of these homes walked daily to work two million women and girls over ten years of age,—over half of the colored female population as against a fifth in the case of white women. These, then, are a group of workers, fighting for their daily bread like men; independent and approaching economic freedom! They furnished a million farm laborers, 80,000 farmers, 22,000 teachers, 600,000 servants and washerwomen, and 50,000 in trades and merchandizing.

The family group, however, which is the ideal of the culture with which these folk have been born, is not based on the idea of an economically independent working mother. Rather its ideal harks back to the sheltered harem with the mother emerging at first as nurse and homemaker, while the man remains the sole breadwinner. What is the inevitable result of the clash of such ideals and such facts in the colored group? Broken families.

Among native white women one in ten is separated from her husband by death, divorce, or desertion. Among Negroes the ratio is one in seven. Is the cause racial? No, it is economic, because there is the same high ratio among the white foreign-born. The breaking up of the present family is the result of modern working and sex conditions and it hits the laborers with terrible force. The Negroes are put in a peculiarly difficult position, because the wage of the male breadwinner is below the standard, while the openings for colored women in certain lines of domestic work, and now in industries, are many. Thus while toil holds the father and brother in country and town at low wages, the sisters and mothers are called to the city. As a result the Negro women outnumber the men nine or ten to eight in many cities, making what Charlotte Gilman bluntly calls "cheap women."

What shall we say to this new economic equality in a great laboring class? Some people within and without the race deplore it. "Back to the homes with the women," they cry, "and higher wage for the men." But how impossible this is has been shown by war conditions. Cessation of foreign migration has raised Negro men's wages, to be sure—but it has not only raised Negro women's wages, it has opened to them a score of new avenues of earning a living. Indeed, here, in microcosm and with differences emphasizing sex equality, is the industrial history of labor in the 19th and 20th centuries. We cannot abolish the new economic freedom of women. We cannot imprison women again in a home or require them all on pain of death to be nurses and housekeepers.

What is today the message of these black women to America and to the world? The uplift of women is, next to the problem of the color line and the peace movement, our greatest modern cause. When, now, two of these movements—woman and color—combine in one, the combination has deep meaning.

In other years women's way was clear: to be beautiful, to be petted, to bear children. Such has been their theoretic destiny and if perchance they have been ugly, hurt, and barren, that has been forgotten with studied silence. In partial compensation for this narrowed destiny the white world has lavished its politeness on its womankind,—its chivalry and bows, its uncoverings and courtesies—all the accumulated homage disused for courts and kings and craving exercise. The revolt of white women against this preordained destiny has in these latter days reached splendid proportions, but it is the revolt of an aristocracy of brains and ability,—the middle class and rank and file still plod on in the appointed path, paid by the homage, the almost mocking homage, of men.

From black women of America, however, (and from some others, too, but chiefly from black women and their daughters' daughters) this gauze has been withheld and without semblance of such apology they have been frankly trodden under the feet of men. They are and have been objected to, apparently for reasons peculiarly exasperating to reasoning human beings. When in this world a man comes forward with a thought, a deed, a vision, we ask not, how does he look,—but what is his message? It is of but passing interest whether or not the messenger is beautiful or ugly,—the *message* is the thing. This, which is axiomatic among men, has been in past ages but partially true if the messenger was a woman. The world still wants to ask that a woman primarily be pretty and if she is not, the mob pouts and asks querulously, "What else are women for?" Beauty "is its own excuse for being," but there are other excuses, as most men know, and when the white world objects to black women because it does not consider them beautiful, the black world of right asks two questions: "What is beauty?" and, "Suppose you think them ugly, what then? If ugliness and unconventionality and eccentricity of face and deed do not hinder men from doing the world's work and reaping the world's reward, why should it hinder women?"

Other things being equal, all of us, black and white, would prefer to be beautiful in face and form and suitably clothed; but most of us are not so, and one of the mightiest revolts of the century is against the devilish decree that no woman is a woman who is not by present standards a beautiful woman. This decree the black women of America have in large measure escaped from the first. Not being expected to be merely ornamental, they have girded themselves for work, instead of adorning their bodies only for play. Their sturdier minds have concluded that if a woman be clean, healthy, and educated, she is as pleasing as God wills and far more useful than most of her sisters. If in addition to this she is pink and white and straight-haired, and some of her fellow-men prefer this, well and good; but if she is black or brown and crowned in curled mists (and this to us is the most beautiful thing on earth), this is surely the flimsiest excuse for spiritual incarceration or banishment.

The very attempt to do this in the case of Negro Americans has strangely over-reached itself. By so much as the defective eyesight of the white world rejects black women as beauties, by so much the more it needs them as human beings,—an enviable alternative, as many a white woman knows. Consequently, for black women alone, as a group, "handsome is that handsome does" and they are asked to be no more beautiful than God made them, but they are asked to be efficient, to be strong, fertile, muscled, and able to work. If they marry, they must as independent workers be able to help support their children, for their men are paid on a scale which makes sole support of the family often impossible.

On the whole, colored working women are paid as well as white working women for similar work, save in some higher grades, while colored men get from one-fourth to three-fourths less than white men. The result is curious and three-fold: the economic independence of black women is increased, the breaking up of Negro families must be more frequent, and the number of illegitimate children is decreased more slowly among them than other evidences of culture are increased, just as was once true in Scotland and Bavaria.

What does this mean? It forecasts a mighty dilemma which the whole world of civilization, despite its will, must one time frankly face: the unhusbanded mother or the childless wife. God send us a world with woman's freedom and married motherhood inextricably wed, but until He sends it, I see more of future promise in the betrayed girl-mothers of the black belt than in the childless wives of the white North, and I have more respect for the colored servant who yields to her frank longing for motherhood than for her white sister who offers up children for clothes. Out of a sex freedom that today makes us shudder will come in time a day when we will no longer pay men for work they do not do, for the sake of their harem; we will pay women what they earn and insist on their working and earning it; we will allow those persons to vote who know enough to vote, whether they be black or female, white or male; and we will ward race suicide, not by further burdening the over-burdened, but by honoring mother-hood, even when the sneaking father shirks his duty.

"Wait till the lady passes," said a Nashville white boy.

"She's no lady; she's a nigger," answered another.

So some few women are born free, and some amid insult and scar-let letters achieve freedom; but our women in black had freedom thrust contemptuously upon them. With that freedom they are buying an un-trammeled independence and dear as is the price they pay for it, it will in the end be worth every taunt and groan. Today the dreams of the mothers are coming true. We have still our poverty and degradation, our lewdness and our cruel toil; but we have, too, a vast group of women of Negro blood who for strength of character, cleanness of soul, and unselfish devotion of purpose, is today easily the peer of any group of women in the civilized world. And more than that, in the great rank and file of our five million women we have the up-working of new revolutionary ideals, which must in time have vast influence on the thought and action of this land.

For this, their promise, and for their hard past, I honor the women of my race. Their beauty,—their dark and mysterious beauty of mid-night eyes, crumpled hair, and soft, full-featured faces—is perhaps more to me than to you, because I was born to its warm and subtle spell; but their worth is yours as well as mine. No other women on earth could have emerged from the hell of force and temptation which once engulfed and still surrounds black women in America with half the modesty and womanliness that they retain. I have always felt like bowing myself before them in all abasement, searching to bring some tribute to these long-suffering victims, these burdened sisters of mine, whom the world, the wise, white world, loves to affront and ridicule and wantonly to insult. I have known the women of many lands and nations,—I have known and seen and lived beside them, but none have I known more sweetly feminine, more unswervingly loyal, more desperately earnest, and more instinctively pure in body and in soul than the daughters of my black mothers. This, then,—a little thing—to their memory and inspiration.

Children of the Moon

I am dead;
Yet somehow, somewhere,
In Time's weird contradiction, I
May tell of that dread deed, wherewith
I brought to Children of the Moon
Freedom and vast salvation.

I was a woman born,
And trod the streaming street,
That ebbs and flows from Harlem's hills,
Through caves and cañons limned in light,
Down to the twisting sea.

That night of nights,
I stood alone and at the End,
Until the sudden highway to the moon,
Golden in splendor,
Became too real to doubt.

Dimly I set foot upon the air,
I fled, I flew, through thrills of light,
With all about, above, below, the whirring
Of almighty wings.

I found a twilight land,
Where, hardly hid, the sun
Sent softly-saddened rays of
Red and brown to burn the iron soil
And bathe the snow-white peaks
In mighty splendor.

Black were the men,
Hard-haired and silent-slow,
Moving as shadows,
Bending with face of fear to earthward;
And women there were none.

"Woman, woman, woman!"
I cried in mounting terror.
"Woman and Child!"
And the cry sang back
Through heaven, with the
Whirring of almighty wings.

Wings, wings, endless wings,—
Heaven and earth are wings;
Wings that flutter, furl, and fold,
Always folding and unfolding,
Ever folding yet again;
Wings, veiling some vast
And veiléd face,

577

In blazing blackness,
Behind the folding and unfolding,
The rolling and unrolling of
Almighty wings!

I saw the black men huddle,
Fumed in fear, falling face downward;
Vainly I clutched and clawed,
Dumbly they cringed and cowered,
Moaning in mournful monotone:

> O Freedom, O Freedom,
> O Freedom over me;
> Before I'll be a slave,
> I'll be buried in my grave,
> And go home to my God,
>   And be free.

It was an angel-music
From the dead,
And ever, as they sang,
Some wingéd thing of wings, filling all heaven,
Folding and unfolding, and folding yet again,
Tore out their blood and entrails,
'Til I screamed in utter terror;
And a silence came,—
A silence and the wailing of a babe.

Then, at last, I saw and shamed;
I knew how these dumb, dark, and dusky things
Had given blood and life,
To fend the caves of underground,
The great black caves of utter night,
Where earth lay full of mothers
And their babes.

Little children sobbing in darkness,
Little children crying in silent pain,
Little mothers rocking and groping and strug-
    gling,
Digging and delving and groveling,
Amid the dying-dead and dead-in-life
And drip and dripping of warm, wet blood,
Far, far beneath the wings,—
The folding and unfolding of almighty wings.

I bent with tears and pitying hands,
Above these dusky star-eyed children,—
Crinkly-haired, with sweet-sad baby voices,
Pleading low for light and love and living—
And I crooned:

"Little children weeping there,
God shall find your faces fair;

Guerdon for your deep distress,
He shall send His tenderness;
For the tripping of your feet
Make a mystic music sweet
In the darkness of your hair;
Light and laughter in the air—
Little children weeping there,
God shall find your faces fair!"

I strode above the stricken, bleeding men,
The rampart 'ranged against the skies,
And shouted:
"Up, I say, build and slay;
Fight face foremost, force a way,
Unloose, unfetter, and unbind;
Be men and free!"

Dumbly they shrank,
Muttering they pointed toward that peak,
Then vastness vaster,
Whereon a darkness brooded,
"Who shall look and live," they sighed;
And I sensed
The folding and unfolding of almighty wings.

Yet did we build of iron, bricks, and blood;
We built a day, a year, a thousand years,
Blood was the mortar,—blood and tears,
And, ah, the Thing, the Thing of wings,
The winged, folding Wing of Things
Did furnish much mad mortar
For that tower.

Slow and ever slower rose the towering task,
And with it rose the sun,
Until at last on one wild day,
Wind-whirled, cloud-swept and terrible
I stood beneath the burning shadow
Of the peak,
Beneath the whirring of almighty wings,
While downward from my feet
Streamed the long line of dusky faces
And the wail of little children sobbing under
    earth.

Alone, aloft,
I saw through firmaments on high
The drama of Almighty God,
With all its flaming suns and stars.
"Freedom!" I cried.
"Freedom!" cried heaven, earth, and stars;
And a Voice near-far,

Amid the folding and unfolding of almighty
    wings,
Answered, "I am Freedom—
Who sees my face is free—
He and his."

I dared not look;
Downward I glanced on deep-bowed heads and
    closéd eyes,
Outward I gazed on flecked and flaming blue—
But ever onward, upward flew
The sobbing of small voices,—
Down, down, far down into the night.

Slowly I lifted livid limbs aloft;
Upward I strove: the face! the face!
Onward I reeled: the face! the face!
To beauty wonderful as sudden death,
Or horror horrible as endless life—
Up! Up! the blood-built way;
(Shadow grow vaster!
Terror come faster!)
Up! Up! to the blazing blackness
Of one veiléd face.
And endless folding and unfolding,
Rolling and unrolling of almighty wings.
The last step stood!
The last dim cry of pain
Fluttered across the stars,
And then—
Wings, wings, triumphant wings,
Lifting and lowering, waxing and waning,
Swinging and swaying, twirling and whirling,
Whispering and screaming, streaming and
    gleaming,
Spreading and sweeping and shading and flam-
    ing—
Wings, wings, eternal wings,
'Til the hot, red blood,
Flood fleeing flood,
Thundered through heaven and mine ears,
While all across a purple sky,
The last vast pinion.
Trembled to unfold.

I rose upon the Mountain of the Moon,—
I felt the blazing glory of the Sun;
I heard the Song of Children crying, "Free!"
I saw the face of Freedom—
And I died.

CHAPTER **VIII**

The Immortal Child

If a man die shall he live again? We do not know. But this we do know, that our children's children live forever and grow and develop toward perfection as they are trained. All human problems, then, center in the Immortal Child and his education is the problem of problems. And first for illustration of what I would say may I not take for example, out of many millions, the life of one dark child.

It is now nineteen years since I first saw Coleridge-Taylor. We were in London in some somber hall where there were many meeting, men and women called chiefly to the beautiful World's Fair at Paris; and then a few slipping over to London to meet Pan-Africa. We were there from Cape Colony and Liberia, from Haiti and the States, and from the Islands of the Sea. I remember the stiff, young officer who came with credentials from Menelik of Abyssinia; I remember the bitter, black American who whispered how an army of the Soudan might some day cross the Alps; I remember Englishmen, like the Colensos, who sat and counseled with us; but above all, I remember Coleridge-Taylor.

He was a little man and nervous, with dark-golden face and hair that bushed and strayed. His fingers were always nervously seeking hidden keys and he was quick with enthusiasm,—instinct with life. His bride of a year or more,—dark, too, in her whiter way,—was of the calm and quiet type. Her soft contralto voice thrilled us often as she sang, while her silences were full of understanding.

Several times we met in public gatherings and then they bade me to their home,—a nest of a cottage, with gate and garden, hidden in London's endless rings of suburbs. I dimly recall through these years a room in cozy disorder, strewn with music—music on the floor and music on the chairs, music in the air as the master rushed to the piano now and again to make some memory melodious—some allusion real.

And then at last, for it was the last, I saw Coleridge-Taylor in a mighty throng of people crowding the Crystal Palace. We came in facing the stage and scarcely dared look around. On the stage were a full orchestra, a chorus of eight hundred voices, and some of the world's famous soloists. He left his wife sitting beside me, and she was very silent as he went forward to lift the conductor's baton. It was one of the earliest renditions of "Hiawatha's Wedding Feast." We sat at rapt attention and when the last, weird music died, the great chorus and orchestra rose as a man to acclaim the master; he turned toward the audience and then we turning for the first time saw that sea of faces behind,—the misty thousands whose voices rose to one strong shout of joy! It was a moment such as one does not often live. It seemed, and was, prophetic.

This young man who stepped forth as one of the most notable of modern English composers had a simple and uneventful career. His father was a black surgeon of Sierra Leone who came to London for study. While there he met an English girl and this son was born, in London, in 1875.

Then came a series of chances. His father failed to succeed and disappeared back to Africa leaving the support of the child to the poor working mother. The child showed evidences of musical talent and a friendly workingman gave him a little violin. A musician glancing from his window saw a little dark boy playing marbles on the street with a tiny violin in one hand; he gave him lessons. He happened to gain entrance into a charity school with a master of understanding mind who recognized genius when he saw it; and finally his beautiful child's treble brought him to the notice of the choirmaster of St. George's, Croyden.

So by happy accident his way was clear. Within his soul was no hesitation. He was one of those fortunate beings who are not called to *Wander-Jahre,* but are born with sails set and seas charted. Already the baby of four little years was a musician, and as choir-boy and violinist he walked unhesitatingly and surely to his life work. He was graduated with honors from the Royal Academy of Music in 1894, and married soon after the daughter of one of his professors. Then his life began, and whatever it lacked of physical adventure in the conventional round of a modern world-city, it more than gained in the almost tempestuous outpouring of his spiritual nature. Life to him was neither meat nor drink,—it was creative flame; ideas, plans, melodies glowed within him. To create, to do, to accomplish; to know the white glory of mighty midnights and the pale Amen of dawns was his day of days. Songs, pianoforte and violin pieces, trios and quintets for strings, incidental music, symphony, orchestral, and choral works rushed from his fingers. Nor were they laboriously contrived or light, thin things made to meet sudden popularity. Rather they were the flaming bits that must be said and sung,—that could not wait the slower birth of years, so hurried to the world as though their young creator knew that God gave him but a day. His whole active life was scarcely more than a decade and a half, and yet in that time, without wealth, friends, or influence, in the face of perhaps the most critical and skeptical and least imaginative civilization of the modern world, he wrote his name so high as a creative artist that it cannot soon be forgotten.

And this was but one side of the man. On the other was the sweet-tempered, sympathetic comrade, always willing to help, never knowing how to refuse, generous with every nerve and fiber of his being. Think of a young musician, father of a family, who at the time of his death held positions as Associate of the Royal College of Music, Professor in Trinity College and Crystal Palace, Conductor of the Handel Choral Society and the Rochester Choral Society, Principal of the

Guildhall School of Music, where he had charge of the choral choir, the orchestra, and the opera. He was repeatedly the leader of music festivals all over Great Britain and a judge of contests. And with all this his house was open in cheering hospitality to friends and his hand ever ready with sympathy and help.

When such a man dies, it must bring pause to a reasoning world. We may call his death-sickness pneumonia, but we all know that it was sheer overwork,—the using of a delicately-tuned instrument too commonly and continuously and carelessly to let it last its normal life. We may well talk of the waste of wood and water, of food and fire, but the real and unforgivable waste of modern civilization is the waste of ability and genius,—the killing of useful, indispensable men who have no right to die; who deserve, not for themselves, but for the world, leisure, freedom from distraction, expert medical advice, and intelligent sympathy.

Coleridge-Taylor's life work was not finished,—it was but well begun. He lived only his first period of creative genius, when melody and harmony flashed and fluttered in subtle, compelling, and more than promising profusion. He did not live to do the organized, constructive work in the full, calm power of noonday,—the reflective finishing of evening. In the annals of the future his name must always stand high, but with the priceless gift of years, who can say where it might not have stood.

Why should he have worked so breathlessly, almost furiously? It was, we may be sure, because with unflinching determination and with no thought of surrender he faced the great alternative,—the choice which the cynical, thoughtless, busy, modern world spreads grimly before its greater souls—food or beauty, bread and butter, or ideals. And continually we see worthier men turning to the pettier, cheaper thing—the popular portrait, the sensational novel, the jingling song. The choice is not always between the least and the greatest, the high and the empty, but only too often it is between starvation and something. When, therefore, we see a man, working desperately to earn a living and still stooping to no paltry dickering and to no unworthy work, handing away a "Hiawatha" for less than a song, pausing for glimpses of the stars when a world full of charcoal glowed far more warmly and comfortably, we know that such a man is a hero in a sense never approached by the swashbuckling soldier or the lying patriot.

Deep as was the primal tragedy in the life of Coleridge-Taylor, there lay another still deeper. He smiled at it lightly, as we all do,—we who live within the veil,—to hide the deeper hurt. He had, with us, that divine and African gift of laughter, that echo of a thousand centuries of suns. I mind me how once he told of the bishop, the well-groomed English bishop, who eyed the artist gravely, with his eye-glass—hair and color and figure,—and said quite audibly to his friends, "Quite interesting—looks intelligent,—yes—yes!"

Fortunate was Coleridge-Taylor to be born in Europe and to speak a universal tongue. In America he could hardly have had his career. His genius was, to be sure, recognized (with some palpitation and consternation) when it came full-grown across the seas with an English imprint; but born here, it might never have been permitted to grow. We know in America how to discourage, choke, and murder ability when it so far forgets itself as to choose a dark skin. England, thank God, is slightly more civilized than her colonies; but even there the path of this young man was no way of roses and just a shade thornier than that of whiter men. He did not complain at it,—he did not

"Wince and cry aloud."

Rather the hint here and there of color discrimination in England aroused in him deeper and more poignant sympathy with his people throughout the world. He was one with that great company of mixed-blooded men: Pushkin and Dumas, Hamilton and Douglass, Browning and many others; but he more than most of these men knew the call of the blood when it came and listened and answered. He came to America with strange enthusiasm. He took with quite simple and unconscious grace the conventional congratulations of the musical world. He was used to that. But to his own people—to the sad sweetness of their voices, their inborn sense of music, their broken, half-articulate voices,—he leapt with new enthusiasm. From the fainter shadowings of his own life, he sensed instinctively the vaster tragedy of theirs. His soul yearned to give voice and being to this human thing. He early turned to the sorrow songs. He sat at the faltering feet of Paul Laurence Dunbar and he asked (as we sadly shook our heads) for some masterpiece of this world-tragedy that his soul could set to music. And then, so characteristically, he rushed back to England, composed a half-dozen exquisite harmonies haunted by slave-songs, led the Welsh in their singing, listened to the Scotch, ordered great music festivals in all England, wrote for Beerbohm Tree, took on another music professorship, promised a trip to Germany, and at last, staggering home one night, on his way to his wife and little boy and girl, fell in his tracks and in four days was dead, at the age of thirty-seven. They say that in his death-throe he arose and facing some great, ghostly choir raised his last baton, while all around the massive silence rang with the last mist-music of his dying ears.

He was buried from St. Michael's on September 5, 1912, with the acclaim of kings and music masters and little children and to the majestic melody of his own music. The tributes that followed him to his grave were unusually hearty and sincere. The head of the Royal College calls the first production of "Hiawatha" one of the most remarkable events in modern English musical history and the trilogy one of the most universally-beloved works of modern English music. One critic calls Taylor's a name "which with that of Elgar represented the nation's most individual output" and calls his "Atonement" "perhaps the finest passion music of modern times." Another critic speaks of his originality: "Though surrounded by the influences that are at work in Europe today, he retained his individuality to the end, developing his style, however, and evincing new ideas in each succeeding work. His untimely death at the age of thirty-seven, a short life—like those of Schubert, Mendelssohn, Chopin, and Hugo Wolf—has robbed the world of one of its noblest singers, one of those few men of modern times who found expression in the language of musical song, a lyricist of power and worth."

But the tributes did not rest with the artist; with peculiar unanimity they sought his "sterling character," "the good husband and father," the "staunch and loyal friend." And perhaps I cannot better end these hesitating words than with that tribute from one who called this master, friend, and whose lament cried in the night with more of depth and passion than Alfred Noyes is wont in his self-repression to voice:

> "Through him, his race, a moment, lifted up
> Forests of hands to beauty, as in prayer,
> Touched through his lips the sacramental cup
> And then sank back, benumbed in our bleak air."

Yet, consider: to many millions of people this man was all wrong. *First*, he ought never to have been born, for he was the mulatto son of a white woman. *Secondly*, he should never have been educated as a musician,—he should have been trained for his "place" in the world and to make him satisfied therewith. *Thirdly*, he should not have married the woman he loved and who loved him, for she was white and the niece of an Oxford professor. *Fourthly*, the children of such a union—but why proceed? You know it all by heart.

If he had been black, like Paul Laurence Dunbar, would the argument have been different? No. He should never have been born, for he is a "problem." He should never be educated, for he cannot be educated. He should never marry, for that means children and there is no place for black children in this world.

In the treatment of the child the world foreshadows its own future and faith. All words and all thinking lead to the child,—to that vast immortality and wide sweep of infinite possibility which the child represents. Such thought as this it was that made the Master say of old as He saw baby faces:

"And whosoever shall offend one of these little ones, it is better for him that a millstone were hanged about his neck and he were cast into the sea."

And yet the mothers and fathers and the men and women of my race must often pause and ask: Is it worth while? Ought children be born to us? Have we any right to make human souls face what we face today? The answer is clear: If the great battle of human right against poverty, against disease, against color prejudice is to be won, it must be won, not in our day, but in the day of our children's children. Ours is the blood and dust of battle; theirs the rewards of victory. If, then, they are not there because we have not brought them into the world, we have been the guiltiest factor in conquering ourselves. It is our duty, then, to accomplish the immortality of black blood, in order that the day may come in this dark world when poverty shall be abolished, privilege be based on individual desert, and the color of a man's skin be no bar to the outlook of his soul.

If it is our duty as honest colored men and women, battling for a great principle, to bring not aimless rafts of children to the world, but as many as, with reasonable sacrifice, we can train to largest manhood, what in its inner essence shall that training be, particularly in its beginning?

The first temptation is to shield the child,—to hedge it about that it may not know and will not dream of the color line. Then when we can no longer wholly shield, to indulge and pamper and coddle, as though in this dumb way to compensate. From this attitude comes the multitude of our spoiled, wayward, disappointed children. And must we not blame ourselves? For while the motive was pure and the outer menace undoubted, is shielding and indulgence the way to meet it?

Some Negro parents, realizing this, leave their children to sink or swim in this sea of race prejudice. They neither shield nor explain, but thrust them forth grimly into school or street and let them learn as they may from brutal fact. Out of this may come strength, poise, self-dependence, and out of it, too, may come bewilderment, cringing deception, and self-distrust. It is, all said, a brutal, unfair method, and in its way it is as bad as shielding and indulgence. Why not, rather, face the facts and tell the truth? Your child is wiser than you think.

The truth lies ever between extremes. It is wrong to introduce the child to race consciousness prematurely; it is dangerous to let that consciousness grow spontaneously without intelligent guidance. With every step of dawning intelligence, explanation—frank, free, guiding explanation—must come. The day will dawn when mother must explain gently but clearly why the little girls next door do not want to play with "niggers"; what the real cause is of the teachers' unsympathetic attitude; and how people may ride in the backs of street cars and the smoker end of trains and still be people, honest high-minded souls.

Remember, too, that in such frank explanation you are speaking in

nine cases out of ten to a good deal clearer understanding than you
think and that the child-mind has what your tired soul may have lost
faith in,—the Power and the Glory.

Out of little, unspoiled souls rise up wonderful resources and healing balm. Once the colored child understands the white world's attitude and the shameful wrong of it, you have furnished it with a great
life motive,—a power and impulse toward good which is the mightiest
thing man has. How many white folk would give their own souls if
they might graft into their children's souls a great, moving, guiding
ideal!

With this Power there comes, in the transfiguring soul of childhood, the Glory: the vision of accomplishment, the lofty ideal. Once
let the strength of the motive work, and it becomes the life task of the
parent to guide and to shape the ideal; to raise it from resentment and
revenge to dignity and self-respect, to breadth and accomplishment, to
human service; to beat back every thought of cringing and surrender.

Here, at last, we can speak with no hesitation, with no lack of
faith. For we know that as the world grows better there will be realized
in our children's lives that for which we fight unfalteringly, but vainly
now.

So much for the problem of the home and our own dark children.
Now let us look beyond the pale upon the children of the wide world.
What is the real lesson of the life of Coleridge-Taylor? It is this: humanly speaking it was sheer accident that this boy developed his genius. We have a right to assume that hundreds and thousands of boys
and girls today are missing the chance of developing unusual talents
because the chances have been against them; and that indeed the majority of the children of the world are not being systematically fitted for
their life work and for life itself. Why?

Many seek the reason in the content of the school program. They
feverishly argue the relative values of Greek, mathematics, and manual
training, but fail with singular unanimity in pointing out the fundamental cause of our failure in human education: That failure is due to
the fact that we aim not at the full development of the child, but that
the world regards and always has regarded education first as a means
of buttressing the established order of things rather than improving it.
And this is the real reason why strife, war, and revolution have
marked the onward march of humanity instead of reason and sound
reform. Instead of seeking to push the coming generation ahead of our
pitiful accomplishment, we insist that it march behind. We say, morally, that high character is conformity to present public opinion; we say
industrially that the present order is best and that children must be
trained to perpetuate it.

But, it is objected, what else can we do? Can we teach Revolution
to the inexperienced in hope that they may discern progress? No, but
we may teach frankly that this world is not perfection, but develop-

ment: that the object of education is manhood and womanhood, clear reason, individual talent and genius and the spirit of service and sacrifice, and not simply a frantic effort to avoid change in present institutions; that industry is for man and not man for industry and that while we must have workers to work, the prime object of our training is not the work but the worker—not the maintenance of present industrial caste but the development of human intelligence by which drudgery may be lessened and beauty widened.

Back of our present educational system is the philosophy that sneers at the foolish Fathers who believed it self-evident, "that all men were created free and equal." Surely the overwhelming evidence is today that men are slaves and unequal. But is it not education that is the creator of this freedom and equality? Most men today cannot conceive of a freedom that does not involve somebody's slavery. They do not want equality because the thrill of their happiness comes from having things that others have not. But may not human education fix the fine ideal of an equal maximum of freedom for every human soul combined with that minimum of slavery for each soul which the inexorable physical facts of the world impose—rather than complete freedom for some and complete slavery for others; and, again, is not the equality toward which the world moves an equality of honor in the assigned human task itself rather than equal facility in doing different tasks? Human equality is not lack of difference, nor do the infinite human differences argue relative superiority and inferiority. And, again, how new an aspect human differences may assume when all men are educated. Today we think of apes, semi-apes, and human beings; tomorrow we may think of Keir Hardies, Roosevelts, and Beethovens—not equals but men. Today we are forcing men into educational slavery in order that others may enjoy life, and excuse ourselves by saying that the world's work must be done. We are degrading some sorts of work by honoring others, and then expressing surprise that most people object to having their children trained solely to take up their father's tasks.

Given as the ideal the utmost possible freedom for every human soul, with slavery for none, and equal honor for all necessary human tasks, then our problem of education is greatly simplified: we aim to develop human souls; to make all intelligent; to discover special talents and genius. With this course of training beginning in early childhood and never ceasing must go the technical training for the present world's work according to carefully studied individual gifts and wishes.

On the other hand, if we arrange our system of education to develop workmen who will not strike and Negroes satisfied with their present place in the world, we have set ourselves a baffling task. We find ourselves compelled to keep the masses ignorant and to curb our own thought and expression so as not to inflame the ignorant. We force moderate reformers and men with new and valuable ideas to become red radicals and revolutionists, since that happens to be the only way to make the world listen to reason. Consider our race problem in the South: the South has invested in Negro ignorance; some Northerners proposed limited education, not, they explained, to better the Negro, but merely to make the investment more profitable to the present beneficiaries. They thus gained wide Southern support for schools like Hampton and Tuskegee. But could this program be expected long to satisfy colored folk? And was this shifty dodging of the real issue the wisest statesmanship? No! The real question in the South is the question of the permanency of present color caste. The problem, then, of the formal training of our colored children has been strangely complicated by the strong feeling of certain persons as to their future in America and the world. And the reaction toward this caste education has strengthened the idea of caste education throughout the world.

Let us then return to fundamental ideals. Children must be trained in a knowledge of what the world is and what it knows and how it does its daily work. These things cannot be separated: we cannot teach pure knowledge apart from actual facts, or separate truth from the human mind. Above all we must not forget that the object of all education is the child itself and not what it does or makes.

It is here that a great movement in America has grievously sinned against the light. There has arisen among us a movement to make the Public School primarily the hand-maiden of production. America is conceived of as existing for the sake of its mines, fields and factories, and not those factories, fields and mines as existing for America. Consequently, the public schools are for training the mass of men as servants and laborers and mechanics to increase the land's industrial efficiency.

Those who oppose this program, especially if they are black, are accused of despising common toil and humble service. In fact, we Negroes are but facing in our own children a world problem: how can we, while maintaining a proper output of goods and furnishing needed services, increase the knowledge of experience of common men and conserve genius for the common weal? Without wider, deeper intelligence among the masses Democracy cannot accomplish its greater ends. Without a more careful conservation of human ability and talent the world cannot secure the services which its greater needs call for. Yet today who goes to college, the Talented or the Rich? Who goes to high school, the Bright or the Well-to-Do? Who does the physical work of the world, those whose muscles need the exercise or those whose souls and minds are stupefied with manual toil? How is the drudgery of the world distributed, by thoughtful justice or the lash of Slavery?

We cannot base the education of future citizens on the present inexcusable inequality of wealth nor on physical differences of race. We must seek not to make men carpenters but to make carpenters men.

Colored Americans must then with deep determination educate

their children in the broadest, highest way. They must fill the colleges with the talented and fill the fields and shops with the intelligent. Wisdom is the principal thing. Therefore, get wisdom.

But why am I talking simply of "colored" children? Is not the problem of their education simply an intensification of the problem of educating all children? Look at our plight in the United States, nearly 150 years after the establishment of a government based on human intelligence.

If we take the figures of the Thirteenth Census, we find that there were five and one-half million illiterate Americans of whom 3,184,633 were white. Remembering that illiteracy is a crude and extreme test of ignorance, we may assume that there are in the United States ten million people over ten years of age who are too ignorant either to perform their civic duties or to teach industrial efficiency. Moreover, it does not seem that this illiteracy is disappearing rapidly.

For instance, nine per cent of American children between ten and nineteen years of age cannot read and write. Moreover, there are millions of children who, judging by the figures for the school year 1909–10, are not going to learn to read and write, for of the Americans six to fourteen years of age there were 3,125,392 who were not in school a single day during that year. If we take the eleven million youths fifteen to twenty years of age for whom vocational training is particularly adapted, we find that nearly five per cent of these, or 448,414, are absolutely illiterate; it is not too much to assume that a million of them have not acquired enough of the ordinary tools of intelligence to make the most of efficient vocational training.

Confining ourselves to the white people, over fifteen per cent of the white children six to fourteen years of age, or 2,253,198, did not attend school during the school year 1909–10. Of the native white children of native parents ten to fourteen years of age nearly a tenth were not in school during that year; 121,878 native white children of native parents, fifteen to nineteen years of age, were illiterate.

If we confine our attention to the colored children, the case is, of course, much worse.

We cannot hope to make intelligent workmen and intelligent citizens of a group of people, over forty per cent of whose children six to fourteen years of age were not in school a single day during 1909–10; for the other sixty per cent the school term in the majority of cases was probably less than five months. Of the Negro children ten to fourteen years of age 18.9 per cent were illiterate; of those fifteen to nineteen years of age 20.3 per cent were illiterate; of those ten to fourteen years of age 31.4 per cent. did not go to school a single day in 1909–10.

What is the trouble? It is simple. We are spending one dollar for education where we should spend ten dollars. If tomorrow we multiplied our effort to educate the next generation ten-fold, we should but begin our bounden duty. The heaven that lies about our infancy is but the ideals come true which every generation of children is capable of bringing; but we, selfish in our own ignorance and incapacity, are making of education a series of miserable compromises: How ignorant can we let a child grow to be in order to make him the best cotton mill operative? What is the least sum that will keep the average youth out of jail? How many months saved on a high school course will make the largest export of wheat?

If we realized that children are the future, that immortality is the present child, that no education which educates can possibly be too costly, then we know that the menace of Kaiserism which called for the expenditure of more than 332 thousand millions of dollars was not a whit more pressing than the menace of ignorance, and that no nation tomorrow will call itself civilized which does not give every single human being college and vocational training free and under the best teaching force procurable for love or money.

This world has never taken the education of children seriously. Misled by selfish dreamings of personal life forever, we have neglected the true and practical immortality through the endless life of children's children. Seeking counsels of our own souls' perfection, we have despised and rejected the possible increasing perfection of unending generations. Or if we are thrown back in pessimistic despair from making living folk decent, we leap to idle speculations of a thousand years hereafter instead of working steadily and persistently for the next generation.

All our problems center in the child. All our hopes, our dreams are for our children. Has our own life failed? Let its lesson save the children's lives from similar failure. Is democracy a failure? Train up citizens that will make it succeed. Is wealth too crude, too foolish in form, and too easily stolen? Train up workers with honor and consciences and brains. Have we degraded service with menials? Abolish the mean spirit and implant sacrifice. Do we despise women? Train them as workers and thinkers and not as playthings, lest future generations ape our worst mistake. Do we despise darker races? Teach the children its fatal cost in spiritual degradation and murder, teach them that to hate "niggers" or "chinks" is to crucify souls like their own. Is there anything we would accomplish with human beings? Do it with the immortal child, with a stretch of endless time for doing it and with infinite possibilities to work on.

Is this our attitude toward education? It is not—neither in England nor America—in France nor Germany—with black nor white nor yellow folk. Education to the modern world is a burden which we are driven to carry. We shirk and complain. We do just as little as possible and only threat or catastrophe induces us to do more than a minimum. If the ignorant mass, panting to know, revolts, we dole them gingerly enough knowledge to pacify them temporarily. If, as in the Great War, we discover soldiers too ignorant to use our machines of murder and destruction, we train them—to use machines of murder and destruction. If mounting wealth calls for intelligent workmen, we rush tumultuously to train workers—in order to increase our wealth. But of great, broad plans to train all men for all things—to make a universe intelligent, busy, good, creative and beautiful—where in this wide world is such an educational program? To announce it is to invite gasps or Brobdingnagian laughter. It cannot be done. It will cost too much.

What has been done with man can be done with men, if the world tries long enough and hard enough. And as to the cost—all the wealth of the world, save that necessary for sheer decent existence and for the maintenance of past civilization, is, and of right ought to be, the property of the children for their education.

I mean it. In one year, 1917, we spent $96,700,000,000 for war. We blew it away to murder, maim, and destroy! Why? Because the blind, brutal crime of powerful and selfish interests made this path through hell the only visible way to heaven. We did it. We had to do it, and we are glad the putrid horror is over. But, now, are we prepared to spend less to make a world in which the resurgence of such devilish power will be impossible?

Do we really want war to cease?

Then educate the children of this generation at a cost no whit less and if necessary a hundred times as great as the cost of the Great War.

Last year, 1917, education cost us $915,000,000.

Next year it ought to cost us at least two thousand million dollars. We should spend enough money to hire the best teaching force possible—the best organizing and directing ability in the land, even if we have to strip the railroads and meat trust. We should dot city and country with the most efficient, sanitary, and beautiful school-houses the world knows and we should give every American child common school, high school, and college training and then vocational guidance in earning a living.

Is this a dream?

Can we afford less?

Consider our so-called educational "problems": "How may we keep pupils in the high school?" Feed and clothe them. "Shall we teach Latin, Greek, and mathematics to the 'masses'?" If they are worth teaching to anybody, the masses need them most. "Who shall go to college?" Everybody. "When shall culture training give place to technical education for work?" Never.

These questions are not "problems." They are simply "excuses" for spending less time and money on the next generation. Given ten millions of dollars a year, what can we best do with the education of a million children? The real answer is—kill nine hundred and ninety thousand of them quickly and not gradually, and make thoroughly-trained men and women of the other ten thousand. But who set the limit of ten million dollars? Who says it shall not be ten thousand millions, as it ought to be? You and I say it, and in saying it we sin against the Holy Ghost.

We sin because in our befuddled brains we have linked money and education inextricably. We assume that only the wealthy have a real right to education when, in fact, being born is being given a right to college training. Our wealth today is, we all know, distributed mainly by chance inheritance and personal favor and yet we attempt to base the right to education on this foundation. The result is grotesque! We bury genius; we send it to jail; we ridicule and mock it, while we send mediocrity and idiocy to college, gilded and crowned. For three hundred years we have denied black Americans an education and now we exploit them before a gaping world: See how ignorant and degraded they are! All they are fit for is education for cotton-picking and dishwashing. When Dunbar and Taylor happen along, we are torn between something like shamefaced anger or impatient amazement.

A world guilty of this last and mightiest war has no right to enjoy or create until it has made the future safe from another Arkansas or Rheims. To this there is but one patent way, proved and inescapable, Education, and that not for me or for you but for the Immortal Child. And that child is of all races and all colors. All children are the children of all and not of individuals and families and races. The whole generation must be trained and guided and out of it as out of a huge reservoir must be lifted all genius, talent, and intelligence to serve all the world.

Almighty Death

Softly, quite softly—
For I hear, above the murmur of the sea,
Faint and far-fallen footsteps, as of One
Who comes from out beyond the endless ends of Time,
With voice that downward looms thro' singing stars;
Its subtle sound I see thro' these long-darkened eyes,
I hear the Light He bringeth on His hands—
Almighty Death!
Softly, oh, softly, lest He pass me by,
And that unquivering Light toward which my longing
    soul
And tortured body through these years have writhed,
Fade to the dun darkness of my days.

Softly, full softly, let me rise and greet
The strong, low luting of that long-awaited call;
Swiftly be all my good and going gone,
And this vast veiled and vanquished vigor of my soul
Seek somehow otherwhere its rest and goal,

Where endless spaces stretch,
Where endless time doth moan,
Where endless light doth pour
Thro' the black kingdoms of eternal death.

Then haply I may see what things I have not seen,
Then I may know what things I have not known;
Then may I do my dreams.
Farewell! No sound of idle mourning let there be
To shudder this full silence—save the voice
Of children—little children, white and black,
Whispering the deeds I tried to do for them;
While I at last unguided and alone
Pass softly, full softly.

CHAPTER **IX**

Of Beauty and Death

For long years we of the world gone wild have looked into the face of death and smiled. Through all our bitter tears we knew how beautiful it was to die for that which our souls called sufficient. Like all true beauty this thing of dying was so simple, so matter-of-fact. The boy clothed in his splendid youth stood before us and laughed in his own jolly way,—went and was gone. Suddenly the world was full of the fragrance of sacrifice. We left our digging and burden-bearing; we turned from our scraping and twisting of things and words; we paused from our hurrying hither and thither and walking up and down, and asked in half-whisper: this Death—is this Life? And is its beauty real or false? And of this heart-questioning I am writing.

My friend, who is pale and positive, said to me yesterday, as the tired sun was nodding:

"You are too sensitive."

I admit, I am—sensitive. I am artificial. I cringe or am bumptious or immobile. I am intellectually dishonest, art-blind, and I lack humor.

"Why don't you stop all this?" she retorts triumphantly.

You will not let us.

"There you go, again. You know that I—"

Wait! I answer. Wait!

I arise at seven. The milkman has neglected me. He pays little attention to colored districts. My white neighbor glares elaborately. I walk softly, lest I disturb him. The children jeer as I pass to work. The women in the street car withdraw their skirts or prefer to stand. The policeman is truculent. The elevator man hates to serve Negroes. My job is insecure because the white union wants it and does not want me. I try to lunch, but no place near will serve me. I go forty blocks to Marshall's, but the Committee of Fourteen closes Marshall's; they say white women frequent it.

"Do all eating places discriminate?"

No, but how shall I know which do not—except—

I hurry home through crowds. They mutter or get angry. I go to a mass-meeting. They stare. I go to a church. "We don't admit niggers!"

Or perhaps I leave the beaten track. I seek new work. "Our employees would not work with you; our customers would object."

I ask to help in social uplift.

"Why—er—we will write you."

I enter the free field of science. Every laboratory door is closed and no endowments are available.

I seek the universal mistress, Art; the studio door is locked.

I write literature. "We cannot publish stories of colored folks of that type." It's the only type I know.

This is my life. It makes me idiotic. It gives me artificial problems. I hesitate, I rush, I waver. In fine,—I am sensitive!

My pale friend looks at me with disbelief and curling tongue.

"Do you mean to sit there and tell me that this is what happens to you each day?"

Certainly not, I answer low.

"Then you only fear it will happen?"

I fear!

"Well, haven't you the courage to rise above a—almost a craven fear?"

Quite—quite craven is my fear, I admit; but the terrible thing is—these things do happen!

"But you just said—"

They do happen. Not all each day,—surely not. But now and then—now seldom, now, sudden; now after a week, now in a chain of awful minutes; not everywhere, but anywhere—in Boston, in Atlanta. That's the hell of it. Imagine spending your life looking for insults or for hiding places from them—shrinking (instinctively and despite desperate bolsterings of courage) from blows that are not always but ever; not each day, but each week, each month, each year. Just, perhaps, as you have choked back the craven fear and cried, "I am and will be the master of my—"

"No more tickets downstairs; here's one to the smoking gallery."

You hesitate. You beat back your suspicions. After all, a cigarette with Charlie Chaplin—then a white man pushes by—

"Three in the orchestra."

"Yes, sir." And in he goes.

Suddenly your heart chills. You turn yourself away toward the golden twinkle of the purple night and hesitate again. What's the use? Why not always yield—always take what's offered,—always bow to force, whether of cannon or dislike? Then the great fear surges in your soul, the real fear—the fear beside which other fears are vain imaginings; the fear lest right there and then you are losing your own soul; that you are losing your own soul and the soul of a people; that millions of unborn children, black and gold and mauve, are being there and then despoiled by you because you are a coward and dare not fight!

Suddenly that silly orchestra seat and the cavorting of a comedian with funny feet become matters of life, death, and immortality; you grasp the pillars of the universe and strain as you sway back to that befrilled ticket girl. You grip your soul for riot and murder. You choke and sputter, and she seeing that you are about to make a "fuss" obeys her orders and throws the tickets at you in contempt. Then you slink to your seat and crouch in the darkness before the film, with every tissue burning! The miserable wave of reaction engulfs you. To think of compelling puppies to take your hard-earned money; fattening hogs to hate you and yours; forcing your way among cheap and tawdry idiots—God! What a night of pleasure!

Here, then, is beauty and ugliness, a wide vision of world-sacrifice, a fierce gleam of world-hate. Which is life and what is death and how shall we face so tantalizing a contradiction? Any explanation must necessarily be subtle and involved. No pert and easy word of encouragement, no merely dark despair, can lay hold of the roots of these things. And first and before all, we cannot forget that this world is beautiful. Grant all its ugliness and sin—the petty, horrible snarl of its putrid threads, which few have seen more near or more often than I—notwithstanding all this, the beauty of this world is not to be denied.

Casting my eyes about I dare not let them rest on the beauty of Love and Friend, for even if my tongue were cunning enough to sing this, the revelation of reality here is too sacred and the fancy too untrue. Of one world-beauty alone may we at once be brutally frank and that is the glory of physical nature; this, though the least of beauties, is divine!

And so, too, there are depths of human degradation which it is not fair for us to probe. With all their horrible prevalence, we cannot call them natural. But may we not compare the least of the world's beauty with the least of its ugliness—not murder, starvation, and rapine, with love and friendship and creation—but the glory of sea and sky and city, with the little hatefulnesses and thoughtlessnesses of race prejudice, that out of such juxtaposition we may, perhaps, deduce some rule of beauty and life—or death?

There mountains hurl themselves against the stars and at their feet lie black and leaden seas. Above float clouds—white, gray, and inken, while the clear, impalpable air springs and sparkles like new wine. Last night we floated on the calm bosom of the sea in the southernmost haven of Mount Desert. The water flamed and sparkled. The sun had gone, but above the crooked back of cumulus clouds, dark and pink with radiance, and on the other sky aloft to the eastward piled the gorgeous-curtained mists of evening. The radiance faded and a shadowy velvet veiled the mountains, a humid depth of gloom behind which lurked all the mysteries of life and death, while above, the clouds hung ashen and dull; lights twinkled and flashed along the shore, boats glided in the twilight, and the little puffing of motors droned away. Then was the hour to talk of life and the meaning of life, while above gleamed silently, suddenly, star on star.

Bar Harbor lies beneath a mighty mountain, a great, bare, black mountain that sleeps above the town; but as you leave, it rises suddenly, threateningly, until far away on Frenchman's Bay it looms above the town in withering vastness, as if to call all that little world petty save itself. Beneath the cool, wide stare of that great mountain, men cannot live as giddily as in some lesser summer's playground. Before the unveiled face of nature, as it lies naked on the Maine coast, rises a certain human awe.

God molded his world largely and mightily off this marvelous coast and meant that in the tired days of life men should come and worship here and renew their spirit. This I have done and turning I go to work again. As we go, ever the mountains of Mount Desert rise and greet us on our going—somber, rock-ribbed and silent, looking unmoved on the moving world, yet conscious of their everlasting strength.

About us beats the sea—the sail-flecked, restless sea, humming its tune about our flying keel, unmindful of the voices of men. The land sinks to meadows, black pine forests, with here and there a blue and wistful mountain. Then there are islands—bold rocks above the sea, curled meadows; through and about them roll ships, weather-beaten and patched of sail, strong-hulled and smoking, light gray and shining. All the colors of the sea lie about us—gray and yellowing greens and doubtful blues, blacks not quite black, tinted silvers and golds and dreaming whites. Long tongues of dark and golden land lick far out into the tossing waters, and the white gulls sail and scream above them. It is a mighty coast—ground out and pounded, scarred, crushed, and carven in massive, frightful lineaments. Everywhere stand the pines—the little dark and steadfast pines that smile not, neither weep, but wait and wait. Near us lie isles of flesh and blood, white cottages, tiled and meadowed. Afar lie shadow-lands, high mist-hidden hills, mountains boldly limned, yet shading to the sky, faint and unreal.

We skirt the pine-clad shores, chary of men, and know how bitterly winter kisses these lonely shores to fill yon row of beaked ice houses that creep up the hills. We are sailing due westward and the sun, yet two hours high, is blazoning a fiery glory on the sea that spreads and gleams like some broad, jeweled trail, to where the blue and distant shadow-land lifts its carven front aloft, leaving, as it gropes, shades of shadows beyond.

Why do not those who are scarred in the world's battle and hurt by its hardness travel to these places of beauty and drown themselves in the utter joy of life? I asked this once sitting in a Southern home. Outside the spring of a Georgia February was luring gold to the bushes and languor to the soft air. Around me sat color in human flesh—brown that crimsoned readily; dim soft-yellow that escaped description; cream-like duskiness that shadowed to rich tints of autumn leaves. And yet a suggested journey in the world brought no response.

"I should think you would like to travel," said the white one.

But no, the thought of a journey seemed to depress them.

Did you ever see a "Jim-Crow" waiting-room? There are always exceptions, as at Greensboro—but usually there is no heat in winter and no air in summer; with undisturbed loafers and train hands and broken, disreputable settees; to buy a ticket is torture; you stand and stand and wait and wait until every white person at the "other window" is waited on. Then the tired agent yells across, because all the tickets and money are over there—

"What d'ye want? What? Where?"

The agent browbeats and contradicts you, hurries and confuses the ignorant, gives many persons the wrong change, compels some to purchase their tickets on the train at a higher price, and sends you and me out on the platform, burning with indignation and hatred!

The "Jim-Crow" car is up next the baggage car and engine. It stops out beyond the covering in the rain or sun or dust. Usually there is no step to help you climb on and often the car is a smoker cut in two and you must pass through the white smokers or else they pass through your part, with swagger and noise and stares. Your compartment is a half or a quarter or an eighth of the oldest car in service on the road. Unless it happens to be a through express, the plush is caked with dirt, the floor is grimy, and the windows dirty. An impertinent white newsboy occupies two seats at the end of the car and importunes you to the point of rage to buy cheap candy, Coco-Cola, and worthless, if not vulgar, books. He yells and swaggers, while a continued stream of white men saunters back and forth from the smoker to buy and hear. The white train crew from the baggage car uses the "Jim-Crow" to lounge in and perform their toilet. The conductor appropriates two seats for himself and his papers and yells gruffly for your tickets before the train has scarcely started. It is best not to ask him for information even in the gentlest tones. His information is for white persons chiefly. It is difficult to get lunch or clean water. Lunch rooms either don't serve niggers or serve them at some dirty and ill-attended hole in the wall. As for toilet rooms,—don't! If you have to change cars, be wary of junctions which are usually without accommodation and filled with quarrelsome white persons who hate a "darky dressed up." You are apt to have the company of a sheriff and a couple of meek or sullen black prisoners on part of your way and dirty colored section hands will pour in toward night and drive you to the smallest corner.

"No," said the little lady in the corner (she looked like an ivory cameo and her dress flowed on her like a caress), "we don't travel much."

Pessimism is cowardice. The man who cannot frankly acknowledge the "Jim-Crow" car as a fact and yet live and hope is simply afraid either of himself or of the world. There is not in the world a more disgraceful denial of human brotherhood than the "Jim-Crow" car of the southern United States; but, too, just as true, there is nothing more beautiful in the universe than sunset and moonlight on Montego Bay in far Jamaica. And both things are true and both belong to this our world, and neither can be denied.

The sun, prepared to cross that awful border which men call Night and Death, marshals his hosts. I seem to see the spears of mighty horsemen flash golden in the light; empurpled banners flame afar, and the low thunder of marching hosts thrills with the thunder of the sea. Athwart his own path, screening a face of fire, he throws cloud masses, masking his trained guns. And then the miracle is done. The host passes with roar too vast for human ear and the sun is set, leaving the frightened moon and blinded stars.

In the dusk the green-gold palms turn their star-like faces and stretch their fan-like fingers, lifting themselves proudly, lest any lordly leaf should know the taint of earth.

Out from the isle the serpent hill thrusts its great length around the bay, shouldering back the waters and the shadows. Ghost rains sweep down, smearing his rugged sides, yet on he writhes, undulant with pine and palm, gleaming until his low, sharp head and lambent tongue, grown gray and pale and silver in the dying day, kisses the molten gold of the golden sea.

Then comes the moon. Like fireflies nesting in the hand of God gleams the city, dim-swathed by fairy palms. A long, thin thumb, mist-mighty, points shadowy to the Spanish Main, while through the fingers foam the Seven Seas. Above the calm and gold-green moon, beneath the wind-wet earth; and here, alone, my soul enchained, enchanted!

From such heights of holiness men turn to master the world. All the pettiness of life drops away and it becomes a great battle before the Lord. His trumpet,—where does it sound and whither? I go. I saw Montego Bay at the beginning of the World War. The cry for service as high as heaven, as wide as human feeling, seemed filling the earth.

What were petty slights, silly insults, paltry problems, beside this call to do and dare and die? We black folk offered our services to fight. What happened? Most Americans have forgotten the extraordinary series of events which worked the feelings of black America to fever heat.

First was the refusal to accept Negro volunteers for the army, except in the four black regiments already established. While the nation was combing the country for volunteers for the regular army, it would not let the American Negro furnish even his proportionate quota of regular soldiers. This led to some grim bantering among Negroes:

"Why do you want to volunteer?" asked many. "Why should you fight for this country?"

Before we had chance to reply to this, there came the army draft bill and the proposal by Vardaman and his ilk to except Negroes. We protested to Washington in various ways, and while we were insisting that colored men should be drafted just as other citizens, the bill went through with two little "jokers."

First, it provided that Negroes should be drafted, but trained in "separate" units; and, secondly, it somewhat ambiguously permitted men to be drafted for "labor."

A wave of fear and unrest spread among Negroes and while we were looking at both these provisions askance, suddenly we received the draft registration blank. It directed persons "of African descent" to "tear off the corner!" Probably never before in the history of the United States has a portion of the citizens been so openly and crassly discriminated against by action of the general government. It was disheartening, and on top of it came the celebrated "German plots." It was alleged in various parts of the country with singular unanimity that Germans were working among the Negroes, and it was further intimated that this would make the Negroes too dangerous an element to trust with guns. To us, of course, it looked as though the discovery and the proposition came from the same thinly-veiled sources.

Considering carefully this series of happenings the American Negro sensed an approaching crisis and faced a puzzling dilemma. Here was evidently preparing fertile ground for the spread of disloyalty and resentment among the black masses, as they were forced to choose apparently between forced labor or a "Jim-Crow" draft. Manifestly when a minority group is thus segregated and forced out of the nation, they can in reason do but one thing—take advantage of the disadvantage. In this case we demanded colored officers for the colored troops.

General Wood was early approached and asked to admit suitable candidates to Plattsburg. He refused. We thereupon pressed the government for a "separate" camp for the training of Negro officers. Not only did the War Department hesitate at this request, but strong opposition arose among colored people themselves. They said we were going too far. "We will obey the law, but to ask for voluntary segregation is to insult ourselves." But strong, sober second thought came to our rescue. We said to our protesting brothers: "We face a condition, not a theory. There is not the slightest chance of our being admitted to white camps; therefore, it is either a case of a 'Jim-Crow' officers' training camp or no colored officers. Of the two things no colored officers would be the greater calamity."

Thus we gradually made up our minds. But the War Department still hesitated. It was besieged, and when it presented its final argument, "We have no place for such a camp," the trustees of Howard University said: "Take our campus." Eventually twelve hundred colored cadets were assembled at Fort Des Moines for officers' training.

The city of Des Moines promptly protested, but it finally changed its mind. Des Moines never before had seen such a class of colored men. They rapidly became popular with all classes and many encomiums were passed upon their conduct. Their commanding colonel pronounced their work first class and declared that they presented excellent material for officers.

Meantime, with one accord, the thought of the colored people turned toward Colonel Young, their highest officer in the regular army. Charles Young is a heroic figure. He is the typical soldier,—silent, uncomplaining, brave, and efficient! From his days at West Point throughout his thirty years of service he has taken whatever task was assigned him and performed it efficiently; and there is no doubt but that the army has been almost merciless in the requirements which it has put upon this splendid officer. He came through all with flying colors. In Haiti, in Liberia, in western camps, in the Sequoia Forests of California, and finally with Pershing in Mexico,—in every case he triumphed. Just at the time we were looking to the United States government to call him to head the colored officers' training at Des Moines, he was retired from the army, because of "high blood pressure!" There is no disputing army surgeons and their judgment in this case may be justified, but coming at the time it did, nearly every Negro in the United States believed that the "high blood pressure" that retired Colonel Young was in the prejudiced heads of the Southern oligarchy who were determined that no American Negro should ever wear the stars of a General.

To say that Negroes of the United States were disheartened at the retirement of Colonel Young is to put it mildly,—but there was more trouble. The provision that Negroes must be trained separately looked simple and was simple in places where there were large Negro contingents, but in the North with solitary Negroes drafted here and there we had some extraordinary developments. Regiments appeared with one Negro where the Negro had to be separated like a pest and put into a house or even a village by himself while the commander frantically telegraphed to Washington. Small wonder that one poor fellow in

601

Ohio solved the problem by cutting his throat. The whole process of drafting Negroes had to be held up until the government could find methods and places for assembling them.

Then came Houston. In a moment the nation forgot the whole record of one of the most celebrated regiments in the United States Army and its splendid service in the Indian Wars and in the Philippines. It was the first regiment mobilized in the Spanish-American War and it was the regiment that volunteered to a man to clean up the yellow fever camps when others hesitated. It was one of the regiments to which Pershing said in December:

"Men, I am authorized by Congress to tell you all that our people back in the States are mightily glad and proud at the way the soldiers have conducted themselves while in Mexico, and I, General Pershing, can say with pride that a finer body of men never stood under the flag of our nation than we find here tonight."

The nation, also, forgot the deep resentment mixed with the pale ghost of fear which Negro soldiers call up in the breasts of the white South. It is not so much that they fear that the Negro will strike if he gets a chance, but rather that they assume with curious unanimity that he has *reason* to strike, that any other persons in his circumstances or treated as he is would rebel. Instead of seeking to relieve the cause of such a possible feeling, most of them strain every effort to bottle up the black man's resentment. Is it inconceivable that now and then it bursts all bounds, as at Brownsville and Houston?

So in the midst of this mental turmoil came Houston and East St. Louis. At Houston black soldiers, goaded and insulted, suddenly went wild and "shot up" the town. At East St. Louis white strikers on war work killed and mobbed Negro workingmen, and as a result 19 colored soldiers were hanged and 51 imprisoned for life for killing 17 whites at Houston, while for killing 125 Negroes in East St. Louis, 20 white men were imprisoned, none for more than 15 years, and 10 colored men with them.

Once upon a time I took a great journey in this land to three of the ends of our world and over seven thousand mighty miles. I saw the grim desert and the high ramparts of the Rocky Mountains. Three days I flew from the silver beauty of Seattle to the somber whirl of Kansas City. Three days I flew from the brute might of Chicago to the air of the Angels in California, scented with golden flowers, where the homes of men crouch low and loving on the good, broad earth, as though they were kissing her blossoms. Three days I flew through the empire of Texas, but all these shall be tales untold, for in all this journey I saw but one thing that lived and will live eternal in my soul,— the Grand Cañon.

It is a sudden void in the bosom of earth, down to its entrails—a wound where the dull titanic knife has turned and twisted in the hole, leaving its edges livid, scarred, jagged, and pulsing over the white, and red, and purple of its mighty flesh, while down below—down, down below, in black and severed vein, boils the dull and sullen flood of the Colorado.

It is awful. There can be nothing like it. It is the earth and sky gone stark and raving mad. The mountains up-twirled, disbodied and inverted, stand on their peaks and throw their bowels to the sky. Their earth is air; their ether blood-red rock engreened. You stand upon their roots and fall into their pinnacles, a mighty mile.

Behold this mauve and purple mocking of time and space! See yonder peak! No human foot has trod it. Into that blue shadow only the eye of God has looked. Listen to the accents of that gorge which mutters: "Before Abraham was, I am." Is yonder wall a hedge of black or is it the rampart between heaven and hell? I see greens,—is it moss or giant pines? I see specks that may be boulders. Ever the winds sigh and drop into those sun-swept silences. Ever the gorge lies motionless, unmoved, until I fear. It is a grim thing, unholy, terrible! It is human— some mighty drama unseen, unheard, is playing there its tragedies or mocking comedy, and the laugh of endless years is shrieking onward from peak to peak, unheard, unechoed, and unknown.

One throws a rock into the abyss. It gives back no sound. It falls on silence—the voice of its thunders cannot reach so far. It is not—it cannot be a mere, inert, unfeeling, brute fact—its grandeur is too serene—its beauty too divine! It is not red, and blue, and green, but, ah! the shadows and the shades of all the world, glad colorings touched with a hesitant spiritual delicacy. What does it mean—what does it mean? Tell me, black and boiling water!

It is not real. It is but shadows. The shading of eternity. Last night yonder tesselated palace was gloom—dark, brooding thought and sin, while hither rose the mountains of the sun, golden, blazing, ensanguined. It was a dream. This blue and brilliant morning shows all those burning peaks alight, while here, shapeless, mistful, brood the shadowed towers.

I have been down into the entrails of earth—down, down by straight and staring cliffs—down by sounding waters and sun-strewn meadows; down by green pastures and still waters, by great, steep chasms—down by the gnarled and twisted fists of God to the deep, sad moan of the yellow river that did this thing of wonder,—a little winding river with death in its depth and a crown of glory in its flying hair.

I have seen what eye of man was never meant to see. I have profaned the sanctuary. I have looked upon the dread disrobing of the Night, and yet I live. Ere I hid my head she was standing in her cavern halls, glowing coldly westward—her feet were blackness: her robes, empurpled, flowed mistily from shoulder down in formless folds of folds; her head, pine-crowned, was set with jeweled stars. I turned away and dreamed—the cañon,—the awful, its depths called; its heights shuddered. Then suddenly I arose and looked. Her robes were falling. At dim-dawn they hung purplish-green and black. Slowly she stripped them from her gaunt and shapely limbs—her cold, gray garments shot with shadows stood revealed. Down dropped the black-blue robes, gray-pearled, and slipped, leaving a filmy, silken, misty thing, and underneath I glimpsed her limbs of utter light.

My God! For what am I thankful this night? For nothing. For nothing but the most commonplace of commonplaces; a table of gentlewomen and gentlemen—soft-spoken, sweet-tempered, full of human sympathy, who made me, a stranger, one of them. Ours was a fellowship of common books, common knowledge, mighty aims. We could laugh and joke and think as friends—and the Thing—the hateful, murderous, dirty Thing which in America we call "Nigger-hatred" was not only not there—it could not even be understood. It was a curious monstrosity at which civilized folk laughed or looked puzzled. There was no elegant and elaborate condescension of—"We once had a colored servant"—"My father was an Abolitionist"—"I've always been interested in *your people*"—there was only the community of kindred souls, the delicate reverence for the Thought that led, the quick deference to the guest. You left in quiet regret, knowing that they were not discussing you behind your back with lies and license. God! It was simply human decency and I had to be thankful for it because I am an American Negro, and white America, with saving exceptions, is cruel to everything that has black blood—and this was Paris, in the years of salvation, 1919. Fellow blacks, we must join the democracy of Europe.

Toul! Dim through the deepening dark of early afternoon, I saw its towers gloom dusky toward the murk of heaven. We wound in misty roads and dropped upon the city through the great throats of its walled bastions. There lay France—a strange, unknown, unfamiliar France. The city was dispossessed. Through its streets—its narrow, winding streets, old and low and dark, carven and quaint,—poured thousands upon thousands of strange feet of khaki-clad foreigners, and the echoes threw back awkward syllables that were never French. Here was France beaten to her knees yet fighting as never nation fought before, calling in her death agony across the seas till her help came and with all its strut and careless braggadocio saved the worthiest nation of the world from the wickedest fate ever plotted by Fools.

Tim Brimm was playing by the town-pump. Tim Brimm and the bugles of Harlem blared in the little streets of Maron in far Lorraine. The tiny streets were seas of mud. Dank mist and rain sifted through the cold air above the blue Moselle. Soldiers—soldiers everywhere—black soldiers, boys of Washington, Alabama, Philadelphia, Mississippi. Wild and sweet and wooing leapt the strains upon the air. French children gazed in wonder—women left their washing. Up in the window stood a black Major, a Captain, a Teacher, and I—with tears behind our smiling eyes. Tim Brimm was playing by the town-pump.

The audience was framed in smoke. It rose ghost-like out of memories—bitter memories of the officer near dead of pneumonia whose pain was lighted up by the nurses waiting to know whether he must be "Jim-Crowed" with privates or not. Memories of that great last morning when the thunders of hell called the Ninety-second to its last drive. Memories of bitter humiliations, determined triumphs, great victories, and bugle-calls that sounded from earth to heaven. Like memories framed in the breath of God, my audience peered in upon me—good, brown faces with great, kind, beautiful eyes—black soldiers of America rescuing beloved France—and the words came in praise and benediction there in the "Y," with its little stock of cigarettes and candies and its rusty wood stove.

"*Alors,*" said Madame, "*quatre sont morts*"—four dead—four tall, strong sons dead for France—sons like the sweet and blue-eyed daughter who was hiding her brave smile in the dusk. It was a tiny stone house whose front window lipped the passing sidewalk where ever tramped the feet of black soldiers marching home. There was a cavernous wardrobe, a great fireplace invaded by a new and jaunty iron stove. Vast, thick piles of bedding rose in yonder corner. Without was the crowded kitchen and up a half-stair was our bedroom that gave upon a tiny court with arched stone staircase and one green tree. We were a touching family party held together by a great sorrow and a great joy. How we laughed over the salad that got brandy instead of vinegar—how we ate the golden pile of fried potatoes and how we pored over the post-card from the Lieutenant of the Senegalese—dear little vale of crushed and risen France, in the day when Negroes went "over the top" at Pont-à-Mousson.

Paris, Paris by purple façade of the opera, the crowd on the Boulevard des Italiens and the great swing of the Champs Elysées. But not the Paris the world knows. Paris with its soul cut to the core—feverish, crowded, nervous, hurried; full of uniforms and mourning bands, with cafés closed at 9:30—no sugar, scarce bread, and tears so interwined with joy that there is scant difference. Paris has been dreaming a nightmare, and though she awakes, the grim terror is upon her—it lies on the sand-closed art treasures of the Louvre. Only the flowers are there, always the flowers, the Roses of England and the Lilies of France.

New York! Behind the Liberty that faces free France rise the white cliffs of Manhattan, tier on tier, with a curving pinnacle, towers square and twin, a giant inkwell daintily stoppered, an ancient pyramid enthroned; beneath, low ramparts wide and mighty; while above, faint-limned against the turbulent sky, looms the vast grace of that Cathedral of the Purchased and Purchasing Poor, topping the world and pointing higher.

Yonder the gray cobwebs of the Brooklyn bridges leap the sea, and here creep the argosies from all earth's ends. We move to this swift home on dun and swelling waters and hear as we come the heartbeats of the new world.

New York and night from the Brooklyn Bridge: The bees and fireflies flit and twinkle in their vast hives; curved clouds like the breath of gods hover between the towers and the moon. One hears the hiss of lightnings, the deep thunder of human things, and a fevered breathing as of some attendant and invincible Powers. The glow of burning millions melts outward into dim and fairy outlines until afar the liquid music born of rushing crowds drips like a benediction on the sea.

New York and morning: the sun is kissing the timid dew in Central Park, and from the Fountain of Plenty one looks along that world street, Fifth Avenue, and walks toward town. The earth lifts and curves graciously down from the older mansions of princes to the newer shops of luxury. Egypt and Abyssinia, Paris and Damascus, London and India caress you by the way; churches stand aloof while the shops swell to emporiums. But all this is nothing. Everything is mankind. Humanity stands and flies and walks and rolls about—the poor, the priceless, the world-known and the forgotten; child and grandfather, king and leman—the pageant of the world goes by, set in a frame of stone and jewels, clothed in scarlet and rags. Princes Street and the Elysian Fields, the Strand and the Ringstrasse—these are the Ways of the World today.

New York and twilight, there where the Sixth Avenue "L" rises and leaps above the tenements into the free air at 110th Street. It circles like a bird with heaven and St. John's above and earth and the sweet green and gold of the Park beneath. Beyond lie all the blue mists and mysteries of distance; beneath, the city rushes and crawls. Behind echo all the roar and war and care and maze of the wide city set in its sullen darkening walls, flashing weird and crimson farewells. Out at the sides the stars twinkle.

Again New York and Night and Harlem. A dark city of fifty thousand rises like magic from the earth. Gone is the white world, the pale lips, the lank hair; gone is the West and North—the East and South is here triumphant. The street is crowd and leisure and laughter. Everywhere black eyes, black and brown, and frizzled hair curled and sleek, and skins that riot with luscious color and deep, burning blood. Humanity is packed dense in high piles of close-knit homes that lie in layers above gray shops of food and clothes and drink, with here and there a moving-picture show. Orators declaim on the corners, lovers lark in the streets, gamblers glide by the saloons, workers lounge wearily home. Children scream and run and frolic, and all is good and human and beautiful and ugly and evil, even as Life is elsewhere.

And then—the Veil. It drops as drops the night on southern seas— vast, sudden, unanswering. There is Hate behind it, and Cruelty and Tears. As one peers through its intricate, unfathomable pattern of ancient, old, old design, one sees blood and guilt and misunderstanding. And yet it hangs there, this Veil, between Then and Now, between Pale and Colored and Black and White—between You and Me. Surely it is a thought-thing, tenuous, intangible; yet just as surely is it true and terrible and not in our little day may you and I lift it. We may feverishly unravel its edges and even climb slow with giant shears to where its ringed and gilded top nestles close to the throne of God. But as we work and climb we shall see through streaming eyes and hear with aching ears, lynching and murder, cheating and despising, degrading and lying, so flashed and fleshed through this vast hanging darkness that the Doer never sees the Deed and the Victim knows not the Victor and Each hates All in wild and bitter ignorance. Listen, O Isles, to these Voices from within the Veil, for they portray the most human hurt of the Twentieth Cycle of that poor Jesus who was called the Christ!

There is something in the nature of Beauty that demands an end. Ugliness may be indefinite. It may trail off into gray endlessness. But Beauty must be complete—whether it be a field of poppies or a great life,—it must end, and the End is part and triumph of the Beauty. I know there are those who envisage a beauty eternal. But I cannot. I can dream of great and never-ending processions of beautiful things and visions and acts. But each must be complete or it cannot for me exist.

On the other hand, Ugliness to me is eternal, not in the essence but in its incompleteness; but its eternity does not daunt me, for its eternal unfulfilment is a cause of joy. There is in it nothing new or unexpected; it is the old evil stretching out and ever seeking the end it cannot find; it may coil and writhe and recur in endless battle to days without end, but it is the same human ill and bitter hurt. But Beauty is fulfilment. It satisfies. It is always new and strange. It is the reasonable thing. Its end is Death—the sweet silence of perfection, the calm and balance of utter music. Therein is the triumph of Beauty.

So strong is the spell of beauty that there are those who, contradicting their own knowledge and experience, try to say that all is beauty. They are called optimists, and they lie. All is not beauty. Ugliness and hate and ill are here with all their contradiction and illogic;

they will always be here—perhaps, God send, with lessened volume and force, but here and eternal, while beauty triumphs in its great completion—Death. We cannot conjure the end of all ugliness in eternal beauty, for beauty by its very being and definition has in each definition its ends and limits; but while beauty lies implicit and revealed in its end, ugliness writhes on in darkness forever. So the ugliness of continual birth fulfils itself and conquers gloriously only in the beautiful end, Death.

At last to us all comes happiness, there in the Court of Peace, where the dead lie so still and calm and good. If we were not dead we would lie and listen to the flowers grow. We would hear the birds sing and see how the rain rises and blushes and burns and pales and dies in beauty. We would see spring, summer, and the red riot of autumn, and then in winter, beneath the soft white snow, sleep and dream of dreams. But we know that being dead, our Happiness is a fine and finished thing and that ten, a hundred, and a thousand years, we shall lie at rest, unhurt in the Court of Peace.

The Prayers of God

Name of God's Name!
Red murder reigns;
All hell is loose;
On gold autumnal air
Walk grinning devils, barbed and hoofed;
While high on hills of hate,
Black-blossomed, crimson-sky'd,
Thou sittest, dumb.

Father Almighty!
This earth is mad!
Palsied, our cunning hands;
Rotten, our gold;
Our argosies reel and stagger
Over empty seas;
All the long aisles
Of Thy Great Temples, God,
Stink with the entrails
Of our souls.
And Thou art dumb.

Above the thunder of Thy Thunders, Lord,
Lightening Thy Lightnings,
Rings and roars
The dark damnation

Of this hell of war.
Red piles the pulp of hearts and heads
And little children's hands.

Allah!
Elohim!
Very God of God!
Death is here!
Dead are the living; deep-dead the dead.
Dying are earth's unborn—
The babes' wide eyes of genius and of joy,
Poems and prayers, sun-glows and earth-songs,
Great-pictured dreams,
Enmarbled phantasies,
High hymning heavens—all
In this dread night
Writhe and shriek and choke and die
This long ghost-night—
While Thou art dumb.

Have mercy!
Have mercy upon us, miserable sinners!
Stand forth, unveil Thy Face,
Pour down the light
That seethes above Thy Throne,
And blaze this devil's dance to darkness!
Hear!
Speak!
In Christ's Great Name—

I hear!
Forgive me, God!
Above the thunder I hearkened;
Beneath the silence, now,—
I hear!

(Wait, God, a little space.
It is so strange to talk with Thee—
Alone!)

This gold?
I took it.
Is it Thine?
Forgive; I did not know.

Blood? Is it wet with blood?
'Tis from my brother's hands.
(I know; his hands are mine.)
It flowed for Thee, O Lord.

War? Not so; not war—
Dominion, Lord, and over black, not white;

Black, brown, and fawn,
And not Thy Chosen Brood, O God,
We murdered.
To build Thy Kingdom,
To drape our wives and little ones,
And set their souls a-glitter—
For this we killed these lesser breeds
And civilized their dead,
Raping red rubber, diamonds, cocoa, gold!

For this, too, once, and in Thy Name,
I lynched a Nigger—

 (He raved and writhed,
 I heard him cry,
 I felt the life-light leap and lie,
 I saw him crackle there, on high,
 I watched him wither!)

Thou?
Thee?
I lynched Thee?

Awake me, God! I sleep!
What was that awful word Thou saidst?
That black and riven thing—was it Thee?
That gasp—was it Thine?
This pain—is it Thine?
Are, then, these bullets piercing Thee?
Have all the wars of all the world,
Down all dim time, drawn blood from Thee?
Have all the lies and thefts and hates—
Is this Thy Crucifixion, God,
And not that funny, little cross,
With vinegar and thorns?
Is this Thy kingdom here, not there,
This stone and stucco drift of dreams?

Help!
I sense that low and awful cry—
Who cries?
Who weeps?
With silent sob that rends and tears—
Can God sob?

Who prays?
I hear strong prayers throng by,
Like mighty winds on dusky moors—
Can God pray?

Prayest Thou, Lord, and to me?
Thou needest me?
Thou *needest* me?

Thou needest *me*?
Poor, wounded soul!
Of this I never dreamed. I thought—

Courage, God,
I come!

CHAPTER X

The Comet

He stood a moment on the steps of the bank, watching the human river that swirled down Broadway. Few noticed him. Few ever noticed him save in a way that stung. He was outside the world—"nothing!" as he said bitterly. Bits of the words of the walkers came to him.

"The comet?"

"The comet—"

Everybody was talking of it. Even the president, as he entered, smiled patronizingly at him, and asked:

"Well, Jim, are you scared?"

"No," said the messenger shortly.

"I thought we'd journeyed through the comet's tail once," broke in the junior clerk affably.

"Oh, that was Halley's," said the president; "this is a new comet, quite a stranger, they say—wonderful, wonderful! I saw it last night. Oh, by the way, Jim," turning again to the messenger, "I want you to go down into the lower vaults today."

The messenger followed the president silently. Of course, they wanted *him* to go down to the lower vaults. It was too dangerous for more valuable men. He smiled grimly and listened.

"Everything of value has been moved out since the water began to seep in," said the president; "but we miss two volumes of old records. Suppose you nose around down there,—it isn't very pleasant, I suppose."

"Not very," said the messenger, as he walked out.

"Well, Jim, the tail of the new comet hits us at noon this time," said the vault clerk, as he passed over the keys; but the messenger passed silently down the stairs. Down he went beneath Broadway, where the dim light filtered through the feet of hurrying men; down to the dark basement beneath; down into the blackness and silence beneath that lowest cavern. Here with his dark lantern he groped in the bowels of the earth, under the world.

He drew a long breath as he threw back the last great iron door and stepped into the fetid slime within. Here at last was peace, and he groped moodily forward. A great rat leaped past him and cobwebs crept across his face. He felt carefully around the room, shelf by shelf, on the muddied floor, and in crevice and corner. Nothing. Then he went back to the far end, where somehow the wall felt different. He sounded and pushed and pried. Nothing. He started away. Then something brought him back. He was sounding and working again when suddenly the whole black wall swung as on mighty hinges, and blackness yawned beyond. He peered in; it was evidently a secret vault—some hiding place of the old bank unknown in newer times. He entered hesitatingly. It was a long, narrow room with shelves, and at the far end, an old iron chest. On a high shelf lay the two missing volumes of records, and others. He put them carefully aside and stepped to the chest. It was old, strong, and rusty. He looked at the vast and old-fashioned lock and flashed his light on the hinges. They were deeply incrusted with rust. Looking about, he found a bit of iron and began to pry. The rust had eaten a hundred years, and it had gone deep. Slowly, wearily, the old lid lifted, and with a last, low groan lay bare its treasure—and he saw the dull sheen of gold!

"Boom!"

A low, grinding, reverberating crash struck upon his ear. He started up and looked about. All was black and still. He groped for his light and swung it about him. Then he knew! The great stone door had swung to. He forgot the gold and looked death squarely in the face. Then with a sigh he went methodically to work. The cold sweat stood on his forehead; but he searched, pounded, pushed, and worked until after what seemed endless hours his hand struck a cold bit of metal and the great door swung again harshly on its hinges, and then, striking against something soft and heavy, stopped. He had just room to squeeze through. There lay the body of the vault clerk, cold and stiff. He stared at it, and then felt sick and nauseated. The air seemed unaccountably foul, with a strong, peculiar odor. He stepped forward, clutched at the air, and fell fainting across the corpse.

He awoke with a sense of horror, leaped from the body, and groped up the stairs, calling to the guard. The watchman sat as if asleep, with the gate swinging free. With one glance at him the messenger hurried up to the sub-vault. In vain he called to the guards. His voice echoed and re-echoed weirdly. Up into the great basement he rushed. Here another guard lay prostrate on his face, cold and still. A fear arose in the messenger's heart. He dashed up to the cellar floor, up into the bank. The stillness of death lay everywhere and everywhere bowed, bent, and stretched the silent forms of men. The messenger paused and glanced about. He was not a man easily moved; but the sight was appalling! "Robbery and murder," he whispered slowly to himself as he saw the twisted, oozing mouth of the president where he lay half-buried on his desk. Then a new thought seized him: If they found him here alone—with all this money and all these dead men—what would his life be worth? He glanced about, tiptoed cautiously to a side door, and again looked behind. Quietly he turned the latch and stepped out into Wall Street.

How silent the street was! Not a soul was stirring, and yet it was high-noon—Wall Street? Broadway? He glanced almost wildly up and down, then across the street, and as he looked, a sickening horror froze in his limbs. With a choking cry of utter fright he lunged, leaned giddily against the cold building, and stared helplessly at the sight.

In the great stone doorway a hundred men and women and children lay crushed and twisted and jammed, forced into that great, gaping doorway like refuse in a can—as if in one wild, frantic rush to safety, they had crushed and ground themselves to death. Slowly the messenger crept along the walls, wetting his parched mouth and trying to comprehend, stilling the tremor in his limbs and the rising terror in his heart. He met a business man, silk-hatted and frock-coated, who had crept, too, along that smooth wall and stood now stone dead with wonder written on his lips. The messenger turned his eyes hastily away and sought the curb. A woman leaned wearily against the signpost, her head bowed motionless on her lace and silken bosom. Before her stood a street car, silent, and within—but the messenger but glanced and hurried on. A grimy newsboy sat in the gutter with the "last edition" in his uplifted hand: "Danger!" screamed its black headlines. "Warnings wired around the world. The Comet's tail sweeps past us at noon. Deadly gases expected. Close doors and windows. Seek the cellar." The messenger read and staggered on. Far out from a window above, a girl lay with gasping face and sleevelets on her arms. On a store step sat a little, sweet-faced girl looking upward toward the skies, and in the carriage by her lay—but the messenger looked no longer. The cords gave way—the terror burst in his veins, and with one great, gasping cry he sprang desperately forward and ran,—ran as only the frightened run, shrieking and fighting the air until with one last wail of pain he sank on the grass of Madison Square and lay prone and still.

When he arose, he gave no glance at the still and silent forms on the benches, but, going to a fountain, bathed his face; then hiding himself in a corner away from the drama of death, he quietly gripped himself and thought the thing through: The comet had swept the earth and this was the end. Was everybody dead? He must search and see.

He knew that he must steady himself and keep calm, or he would go insane. First he must go to a restaurant. He walked up Fifth Avenue to a famous hostelry and entered its gorgeous, ghost-haunted halls. He beat back the nausea, and, seizing a tray from dead hands, hurried into the street and ate ravenously, hiding to keep out the sights.

"Yesterday, they would not have served me," he whispered, as he forced the food down.

Then he started up the street,—looking, peering, telephoning, ringing alarms; silent, silent all. Was nobody—nobody—he dared not think the thought and hurried on.

Suddenly he stopped still. He had forgotten. My God! How could he have forgotten? He must rush to the subway—then he almost laughed. No—a car; if he could find a Ford. He saw one. Gently he lifted off its burden, and took his place on the seat. He tested the throttle. There was gas. He glided off, shivering, and drove up the street. Everywhere stood, leaned, lounged, and lay the dead, in grim and awful silence. On he ran past an automobile, wrecked and overturned; past another, filled with a gay party whose smiles yet lingered on their death-struck lips; on past crowds and groups of cars, pausing by dead policemen; at 42nd Street he had to detour to Park Avenue to avoid the dead congestion. He came back on Fifth Avenue at 57th and flew past the Plaza and by the park with its hushed babies and silent throng, until as he was rushing past 72nd Street he heard a sharp cry, and saw a living form leaning wildly out an upper window. He gasped. The human voice sounded in his ears like the voice of God.

"Hello—hello—help, in God's name!" wailed the woman. "There's a dead girl in here and a man and—and see yonder dead men lying in the street and dead horses—for the love of God go and bring the officers—" And the words trailed off into hysterical tears.

He wheeled the car in a sudden circle, running over the still body of a child and leaping on the curb. Then he rushed up the steps and tried the door and rang violently. There was a long pause, but at last the heavy door swung back. They stared a moment in silence. She had not noticed before that he was a Negro. He had not thought of her as white. She was a woman of perhaps twenty-five—rarely beautiful and richly gowned, with darkly-golden hair, and jewels. Yesterday, he thought with bitterness, she would scarcely have looked at him twice. He would have been dirt beneath her silken feet. She stared at him. Of all the sorts of men she had pictured as coming to her rescue she had not dreamed of one like him. Not that he was not human, but he dwelt in a world so far from hers, so infinitely far, that he seldom even entered her thought. Yet as she looked at him curiously he seemed quite commonplace and usual. He was a tall, dark workingman of the better class, with a sensitive face trained to stolidity and a poor man's clothes and hands. His face was soft and slow and his manner at once cold and nervous, like fires long banked, but not out.

So a moment each paused and gauged the other; then the thought of the dead world without rushed in and they started toward each other.

"What has happened?" she cried. "Tell me! Nothing stirs. All is silence! I see the dead strewn before my window as winnowed by the breath of God,—and see—" She dragged him through great, silken hangings to where, beneath the sheen of mahogany and silver, a little

French maid lay stretched in quiet, everlasting sleep, and near her a butler lay prone in his livery.

The tears streamed down the woman's cheeks and she clung to his arm until the perfume of her breath swept his face and he felt the tremors racing through her body.

"I had been shut up in my dark room developing pictures of the comet which I took last night; when I came out—I saw the dead!

"What has happened?" she cried again.

He answered slowly:

"Something—comet or devil—swept across the earth this morning and—many are dead!"

"Many? Very many?"

"I have searched and I have seen no other living soul but you."

She gasped and they stared at each other.

"My—father!" she whispered.

"Where is he?"

"He started for the office."

"Where is it?"

"In the Metropolitan Tower."

"Leave a note for him here and come."

Then he stopped.

"No," he said firmly—"first, we must go—to Harlem."

"Harlem!" she cried. Then she understood. She tapped her foot at first impatiently. She looked back and shuddered. Then she came resolutely down the steps.

"There's a swifter car in the garage in the court," she said.

"I don't know how to drive it," he said.

"I do," she answered.

In ten minutes they were flying to Harlem on the wind. The Stutz rose and raced like an airplane. They took the turn at 110th Street on two wheels and slipped with a shriek into 135th.

He was gone but a moment. Then he returned, and his face was gray. She did not look, but said:

"You have lost—somebody?"

"I have lost—everybody," he said, simply—"unless—"

He ran back and was gone several minutes—hours they seemed to her.

"Everybody," he said, and he walked slowly back with something film-like in his hand which he stuffed into his pocket.

"I'm afraid I was selfish," he said. But already the car was moving toward the park among the dark and lined dead of Harlem—the brown, still faces, the knotted hands, the homely garments, and the silence—the wild and haunting silence. Out of the park, and down Fifth Avenue they whirled. In and out among the dead they slipped and quivered, needing no sound of bell or horn, until the great, square

Metropolitan Tower hove in sight. Gently he laid the dead elevator boy aside; the car shot upward. The door of the office stood open. On the threshold lay the stenographer, and, staring at her, sat the dead clerk. The inner office was empty, but a note lay on the desk, folded and addressed but unsent:

Dear Daughter:
    I've gone for a hundred mile spin in Fred's new Mercedes. Shall not be back before dinner. I'll bring Fred with me.

                                         J. B. H.

"Come," she cried nervously. "We must search the city."

Up and down, over and across, back again—on went that ghostly search. Everywhere was silence and death—death and silence! They hunted from Madison Square to Spuyten Duyvel; they rushed across the Williamsburg Bridge; they swept over Brooklyn; from the Battery and Morningside Heights they scanned the river. Silence, silence everywhere, and no human sign. Haggard and bedraggled they puffed a third time slowly down Broadway, under the broiling sun, and at last stopped. He sniffed the air. An odor—a smell—and with the shifting breeze a sickening stench filled their nostrils and brought its awful warning. The girl settled back helplessly in her seat.

"What can we do?" she cried.

It was his turn now to take the lead, and he did it quickly.

"The long distance telephone—the telegraph and the cable—night rockets and then—flight!"

She looked at him now with strength and confidence. He did not look like men, as she had always pictured men; but he acted like one and she was content. In fifteen minutes they were at the central telephone exchange. As they came to the door he stepped quickly before her and pressed her gently back as he closed it. She heard him moving to and fro, and knew his burdens—the poor, little burdens he bore. When she entered, he was alone in the room. The grim switchboard flashed its metallic face in cryptic, sphinx-like immobility. She seated herself on a stool and donned the bright earpiece. She looked at the mouthpiece. She had never looked at one so closely before. It was wide and black, pimpled with usage; inert; dead; almost sarcastic in its unfeeling curves. It looked—she beat back the thought—but it looked,— it persisted in looking like—she turned her head and found herself alone. One moment she was terrified; then she thanked him silently for his delicacy and turned resolutely, with a quick intaking of breath.

"Hello!" she called in low tones. She was calling to the world. The world *must* answer. Would the world *answer*? Was the world—

Silence!

She had spoken too low.

"Hello!" she cried, full-voiced.

She listened. Silence! Her heart beat quickly. She cried in clear, distinct, loud tones: "Hello—hello—hello!"

What was that whirring? Surely—no—was it the click of a receiver?

She bent close, she moved the pegs in the holes, and called and called, until her voice rose almost to a shriek, and her heart hammered. It was as if she had heard the last flicker of creation, and the evil was silence. Her voice dropped to a sob. She sat stupidly staring into the black and sarcastic mouthpiece, and the thought came again. Hope lay dead within her. Yes, the cable and the rockets remained; but the world—she could not frame the thought or say the word. It was too mighty—too terrible! She turned toward the door with a new fear in her heart. For the first time she seemed to realize that she was alone in the world with a stranger, with something more than a stranger,— with a man alien in blood and culture—unknown, perhaps unknowable. It was awful! She must escape—she must fly; he must not see her again. Who knew what awful thoughts—

She gathered her silken skirts deftly about her young, smooth limbs—listened, and glided into a side-hall. A moment she shrank back: the hall lay filled with dead women; then she leaped to the door and tore at it, with bleeding fingers, until it swung wide. She looked out. He was standing at the top of the alley,—silhouetted, tall and black, motionless. Was he looking at her or away? She did not know— she did not care. She simply leaped and ran—ran until she found herself alone amid the dead and the tall ramparts of towering buildings.

She stopped. She was alone. Alone! Alone on the streets—alone in the city—perhaps alone in the world! There crept in upon her the sense of deception—of creeping hands behind her back—of silent, moving things she could not see,—of voices hushed in fearsome conspiracy. She looked behind and sideways, started at strange sounds and heard still stranger, until every nerve within her stood sharp and quivering, stretched to scream at the barest touch. She whirled and flew back, whimpering like a child, until she found that narrow alley again and the dark, silent figure silhouetted at the top. She stopped and rested; then she walked silently toward him, looked at him timidly; but he said nothing as he handed her into the car. Her voice caught as she whispered:

"Not—that."

And he answered slowly: "No—not that!"

They climbed into the car. She bent forward on the wheel and sobbed, with great, dry, quivering sobs, as they flew toward the cable office on the east side, leaving the world of wealth and prosperity for the world of poverty and work. In the world behind them were death and silence, grave and grim, almost cynical, but always decent; here it was hideous. It clothed itself in every ghastly form of terror, struggle, hate, and suffering. It lay wreathed in crime and squalor, greed and lust. Only in its dread and awful silence was it like to death everywhere.

Yet as the two, flying and alone, looked upon the horror of the world, slowly, gradually, the sense of all-enveloping death deserted them. They seemed to move in a world silent and asleep,—not dead. They moved in quiet reverence, lest somehow they wake these sleeping forms who had, at last, found peace. They moved in some solemn, world-wide *Friedhof*, above which some mighty arm had waved its magic wand. All nature slept until—until, and quick with the same startling thought, they looked into each other's eyes—he, ashen, and she, crimson, with unspoken thought. To both, the vision of a mighty beauty—of vast, unspoken things, swelled in their souls; but they put it away.

Great, dark coils of wire came up from the earth and down from the sun and entered this low lair of witchery. The gathered lightnings of the world centered here, binding with beams of light the ends of the earth. The doors gaped on the gloom within. He paused on the threshold.

"Do you know the code?" she asked.

"I know the call for help—we used it formerly at the bank."

She hardly heard. She heard the lapping of the waters far below,— the dark and restless waters—the cold and luring waters, as they called. He stepped within. Slowly she walked to the wall, where the water called below, and stood and waited. Long she waited, and he did not come. Then with a start she saw him, too, standing beside the black waters. Slowly he removed his coat and stood there silently. She walked quickly to him and laid her hand on his arm. He did not start or look. The waters lapped on in luring, deadly rhythm. He pointed down to the waters, and said quietly:

"The world lies beneath the waters now—may I go?"

She looked into his stricken, tired face, and a great pity surged within her heart. She answered in a voice clear and calm, "No."

Upward they turned toward life again, and he seized the wheel. The world was darkening to twilight, and a great, gray pall was falling mercifully and gently on the sleeping dead. The ghastly glare of reality seemed replaced with the dream of some vast romance. The girl lay silently back, as the motor whizzed along, and looked half-consciously for the elf-queen to wave life into this dead world again. She forgot to wonder at the quickness with which he had learned to drive her car. It seemed natural. And then as they whirled and swung into Madison Square and at the door of the Metropolitan Tower she gave a low cry, and her eyes were great! Perhaps she had seen the elf-queen?

The man led her to the elevator of the tower and deftly they ascended. In her father's office they gathered rugs and chairs, and he wrote a note and laid it on the desk; then they ascended to the roof and he made her comfortable. For a while she rested and sank to dreamy somnolence, watching the worlds above and wondering. Below lay the dark shadows of the city and afar was the shining of the sea. She glanced at him timidly as he set food before her and took a shawl and wound her in it, touching her reverently, yet tenderly. She looked up at him with thankfulness in her eyes, eating what he served. He watched the city. She watched him. He seemed very human,—very near now.

"Have you had to work hard?" she asked softly.

"Always," he said.

"I have always been idle," she said. "I was rich."

"I was poor," he almost echoed.

"The rich and the poor are met together," she began, and he finished:

"The Lord is the Maker of them all."

"Yes," she said slowly; "and how foolish our human distinctions seem—now," looking down to the great dead city stretched below, swimming in unlightened shadows.

"Yes—I was not—human, yesterday," he said.

She looked at him. "And your people were not my people," she said; "but today—" She paused. He was a man,—no more; but he was in some larger sense a gentleman,—sensitive, kindly, chivalrous, everything save his hands and—his face. Yet yesterday—

"Death, the leveler!" he muttered.

"And the revealer," she whispered gently, rising to her feet with great eyes. He turned away, and after fumbling a moment sent a rocket into the darkening air. It arose, shrieked, and flew up, a slim path of light, and, scattering its stars abroad, dropped on the city below. She scarcely noticed it. A vision of the world had risen before her. Slowly the mighty prophecy of her destiny overwhelmed her. Above the dead past hovered the Angel of Annunciation. She was no mere woman. She was neither high nor low, white nor black, rich nor poor. She was primal woman; mighty mother of all men to come and Bride of Life. She looked upon the man beside her and forgot all else but his manhood, his strong, vigorous manhood—his sorrow and sacrifice. She saw him glorified. He was no longer a thing apart, a creature below, a strange outcast of another clime and blood, but her Brother Humanity incarnate, Son of God and great All-Father of the race to be.

He did not glimpse the glory in her eyes, but stood looking outward toward the sea and sending rocket after rocket into the unanswering darkness. Dark-purple clouds lay banked and billowed in the west. Behind them and all around, the heavens glowed in dim, weird radiance that suffused the darkening world and made almost a minor music. Suddenly, as though gathered back in some vast hand, the great cloud-curtain fell away. Low on the horizon lay a long, white star—mystic, wonderful! And from it fled upward to the pole, like some wan bridal veil, a pale, wide sheet of flame that lighted all the world and dimmed the stars.

In fascinated silence the man gazed at the heavens and dropped his rockets to the floor. Memories of memories stirred to life in the dead recesses of his mind. The shackles seemed to rattle and fall from his soul. Up from the crass and crushing and cringing of his caste leaped the lone majesty of kings long dead. He arose within the shadows, tall, straight, and stern, with power in his eyes and ghostly scepters hovering to his grasp. It was as though some mighty Pharaoh lived again, or curled Assyrian lord. He turned and looked upon the lady, and found her gazing straight at him.

Silently, immovably, they saw each other face to face—eye to eye. Their souls lay naked to the night. It was not lust; it was not love—it was some vaster, mightier thing that needed neither touch of body nor thrill of soul. It was a thought divine, splendid.

Slowly, noiselessly, they moved toward each other—the heavens above, the seas around, the city grim and dead below. He loomed from out the velvet shadows vast and dark. Pearl-white and slender, she shone beneath the stars. She stretched her jeweled hands abroad. He lifted up his mighty arms, and they cried each to the other, almost with one voice, "The world is dead."

"Long live the—"

"Honk! Honk!" Hoarse and sharp the cry of a motor drifted clearly up from the silence below. They started backward with a cry and gazed upon each other with eyes that faltered and fell, with blood that boiled.

"Honk! Honk! Honk! Honk!" came the mad cry again, and almost from their feet a rocket blazed into the air and scattered its stars upon them. She covered her eyes with her hands, and her shoulders heaved. He dropped and bowed, groped blindly on his knees about the floor. A blue flame spluttered lazily after an age, and she heard the scream of an answering rocket as it flew.

Then they stood still as death, looking to opposite ends of the earth.

"Clang—crash—clang!"

The roar and ring of swift elevators shooting upward from below made the great tower tremble. A murmur and babel of voices swept in upon the night. All over the once dead city the lights blinked, flickered, and flamed; and then with a sudden clanging of doors the entrance to the platform was filled with men, and one with white and flying hair rushed to the girl and lifted her to his breast. "My daughter!" he sobbed.

Behind him hurried a younger, comelier man, carefully clad in motor costume, who bent above the girl with passionate solicitude and gazed into her staring eyes until they narrowed and dropped and her face flushed deeper and deeper crimson.

"Julia," he whispered; "my darling, I thought you were gone forever."

She looked up at him with strange, searching eyes.

"Fred," she murmured, almost vaguely, "is the world—gone?"

"Only New York," he answered; "it is terrible—awful! You know,—but you, how did you escape—how have you endured this horror? Are you well? Unharmed?"

"Unharmed!" she said.

"And this man here?" he asked, encircling her drooping form with one arm and turning toward the Negro. Suddenly he stiffened and his hand flew to his hip. "Why!" he snarled. "It's—a—nigger—Julia! Has he—has he dared—"

She lifted her head and looked at her late companion curiously and then dropped her eyes with a sigh.

"He has dared—all, to rescue me," she said quietly, "and I—thank him—much." But she did not look at him again. As the couple turned away, the father drew a roll of bills from his pockets.

"Here, my good fellow," he said, thrusting the money into the man's hands, "take that,—what's your name?"

"Jim Davis," came the answer, hollow-voiced.

"Well, Jim, I thank you. I've always liked your people. If you ever want a job, call on me." And they were gone.

The crowd poured up and out of the elevators, talking and whispering.

"Who was it?"

"Are they alive?"

"How many?"

"Two!"

"Who was saved?"

"A white girl and a nigger—there she goes."

"A nigger? Where is he? Let's lynch the damned—"

"Shut up—he's all right—he saved her."

"Saved hell! He had no business—"

"Here he comes."

Into the glare of the electric lights the colored man moved slowly, with the eyes of those that walk and sleep.

"Well, what do you think of that?" cried a bystander; "of all New York, just a white girl and a nigger!"

The colored man heard nothing. He stood silently beneath the glare of the light, gazing at the money in his hand and shrinking as he gazed; slowly he put his other hand into his pocket and brought out a baby's filmy cap, and gazed again. A woman mounted to the platform and looked about, shading her eyes. She was brown, small, and toil-worn, and in one arm lay the corpse of a dark baby. The crowd parted and her eyes fell on the colored man; with a cry she tottered toward him.

"Jim!"
He whirled and, with a sob of joy, caught her in his arms.

A Hymn to The Peoples

O Truce of God!
And primal meeting of the Sons of Man,
Foreshadowing the union of the World!
From all the ends of earth we come!
Old Night, the elder sister of the Day,
Mother of Dawn in the golden East,
Meets in the misty twilight with her brood,
Pale and black, tawny, red and brown,
The mighty human rainbow of the world,
Spanning its wilderness of storm.

Softly in sympathy the sunlight falls,
Rare is the radiance of the moon;
And on the darkest midnight blaze the stars—
The far-flown shadows of whose brilliance
Drop like a dream on the dim shores of Time,
Forecasting Days that are to these
As day to night.

So sit we all as one.
So, gloomed in tall and stone-swathed groves,
The Buddha walks with Christ!
And Al-Koran and Bible both be holy!

Almighty Word!
In this Thine awful sanctuary,
First and flame-haunted City of the Widened World,
Assoil us, Lord of Lands and Seas!

We are but weak and wayward men,
Distraught alike with hatred and vainglory;
Prone to despise the Soul that breathes within—
High visioned hordes that lie and steal and kill,
Sinning the sin each separate heart disclaims,
Clambering upon our riven, writhing selves,
Besieging Heaven by trampling men to Hell!

We be blood-guilty! Lo, our hands be red!
Not one may blame the other in this sin!
But here—here in the white Silence of the Dawn,
Before the Womb of Time,
With bowéd hearts all flame and shame,
We face the birth-pangs of a world:
We hear the stifled cry of Nations all but born—
The wail of women ravished of their stunted brood!
We see the nakedness of Toil, the poverty of Wealth,

We know the Anarchy of Empire, and doleful Death
   of Life!
And hearing, seeing, knowing all, we cry:

Save us, World-Spirit, from our lesser selves!
Grant us that war and hatred cease,
Reveal our souls in every race and hue!
Help us, O Human God, in this Thy Truce,
To make Humanity divine!

CHAPTER 7

Africa and Colonialism

everal of Du Bois's major works, including *The Negro* (1915), *Darkwater* (1920), and *Black Folk Then and Now* (1939), contain a great deal of material on Africa, and the later volume *The World and Africa* (1947; revised 1965) brings his long-evolving history of Africa and the African diaspora up to date at the end of his life. Beginning with an Afrocentric romanticism that was characteristic of his early essays and verse, Du Bois over time adopted a critique of colonialism grounded in a socialist interpretation of traditional African tribal communities. His interest in the links between African American rights and the struggle against colonialism in Africa dates from his participation in the Pan-African conferences that began in 1900 and lasted throughout the post–World War II period. In *Dusk of Dawn* (1940) and other later works, Du Bois stressed his Marxist-inspired view that the "primitive" communal organization of African villages offered an antidote to capitalized, industrialized models of Western life. At the same time, he continued to advance the thesis, derived from late-nineteenth-century writings on Africa and later revived in Afrocentric arguments of the late twentieth century, that Africa was the cradle of modern civilization, as well as the source of many of its artistic and industrial achievements, and that the continent's natural development had been destroyed by the slave trade and European colonialism. An early version of these theories, drawn from portions of *The Negro,* appears here under the title "Africa and the Slave Trade."

"To the Nations of the World" (1900) is Du Bois's portion of the *Report on the Pan-African Conference* of 1900, which, like the "Manifesto of the Second Pan-African Congress" (1921)—a conference held in 1919 is usually referred to as the "first" Pan-African Congress—presents a political and economic agenda that would be reiterated at many such meetings by African, American, and Caribbean black intellectuals and politicians held to protest and organize against colonialism. The same conference prompted a series of letters to *The Crisis* in which Du Bois outlined his theory that Pan-Africanism might have something in common with Jewish Zionism. Like Du Bois's poem of racial pride "The Song of the Smoke," "A Day in Africa" (1908) fantasizes about a beatific pastoral Africa and thus looks ahead to the romanticized "Little Portraits of Africa" that Du Bois would sketch for readers of *The Crisis* during his first visit to Africa in 1924. Du

Bois's contribution to a 1926 volume of the same name, "What Is Civilization?", develops a concise argument about African prehistory, the village as a model of a socialized economy, and the relationships between African and African American culture. Some of the same ideas are elaborated in more detail in the 1943 essay "The Realities in Africa," in which Du Bois analyzes the combat between indigenous African economic development and European exploitation against the political and military backdrop of the two world wars.

Although he was unable to attend the All-African People's Conference in Accra in 1958, Du Bois's wife, Shirley Graham Du Bois, read "The Future of Africa," an address he had composed for the occasion. Here, autobiographical reflections, socialist theory, and celebratory anticipation of speading African independence are mixed together even as Du Bois cites once more a phrase from Goethe (*"Entbehren sollst du, sollst entbehren"*—"Thou shalt forego, shalt do without") that had first appeared half a century earlier in *The Souls of Black Folk* as an admonition that political struggle requires sacrifice for the common good. In "Whites in Africa After Negro Autonomy" (1962), Du Bois meditates on both the achievements and the disasters of European colonialism, contrasting his thoughts about Africa to what he took to be the decadence of contemporary American culture at midcentury.

TO THE NATIONS OF THE WORLD

In the metropolis of the modern world, in this the closing year of the nineteenth century, there has been assembled a congress of men and women of African blood, to deliberate solemnly upon the present situation and outlook of the darker races of mankind. The problem of the twentieth century is the problem of the colour line, the question as to how far differences of race, which show themselves chiefly in the colour of the skin and the texture of the hair, are going to be made, hereafter, the basis of denying to over half the world the right of sharing to their utmost ability the opportunities and privileges of modern civilisation.

To be sure, the darker races are to-day the least advanced in culture according to European standards. This has not, however, always been the case in the past, and certainly the world's history, both ancient and modern, has given many instances of no despicable ability and capacity among the blackest races of men.

In any case, the modern world must needs remember that in this age, when the ends of the world are being brought so near together, the millions of black men in Africa, America, and the Islands of the Sea, not to speak of the brown and yellow myriads elsewhere, are bound to have great influence upon the world in the future, by reason of sheer numbers and physical contact. If now the world of culture bends itself towards giving Negroes and other dark men the largest and broadest opportunity for education and self-development, then this contact and influence is bound to have a beneficial effect upon the world and hasten human progress. But if, by reason of carelessness, prejudice, greed and injustice, the black world is to be exploited and ravished and degraded, the results must be deplorable, if not fatal, not simply to them, but to the high ideals of justice, freedom, and culture which a thousand years of Christian civilisation have held before Europe.

And now, therefore, to these ideals of civilisation, to the broader humanity of the followers of the Prince of Peace, we, the men and women of Africa in world congress assembled, do now solemnly appeal:—

Let the world take no backward step in that slow but sure progress which has successively refused to let the spirit of class, of caste, of privilege, or of birth, debar from like liberty and the pursuit of happiness a striving human soul.

Let not mere colour or race be a feature of distinction drawn between white and black men, regardless of worth or ability.

Let not the natives of Africa be sacrificed to the greed of gold, their liberties taken away, their family life debauched, their just aspirations repressed, and avenues of advancement and culture taken from them.

Let not the cloak of Christian missionary enterprise be allowed in the future, as so often in the past, to hide the ruthless economic exploitation and political downfall of less developed nations, whose chief fault has been reliance on the plighted faith of the Christian church.

Let the British nation, the first modern champion of Negro freedom, hasten to crown the work of Wilberforce, and Clarkson, and Buxton, and Sharpe, Bishop Colenso, and Livingstone, and give, as soon as practicable, the rights of responsible government to the black colonies of Africa and the West Indies.

Let not the spirit of Garrison, Phillips, and Douglas wholly die out in America; may the conscience of a great nation rise and rebuke all dishonesty and unrighteous oppression toward the American Negro, and grant to him the right of franchise, security of person and property, and generous recognition of the great work he has accomplished in a generation toward raising nine millions of human beings from slavery to manhood.

Let the German Empire, and the French Republic, true to their great past, remember that the true worth of colonies lies in their prosperity and progress, and that justice, impartial alike to black and white, is the first element of prosperity.

Let the Congo Free State become a great central Negro State of the world, and let its prosperity be counted not simply in cash and commerce, but in the happiness and true advancement of its black people.

Let the nations of the World respect the integrity and independence of the free Negro States of Abyssinia, Liberia, Hayti, etc., and let the inhabitants of these States, the independent tribes of Africa, the Negroes of the West Indies and America, and the black subjects of all nations take courage, strive ceaselessly, and fight bravely, that they may prove to the world their incontestable right to be counted among the great brotherhood of mankind.

Thus we appeal with boldness and confidence to the Great Powers of the civilised world, trusting in the wide spirit of humanity, and the deep sense of justice of our age, for a generous recognition of the righteousness of our cause.

A DAY IN AFRICA

I rose to sense the incense of the hills,
The royal sun sent crimsoned heralds to the dawn
She glowed beneath her bridal veil of mist—
I felt her heart swell while the king
Paused on the world's rough edge,
And thousand birds did pour their little hearts
To maddened melody.
I leapt and danced, and found
My breakfast poised aloft,
All served in living gold.

In purple flowered fields I wandered
Wreathed in crimson, blue and green.
My noon-tide meal did fawn about my feet
In striped sleekness.
I kissed it ere I killed it,
And slept away the liquid languor of the noon;
Then rose and chased a wild new creature
Down the glen, till suddenly
It wheeled and fetched its fangs
Across my breast. I poised my spear:
Then saw its fear-mad piteous eyes,
And gave it life and food.

The sun grew sad. I watched
The mystic moon-dance of the elves
Amid the mirth-mad laughter of the stars;
Till far away some voice did wind

627

The velvet trumpet of the night—
And then in glooming caves
I laid me with the lion,
And I slept.

AFRICA AND THE SLAVE TRADE

Africa is at once the most romantic and the most tragic of continents. Its very names reveal its mystery and wide-reaching influence. It is the "Ethiopia" of the Greek, the "Kush" and "Punt" of the Egyptian, and the Arabian "Land of the Blacks." To modern Europe it is the "Dark Continent" and "Land of Contrasts"; in literature it is the seat of the Sphinx and the lotus eaters, the home of the dwarfs, gnomes, and pixies, and the refuge of the gods; in commerce it is the slave mart and the source of ivory, ebony, rubber, gold, and diamonds. What other continent can rival in interest this Ancient of Days?

There are those, nevertheless, who would write universal history and leave out Africa. But how, asks Ratzel, can one leave out the land of Egypt and Carthage? and Frobenius declares that in future Africa must more and more be regarded as an integral part of the great movement of world history. Yet it is true that the history of Africa is unusual, and its strangeness is due in no small degree to the physical peculiarities of the continent. With three times the area of Europe it has a coast line a fifth shorter. Like Europe it is a peninsula of Asia, curving southwestward around the Indian Sea. It has few gulfs, bays, capes, or islands. Even the rivers, though large and long, are not means of communication with the outer world, because from the central high plateau they plunge in rapids and cataracts to the narrow coastlands and the sea.

The general physical contour of Africa has been likened to an inverted plate with one or more rows of mountains at the edge and a low coastal belt. In the south the central plateau is three thousand or more feet above the sea, while in the north it is a little over one thousand feet. Thus two main divisions of the continent are easily distinguished: the broad northern rectangle, reaching down as far as the Gulf of Guinea and Cape Guardafui, with seven million square miles; and the peninsula which tapers toward the south, with five million square miles.

Four great rivers and many lesser streams water the continent. The greatest is the Congo in the center, with its vast curving and endless estuaries; then the Nile, draining the cluster of the Great Lakes and flowing northward "like some grave, mighty thought, threading a dream"; the Niger in the northwest, watering the Sudan below the Sahara; and, finally, the Zambesi, with its greater Niagara in the southeast. Even these waters leave room for deserts both south and north, but the greater ones are the three million square miles of sand wastes in the north.

More than any other land, Africa lies in the tropics, with a warm, dry climate, save in the central Congo region, where rain at all seasons brings tropical luxuriance. The flora is rich but not wide in variety, including the gum acacia, ebony, several dye woods, the kola nut, and probably tobacco and millet. To these many plants have been added in historic times. The fauna is rich in mammals, and here, too, many from other continents have been widely introduced and used.

Primarily Africa is the Land of the Blacks. The world has always been familiar with black men, who represent one of the most ancient of human stocks. Of the ancient world gathered about the Mediterranean, they formed a part and were viewed with no surprise or dislike, because this world saw them come and go and play their part with other men. Was Clitus the brother-in-law of Alexander the Great less to be honored because he happened to be black? Was Terence less famous? The medieval European world, developing under the favorable physical conditions of the north temperate zone, knew the black man chiefly as a legend or occasional curiosity, but still as a fellow man—an Othello or a Prester John or an Antar.

The modern world, in contrast, knows the Negro chiefly as a bond slave in the West Indies and America. Add to this the fact that the darker races in other parts of the world have, in the last four centuries, lagged behind the flying and even feverish footsteps of Europe, and we face to-day a widespread assumption throughout the dominant world that color is a mark of inferiority.

The result is that in writing of this, one of the most ancient, persistent, and widespread stocks of mankind, one faces astounding prejudice. That which may be assumed as true of white men must be proven beyond peradventure if it relates to Negroes. One who writes of the development of the Negro race must continually insist that he is writing of a normal human stock, and that whatever it is fair to predicate of the mass of human beings may be predicated of the Negro. It is the silent refusal to do this which has led to so much false writing on Africa and of its inhabitants. Take, for instance, the answer to the apparently simple question "What is a Negro?" We find the most extraordinary confusion of thought and difference of opinion. There is a certain type in the minds of most people which, as David Livingstone said, can be found only in caricature and not in real life. When scientists have tried to find an extreme type of black, ugly, and woolly-haired Negro, they have been compelled more and more to limit his home even in Africa. At least nine-tenths of the African people do not at all conform to this type, and the typical Negro, after being denied a dwelling place in the Sudan, along the Nile, in East Central Africa, and in South Africa, was finally given a very small country between the Senegal and the Niger, and even there was found to give trace of many stocks. As Winwood Reade says, "The typical Negro is a rare variety even among Negroes."

As a matter of fact we cannot take such extreme and largely fanciful stock as typifying that which we may fairly call the Negro race. In the case of no other race is so narrow a definition attempted. A "white" man may be of any color, size, or facial conformation and have endless variety of cranial measurement and physical characteristics. A "yellow" man is perhaps an even vaguer conception.

In fact it is generally recognized to-day that no scientific definition of race is possible. Differences, and striking differences, there are between men and groups of men, but they fade into each other so insensibly that we can only indicate the main divisions of men in broad outlines. As Von Luschan says, "The question of the number of human races has quite lost its *raison d'être* and has become a subject rather of philosophic speculation than of scientific research. It is of no more importance now to know how many human races there are than to know how many angels can dance on the point of a needle. Our aim now is to find out how ancient and primitive races developed from others and how races changed or evolved through migration and inter-breeding."

The mulatto (using the term loosely to indicate either an intermediate type between white and black or a mingling of the two) is as typically African as the black man and cannot logically be included in the "white" race, especially when American usage includes the mulatto in the Negro race.

It is reasonable, according to fact and historic usage, to include under the word "Negro" the darker peoples of Africa characterized by a brown skin, curled or "frizzled" hair, full and sometimes everted lips, a tendency to a development of the maxillary parts of the face, and a dolichocephalic head. This type is not fixed or definite. The color varies widely; it is never black or bluish, as some say, and it becomes often light brown or yellow. The hair varies from curly to a wool-like mass, and the facial angle and cranial form show wide variation.

It is as impossible in Africa as elsewhere to fix with any certainty the limits of racial variation due to climate and the variation due to intermingling. In the past, when scientists assumed one unvarying Negro type, every variation from that type was interpreted as meaning mixture of blood. To-day we recognize a broader normal African type which, as Palgrave says, may best be studied "among the statues of the Egyptian rooms of the British Museum; the larger gentle eye, the full but not over-protruding lips, the rounded contour, and the good-natured, easy, sensuous expression. This is the genuine African model." To this race Africa in the main and parts of Asia have belonged since prehistoric times.

The color of this variety of man, as the color of other varieties, is due to climate. Conditions of heat, cold, and moisture, working for thousands of years through the skin and other organs, have given men their differences of color. This color pigment is a protection against sunlight and consequently varies with the intensity of the sunlight. Thus in Africa we find the blackest men in the fierce sunlight of the desert, red pygmies in the forest, and yellow Bushmen on the cooler southern plateau.

Next to the color, the hair is the most distinguishing characteristic of the Negro, but the two characteristics do not vary with each other. Some of the blackest of the Negroes have curly rather than woolly hair, while the crispest, most closely curled hair is found among the yellow Hottentots and Bushmen. The difference between the hair of the lighter and darker races is a difference of degree, not of kind, and can be easily measured. If the hair follicles of a Chinaman, a European, and a Negro are cut across transversely, it will be found that the diameter of the first is 100 by 77 to 85, the second 100 by 62 to 72, while that of the Negro is 100 by 40 to 60. This elliptical form of the Negro's hair causes it to curl more or less tightly.

There have been repeated efforts to discover, by measurements of various kinds, further and more decisive differences which would serve as really scientific determinants of race. Gradually these efforts have been given up. To-day we realize that there are no hard and fast racial types among men. Race is a dynamic and not a static conception, and the typical races are continually changing and developing, amalgamating and differentiating. In this little book, then, we are studying the history of the darker part of the human family, which is separated from the rest of mankind by no absolute physical line, but which nevertheless forms, as a mass, a social group distinct in history, appearance, and to some extent in spiritual gift. . . .

Color was never a badge of slavery in the ancient or medieval world, nor has it been in the modern world outside of Christian states. Homer sings of a black man, a "reverend herald"

> Of visage solemn, sad, but sable hue,
> Short, woolly curls, o'erfleeced his bending head, . . .
> Eurybiates, in whose large soul alone,
> Ulysses viewed an image of his own.

Greece and Rome had their chief supplies of slaves from Europe and Asia. Egypt enslaved races of all colors, and if there were more blacks than others among her slaves, there were also more blacks among her nobles and Pharaohs, and both facts are explained by her racial origin and geographical position. The fall of Rome led to a cessation of the slave trade, but after a long interval came the white slave trade of the Saracens and Moors, and finally the modern trade in Negroes.

Slavery as it exists universally among primitive people is a system whereby captives in war are put to tasks about the homes and in the fields, thus releasing the warriors for systematic fighting and the women for leisure. Such slavery has been common among all peoples and was wide-spread in Africa. The relative number of African slaves under these conditions was small and the labor not hard; they were members of the family and might and did often rise to high position in the tribe.

Remembering that in the fifteenth century there was no great disparity between the civilization of Negroland and that of Europe, what made the striking difference in subsequent development? European civilization, cut off by physical barriers from further incursions of barbaric races, settled more and more to systematic industry and to the domination of one religion; African culture and industries were threatened by powerful barbarians from the west and central regions of the continent and by the Moors in the north, and Islam had only partially converted the leading peoples.

When, therefore, a demand for workmen arose in America, European exportation was limited by religious ties and economic stability. African exportation was encouraged not simply by the Christian attitude toward heathen, but also by the Moslem enmity toward the unconverted Negroes. Two great modern religions, therefore, agreed at least in the policy of enslaving heathen blacks, while the overthrow of black Askias by the Moors at Tenkadibou brought that economic chaos among the advanced Negro peoples and movement among the more barbarous tribes which proved of prime advantage to the development of a systematic trade in men.

The modern slave trade began with the Mohammedan conquests in Africa, when heathen Negroes were seized to supply the harems, and as soldiers and servants. They were bought from the masters and seized in war, until the growing wealth and luxury of the conquerors demanded larger numbers. Then Negroes from the Egyptian Sudan, Abyssinia, and Zanzibar began to pass into Arabia, Persia, and India in increased numbers. As Negro kingdoms and tribes rose to power they found the slave trade lucrative and natural, since the raids in which slaves were captured were ordinary inter-tribal wars. It was not until the eighteenth and nineteenth centuries that the demand for slaves in Christian lands made slaves the object, and not the incident, of African wars.

In Mohammedan countries there were gleams of hope in slavery. In fiction and in truth the black slave had a chance. Once converted to Islam, he became a brother to the best, and the brotherhood of the faith was not the sort of idle lie that Christian slave masters made it.

In Arabia black leaders arose like Antar; in India black slaves carved out principalities where their descendants still rule.

Some Negro slaves were brought to Europe by the Spaniards in the fourteenth century, and a small trade was continued by the Portuguese, who conquered territory from the "tawny" Moors of North Africa in the early fifteenth century. Later, after their severe repulse at Al-Kasr-Al-Kabu, the Portuguese began to creep down the west coast in quest of trade. They reached the River of Gold in 1441, and their story is that their leader seized certain free Moors and the next year exchanged them for ten black slaves, a target of hide, ostrich eggs, and some gold dust. The trade was easily justified on the ground that the Moors were Mohammedans and refused to be converted to Christianity, while heathen Negroes would be better subjects for conversion and stronger laborers. In the next few years a small number of Negroes continued to be imported into Spain and Portugal as servants. We find, for instance, in 1474, that Negro slaves were common in Seville. There is a letter from Ferdinand and Isabella in the year 1474 to a celebrated Negro, Juan de Valladolid, commonly called the "Negro Count" (El Conde Negro), nominating him to the office of "mayoral of the Negroes" in Seville. The slaves were apparently treated kindly, allowed to keep their own dances and festivals, and to have their own chief, who represented them in the courts, as against their own masters, and settled their private quarrels.

Between 1455 and 1492 little mention is made of slaves in the trade with Africa. Columbus is said to have suggested Negroes for America, but Ferdinand and Isabella refused. Nevertheless, by 1501, we have the first incidental mention of Negroes going to America in a declaration that Negro slaves "born in the power of Christians were to be allowed to pass to the Indies, and the officers of the royal revenue were to receive the money to be paid for their permits."

About 1501 Ovando, Governor of Spanish America, was objecting to Negro slaves and "solicited that no Negro slaves should be sent to Hispaniola, for they fled amongst the Indians and taught them bad customs, and never could be captured." Nevertheless a letter from the king to Ovando, dated Segovia, the fifteenth of September, 1505, says, "I will send more Negro slaves as you request; I think there may be a hundred. At each time a trustworthy person will go with them who may have some share in the gold they may collect and may promise them ease if they work well." There is a record of a hundred slaves being sent out this very year, and Diego Columbus was notified of fifty to be sent from Seville for the mines in 1510.

After this time frequent notices show that Negroes were common in the new world. When Pizarro, for instance, had been slain in Peru, his body was dragged to the cathedral by two Negroes. After the battle of Anaquito the head of the viceroy was cut off by a Negro, and during the great earthquake in Guatemala a most remarkable figure was a gigantic Negro seen in various parts of the city. Nunez had thirty Negroes with him on the top of the Sierras, and there was rumor of an aboriginal tribe of Negroes in South America. One of the last acts of King Ferdinand was to urge that no more Negroes be sent to the West Indies, but under Charles V, Bishop Las Casas drew up a plan of assisted migration to America and asked in 1517 the right for immigrants to import twelve Negro slaves, in return for which the Indians were to be freed.

Las Casas, writing in his old age, owns his error: "This advice that license should be given to bring Negro slaves to these lands, the Clerigo Casas first gave, not considering the injustice with which the Portuguese take them and make them slaves; which advice, after he had apprehended the nature of the thing, he would not have given for all he had in the world. For he always held that they had been made slaves unjustly and tyrannically; for the same reason holds good of them as of the Indians."

As soon as the plan was broached a Savoyard, Lorens de Gomenot, Governor of Bresa, obtained a monopoly of this proposed trade and shrewdly sold it to the Genoese for twenty-five thousand ducats. Other monopolies were granted in 1523, 1527, and 1528. Thus the American trade became established and gradually grew, passing successively into the hands of the Portuguese, the Dutch, the French, and the English.

At first the trade was of the same kind and volume as that already passing northward over the desert routes. Soon, however, the American trade developed. A strong, unchecked demand for brute labor in the West Indies and on the continent of America grew until it culminated in the eighteenth century, when Negro slaves were crossing the Atlantic at the rate of fifty to one hundred thousand a year. This called for slave raiding on a scale that drew upon every part of Africa—upon the west coast, the western and Egyptian Sudan, the valley of the Congo, Abyssinia, the lake regions, the east coast, and Madagascar. Not simply the degraded and weaker types of Negroes were seized, but the strong Bantu, the Mandingo and Songhay, the Nubian and Nile Negroes, the Fula, and even the Asiatic Malay, were represented in the raids.

There was thus begun in modern days a new slavery and slave trade. It was different from that of the past, because more and more it came in time to be founded on racial caste, and this caste was made the foundation of a new industrial system. For four hundred years, from 1450 to 1850, European civilization carried on a systematic trade in human beings of such tremendous proportions that the physical, economic, and moral effects are still plainly to be remarked throughout the world. To this must be added the large slave trade of Mussulman lands, which began with the seventh century and raged almost unchecked until the end of the nineteenth century.

These were not days of decadence, but a period that gave the world Shakespeare, Martin Luther, and Raphael, Haroun-al-Raschid and Abraham Lincoln. It was the day of the greatest expansion of two of the world's most pretentious religions and of the beginnings of the modern organization of industry. In the midst of this advance and up-lift this slave trade and slavery spread more human misery, inculcated more disrespect for and neglect of humanity, a greater callousness to suffering, and more petty, cruel, human hatred than can well be calculated. We may excuse and palliate it, and write history so as to let men forget it; it remains the most inexcusable and despicable blot on modern human history. . . .

The slave trade thus begun by the Portuguese, enlarged by the Dutch, and carried to its culmination by the English centered on the west coast near the seat of perhaps the oldest and most interesting culture of Africa. It came at a critical time. The culture of Yoruba, Benin, Mossiland, and Nupe had exhausted itself in a desperate attempt to stem the on-coming flood of Mohammedan culture. It has succeeded in maintaining its small, loosely federated city-states suited to trade, industry, and art. It had developed strong resistance toward the Sudan state builders toward the north, as in the case of the fighting Mossi; but behind this warlike resistance lay the peaceful city life which gave industrial ideas to Byzantium and shared something of Ethiopian and Mediterranean culture.

The first advent of the slave traders increased and encouraged native industry, as is evidenced by the bronze work of Benin; but soon this was pushed into the background, for it was not bronze metal but bronze flesh that Europe wanted. A new tyranny, bloodthirsty, cruel, and built on war, forced itself forward in the Niger delta. The powerful state of Dahomey arose early in the eighteenth century and became a devastating tyranny, reaching its highest power early in the nineteenth century. Ashanti, a similar kingdom, began its conquests in 1719 and grew with the slave trade. Thus state building in West Africa began to replace the city economy, but it was a state built on war and on war supported and encouraged largely for the sake of trade in human flesh. The native industries were changed and disorganized. Family ties and government were weakened. Far into the heart of Africa this devilish disintegration, coupled with Christian rum and Mohammedan raiding, penetrated. The face of Africa was turned south on these slave traders instead of northward toward the Mediterranean, where for two thousand years and more Europe and Africa had met in legitimate trade and mutual respect. The full significance of the battle of Tenkadibou, which overthrew the Askias, was now clear. Hereafter Africa for centuries was to appear before the world, not as the land of gold and ivory, of Mansa Musa and Meroe, but as a bound and captive slave, dumb and degraded. . . .

Such a large number of slaves could be supplied only by organized slave raiding in every corner of Africa. The African continent gradually became revolutionized. Whole regions were depopulated, whole tribes disappeared; villages were built in caves and on hills or in forest fast-nesses; the character of peoples like those of Benin developed their worst excesses of cruelty instead of the already flourishing arts of peace. The dark, irresistible grasp of fetish took firmer hold on men's minds.

Further advances toward civilization became impossible. Not only was there the immense demand for slaves which had its outlet on the west coast, but the slave caravans were streaming up through the desert to the Mediterranean coast and down the valley of the Nile to the centers of Mohammedanism. It was a rape of a continent to an extent never paralleled in ancient or modern times.

In the American trade there was not only the horrors of the slave raid, which lined the winding paths of the African jungles with bleached bones, but there was also the horrors of what was called the "middle passage," that is, the voyage across the Atlantic. As Sir William Dolben said, "The Negroes were chained to each other hand and foot, and stowed so close that they were not allowed above a foot and a half for each in breadth. Thus crammed together like herrings in a barrel, they contracted putrid and fatal disorders; so that they who came to inspect them in a morning had occasionally to pick dead slaves out of their rows, and to unchain their carcases from the bodies of their wretched fellow-sufferers to whom they had been fastened."

It was estimated that out of every one hundred lot shipped from Africa only about fifty lived to be effective laborers across the sea, and among the whites more seamen died in that trade in one year than in the whole remaining trade of England in two. The full realization of the horrors of the slave trade was slow in reaching the ears and conscience of the modern world, just as to-day the treatment of dark natives in European colonies is brought to publicity with the greatest difficulty. The first move against the slave trade in England came in Parliament in 1776, but it was not until thirty-one years later, in 1807, that the trade was banned through the arduous labors of Clarkson, Wilberforce, Sharpe, and others.

Denmark had already abolished the trade, and the United States attempted to do so the following year. Portugal and Spain were induced to abolish the trade between 1815 and 1830. Notwithstanding these laws, the contraband trade went on until the beginning of the Civil War in America. The reasons for this were the enormous profit of the trade and the continued demand of the American slave barons, who had no sympathy with the efforts to stop their source of cheap labor supply.

However, philanthropy was not working alone to overthrow Negro slavery and the slave trade. It was seen, first in England and later in other countries, that slavery as an industrial system could not be made to work satisfactorily in modern times. Its cost was too great, and one of the causes of this cost was the slave insurrections from the very beginning, when the slaves rose on the plantation of Diego Columbus down to the Civil War in America. Actual and potential slave insurrection in the West Indies, in North and South America, kept the slave owners in apprehension and turmoil, or called for a police system difficult to maintain. In North America revolt finally took the form of organized running away to the North, and this, with the growing scarcity of suitable land and the moral revolt, led to the Civil War and the disappearance of the American slave trade.

There was still, however, the Mohammedan slave trade to deal with, and this has been the work of the nineteenth and early twentieth centuries. In the last quarter of the nineteenth century ten thousand slaves annually were being distributed on the southern and eastern coast of the Mediterranean and at the great slave market in Bornu.

On the east coast of Africa in 1862 nineteen thousand slaves were passed into Zanzibar and thence into Arabia and Persia. As late as 1880, three thousand annually were being thus transplanted, but now the trade is about stopped. To-day the only centers of actual slave trading may be said to be the cocoa plantations of the Portuguese Islands on the west coast of Africa, and the Congo Free State.

Such is the story of the Rape of Ethiopia—a sordid, pitiful, cruel tale. Raphael painted, Luther preached, Corneille wrote, and Milton sung; and through it all, for four hundred years, the dark captives wound to the sea amid the bleaching bones of the dead; for four hundred years the sharks followed the scurrying ships; for four hundred years America was strewn with the living and dying millions of a transplanted race; for four hundred years Ethiopia stretched forth her hands unto God.

AFRICA, COLONIALISM, AND ZIONISM

Europe had begun to look with covetous eyes toward Africa as early as 1415 when the Portuguese at the Battle of Ceuta gained a foothold in Morocco. Thereafter Prince Henry of Portugal instituted the series of explorations which resulted not only in the discovery of Cape Verde, the Guinea Coast and the Cape of Good Hope, but by 1487 gave to Portugal the possession of a very fair slice of the African East Coast. This was the beginning of the Portuguese Colonies of Guinea, Angola and East Africa. Other European nations, France, Holland, Spain, England and Denmark, followed and set up trading stations along the African coast whose chief reason for existence was the fostering of the slave trade.

But the partition of Africa as we know it is much more recent and begins with the founding in 1884 of the Congo Free State whose inception was so zealously fostered by Leopold of Belgium and which in 1908 was annexed to Belgium. The "scramble" for African colonies was on and within a quarter of a century Africa was virtually in the hands of Europe.

In this division the British Empire gained a network of possessions extending from the Anglo-Egyptian Sudan down to South Africa with valuable holdings on the East Coast and in Somaliland. France came next with an actually larger area, but with a smaller population. Her spoils reached from Morocco and Algeria, including the Algerian Sahara, to the French Congo, and on the Eastern Coast comprised Madagascar and French Somaliland. Germany, who was late in entering the game of colonization, contrived none the less to become mistress of four very valuable colonies, Togoland, Kamerun, South-West Africa and East Africa. Italy's and Spain's possessions were relatively unimportant, embracing for the former, Eritrea and Italian Somaliland, and for the latter Rio de Oro and the Muni River settlements.

This was the state of affairs when the war broke out in 1914. In Africa the only independent states were the Republic of Liberia, and the kingdom of Abyssinia which, according to history, has been independent since the days of Menelek, the reputed Son of Solomon, and the Queen of Sheba. The number of souls thus under the rule of aliens is astounding, amounting in the case of England, France, Germany and Belgium to more than 110,000,000. During the course of the war Germany lost all four of her African colonies with a population estimated at 13,420,000. It is the question of the reapportionment of this vast number of human beings which has started the Pan-African movement. Colored America is indeed involved.

> "If we do not feel the chain
> When it works another's pain,
> Are we not base slaves indeed,
> Slaves unworthy to be freed?"

The suggestion has been made that these colonies which Germany has lost should not be handed over to any other nation of Europe but should, under the guidance of *organized civilization*, be brought to a point of development which shall finally result in an autonomous state. This plan has met with much criticism and ridicule. Let the natives develop along their own lines and they will "go back," has been the cry. Back to what, in Heaven's name?

Is a civilization naturally backward because it is different? Outside of cannibalism, which can be matched in this country, at least, by lynching, there is no vice and no degradation in native African customs which can begin to touch the horrors thrust upon them by white masters. Drunkenness, terrible diseases, immorality, all these things have been the gifts of European civilization. There is no need to dwell on German and Belgian atrocities, the world knows them too well. Nor have France and England been blameless. But even supposing that these masters had been models of kindness and rectitude, who shall say that any civilization is in itself so superior that it must be superimposed upon another nation without the expressed and intelligent consent of the people most concerned. The culture indigenous to a country, its folk-customs, its art, all this must have free scope or there is no such thing as freedom for the world.

The truth is, white men are merely juggling with words—or worse—when they declare that the withdrawal of Europeans from Africa will plunge that continent into chaos. What Europe, and indeed only a small group in Europe, wants in Africa is not a field for the spread of European civilization, but a field for exploitation. They covet the raw materials,—ivory, diamonds, copper and rubber in which the land abounds, and even more do they covet cheap native labor to mine and produce these things. Greed,—naked, pitiless lust for wealth and power, lie back of all of Europe's interest in Africa and the white world knows it and is not ashamed.

Any readjustment of Africa is not fair and cannot be lasting which does not consider the interests of native Africans and peoples of African descent. Prejudice, in European colonies in Africa, against the ambitious Negro is greater than in America, and that is saying much. But with the establishment of a form of government which shall be based on the concept that Africa is for Africans, there would be a chance for the colored American to emigrate and to go as a pioneer to a country which must, sentimentally at least, possess for him the same fascination as England does for Indian-born Englishmen.

This is not a "separatist" movement. There is no need to think that those who advocate the opening up of Africa for Africans and those of African descent desire to deport any large number of colored Americans to a foreign and, in some respects, inhospitable land. Once for all, let us realize that we are Americans, that we were brought here with the earliest settlers, and that the very sort of civilization from which we came made the complete adoption of western modes and customs imperative if we were to survive at all. In brief, there is nothing so indigenous, so completely "made in America" as we. It is as absurd to talk of a return to Africa, merely because that was our home 300 years ago, as it would be to expect the members of the Caucasian race to return to the fastnesses of the Caucasus Mountains from which, it is reputed, they sprang.

But it is true that we as a people are not given to colonization, and that thereby a number of essential occupations and interests have been closed to us which the redemption of Africa would open up. The African movement means to us what the Zionist movement must mean to the Jews, the centralization of race effort and the recognition of a racial fount. To help bear the burden of Africa does not mean any lessening of effort in our own problem at home. Rather it means increased interest. For any ebullition of action and feeling that results in an amelioration of the lot of Africa tends to ameliorate the condition of colored peoples throughout the world. And no man liveth to himself.

MANIFESTO OF THE SECOND PAN-AFRICAN CONGRESS

The absolute equality of races,—physical, political and social—is the founding stone of world peace and human advancement. No one denies great differences of gift, capacity and attainment among individuals of all races, but the voice of science, religion and practical politics is one in denying the God-appointed existence of super-races, or of races naturally and inevitably and eternally inferior.

That in the vast range of time, one group should in its industrial technique, or social organization, or spiritual vision, lag a few hundred years behind another, or forge fitfully ahead, or come to differ decidedly in thought, deed and ideal, is proof of the essential richness and variety of human nature, rather than proof of the co-existence of demigods and apes in human forms. The doctrine of racial equality does not interfere with individual liberty, rather, it fulfills it. And of all the various criteria by which masses of men have in the past been prejudged and classified, that of the color of the skin and texture of the hair, is surely the most adventitious and idiotic.

It is the duty of the world to assist in every way the advance of the backward and suppressed groups of mankind. The rise of all men is a menace to no one and is the highest human ideal; it is not an altruistic benevolence, but the one road to world salvation.

For the purpose of raising such peoples to intelligence, self-knowledge and self-control, their intelligentsia of right ought to be recognized as the natural leaders of their groups.

The insidious and dishonorable propaganda, which, for selfish ends, so distorts and denies facts as to represent the advancement and development of certain races of men as impossible and undesirable, should be met with widespread dissemination of the truth. The experiment of making the Negro slave a free citizen in the United States is not a failure; the attempts at autonomous government in Haiti and Liberia are not proofs of the impossibility of self-government among black men; the experience of Spanish America does not prove that mulatto democracy will not eventually succeed there; the aspirations of Egypt and India are not successfully to be met by sneers at the capacity of darker races.

We who resent the attempt to treat civilized men as uncivilized, and who bring in our hearts grievance upon grievance against those who lynch the untried, disfranchise the intelligent, deny self-government to educated men, and insult the helpless, we complain; but not simply or primarily for ourselves—more especially for the millions of our fellows, blood of our blood, and flesh of our flesh, who have not even what we have—the power to complain against monstrous wrong, the power to see and to know the source of our oppression.

How far the future advance of mankind will depend upon the social contact and physical intermixture of the various strains of human blood is unknown, but the demand for the interpenetration of countries and intermingling of blood has come in modern days, from the white race alone, and has been imposed upon brown and black folks mainly by brute force and fraud. On top of this, the resulting people of mixed race have had to endure innuendo, persecution, and insult, and the penetrated countries have been forced into semi-slavery.

If it be proven that absolute world segregation by group, color or historic affinity is best for the future, let the white race leave the dark world and the darker races will gladly leave the white. But the proposition is absurd. This is a world of men, of men whose likenesses far outweigh their differences; who mutually need each other in labor and thought and dream, but who can successfully have each other only on terms of equality, justice and mutual respect. They are the real and only peacemakers who work sincerely and peacefully to this end.

The beginning of wisdom in interracial contact is the establishment of political institutions among suppressed peoples. The habit of democracy must be made to encircle the earth. Despite the attempt to prove that its practice is the secret and divine gift of the few, no habit is more natural or more widely spread among primitive people, or more easily capable of development among masses. Local self-government with a minimum of help and oversight can be established tomorrow in Asia, in Africa, in America and in the Isles of the Sea. It will in many instances need general control and guidance, but it will fail only when that guidance seeks ignorantly and consciously its own selfish ends and not the people's liberty and good.

Surely in the 20th century of the Prince of Peace, in the millennium of Buddha and Mahmoud, and in the mightiest Age of Human Reason, there can be found in the civilized world enough of altruism, learning and benevolence to develop native institutions for the native's good, rather than continue to allow the majority of mankind to be brutalized and enslaved by ignorant and selfish agents of commercial institutions, whose one aim is profit and power for the few.

And this brings us to the crux of the matter: It is the shame of the world that today the relation between the main groups of mankind and their mutual estimate and respect is determined chiefly by the degree in which one can subject the other to its service, enslaving labor, making ignorance compulsory, uprooting ruthlessly religion and customs, and destroying government, so that the favored Few may luxuriate in the toil of the tortured Many. Science, Religion and Philanthropy have thus been made the slaves of world commerce and industry, and bodies, minds, souls of Fiji and Congo, are judged almost solely by the quotations on the Bourse.

The day of such world organization is past and whatever excuse be made for it in other ages, the 20th century must come to judge men as men and not as material and labor.

The great industrial problem which has hitherto been regarded as the domestic problem of culture lands, must be viewed far more broadly, if it is ever to reach just settlement. Labor and capital in England, France, and America can never solve their problem as long as a similar and vastly greater problem of poverty and injustice marks the relations of the whiter and darker peoples. It is shameful, unreligious, unscientific and undemocratic that the estimate, which half the peoples of earth put on the other half, depends mainly on their ability to squeeze profit out of them.

If we are coming to recognize that the great modern problem is to correct maladjustment in the distribution of wealth, it must be remembered that the basic maladjustment is in the outrageously unjust distribution of world income between the dominant and suppressed peoples; in the rape of land and raw material, and monopoly of technique and culture. And in this crime white labor is *particeps criminis* with white capital. Unconsciously and consciously, carelessly and deliberately, the vast power of the white labor vote in modern democracies has been cajoled and flattered into imperialistic schemes to enslave and debauch black, brown and yellow labor, until with fatal retribution, they are themselves today bound and gagged and rendered impotent by the resulting monopoly of the world's raw material in the hands of a dominant, cruel and irresponsible few.

And, too, just as curiously, the educated and cultured of the world, the well-born and well-bred, and even the deeply pious and philanthropic, receive their training and comfort and luxury, the ministrations of delicate beauty and sensibility, on condition that they neither inquire into the real source of their income and the methods of distribution or interfere with the legal props which rest on a pitiful human foundation of writhing white and yellow and brown and black bodies.

We claim no perfectness of our own nor do we seek to escape the blame which of right falls on the backward for failure to advance, but *noblesse oblige*, and we arraign civilization and more especially the colonial powers for deliberate transgressions of our just demands and their own better conscience.

England, with her Pax Britannica, her courts of justice, established commerce and a certain apparent recognition of native law and customs, has nevertheless systematically fostered ignorance among the natives, has enslaved them and is still enslaving some of them, has usually declined even to try to train black and brown men in real self-government, to recognize civilized black folks as civilized, or to grant to colored colonies those rights of self-government which it freely gives to white men.

Belgium is a nation which has but recently assumed responsibility for her colonies, and has taken some steps to lift them from the worst abuses of the autocratic regime; but she has not confirmed to the people the possession of their land and labor, and she shows no disposition to allow the natives any voice in their own government, or to provide for their political future. Her colonial policy is still mainly dominated by the banks and great corporations. But we are glad to learn that the present government is considering a liberal program of reform for the future.

Portugal and Spain have never drawn a legal caste line against persons of culture who happen to be of Negro descent. Portugal has a humane code for the natives and has begun their education in some regions. But, unfortunately, the industrial concessions of Portuguese Africa are almost wholly in the hands of foreigners whom Portugal cannot or will not control, and who are exploiting land and re-establishing the African slave trade.

The United States of America after brutally enslaving millions of black folks suddenly emancipated them and began their education; but it acted without system or forethought, throwing the freed men upon the world penniless and landless, educating them without thoroughness and system, and subjecting them the while to lynching, lawlessness, discrimination, insult and slander, such as human beings have seldom endured and survived. To save their own government, they enfranchised the Negro and then when danger passed, allowed hundreds of thousands of educated and civilized black folk to be lawlessly disfranchised and subjected to a caste system; and, at the same time, in 1776, 1812, 1861, 1897, and 1917, they asked and allowed thousands of black men to offer up their lives as a sacrifice to the country which despised and despises them.

France alone of the great colonial powers has sought to place her cultured black citizens on a plane of absolute legal and social equality with her white and given them representation in her highest legislature. In her colonies she has a widespread but still imperfect system of state education. This splendid beginning must be completed by widening the political basis of her native government, by restoring to the indigenes the ownership of the soil, by protecting native labor against the aggression of established capital and by asking no man, black or white, to be a soldier unless the country gives him a voice in his own government.

The independence of Abyssinia, Liberia, Haiti and San Domingo, is absolutely necessary to any sustained belief of the black folk in the sincerity and honesty of the white. These nations have earned the right to be free, they deserve the recognition of the world: notwithstanding all their faults and mistakes, and the fact that they are behind the most advanced civilization of the day, nevertheless they compare favorably with the past, and even more recent, history of most European nations, and it shames civilization that the treaty of London practically invited Italy to aggression in Abyssinia, and that free America has unjustly and cruelly seized Haiti, murdered and for a time enslaved her workmen, overthrown her free institutions by force and has so far failed in return to give her a single bit of help, aid or sympathy.

What do those wish who see these evils of the color line and racial discrimination and who believe in the divine right of suppressed and backward peoples to learn and aspire and be free?

The Negro race through its thinking intelligentsia is demanding:

I—The recognition of civilized men as civilized despite their race or color

II—Local self government for backward groups, deliberately rising as experience and knowledge grow to complete self government under the limitations of a self-governed world

III—Education in self knowledge, in scientific truth and in industrial technique, undivorced from the art of beauty

IV—Freedom in their own religion and social customs, and with the right to be different and non-conformist

V—Co-operation with the rest of the world in government, industry and art on the basis of Justice, Freedom and Peace

VI—The ancient common ownership of the land and its natural fruits and defence against the unrestrained greed of invested capital

VII—The establishment under the League of Nations of an international institution for the study of Negro problems

VIII—The establishment of an international section in the Labor Bureau of the League of Nations, charged with the protection of native labor.

The world must face two eventualities: either the complete assimilation of Africa with two or three of the great world states, with political, civil and social power and privileges absolutely equal for its black and white citizens, or the rise of a great black African state founded in Peace and Good Will, based on popular education, natural art and industry and freedom of trade; autonomous and sovereign in its internal policy, but from its beginning a part of a great society of peoples in which it takes its place with others as co-rulers of the world.

In some such words and thoughts as these we seek to express our will and ideal, and the end of our untiring effort. To our aid we call all men of the Earth who love Justice and Mercy. Out of the depths we have cried unto the deaf and dumb masters of the world. Out of the depths we cry to our own sleeping souls.

The answer is written in the stars.

LITTLE PORTRAITS OF AFRICA

The Place, The People

Africa is vegetation. It is the riotous, unbridled bursting life of leaf and limb. It is sunshine—pitiless shine of blue rising from morning mists and sinking to hot night shadows. And then the stars—very near are the stars to Africa, near and bright and curiously arrayed. The tree is Africa. The strong, blinding strength of it—the wide deep shade, the burly lavish height of it. Animal life is there wild and abundant—perhaps in the inner jungle I should note it more but here the herb is triumphant, savagely sure—such beautiful shrubbery, such splendor of leaf and gorgeousness of flower I have never seen.

And the people! Last night I went to Kru-town and saw a Christmas masque. There were young women and men of the color of warm ripe horse chestnuts, clothed in white robes and turbaned. They played the Christ story with sincerity, naiveté and verve. Conceive "Silent Night" sung in Kru by this dark white procession with flaming candles; the little black mother of Christ crossing with her baby, in figured blue, with Joseph in Mandingan fez and multi-colored cloak and beside them on her worshipping knees the white wreathed figure of a solemn dark angel. The shepherds watched their flocks by night, the angels sang; and Simeon, raising the baby high in his black arms, sang with my heart in English Kru-wise, *"Lord now lettest thou thy servant depart in peace for mine eyes have seen thy salvation!"*

Liberia is gay in costume—the thrifty Krus who burst into color of a holiday; the proud Veys always well-gowned; the Liberian himself often in white. The children sometimes in their own beautiful skins.

SUNDAY, JANUARY 13, 1924

I have walked three hours in the African bush. In the high bush mighty trees arose draped, with here and there the flash of flower and call of bird. The monkey sentinel cried and his fellows dashed down the great tree avenues. The way was marked—yonder the leopard that called last night under the moon, a bush cow's hoof; a dainty tread of antelope. We leaped the trail of driver ants and poked at the great houses of the white ants. The path rose and wound and fell now soft in green glow, now golden, now shimmery through the water as we balanced on a bare log. There was whine of monkey, scramble of timid unseen life, glide of dark snake. Then came the native farms—coffee, cocoa, plantain, cassava. Nothing is more beautiful than an African village—its harmonious colorings—its cleanliness, its dainty houses with the kitchen palaver place of entertainment, its careful delicate decorations and then the people. I believe that the African form in color and curve is the beautifulest thing on earth; the face is not so lovely—though often comely with perfect teeth and shining eyes,—but the form of the slim limbs, the muscled torso, the deep full breasts!

The bush is silence. Silence of things to be, silence vocal with infinite minor music and flutter and tremble—but silence, deep silence of the great void of Africa.

And the palms; some rose and flared like green fine work; some flared before they rose; some soared and drooped; some were stars and some were sentinels; then came the ferns—the feathery delicate things of grottos and haunts with us, leapt and sang in the sun—they thrust their virgin tracery up and out and almost to trees. Bizarre shapes of grass and shrub and leaf greeted us as though some artist all Divine was playing and laughing and trying every trick of his bewitched pencil above the mighty buildings of the ants.

I am riding on the singing heads of black boys swinging in a hammock. The smooth black bodies swing and sing, the neck set square, the hips sway. O lovely voices and sweet young souls of Africa!

Monrovia

Monrovia is a city set upon a hill. With coy African modesty her face is half turned from the bold and boisterous ocean and her wide black eyes gaze dreamfully up the Stockton and St. Paul. Her color is white and green and her head of homes rises slowly and widely in spacious shading verandah toward the great headland of Mesurado where the lighthouse screams to wandering ships. Her hair is plaited decently on mighty palm leaves and mangoes; her bare feet, stained with travel, torn with ancient cicatriced wounds drabble in the harbor waters down on Water Street and shun the mud town Plymouth Rock which is Providence Island. Her feet are ugly and old, but oh her hands, her smooth and black and flying hands are beautiful and they linger on roof and porch, in wide-throated grassy street and always they pat and smooth her hair, the green and sluggish palms of her heavy beautiful hair. And there is gold in her hair.

Africa

The spell of Africa is upon me. The ancient witchery of her medicine is burning my drowsy, dreamy blood. This is not a country, it is a world—a universe of itself and for itself, a thing Different, Immense, Menacing, Alluring. It is a great black bosom where the Spirit longs to die. It is life so burning, so fire encircled that one bursts with terrible soul inflaming life. One longs to leap against the sun and then calls, like some great hand of fate, the slow, silent crushing power of almighty sleep—of Silence, of immovable Power beyond, within, around. Then comes the calm. The dreamless beat of midday stillness at dusk, at dawn, at noon, always. Things move—black shiny bodies, perfect bodies, bodies of sleek unearthly poise and beauty. Eyes languish, black eyes—slow eyes, lovely and tender eyes in great dark formless faces. Life is slow here. Impetuous Americans quiver in impetuous graves. I saw where the ocean roars to the soul of Henry Highland Garnet. Life slows down and as it slows it deepens; it rises and descends to immense and secret places. Unknown evil appears and unknown good. Africa is the Spiritual Frontier of human kind—oh the wild and beautiful adventures of its taming! But oh! the cost thereof—the endless, endless cost! Then will come a day—an old and ever, ever young day when there will spring in Africa a civilization without coal, without noise, where machinery will sing and never rush and roar, and where men will sleep and think and dance and lie prone before the rising sons, and women will be happy.

The objects of life will be revolutionized. Our duty will not consist in getting up at seven, working furiously for six, ten and twelve hours, eating in sullen ravenousness or extraordinary repletion. No—We shall dream the day away and in cool dawns, in little swift hours, do all our work.

WHAT IS CIVILIZATION?

Three things Africa has given the world, and they form the essence of African culture: Beginnings, the village unit, and art in sculpture and music.

Long before the last two thousand years, which we call the years of modern civilization, lay the beginnings of human culture. For ten thousand years,—perhaps fifty thousand years and more,—mankind struggled with the first steps of advance; struggled and wavered, forged forward, retreated, fell, and arose again. This was a period fateful for all mankind,—for all culture. It was far more tremendous in its ultimate significance than anything that has happened since.

It was during these years that the black race, in its own land, Africa, and in all the paths by which it wended its way thither, seems always to have been first. Wherever one sees the first faint steps of human culture, the first successful fight against wild beasts, the striving against weather and disease, there one sees black men. To be sure, they were not the only beginners, but they seem to have been the successful and the persistent ones. Thus Africa appears as the Father of mankind, and the people who eventually settled there, wherever they may have wandered before and since,—along the Ganges, the Euphrates, and the Nile, in Cyprus and about the Mediterranean shores,—form the largest and often the only group of human beings successfully advancing from animal savagery toward primitive civilization. The ancient world looked upon them continually as creators of human culture and rang with their tributes. Hammurabi, law giver of Babylonia, is called "to go forth like the sun over the Black race." The Greeks sent Zeus and Poseidon to feast annually with the "Blameless Blacks," and the Roman historians tell us that the Blacks "conceive themselves to be of greater antiquity than any other nation. They suppose themselves also to be the inventors of divine worship, of festivals, of solemn assemblies, of sacrifices, and every religious practice. They affirm that the Egyptians are one of their colonies."

Out of many things that these beginnings emphasize we may select one: the discovery of the use of iron. Probably the properties of iron have been discovered in the world many times and in many places, but it seems likely that while Europe was still in its stone age and while neither Egypt nor Western Asia nor ancient China knew iron, the black Africans had invented the art of smelting. It was a moment big with promise for the uplift of the human race. No effective industry, no sure defense was possible for mankind with laboriously chipped stone tools. Copper and bronze made great advance over stone, but only hard iron founded modern industry; and this marvelous discovery was made by African Negroes.

The second thing that came out of the early strife of black folk was the village unit. I shall never forget my first glimpse of an African village. The night before, we had ridden the bar in the moonlight with the curious singing of lithe black boys. Above on the great headland twinkled Monrovia; below lay the black and silent forests beside a sombre sea. But this morning down by the sea and down by the forests suddenly we walked out into a little town. It was a town of the Vais. It was a thing of clay, colored cream and purple, clean, quiet, small, with perhaps a dozen or more homes. Authority was here and religion, industry and trade, education and art. It was not a complete thing from a modern point of view. It had little or no machinery; it lay almost defenseless against surrounding malaria. Of news service with the greater world, there was none. Though its whole inner being had been changed and in some respects upset by a new surrounding and invading economy, this little village was a mighty thing; it had come down from a mighty past. Its beginning stretched back in time thousands of thousands of years; it gathered to itself traditions and customs springing almost from the birth of the world. In space alone it stretched back along a path leading from the low thunder of the sea on the black West Coast to the great central plateau of Africa with forest, lake, and sand, two hundred miles away. Perhaps the great successive movements of this vast continent, so veiled today in mystery, had brought it even further seaward from the regions of the Mountains of the moon, past Ethiopia and Nubia, Melle and Songhay, Haussaland and Benin, those shadowy empires of the past. Perhaps even this little village here once knew Atlantis itself, and Greece and Phoenicia.

No matter whence the African village came and how it is to-day distorted and changed, and has been in the past glorified and degraded, it is a singularly persistent and eternal thing. Again and again this village with its conical huts, its central fire, its grassy streets, its fields of grain and fruit, and its cattle has been reborn in Africa and has spread itself over the endless miles of the continent. Even the African city as it rose time and time again was a city of villages. Ancient Jenne, whence comes our modern word Guinea, "had seven thousand villages so near to one another that the chief of Jenne had no need of messengers," but cried his messages from gate to gate and village to village until within a few moments they had gone a hundred miles to Lake Dibo.

We know the village unit the world over and among all people, but among most folk the village early lost itself in some larger unit, and civilization became a matter of city and state and nation. But the African village, because of geography and climate, because perhaps of some curious inner tenacity and strength of tradition, persisted and did on a small scale what the world has continually attempted on a wider scale and never satisfactorily accomplished. The African village socialized the individual completely, and yet because the village was small this socialization did not submerge and kill individuality. When the city socializes the modern man he becomes mechanical, and cities tend to be all alike. When the nation attempts to socialize the modern man the result is often a soulless Leviathan. The African village attempted a small part of the task of the modern city and state, and accomplished that part more successfully. It lost thereby breadth and power, it failed to integrate into a larger permanent imperialism. It never succumbed wholly to a militarism of its own but for that very reason it tasted slavery of every sort to others. But it was and is and perhaps will long be in its limited way a perfect human thing.

In the African village were bred religion, industry, government, education, and art, and these were bred as integral inter-related things. The primitive religion of Africa as developed by the African village underlies the religions of the world. Egyptian religion was in its beginning and later development of purely Negro character, and mulatto Egyptian priests on the stones of Egypt continually receive their symbols of authority from the black priests of Ethiopia. The Negro religion thus developed had something about it that was grim and terrible, and for that very reason it powerfully expressed the feelings of the first fighters in the world. The fire and desert, water and jungle of Africa, the beast and bird and serpent, the devil of disease with his flies and insects and worms and the infinitesimal germs that creep in the skin and veins and marrow of men,—all these are personified by the African Fetish. Fetish is a primitive philosophy of life. It is a spiritual explanation of physical evil and it explains by making all things spirit, both the good and the bad, and by seeking spiritual cure for physical ill.

The religion of the black man spread among all the Mediterranean races. Shango, god of the West Coast, hurler of thunder-bolts and lord of the storms, render of trees and slayer of men, cruel and savage and yet beneficent, was prototype of Zeus and Jupiter and Thor.

The African villagers from early days wove cloth, baked earthenware, manufactured instruments and arms, baskets and shoes, soap and glass. They worked in iron, copper, brass, bronze, gold, silver, bone, and ivory. They built in fibre, wood, and stone. They developed an original division of industry, a division first by families and clans, so that even the militarized Zulus are to this day divided according to ancient industrial designation like "the men of iron" and "sons of corn cleaners." Beyond that, division of industry appeared among the villages so that they were grouped according to their reciprocal activities and became complements one to another. One village specialized in fishing, another in wine, another in metals, and still another in trade,—importing from without. Sometimes the division was even more delicate: One Congo village carves elephant tusks, another makes a particular style of hat, and others swords, copper rings, wood carvings, and burnt clay pitchers.

Out of this industry developed the African market-place which knit the continent together with paths and trade centres, from the Gulf of Guinea to Zanzibar and from Walfish Bay to Lake Chad, long before the modern coming of Europe. The trade of African villages early reached the world,—Egypt, Persia, and India, Cyprus, Greece, and Rome, Byzantium, Spain, and Italy.

What the village system lacked in breadth and vision it gained in depth and personal knowledge. There was no monopoly, no poverty, no prostitution, and the only privilege was the definite, regulated, and usually limited privilege of the chief and head men, given in return for public service and revocable for failure. This primal village life has to-day largely disintegrated before the white invader, before machine goods and imperial compulsion, but it played its part in the world and was a rare contribution to civilization.

For stubbornly clinging to this fine and narrow village type of government and association, Africa has paid with dispersion and slavery. Dispersion came because the Village could not corral and hold its strongly developed individualities as could the state and empire. So that from days before the dawn of history down to our era a stream of black men have passed out of black Africa and into the world and profoundly influenced civilization by their genius. There was Nefertari, the black queen of Egypt who drove out the Hyksos and was, as Flinters Petrie says, "the most venerated figure of Egyptian history"; there was the black Mutemua, mother of the great Amen-hote III who built the temple at Luxor and whose direct descendant was the royal princess who by marriage made Tut-ankh-amen Pharaoh of Egypt. As the late Professor [A. F.] Chamberlain wrote: "Besides these marked individual instances, there is the fact that the Egyptian race itself in general had a considerable element of Negro blood, and one of the prime reasons why no civilization of the type of that of the Nile arose in other parts of the continent, if such a thing were possible, was that Egypt acted as a sort of channel by which the genius of Negroland was drafted off into the service of Mediterranean and Asiatic culture."

The second and more terrible way in which Africa paid for her individualistic village culture was by the slave trade; Christian Europe traded in human beings for four hundred years. The slave trade alone cost Africa in dead and stolen nearly one hundred million souls. And yet people to-day ask the cause of the stagnation of culture in that land since 1600!

Nevertheless for all this there was compensation, and this compensation was African art. The sense of beauty is the last and best gift of Africa to the world and the true essence of the black man's soul. African art is the offspring of the African climate and the Negro soul. The sunshine of central Africa cloaks you like a golden blanket; it hangs heavy about your shoulders; it envelopes you; it smothers you in a soft but mighty embrace. The rain of Africa is a consuming flood, a river pouring out of heaven, without banks or current. In Africa the swift, the energetic are the dead. In Africa the "lazy" survive and live. This African laziness is several things; it is shelter from the penetrating rain; it is defense from malaria. And it brings with it leisure and dreams and human intercourse.

Deep in forest fastness and by the banks of low, vast rivers, in the deep tense quiet of the endless jungle, the human soul whispered its folk tales, carved its pictures, sang its rhythmic songs, and danced and danced. The languages of Africa grew and developed for their unique work, "so simple and clear in their phonology, so logical in their syntax." From these has descended one of the richest masses of oral tradition of poetry and folk lore which the world knows. To this was early added the art of sculpture.

We have long known of the African artist. Traces of his work have been found in prehistoric Europe, in parts of Asia, and of course in Egypt. Later rich centres of African art were brought to European knowledge on the African western coast. It was long customary to think of this art first as imitation, secondly as inexpressibly crude and funny; but to-day more recent interpretations show that the primitive art of Africa is one of the greatest expressions of the human soul in all time, "that black men invented art as they invented fire," that they spread their ideas of art among their white neighbors, and that their earliest expressions had an originality and fidelity of purpose that the primitive world never surpassed.

Finally, out of Africa and out of the soul of Black folk came music and rhythm. The African not only sang beautiful melodies but he invented part singing, and his instinct for rhythm developed syncopation. He early made musical instruments, and especially did he make the drum a living and speaking thing. His songs "rich as is their weave of rhythm and polyphony are not the only music of the African, but through other instruments of his own invention the black man achieves the independence of human voice that presupposes a conception of music as an art, demanding an understanding of tome qualities and again a sense for the structural building of rhythmic and melodic balances of sound."

What is African music? Have you heard the tom-tom in O'Neill's "Emperor Jones?" Below this ecstasy of fear runs that rhythmic obligato,—low, sombre, fateful, tremendous; full of deep expression and infinite meaning; have you dancing in your soul and have you heard a Negro orchestra playing jazz? Your head may revolt, your ancient conventions scream in protest, but your heart and body leap to rhythm. It is a new and mighty art which Africa gave America and America is giving the world. It has circled the world, it has set hundreds of millions of feet a-dancing,—it is a "new" and "American" art which has already influenced all music and is destined to do more. Or again, have you heard the Sorrow Song?

Once upon a time,—I was a youth of eighteen,—I taught school in the hills of Tennessee. I was new to section and people; and on a soft and dark and lovely night, I went out under the stars. And there rolling down across the valley came music. It was as the Voice of Angels upon the Hills of God. It was the sorrow of riven souls suddenly articulate; it was the tears of slaves, the sobs of raped daughters, the quiver of murdered bodies, the defiance of deathless hope. I shivered and ran. I hurried along the stony creek, and up hard hills, and through the gray and twinkling village. And ever as I ran the music, the terrible, beautiful music swept nearer. It became more human, louder, pulsating with life and vigor and yet more poignantly sweet.

There was a building set upon a hill,—a dim, dilapidated thing, half-furnished with bench and board and far-flung door and window. There within swayed and danced a people mad with song. It was the demoniac possession of infinite music. Wild arms waved in air, wild feet beat out the time, wild faces, dark, sweat-creased, stared up to God and wild and wilder words cut the night:—

"Stand the storm, it won't be long, we'll anchor by and by!"

"Oh, the stars of the elements are falling and the moon drips away into blood,—!"

"Roll, Jordan, roll!"

Oh, it was bizarre,—the people were black and dirty and funny but I stood and wept, and when, in a flash of silence, a woman leaped into the air and shrieked as the dying shriek I sat down cold with terror and hot with new ecstasy.

Again and yesterday I sat in old St. George's, New York, and heard a whole service intoned to the music set by a Negro composer, built on Negro themes and sung by a white choir. The audience within was spellbound and, without, a thousand friends of Harry Burleigh clamored for admittance in vain.

And finally, last Christmas, I looked out of my window. The moonlight drifted down on palm and mango. Strange blossoms spread their scent on the soft hot breeze. I could hear the dull roar of the Atlantic beyond Cape Mesurado. I could hear music,—songs that rose and rolled nearer. Words half English, half Vai, tunes that were once gospel hymns, but Africa had taken them. Africa had given them rhythm and syncopation; high soared the soprano obligato, low rolled the strong big voices of men. It was the strangest combination, re-weaving, new-birthing of an old thing, I had ever heard. Such is the gift of music which Africa is still giving the world.

The essence of African culture then lies in its initial strife which began all culture; in its development of the village unit in religion, industry, and government; and finally in its art,—its realization of beauty in folk lore, sculpture, and music. All this Africa has given the modern world together with its suffering and its woe.

THE REALITIES IN AFRICA

In modern times two great world movements have hinged on the relation of Africa to the other continents: the African slave trade, which transferred perhaps ten million laborers from Africa to America and played a major rôle in the establishment of capitalism in England and Europe based on sugar and cotton; and the partitioning of Africa after the Franco-Prussian War which, with the Berlin Conference of 1884, brought colonial imperialism to flower.

The primary reality of imperialism in Africa today is economic. Since 1884 there has been invested in that continent a sum larger than the total gold reserve of the British Empire and France in 1939. Due to this investment there were exported annually from Africa, just before the present war, seven hundred million dollars' worth of products. And this valuation of African exports is abnormally low, since in a market controlled by the manufacturers the labor cost is depressed so as to yield high profit; the potential value of African raw materials runs into the billions.

These, then, are the two facts to keep in mind in our discussions of the future of Africa—that in the nineteenth century the African trade in men changed to a trade in raw materials; and that thenceforth the political domination which insured monopoly of raw materials to the various contending empires was predicated on the exploitation of African labor inside the continent. The integration of Africa into the world economic organization since the Industrial Revolution has been of far greater significance than social scientists like to admit. A quite natural reticence regarding the immense extent of the slave trade fostered the tendency to treat that question as an incidental moral lapse which was overshadowed and atoned for by the abolitionist crusade of 1800–1860. But an understanding of the economic background of that crusade is basic to the correct interpretation of the twentieth century and its two world wars.

In the eighteenth century England became the great slave-trading nation of the world and made America a land of chattel slavery. But in the nineteenth century England appears as the emancipator, who stopped the slave trade at great cost, abolished slavery in her own territories and stimulated the reaction against Negro slavery throughout the world. How do these attitudes harmonize? The rise of liberal and philanthropic thought in the latter part of the eighteenth century accounts, of course, for no little of the growth of opposition to slavery and the slave trade; but it accounts for only a part of it. Other and dominant factors were the diminishing returns of the African slave trade itself, the bankruptcy of the West Indian sugar economy through the Haitian revolution, the interference of Napoleon and the competition of Spain. Without this pressure of economic forces, Parliament would not have yielded so easily to the abolition crusade. Moreover, new fields of investment and profit were being opened to Englishmen by the consolidation of the empire in India and by the acquisition of new spheres of influence in China and elsewhere. In Africa, British rule was actually strengthened by the anti-slavery crusade, for new territory was annexed and controlled under the aegis of emancipation. It would not be right to question for a moment the sincerity of Sharpe, Wilberforce, Buxton and their followers. But the moral force they represented would have met with greater resistance had it not been working along lines favorable to English investment and colonial profit.

There followed a brief but interesting period of readjustment. For a while after the triumph of the abolition movement the idea was fairly widespread in England that Africa was to be allowed its own development so long as trade was free. Sierra Leone, the British Negro settlement, was promised eventual autonomy; and when Napier overthrew Theodore of Ethiopia in 1868, he withdrew without even attempting permanent control or annexation. But soon the investing countries realized that strong political control in African and Asiatic colonies would result in such a monopoly of labor and raw material as to insure magnificent profits. The slave trade and slavery would not only be unnecessary; they were actually a handicap to profitable investment.

The process of strengthening control over the people of Africa was therefore developed in the name of stopping the slave trade and abolishing slavery. For a while, English philanthropy and English imperialism seemed to have found one of those pre-established harmonies in economic life upon which Bentham and the Physiocrats had loved to expatiate. Increased trade and stable government in Africa was going to be the best way of civilizing the natives and lifting them toward self-government. Philanthropy, guided by men like Livingstone, envisaged the raising of the status of black labor in Africa as not only compatible with industrial profit, but practically synonymous with it. It was equally clear that unless there was political domination of these colonies to insure a virtual monopoly of material and labor, the colonial investment there would not be secure. The almost complete partition of Africa followed, settling in the hands of England a vast colonial empire and yielding to France and to Germany less valuable but nevertheless large imperial domains.

A technique of domination was gradually developed. Physical force backed by superior firearms was used in the Sudan. In South Africa, economic pressure was applied by land monopoly, supplemented by a head tax which meant compulsory labor. A caste system of Negroes subordinated to whites was widely instituted, but to some extent modified by cultural segregation, sometimes called "Indirect Rule," by which the cultural integrity of African tribes was within limits permitted for local government, but their economic activities guided by the interests of investment in the hands of the governing country. Just as European peasants did not get a cent of compensation for the three and a half million acres of common land taken from them between 1801 and 1831, so in the Union of South Africa the natives who formed eighty percent of the population came to possess only eight percent of the land. In Kenya 3,000,000 natives are confined today to 50,000 square miles of the poorest land; the best land has been given to Europeans, often at a nominal price, in estates so large that they can only be cultivated by hired labor. Again and again forced labor has been legalized in Kenya; and it is legal today. Labor in the mines of South Africa was long removed only a step from serfdom, and labor conditions there now allow a native wage of $15 a month. In the Belgian Congo and French Equatorial Africa there has been a sordid history of cruelty, extermination and exploitation.

We must not blink the fact that in the past it has been profitable to a mother country to possess colonies. One sometimes hears that colonies represent a sort of philanthropic enterprise. The colonial system is commended for whatever education and social services it has given to the natives and is not blamed if these social services have been miserably inadequate as compared to the need. The fact is that so far as government investment is concerned, the money which Great Britain,

France, Portugal and Germany *as governments* have invested in Africa has yielded small returns in taxes and revenues. But this governmental investment and its concomitant political control have been the basis upon which private investors have built their private empires, being thus furnished free capital by home taxation; and while the mass of people in the mother country have been taxed and often heavily for this governmental gift abroad, the private capitalist who has invested in the colonies has reaped not only interest from his own investment but returns from investments which he did not make and which are protected by armies and navies which he only partially supported. Immense sums have been derived from raw material and labor whose price has been depressed to a minimum while the resulting goods processed in the mother country are sold at monopoly prices. The profits have not been evenly distributed at home; but the net return to the white races for their investment in colored labor and raw material in Africa has been immense. That, very briefly, is the fundamental fact of the situation which confronts us in Africa today.

II

For convenience we refer to "Africa" in a word. But we should remember that there is no one "Africa." There is in the continent of Africa no unity of physical characteristics, of cultural development, of historical experience, or of racial identity.

We may distinguish today at least eleven "Africas." There is North Africa—though Algeria and Libya are in large degree a part of southern Europe. There is French West Africa, a vast and loosely integrated region, in one small part of which an educational and cultural development of the natives is in evidence and where there has been some economic progress. There is Egypt, which is still a political and economic satellite in the British Empire; but from Egypt the Anglo-Egyptian Sudan has been cut off and presents a different economy and faces a different destiny. To the south lies Ethiopia, whose long and tragic history foreshadowed the present war. Turning westward again, we have French Equatorial Africa, an economic echo of the Belgian Congo, the seat in the past of terrible exploitation and in the present of a new arming of blacks for European wars.

Then there is British West Africa. It consists of four colonies and demonstrates the most advanced possibilities of the Negro race in Africa; even here those possibilities are held in check by the limited application of the democratic methods and by carefully organized exploitation. There is the Belgian Congo, whose astonishing history is known to all. There is British East Africa, consisting of Uganda, Kenya and Tanganyika, combining an advanced native state, an extreme example of European land-aggression in Kenya, and the former German colony of Tanganyika. There is Portuguese Africa, almost split in two by British territory and dependent mainly upon British economic organization. Finally, there are South Africa and the Rhodesias, where 3,000,000 white people are holding 10,000,000 darker folk in economic serfdom. This is preëminently the land of gold, jewels and metals.

Current world opinion makes little distinction among these groups. Berbers of North Africa are usually classed as "white" peoples; Abyssinians are now and then declared not to be Negroes; but on the whole, all Africans, save recent white European immigrants and their offspring, are classed among the peoples of the earth who are inferior in status and in kind.

This decree of inferiority is not based on scientific study—indeed the careful anthropological and social study of Africa has only just begun. Again we must come back to dollars, pounds, marks and francs. The judgment on Africa was rendered on economic grounds (although, of course, pseudo-scientific dogma were adduced to bolster it). Liberal thought and violent revolution in the eighteenth and early nineteenth centuries shook the foundations of a social hierarchy in Europe based on unchangeable class distinctions. But in the nineteenth and early twentieth centuries the Color Line was drawn as at least a partial substitute for this stratification. Granting that all white men were born free and equal, was it not manifest—ostensibly after Gobineau and Darwin, but in reality after James Watt, Eli Whitney, Warren Hastings and Cecil Rhodes—that Africans and Asiatics were born slaves, serfs or inferiors? The real necessity of this fantastic rationalization was supplied by the demands of modern colonial imperialism. The process of exploitation that culminated in the British, French and German empires before the First World War turned out to be an investment whose vast returns depended on cheap labor, under strict political control, without too much interference from mawkish philanthropy.

Philanthropy has fought stout battles for a liberalization of imperialistic rule in the past. The focus of those battles has usually been the question of education of the peoples of Africa; it was the difference of opinion on this issue which awoke philanthropy from its dream of foreordained harmony between the cohorts of Christianity and business. The painful question inevitably arose: to what degree should native people be allowed an education, in view of the fact that educated men do not make cheap and docile laborers? Sharp disputes took place between missionaries and administrative officials over the missionaries' plans for schools and for the training of skilled artisans, civil servants, and professional men such as physicians. In some cases, at least, the insistence of the missionaries was so great that government was forced to yield.

The cultural possibilities of the African native are undeniable. It is admitted even in South Africa today that the native is not being kept out of skilled labor because he is incapable. And his capacity for political self-rule is shown by the success of the native states of the West Coast, the Bunga of the Transkei and other such experiments. Missionaries, travellers, and now many government agents agree that it would be possible to place centers of education in Africa which would in a few generations train an intelligentsia capable eventually of taking fairly complete charge of the social development of the continent. There are beginnings of such centers today at Fort Hare, South Africa; Achimota and Fourah Bay, West Africa; and Makerere, Uganda.

Cutting across this whole question comes the issue of the use of Negroes in war. The Civil War in the United States was fought with the help of 200,000 black troops with a growing possibility of enlisting a majority of the slaves; and their use made further slavery unthinkable. The First World War was fought with the help of black troops which France brought to Europe to ward off annihilation; the blacks of French West Africa were armed on a large scale and became an effective fighting force in Europe. Europe protested—the English in South Africa as well as the Germans in Europe. If armed natives were going to be used in European disputes, would not native colonial revolt be only a matter of years? Today the Free French are not only using black troops but using them under a black governor of French Equatorial Africa, while Senegalese troops of French West Africa and colored troops of North Africa are used in increasing numbers.

Unless this question of racial status is frankly and intelligently faced it will become a problem not simply of Africa but of the world. More than the welfare of the blacks is involved. As long as there is in the world a reservoir of cheap labor that can raise necessary raw materials, and as long as arrangements can be made to transport these raw materials to manufacturing countries, this body of cheap labor will compete directly or indirectly with European labor and will be often substituted for European labor. This situation will increase the power of investors and employers over the political organization of the state, leading to agitation and revolt within the state on the part of the laboring classes and to wars between states which are competing for domination over these sources of profit. And if the fiction of inferiority is maintained, there will be added to all this the revolt of the suppressed races themselves, who, because of their low wages, are the basic cause of the whole situation.

The World War of 1914–1918 was caused in part by the German demand for a larger share in the domination over labor and in the exploitation of raw materials in Asia and Africa. An important aspect of the World War of 1939 is the competition for the profit of Asiatic labor and materials—competition in part between European countries, in part between those countries and Japan. Submerged labor is revolting in the East Indies, Burma and India itself. It would be a grave mistake to think that Africans are not asking the same questions that Asiatics are: "Is it a white man's war?"

The social development of Africa for the welfare of the Africans, with educated Africans in charge of the program, would certainly interfere with the private profits of foreign investment and would ultimately change the entire relationship of Africa to the modern world. Is the development of Africa for the welfare of Africans the aim? Or is the aim a world dominated by Anglo-Saxons, or at least by the stock of white Europe? If the aim is to keep Africa in subjection just as long as possible, will this not plant the seeds of future hatreds and more war?

III

One would think that Africa, so important in world trade and world industrial organization and containing at least 125,000,000 people, would be carefully considered today in any plan for post-war reconstruction. This does not seem to be the case. When we examine the plans which have been published we find either no mention of Africa or only vague references. In President Roosevelt's "four freedoms" speech in January 1941, he did not seem to be thinking of Africa when he mentioned freedom of speech, freedom from want and freedom from fear. When Pope Pius XII spoke in June 1941 on "Peace and the Changing Social Order" his only phrase which could have referred to Africa was "the more favorable distribution of men on the earth's surface." The British Christian leaders in May 1941 made ten proposals for a lasting peace. The tenth reference was to the resources of the earth which "should be used as God's gifts to the whole human race." The American Friends Service Committee in June 1941 similarly asked that all nations be assured "equitable access to markets." That refers to Africa—but it is an ominous reference. The eight points of the Atlantic Charter were so obviously aimed at European and North American conditions that Winston Churchill frankly affirmed this to be the case, although he was afterward contradicted by President Roosevelt. The proposals which have been made by publicists like Clarence Streit and Henry Luce imply a domination of the world by English-speaking peoples, with only passing consideration of black folk. Only in the recent report on "The Atlantic Charter and Africa from an American Standpoint," by the Committee on Africa, the War, and Peace Aims, is a more realistic attitude toward Africa manifest. The Committee insists "That Africa today should be the subject of intelligent study in this country for many reasons, but especially because it is the ancestral home of one-tenth of our population, and that it is a continent of vast possibilities and difficult problems, and of vital concern to the United Nations in the present war . . . that Africa still represents the largest underdeveloped area in the world, with mineral deposits, agricultural land, waterpower, forest and wild life, resources of importance, all of which are decreasing in value because of careless or reckless use or exploitation; and that these resources need development for its own defense and welfare."

The largest undeveloped area in the world! Is that phrase, spoken frankly by a body particularly conscious of African problems, the clue to the reticence of the other postwar statements on the subject of Africa? I do not mean to be unduly pessimistic; but realism demands that we face the fact that after this war the United Nations will be almost irresistibly tempted to consider Africa from an industrial and commercial point of view as a means of helping pay war costs and reëstablishing prosperity.

If the treatment of Africa in postwar planning begins or ends here the results will be tragic. One can see in all these postwar plans—although often, I know, the implication is not intentional or even suspected—the persistence of the old pattern of thought: the white man's need of African labor and raw materials and the assumption that these must be cheap in order to yield maximum profits. Above all, and most tragically, appears the assumption that the only problem so far as Africa is concerned is that the various dominating nations of the world must henceforth be treated equitably in sharing the material and the labor.

The memorable phrase of the First World War, the German demand for "a place in the sun," meant that Germany demanded metals, vegetable oils, fibres and foods from Africa on equal terms with England, either by pooling or preferably by dividing up Africa's land, labor and resources afresh. To return to such a plan after a generation of indecision, after another ghastly war, and in a period bursting with the components of still another and vaster war, would be blindness indeed. Yet this is precisely what many have in mind. If the rivalry of dominant European nations for colonial profit can be composed by a more equitable distribution of raw materials and labor, they say, then peace will be assured in the world. When they say nothing about the aspirations of the peoples of Africa themselves, what they are actually saying is that peace will be assured if we will all merely return to the eighteenth century.

IV

The first National Congress of British West Africa met in Accra, capital of the Gold Coast Colony, in mid-March, 1920. The Congress, composed of delegates from Nigeria, the Gold Coast, Sierra Leone and Gambia, drafted a memorial to His Majesty the King which is a worthy and remarkable document:

In presenting the case for the franchise for the different colonies composing British West Africa, namely, the Gambia, Sierra Leone, the Gold Coast and Nigeria, it is important to remember that each of these colonies is at present governed under the Crown Colony System. By that is meant that the power of selecting members for the legislative councils is in the Governor of each colony and not dependable upon the will of the people through an elective system. In the demand for the franchise by the people of British West Africa, it is not to be supposed that they are asking to be allowed to copy a foreign institution. On the contrary, it is important to notice that the principle of electing representatives to local councils and bodies is inherent in all the systems of British West Africa. According to African institutions every member of a community belongs to a given family with its duly accredited head, who represents that family in the village council, naturally composed of the heads of the several families. Similarly in a district council the different representatives of each village or town would be appointed by the different villages and towns, and so with the Provincial Council until, by the same process, we arrive at the Supreme Council, namely, the State Council, presided over by the Paramount Chief. . . .

The Congress presses for the appointment of duly qualified and experienced legal men to judicial appointments in British West Africa no matter how high the emolument might be. It also presses for the appointment of African barristers of experience, many of whom as jurists and legislative councillors are found along the West Coast, to appointments on the judicial bench as well as other judicial appointments. The Congress contends that there are African legal men of experience capable of holding any judicial office in British West Africa. It may be mentioned that in Sierra Leone years ago the late Hon. Sir Samuel Lewis, Knight, C. M. G., an African, held the appointment of Acting Chief Justice; the late Mr. J. Renner Maxwell of Oxford University, an African, held the office of Chief Magistrate of the Gambia, which was equivalent then to the office of Chief Justice; that His Honour the late Mr. Justice Francis Smith, an African, was the Senior Puisne Judge of the Gold Coast, and on several occasions held the appointment of Acting Chief Justice; that the late Mr. James A. McCarthy, an African, was for many years the Queen's Advocate of Sierra Leone, which was then equivalent to the post of Attorney General, and on many occasions acted as Chief Justice of that Colony. Subsequently he became the Solicitor General of the Gold Coast, and acted as Puisne Judge on several occasions in that Colony. Further, the late Sir Conrad Reeves, an African, was Chief Rustice of Jamaica for many years. Therefore it is no new thing to suggest that worthy Africans should be admitted to the highest judicial offices in the judicial service of British West Africa. It is worthy of note that so renowned is the forensic ability of the African legal practitioner, generally a barrister of one of the Inns of Court in London, that they usually control all the practice in British West Africa and the percentage of European practitioners is hardly three.

It must be remembered that this clear and concise demand for elementary democratic rights among the black people of British West Africa was drafted by native-born Africans of Negro descent. In response to it an elective element was admitted to the governors' councils in four colonies. The governor retained the selection of a majority of the council. Any legislation which he wished was guaranteed passage. In these same councils, in all the colonies, sat men representing business and industry directly, that is, voting in the name of and for foreign investors. They still do.

It should be noted also that many of the preferments listed by the Congress came in that period when, under the triumph of philanthropy, England was hesitating between a policy of slavery and colonial autonomy. Soon, as we have seen, the die was cast.

Beside this document, now, place a statement made in 1923 by the white settlers of Kenya. It is the voice of triumphant commercialism, formulating a racial philosophy for the modern world:

> It has been shown that the Black Race possesses initiative but lacks constructive powers, characteristics which justify Lugard's judgment that for the native African "the era of complete independence is not yet visible on the horizon of time." The controlling powers may, therefore, aim at advancing the black race as far along the road of progress as its capacity allows, without misgivings that the success of their endeavours will lead to a demand for their withdrawal, entailing loss of prestige and trade. The development of British territories in Africa opens up a vista of commercial expansion so endless that calculated description is difficult. The bare facts are that the area of these territories is 4,000,000 square miles, as compared with India's 1,900,000; that India's overseas trade is about £350,000,000 and British Africa's (excluding Egypt) is about £292,000,000; that the non-self-governing territories, whose total area is 2,628,498 square miles, already produce an overseas trade of £76,500,000, although their development can hardly be said to have begun; that the average fertility and mineral wealth of their soil are at least equal to those of any other great land mass; that they hold an intelligent fast-breeding native population of about 60 millions, waiting for guidance to engage in the production of the raw materials of industry and foodstuffs; and that white settlement coöperating with the native populations does stimulate production many hundreds of times, and does bring about a demand for manufactured articles out of all proportion to its numerical strength.

Here, then, is the African question: European profit—or Negro development? There is no denying that the training of an African intelligentsia implies most difficult problems—the problem of preserving rather than destroying the native cultural patterns and all the problems that come with inexperienced social leadership. The point is that the decision in these matters must not be left to those interested primarily in financial gain, or to white people alone. If there is to be real Negro development there must be created some organ of international trust-eeship and the native intelligence of Africa must be represented on the guiding boards. Can we expect Europe and America to approach this question in a way that promises a solution? We could not expect it under ordinary circumstances; but the circumstances today are not ordinary.

If I were to try to state summarily the objectives of postwar planning for Africa, looking toward the achievement of the world peace which we all so deeply feel must follow this world war, I would say first that it is necessary to renounce the assumption that there are a few large groups of mankind called races, with hereditary differences shown by color, hair and measurements of the bony skeleton which fix forever their relations to each other and indicate the possibilities of their individual members. There is no proof that persons and groups in Africa are not as capable of useful lives and effective progress as peoples in Europe and America.

I would say, second, that we must repudiate the more or less conscious feeling, widespread among the white peoples of the world, that other folk exist not for themselves, but for their uses to Europe; that white Europe and America have the right to invade the territory of colored peoples, to force them to work and to interfere at will with their cultural patterns, while demanding for whites themselves a preferred status and seriously and arbitrarily restricting the contacts of colored folk with other and higher culture. The most dangerous excuse for this situation is the relation between European capital and colored labor involving high profit, low wages and cheap raw material. It places the strong motive of private profit in the foreground of our inter-racial relations, while the greater objects of cultural understanding and moral uplift are pushed into the background.

I would say, third, that it must be agreed that in Africa the land and the natural resources belong primarily to the native inhabitants. The necessary capital for the development of Africa's resources should be gradually and increasingly raised from savings of the African natives which a higher wage and a just incidence of taxation would make possible. I would say, fourth, that a systematic effort must be begun to train an educated class among the natives, and that class must be allowed to express its opinions and those opinions be given due weight. And I would say, finally, that political control must be taken away from commercial and business interests owned and conducted in the foreign nations which dominate the continent, and this control be vested provisionally in an international mandates commission.

These, in simplest form, are the proposals for the future which correspond to the present realities in Africa.

THE FUTURE OF AFRICA

Fellow Africans: About 1735, my great-great grandfather was kidnapped on this coast of West Africa and taken by the Dutch to the colony of New York in America, where he was sold in slavery. About the same time a French Huguenot, Jacques Du Bois, migrated from France to America and his great-grandson, born in the West Indies and with Negro blood, married the great-great granddaughter of my black ancestor. I am the son of this couple, born in 1868, hence my French name and my African loyalty.

As a boy I knew little of Africa save legends and some music in my family. The books which we studied in the public school had almost no information about Africa, save of Egypt, which we were told was not Negroid. I heard of few great men of Negro blood, but I built up in my mind a dream of what Negroes would do in the future even though they had no past.

Then happened a series of events: In the last decade of the 19th century, I studied two years in Europe, and often heard Africa mentioned with respect. Then, as a teacher in America, I had a few African students. Later at Atlanta University a visiting professor, Franz Boaz, addressed the students and told them of the history of the Black Sudan. I was utterly amazed and began to study Africa for myself. I attended the Paris Exposition in 1900, and met with West Indians in London in a Pan-African Conference. This movement died, but in 1911 I attended a Races Congress in London which tried to bring together representatives from all races of the world. I met distinguished Africans and was thrilled. However, World War killed this movement.

We held a small meeting in 1919 in Paris. After peace was declared, in 1921, we called a much larger Pan-African Congress in London, Paris and Brussels. The 200 delegates at this congress aroused the fury of the colonial powers and all our efforts for third, fourth and fifth congresses were only partially successful because of their opposition. We tried in vain to convene a congress in Africa itself.

The great depression of the 'thirties then stopped our efforts for 15 years. Finally in 1945 black trade union delegates to the Paris meeting of trade unions called for another Pan-African Congress. This George Padmore organized and, at his request, I came from America to attend the meeting at Manchester, England. Here I met Kwame Nkrumah, Jomo Kenyatta, Johnson of Liberia and a dozen other young leaders.

The program of Pan-Africa as I have outlined it was not a plan of action, but of periodical conferences and free discussion. And this was a necessary preliminary to any future plan of united or separate action. However, in the resolutions adopted by the successive Congresses were many statements urging united action, particularly in the matter of race discrimination. Also, there were other men and movements urging specific work.

World financial depression interferred with all these efforts and suspended the Pan-African Congresses until the meeting in Manchester in 1945. Then, it was reborn and this meeting now in Accra is the sixth effort to bring this great movement before the world and to translate its experience into action.

My only role in this meeting is one of advice from one who has lived long, who has studied Africa and has seen the modern world.

In this great crisis of the world's history, when standing on the highest peaks of human accomplishment we look forward to Peace and backward to War, when we look up to Heaven and down to Hell, let us mince no words. We face triumph or tragedy without alternative.

Africa, ancient Africa, has been called by the world and has lifted up her hands! Africa has no choice between private capitalism and socialism. The whole world, including capitalist countries, is moving toward socialism, inevitably, inexorably. You can choose between blocs of military alliance, you can choose between groups of political union; you cannot choose between socialism and private capitalism because private capitalism is doomed!

But what is socialism? It is a disciplined economy and political organization to which the first duty of a citizen is to serve the state; and the state is not a selected aristocracy, or a group of self-seeking oligarchs who have seized wealth and power. No! The mass of workers with hand and brain are the ones whose collective destiny is the chief object of all effort.

Gradually, every state is coming to this concept of its aim. The great Communist states like the Soviet Union and China have surrendered completely to this idea. The Scandinavian states have yielded partially; Britain has yielded in some respects, France in part, and even the United States adopted the New Deal which was largely socialism; though today further American socialism is held at bay by 60 great groups of corporations who control individual capitalists and the trade union leaders.

On the other hand, the African tribe, whence all of you sprung, was communistic in its very beginnings. No tribesman was free. All were servants of the tribe of whom the chief was father and voice.

When now, with a certain suddenness, Africa is whirled by the bitter struggle of dying private capitalism into the last great battleground of its death throes, you are being tempted to adopt at least a passing private capitalism as a step to some partial socialism. This would be a grave mistake.

For 400 years Europe and North America have built their civilization and comfort on theft of colored labor and the land and materials which rightfully belong to these colonial peoples.

The dominant exploiting nations are willing to yield more to the demands of the mass of men than were their fathers. But their yielding takes the form of sharing the loot—not of stopping the looting. It takes the form of stopping socialism by force and not of surrendering the fatal mistakes of private capitalism. Either capital belongs to all or power is denied all.

Here then, my Brothers, you face your great decision: Will you for temporary advantage—for automobiles, refrigerators and Paris gowns—spend your income in paying interest on borrowed funds; or will you sacrifice your present comfort and the chance to shine before your neighbors, in order to educate your children, develop such industry as best serves the great mass of people and make your country strong in ability, self-support and self-defense? Such union of effort for strength calls for sacrifice and self-denial, while the capital offered you at high price by the colonial powers like France, Britain, Holland, Belgium and the United States, will prolong fatal colonial imperialism, from which you have suffered slavery, serfdom and colonialism.

You are not helpless. You are the buyers and to continue existence as sellers of capital, these great nations, former owners of the world, must sell or face bankruptcy. You are not compelled to buy all they offer now. You can wait. You can starve a while longer rather than sell your great heritage for a mess of Western capitalist pottage. You can not only beat down the price of capital as offered by the united and monopolized Western private capitalists, but at last today you can compare their offers with those of socialist countries like the Soviet Union and China, which with infinite sacrifice and pouring out of blood and tears, are at last able to offer weak nations needed capital on better terms than the West.

The supply which socialist nations can at present spare is small as compared with that of the bloated monopolies of the West, but it is large and rapidly growing. Its acceptance involves no bonds which a free Africa may not safely assume. It certainly does not involve slavery and colonial control which the West has demanded and still demands. Today she offers a compromise, but one of which you must beware:

She offers to let some of your smarter and less scrupulous leaders become fellow capitalists with the white exploiters if in turn they induce the nation's masses to pay the awful costs. This happened in the West Indies and in South America. This may yet happen in the Middle East and Eastern Asia. Strive against it with every fibre of your bodies and souls. A body of local private capitalists, even if they are black, can never free Africa; they will simply sell it into new slavery to old masters overseas.

As I have said, this is a call for sacrifice. Great Goethe sang, "Entbehren sollst du, sollst entbehren"—"Thou shalt forego, shalt do without." If Africa unites, it will be because each part, each nation, each tribe gives up a part of its heritage for the good of the whole. That is what union means; that is what Pan-Africa means: When the child is born into the tribe the price of his growing up is giving a part of his freedom to the tribe. This he soon learns or dies. When the tribe becomes a union of tribes, the individual tribe surrenders some part of its freedom to the paramount tribe.

When the nation arises, the constituent tribes, clans and groups must each yield power and some freedom to the demands of the nation or the nation dies before it is born. Your local tribal, much-loved languages must yield to the few world tongues which serve the largest number of people and promote understanding and world literature.

This is the great dilemma which faces Africans today, faces one and all: Give up individual rights for the needs of Mother Africa; give up tribal independence for the needs of the nation.

Forget nothing, but set everything in its rightful place; the glory of the six Ashanti wars against Britain; the wisdom of the Fanti Confederation; the growth of Nigeria; the song of the Songhay and Hausa; the rebellion of the Mahdi and the hands of Ethiopia; the greatness of the Basuto and the fighting of Chaka; the revenge of Mutessi, and many other happenings and men; but above all—Africa, Mother of Men.

Your nearest friends and neighbors are the colored people of China and India, the rest of Asia, the Middle East and the sea isles, once close bound to the heart of Africa and now long severed by the greed of Europe. Your bond is not mere color of skin but the deeper experience of wage slavery and contempt. So too, your bond with the white world is closest to those who support and defend China and help India and not those who exploit the Middle East and South America.

Awake, awake, put on thy strength, O Zion! Reject the weakness of missionaries who teach neither love nor brotherhood, but chiefly the virtues of private profit from capital, stolen from your land and labor. Africa, awake! Put on the beautiful robes of Pan-African socialism.

You have nothing to lose but your chains! You have a continent to regain! You have freedom and human dignity to attain!

WHITES IN AFRICA AFTER NEGRO AUTONOMY

A rather curious change of emphasis has caught my attention recently. Negroes are being accused of racism, that is, of unduly emphasizing racial differences and of advocating racial separation. This would be laughable if it did not have so serious a side. A shattered and almost fatally divided world, now making desperate effort to envision a humanity bound together in peace and at least with some approach to brotherhood, is being warned that its worst victims are contemplating resurgence of race hate!

Of the debt which the white world owes Africa, there can be no doubt. No black man can recall it without a shudder of disgust and hate. The white followers of the meek and lowly Jesus stole fifteen million men, women, and children from Africa from 1400 to 1900 A. D. and made them working cattle in America; they left eighty-five million black corpses to mark their trail of blood and tears; then from 1800 to this day their scientists, historians, and ministers of the Gospel preached, wrote, and taught the world that a black man was by the grace of God and law of nature so evil and inferior that slavery, insult, and exploitation were too good for him and that the virgin purity of white women could only be secure if mulatto bastards were strewn from the Atlantic to the Pacific and from the North to the South pole. Harsh words?—but dismal truth. So what? Can bitter revenge erase all this? If Sir John Hawkins could be caught in West Africa today, even I shudder to think what Ghana might do to this blasphemous hypocrite. But he is beyond hurt today.

When I began my active life, nearly seventy years ago, the open and active contempt shown by white civilization for Negroes in the United States was almost incredible. My friend, a black Oxford man, clergyman of the Episcopal church, and of high and singularly fine character, was once in the home of a white American clergyman who introduced him to his brother. The brother refused to receive an introduction to a Negro. My friend, Alexander Crummell, applied for a colored church in Philadelphia to the presiding bishop. Bishop Onderdonk read the letter hastily and frowned. Fortunately, his mind was already clear on this point, and he cleared his brow and looked at Crummell. Then he said, slowly and impressively, "I will receive you into this diocese on one condition: no Negro priest can sit in my church convention, and no Negro church must ask for representation there."

In 1910 I could not buy an orchestra seat in any New York theater. I could eat in no restaurant downtown. Today, in the southern states of America no white man can marry the colored mother of his child. Most southern Negroes cannot vote, no matter what their education or character. All Negroes belong to a segregated inferior caste. The Supreme Court has ordered segregation to cease in public schools, but most of the former slaves states have refused to obey the law.

In Africa itself color caste is still the rule. In Sierra Leone, when I was there in 1928, a black physician with the same training as his white colleague was paid a salary 25 percent less than the white man; he lived by compulsion in poorer quarters and had curtailed allowances. More money was spent on the white golf courses than on Negro schools.

I need hardly mention the status of Negroes in the Union of South Africa, and in Rhodesia, Kenya, and Tanganyika, as compared with that of whites. White missionaries have long worked among Negroes, but they did what white business allowed, in the long run, or else they were replaced. Missionaries gave Africa schools, but they also helped to furnish cheap labor and free lands to white exploiters. These missionaries usually broke down native culture patterns, replacing them in most respects, by color caste. They lived separately from the natives, used them as servants, and limited their education so as to keep them inferior to whites and to prepare them for cheap labor, from which whites could profit. To this program there were notable exceptions, but those missionaries who insisted on Negro equality were soon recalled. The white missionaries to Africa became in the end the chief guides to colonial imperialism.

Even today and in the case of Dr. Schweitzer, whose valuable work in medicine all acknowledge, there is the charge that Dr. Schweitzer apparently does not always remember that, needed as medicine is and despite the continuous fight against disease in Africa, what is needed more is free, intelligent manhood and the abolition of that exploitation so often carried on by the very persons who contribute to hospitals while they allow their agents to steal for them in the colony the moneys which support their charities.

In Africa the political liberation of its nations has begun, until we recognize in the United Nations today more than twenty independent African nations. In the Union of South Africa and the Rhodesias there is still the firm determination of a minority of whites to rule the majority of Negroes and colored folk. In Kenya land monopoly is slipping, but still persists. In the Belgian Congo we have had the greatest surprise. Belgium, after depriving the Congolese of everything beyond primary education, has suddenly been forced to yield to a demand of the Congolese for independence. Then the Congolese prime minister was slain. Disaster followed, and yet the Congo is to become an independent Negro state. In spite of this, Europe and North America have by no means surrendered their determination to shape Africa through invested capital owned by Europeans or by such black allies as they are able to obtain among the African inhabitants.

In fine, West Europe is still determined to base its culture and comfort on underpaid labor and the virtual theft of land and materials by white investors. The prosperity of South Africa and Rhodesias is due to the wealth invested there by Britain and America, which makes huge profits because of the low wage paid black labor and the seizure of materials without any recognition of native rights. So long as this method of business and industry persists, the Africans must fight back. They will not fight the dead past, but the living present.

Naturally, this world treatment of men with black skins has embittered them and made them resentful of the assumptions of white men. In my own writings, I have often expressed this feeling. Today my resentment at the doctrine of race superiority, as preached and practiced by the white world for the last 250 years, has been pointed to with sharp criticism and contrasted with the charity of Gandhi and of the colored minister [Dr. Martin Luther King, Jr.] who led the recent boycott in Alabama. I am quite frank: I do not pretend to "love" white people. I think that as a race they are the most selfish of any on earth. I think that the history of the world for the last thousand years proves this beyond doubt, and it is more than proven today by the Salvation Army tactics of Toynbee and his school of history. Current history has tried desperately to ignore Africa and its contribution to civilization. Honesty and clarity in historical writing and research are certainly gaining, but are still lacking in the study of Negro history.

To many students of race relations the work of missionaries, especially in Africa, is a matter of congratulation and hope. In some of their satisfaction I share. I have just read Seaver's story of David Livingstone. I know of the fine efforts of Dr. Schweitzer to rid Africa of disease—that Africa which my friend, Sir Harry Johnston, rightly called "the chief stronghold of the real Devil—the reactionary forces of Nature hostile to the uprise of Humanity. Here Beelzebub, King of the Flies, marshals his vermiform and arthropod hosts—insects, ticks, and nematode worms—which more than on other continents . . . convey to the skin, veins, intestines, and spinal marrow of men and other vertebrates the micro-organisms which cause deadly, disfiguring, or debilitating diseases, or themselves create the morbid condition of the persecuted human being."

What now has this to do with the prospects of the future? If following Ethiopia, the Sudan, Liberia, Ghana, the new black French states, and the Congo, the peoples of Africa assert themselves and are able to maintain their autonomy, what is going to happen to white Europeans and to North Americans who live in Africa? Quite naturally, white thinkers are apt to be panic-stricken when this question arises. They remember some shameful episodes in the recent past—the action of a great British general in punishing the Mahdi who ran England out of the Sudan for a generation. Kitchener dug the dead body of this black man from its grave and fed it to the crocodiles of the Nile to prove the superiority of the white race. Even Churchill called this "a foul deed." But Britain made Kitchener a viscount. So Frederick Lugard, after a shameful career of murder in Uganda, became a noble British lord and authority on Africa. Chinese Gordon arose from scoundrel in China almost to a saint in the British Sudan.

White Belgians slaughtered natives of the Congo when yesterday they demanded some of the rights of white men. The Union of South Africa has acted like wild beasts toward black folk, and the story of Kenya is a disgrace to Britain. Quite naturally, then, white Europe is asking what Europeans can expect if ever Africans become free.

Yet no program of revenge may occur. And this not because the Christianity taught Africans by whites, while whites enslaved and raped them, will prove to be more efficacious in black consciences than in white, but simply because the black leaders of present Africa are not fools. Haile Selassie, Nkrumah, Azikiwe, Touré, and even Tubman are men of reason. They are well aware that the worst oppressors and enslavers of Africa are in vast majority dead, and cannot today be harmed by belated revenge. They know that there are white people in France, Britain, and America who can be just, and Negroes see also that the Soviet Union, China, Poland, and Czechoslovakia have proved that some white nations can treat colored people as brothers—can view men as men even though they are black, yellow, or red as Russia. They see and feel each day the mighty flood rolling toward socialism and to a real communism of mankind, and that in no far distant day. These leaders, and others being trained to succeed them, will act with reason if permitted—not without difficulties, not without seeing many of their dark fellows yield to the seductions of Western capitalism, which once lured Tunis, Morocco, and Algeria to their doom, and today have a stranglehold on Liberia and are seeking investments in South, Central, and West Africa.

But there is a wise portion of the peoples of Africa of Ghana and Nigeria, of South African blacks, and of American Negroes who glimpse a straight path. Africa needs capital goods to promote industry and break the capitalistic fetters on cheap crops and labor, and the processing of goods abroad and resale to the natives in the form of gin and baubles at fabulous prices. Africa needs sanitation and medicine; she needs agriculture for crops suited to her own wants and the conservation of power for her own factories. This capital she can borrow— she is begged today to borrow it from Britain and the United States at 10 or even 100 percent interest; but *there* lies disaster, and this Africa is beginning to realize. This capital she can herself save in part, but at cruel sacrifice and amid the cheerful sneers of white tourists and students. Yet if Africa saves its own capital in part, or borrows it from lands like the Soviet Union and China at rates far below the debt slavery offered by the United States, Britain, and West Germany, her chances of survival are good. That this is possible, China can tell her: Egypt is learning; even India begins to suspect. Africa knows that this kind of revenge on her traducers will far exceed in satisfaction any petty deeds inspired by hate of the dead and the dying—of the dead slave-traders and of the dying corporations of exploiters and thieves who are working today.

What, then, will happen to white folk in Africa when black folk rule their own territory depends on what white folks do, and do now. And the whites to whom I refer are not the dead nor simply those living in Africa. I refer to the white world as a whole. We are come to a time when the sins and mistakes of the whole group must be considered and judged, not simply small localities or single individuals. Perhaps in the fifteenth century, slavery of Negroes was the guilt mainly of certain individuals. But today, the poverty of the majority of human beings, the war, murder, and destruction due to colonial imperialism, cannot be charged simply against the Union of South Africa, or the white owners of Kenya land, or the Dutch monopolists of Indonesia. No. The real culprits are the British and American shareholders in corporations, the rich cartel owners who form the aristocracy of France and Germany, and the well-paid leaders of labor unions who exclude or segregate Negroes and other colonial folk.

It is folk like these who finance race hate in Africa: grow rich on coffee, fruit, and sugar in Central and South America; and plead innocence of wrong because they "do not know" what investment, incorporated business, stock markets, and world trade are doing to mankind. It is their business to know the crime which is devastating the earth. It is hard to point to examples of this in business and industry. Individual income and profit are the closely guarded secrets of the modern world. Yet here is one instance revealed in the soliciting of further investment: in one year Northern Rhodesia sold its copper product for $36,000,000. Of this income, one half went to British and American shareholders, part based on old but quite baseless claims of "ownership" and part on "investment" and stock gambling. Two and one-half million dollars went to 1,690 white artisans, at $15,000 each for the year. They worked as trained technicians, but most of their actual toil and part of their skill was performed by Negro helpers. The whites lived like little lords and had all the cheap house service which they wanted, with modern homes and the right to vote. They had a recognized union, to which no Negro could belong. Less than 2 percent of the total 36 millions of income from copper, $632,000, or $37 each a year, was paid to 17,000 African laborers, who did the bulk of the toil and whose fathers had once owned land and its fruits. The nations and individuals whose life, culture, power, and luxury rest on this colossal theft are the persons responsible for the present plight of Rhodesia.

This is abundantly proven in the case of the Congo. The Congo needed technical leadership and professional knowledge. Particularly were physicians needed; but when the Belgians contemplated medical schools, they found that their system of education had not furnished enough training so that educated Congolese could be given a course in modern medicine; and of course neither Belgium nor Europe could spare white physicians for black Africa in any adequate numbers.

The persons who saw Liverpool virtually built on the bodies of black slaves may not have realized who the people were committing this crime; but the rich and respectable folk who today see the open attempt of two and a half million white South Africans to rule ten million black and colored folk, and know the demand of 215,000 whites of the Rhodesias and Nyasaland to control the land and labor of seven million Negroes and Asiatics, those Europeans who base their own support, comfort, art, and culture on the profits which accrue from this outrageous denial of elementary democracy, must be conscious of what is happening. Western Europe in fact knows this, North America knows it, and yet they make small attempt to stop it. On the contrary, the flow of capital into these lands continues, year by year.

As black Africa grows in strength, unity, and intelligence, this plan of building white wealth and culture on Negro poverty and exploitation must cease. It may cease as a result of study, the spread of conference, and the strengthening of moral fiber in the world. Or it may come from the lessening of profit on African exploitation and monopoly, and the realization, due to African organization and intelligence, that in the future European civilization will depend on European labor and not on cheap colored labor abroad.

Progress may be helped by the realization on the part of Africans that their freedom will not come as a gift from white folk, but as a result of what they themselves sacrifice and do. Or again maybe the only way to bring South Africa to its senses is for West Africa to drop atom bombs on Cape Town, Johannesburg, and Salisbury, secure in the hope that Britain and the United States will not dare to interfere because of the Soviet Union and China. God forbid that this awful catastrophe should ever threaten; but if it does, the best people of Europe and America, living and carousing on the degradation of Africa, will bear the blame.

It is more likely that reason and decency will prevail. For this, we may count on present African leadership. Every current black leader begs for reform by consultation, compromise, peace, and the rule of right. The great All-African meeting at Accra, West Africa, which culminated five Pan-African congresses held in Europe, 1919 to 1945, indicated a settled determination on the part of the Africans from Algeria and Egypt to the Cape of Good Hope to be free of foreign domination and to unite to secure this great end. I was invited to attend but could not. I sent a message by my wife, Shirley Graham, which was read to the conference amid applause. In this message I said: "Avoid western investment so far as possible; sacrifice and save your own capital; when possible, borrow from the Soviet Union and China such capital as they can spare, at the low rates which only socialist lands can afford."

This conference was an outstanding success. There prevailed a spirit of brotherhood and co-operation with all the world. But let us not count on this attitude lasting forever. As Mboya, the remarkable young Kenyan chairman, said: "We have been slapped down; we have turned the other cheek; there is no third cheek!" For continuance of this spirit of compromise, then, must come action and thought, investigation and research, and that not by Europeans alone but by African scholars and thinkers. There must rise in America a new crop of men of courage to supplant the present plethora of cowards and pussyfooters in high places. The "Church of Christ" must become a Church of Man, organized for honesty and right doing—and not for dogma, miracles, and show. Above all, civilized man must learn and acknowledge that not individual wealth, but decent living for the masses is the chief end of man.

There was a day when the world rightly called Americans honest, even if crude—earning their living by hard work, telling the truth no matter whom it hurt, and going to war only for what they believed in, a just cause, after nothing but force seemed possible. Today millions of us are lying, stealing, and killing. We call all this by finer names: Advertising, Free Enterprise, and National Defense. But names in the end deceive no one; today we use science to help us deceive our fellows; we take wealth that we never earned; and we are devoting our vast energy to prepare ourselves to kill, maim, and drive insane—men, women, and children who dare refuse to do what we want done. Some profess to know why we fail. They say we haven't taught our children mathematics and physics. No, it is because we have not taught our children to read and write or to behave like human beings and not like hoodlums. Every child on the street is whooping it up with toy guns, and the big boys with real pistols. When Elvis Presley goes through his suggestive motions on the public stage, it takes the city police force to hold back teen-age children from hysteria. The story of the rigged TV quizzes completes the picture of our spiritual decadence.

The highest ambition of an American boy today is to be a millionaire. The highest ambition of an American girl is to be a movie star. Of the ethical aims which lie back of these ideals, little is said or learned. What are we doing about it? Half the Christian churches of New York are trying to ruin the free public schools in order to install religious dogma in them, and the other half are too interested in Venezuelan oil to prevent the best center in Brooklyn from fighting youthful delinquency, or to stop a bishop from kicking William Howard Melish into the street and closing his church. Which of the hundreds of churches sitting half empty protests about this? They hire Billy Graham to replace the circus in Madison Square Garden.

On the other hand, the plea for peace comes today mainly from Communists. The spread of education and science comes from Communists. The saner distribution of wealth is the object of Communism. Is this why we hate Communism and persecute its followers? The greatest threat of war comes from the United States and from its support of colonial imperialism. Why is this? Is it because the United States built its wealth on the blood and slavery of Africans? Is this why color caste and race hate persist among us as it fades among the rest of mankind? We may not delude ourselves into silence based on undoubted progress in American race relations during the last fifty years, culminating in a Supreme Court decision which is not yet enforced, or on favors to Negroes in return for their acquiescence in national policies which continue to spell ruin for the colored peoples of the world. Not freedom to exploit each other is the salvation of black America, but understanding and fellowship with the oppressed laborers of all the world. If this is true, then on the United States more than on any nation in the world lies the burden of effort for "peace on earth." The freedom of Africa depends on us, and to this end, all Americans, Negroes as well as whites, should prepare for action.

This word of mine is no effort to detract from the beneficial work of missionaries. They have done good and harm. The work of men like Dr. Schweitzer in medicine deserves all praise. The missionary of medicine is sorely needed in Africa. But the defenders of manhood are needed even more.

I look for peace and good will as Africa strives for freedom. I firmly believe that this day will come. But it will come and succeed only if the white world honestly co-operates, only if the European itch for profits at any price dies away and a broader, better ideal of human relations succeeds. I hope this change will come, but its coming will not be automatic; it will be in great part because men like Dr. Schweitzer aid and openly and clearly advocate it. It will be because Dr. Schweitzer would not only treat disease but train Negroes as assistants and helpers, surround himself with a growing African staff of scientifically educated natives who can in time carry on and spread his work and see that it is supported by the new African states and does not continue to be dependent on European charity. This would be fundamental and lasting missionary work and not mere almsgiving and paternalistic feeding of children from a silver spoon.

I have just returned from six weeks in West Africa. I have lived in the land of black folk and under a culture which they created. I have seen a black man [Kwame Nkrumah] with ancient and beautiful ceremony installed as the head of an independent African state, and I have seen him send his black soldiers to save the struggling Congolese from being overwhelmed by Belgian and American capitalists. I am thrilled and hopeful from all this which I have seen.

Bibliography

The following bibliography includes both works cited in the Introduction and other important studies of W. E. B. Du Bois or the African American history and culture of his era.

Achebe, Chinua. *Hopes and Impediments: Selected Essays*. New York: Doubleday, 1989.

Andrews, William L., ed. *Critical Essays on W. E. B. Du Bois*. Boston: G. K. Hall, 1985.

Appiah, Kwame Anthony. *In My Father's House: Africa in the Philosophy of Culture*. New York: Oxford University Press, 1992.

Aptheker, Herbert. Introduction. W. E. B. Du Bois. *The Souls of Black Folk*. 1903; rpt. Millwood, N.Y.: Kraus-Thomson, 1973.

Ayers, Edward L. *The Promise of the New South: Life After Reconstruction*. New York: Oxford University Press, 1992.

Baker, Houston A. *Modernism and the Harlem Renaissance*. Chicago: University of Chicago Press, 1987.

Baldwin, James. *Nobody Knows My Name*. New York: Dell, 1961.

Bhabha, Homi K. *The Location of Culture*. New York: Routledge, 1994.

Blight, David W. "W. E. B. Du Bois and the Struggle for American History Memory." In *History and Memory in African-American Culture*, ed. Genevieve Fabre and Robert O'Meally. New York: Oxford University Press, 1994, 45–71.

Blyden, Edward W. *Christianity, Islam, and the Negro Race*. London: Whittingham, 1887.

Bourne, Randolph. *History of a Literary Radical and Other Essays*. New York: B. W. Huebsch, 1920.

Broderick, Francis L. *W. E. B. Du Bois: Negro Leader in a Time of Crisis*. Stanford, Calif.: Stanford University Press, 1959.

Byerman, Keith E. *Seizing the Word: History, Art, and Self in the Work of W. E. B. Du Bois*. Athens: University of Georgia Press, 1994.

Casely Hayford, J. E. *Ethiopia Unbound: Studies in Race Emancipation*. 1911; rpt. London: Frank Case, 1969.

Césaire, Aimé. *Discourse on Colonialism*. 1955, trans. Joan Prinkham, Rpt. New York: Monthly Review Press, 1975.

Clarke, John Henrik, ed. *Black Titan: W. E. B. Du Bois*. Boston: Beacon Press, 1970.

Contee, Clarence G. *W. E. B. Du Bois and African Nationalism, 1914–1945*. Doctoral dissertation, American University, 1969.

Cruse, Harold. *The Crisis of the Negro Intellectual: A Historical Analysis of the Failure of Black Leadership*. 1967; rpt. New York: Quill, 1984.

Davis, Allison. *Leadership, Love, and Aggression*. New York: Harcourt Brace Jovanovich, 1983.

Du Bois, Shirley Graham. *His Day Is Marching On: A Memoir of W. E. B. Du Bois*. Philadelphia: Lippincott, 1971.

Du Bois, W. E. B. *The Autobiography of W. E. B. Du Bois: A Soliloquy on Viewing My Life from the Last Decades of Its First Century*. New York: International, 1968.

—— *Black Folk Then and Now*, ed. Herbert Aptheker. 1924; rpt. Millwood, N.Y.: Kraus-Thomson, 1975.

—— *Black Reconstruction in America, 1860–1880*. New York: Harcourt, Brace, 1935.

—— *Correspondence of W. E. B. Du Bois*, 3 vols., ed. Herbert Aptheker. Amherst: University of Massachusetts Press, 1973.

—— *Darkwater: Voices from Within the Veil*. New York: Harcourt, Brace, 1920.

—— *Dusk to Dawn: An Essay Toward an Autobiography of a Race Concept*. 1940; rpt. New York: Schocken, 1968.

—— *The Gift of Black Folk: The Negroes in the Making of America*. Boston: Stratford, 1924.

—— *John Brown*. 1906; rpt. New York: International, 1972.

—— *The Negro*. 1915; rpt. New York: Oxford University Press, 1970.

—— *The Souls of Black Folk*. Chicago: A. C. McClurg, 1903.

—— "The Talented Tenth," in *The Negro Problem: A Series of Articles by Representative American Negroes of Today*. New York: James Potts, 1903, 33–75.

—— *The World and Africa*. 1946; rpt. rev. ed. New York: International, 1965.

—— *Writings by W. E. B. Du Bois in Periodicals Edited by Others*, 4 vols., ed. Herbert Aptheker. Millwood, N.Y.: Kraus-Thomson, 1982.

Early, Gerald, ed. *Lure and Loathing: Essays on Race, Identity, and the Ambivalence of Assimilation*. New York: Penguin, 1993.

Esedebe, P. Olisanwuche. *Pan-Africanism: The Idea and Movement, 1776–1963*. Washington, D.C.: Howard University Press, 1982.

Essien-Udom, E. U. *Black Nationalism: A Search for an Identity in America*. Chicago: University of Chicago Press, 1963.

Ferris, William H. *The African Abroad, Or His Evolution in Western Civilization*, 2 vols. New Haven, Conn.: Tuttle, Morehouse, and Taylor, 1913.

Fredrickson, George M. *Black Liberation: A Comparative History of Black Ideologies in the United States and South Africa*. New York: Oxford University Press, 1995.

Friedman, Murray. *What Went Wrong? The Creation and Collapse of the Black-Jewish Alliance*. New York: Free Press, 1995.

Fullinwider, S. P. *The Mind and Mood of Black America: Twentieth-Century Thought*. Homewood, Ill.: Dorsey, 1969.

Garvey, Marcus. *Philosophy and Opinions of Marcus Garvey*, ed. Amy Jacques-Garvey. 2 vols. in one. 1923, 1925; rpt. New York: Atheneum, 1971.

Gates, Henry Louis, Jr. *Figures in Black: Words, Signs, and the "Racial" Self*. New York: Oxford University Press, 1987.

Geiss, Immanuel. *The Pan-African Movement: A History of Pan-Africanism in America, Europe, and Africa*, trans. Ann Keep. 1968; rpt. New York: Africana Publishing, 1974.

Gilroy, Paul. *The Black Atlantic: Modernity and Double-Consciousness*. Cambridge, Mass.: Harvard University Press, 1993.

Gossett, Thomas S. *Race: The History of an Idea in America*. 1963; rpt. New York: Schocken, 1965.

Henry, Charles P. *Culture and African American Politics*. Bloomington: Indiana University Press, 1990.

Higham, John. *Strangers in the Land: Patterns of American Nativism, 1860–1925*. 1955; rpt. New York: Atheneum, 1963.

Horne, Gerald. *Black and Red: W. E. B. Du Bois and the Afro-American Response to the Cold War, 1944–1963*. Albany: State University of New York Press, 1986.

Huggins, Nathan. *Harlem Renaissance*. New York: Oxford University Press, 1971.

Hurston, Zora Neale. "Spirituals and Neo-Spirituals." In *Negro: An Anthology*, ed. Nancy Cunard. Abridged ed. by Hugh Ford. 1933; rpt. New York: Frederick Ungar, 1970, 223–25.

Johnson, James Weldon. *Along This Way: The Autobiography of James Weldon Johnson*. 1933; rpt. New York: Viking, 1968.

Kellogg, Charles Flint. *NAACP: A History of the National Association for the Advancement of Colored People*. Baltimore: Johns Hopkins University Press, 1967.

King, Martin Luther, Jr. "Honoring Dr. Du Bois." In *W. E. B. Du Bois Speaks: Speeches and Addresses, 1890–1919*, ed. Philip S. Foner. New York: Pathfinder Press, 1970, 12–20.

Kluger, Richard. *Simple Justice: The History of Brown v. Board of Education and Black America's Struggle for Equality*. New York: Random House, 1975.

Kull, Andrew. *The Color-Blind Constitution*. Cambridge, Mass.: Harvard University Press, 1992.

Lamming, George. *The Pleasures of Exile*. 1960; rpt. Ann Arbor: University of Michigan Press, 1992.

Langley, J. Ayodele. *Pan-Africanism and Nationalism in West Africa, 1900–1945: A Study in Ideology and Social Classes*. Oxford: Clarendon Press, 1973.

Legum, Colin. *Pan-Africanism: A Short Political Guide*. London: Pall Mall Press, 1962.

Levine, Lawrence W. *Black Culture and Black Consciousness: Afro-American Folk Thought from Slavery to Freedom*. New York: Oxford University Press, 1977.

Lewis, David Levering. *W. E. B. Du Bois: Biography of a Race, 1868–1919*. New York: Henry Holt, 1993.

Locke, Alain, ed. *The New Negro: Voices of the Harlem Renaissance*. 1925; rpt. New York: Atheneum, 1992.

Lovell, John, Jr. *Black Song: The Forge and the Flame. The Story of How the Afro-American Spiritual Was Hammered Out*. New York: Macmillan, 1972.

Marable, Manning. *W. E. B. Du Bois: Black Radical Democrat*. Boston: Twayne, 1986.

Martin, Tony. *Race First: The Ideology and Organizational Struggles of Marcus Garvey and the Universal Negro Improvement Association*. Westport, Conn.: Greenwood Press, 1776.

McAdam, Doug. *Political Process and the Development of Black Insurgency, 1930–1970*. Chicago: University of Chicago Press, 1982.

McCarthy, Michael. *Dark Continent: Africa as Seen by Americans*. Westport, Conn.: Greenwood Press, 1983.

McKay, Claude. *A Long Way from Home: An Autobiography*. 1937; rpt. New York: Harcourt, Brace and World, 1970.

McPherson, James M. *The Abolitionist Legacy: From Reconstruction to the NAACP*. Princeton, N.J.: Princeton University Press, 1975.

Meier, August. *Negro Thought in America, 1880–1915: Racial Ideologies in the Age of Booker T. Washington*. Ann Arbor: University of Michigan Press, 1963.

Miller, Loren. *The Petitioners: The Story of the Supreme Court and the Negro*. Cleveland: Meridian, 1967.

Moses, Wilson J. *The Golden Age of Black Nationalism*. 1978; rpt. New York: Oxford University Press, 1988.

Ngugi wa Thiong'o. *Moving the Centre: The Struggle for Cultural Freedom*. London: James Currey, 1993.

Phillips, Ulrich B. *Life and Labor in the Old South*. 1929; rpt. Boston: Little, Brown, 1963.

Pinckney, Alphonso. *Red, Black, and Green: Black Nationalism in the United States*. New York: Cambridge University Press, 1976.

Rampersad, Arnold. *The Art and Imagination of W. E. B. Du Bois*. Cambridge, Mass.: Harvard University Press, 1976.

Retamar, Roberto Fernández. *Caliban and Other Essays*, trans. Edward Baker. Minneapolis: University of Minnesota Press, 1989.

Rudwick, Elliott M. *W. E. B. Du Bois: Propagandist of the Negro Protest*. 1960; rpt. New York: Atheneum, 1968.

Said, Edward. "Reflections on Exile." In *Out There: Marginalization and Contemporary Cultures*, ed. Russell Ferguson et al. Cambridge, Mass.: MIT Press, 1990, 357–66.

Senghor, Léopold Sédar. "The Struggle for *Négritude*." In *Prose and Poetry*, trans. John Reed and Clive Wake. London: Oxford University Press, 1965.

Sitkoff, Harvard. *A New Deal for Blacks: The Emergence of Civil Rights as an Issue*. New York: Oxford University Press, 1978.

Solomon, Mark I. *Red and Black: Communism and Afro-Americans, 1929–1935*. New York: Garland, 1988.

Stepto, Robert B. *From Behind the Veil: A Study of Afro-American Narrative*. Urbana: University of Illinois Press, 1979.

Stuckey, Sterling. *Slave Culture: Nationalist Theory and the Foundations of Black America*. New York: Oxford University Press, 1987.

Sundquist, Eric J. *To Wake the Nations: Race in the Making of American Literature*. Cambridge, Mass.: Harvard University Press, 1993.

Toll, William. *The Resurgence of Race: Black Social Theory from Reconstruction to the Pan-African Conferences*. Philadelphia: Temple University Press, 1979.

Turner, Henry M. "The American Negro and the Fatherland." In *Africa and the Negro: Addresses and Proceeding of the Congress on Africa*. Atlanta: Gammon Theological Seminary, 1896, 195–98.

Watkins, Mel. *On the Real Side: Laughing, Lying, and Signifying: The Underground Tradition of African-American Humor*. New York: Simon and Schuster, 1994.

Weisbord, Robert. *Ebony Kinship: Africa, Africans, and the Afro-American*. Westport, Conn.: Greenwood Press, 1973.

West, Cornel. *The American Evasion of Philosophy: A Genealogy of Pragmatism.* Madison: University of Wisconsin Press, 1989.

Williamson, Joel. *The Crucible of Race: Black-White Relations in the American South Since Emancipation.* New York: Oxford University Press, 1984.

Woodward, C. Vann. *The Strange Career of Jim Crow.* Rev. ed. New York: Oxford University Press, 1966.

Zamir, Shamoon. *W. E. B. Du Bois and American Thought, 1888–1903.* Chicago: University of Chicago Press, 1995.

AUG 2 3 2019

CPSIA information can be obtained
at www.ICGtesting.com
Printed in the USA
LVHW080016060819
626671LV00002B/21/P